Communications in Computer and Information Science   **617**

Commenced Publication in 2007
Founding and Former Series Editors:
Alfredo Cuzzocrea, Dominik Ślęzak, and Xiaokang Yang

More information about this series at http://www.springer.com/series/7899

Constantine Stephanidis (Ed.)

HCI International 2016 – Posters' Extended Abstracts

18th International Conference, HCI International 2016
Toronto, Canada, July 17–22, 2016
Proceedings, Part I

 Springer

Editor
Constantine Stephanidis
University of Crete / Foundation
for Research & Technology - Hellas
(FORTH)
Heraklion, Crete
Greece

ISSN 1865-0929   ISSN 1865-0937 (electronic)
Communications in Computer and Information Science
ISBN 978-3-319-40547-6   ISBN 978-3-319-40548-3 (eBook)
DOI 10.1007/978-3-319-40548-3

Library of Congress Control Number: 2016941295

Printed on acid-free paper

This Springer imprint is published by Springer Nature
The registered company is Springer International Publishing AG Switzerland

Foreword

The 18th International Conference on Human-Computer Interaction, HCI International 2016, was held in Toronto, Canada, during July 17–22, 2016. The event incorporated the 15 conferences/thematic areas listed on the following page.

A total of 4,354 individuals from academia, research institutes, industry, and governmental agencies from 74 countries submitted contributions, and 1,287 papers and 186 posters have been included in the proceedings. These papers address the latest research and development efforts and highlight the human aspects of the design and use of computing systems. The papers thoroughly cover the entire field of human-computer interaction, addressing major advances in knowledge and effective use of computers in a variety of application areas. The volumes constituting the full 27-volume set of the conference proceedings are listed on pages IX and X.

I would like to thank the program board chairs and the members of the program boards of all thematic areas and affiliated conferences for their contribution to the highest scientific quality and the overall success of the HCI International 2016 conference.

This conference would not have been possible without the continuous and unwavering support and advice of the founder, Conference General Chair Emeritus and Conference Scientific Advisor Prof. Gavriel Salvendy. For his outstanding efforts, I would like to express my appreciation to the communications chair and editor of *HCI International News*, Dr. Abbas Moallem.

April 2016   Constantine Stephanidis

HCI International 2016 Thematic Areas
and Affiliated Conferences

Thematic areas:

- Human-Computer Interaction (HCI 2016)
- Human Interface and the Management of Information (HIMI 2016)

Affiliated conferences:

- 13th International Conference on Engineering Psychology and Cognitive Ergonomics (EPCE 2016)
- 10th International Conference on Universal Access in Human-Computer Interaction (UAHCI 2016)
- 8th International Conference on Virtual, Augmented and Mixed Reality (VAMR 2016)
- 8th International Conference on Cross-Cultural Design (CCD 2016)
- 8th International Conference on Social Computing and Social Media (SCSM 2016)
- 10th International Conference on Augmented Cognition (AC 2016)
- 7th International Conference on Digital Human Modeling and Applications in Health, Safety, Ergonomics and Risk Management (DHM 2016)
- 5th International Conference on Design, User Experience and Usability (DUXU 2016)
- 4th International Conference on Distributed, Ambient and Pervasive Interactions (DAPI 2016)
- 4th International Conference on Human Aspects of Information Security, Privacy and Trust (HAS 2016)
- Third International Conference on HCI in Business, Government, and Organizations (HCIBGO 2016)
- Third International Conference on Learning and Collaboration Technologies (LCT 2016)
- Second International Conference on Human Aspects of IT for the Aged Population (ITAP 2016)

Conference Proceedings Volumes Full List

1. LNCS 9731, Human-Computer Interaction: Theory, Design, Development and Practice (Part I), edited by Masaaki Kurosu
2. LNCS 9732, Human-Computer Interaction: Interaction Platforms and Techniques (Part II), edited by Masaaki Kurosu
3. LNCS 9733, Human-Computer Interaction: Novel User Experiences (Part III), edited by Masaaki Kurosu
4. LNCS 9734, Human Interface and the Management of Information: Information, Design and Interaction (Part I), edited by Sakae Yamamoto
5. LNCS 9735, Human Interface and the Management of Information: Applications and Services (Part II), edited by Sakae Yamamoto
6. LNAI 9736, Engineering Psychology and Cognitive Ergonomics, edited by Don Harris
7. LNCS 9737, Universal Access in Human-Computer Interaction: Methods, Techniques, and Best Practices (Part I), edited by Margherita Antona and Constantine Stephanidis
8. LNCS 9738, Universal Access in Human-Computer Interaction: Interaction Techniques and Environments (Part II), edited by Margherita Antona and Constantine Stephanidis
9. LNCS 9739, Universal Access in Human-Computer Interaction: Users and Context Diversity (Part III), edited by Margherita Antona and Constantine Stephanidis
10. LNCS 9740, Virtual, Augmented and Mixed Reality, edited by Stephanie Lackey and Randall Shumaker
11. LNCS 9741, Cross-Cultural Design, edited by Pei-Luen Patrick Rau
12. LNCS 9742, Social Computing and Social Media, edited by Gabriele Meiselwitz
13. LNAI 9743, Foundations of Augmented Cognition: Neuroergonomics and Operational Neuroscience (Part I), edited by Dylan D. Schmorrow and Cali M. Fidopiastis
14. LNAI 9744, Foundations of Augmented Cognition: Neuroergonomics and Operational Neuroscience (Part II), edited by Dylan D. Schmorrow and Cali M. Fidopiastis
15. LNCS 9745, Digital Human Modeling and Applications in Health, Safety, Ergonomics and Risk Management, edited by Vincent G. Duffy
16. LNCS 9746, Design, User Experience, and Usability: Design Thinking and Methods (Part I), edited by Aaron Marcus
17. LNCS 9747, Design, User Experience, and Usability: Novel User Experiences (Part II), edited by Aaron Marcus
18. LNCS 9748, Design, User Experience, and Usability: Technological Contexts (Part III), edited by Aaron Marcus
19. LNCS 9749, Distributed, Ambient and Pervasive Interactions, edited by Norbert Streitz and Panos Markopoulos
20. LNCS 9750, Human Aspects of Information Security, Privacy and Trust, edited by Theo Tryfonas

HCI International 2016 Conference

The full list with the program board chairs and the members of the program boards of all thematic areas and affiliated conferences is available online at:

http://www.hci.international/2016/

HCI International 2017

The 19th International Conference on Human-Computer Interaction, HCI International 2017, will be held jointly with the affiliated conferences in Vancouver, Canada, at the Vancouver Convention Centre, July 9–14, 2017. It will cover a broad spectrum of themes related to human-computer interaction, including theoretical issues, methods, tools, processes, and case studies in HCI design, as well as novel interaction techniques, interfaces, and applications. The proceedings will be published by Springer. More information will be available on the conference website: http://2017.hci.international/.

General Chair
Prof. Constantine Stephanidis
University of Crete and ICS-FORTH
Heraklion, Crete, Greece
E-mail: general_chair@hcii2017.org

http://2017.hci.international/

Contents – Part I

Cognitive Issues in HCI

Information Presentation and Visualization

Interaction Design

Human Modelling and Ergonomics

Contents – Part II

Gesture and Motion-Based Interaction

Expressions and Emotions Recognition and Psychophisiological Monitoring

Technologies for Learning and Creativity

Health Applications

Location-based and Navigation Applications

Smart Environments and the Internet of Things

Design and Evaluation Case Studies

Design Thinking, Education
and Expertise

Exposing American Undergraduates to *Monozukuri* and Other Key Principles in Japanese Culture, Design, Technology and Robotics

Dave Berque[1](✉) and Hiroko Chiba[2]

[1] Computer Science Department, DePauw University, Greencastle, USA
dberque@depauw.edu
[2] Modern Languages Department, DePauw University, Greencastle, USA
hchiba@depauw.edu

Abstract. Exposure to varied cultures and related design principles has the potential to impact designers in a positive way. However, despite the potential for cross-cultural experiences to influence designers, American undergraduate liberal arts colleges do not typically include these topics as part of the standard computer science curriculum or as part of their general education requirements. We present a case study in exposing undergraduate students at an American liberal arts college to Japanese culture, technology and design through an immersive three-week course that includes two weeks of study in Japan. Through this cross-cultural course, students learn about Japanese culture, technology and design with an emphasis on the way these three areas are interrelated.

Keywords: Cultural differences · Developing HCI expertise and capability worldwide · Education · *Monozukuri*

1 Introduction

Exposure to varied cultures and design principles has the potential to impact designers in a positive way. For example, Steve Jobs took an approach to Human Computer Interaction and design that was heavily influenced by the time he spent in Japan and by his study of Japanese culture [4]. However, despite the potential for cross-cultural experiences to influence designers, American undergraduate liberal arts colleges do not typically include these topics as part of the standard computer science curriculum or as part of their general education requirements.

We present a case study in exposing undergraduate students at an American liberal arts college to Japanese culture, technology and design through an immersive three-week course that includes two weeks of study in Japan. Through this cross-cultural course, students learn about Japanese history, language, culture, technology and design with an emphasis on the way these three areas are interrelated. The course was offered in January 2013 and again in January 2015 with a third offering scheduled for January 2017. The course is co-taught by the co-authors, which allows us

© Springer International Publishing Switzerland 2016
C. Stephanidis (Ed.): HCII 2016 Posters, Part I, CCIS 617, pp. 3–8, 2016.
DOI: 10.1007/978-3-319-40548-3_1

to combine experience with computer science, human computer interaction, design, and robotics (first author) and Japanese language, Japanese culture and Japanese history (second author). The most recent offerings of the course includes a multi-day on-campus orientation, approximately two weeks on-site in Japan, and an on-campus follow-up component.

The Japanese concept of *monozukuri*, which literally means "making things," [3, 5] serves as the central theme of the course. *Monozukuri* is one of the key concepts that inspire product manufacturing in contemporary Japanese industry. The concept implies the spirit or determination to produce excellent products and the ability to constantly improve the products. The spirit of craftsmanship has been the driving force behind traditional art and craft-making throughout Japanese history. In contemporary society, it is one of the foundations for the production of products from cars to robots to video games. As such, the spirit of *monozukuri* can also be seen in small items commonly found in a regular household as well as in Japanese civil, industrial, and technology design projects.

Each offering of the course enrolled students from multiple majors, although most students in the course had prior course work in computer science and/or Japanese language or culture. For example, of the 25 students who enrolled in the course in January 2015, 18 were computer science majors and 12 had completed courses in Japanese language, history, and/or culture. There was some overlap between these groups, such that 7 students had studied computer science as well as Japanese language, history, and/or culture. Only two students had no prior academic background in any of these areas.

2   Course Organization

2.1   On-Campus Orientation

The course began on-campus to provide all students, regardless or prior coursework, with background related to design principles, robotics (including introduction to programming Scribbler robots), Japanese history and geography and their influence on Japanese culture, and basic Japanese language. Students completed several readings on these topics, which were also discussed during class sessions. Additionally, each student spent time identifying a topic to write about in a final paper that would explore how the Japanese principle of *monozukuri* is manifested in an area of interest to the student. The time in Japan spanned about two weeks and included several destinations that provided students with the opportunity to study *monozukuri* in various contexts. The major destinations and themes are described in the remainder of this section.

2.2   Three-Day Homestay in Itakura

We began our time in Japan with a three-day homestay in a small town called Itakura where the students learned about Japanese design and culture in daily life, and participated in activities at Toyo University's Itakura campus as well as cultural activities including a tea ceremony and traditional Japanese dance and Taiko music. Through the homestay, the students could see how common household items were designed and could consider aspects of Japanese daily life, including the art of hosting guests, through the lens of *monozukuri*.

2.3 Tokyo Visit

After departing Itakura, we moved to Tokyo for a five-day visit that focused on the design of modern technology, including a one-day city overview, a visit to the National Museum of Emerging Science and Innovation, and a full-day visit to the department of Advanced Robotics at the Chiba Institute of Technology.

Along with the homestay, the visit to the Chiba Institute of Technology (CIT) was a highlight of the course for most students. The visit, which included significant interaction with CIT students and faculty, took place at two locations. First, we stopped at the CIT Skytree Town Satellite Campus to visit a robotics showcase that is jointly sponsored by CIT and the Future Robotics Technology Center (fuRo), a research lab affiliated with CIT. While visiting the joint CIT/fuRo showcase, we participated in hands-on demonstrations of robotics technology, including a demonstration of, and chance to drive, the disaster response robot that was sent to the Fukushima disaster area in 2011.

From the Skytree Town Satellite Campus we continued on to CIT's main campus in Chiba Prefecture where we visited the Department of Advanced Robotics. We were welcomed to the department with a presentation about Japanese robotics in general, and the work that is being done at CIT in particular. The welcome was followed by an extensive and fascinating series of small-group laboratory demonstrations by various CIT faculty members and students. Our students were amazed by the wide array of highly advanced technologies we saw, as well as by the design process that the research teams followed. At CIT, students also learned how Japanese roboticists conceive of robot-making within the context of Japanese culture and society. For example, the students learned that Japan's aging population has influenced roboticists to consider ways that robots can be used in healthcare. The students also learned that the Japanese have pioneered the notion of kansei engineering, which means that emotions and affection are incorporated into products and services [1]. This approach to engineering was reflected in the demonstrations that the students saw at CIT.

The CIT visit culminated with a Presidential reception that included a wonderful dinner and the opportunity to play traditional Japanese games with our hosts. This event once again exposed our students to the role *monozukuri* plays in hosting guests in Japan as well as to principles of game design.

2.4 Nagoya Visit

We departed Tokyo for Kyoto, but stopped in route for a one-day visit to Nagoya where we learned about industrial development in Japan through a visit to the Toyota Commemorative Museum of Industry and Technology as well as the Noritake Museum. During this part of the course, students focused on understanding how companies have used iterative design philosophies to adapt to changing conditions and to take advantage of new opportunities.

At the Noritake Museum, we learned about the history of Noritake and the approach the company takes to designing and crafting ceramics. Much of the Noritake Museum was designed as a working exhibit, which allowed us to watch craftspeople carrying out the various stages of the ceramics design and production process. While Noritake is best known for designing and manufacturing china and tableware, the company has more recently moved into high-tech areas including the design of circuit substrates and engineering ceramics [2].

Next, we visited to the Toyota Commemorative Museum of Industry and Technology. Toyota originally started out as a textiles company [6] and the museum visit showed how the company had moved through a series of technological improvements to continually innovate with regard to the process of continuously producing higher quality materials. The museum then traced the company's path into the automotive industry, and showed how Toyota more recently became an innovator in producing environmentally friendly cars, as well as in using advanced manufacturing techniques such as robots. These themes gave the students another opportunity to think about *monozukuri* and also connected nicely to the robotics demonstrations we had seen previously at CIT.

2.5   Kyoto Visit

Our stay in Tokyo was followed by a four-day visit to Kyoto to study traditional Japanese craftsmanship, in part through visits to several city highpoints. Specifically, the group visited the Golden Pavilion, Nijo Castle, the Imperial Palace, the Heian Shrine, Sanjusangendo Hall, and the Kiyomizu Temple. Exploring these important historical areas, and thinking about how they were designed, gave students the chance to think about *monozukuri* in a historical and cultural context. For example, a number of these historical sites housed traditional Japanese gardens whose design was influenced by Zen philosophy. In contemporary times, the design of products, both inside and outside of Japan, including Apple products, has been influenced by similar principles [4].

2.6   Hiroshima and Miyajima Visit

During our time in Kyoto, we took a day-trip to Hiroshima to learn about the potential negative consequences of design and technology. We began this visit at the Hiroshima Peace Memorial Museum, which the entire group found to be incredibly powerful, meaningful and important. While the message of the museum was the central focus of our visit, we were also able to think about the crafting of the museum displays from the vantage point of *monozukuri*. From the museum, we moved to the Itsukushima Shrine in Miyajima, which we were fortunate to see at high tide. This site also afforded several opportunities to consider design from a cultural and historical perspective.

3 Student Paper Topics and Conclusion

During their time in Japan, students made periodic on-line journal entries, further developed ideas for their final papers, and took photographs to incorporate into their papers. Upon return to campus, students participated in a debriefing, demonstrated what they learned through a final examination, and completed their final papers. Students wrote on topics including:

- The Influence of *Monozukuri* in Japanese Technology
- *Monozukuri* and its Effect on Commercial Japanese Restrooms
- *Monozukuri* and the Influence of Hospitality on Japanese Design
- *Monozukuri*: The Creation of a Modern World With a Historic Foundation
- *Toyotazukuri*: Evolution versus Revolution
- *Monozukuri* in the Creating of Living Spaces and Household Products
- *Monozukuri* in Design and Industry: Innovation by Adaptive Repetition, Inspiration and Tradition
- *Monozukuri*: The Wabi Sabi Influence On Presentation in Japan
- Domestic Design: How *Monozukuri* Affects Personal Relationships in Japan
- *Monozukuri* and the Changing Face of Buddhism

While many of the students chose to relate *monozukuri* directly to technology and design, some students opted to explore other topics. However, when taken as a set, these papers clearly demonstrated that students had learned a lot about the significant impact culture can have on design and the importance of *monozukuri* in Japanese culture. One student summarized the course this way: "I learned so much about Japanese culture, technology, and design, and about how they are all intimately linked together" while a second wrote: "the trip increased and established open mindedness to other cultures, basic Japanese fluency, and new ways of approaching design challenges."

Based on the paper topics and content, as well as on student feedback, we believe this course was successful in helping students understand the impact that culture has on technology and design. We also believe that the course was successful in helping students understand the importance of considering cultural differences when designing products and services.

Acknowledgements. The initial offering of the course described in this paper was supported by a generous grant from the Japan Foundation. The authors also thank the town of Itakura, Toyo University, and Chiba Institute of Technology for hosting us during our visits.

References

1. Kansei Robotics: bridging human beings and electronic gadgets through kansei engineering, The Japan News, Chuo. www.yomiuri.co.jp/adv/chuo/dy/research/20100430.html
2. Noritake Electronics Web Site. www.noritake-elec.com/about_us/about.htm

3. Recapturing *Monozukuri* in Toyota's Manufacturing Process, MIT Sloan Management Review. http://sloanreview.mit.edu/article/recapturing-monozukuri-in-toyotas-manufacturing-ethos/

4. Steve Jobs and Japan, nippon.com. www.nippon.com/en/currents/d00010/

5. The Mindset of *Monozukuri*, Education in Japan. https://educationinjapan.wordpress.com/2009/04/14/the-mindset-of-monozukuri-from-mechanical-dolls-to-vending-machines-and-house-bots/

6. Toyota Global Web Site. www.toyota-global.com/company/history_of_toyota/1867-1939.html

Program for the Application of Innovative Design Thinking: Assessment of Product Opportunity Gaps of Classroom Furniture

Chin-Chuan Chen[1(✉)] and Tien-Li Chen[2]

[1] Doctoral Program in Design,
National Taipei University of Technology, Taipei, Taiwan
Hugochen44@gmail.com
[2] Department of Industrial Design,
National Taipei University of Technology, Taipei, Taiwan
chentl@ntut.edu.tw

Abstract. The objective of this research was to investigate the different product opportunities related to innovative design thinking courses. The study was done at the teaching spaces in National Taipei University of Technology. 27 students were interviewed and their behaviors observed. Research results include findings on item storage, desktop space expansion, manual operation and light weighting. Our results show that the best scenario is to give lectures and encourage small group discussions in a flexible and private space.

Keywords: Design thinking · Work shop · Product opportunity gaps · Classroom furniture

1 Introduction

When companies do business or bring new products to market, they face stiff competition and complicated problems. They need to work with other cross-industry professionals to resolve those issues. For the past 20 years, Bill Moggridge, Founder of IDEO Design Consulting Company and Time Brown have developed various theories on innovative design thinking [1].

To address the challenges of our changing times, there are new teaching methods such as innovative design thinking courses and using existing furniture to organize workshops. These type of research normally target classroom furniture ergonomics and operations [2], not so much on course activities or space requirements for the various stages of classroom space equipment design. Liang You Zhou mentioned the need to learn from potential customers, foundries and end consumers. It is also necessary to potential problems from user's point of view and finds innovative product designs via different perspectives.

The objective of this research were to study students in innovative design thinking camps, the teaching activities at every stage, the methods used, user behaviors, the opportunities and demand importance for classroom space products.

© Springer International Publishing Switzerland 2016
C. Stephanidis (Ed.): HCII 2016 Posters, Part I, CCIS 617, pp. 9–14, 2016.
DOI: 10.1007/978-3-319-40548-3_2

2   Literature Review

2.1   Curriculum Theories

Courses have a 4-step curriculum: (1) Objectives, (2) Designs, (3) Implementations and (4) Evaluations [3]. They are designed for an entire teaching system or curriculum, integrated with systems and logic. Courses include behavior, actions and level learning.. Teachers must plan activities that allowing students to understand the purpose and value of learning [4]. All the courses and activities must complement available equipment, tools, materials, content etc. Normally, teachers will have a unilateral relationship with their students. There are fewer opportunities for the former to interact with their students.. It is advised to use case studies and innovative design thinking methods to guide students into the professional architectural design industry. This is to reduce differences stemmed from students' diverse backgrounds [5]. This research will study the opinions and attitudes of the different interior design course teaching methods and evaluation platforms.

2.2   Design Thinking

The structure and process of USA's Stanford University D School Innovative Design Thinking course is as follow: (1) Empathize, (2) Define, (3) Ideate, (4) Prototype and (5) Test. They teach via workshops, provide stationary paper, poster paper, pens, color papers and encourage projects etc. They also well-utilize university discussion rooms, space, tables, furniture and other equipment etc [6].

Innovative design thinking is a type of concept development, design concept and implementation process. (1). National Taiwan University of Science and Technology opened courses on innovative design thinking and teaching methods include lectures, small group activities, concept development, presentation etc., to achieve teaching goals.

The research also investigates ways to utilize design thinking concepts on consumer products, services, systems etc. There must be training to seek effective innovative thinking paths suitable for develop pattern design courses. This will help in the area of maximizing functionality. The challenge is creating an aesthetical but effective method [7]. In the area of print design, we must harness the power of design thinking knowledge to bring cross-industry professionals together. In the innovative model of artistic design. There are an increasing number of teachers who participate in workshops gearing towards more creation-oriented and imaginative presentations [8]. For example, there is a need to integrate more open teaching design workshop partnership models, cultivate students' development of innovative working capabilities. If we apply design thinking on architectural design and operations, we will be able to help students realizing and achieving outstanding results in space and construction designs [9]. We will be able to achieve innovation in teaching when we are aware of the positive impacts of innovative design thinking on print, artistic, architectural designs etc.

2.3 Space Allocation

The physical environment refers to the surroundings and things in a person's surroundings [10]. Space and time form the two basic elements of motion and matter. People have provided research on venues, interpersonal relationship distances. There are studies on logistical operations and adjacency analysis of space which involves flow lines, functional space abuts, humanity scale, furniture and equipment configuration [11].

It is recommended to have three to four classes for every topic. This helps in cultivating students' learning autonomy, collaborative learning ability, interpersonal relationships and creating a blissful and happy learning environment. [12] Spatial design can impact students' behaviors during learning activities and space will affect their comfort level. A multi-faceted learning group and resource group design can give a flexible and ergonomic teaching environment. There are several innovative teaching models: Breaking away from traditional spatial allocation, effectively utilizing space to incorporate classroom tables, chairs, discussion walls and using sounds to create atmosphere, encouraging privacy between small groups in discussion etc. These are important factors in encouraging interactive teaching and learning between workshop teachers and students [13].

In view of the above, it is obvious that there is a positive relationship between innovative design thinking courses and an ideal classroom spatial arrangement. This includes organizing workshop learning activities, lectures, small group activities, concept development, product presentations etc. The relationship between the behaviors of users in classroom teaching activities and space and equipment is depicted clearly in the below table (Table 1).

3 Research Methods

The observation was adopted in this study Theresa L. White & Donald H. McBurney, [14], the targets of observation were the students participating in the innovative design-thinking program and the place was the multiple-function lecture hall of National Taipei University of Science and Technology. The students were members with background in design and engineering. There were 27 students (21 males and 6 females). The equipment for observation, 1. Camera; 2. Camera recorder, 3. Notebook, 4. Observation. These tools were adopted for tracking the behaviors of the students in the classroom. The original setting of this lecture hall was prepared for the students with design major and the chairs and desks are arranged in three rows (Fig. 1A). Now, this arrangement could not satisfy the needs of the activities of the workshop. The chairs and the desks were rearranged in the lecture hall for meeting the needs in the activities of the innovative design-thinking workshop, which was shown in the floor plan (Fig. 1B). The students were organized into groups of 6 to 8 persons for the workshop participation. They participated in the activities of the program, and the methods of teaching in the space.

Table 1. Observation of the relation between behaviors, space, and classroom furniture

Teaching activities	Space	Human behaviors	Demand for classroom furniture
Explaining of the theme	Students are scattered all over in the classroom	Teacher presents the lecture. Students make note at the desk.	Writing on horizontal plane, enlargement of the desktop size.
Group discussion and brain storming	Students are organized into groups in different areas of the classroom	Teacher gives instruction in motion. Students are either sitting of standing in the course of discussion.	Adhesive tape, writing on white board, vertical surface, plane urface, partition. Enlargement of desktop size.
Development of ideas	Students are organized into groups in different areas of the classroom	Teacher gives instruction in motion. Students are either sitting of standing in the course of idea development.	White board function, enlargement of desktop size.
Group briefing	Group briefing. Other students are sitting or standing as they listen.	Teacher gives instruction and evaluation. Group briefing.	Writing on plane surface, use of vertical surface, mobile.
Group briefing	Group briefing. Other students are sitting or standing as they listen.	Teacher gives instruction and evaluation. Group briefing.	Writing on plane surface, use of vertical surface, mobile.

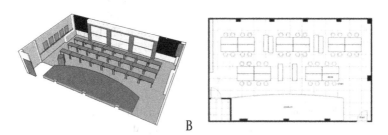

B

Fig. 1. The layout of the lecture hall before (A) and the layout of the lecture hall after (B)

4   Conclusion and Discussion

The research was done via semi-structured interviews and observations, and it helped us to understand the opportunistic demands of classroom spatial equipment. It was discovered that there are instances of untidy spatial planning and irregular wall specifications, irregular distances between spatial equipment and tables and chairs, messy flow lines, tables, chairs, and furniture placed in class room were not suitable for small group student discussion, noisy atmospheres and no sense of privacy, stationary, papers, laptops placed messily on tables etc. **Result Findings**: Currently, there were transformations of student workshop activities in current classroom environments, spatial allocation, furniture equipment and wall usage. Previously, it was rigid and unable to fulfill workshop teaching and learning activity needs. Thus, furniture equipment design and spatial allocation could enable teachers and students to achieve their course goals and course structure, furniture design specifications must fulfill those purposes [15]. Regardless if it was static or dynamic environment spaces, it is spatial format transformation that defines them. There were furniture product opportunities, complementing workshop activities for learning and teaching, to elevate course effectiveness.

Limitations: Current research focuses only the current situations in National Technological University of Taiwan, their teachers and students' teaching and learning activities, space dynamics and case studies. Thus this study might be skewed and biased to some extent.

5   Result

This research studies innovative design thinking courses workshops, learning and teaching activities, space, furniture structure. We also observed human behaviors for example by monitoring teachers and students who participate in teaching and learning activities. We saw functional demands and opportunities in classroom furniture in the areas of writing, doing presentations, whiteboard functions, sticky notes, moving, enlarged table space, putting in a separator etc. Research results included findings on item storage, desktop space expansion, manual operation and light weighting. The best scenario was to give lectures and encourage small group discussions in a flexible and private space. Course curriculum's activities, methods, behaviors and classroom space is known to affect each other. Thus, there are demands on furniture and equipment. To maximize teachers and students' dynamics, activity space size, movement flow, physical static, it is best to arrange groups of 6 to 8 people. With storage capabilities, flexible change and compartment use, and internal space furniture during learning activities.

The results of the study recommends that future research can utilize corporate office environments and residences, to study opportunities in different environment space furniture products.

Acknowledgement. We are grateful to the Executive Yuan and Ministry of Science and Technology for funding under project No.103-2511-S-027-002-MY3.

References

1. Brown, T.: Chang by Design How Design Thinking Transforms, Press. New York (2009)
2. Gouvali, M.K., Boudolos, K.: Match between school furniture dimensions and children's anthropometry. Appl. Ergonomics **37**, 765–773 (2006)
3. Wiles, J., Bondi, J.: Curriculum Development: A Guide to Practice, 6th edn, p. 131. Merrill, Columbus (2002)
4. Zhang Q.B.: Teaching Principles and Practices. Taipei City, Wu Nan (2009)
5. Borich, G.D.: Aspects of Effective Teaching (Translated by Hao Yong Wei). Pro-Ed Publishing, Taipei City (2014)
6. Xuan, X.M.: Study on Architectural Design Curriculum and its Teaching Methods (Master's Degree), National Taipei University of Technology, Taipei City (2014)
7. D school.stanford.edu. http://dschool.stanford.edu/
8. Nobuyuki, U., Takeo, I., Mitra, N.J.: Guided exploration of physically valid shapes for furniture design. Commun. ACM **58**(9), 116–124 (2015). doi:10.1145/2801945
9. Xia, C.Y., Ling, Z.Y., Zhi, C.X.: The effect evaluation of teacher empowerment workshop of creative tendencies and imagination. Creation J. **5**(1), 65–86 (2014). in Chinese
10. Yu, Z., Hong, Z., & College of Architecture, Dong Nan University, South, 210096. Design Practice at Teacher's Workshop on "Space-tectonics": Attempt at One New Method for Design and Teaching. College of Architecture Newsletter, pp. 20–23. June 2011
11. Analysis of Space Adjacency (Translated by Lin Zheng Da, Lin Jian Xia) Liu He Publisher, Taipei City (1999)
12. Study on the Use of Lin Yue Yuan Group Classroom Space in National Elementary Schools-Using Ji Mei Elementary School in New Taipei City as Case Study- Graduate School of Architecture, Master's Degree thesis, Hua Fan University (2011)
13. Workshop Research from Students of National Taipei University of Technology, (Lin Bing Han, Wu Cang Ru etc) (2014)
14. Theresa, L., White & Donald, H., McBurney.: Design Research Methods, 6th Edition (2013)
15. Roozenburg, N.F.M., Eekels, J.: Product Design: Fundamentals and Methods. Delft University of Technology, The Netherlands (1991)

Message Delivery of Cultural and Creative Products Under Cultural Industries

Chi-Hsiung Chen[1,2] and Shih-Ching Lin[2(✉)]

[1] Department of Product Design, Chungyu Institute of Technology,
No. 40, Yi 7th Rd., Keelung 20103, Taiwan, ROC
chenchs@cit.edu.tw
[2] Graduate School of Design, Doctoral Program,
National Yunlin University of Science and Technology, No.123,
University Rd., Sec. 3, Douliou 64002, Yunlin, Taiwan, ROC
malinda0810@gmail.com

Abstract. Taiwanese culture is diverse, rich and sophisticated. After a long-term accumulation, it also has acquired solid cultural capacity. In the meantime, in recent years, the government has actively promoted policies on the cultural and creative industry, which has stimulated the developmental trends of creative industries and created new opportunities for many cultural and creative products. As a result, it has brought a lot of negative phenomena of "cultural industry" to Taiwan. Consequently, the initially good intention of the government in promoting the cultural and creative industry has eroded away the subjectivity and creativity of culture. Therefore, the purpose of this study is to explore and find the balance between two aspects – "commercialization" and "preservation of the spirit of cultural connotation" – in the process of developing cultural and creative products. Through case studies and fieldwork survey, this study performed analysis based on observations of special cultural activities and sceneries in Taiwan. Questionnaires were designed through the three-level theory of cultural coding. Design patterns and indicators of cultural and creative products were formulated based on visitors' feedbacks and will be provided as a basis of reference for future designers of cultural and creative products. There are three findings obtained from this study: (1) High degree of correlation between cultural and creative product designs and cultural activities is fundamental and will create a memory connection with the products in a consumer's brain. (2) Experiential models and handmade designs can enhance consumers' understanding of culture. (3) Through the three-level theory of model design – integrated thinking of the strategic level, the connotative level, and the technical level – cultural products can effectively deliver cultural messages to consumers and at the same time create cultural styles.

Keywords: Cultural and creative products · Cultural industry · Consumer psychology · Message delivery introduction

© Springer International Publishing Switzerland 2016
C. Stephanidis (Ed.): HCII 2016 Posters, Part I, CCIS 617, pp. 15–23, 2016.
DOI: 10.1007/978-3-319-40548-3_3

1   Introduction

The rise of a cultural economy has brought forth the development of a global cultural industry that reinterprets and transforms local cultures into cultural symbols to be applied in product design, giving birth to various cultural merchandises. In the supply aspect, the features of the merchandise of cultural creative are their differentiation and uniqueness, which are promoted in the market with highly competitive marketing strategies. In the demand aspect, the consumers' needs tend to be unstable and unpredictable.

Various types of consumers in today's market are all different; hence a barrier in communication exists when products of cultural creative merchandisers intend to enter the consumers' lives with their cultural spirit. Thus, in order to build a perfect bridge to connect the cultural connotation and the consumers' resonance, we need to find out effective models for various cultural merchandise that target different groups of consumers, and further apply these findings accordingly in product design to fulfill the consumers' expectations about these merchandise of cultural creativity.

2   Literature Review

2.1   Design and Cultural Economy

The 21st century is the time for culture, and the arrival of the age of cultural economy means the impact of culture to contemporary society is more widespread and in-depth. "Culture" and "economy," two fields that used to be considered incompatible, began to overlap, thus the rise of "Cultural Economics." This indicates that culture and economy were two unintegrated major fields, but the development of a cultural creative industry has been accelerated due to changes in society and the pressure of global culture.

Whether to increase cultural elements in some industries or industrialize certain cultures, the economic value generated by culture has impressed many, as the reviving culture brings forth prosperous economic visions, and further become important goals for a nation's cultural strategies and economics. Zukin (1995) emphasized that culture is not only capable for propelling the industries in terms of the economic aspect, but can also be used as the basis of the economy, providing product concepts for an entire line of products; the relationship between culture and economy has transformed from traditionally contradictory to mutual beneficial. Lash Urry (1994) had the same idea, indicating that a mutual beneficial relationship exists between culture and economy; culture is presented as merchandise because of economy, and economy is enhanced through culture in terms of beautification and embedded connotation, and elevates life quality and cultural recognition (Liang and Zhang 1995). Product design plays the role of cultural messenger in cultural economy, delivering cultural messages to the consumers through symbolic cultural codes and semantic con-version, such cultural merchandise also allows the consumers to foster affection toward local culture and boosts the value of culture.

2.2 Three-Level Theory of Cultural Codes

Design is a kind of communication; culture is the symbolic messages of products (Yang 1989). Based on research on the relationship among the three aspects of "design," "symbols," and "communication," cultural symbolism for design is constructed, and the three-level theory was raised in design, namely a "technical level," "connotation level," and "strategic level," as shown in Fig. 1.

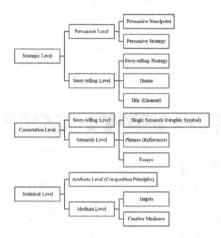

Fig. 1. Three-level Theory of Cultural Codes (Yang 1989, Illustration by the Researcher)

2.3 Consumer Psychology

According to the EBM model (shown in Fig. 2) constructed by Engle et al. (2001), consumers' behaviors are the activities people engage when they acquire, consume and dispose products and services. The EBM model divides consumers' decision-making process into seven main phases, namely, need recognition, search for information, pre-purchase alternative evaluation, purchase, consumption, post-consumption evaluation and divestment.

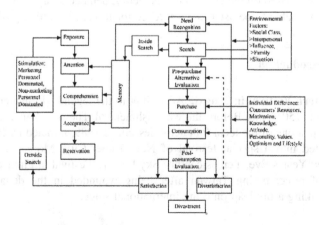

Fig. 2. Entire Model of Consumers' Decision-making Process (Engle et al. 2001)

3   Research Design

This study aims to explore unique Taiwanese cultural activities in depth. At the same time, analysis was conducted on three cultural events – The Sky Lantern Festival in Pingxi, Sanyi Wood Carving Festival, and The Hakka Tung Blossom Festival, which were chosen and announced by Taiwan Tourism Bureau as unique Taiwanese cultural events. Cultural meanings and cultural elements were studied based on these three events. Field research method was used to visit and retrieve on-site relevant cultural elements. On top of that, in-depth interview was conducted with consumers to understand their cultural interpretation and awareness. After compilation and analysis, modifications on the actual design and design model were carried out. The study process flowchart is shown in Fig. 3.

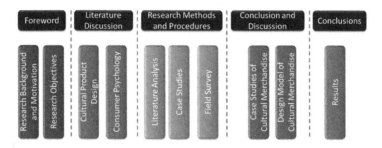

Fig. 3. Study process flowchart

4   Results and Discussion

According to the three major unique cultures selected by Taiwan Tourism Bureau, this study conducted case analysis on The Sky Lantern Festival in Pinxi, Sanyi Wood Carving Festival, and The Hakka Tung Blossom Festival. Through on-site visit and investigation and literature review and collection, their cultural elements were understood. In addition, based on the cultural codes theory, detailed analysis was conducted, which will be available to be used as a reference for future innovative product design.

4.1   Case Introduction

The Sky Lantern Festival in Pingxi. According to the legend, sky lanterns have the history of about 150 years. Before the establishment of The Sky Lantern Festival in Pingxi, it was just one of the local folk activities. Since 1989, initiated by local people, it was promoted into a special festival of New Taipei City. Moreover, during the millennial New Year's Eve, a cross-century Sky Lantern Festival in Pinxi was held for the thought of remembering Taiwan after being wounded in the devastating 921 earthquake, making a big leap onto the international stage.

Sanyi Wood Carving Festival. Sanyi Village, Miaoli County, is an internationally renowned woodcarving village, originated in the 1920 s. In the early time, carvings were mainly made out of natural, rare wood. In early 1970, Sanyi woodcarving reached its peak period. Having won fame both at home and abroad, most products were exported. In the 1980 s, due to poor economy resulted from international energy crisis, the woodcarving industry reflected upon how woodcarving products could be leveled up into artworks. The establishment of Sanyi Wood Sculpture Museum in 1995 has gathered woodcarving practitioners from around the country to this village to learn and observe each other, from which a village that is known for its sculptures has formed.

The Hakka Tung Blossom Festival. Every year during the transition between spring and summer, from the north mountainous area of Changhua, Taiwan, to Hualien, Taitung in the eastern region, beautiful snow-white sceneries of Tung blossoms are seen everywhere on mountains. Especially in the Hakka villages in Taoyuan, Hsinchu, Miaoli in April and May, fluttering of snow-white pedals has formed the most beautiful scenery in Taiwan.

4.2 Results of Interview Questionnaire

Based on the locations of the cultural events, this study conducted field research and analysis for three times. In addition, the design of questionnaire and in-depth consumer interview are based on the cultural codes theory and cultural and creative product design model. Random sampling method was used separately in Pingxi District in New Taipei City, Sanyi Village in Miaoli County, and Nanzhuang Village in Miaoli County to conduct interviews with consumers who went there to participate in the cultural activities. After the results of the interviews were compiled and analyzed, a structure was created as seen in Fig. 4.

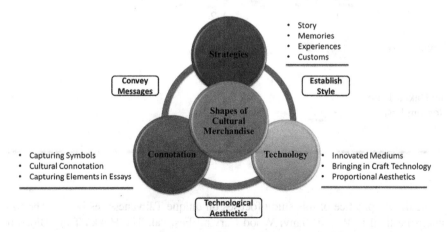

Fig. 4. A structural diagram of consumer cultural elements

According to the cultural and creative product design model, this study conducted relevant questionnaire interview to understand consumers' interpretation of cultural products. In general, the questionnaire is divided into three properties - style aesthetics, message transmission, and craft aesthetics – to carry out in-depth interviews. Consumers have fixed impressions toward certain cultural styles. Therefore, regarding style aesthetics, the interpretation of cultural elements and the application of shapes and colors will influence consumers' perception of cultures. In terms of message transmission, in response to the direct presentation of cultures, consumers experience awakening of their past memories. In terms of craft aesthetics, creative design thinking, introduction of traditional crafts, and introduction of innovative technologies are the main factors that attract consumers' attention.

4.3   The Retrieve and Application of Cultural Codes

Through literature analysis and the three-level theory of cultural codes, this study chose three unique Taiwanese festivals – the Sky Lantern Festival in Pingxi, Sanyi Wood Carving Festival, and the Hakka Tung Blossom Festival – and conducted in-depth study. Through field research investigation, on-site participation of cultural activities, and in-depth interviews, relevant cultural codes were retrieved to carry out product design and numbering as shown in Table 1. In addition, their design concepts were organized as shown in Table 2.

Table 1. Design and numbers of the cultural products

Cultural events	Design practices		
The Sky Lantern Festival in Pingxi	A-1	A-2	
Sanyi Wood Carving Festival	B-1	B-2	
The Hakka Tung Blossom Festival	C-1	C-2	

The design practice of this study focuses on unique Taiwanese festivals – The Sky Lantern Festival in Pingxi, Sanyi Wood Carving Festival, The Hakka Tung Blossom Festival to conduct product design. The design direction of The Sky Lantern Festival in Pingxi products uses sky lanterns as the main design element. The implications of

Table 2. Design concepts of the cultural products (source of data: organized by this study)

NO.	Name	Design concept
A-1	Sky Lantern Wall Lamp With Key Hooks	Utilizing the prayer image of sky lanterns with the design of wall lamp, it symbolizes leaving a light for people who come home late. It also conveys a meaning of wishing people safe wherever they go.
A-2	Sky Lantern Style Lamp For Reading	When sky lanterns rise into the sky, it symbolizes people's wishes have reached the heaven. It uses magnetic floating method to increase cultural interest.
B-1	Ruins of Long-teng Bridge Lunch Box	Having railroad meal on railway trains is a shared memory of Taiwanese people. Manufactured by Sanyi traditional carpenters, the local well-known tourist attractions are integrated on both sides based on the design of "Ruins of Long-teng Bridge". It can be used for placing chopsticks. Both the chopsticks and lid are printed with rail tracks so that consumers can associate with the historic glorious appearance of the Ruins of Long-teng Bridge.
B-2	Ruins of Long-teng Bridge Sauce Dish	Sauces are one of the soul elements of the Taiwanese gourmet snacks. Most Taiwanese people have the habit of dipping sauces while having meals. On both sides of the dish, there are "Ruins of Long-teng Bridge" chopstick stands. Using latch structure combined with the dish, when not in use, it can be easily disassembled and stored.
C-1	Tung Blossom Color Changing Cup	The design is based on the image of falling Tung flowers. Using the method of color changing to create the gradient effect.
C-2	Tung Blossom Notebook	Using Hakka dying techniques, a link of memory is made through the color changing Tung blossoms. It symbolizes the image of endless life after flowers fall off.

blessings and prayers of sky lanterns are incorporated into the product design, through which the connectivity between the cultural product and local features is enhanced. Moreover, the special significance of "bringing wishes and blessings home" increases consumers' willingness to purchase. The design direction of Sanyi wood carving products integrates the local landscape "Ruins of Long-teng Bridge" into the design process. Woodcarving and wood material decorations are moderately incorporated onto parts of the products to integrate woodcarving art with traveling experience, enhancing tourists' memory connection. The design direction of the Hakka Tung Blossom Festival products is based on the most direct way of reference, with which the image of Tung blossoms is applied onto products. In addition to the application of totems, this allows consumers to associate the products with the romantic vibe of Tung blossom rain.

4.4   The Model Construction of Cultural and Creative Product Design

Based on the three-level theory of cultural codes, through participation of the cultural activities and in-depth interviews, this study aims to understand consumers' understanding and interpretation of local cultures so that the practical design of cultural products can be reestablished. According to the research results of in-depth interviews and practical design, this study focuses on the three-level theory of cultural codes and the results of design research. Based on the correlated development of the three levels – style aesthetics, message transmission, and craft techniques, through in-depth interviews, other individual factors are compiled and the model of cultural and creative product design is constructed, which is shown in Fig. 5.

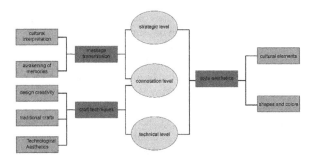

Fig. 5. The model of cultural product design

5   Conclusion

In the process of designing cultural products, through understanding consumers' interpretation of cultures, design conception is conducted focusing on the understanding and concepts of cultural implications. In addition to the increased intensity of cultural message transmission, customers can better resonate with the products. Through the three-level theory of cultural codes, this study conducted in-depth interviews and studies with consumers to re-examine the design model of cultural products, through which practical design is carried out. Through the results of the practical design, the study compiled the following three points of conclusion.

1. There is a high degree of correlation between cultural and creative product design and cultural activities, which enable consumers to make memory links based on products.
2. Through the integrated conception of the three-level theory model, in terms of style aesthetics, cultural product design must place emphasis on the application of cultural elements and the configuration of highly relevant shapes and colors. Regarding message transmission, cultural interpretation and memory linking must be emphasized. As for craft techniques, emphasis should be placed on design creativity, the application of traditional crafts and the introduction of innovative technologies to enhance the value, with regard to cultural spirit and industrial economic aspects, of cultural products.

3. Through the comprehensive conception of cultural product design, based on consumers' understanding and interpretation, a more accurate design can be created to effectively transmit cultural meanings.

References

Wang, H., Ruilin, H.: J. Des. **16**(4) (2011)

Yang, Y.: Cultural Foundation of Design: Design, Symbols and Communication. Pacific (1989)

Zukin, S.: The Culture of Cities, pp. 1–48. Blackwell, London (1995)

Liang, B., Changyi, Z.: J. Geogr. Sci. **39**, 31–51 (2005)

Feng, J.: Culture is Good Business, Design Culture Guided Reading (2002)

Taiwan Tourism Bureau, Ministry of Transportation. http://www.taiwan.net.tw/w1.aspx

Using MURAL to Facilitate Un-Moderated Formative User Experience Research Activities

Edward S. De Guzman[✉]

Autodesk, Inc., One Market Street, Suite 500, San Francisco, CA 94105, USA
Edward.DeGuzman@autodesk.com

Abstract. Un-moderated user research platforms such as Usertesting.com [1] or UserZoom [2] are gaining popularity with user experience research practitioners for several reasons. It is more efficient from a logistics standpoint, most platforms allow the researcher to easily collect user experience metrics and for some metrics the data collected is comparable to data collected in a lab study. Un-moderated user research platforms have typically been used to facilitate *evaluative* user experience research studies. There has been little exploration in the HCI literature on the use of these platforms for *formative* user experience research activities. MURAL (http://mural.ly) is a visual workspace used by creative teams to share inspiration, discover new insights, brainstorm and organize ideas and define solutions. In this paper, we describe how MURAL can be used as a platform to facilitate un-moderated formative user experience research activities.

Keywords: User research · Remote research · Formative research methods

1 Introduction

Un-moderated user research studies such as Usertesting.com or UserZoom are gaining popularity with user experience research practitioners for several reasons. It is more efficient from a logistics standpoint, most platforms allow the researcher to easily collect user experience metrics and for some metrics (e.g., self-reported overall ease), the data collected is comparable to data collected in a lab study.

1.1 Un-Moderated User Experience (UX) Research

In a remote un-moderated research study, researchers use an online software program to automate their study. The research participants get a list of pre-determined tasks to perform on their own. In some testing platforms the participant's screen and voice are recorded. Since the testing platform is cloud-based, participants are able to complete the tasks in their own environment at a time that is convenient for them. There is no moderator present; when the participant has completed the tasks, the results are sent to the researcher. Data available from these software platforms can include: task success ratios, time on task, clickstreams, heat maps, video, audio, facial expressions, mouse

© Springer International Publishing Switzerland 2016
C. Stephanidis (Ed.): HCII 2016 Posters, Part I, CCIS 617, pp. 24–29, 2016.
DOI: 10.1007/978-3-319-40548-3_4

movements, or responses to a follow-up questionnaire. The research can access results through an dashboard, or export the results to a file format that can be read offline.

Un-moderated research is recommended for evaluative research studies where the goal is to collect feedback on specific tasks. It is important that the tasks are designed so that the participant is unlikely to navigate far from the research materials. If the research method relies on a large sample size for arriving at conclusive results, an un-moderated research study is recommended since a moderator does not need to be present during each session. Since this style of research allows the participant to participate on their own time and in their own environment, un-moderated research studies minimize the bias introduced by conducting studies in artificial laboratory setting.

1.2   Un-Moderated UX Research: Pros and Cons

User experience research practitioners receive several benefits from un-moderated user research platforms. Since the researcher does not need to be present for the duration of the study, the number of person-hours needed to execute the study is reduced. This is a significant benefit for research studies requiring large sample sizes. The "on-demand" aspect of the study allows multiple sessions to facilitated concurrently. As a result, it becomes more feasible to collect large sample sizes which, in turn, reduces the margin of error and allows the researcher to arrive at conclusions with a higher degree of significance.

In addition to making it easier to execute a research study with large sample size, the logistics of setting up the study become easier. There's no need to schedule appointments or travel to a research facility to conduct the sessions. By eliminating travel it becomes easier to get broader geographic coverage in the research study participant profile. By allowing participants to participate at a time that is convenient for them and on their choice of equipment, the chance to observe more natural behavior is higher compared to an artificial lab setting with a researcher observing the participant complete the tasks.

There are several limitations to this approach for answering research questions. First, there is an emphasis on using un-moderated research studies for *evaluative* research, where the objective is to get feedback on an existing design or information architecture. Common types of activities include: task-based usability testing, prototype and wireframe testing, click testing, timeout testing (e.g., 5-s test), card sorting and tree testing. These platforms have not been used for conducting *formative* research studies. In these studies, the objective is often to collect data to inform the design of an experience, to explore a new product concept or direction with users or to learn more about a specific target user. Examples of formative research methods can include: semi-structured interviews, focus groups, diary studies, collaging, feature prioritization exercises, stakeholder mapping and experience diagramming.

One reason why un-moderated research platforms are not used for formative research lies in the mechanisms that these systems have for collecting feedback from the participants. In evaluative research, common metrics include objective measures such as task success rate, time on task and subjective measures such as the participant's self-reported response to follow-up survey questions after a task. Un-moderated research platforms are well-designed to collect these measures. In formative research, the data is less structured. For example, in an experience diagramming exercise, the participant produces a visual artifact showing a progression of events and a reflection of the experience at each event. In a focus group, multiple participants are engaged in conversation in real-time. In a stakeholder map, the participant produces a visual artifact representing a network of people and the connections between them. As a consequence of the un-structured nature of the data in formative research activities, researchers shy away from cloud based un-moderated platforms because it is difficult to collect the participant data. Un-moderated research platforms today are optimized for collecting structured data. In this paper, we propose an existing tool that eases some of the tensions introduced by the limitations of today's un-moderated research platforms. We present examples of how this brainstorming tool can be used to conducted un-moderated formative user experience research.

2   MURAL as a Platform for Un-Moderated UX Research

MURAL (http://mural.ly) is a visual workspace used by creative teams to share inspiration, discover new insights, brainstorm and organize ideas and define solutions. In this paper, we describe how MURAL can be used as a platform to facilitate un-moderated formative user experience research activities. While MURAL already supports traditional formative research and analysis methods such as experience diagramming, feature prioritization and affinity clustering, we present innovative ways of using the platform.

Card Sorting Card sorting is a technique to understand and assess expectations and understanding about a set of topics. The participant is a given a set of topics/concepts/ideas as "cards" and organizes the cards into categories which can be defined by the participant or the researcher.

Example. In Fig. 1, participants are asked to drag a set of concepts into one of two categories:

- Table Stakes: features or experiences that earn trust and respect from customers as a provider of design software and services across desktop, web and mobile
- Differentiating Value: opportunities to develop unique industry expertise and deliver unique value for customers

While there are other web-based platforms for doing online card sorting (e.g., OptimalSort), the service provides a limited set of capabilities for providing feedback (if any). Using MURAL's platform for conducting a card sort exercise, participants can create additional sticky notes to explain how they sorted the cards. They can also draw shapes and lines to more visually describe their sorting rationale (Figs. 2 and 3).

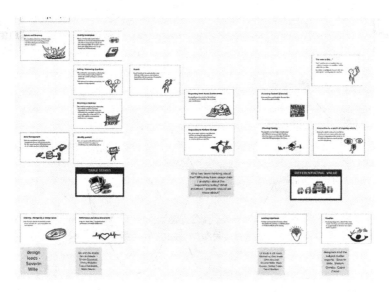

Fig. 1. Card sorting exercise facilitated using MURAL

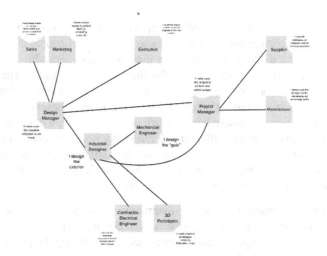

Fig. 2. Use of MURAL to conduct a Stakeholder Mapping exercise

Stakeholder Mapping Stakeholder mapping [needs ref] is a way of diagramming the network of people who are involved in a given work process. For example, an industrial designer needs to work with several types of stakeholders: other industrial designers, a manager/executive persona, a mechanical engineer and external vendors such as physical prototypers and manufacturers. Stakeholder maps allow the researcher to see the entire landscape of people involved in a complex process. This may influence where UX effort is focused or it may uncover UX opportunities that were not visible due to a limited view of the entire process.

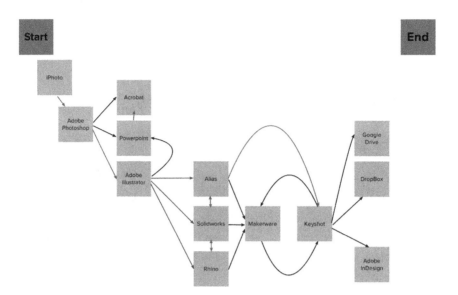

Fig. 3. Use of MURAL to conduct an experience diagramming exercise

In the above example, the stakeholder mapping exercise is presented in two stages. In the first stage, the participant is asked to brainstorm a list of people that are part of a specific process (e.g., if the participant is an industrial designer, who are people that you have to interact with at some point in the lifecycle of a project?). The participant creates one sticky note for each person. Then the sticky notes are arranged in a way that the participant can draw connections using the line tools. These lines can also be labeled to describe the relationship between two people. In a more detailed stakeholder diagram, the participant can use different colored sticky notes to denote different types of stakeholders. After constructing the diagram, the participant can use an additional sticky note as a speech-bubble to describe the stakeholder's mindset or the participant's most common pain point when interacting with this stakeholder.

Experience Diagramming Experience diagramming [needs ref] is a method to visualize a process or workflow that can be broken down into phases or events. When used as a formative research method, experience diagramming helps the researcher understand the impact of each event from the user's perspective.

In the above example, the experience diagramming exercise is being used to understand how data moves between applications across the duration of a project. The researcher prepares the workspace by placing "START" and "END" sticky notes on the right and left sides of the MURAL. The participant is asked to brainstorm and generate a list of major software tools used in a project for design or collaboration. Each individual application is written on a sticky note and placed sequentially along the start/end timeline. Next, the participant draws arrows to the direction of data flow. Finally, the participant uses changes the stroke color of the arrows to green to indicate a smooth transition. Similarly, the stroke color of the arrows is changed to red to indicate when a transition is inefficient or frustrating. When needed, the participant can give more detailed explanations on additional green sticky notes.

3 Conclusion

As un-moderated research grows in popularity among the user experience researcher community, an open area of investigation is in which research methods can be executed using an un-moderated research platform. In this paper we describe how MURAL can be used as a platform for conducting formative user research activities. Because MURAL supports richer forms of feedback than most other platforms, the flexibility makes it a better tool than existing platforms for conducting formative user experience research. As a case study, we demonstrate how MURAL can be used to execute three different types of research activities: card sorting, stakeholder mapping and experience diagramming.

References

1. Usertesting.com. http://www.usertesting.com/
2. UserZoom. http://www.userzoom.com

Pet Empires: Combining Design Thinking, Lean Startup and Agile to Learn from Failure and Develop a Successful Game in an Undergraduate Environment

Danielly F.O. de Paula[✉] and Cristiano C. Araújo

Post-Graduate Program in Computer Science, Universidade Federal de
Pernambuco Center of Informatics (CIn), Recife-PE, Brazil
{dfop2, cca2}@cin.ufpe.br

Abstract. Startups are able to produce software products with a strong impact on the market, significantly contribution to the global economy. However, eight of ten software startups fail within their first three years - the main failure is caused by the high cost of getting the first customer and the even higher cost of getting the product wrong. In order to reduce these failures, more recent research has focused on combining the approaches of Design Thinking (DT), Lean Startup and Agile to develop and scale new products. This research aims to offer new insights on how startups can benefit by combing the approaches above to developing new software products. As a result, this paper provides a model which demonstrated good potential to be used by startups.

Keywords: Design thinking · Len startup · Agile methodology · Software development

1 Introduction

Nowadays, Design Thinking has been implemented in many different organizational settings, most notably Information Technology (IT). However, we still don't know how the appropriate combinations of design thinking with common IT development models look like (Lindberg et al. 2011). To address this gap, this article aims to analyze the introduction of Design Thinking practices to IT development in a startup environment. Initially, the team followed an existing model to develop a mobile game, and then to better fit in a startup context the model was adapted.

In order to introduce the DT concepts, the Nordstrom model (Grossman-kahn and Rosensweig 2012) was chosen because it seemed to be an easy way to introduce DT practices in IT teams using just a few steps. Furthermore, its features included the more recommended practices, such as Design Thinking, Lean Startup and Agile, for developing new software products in a startup environment (Paternoster et al. 2014) (Grossman-kahn and Rosensweig 2012). The startup was composed by three computer science undergraduate students working at BlackBerry Tech Center Recife (TC). The TC aimed to offer a place where undergraduate students could learn how to create innovative software solutions by experiencing a simulation of a startup environment.

© Springer International Publishing Switzerland 2016
C. Stephanidis (Ed.): HCII 2016 Posters, Part I, CCIS 617, pp. 30–34, 2016.
DOI: 10.1007/978-3-319-40548-3_5

They used to work with Lean Startup and Scrum, but had no experience with DT. Thus, the team faced two big challenges: learning how to work with DT and developing their first game. Overall, this study contributes to the HCI literature by presenting new insights on how to introduce DT practices in IT undergraduate teams that already follow Scrum and Lean Startup. In addition, it contributes to the improvement of the Nordstrom model by putting more emphasis on the use of DT.

2 Background and Related Work

2.1 Combining Design Thinking, Agile Methodology and Lean Startup

Ever since Design Thinking (DT) was used as the title of Rowe's 1987 book many researchers have attempted to validate the nature of design thinking in the business context (Martin 1995). Brown (2009) has defined design thinking as "bringing designers' principles, approaches, methods, and tools to problem-solving". The idea behind this approach is to employ practices that help organizational participants to reevaluate fundamental assumptions about the way their organization's function and to develop thus appropriate solutions to novel problems (Boland and Collopy 2004).

In comparison with design thinking, agile shows some strong parallels: core features like iterative learning and development processes, and extensive team communication (Lindberg et al. 2011). However, agile has some restrictions: (a) there is less emphasis on interdisciplinary creative collaboration than in design thinking; (b) agile seems to have a tendency to avoid divergent thinking in order to maintain the overall view on what to do next and (c) Agile assumes that teams already start with a product vision and a product backlog without a clear picture as to where that vision will come from (Lindberg et al. 2011).

Similar to design thinking, lean is also focusing on users or customers; however, does not provide guiding principles on how to find out what is valuable to the customer (Kowark et al. 2014). There are good reasons why both Lean and design thinking make particular sense together: (a) developers in business software companies are often not actual users of their own products. Hence, the empathy phase from DT is needed (Kowark et al. 2014). There is still no model widely accepted by the literature; however Grossman-kahn et al. (2012) recently released a model combining the three approaches.

The Nordstrom Model. Grossman-kahn et al. (2012) argue that the development of a new product must start with practices of Design Thinking, because the team needs at the earliest find out the needs of users, identify problems and propose solutions (Fig. 1).

All practices of Design Thinking follow the Human Centered Design Toolkit[1] from IDEO. Only after performing step-by-step manual of IDEO, the team is able to start the practices of Agile, following the philosophy of Lean. The model was positively validated by the laboratory team of Nordstrom.

---

[1] http://www.designkit.org/.

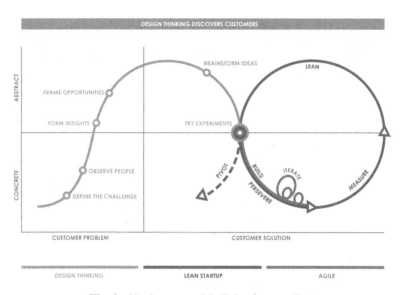

Fig. 1. Nordstrom model (Color figure online)

3   Method

This study aims to offer new insights on how startups can benefit by combing Design Thinking, Lean Startup and Agile Methodology to develop new software products. The following questions served as guide to conduct the research:

RQ1: What are the challenges of introducing the Nordstrom model to an IT team?
RQ2: How can we improve the Nordstrom model to fit better in an undergraduate environment?
RQ3: What is the impact of applying DT, Lean and Agile in an IT team?

In order to answer these questions, the Nordstrom Model was introduced in one IT team which was incubated at BlackBerry Tech Center Recife (Brazil). The team was composed of two developers and one designer. The Tech Center was chosen because of the possibility to monitor teams in daily activities for one year. Although the research was carried on a small sample, the authors were present in all phases of the development process. The decision of having a small sample was made because the authors would like to be as close as possible to the team in order to evaluate better the introduction of the model.

An action research (Susman and Evered 1978) was carried out because it emphasizes collaboration between researchers and practitioners. In addition, the action researcher is concerned to create organizational change and simultaneously to study the process. The Nordstrom Model was chosen because it uses DT, Agile and Lean to cover the entire process of developing software. The team followed this model to develop a mobile game - Pet Empire game.

4 Testing the Model

4.1 Pet Empires – 1st Cycle

The first cycle lasted three months, and the startup followed the Nordstrom model. In this time, the team didn't receive a brief from Blackberry. Thus, they had to think what challenge would be addressed. The option chosen was: How can we develop an interesting game?

The team went through all the model's steps. As a result, a mobile game was developed in which cats and dogs would fight against each other in turns (similar to chess). The value proposition was to deliver a quick game for people who have little time available to play. To verify if the final product was good enough to be released, the game was presented to the International Game Developers Association Recife (a local group of game developers). Pet Empires received a bad evaluation by the community due to its poor gameplay. The team analyzed the reasons that led to the errors pointed out.

Firstly, the team noticed the gameplay was very complex, and one match could last weeks. This result contradicts with the game's value proposition which was to deliver a quick and easy game for busy people. Secondly, the team analyzed the development process to find out what exactly pushed them away from the users' need. Further analysis showed that the team did not consider the users' needs throughout the implementation phase. This was caused mainly because the Nordstrom model did not offer enough support to contrast the new findings against previous reports about the users.

4.2 Pet Empires – 2nd Cycle

The second cycle aimed to solve the previous problems, this time the Nordstrom model was modified to use DT practices in the entire process, not only in the beginning. The game was released in four months, and it is available on Kongregate. To evaluate the game, the team organized a launch event where more than 40 people who no previous knowledge of the game had participated in a competition. All those people who attended the event completed a questionnaire about the game. Moreover, they were observed while playing to identify facial expressions of satisfaction or dissatisfaction. A total of 93 % users would play again which shows how the user experience was highly positive. In addition, the game was challenge and difficulty in a right level to a casual game. Because of that, most of the users felt satisfied with the game.

Although the second cycle took more time, the result was better than the first one. The use of design thinking in the entire process offered a better way to solve micro problems since it provides a set of techniques on how to approach the users in case of doubts. Thus, the team stopped guessing, then started to collect more precisely answers. The modifications done in the Nordstrom model resulted in (a) game with greater acceptance from the users, and (b) an easier way to understand the "insights" and "frame opportunities" phases.

5   Conclusion

This study investigated the challenges of applying the Nordstrom Innovation Lab's Model to IT development. The model was used by a team of three Computer science undergraduate students to develop a game. The main results suggest that: (a) during the prototype phase the team should validate the user experience by using an interface that is closest to the final product, and (b) Design thinking should be used in the entire process of the Nordstrom Model. Understanding the challenges faced by IT teams to combine Design Thinking, Agile and Lean Startup is critical to help the industry and literature on how to improve software development. For IT teams, knowing how to overcome the challenges when adopting design thinking will help them to improve their software development processes and launch more innovative products. For the literature, this study contributes on (a) how a combination of design thinking with IT development would look like; (b) the implications of the adoption of design by undergraduate students; (c) the improvement of the Nordstrom Innovation Lab's model.

Future work should focus on using the model to develop new software, thinking about monetization, hence try to sell it. Besides that, to help teams understand design thinking, a set of tools should be developed to teach and support the process.

Acknowledgement. Authors would like to thank BlackBerry and the entire staff of BlackBerry Tech Center Recife, especially Pet Empires development team: Alexandre Cisneiros, Luiz Araujo and Pedro Dias.

References

Brown, T.: Change by Design: How Design Thinking Transforms Organizations and Inspires Innovation. Harper Business, New York (2009)

Boland Jr., R.J., Collopy, F.: Design matters for management. In: Boland Jr., R.J., Collopy, F. (eds.) Managing as Designing, pp. 3–18. Stanford University Press, Stanford (2004)

Grossman-kahn, B., Rosensweig, R.: Skip the silver bullet: driving innovation through small bets and diverse practices. In: Leading Through Design, 815 p. (2012)

Kowark, T., Hger, F., Gehrer, R., Krger, J.: A research plan for the integration of design thinking with large scale software development projects. In: Leifer, L., Plattner, H., Meinel, C. (eds.) Design Thinking Research. Understanding Innovation, pp. 183–202. Springer International Publishing, Switzerland (2014)

Lindberg, T., Meinel, C., Wagner, R.: Design thinking: a fruitful concept for it development? In: Meinel, C., Leifer, L., Plattner, H. (eds.) Design Thinking. Understanding Innovation, pp. 3–18. Springer, Heidelberg (2011)

Martin, R.: The Design of Business: Why Design Thinking Is the Next Competitive Advantage. Harvard Business School Press, Boston (1995)

Paternoster, N., et al.: Software development in startup companies: a systematic mapping study. Inf. Softw. Technol. **56**(10), 1200–1218 (2014). Elsevier

Susman, G.I., Evered, R.D.: An assessment of the scientific merits of action research. Adm. Sci. Q. **23**, 582–603 (1978)

Attracting Consumers' Attention and Interest in Exploring: Does HCI Strategy Matter?

Eugenia Huang[1(✉)], Sheng-Wei Lin[2], and Yu-Han Wu[1]

[1] Department of Management Information Systems,
National Chengchi University, Taipei, Taiwan
huang.eugenia@gmail.com, doraemon13013@gmail.com
[2] Department of Computer Science and Information Management,
Soochow University, Suzhou, Taiwan
larman520@gmail.com

Abstract. The aim of this study is to understand the best approaches for drawing consumers' attention and triggering their interest in exploring marketers' offerings. Human-computer interaction (HCI) strategies, which are widely adopted by online marketers, are categorized into two dimensions: intervention mode and interaction scheme. Intervention mode refers to the way that marketing messages intervene in the activities of online consumers, whereas interaction scheme refers to the communication acts required from consumers after the initial intervention. A within-subjects experiment is used in this study.

Keywords: HCI strategy · Intervention mode · Interaction scheme · Consumer attention · Online advertising · Exploring interest

1 Introduction

Business companies try to communicate with consumers through various marketing channels. Advances in Web technology have enabled marketers to use more aggressive ways of contacting potential customers in the online environment. Online users are exposed to massive amounts of information with either active or passive intentions. Aiming to understand what kind of approach can better draw consumers' attention and trigger their interest in exploring marketers' offerings, this study investigates the human-computer interaction (HCI) strategies that are widely adopted by marketers. We argue that HCI strategies have an important effect on consumers' reactions. Rather than measuring advertising effectiveness, we narrow the research scope to observe the relationship between advertising and real-time reactions, i.e. how to attract customers' attention and interest in exploring. Focusing on real-time reactions provides a more in-depth understanding of how advertising affects the explosion of advertising (Fig. 1).

Electronic devices have a revolutionary evolution in both functionality and usability. The penetration of mobile devices and services has led to the transformation of online business from e-commerce to m-commerce. Traditional electronic devices and mobile devices differ not only in their physical size, but also in their use of scenarios and HCI methods (physical keyboard vs. touch screen). Providing insight into the distinction is increasingly important, especially for companies who rely on

© Springer International Publishing Switzerland 2016
C. Stephanidis (Ed.): HCII 2016 Posters, Part I, CCIS 617, pp. 35–39, 2016.
DOI: 10.1007/978-3-319-40548-3_6

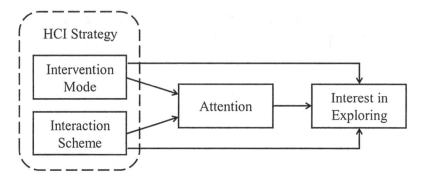

Fig. 1. Research model

online channels. Hence, to understand the HCI strategy in the mobile context, the goals of this research are as follows:

1. What are the dimensions of HCI strategy?
2. How does HCI strategy affect customers' reactions within a mobile context?
3. What combinations of HCI strategy can best draw customers' attention and trigger their interest in exploring?

2 Literature Review

2.1 Communications and HCI Strategy

Communication Model. Marketing is the process of communication between a marketer and consumers or business partners. According to the Shannon-Weaver communication model [1], noise may occur in the communication channel. When mobile electronic devices are used as the channel of communication, the issue of reducing noise is related either to device problems or to the interaction between human and device. Therefore, HCI issues should be considered in communication.

Interactivity. William et al. [2] proposed that interactivity has three characteristics: control of the content and subsequent communication, the sender and receiver can exchange roles and they have the potential to converse with each other. A new approach to online advertising, referred to as "call to action" (CTA), displays a button in an advert that invites receivers to click if they want more information. The design of CTA makes it possible for marketers to control the content and subsequent steps. When the receiver pushes the CTA button, the message "I'm willing to learn more" is sent back and a conversation begins between the two parties.

Intervention. Ducoffe [3] found that irritation had a negative effect on advertising value and attitudes toward advertising. Other researchers have found similar results. Edwards et al. [4] suggest that advertising intrusiveness increases advertising avoidance. Furthermore, Tsang et al. [5] state that attitudes toward advertising are only positive if advertising is permitted by customers. These results emphasize the intervention aspect of advertising. Rather than using the terms irritation and intrusiveness, we prefer to use "intervention" to represent our meaning, as we approach this issue from an HCI perspective.

HCI Strategy. To identify HCI strategies, two dimensions are considered: intervention mode and interaction scheme. Intervention mode refers to the way that marketing messages intervene in the activities of online consumers, whereas interaction scheme refers to the communication acts required from the consumers after the initial intervention.

After viewing a wide range of advertising, we categorize the intervention mode into three types based on how the advertising intervenes in the customer experience: vertical, parallel and overlap modes. In the vertical mode, advertising interrupts the customer's surfing experience fully or partially, as in a pop-up window or must-read advert, he/she has no choice about being exposed to the advertising, like two streams (advertising stream and customer experience stream) that intersect and conflict. Banner advertising and title sponsorship belong to the parallel mode because this type of advertising does not interrupt customers' surfing experience but occupies and exists parallel to customer experience. In the overlap mode, the advertising overlaps with the customer's experience, neither forced exposure nor occupied an area, adverts merge with the customer's experience. To be more specific, native advertising and placement advertising can be classified into the overlap mode.

We divide interaction scheme into two types based on the communication acts required from consumers and refer to them as read-oriented and action-oriented. CTA can be categorized in the action-oriented scheme because it is designed to make the customer perform an action (click action) on the advertising. Traditional graphic design, which is still widely used in the online environment, can be categorized as a read-oriented scheme because the only communication act required from the consumer is reading.

2.2 Information Processing and Customer Behavior Model

Information Processing Model. An information processing model is used to describe the human processing that takes place after receiving information. McGuire [6] proposed six stages of human information processing: presentation, attention, comprehension, yielding, retention and behavior. We focus on the presentation and attention processes because they are involved in HCI in advertising.

Customer Behavior Model. Hall [7] proposed the AIDMA (Attention, Interest, Desire, Memory, Action) customer behavior model. With the growth of the Internet, Dentsu [8] adapted the model to the AISAS (Attention, Interest, Search, Action, Share) model to fit the Web 2.0 era. The attention and interest stages are an essential part of both models, regardless of the progress in technology.

Attention and Interest in Exploring. Attention has become a scarce resource since people have become used to living with an information glut due to the growth of information technology. Besides attracting customers' attention, as a bridge between attention and searching, it is also important to trigger customers' interest in exploring. Because arousing curiosity is a common and efficient way of inducing an interest in exploring, a CTA scheme offers not only interactivity but also partial information exposure, which is one of the factors that induces curiosity [9].

3   Research Methodology

3.1   Research Framework

Drawing on existing theories and literature, a research model is developed to explain the relationships between HCI strategies, consumers' attention and consumers' interest in exploring.

3.2   Research Design

This study aims to identify HCI strategies in online advertising within a mobile context. Because every Internet user is exposed to online advertising, we examine our model in a general sample. To ensure the external validity in this study, we conduct a field experiment as our research method rather than laboratory experiment.

Experiment Design. This study followed a 3 × 2 within-subjects factorial design. The three levels of intervention mode (vertical, parallel and overlap mode) were represented as pop-up advertising, banner advertising and native advertising, respectively. The two levels of interaction scheme (read-oriented and action-oriented scheme) were manipulated as graphic advertising with detailed information and CTA advertising with simple information and an action button. Eligible participants were those who used mobile devices to surf the Internet. To avoid advertising bias between participants, a within-subjects experiment was used.

Experiment Procedure. First, we provided some basic instructions about the experiment, such as "We need participants in a mobile context," "Participants who surf the Internet using mobile devices are suitable for this research," "You will be invited to a webpage, please enjoy using it as you usually would." To confirm the manipulation of the mobile context, the webpages were designed to fit a mobile screen size. In addition to the webpage design, we recorded the exposure time on the experiment page and the participants' device features using programming language as one of the manipulation checks. After viewing the experimental material, the participants were required to answer manipulation check questions and were then invited to answer some questions and provide demographic information.

4 Discussions

This study aimed to categorize online advertising from an HCI perspective. After reviewing the literature, HCI strategies were categorized into intervention mode and interaction scheme. Our findings suggest that marketers should consider their HCI strategy while planning online advertising or digital marketing. Furthermore, while HCI plays an important role in the computer field, our study shows that the marketing field should not overlook the importance of HCI issues, which are important for gaining customers' attention and interest in exploring.

References

1. Shannon, C.E., Weaver, W.: The mathematical theory of information (1949)
2. Williams, F., Rice, R.E., Rogers, E.M.: Research Methods and the New Media. Simon and Schuster, New York (1988)
3. Ducoffe, R.H.: Advertising value and advertising on the web. J. Advert. Res. **36**(5), 21–35 (1996)
4. Edwards, S.M., Li, H., Lee, J.H.: Forced exposure and psychological reactance: antecedents and consequences of the perceived intrusiveness of pop-up ads. J. Advert. **31**(3), 83–95 (2002)
5. Tsang, M.M., Ho, S.C., Liang, T.P.: Consumer attitudes toward mobile advertising: an empirical study. Int. J. Electron. Commer. **8**(3), 65–78 (2004)
6. McGuire, W.J.: Personality and attitude change: an information-processing theory. In: Psychological Foundations of Attitudes, pp. 171–196 (1968)
7. Hall, S.R.: The advertising handbook; a reference work covering the principles and practices of advertising (1921)
8. Dentsu Inc.: Digitization changing the consumer purchasing process: From AIDMA to AISAS. http://www.dentsu.com/ir/marketing/pdf/AR2006_E6.pdf. Accessed 15 October
9. Berlyne, D.E.L.: Conflict, Arousal, and Curiosity. McGraw-Hill Book Co, Maidenherd (1960)

Reflecting on Expertise, a Key Factor When Designing for Professional Development in Informal Science Institutions

Priscilla F. Jimenez Pazmino[1]([⊠]), Leilah Lyons[1,2], Brian Slattery[2], and Benjamin Hunt[2]

[1] Department of Computer Science,
University of Illinois – Chicago, Chicago, USA
{pjimen5,llyons}@uic.edu
[2] Learning Sciences Research Institute,
University of Illinois – Chicago, Chicago, USA
{bslatt2,bhunt7}@uic.edu

Abstract. Informal Science Institutions (ISIs) like museums and zoos are increasingly employing mobile technology to support their interpretive staff (explainers). One approach to designing technology to support existing tasks is participatory design (PD), where end-users are involved as experts in the task domain who can help envision the application of technology. Our participatory design sessions engaged explainers from two different ISIs, with different levels of expertise and age (youth and adults). We implemented a socio-technical PD approach in engaging participants in examining and proposing features for a Facilitation, Reflection, and Augmented Interpretation Mobile System (FRAIMS). Involving novices and emerging professionals in participatory design is as important as involving experienced and expert participants, especially when designing in supports for professional development. Our analysis highlights the benefit of considering the level of expertise of participants as a key factor that shapes a design, having as a result, different supports for the design of the mobile interpretation application.

Keywords: Participatory design · Mobile tools · Museums · Interpreters · Expertise · Professional development

1 Introduction

Our research group has studied how mobile technology can be adopted to improve interpretation at Informal Science Institutions (ISIs), like museums and zoos. Since explainers are a diverse population in terms of expertise and age, we had to think about how our designs would serve users with different levels of professional expertise, and in turn, what design methods we should use to elicit design requirements from users with different levels of professional expertise.

One approach to designing technology to support existing tasks is participatory design methods, where end-users are involved as experts in the task domain who can help envision the application of technology. However, novices and emerging

© Springer International Publishing Switzerland 2016
C. Stephanidis (Ed.): HCII 2016 Posters, Part I, CCIS 617, pp. 40–45, 2016.
DOI: 10.1007/978-3-319-40548-3_7

professionals have unique needs even though they lack advanced expertise with the task domain. Involving them in design is important, but (as other HCI researchers have noted) the design process may need to be altered to support their successful participation. In our prior work, we examined how the structure of Participatory Design sessions could impact the design contributions made by non-experts [7]. In this paper, we examine in more depth the types of design requirements generated by participants with varying levels of professional expertise. Although it might seem controversial, since by definition non-experts may not have a deep understanding of their work tasks, through this work we have come to consider non-expert explainers to be an important and distinct group of participants who could share their perspectives and add to the design. This work describes the results of including of youth novices and emerging professionals in participatory design sessions.

For the purpose of this research, we differentiated novices, emerging professionals and experts based on the years and frequency they had worked as explainers. An explainer is labeled as novice when he/she has performed interpretation for visitors for less than one year in an ISI. We stress the word youth when the novices are enrolled in high school/college and are less than 21 years old. They are labeled as experts when they have worked in the ISI as a full staff member for more than two years and performed as explainers in a daily basis or equivalent, or they are responsible for the training and supervision of the ISI interpretive programs. An emerging professional is anything in between a novice and an expert.

2 Background and Prior Work

2.1 Museum Context: Challenges of Supporting Interpretation in Informal Learning Science Institutions

Explainers are front-line informal educators—often a mix of adult full-time and youth part-time employees—who help museum guests learn from exhibits at ISIs, while also introducing additional learning goals that deepen guests' engagement [9]. Explainers scaffold guest learning through the use of analogies, visual aids, or simplified thematic statements [5]. However, novice and volunteer explainers generally lack the rich knowledge of exhibit content [4], or the pedagogical content knowledge [10] necessary to engage in these practices. Unfortunately, explainers have little time for structured professional development, and are rarely the focus of evaluation. Most of their professional development occurs in fleeting on-the-job conversations [8], which represents missed opportunities for reflecting and building on explainers' experiences at a programmatic level. Explainers need extensive exposure to gain understanding of the diversity and range of guest backgrounds, interests, and behaviors [4], which creates gaps between more novice and more expert explainers.

2.2 Participatory Design Methods

In the museum context, few researchers have seen the value of including participants such as teenagers or children in the design process [2, 6, 11] alongside curators and museum staff. In [11], researchers found that youth participants—including youth explainers—had trouble taking control in projects involving adults and supervisors. These difficulties only faded after extensive time was spent on the project, which is a luxury of time that few youth-collaborative projects have available. Our methodological approach involves centering the contributions of youth novice explainers, in sessions where they are perceived as the main contributors of design ideas. This approach is meant to elicit explainers' contributions as both employees and users, by having them reflect on their own prior practice. Youth explainers are seen as experts about their own professional context, as they face unique challenges that might not be noticed by their more expert peers.

2.3   How Novices Are Different from Other Target Populations

Novices can be distinguished from experts by their relatively shallow training, lack of experience, disorganized domain knowledge, and insufficient metacognitive skills [3]. Explainers, like other learners, need support with noticing problems with their learning process, reflecting on what they do and don't know, and adjusting their behavior based on these determinations. Developing these metacognitive skills is highly important for explainers' professional development. With the characteristics of novice explainers as a guide, we designed participatory design sessions that should support explainers' focus and ability to express rich design contributions. We applied Socio-technical Systems (STS) theory [1] to craft participatory design sessions incorporating sociotechnical strategies such as role-play (e.g. demonstrations of the intersecting technical and social aspects of working designs), well-defined task-focused activities (e.g. technology-supported brainstorming and design activities around specific goals) and expert scaffolding for idea organization (ensuring that discussion is goal-aligned, without overriding or evaluating participants' design contributions). In this way, our participatory design approach should hopefully yield desirable and practical design recommendations that benefit novice interpreters.

3   Design Studies

We devised a participatory design approach to better elicit design contributions from non-expert participants using a socio-technical framework, detailed further in [7]. We enacted this participatory design approach in two different ISIs: a large zoo and a medium-sized science center, each located in a major metropolitan area with a diverse audience. Details of the sessions can be seen in Table 1. The participatory desgin framework – fully implemented in session III – aims to facilitate the elicitation process to take advantage of the inclusion of non-experts in participatory design sessions, by implementing socio-technical strategies: (1) starting the activity with a role-play scenario in a real setting and (2) including an outside expert to scaffold the organization and categorization of ideas.

Table 1. Participatory design sessions

Participatory design sessions	Session I (Zoo)	Session II (Zoo)	Session III (Science Center)
Participants (explainers)	Experts (7 participants) 19–63 years old	Novices (12 participants) 14–17 years old	Novices and in-development (8 participants) 16–22 years old
Initial exhibit example	Introduction of an interactive exhibit that uses a mobile interpretation tool and that the explainers participants have experience facilitating for visitors	Demonstration of a mobile interpretation tool used to start an interactive exhibit/game and to summon digital content that complements the game experience	Role play in-situ to demonstrate the mobile interpretation tool working with an exhibit that display interactive visualization of census data
Help during categorization process	None	Scaffolded by outside expert explainer	Scaffolded by outside expert explainer

3.1 Protocol

The workshops sessions were about 2–3 hours long. Each session began with a short pre-survey to gather information about participants' confidence and comfort sharing ideas, as well as basic demographic information. This was intended to identify differences in the explainers' level of expertise. Next, the facilitators of the session (members of the research team) introduced themselves, the workshop goal, and the general idea behind mobile support to be designed. After this introduction, the facilitators followed the guidelines of the socio-technical framed session; each involved idea generation, idea categorization, paper-prototyping of designs, and sharing of designs with the group. The participants focused on three main areas/themes of the Tablet Support Tool (TST) design: (1) categorization and grouping of resources/features used when having discussions with visitors; (2) ways in which explainers can use the TST to seek help during interpretation; (3) ways in which explainers can use the TST to seek help after interpretation.

4 Data Collected

Participants generated paper prototypes designs of different features, being this a visual way they can communicate their needs. These were drawn on pages showing an outline of an iPad frame, or freehand on blank paper. From the discussions of the design paper prototypes and drawings, a set of 19 unique functional requirements were captured during the workshops, such as: "An interactive map of the venue (along with exhibit information)", "Fun fact category", "List of activities/ideas to share/ask based on age",

"Recording interaction with visitors", "Rating of exhibit material", "Create a virtual space where explainers can chat, message each other, or manage schedules with the mobile," among others. These requirements were categorized and quantified based on the phase of interpretation (Preparation, Enactment, or Reflection) they belong to, see Table 2.

Table 2. Amount of functional requirements by interpretation phase. Columns E:Expert, I: In-development, N:Novice.

Phase of Interpretation	Amount of functional requirements per phase	E	I	N
Preparation	4	1	4	3
Preparation / Enactment	2	-	2	1
Enactment	5	3	5	4
Enactment / Reflection	1	-	1	-
Reflection	6	-	6	1

We can see that the in-development interpreters suggested the majority of the functional requirements, and that these requirements covered all phases of interpretation. Experts reported almost no need for reflection or preparation to be implemented in a mobile tool, even though they are very knowledgeable of reflection time as being important for professional development. Expert explainers expressed that current practices of getting verbal feedback during occasional meetings and right after an enactment are enough – and while this may be enough for *them* to reflect on their practice, it seems that non-experts did not necessarily share this view.

Also, expert explainers did not suggest a significant number of features that would assist them in the preparation phase, in contrast to novice and in-development explainers who reported ideas such as: "Allow access to share documents that everybody can share and edit", "An interactive map of the venue (along with exhibit information)", "Have a diagram of the exhibit with detailed information", among others. This suggests that experts my take for granted their familiarity with the institution's exhibits and their content; whereas non-experts clearly expressed a need for reference material to help them develop this familiarity.

5   Conclusion and Future Work

This paper implemented a theory-derived participatory design technique for eliciting requirements from youth emerging professionals and examined the nature of the design requirements suggested by participants with different degrees of expertise. The performed participatory design sessions used two strategies informed by socio-technical systems theory (role-play scenario in a real setting, and discussion guidance by an expert) to elicit design recommendations from non-experts. Our data shows that participants with different levels of expertise contributed to the generated set of requirements in different ways. Previous work [12] has demonstrated how children's context expertise can influence the resultant designs in participatory design; here, we suggest that "domain expertise" is also an important factor to consider in participants when running participatory design sessions.

We believe novices and emerging professionals are a key population to include as contributors in participatory design sessions for technology that aims to improve their professional development. Although they do not have the same expertise level, the same amount of on-the-job experience, or level of reflection on their practice as experts have, youth non-experts can bring to the discussion perspectives that might be missed by experts. In a sense, novices and emerging professionals are bringing their own kind of "expertise" to the design: their intimate knowledge of the types of supports they need to reach professional goals set for them by their institutions.

References

1. Applebaum, S.: Socio-technical systems theory: an intervention strategy for organizational development. Manag. Decis. **35**(6), 452–463 (1997)
2. Axelsen, L.V., Mygind, L., Bentsen, P.: Designing with children: a participatory design framework for developing interactive exhibitions. Int. J. Incl. Mus. **7**(1), 1–16 (2015)
3. Bransford, J., Brown, A.L., Cocking, R.R., National Research Council (U.S.): How People Learn: Brain, Mind, Experience, and School. National Academy Press, Washington D.C (1999)
4. Diamond, J., John, M.S., Cleary, B., Librero, D.: The exploratorium's explainer program: the long-term impacts on teenagers of teaching science to the public. Sci. Educ. **71**(5), 643–656 (1987)
5. Ham, S.H.: Environmental Interpretation: A Practical Guide for People with Big Ideas and Small Budgets. Fulcrum Publishing, Golden (1992)
6. Iversen, O., Smith, R.: Scandinavian participatory design: dialogic curation with teenagers. In: Proceeding IDC 2012, pp. 106–115. ACM Press (2012)
7. Jimenez Pazmino, P., Slattery, B., Lyons, L., Hunt, B.: Designing for youth interpreter professional development: a socio technologically-framed participatory design approach. In: Proceeding IDC 2015, pp. 1–10. ACM Press
8. Motto, A.: Peer learning: a strategy for practical explainer training. J. Sci. Commun. **7**(4), 1–5 (2008)
9. Pattison, S.A., Dierking, L.D.: Staff-mediated learning in museums: a social interaction perspective. Visit. Stud. **16**(2), 117–143 (2013)
10. Shulman, L.S.: Those who understand: knowledge growth in teaching. Educ. Res. **15**(4), 4–14 (1986)
11. Taxén, G.: Introducing participatory design in museums. In: Proceeding PDC 2004, vol. 1, pp. 204–213. ACM Press (2004)
12. Yip, J., Clegg, T., Bonsignore, E., Gelderblom, H., Rhodes, E., Druin, A.: Brownies or bags-of-stuff? Domain expertise in cooperative inquiry with children. In: Proceeding IDC 2013, pp. 201–210. ACM Press (2013)

Study on the Relationship Between Mental Model of Designer Team and Factors in Remote Collaboration

Wu Jing[(⊠)]

Hangzhou, Zhejiang, China
`wuwuquiet@163.com`

Abstract. At present, the Computer Supported Cooperative Work (CSCW) has been used in many industries, and in the field of design, more and more remote collaborative design requirements of the multinational design resources, also requires a corresponding technical products and systems as a powerful support. The development of related technologies of remote cooperative work, must well consider interactive cognition of team members when work remotely as well as the interrelation between it and the system function, structure, interface, environment and other factors. This paper is aimed to explore and analyze the real relationship between the designer team mental model and the influence factors in the remote collaborative environment.

Keywords: Gray correlation analysis · Mental models · Factors · Design team · Remote collaboration

1 Introduction

The application of cloud technology and the remote communication, which supported by the strong computing power, make it possible to design work in different places. It can be predicted that in the future there will be more and more creative work in different places. And creative activities based on team work, a long-distance real-time, interdisciplinary background of collaborative design work, already are one of the development trends based on mobile networks.

At present the major mainstream Internet companies in the resources to the mobile end of the slant, and strive to replicate the success of the PC side, but the development of mobile Internet time is shorter, interactive design in the short term for mobile devices there are still shadows the PC side, the emergence of mobile device characteristics It does not match the problem, which greatly affects the user experience. For designers, the "move" is full of possibilities, if the design discussed in different places during real time, designers urgent need for high-quality visual experience to interact with the mobile terminal, in time, space be able to experience a different "World."

© Springer International Publishing Switzerland 2016
C. Stephanidis (Ed.): HCII 2016 Posters, Part I, CCIS 617, pp. 46–51, 2016.
DOI: 10.1007/978-3-319-40548-3_8

2 Theoretical Research

2.1 Mental Models

Mental model refers to the individual's environment and its expected behavior of mental representation, including the individual's cognitive structure, knowledge structure or knowledge base [1]. Mental model in an individual growth process through the formation of long-term learning, after the formation of imperceptible change is not easy, it is a way of thinking and ideas implicit in the depths of the individual heart, directly or indirectly affect the individual's behavior. Mental models designers can learn from five aspects [2]:

Designer solved is "no clear design issues that were not clearly defined problem";

Designer style model is to solve the problem "solution focused" (Looking from various aspects, deepening the best solution);

Designer style way of thinking is "creative" (inspiration, unconscious, nonverbal thinking);

Designers use the "code" to convert the abstract demand and figurative forms (Code: graphically oriented, sketches, renderings, models, etc.);

Designers use the "code" to read and write, convert creation language.

2.2 Team Mental Models

The concept of team mental model was first proposed by Cannon-Bowers and Salas [3], they think the team mental model refers to the team members have knowledge of the structure, which allows team members to team work to form a correct interpretation and expected to coordinate their actions in order to meet the needs of teamwork and other team members.

Figure 1 shows the four types of team mental models proposed by Cannon-Bowers and Salas (2000) [3].

Type of mental models	Content	stability	Remark
Equipment or technology	Device Function Operating procedures Limitations equipment Possible failures	high	Most stable mental model, but the effective functioning of this team do not ask
Team task	Task program Accident Task Scenario Tactics Environmental constraints	in	Consistency is critical in highly programmed tasks, team members will agree with each other, in the process of low task, whether it can reach
Team interactions	Role responsibilities Information Sources Interactive mode Communication channels Role Interdependence	in	Its degree of consistency will affect the level of the team members how to communicate and coordinate, adaptable team doing well in this regard
Teammates	Teammate knowledge Teammate skills Teammate ability Teammate hobby Teammate habit	low	Good knowledge of his teammates can help team members to adjust their behavior to adapt to the characteristics of his teammates

Fig. 1. Four types of team mental models (Source: Cannon-Bowers and Salas 2000)

2.3   Factors of Team Mental Models

Many factors affect the team mental models inside and outside, Kraiger and Wenzel proposed four categories of factors theoretically [4] (Fig. 2):

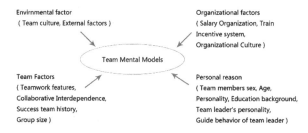

Fig. 2. Factors affecting team mental models (Source: Kraiger and Wenzel [4] and homemade)

It shows the details diagram of factors and team mental models below (Fig. 3).

Factors		Team Mental Models	
Envirnmental factor	Team culture Cultural Orientation External factors Emphasis on team	Device Function Operating procedures Equipment limitations Possible failures	Device
Organizational factors	Organizational Culture Salary Organization Incentive system Train	Teammates knowledge Teammate skills The ability of teammates Teammate hobby Teammate habit The attitude of teammates Teammate faith	Teammates
Team Factors	Teamwork features Collaborative Interdependence Success team history Team set the length of time Group size (Number of members) Team Type	Task procedures accident The Situation Tactics Environmental constraints (remote)	Task
Personal reason	Team members sex, Age Personality Education background Team leader's personality Guide behavior of team leader	Roles Information Sources Interactive mode Communication channels Role Interdependence	Team interaction

Fig. 3. Factors and team mental models (Source: Kraiger and Wenzel [4] and Cannon–Bowers and Salas 2000 and homemade).

2.4   Features Design Activities Under CSCW

CSCW originally proposed by the United States DEC's Paul Cashman and MIT's Irene Grief in 1984 [5], and its main contents for the study of how to use the computer, multimedia technology and network communication technology to support the work of team members to work together in a shared environment, through discussions and exchange, division of labor, work together to complete the task [6]. According CSCW system, teamwork is divided into two dimensions: time and space [7]. As shown below (Fig. 4):

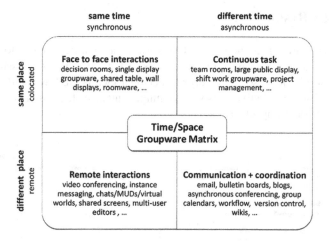

Fig. 4. Collaborative work under CSCW (Source: http://en.wikipedia.org/wiki/CSCW)

3   Research Methods

3.1   Questionnaire Survey

The main problem for the team mental model and influencing factors, the target user: software product designers, ordinary designer based.

Research objectives:

1. Identify the relationship between team mental models and factors.
2. Dig out the potential demand for designer team under remote collaborative environment.

Recycling: The 102 valid questionnaires
Questionnaire design:(Part of the questions)
Part I: basic personal information
Example: Company size: A under 500 B 500–2000 C more than 2000
Part II: Teamwork information
Example: If the company emphasis on team work together
Part III: personal perception of teamwork
Example: Your understanding of the attitude of the team members.

3.2   Grey Correlation Analysis

Gray correlation analysis method, based on the degree of similarity or dissimilarity between the trends of factors, namely the "gray correlation degree", a method as a measure of the degree of association between factors [8]. 102 questionnaires data were analyzed using this method.

4 Research Result

As can be seen from Fig. 5, the influence of various factors. Personal factors, in which the influence of a dominant position, regardless of the "teammates", " team task " or "team interaction." This also can be drawn: personal factors are low stability, dynamic variables; so if some effective personal training, guidance, team mental models will have a more positive impact.

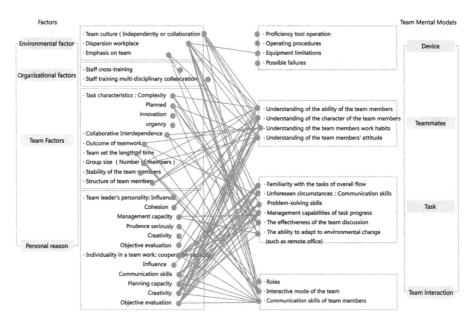

Fig. 5. Factors and team mental models cross-impact diagram (Source: Grey Correlation Analysis and homemade).

Other factors such as environmental factors - "the dispersion of the team work-place", which for equipment and technology have higher requirements, and accordingly, for interactive mode, know each other and communication, have a quite challenge. In addition, the culture, emphasis on collaboration will also affect the team's daily interaction model, understand, implement tasks.

Therefore, the impact factor is the superposition of multiple factors acting on the design team mental models, not one simple influence, if you want to form a highly efficient team mental models, which inevitably from where to find the relevant factors, targeted to guide their influence trend.

References

1. Norman, Donald A.: The Design of Everyday Things. Basic Books, New York (2002)
2. Cross, Nigel: Designerly Ways of Knowing. Springer, London (2006)
3. Cannon-Bowers, J.A., Salas, E.: Shared mental models in expert team decision making. In: Castellan Jr., N.J. (ed.) Individual and Group Decision Making: Current Issues, pp. 221–246. Erlbaum, Hillsdale (1993)
4. Kraiger, K., Wenzel, L.H.: Conceptual development and empirical evaluation of measures of shared mental models as indicators of team effectiveness. In: Brannick, M.T., Salas, E., Prince, C. (eds.) Team Performance Assessment and Measurement, pp. 63–84. Erlbaum, Mahwah (1997)
5. Wilson, Paul: Computer supported cooperative work (CSCW): origins, concepts and research initiatives. Comput. Netw. ISDN Syst. **23**, 91–95 (1991)
6. Grudin, J.: CSCW Introduction. Comm ACM **34**(12) (1991)
7. http://en.wikipedia.org/wiki/CSCW
8. http://baike.baidu.com/link?url=WlxSDoxMjCZySecxvgBiPs6RmDKKJO5VcEuQVa6FeOldqxTyPOBZL0qLM2-t78CtczfRZjYxZ_EmHj5rpYrUxa

A Conceptual Research Agenda and Quantification Framework for the Relationship Between Science-Fiction Media and Human-Computer Interaction

Philipp Jordan[1(✉)], Omar Mubin[2], and Paula Alexandra Silva[3]

[1] University of Hawaii at Manoa, Honolulu, USA
philippj@hawaii.edu
[2] SCEM Western Sydney University, Sydney, Australia
o.mubin@westernsydney.edu.au
[3] Maynooth University, Maynooth, Ireland
paula.alexandra@nuim.ie

Abstract. The use of science-fiction movies and series to stimulate and generate real-world technological innovations and devices is often utilized by Human-Computer Interaction researchers, user experience professionals and science educators. It is widely acknowledged that science-fiction has had an impact on the development of interactive technology. However, this impact has neither been fully conceptually developed nor quantitatively determined. This research aims to provide a conceptual research agenda for the relationship between science-fiction and Human-Computer Interaction. To advance this agenda, we introduce a possible quantification framework utilizing scientometric analysis, in particular, citation- and keyword analysis of peer-reviewed publications in Computer Science to quantify the reciprocal connection of science-fiction media and Human-Computer Interaction.

Keywords: Creativity · Design fiction · Foresight · Future visions · Human-computer interaction · Interaction design · Science-fiction · Science-fiction prototyping · Scientometrics · STS · Technology assessment

1 Introduction

The relationship and synergy between popular science-fiction (Sci-Fi) movies and series and real-world Research and Development (R&D) has been acknowledged within the scientific community, with the latter often using the earlier as inspiration for its projects and endeavors. In this study, we discover traces, identify evidence and review relevant state-of-the-art research in media and academia to recognize synergy effects of this bi-directional relationship Sci-Fi visualizations and real-world science.

In particular, we focus on the field of Human-Computer Interaction (HCI) located within the extensive Computer Science area. In the first part of this research, we give an account of the relationship between Sci-Fi and R&D through explicit referral and examples of Sci-Fi movies and series in popular news as well as scientific proceedings

C. Stephanidis (Ed.): HCII 2016 Posters, Part I, CCIS 617, pp. 52–57, 2016.
DOI: 10.1007/978-3-319-40548-3_9

and publications, extending notions of anecdotal evidence. We further mention applied professional associations and computer science education studies to substantiate an account of the undeniable impact of Sci-Fi media on the inspiration and creativity of scientists and vice-versa. We then condense these recent efforts in a comprehensive, but conceptual research agenda to study, advance and systematically put a figure on this relationship. To do so, we propose a quantification framework and outline measurements to study the charted relationship and conceptual research agenda of HCI and Sci-Fi media.

2 Background

Sci-Fi movies and series have depicted innovative devices and technologies well ahead of their initial conceptualization in R&D. In this section, we draw upon the broad fields of Science, Technology, Engineering and Mathematics (STEM), and in particular the field of Computer Science and HCI to show how these utilize and intersect with Sci-Fi movies and series in a variety of ways.

For instance, Metropolis, a German Sci-Fi dystopia from 1927 shows one of the earliest depictions of a video phone call. Stanley Kubrick's movie, 2001: A Space Odyssey, reportedly engaged multiple science advisors on the production of the movie. According to Kirby's research [12], anthropologists, aeronautical engineers, nuclear physicists as well as statisticians advised on the production of the space epos. In parallel, more than 50 consultations with private companies, government agencies, university groups and research institutions were undertaken by the production staff. The goal was to accurately depict space science and technology, supercomputers, future interfaces and the possible event of a technological singularity. Spielberg's Minority Report is yet another example of this mutual relationship, with the movie depicting highly personalized technologies, such as targeted advertising and biometrics as well as innovate gestural interfaces. The latter are attributed to John Underkoffler, a MIT researcher, whose gestural interfaces in Minority Report have been adopted by Boeing as a *"spatial operating system featuring gestural input and high-definition graphical output to analyze large data sets in real time"* [18]. Christopher Nolan, the director of Interstellar, recently collaborated with the world-renowned theoretical physicist Kip Thorne [25]. Thorne, collaborating as technical advisor and executive producer, helped to accurately portray what life on a Mars space station would be like. Contemporary Sci-Fi movies, such as Her and Ex Machina extend depictions of artificial intelligence, consciousness and humanoids in future societies to both, illustrate forthcoming science, technology and society (STS) issues and question the ethics of probable robot-human relationships.

The improvement and availability of special effects technologies for movies and post-production techniques, such as chroma-keying, computer-generated imagery, computer animation and virtual cinematography become an everyday tool for movie productions. Depending on the budget, Sci-Fi movie productions can draw on an unlimited and unprecedented number of visualizations toolkits and techniques to showcase future societies in Sci-Fi movies and series. For instance, Schmitz et al. [20] determine three key factors contributing to the applicability of interaction design in Sci-Fi movies which are: (i) the available special effects technologies, (ii) the available budget and (iii) the overarching importance of the role of technology within the movie itself. Academic research has gradually recognized the interdisciplinary intersection of HCI, interaction design, Computer Science and STEM fields with Sci-Fi media. As Perkowitz [19, p. 215] states: *"interactions between science and science-fiction involve books as well as movies. Books are better than films at conveying complex ideas [...] but the enormous power of films to reach millions can't be downplayed."*

In conjunction with these links, Kirby [13] presents a series of qualitative studies on the collaboration of film-makers and real-world scientists. Further studies have discussed the emergence of HCI and Sci-Fi movie collaboration frameworks [12, 20] as well as the growing liaison of scientists and filmmakers [22]. Additionally, empirical studies on the topic found correlations between classroom creativity and Sci-Fi media [15] as well as the potential value of Sci-Fi media for computer-science higher education [8].

Likewise, the importance of stories and constraint-free reasoning is discussed extensively by Bleecker [4], Tanenbaum [24], Dunne and Raby [6] and Lindley and Coulton [16] concluding in the emergence of design fiction. Design fiction, although a contested term is generally understood as a method of critical design to develop fictional and narrative scenarios to envision, explain and raise questions about possible futures for design and society while neglecting any technical constraints or feasibility.

In many regards, the technical feasibility of a Sci-Fi technology has not prevented scientists from deductive reasoning and action towards possible real-world implications. For example, physics students calculated the energy necessary for a 'death star' planet destroyer from the world-wide known Star Wars franchise [5]. In a more applied sense, the practicality of the technologies, devices, interfaces and interactions portrayed in Sci-Fi movies and series have been investigated as means to delineate Sci-Fi heuristics and design patterns in multimodal, fictional interfaces [21].

Moreover, professional HCI and interaction design associations, such as the User Experience Professionals Association (UXPA) [26] as well as STEM periodicals, such as the Biochemist Society [3], have published special issues on Sci-Fi and interaction design, design fiction and the utility of Sci-Fi in the classroom and elsewhere.

3   Conclusions

In conclusion, we present both, a conceptual research agenda that combines Sci-Fi media and HCI in addition to a quantification framework of the said agenda.

The center of this agenda constitutes the growing relationship between HCI and Sci-Fi media, which gives an account of a bi-directional synergy between both fields, as outlined in section two. This bidirectional relationship is enclosed in six distinct items. We present and discuss each of these item briefly to reflect on their importance in facilitating innovative HCI research.

In addition, we propose a quantification framework to measure the relationship between Sci-fi movies and series and real-world R&D to quantify and assess aspects of this conceptual research agenda to, for instance, highlight specific fields within STEM which have a stronger or weaker correlation with Sci-Fi production in terms of inspiration, collaboration, economies, pedagogic opportunities and scientific production.

3.1   A Conceptual Research Agenda of HCI Advancement and Sci-Fi Media

First of all, the audiovisual presentation of technologies, interfaces and interactions within a strong narrative to depict potential applications, technologies and futures build the core of our proposed research agenda. The interchange of scientists and film-makers can both, facilitate representations of technology and devices for inspiration and evaluation in HCI research and advance real-world technology as well [18, 21].

Second, we acknowledge and built upon concurrent research programs on this core relationship of HCI in conjunction with Sci-Fi movies and series as well as vice-versa [12, 13, 20]. However, these agendas neglect, or do not consider, any potential methodology, in particular a quantification framework, to measure these relationships across, for instance, Computer Science subtopics.

Third, our research agenda recognizes educational and pedagogical opportunities of Sci-Fi for innovative HCI and Computer Science schooling as evidenced in evolving university curricula, such as Sci-Fi based prototyping courses [14] as well as the advent of new methods, for example design fiction [16] and Sci-Fi prototyping [9].

Fourth, we identify emerging economies and job markets for scientists as the new role of researchers as part of movie productions has been poorly researched. In the context of previous studies which show long-lasting and general collaboration arrangements of scientists and movie producers [12, 13, 22], we identify specific and incremental developments. For example, standardization efforts of the position titles of scientists on Sci-Fi movie credits currently range from 'technical advisor' to 'science consultant' to 'futurist' despite the fact that scientists are occasionally not referred at all.

Fifth, the broader socio-technical impact of Sci-Fi on emerging HCI technologies and subtopics through studies of STS. For example, emerging R&D areas, such as artificial intelligence, robotics or cybersecurity [14] and the cinematic depiction of the said may well be related to the perceived technology readiness of the audience. For instance, Sci-Fi movies and series stereotypically depict either a utopian future vision with seamlessly integrated technologies which benefit the many or society as a whole or – in stark contrast – a dystopian setting, where information and communication technologies are appropriated by a few for base motives such as surveillance or oppression.

Sixth, the recognition and consideration of the dominance of western Sci-Fi movie productions or 'Hollywood' neglecting niche productions from, for instance India, Russia, China or Japan as well as independent studios [17]. The notion of this cultural bias is part of our conceptual research agenda while in the meantime the impact on scientists, audiences and the whole popular culture may well be studied through STS research.

3.2   A Quantification Framework of HCI Research and Sci-Fi Media

Current research lacks of an effective methodology to quantify the outlined bidirectional, multi-faceted relationship between HCI and Sci-Fi in all its aspects and evolutions. Among others, the primary aim of this exploratory study is to establish a ground truth for a quantification framework of the link between HCI and Sci-Fi movies and series. To address this imminent research gap, we aim to deliver a first of a kind measure of the central research question of our conceptual research agenda, that is to say a quantification of the mutual relationship between both fields.

To do so, we propose to use a combination of tools in a pilot study of a selected sample of HCI relevant, peer-reviewed collections. Specifically, we propose using keyword analysis, text mining and citation analysis of a sample of referred publications of established HCI collections. The process is roughly outlined below:

1. In a first step, we propose title and key-word/meta-data analysis through a dictionary (for example Sci-Fi, future visions, movie titles, advisor titles etc.) to identify and filter very closely related papers who inform on the relationship of HCI and Sci-Fi media.
2. In a second step, we intend to use text mining and qualitative content analysis of the sampled papers to understand the context of the cited Sci-Fi concept in relation to the HCI research more detail. For example, we can determine which subtopics of HCI, such as mobile computing, robotics, wearables or virtual reality more frequently refer to Sci-Fi media in comparison to other fields. This should allow us to explore why certain subfields are more prone to mention Sci-Fi movies and series than others.
3. In a final step, we suggest citation analysis of identified publications in the previous steps to trace related research in the publication itself and the domain under review and link, for example, research curricula of authors or institution affiliations to our analysis.

In summary, we believe that a combination of the afore-mentioned approaches will - in an ideal case scenario - provide us with an improved and measurable understanding of the impact and mutual relationship of Sci-Fi media and HCI research.

References

1. Bates, R., Goldsmith, J., Berne, R., Summet, V., Veilleux, N.: Science fiction in computer science education. In: Proceedings of the 43rd ACM Technical Symposium on Computer Science Education (SIGCSE '12), pp. 161–162. ACM, New York (2012). doi:10.1145/2157136.2157184
2. Bergman, E., Lund, A., Dubberly, H., Tognazzini, B., Intille, S.: Video visions of the future. In: Dykstra-Erickson, E., Tscheligi, M. (eds.) Extended Abstracts of the 2004 Conference, p. 1584
3. Biochemical Society: The Biochemist. Science Fact and Science Fiction, vol. 34
4. Bleecker, J.: Design Fiction: From Props to Prototypes (2010)
5. Boulderstone, D., Meredith, C., Clapton, S.: That's no moon. J. Phys. Spec. Top. **9**, 195–196 (2010)
6. Dunne, A., Raby, F.: Speculative Everything. Design, Fiction, and Social Dreaming. MIT Press, Cambridge (2013)
7. Figueiredo, L.S., Gonçalves Maciel Pinheiro, M.G., Vilar Neto, E.X., Teichrieb, V.: An open catalog of hand gestures from Sci-Fi movies. In: Begole, B., Kim, J., Inkpen, K., Woo, W. (eds.) The 33rd Annual ACM Conference Extended Abstracts, pp. 1319–1324
8. Goldsmith, J., Mattei, N.: Fiction as an introduction to computer science research. Trans. Comput. Educ. **14**, 1–14 (2014)

9. Johnson, B.D.: Science Fiction Prototypes Or: How I Learned to Stop Worrying about the Future and Love Science Fiction. In: Callaghan, V., Kameas, A., Reyes, A., Royo, D., Weber, M. (eds.) Intelligent Environments 2009 – Proceedings of the 5th International Conference on Intelligent Environments, pp. 3–8. IOS Press, Barcelona (2009)
10. Johnson, B.D.: Science fiction prototypes or: how I learned to stop worrying about the future and love science fiction (2009)
11. Kaye, J., Dourish, P.: Special issue on science fiction and ubiquitous computing. Pers. Ubiquit. Comput. **18**, 765–766 (2014)
12. Kirby, D.A.: Lab Coats in Hollywood. Science, Scientists, and Cinema. MIT Press, Cambridge (2011)
13. Kirby, D.: The future is now: diegetic prototypes and the role of popular films in generating real-world technological development. Soc. Stud. Sci. **40**, 41–70 (2010)
14. Kohno, T., Johnson, B.D.: Science fiction prototyping and security education. In: Cortina, T. J., Walker, E.L., King, L.S., Musicant, D.R. (eds.) The 42nd ACM Technical Symposium, p. 9
15. Lin, K.-Y., Tsai, F.-H., Chien, H.-M., Chang, L.-T.: Effects of a science fiction film on the technological creativity of middle school students. Eurasia J. Math. Sci. Technol. Educ. **9**, 191–200 (2013)
16. Lindley, J., Coulton, P.: Back to the future. In: Lawson, S., Dickinson, P. (eds.) The 2015 British HCI Conference, pp. 210–211 (2015)
17. Marcus, A.: The history of the future. Interactions **20**, 64 (2013)
18. Overby, S.: Boeing Adopts Sci-Fi Data Manipulation Mode. http://www.cio.com/article/ 2395557/business-intelligence/boeing-adopts-sci-fi-data-manipulation-model.html
19. Perkowitz, S.: Hollywood Science. Movies, Science, and the End of the World. Columbia University Press, New York (2010)
20. Schmitz, M., Endres, C., Butz, A. (eds.): A survey of human-computer interaction design in science fiction movies (2008)
21. Shedroff, N., Noessel, C.: Make It So. Interaction Design Lessons from Science Fiction. Rosenfeld Media, Brooklyn (2012)
22. Smaglik, P.: Entertaining science. Scientific advisers for films and television help to bring credibility to the screen — and take some tangible and intangible benefits back to the lab. Nat. Careers **511**, 113–115 (2014)
23. Stalenhoef, P.: Should films be scientifically accurate? In: RiAus Australia's Science Channel
24. Tanenbaum, J.: Design fictional interactions. Interactions **21**, 22–23 (2014)
25. Thorne, K.S., Nolan, C.: The science of interstellar (2014)
26. User Experience Professionals Association (UXPA): Science fiction. User Exp. Mag. **13**(2)

Technology Roadmap for Realistic Contents: The Korea Case

Sangil Kim[✉]

Korea Institute of S&T Evaluation and Planning, Seoul, Korea
cappy@kistep.re.kr

Abstract. Countries worldwide actively invest in state-of-the-art technology for new market creation to compete in the post-economic crisis era. Due to the advent of new services using smart devices and technology convergence, the importance of content technology is being emphasized. For a systematic response to this situation, systematic strategies and cooperation between government departments that invest in R&D are necessary conditions for maximizing the use of limited government financial resources and return on investment. However, technology roadmaps for realistic contents established by individual ministries lack linkages with national goals and do not provide clear guidance for the separate roles of government departments. Additionally, the existing national technology roadmaps for a realistic contents present only technology trees and timetables, which do not include supporting measures necessary for the practical application or commercialization of technology.

Therefore, this paper is focus on how the roadmap process can be used to develop long-term strategic planning and foster inter-ministry R&D cooperation for securing realistic content technology. In these terms, this paper will suggest an overall process to set up STR (Strategic Technology Roadmaps) for realistic contents, such as a roadmap format including policy-related supporting measures for technology commercialization and government R&D performance (legal systems, human resources training, infrastructure development). Finally, a process was presented to align the realistic content technology roadmap with the coordination of government R&D programs and budget allocation.

Keywords: Technology roadmap · Realistic contents · R&D cooperation · Government R&D

1 Introduction

With the international environment changing rapidly and uncertainty on the rise, state-of-the-art technology is increasingly becoming an essential component in development of the country and increase of competitiveness, not just for Korea and Japan which have limited resources but for the United States and China which have abundant geographical resources. Technology roadmap is a tool to secure state-of-the-art technology and it is used widely not only in private companies but also government ministries and various government-funded research institutes [1–3]. Technology roadmap helps the organization to deduce technologies they need to secure and share

© Springer International Publishing Switzerland 2016
C. Stephanidis (Ed.): HCII 2016 Posters, Part I, CCIS 617, pp. 58–63, 2016.
DOI: 10.1007/978-3-319-40548-3_10

the technological goals within the organization. Moreover, it allows long-term R&D planning and used as a tool for efficient R&D management [4].

Government ministries who process R&D programs implemented R&D roadmaps for each ministry to carry out their duties, however it has been pointed out that there is little connection to the vision and goal of the whole nation, and a lack of systematic assignments of duties among ministries. Despite this, there is not enough research on the activities regarding the government sectors' technology roadmap and utilizing them. Thus, this paper analyzes the strategic technology roadmapping program for the realistic contents technology that is conceived and implemented to promote the inter-ministry R&D cooperation in this Korean context..

2   Design of Strategic Technology Roadmap

In previous studies, the structuralized methodology in developing roadmaps can be divided into preliminary activity, development of TRM, and follow-up activities [5, 6]. In this study, this will be more segmented; there will be 3 stages of the preliminary stage, 8 stages of the development of TRM stage, and lastly the follow-up activities stages, totaling to 11 stages in steps to developing national strategic roadmaps. HCI 1 shows the details of each stage (Table 1).

Table 1. Strategic technology roadmapping process for realistic contents

Category	Steps
Preliminary	1. Definition of STR
	2. Organization of the project teams
Development of STR for inter-ministry R&D cooperation	3. Prospect on environmental changes and analysis of future demand for realistic contents technology
	4. Definition and scope setting of the technology
	5. Market status and prospect, technology status and competition circumstances analysis
	6. Vision and goal setting
	7. Core technology selection and research development goals setting of realistic contents technology
	8. Establishment of technology strategies
	9. Roadmap development
	10. Roadmap verification
Follow-up	11. Provide systematic device for periodic updates and implementation

3   Roadmap Development for Realistic Contents Technology

A simple format was used in the step to write up the roadmap to allow ease of understanding by those who will use the roadmap such as the policymakers of the government, planners for R&D planning, and researchers carrying out R&D in research institutes. Time horizon is over the course of 10 years from 2014 to 2023, divided into the near future until 2018 as stage 1 and 2019–2023 of further future as stage 2. In the near future, the upcoming changes are comparatively easier to predict, whereas the far future is comparatively harder to predict in a precise manner [7]. Also considering the current status of rapid changes in technology development, it is extremely difficult to develop a roadmap predicting the far future. Therefore this study presents a detailed time schedule is presented in stage 1 of near future and only the assumed point in time for technology development and strategy for stage 2. Common symbols used in the roadmap for each technology are shown in Table 2. The point where the bar-shaped arrow starts does not signify the starting point of R&D for the technology, but the necessity of increase in investment because R&D has taken off (Fig. 1).

Table 2. Technology and strategy layer format

Name	Diagram	
	Technology name	
Technology development method	Self-development	◎
	International joint development	●
	International technology implementation	◖
	International outsourcing	◗
Technology development agent	Led by government	G
	Led by private	P
	Collaboration between government and private	G+P
Technology Development stage	Initial	◆
	Application · development	◇
	Commercialization	◈

4 Roadmap Verification

STR encourages cooperation among the 14 ministries that are carrying out government R&D and is used as a guideline for governmental R&D budget distribution and adjustment, so it is very important to secure the objectivity and reliability of the STR.

This stage modifies and supplements to the roadmap written from stages previous to the roadmap implementation processes. Normally a roadmap consists of information collected from various sources and the information presented by each field's experts from the roadmap project team cannot be totally sufficient in predicting the future [7]. Thus the roadmap written by the roadmap establishment team requires multiple reviews and supplementing processes [7]. Especially STR encourages inter-ministry coopera-tion among 14 ministries carrying out R&D and is used in R&D budgeting distribution and adjustment, the securing objectivity and reliability is especially important.

This study carried out authentication work in 5 stages to improve the quality of the STR draft written by the roadmap establishment team. In the first step, the draft written

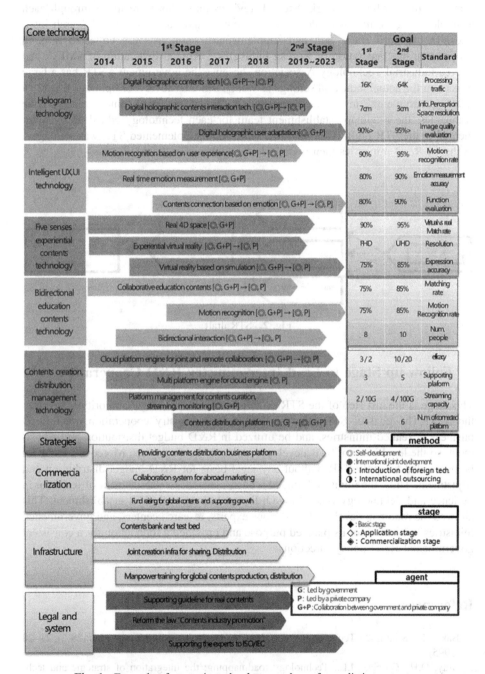

Fig. 1. Example of strategic technology roadmap for realistic contents

by the roadmap establishment team was sent to the 14 R&D governmental ministries to carry out the verification work. Second, reviews and edits were made through each technology's government funded research centers and national/public research institutes. In the third stage, edit and supplementary opinions were collected through cooperation by 'Federation of Korean Industries', 'Korean Federation of SMEs', and 'Korea Industrial Technology Association' because the government's STR has a large impact on the actual industrial settings as well. Then after review of opinions by the 14 R&D governmental ministries, government funded research centers, and private companies, the roadmap establishment team for each technology edited and supplemented to the STR draft. Afterward, the edited and supplemented STR was sent again to the 14 R&D ministries then reviewed and approved in final (Fig. 2).

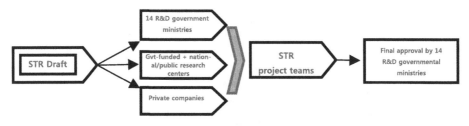

Fig. 2. STR draft

5   Follow-up Stage to Lead Inter-ministry R&D Cooperation

This stage is the last step of the STR establishment where a legal authority is given to the STR. The goal of STR is to encourage inter-ministry cooperation, plan R&D business in related ministries, and be utilized in R&D budget distribution and adjustment, so the legal basis of STR development has to be clearly set. Moreover, it cannot be demanded to apply STR without any legal basis for R&D budget distribution and adjustment. Thus, the ministry founded a basis clause for establishment of roadmap in 'Science and Technology Basic Law Ordinance' along with STR establishment. This allowed the roadmap developed by various experts, research centers, and governmental ministries to be used for its planned purpose and provided a foundation for a consistent governmental R&D policy direction.

References

1. Baker, D., Smith, D.: Technology foresight using roadmaps. Long Range Plan. **28**(2), 21–28 (1995)
2. Bray, O.H., Garcia, M.L.: Technology roadmapping: the integration of strategic and technology planning for competitiveness. In: Proceedings of PICMET 1997, Portland (1997)

3. Willyard, C.H., McClees, C.: Motorola's technology roadmap process. Res. Manag. **30**(5), 13–19 (1987)
4. Lee, S., et al.: Technology roadmapping for R&D planning: the case of the Korean parts and materials industry. Technovation **27**(8), 433–445 (2007)
5. Garcia, M.L., Bray, O.H.: Fundamentals of Technology Roadmapping. Sandia National Laboratories, Albuquerque (1997)
6. Strauss, J., Radnor, M., Peterson, J.: Plotting and navigating a non-linear roadmap: knowledge-based roadmapping for emerging and dynamic environments. In: Proceedings of East Asian Conference on Knowledge Creation Management, Singapore, 6–7 March 1998
7. Lee, J.H., Phaal, R., Lee, S.-H.: An integrated service-device-technology roadmap for smart city development. Technol. Forecast. Soc. Change **80**(2), 286–306 (2013)

Supporting Complex Decisions Through Selection of Appropriate Graphical Layout

Caroline Parker[1][✉] and Kendra DeBusk[2]

[1] Glasgow Caledonian University, Glasgow, UK
c.g.parker@gcal.ac.uk
[2] Genentech Inc., South San Francisco, CA, USA
kendrapad@yahoo.com

Abstract. Decision support tools are designed to improve a user's ability to take complex decisions and the choice of presentation format is highly relevant to this. Many papers have demonstrated a link between graphical format and decision choice but there has been less evaluation within the context of complex decision making and uncertainty. This study examines the impact of data representation (a) within a univariate and continuous choice decision context and (b) within a multivariate context with discrete choices. Participants in each study were randomly allocated to different display conditions and the impact of the display on their performance recorded, in (a) accuracy of the response and (b) the ease of decision making and comfort with the decision choice. The results suggest that while it is possible to identify graphical representations that produce better decision responses in a single-variable problem scenario this is not necessarily true in a multivariate discrete-choice situation.

Keywords: Visual representation · Graphical representation · Decision task · Complex decision-making · Non-expert user · Uncertainty

1 Introduction

Decision Support Tools (DST), defined in their widest sense, exist to support and where possible, improve, decision making. Many real life decisions and particularly those in disciplines such as health, agriculture and financial management are highly complex, multivariate and are taken under conditions of risk and uncertainty. Taking the wrong, or sub-optimal decision may be inconvenient, financially costly or in extreme cases have long lasting health implications. It is particularly important therefore that the information displayed to the decision maker is as clear as it can be. Many modern DST make excellent use of mathematical models to support decision makers in evaluating the implications of choice decisions. The experience of the user in relation to the format of the output from these models may however have an impact on the quality of the decision made.

© Springer International Publishing Switzerland 2016
C. Stephanidis (Ed.): HCII 2016 Posters, Part I, CCIS 617, pp. 64–68, 2016.
DOI: 10.1007/978-3-319-40548-3_11

2   Literature Review

While experts within the field may be familiar with model outputs those called upon to make decisions based on them may not be. In medicine for example, patients with a range of educational backgrounds are becoming increasingly involved in the clinical decision process [1].

Images and graphical representations can reduce cognitive load and increase the efficient processing of information [2] making data more accessible. The nature of the graph employed also has a determining impact on the outcome. Elting et al. [3] demonstrated that in deciding whether or not to continue clinical trials physicians were influenced more by the graphical format than the data.

In an early approach to the type of systematic research that some more recent authors call for [4] Ibrekk and Morgan [5] compared a range of graph types in supporting the decisions of non-experts in conditions of uncertainty. They concluded the best representation depended on the task and hypothesised that the best option might be a combination of cumulative probability density and probability density graphs. The current study tests their hypothesis and then goes on to explore the impact of display type in a more complex, multivariate decision context.

3   Study 1

Methodology
Forty-two non-expert participants (22 males, 20 females) randomly assigned to display conditions were shown graphical displays of meteorological data and asked to judge the likelihood of snowfall and advisability of travel. Six conditions were tested, the five most successful graphical types from the original Ibrekk and Morgan study (bar/column, pie, horizontal shaded probability density, traditional probability density, cumulative probability) and the combination graph Ibrekk and Morgan proposed but did not test (Fig. 1 and Table 1).

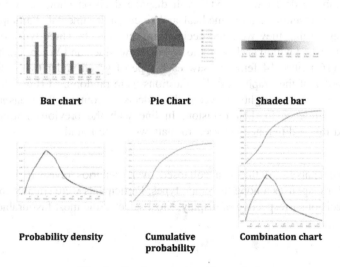

Fig. 1. Graph types tested in study 1

Results

Participants did well estimating the amount of snow using the pie chart, shaded graph, probability density graph, and the combined cumulative probability and probability density graph. Chi-square analysis showed a significant difference in the best estimates among the different types of graphs ($\chi = 45.9$, d.f. = 5, p < .001). There were also significant differences among the graphs for the responses to the probability of having more than a certain amount of snow ($\chi = 39.4$, d.f. = 5, p < .001 and the probability of the amount of snow being between two amounts ($\chi = 33.7$, d.f. = 5, p < .001).

Table 1. Percentage correct responses to questions requiring respondents best estimate, estimation of likelihood of more than given amount or probability between two amounts.

Decision task Display type	Best esti-mate	More than a giv-en amount	Between two amounts
Shade	81	7.1	0
Pie	83.3	59.5	50
Cumulative Prob.	26.2	14.3	19
Bar	59.5	26.2	21.4
Combonation Prob	76.2	26.2	14.3
Prob Density	78.6	14.3	21.4

4   Study 2

Methodology

This study explored the performance of bar, column and line graphs within more complex symbolic decision contexts, with discrete decision choices. A total of six scenarios were developed, three medical and three environmental. Participants were asked to imagine that they were the decision maker in each. Three types of decision question were asked within each scenario: What, How Much and When. Each of the 30 participants (16 males, 14 females) saw each type of graph under two different scenarios: the order of the graphs and the questions were randomized (Fig. 2).

As there is often no 'right' answer in these decision contexts the measure was the individuals confidence in their decision. In line with the previous findings it was hypothesised that a difference between formats would be found.

Results

A Chi-square analysis of the data collapsed over scenarios revealed no significant differences for responses among the graph types. Participants were equally comfortable with their decisions irrespective of display. Most selected the most favourable outcome (Table 2).

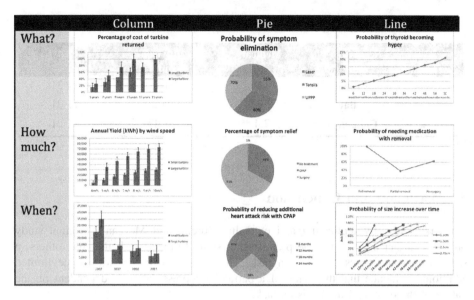

Fig. 2. examples of the graphical display types used in study 2 (Color figure online)

A post-hoc examination of the two types of scenario, environmental and medical did reveal some interesting trends. The data suggested an interaction between graph and scenario type, with a greater degree of confidence being expressed in the environmental scenarios and where a column display was used (Fig. 3).

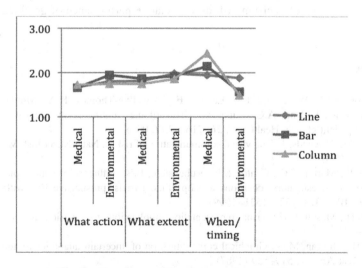

Fig. 3. Showing confidence means for graph types

Table 2. Showing mean scores for confidence for the representation types

Scenario Graph types	Medical	Environ- mental	All
Line	1.9	1.87	11.21
Bar	2.07	1.5	11.21
Column	2.4	1.47	11.21

5   Discussion and Conclusion

The first study, by replicating and extending Ibrekk and Morgan's original study provides further support for the premise that some formats are better than others in supporting some types of decision task. The second study provides some limited additional evidence that the value of a particular representation is dependent on the nature of the data, and the decision task.

It is possible that a ceiling effect may have masked differences between representation formats in the second study. Cognitive load could have been reduced by the participant's emotional engagement with the task, each person having some existing belief or experience which provided a cognitive short cut. However no objective measure of the tasks decision complexity was available and this makes it difficult to clearly interpret the results. Future work could explore this possibility.

These studies, particularly the first, support the work of others in identifying differences between graphical layouts in decision quality and decision confidence and underline the impact of decision task on the relative performance of graphical type.

References

1. O'Connor, A.M., Wennberg, J.E., Legare, F., Llewellyn-Thomas, H.A., Moulton, B.W., Sepucha, K.R., Sodano, A.G., King, J.S.: Toward the 'tipping point': decision aids and informed patient choice. Health Aff. **26**, 716–725 (2007)
2. Lipkus, I.M., Hollands, J.: The visual communication of risk. J. Nat. Cancer Inst. Monogr. **25**, 149–163 (1998)
3. Elting, L.S., Martin, C.G., Cantor, S.B., Rubenstein, E.B.: Influence of data display formats on physician investigators' decisions to stop clinical trials: prospective trial with repeated measures. BMJ **318**, 1527–1531 (1999)
4. Lurie, N.H., Mason, C.H.: Visual representation: implications for decision making. J. Mark. **71**, 160–177 (2007)
5. Ibrekk, H., Morgan, M.G.: Graphical communication of uncertain quantities to nontechnical people. Risk Anal. **7**, 519–529 (1987)

From Real Tombs to Digital Memorials: An Exploratory Study in Multicultural Elements for Communication

Vinicius Carvalho Pereira[1], Cristiano Maciel[2(✉)],
and Carla Faria Leitão[3]

[1] Department of Letters,
Universidade Federal de Mato Grosso (UFMT), Cuiabá, Brazil
viniciuscarpe@gmail.com
[2] Computer Science Institute, LAVI,
Universidade Federal de Mato Grosso (UFMT),
Av. Fernando Corrêa Da Costa, N°2367, Cuiabá, MT 78060-000, Brazil
crismac@gmail.com
[3] Semiotic Engineering Research Group (SERG), Informatics Department,
PUC-Rio, R. Marquês de São Vicente, 225, Rio de Janeiro, RJ 22451-900, Brazil
cfaria@inf.puc-rio.br

Abstract. This research is based on a semiotic analysis of tombs and tombstones in order to discuss elements that might be useful for software design, especially of digital memorials. In this research, Saussurean semiotics was considered.

Keywords: Digital memorials · Semiotics · Multicultural · Cemeteries · Tombstone

1 Introduction

The design of digital artifacts is aided by the use of real-world metaphors, so that elements from different cultures influence the characteristics of those software products. Some web applications have been developed to pay homage to deceased people; they are called digital memorials [2, 12, 19] and they bear some resemblance to physical memorials, which are tributes to specific individuals or groups. Likewise, cemeteries (with their tombs and tombstones) are places where corpses are buried and homages are paid.

By observing tombstones, memorials and cemeteries in various countries, one notices how differently built those tributes are in terms of content and expression. Besides, the objects visitors bring to those spaces, such as flowers and candles, vary from one culture to another, which shows distinct interactive patterns between the living and the dead, and between the living about the dead. Considering this scenario, it is clear that the most famous digital memorials in the web do not meet such cultural diversity.

© Springer International Publishing Switzerland 2016
C. Stephanidis (Ed.): HCII 2016 Posters, Part I, CCIS 617, pp. 69–77, 2016.
DOI: 10.1007/978-3-319-40548-3_12

In HCI, many researches have been carried out focusing on the impact of cultural factors in HCI design and on the support to developing multicultural interfaces and systems [15, 16, 18, 22]. But the study of digital memorials design and development is still new, unexplored and challenging. Therefore, the research project this paper is a part of is aimed at analyzing to what extent can the project of digital memorials allow different settings in terms of expression and content, through the use of diverse semiotic elements, so as to meet users' multiculturalism.

To do so, it is first necessary to adopt a clear and specific perspective towards the concept of culture. In consistency to the semiotic approach of the project, we herein adopt the definition of culture from interpretive or symbolic anthropology, according to Geertz [7], to whom culture is built as a web of significance in which human beings are interwoven and by means of which they are built. Thus, different cultural systems are different sets of meanings shared by a group of people, expressed by different signs. Differently from a universalist approach to culture, more common in HCI [9], cultural analysis is understood in our project as an interpretative process, looking for meanings.

In this initial stage of the process, we carried out a qualitative exploratory case study to better understand the design features of real-world artifacts, by observing photos of tombs and tombstones. Our goal is to identify preliminary interpretative elements by analyzing verbal and non-verbal signs used to describe the dead in those objects. In this stage of the research, Saussurean semiotics was considered [20]. Our intention is that these elements serve as conceptual scaffolds for future studies about the design and evaluation of digital memorials, where it may be possible to identify patterns and communicational paradigms for this domain.

2   Theoretical Background

Digital memorials are increasing in terms of popularity [13], possibly due to the new relationships they enable towards death, the dead and mourners, or maybe due to the fact they can be accessed from anywhere in the world, which differs sharply from the locative nature of physical memorials. Some digital memorials also permit that people leave virtual flowers, candles or even virtual prayers for the dead [13].

Lopes et al. [13] discuss recommendations for the design of software programs for digital memorials. The recommendations are divided into: a. modeling social network elements; b. allowing to pay homage to the deceased; and c. warranting cultural diversity. Based on practical recommendations for the design of digital memorials, prototypes were developed to discuss and improve the proposed recommendations.

However, a challenge upon designing such systems is the need to meet users' different expectations, built through cultural practices, toward death, which is a taboo issue that can even limit software engineers' capacities to find better design solutions to handle death and mortality [14].

For example, in the real world, diverse cultures build tombs with different shapes, sizes and colors, which are features that do not have mere functional reasons, but also semiotic ones [21]. A tomb has a certain size not only for a corpse to fit in it, but also to represent certain ideas of grandeur or unimportance, depending on the social role the deceased played in that society. Also, funerary art is very common in cemeteries of certain cultures [4]. That social practice of visiting cemeteries for aesthetical/cultural appreciation is called necro-tourism. The graveyards that attract most tourists in the world[1] are located in the USA, France, Italy, Czech Republic and Argentina.

Tombstones are also funerary architectural elements of semiotic relevance, as they convey a message from family and/or friends to other visitors of the cemetery, depicting the deceased and paying homage to him or her. Like tombs and funerary art, tombstones also vary a lot from culture to culture, both in terms of what it is said about the deceased (the content of the message) and how it is said (the expression of the message), by means of verbal and non-verbal signs, like colors, shapes and images.

A semiotic approach proves useful to analyze those data in tombstones, as it provides the analyst with conceptual tools to understand representations and meaning-making through signs, irrespective of their domain. Semiotics warrants scientific and systematic lenses for the analysis of signs of all sorts, whether they are visual, verbal, musical etc., so as to capture the processes through which they convey meaning [12]. As every culture is a sign system [11], understanding how meanings are conveyed within every culture and across different cultures allows us to design interfaces which meet different cultural codes, especially when it comes to controversial and taboo issues, such as death and bereavement.

The twentieth century saw the rise of different semiotic schools, and Computer Science, especially Human-Computer Interaction, has incorporated semiotic concepts, especially those from Peirce's [17], Jakobson's [10] and Eco's [5] semiotics, which serve as theoretical tools to understand how meaning is produced in computer interfaces through signs. The research herein carried out, aimed at analyzing the design of tombstones, uses concepts from Saussure's semiotics [20] to describe those objects, as detailed in the methodology section. Our intention is to elicit semiotic features from tombstones so we can apply them to the design of digital memorials in future research.

Saussurean semiotics relies on a bipartite definition of sign, according to Hjelmslev [8], composed of a signifier (an acoustic image, or the expression plane,) and a signified (a concept, or the content plane), which are two faces of the same entity, arbitrarily bound. That means the concept of death (signified) and the color black (signifier) are arbitrarily connected in Brazilian culture, for example, so this color is often used in funerals. However, there is nothing in the color itself that relates to death. The relation between a signifier and its signified is socially constructed.

3   Methodology

Considering the aforementioned concepts, we carried out a semiotic analysis according to the method proposed by Roland Barthes [1], who determined that the first step of a semiotic analysis consists in determining the sample of materials to be analyzed. As we are here conducting an exploratory research, so as to elicit semiotic elements from tombstones for further applications in digital memorials, we decided to make a contrastive analysis of three tombstones, from different countries: Mário de Andrade's, in

---

[1] http://goo.gl/gsxaDX.

Cemitério da Consolação (São Paulo, Brazil); Sarah John's, in the Hollywood Forever Cemetery (Los Angeles, USA); and Edith Piaf's, in the Père Lachaise Cemetery (Paris, France). These tombstones were chosen because they belong to famous deceased people, which might lead their communities to make a more refined use of semiotic symbols to pay homage to their death. Besides, we chose tombstones of people who died in the middle of the twentieth century. We decided to restrict our sample to such a period of time, so that we could compare tombstones from societies with fairly similar technological development in the Western world, so as to reduce the amount of extrinsic variables.

After deciding on the sample, the tombstones photographed were analyzed in the light of Saussurean semiotics [20]. Then, for each photo we mapped out its denotative level, describing its semiotic manifest features in syntagmatic and paradigmatic relations. Then, we outlined possible connotative relations some signs might evoke. In addition to that, we compared the semiotic structures of the three photos in order to identify recurrent patterns in the relation between signifiers and signifieds. Notice that, although Saussurean semiotics was developed with a view to verbal language, it can be used to analyze any kind of signs, since human interpretation of all signs can only occur mediated by language. Therefore, if the objects herein under analysis are not linguistic themselves, the understanding we can make out of them can only be mediated by words, and are therefore semiotically constrained.

4 Analyses and Discussions

In this section, we analyze each tombstone in terms of content and expression (signified and signifier, respectively) and then we proceed to a contrastive analysis between them.

The Brazilian tombstone (Fig. 1) belongs to the modernist writer Mario de Andrade, who participated in the renovation of literary language and forms in the beginning of the twentieth century in Brazil. The author is buried in one of the most traditional cemeteries of the country: Cemitério da Consolação.

Despite his fame, Mário de Andrade's tombstone has no original elements that refer to his contributions to Brazilian literature and arts. All it says is his name, birth date (marked by the symbol of a star) and death date (marked by the symbol of a cross). This is by far the most common template for tombstones in the country, although most contain the deceased's photo. The only original symbol of grandeur in this tomb is the material it is made of (black granite), along with the material the inscription letters are made of (brass). In Brazilian society, both materials connote respect and lordliness.

The non-verbal signs of the star and the cross also have second-level meanings, as each of them has a collateral signified besides indicating birth and death, respectively. The cross is traditionally associated with death in Brazilian society, irrespective of the deceased person's religion, through a metonymic relation with Jesus Christ's death on a cross. However, when placed upon a tombstone, that sign might convey a second-level meaning: the idea that, after death, Mário de Andrade Soul's might go to Heaven, like Christ's soul did, according to biblical discourse.

Moreover, if the cross has a highly conventional meaning in Brazilian societies, the same does not apply to stars, especially in the context of cemeteries. There is no social

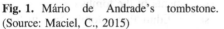

Fig. 1. Mário de Andrade's tombstone. (Source: Maciel, C., 2015)

Fig. 2. Sarah John's tombstone (Source: Maciel, C., 2015).

convention establishing a regular connotation for the sign of a star as a signifier for birth. Nevertheless, due to the linguistic value property, that sign gains meaning in contrast with the cross. If on a tombstone there are two dates and one of them represents the death date, the other one, irrespective of other non-verbal signs, must represent the birth date. Obvious as it may seem, such fact suggests that the representation of death is much more conventionalized in that society through the sign of a cross, so any other sign, in opposition to the cross, would assume the meaning of birth, even if a zero-sign (or no sign) were used before the first date.

In the bottom left corner of the tomb, one can also see a modern device to provide cemetery visitors with information about the deceased: QR-code tags integrated with MemoriAll software[2]. According to Cann [3], "QR codes transfer the dead from the cemetery to the realm of the living by giving the living a connection to the deceased that can be accessed anywhere".

Figure 2 shows Sarah John's tombstone, in the Hollywood Forever Cemetery, where some celebrities from the entertainment industry are buried. In terms of content transmitted by verbal signs, the template of this tombstone is far more open than the previous one: besides the deceased person's name and death date, it describes her job, skills, likes and even her last words. Curiously, it does not show her birth date, although this feature is commonly explicit in North-American tombstones. If we transpose that to digital memorials, it might suggest that the birth date field should not necessarily be filled in by a user building a memorial to a beloved deceased person. On the other hand, the death date should be compulsory, as it is part of the proof someone is really dead (and there is no need to prove someone dead was once born).

As to non-verbal signs, one notices the syntagmatic relation between two Jewish symbols on her tombstone: the seven-branched Menorah (the icon of a candelabrum on the top left corner) and the Star of David; both connotatively state her belonging to the Jew community, even after death. Her identity is also reinforced in the tombstone through a full-body photo, which overlaps meanings with the verbal message, like in the words "gorgeous" and "beautiful", which repeat (and emphasize) signifieds depicted by the photo.

---

[2] http://www.memoriall.com.br/0020X#.VxFm0dIrKUk.

Considering the non-verbal signs, we can also notice a paradigmatic relation between the Star of David in Fig. 2 and the cross in Fig. 3. These signs play homologous semiotic roles in their tombstones, as both mark death dates.

The design of this tombstone also foresees visitors' intention to leave material homages and mementos to the deceased in the brass vases attached to the stone for such purpose. Notice these vases are permanent elements and one of them contains an artificial flower, which also integrates the non-verbal elements of the tombstone.

Figure 3 shows Edith Piaf's tombstone, in the Père Lachaise Cemetery, the most famous graveyard in this country. Piaf was a famous singer of the chanson française genre, and her tomb is frequently adorned by mementos left by visitors, such as flowers or even a shawl, as can be seen in Fig. 3 adorning a vase on her tomb.

Fig. 3. Piaf's tombstone (Source: Maciel, C., 2014)

In terms of verbal elements, this tombstone differs from the others by showing not only the name she was worldwide renown after (Edith Piaf), but also as Madame Laboukas, which was her husband's surname. That suggests people may want tombstones not only to show the deceased's civil names, but also more affectionate terms, such as nicknames, pseudonyms or references to family and friends.

Besides, it is common in France to find tombstones that show full birth and death dates, but there are also those where only the years of birth and death are written. This also suggests the need to make the statement of birth and death dates more flexible in digital memorials.

As to non-verbal signs, this tombstone is made of the same materials (granite and copper) as the one in Fig. 1, again conveying meanings of grandeur and lordliness. In addition to that, one cannot disregard the syntagmatic relations between this tombstone and other architectural features on the tomb whereupon it lays. On Piaf's tomb, there is a big image of Jesus on the Cross, which ascribes the signified of Christianity to the deceased, and indirectly compares the holiness of her destiny to that of Christ's, in heaven, according to biblical discourse. The vase on the tomb, with Edith Piaf's initials carved, is also in a syntagmatic relation with her name on the tombstone, so that it is to Piaf that any flower therein is destined, similarly to the role the little attached vases played in the tombstone of Fig. 3.

A brief comparative analysis of these tombstones points out that tombstones, rather than mere pragmatic function, that is, to state who is buried in that grave, play refined semiotic roles, by allowing the bereaved to express condolences and affectionate feelings for the deceased. Small as the present sample may be, it shows the homages paid to the dead through tombstones is built by a careful sign display, both in terms of content and expression, and digital memorial systems should allow the same.

To begin with, a digital memorial should not present a single way of representing a deceased person's identity, and should have as little compulsory fields to fill in as possible. Issues related to different levels of privacy exposure are relevant to the design of digital memorials, along with the possibility to express different sides of public, familiar or artistic life, through varied signs. Due to the taboos and soft spots concerning death and mourning in different societies, some might want a photo of the deceased person to be available in the memorial; some might not. Likewise, if the field name should be necessarily filled in upon the creation of such a memorial, there should be another field for alternative names, nicknames, pseudonyms etc., as many people are known among their beloved ones by names which are not in civil registers.

This analysis also showed that people might want to add personal information about the deceased, such as likes, personal traits, job and skills. In pragmatic terms, those pieces of information cannot be considered homage to the deceased; instead, they are data about the dead person which are made available for those who had not known him or her. Thus, digital memorials must be designed not only with a view to paying homages, but also to fighting against oblivion, which requires passing information about the dead to people who had not met him or her in life.

Finally, the direct relation between death and religious culture emerges as a conceptual category. The possibility to express (or not) the deceased person's religion, as well as the possibility for mourners to pay homage to the dead through the meaning web of their culture, seem to be important issues in the design of digital memorials. The recommendations by Lopes et al. [13] include religion-related issues.

These analyses also show that the expression of birth and death dates is subject to variation. Although the death date (or year) was found in the three tombstones herein analyzed, the same does not apply to the birth date. The format of displaying these dates (whether in full or just by saying the year) was also variable, which might be considered upon designing digital memorials.

Rather than a merely verbal message, tombstones were also clad with non-verbal signs and surrounded by mementos left by people who visited those tombs. As one can choose the material a tombstone is made of, the font and size the message will be written in, the shape of the stone, symbols that should be added to it etc., digital memorials should allow for similar customization of the interface, as well model the possibility of people virtually performing interactions with the deceased, similar to those of people who visit cemeteries, like lighting candles, leaving flowers, polishing the tombstone, leaving unexpected gifts or praying.

5 Final Remarks

Creating digital memorials automatically based on data from existing profiles, like some social networks have done [6], bypasses the lack of management of the deceased user's profile. However, such automatic processes, like Facebook does, mixes information about the dead and homages paid to the dead, which are clearly separate in physical world memorial and funeral practices, like what is permanently written in a tombstone and the ephemeral discourses people may leave on a tomb, like flowers, paper-based messages or other mementos.

Such elements, along with funerary art in different countries, show habits and beliefs that should be further studied to support the design of spaces in the digital world. For example, how can one incorporate in design that in some Eastern countries stones are placed over tombs as homage? Would that be equivalent to posting the photo of a stone in the deceased person's profile or should this element be modeled within the system?

Finally, and considering the futures advances of this research, encompassing the analyses of cemeteries from other cultures (as well as other semiotic perspectives), we intend to propose requirements for software production in this area. Those recommendations are also expected to permit the customization of settings in such systems to better address users' memorial practices, which are currently carried out in cemeteries through tombstones.

References

1. Barthes, R.: Elements of Semiology. Hill and Wang, New York (1977). Translated by Lavers, A., Smith, C.
2. Brubaker, J.R., Hayes, G.R., Dourish, J.P.: Beyond the grave: facebook as a site for the expansion of death and mourning. The Information Society (in press)
3. Cann, C.K.: Tombstone technology: deathscapes in Asia, the UK and the US. In: Maciel, C., Pereira, V.C. (eds.) Digital legacy and interaction. Human–Computer Interaction Series, pp. 101–113. Springer International Publishing, Switzerland (2013)
4. Cannon, A.: The historical dimension in mortuary expressions of status and sentiment. Curr. Anthropol. **30**(4), 437–458 (1989)
5. Eco, U.: A Theory of Semiotics. Indiana University Press, Bloomington (1979)
6. Facebook Memorialization Request. https://www.facebook.com/help/contact/305593649477 238
7. Geertz, C.: The Interpretation of Cultures: Selected Essays. Basic Books, New York (1973)
8. Hjelmslev, L.: Prolegomena to a theory of language. Indiana University Publications in Anthropology and Linguistics (IJAL Memoir, 7), Baltimore. (2nd OD (slightly rev.), University of Wisconsin Press, Madison (1961)
9. Hofstede, G.H.: Culture's Consequences: International Differences in Work-Related Values. Sage Publications, London (1984)
10. Jakobson, R.: Style in Language (ed. Thomas Sebeok). MIT Press, Cambridge (1960)
11. Salgado, L.C.C., Leitão, C.F., De, S.C.S.: A Journey Through Cultures: Metaphors for Guiding The Design of Cross-Cultural Interactive Systems. Springer, London (2013)
12. Penn, G.: Análise Semiótica de Imagens Paradas. In: Bauer, M.W., Gaskell, G. (org.). Pequisa Qualitativa com texto: imagem e som. 10. Ed. Vozes, Petrópolis, RJ (2012)
13. Lopes, A.D., Maciel, C., Pereira, V.C.: Recomendações para o design de memórias digitais na web social. In: Proceedings of the 13th Brazilian Symposium on Human Factors in Computing Systems. SBC 2014, pp. 275–284 (2014)
14. Maciel, C., Pereira, V.C.: Digital Legacy and Interaction: Post-Mortem Issues. Springer Science & Business Media, Switzerland (2013)
15. Marcus, A.: Global and intercultural user-interface design. In: Jacko, J., Sears, A. (eds.) The Human-Computer Interaction Handbook, pp. 441–463. LEA, Mahwah (2002)
16. Nielsen, J.: Designing User Interfaces for International Use. Elsevier, New York
17. Peirce, C.S.: (CP) Collected Papers of Peirce, C.S., ed. by C. Hartshorne, P., Burks, W.A., 8 volumes, pp. 1931–1958. Harvard University Press, Cambridge, MA

18. Rau, P.: Internationalization, vol. 6775, pp. 94–103. Design and Global Development. Springer, Berlin/Heidelberg (2011)
19. Riechers, A.: The persistence of memory online: digital memorials, fantasy, and grief as entertainment. In: Maciel, C., Pereira, V.C. (eds.) Digital Legacy and Interaction: Post-Mortem Issues. Human–Computer Interaction Series (HCI), 1st edn, pp. 49–61. Springer, Switzerland (2013)
20. De Saussure, F.: Course in General Linguistics. Fontana/Collins, Glasgow (1977)

Capabilities Driving Competitive Advantage in New Product Development: Coordination Capability, Absorptive Capability, and Information Technology Capability

Yi-Ming Tai[1(✉)] and Yi-Cheng Ku[2]

[1] National Pingtung University, No.51, Min-Sheng East Road,
Pingtung 900, Taiwan
ymtai@mail.nptu.edu.tw
[2] Fu Jen Catholic University, No. 510, Zhongzheng Road,
Xinzhuang District, New Taipei 24205, Taiwan
023089@mail.fju.edu.tw

Abstract. Coordinating demand-side and supply-side partners' resources is critical for creating competitive advantage in new product development (NPD). Recently, the interorganizational coordination efforts have been further augmented through complementary investments in product lifecycle management (PLM). PLM provides an integrated collaborative product development platform that enables firms to effectively conduct complex and communication-intensive interorganizational coordination. The capabilities of coordinating demand-side and supply-side partners and of employing PLM system in interorganizational coordination are likely to be critical in determining firms' competitive NPD advantage. Hence, the first purpose of this study is not only to understand what the impact of coordination capability with demand-side and supply-side partners will be on competitive NPD advantage, but also to investigate how IT capability derived from implementing PLM systems shapes the role of coordination capability in creating competitive NPD advantage. Moreover, successful NPD requires firms to have highly developed absorptive capability allowing them to internalize and translate partners' knowledge into product development. Somewhat overlooked has been the moderating effect of absorptive capability on the competitive impact of coordination capability. Hence, this study's second purpose is to understand how absorptive capability shapes the role of coordination capability in creating competitive advantage in NPD.

Keywords: Coordination capability · Competitive advantage in new product development · Product lifecycle management system · Information technology capability · Absorptive capability

1 Introduction

Competitive advantage in new product development (NPD) refers to firms' ability to develop new products that outperform their competitors in the marketplace [12, 19, 23]. NPD involves various complex and interdependent activities, such as generating and

C. Stephanidis (Ed.): HCII 2016 Posters, Part I, CCIS 617, pp. 78–83, 2016.
DOI: 10.1007/978-3-319-40548-3_13

assessing various new product opportunities and ideas, translating product requirements into final design specifications, and launching product to market [8, 13]. Creating
competitive advantage in NPD requires firms to effectively collaborate with
demand-side and supply-side partners. Collaboration involves intense interorganizational processes that use coordination mechanisms to develop mutual understanding
between firms and their partners and to align the partners' activities with the firms'
objectives [1, 12, 24].

In the NPD context, researchers and practitioners have underscored the importance
of coordination capability and information technology (IT) capability to the success of
integrating demand-side and supplier-side partners' resources [8, 10, 14]. When NPD
takes place in supply chain context, the relationships between firms and the firms'
demand-side or supply-side partners have to be restructured to go beyond operational
efficiencies in order to create an environment that enables the firms to leverage their
partners' resources to develop new product [2, 3]. This has in turn created demand for
appropriate interorganizational coordination mechanism to support the complex interaction processes and to ensure information integration with demand-side and
supply-side partners. Coordination capability enables firms to tap into the pool of
external information, expertise and experiences held by demand-side and supply-side
partners help improve NPD performance. The greater coordination with demand and
supply-side partners results in the increased formation processing requirements, leading
to the heavy emphasis on firms' IT capability [3, 20, 25].

Numerous studies have investigated how IT capability and interorganizational
capability contributes to NPD performance (e.g., [8, 12, 13, 18, 23]). However, most of
prior research investigating coordination capability and IT capability has conceived of
them as operating independently with regard to their effect on NPD performance [3].
Less attention has been paid to how coordination capability with demand-side and
supply-side partners will be synergistically complemented by IT capability in their
impact on the creation of competitive advantage in NPD. There is growing doubt that
isolated organizational capabilities, however valuable, may not be effective as a single
asset, especially for complex interorganizational activities such as partner-oriented
NPD. Researcher has found that the value of organizational capabilities emerges from
complementarities [6, 7, 9]. When both IT and coordination capabilities are held, NPD
can benefit from their complementarity. IT capability is regarded as an effective
complement to coordination processes. Whereas firms may have developed strong
coordination capability with external partners, unless complemented by the adequate IT
capability, the firms are unlikely to yield the desired effects on competitive advantage
in NPD. Accordingly, this study first addresses the following question: *What will the
impact of coordination capability with demand-side and supply-side partners be on
competitive advantage in NPD? How does IT capability shape the role of coordination
capability in creating competitive advantage in NPD?*

Moreover, another contribution of this study is the emphasis on absorptive capability as a moderator in the relationship between coordination capability and competitive advantage in NPD. Absorptive capability refers to firms' ability to identify,
assimilate and exploit valuable knowledge received from external sources, such as
demand-side and supply-side partners [5, 22]. This study will address the issue of how
the effects of firms' coordination capability on competitive advantage in NPD can be

moderated by the firms' absorptive capability. Answering this question can make a contribution to the literature on the NPD performance impact. Furthermore, whether firms are able to internalize and translate transferred knowledge into their NPD process may crucially depend on their absorptive capability [11, 15]. Therefore, this study expects that the impact level of firms' coordination capability on competitive advantage in NPD will be moderated by the firms' absorptive capability. With this motivation, the second research question that this study will seek to address is: *How does absorptive capability shape the role of coordination capability in creating competitive advantage in NPD?*

2   Conceptual Background and Research Model

NPD involves various complex and interdependent activities that can be decomposed into discovery, development, and commercialization [8, 13]. Each of the NPD activities has different requirements, including market, design and manufacturing technology information collection and analysis as well as coordination with related NPD participants [3, 23, 24]. NPD success is driven by how demand-side and supply-side partners' resources are integrated and deployed in the NPD process [12, 19, 21]. Integrating partners involves intense interorganizational processes requiring firms to coordinate the partners' activities to ensure interoperability and seamless process synchronization [6, 16, 17]. Firms have to establish appropriate coordination mechanisms for facilitating mutual understanding with NPD partners and aligning the partners' activities with their objectives.

Moreover, successful NPD requires firms to harness new knowledge obtained from external sources (e.g., demand-side and supply-side partners) and to apply the new knowledge to understand market tendencies and to catch market opportunities [2, 4, 22]. Highly developed absorptive capability allows firms not only to find out about technological developments or business trends, but also to integrate external knowledge into their NPD activities [5, 11, 15]. Hence, this study suggests that creating competitive advantage in NPD requires three key organizational capabilities: coordination capability with demand-side partners, coordination capability with supply-side partners, and absorptive capability.

To address the research issues, this study draws on the resource-based view (RBV) to propose a competitive advantage impact model (Fig. 1) of complementary NPD drivers, encompassing coordination capability, absorptive capability, and IT capability. For establishing the impact model, this study will employ an integrated perspective from interorganizational coordination, IT-based business value and organizational learning to investigate how coordination capability with demand-side and supply-side partners influences competitive advantage in NPD and how IT capability and absorptive capability moderates the impact of coordination capability.

When considering interorganizational coordination capability required in the NPD context, the research model focuses on coordination capability with demand-side and supply-side partners. Moreover, absorptive capability and IT capability derived from Web-enabled interorganizational systems are regarded not only as the important factors in creating competitive advantage in NPD but also as the complements to moderate the

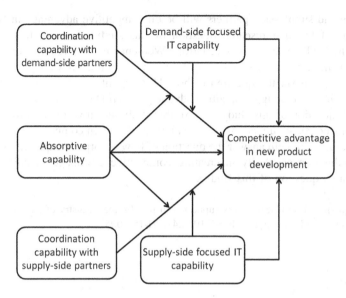

Fig. 1. Research model

effects of coordination capability with demand-side and supply-side. Specifically, the model evaluates (1) the impact of coordination capability with demand-side and supply-side partners on competitive NPD advantage, (2) the impact of IT capability derived from Web-enabled interorganizational systems on competitive NPD advantage, (3) the moderating effect of IT capability derived from Web-enabled interorganizational systems on the impact of coordination capability with demand-side and supply-side partners, (4) the impact of absorptive capability on competitive advantage in NPD, and (5) the moderating effect of absorptive capability on the impact of coordination capability with demand-side and supply-side partners.

3   Anticipated Contributions

This study focuses on investigating what the impact of coordination capability with demand-side and supply-side partners will be on competitive advantage in NPD and how absorptive capability and IT capability of Web-enabled interorganizational systems moderates the impact of coordination capability. For addressing the research issues, this study draws on the RBV to propose a competitive advantage impact model of complementary NPD drivers. Based on the literature analysis and a comprehensive study in the impact of coordination capability on competitive advantage in NPD and the moderating effect of IT capability and absorptive capability, this study will provide several contributions.

First, this study will investigate the ways through which coordination capability with demand-side and supply-side partners affect competitive advantage in NPD. The results will help answer the question of what the impact of coordination capability with demand-side and supply-side partners will be on competitive advantage in NPD (i.e., the first part of the first research question of this study). Second, this study will investigate how IT capability derived from Web-enable interorganizational systems moderates the impact of coordination capability on competitive advantage in NPD. The results will help answer the question of how IT capability shapes the role of coordination capability in creating competitive advantage in NPD (i.e., the second part of the first research question of this study). Third, this study will investigate how absorptive capability moderates the impact of coordination capability on competitive advantage in NPD. The results will help answer the question of how absorptive capability shapes the role of coordination capability in creating competitive advantage in NPD (i.e., the second research question of this study).

Acknowledgment. This research was supported in part by the Ministry of Science and Technology in Taiwan under the grant MOST 104-2410-H-153-005.

References

1. Arakji, R.Y., Lang, K.R.: Digital consumer networks and producer-consumer collaboration: innovation and product development in the video game industry. J. Manag. Inf. Syst. **24**, 195–219 (2007)
2. Bellamy, M.A., Ghosh, S., Hora, M.: The influence of supply network structure on firm innovation. J. Oper. Manag. **32**, 357–373 (2014)
3. Bendoly, E., Bharadwaj, A., Bharadwaj, S.: Complementary drivers of new product development performance: cross-functional coordination, information system capability, and intelligence quality. Prod. Oper. Manag. **21**, 653–667 (2012)
4. Escribano, A., Fosfuri, A., Tribó, J.A.: Managing external knowledge flows: the moderating role of absorptive capacity. Res. Policy **38**, 96–105 (2009)
5. Fabrizio, K.R.: Absorptive capacity and the search for innovation. Res. Policy **38**, 255–267 (2009)
6. Gao, T., Tian, Y.: Mechanism of supply chain coordination cased on dynamic capability framework-the mediating role of manufacturing capabilities. J. Ind. Eng. Manag. **7**, 1250–1267 (2014)
7. He, Y., Lai, K., Sun, H., Chen, Y.: The impact of supplier integration on customer integration and new product performance: the mediating role of manufacturing flexibility under trust theory. Int. J. Prod. Econ. **147**, 260–270 (2014)
8. Hilletofth, P., Eriksson, D.: Coordinating new product development with supply chain management. Ind. Manag. Data Syst. **111**, 264–281 (2011)
9. Johnson, W.H., Filippini, R.: Integration capabilities as mediator of product development practices-performance. J. Eng. Tech. Manag. **30**, 95–111 (2013)
10. Lindgreen, A., Maon, F., Vanhamme, J., Sen, S.: Sustainable Value Chain Management: A Research Anthology. Farnham, Gower (2013)
11. Liu, H., Ke, W., Wei, K.K., Hua, Z.: The impact of IT capabilities on firm performance: the mediating roles of absorptive capacity and supply chain agility. Decis. Supp. Syst. **54**, 1452–1462 (2013)
12. Mishra, A.A., Shah, R.: In union lies strength: collaborative competence in new product development and ITs performance effects. J. Oper. Manag. **27**, 324–338 (2009)

13. Pavlou, P.A., El Sawy, O.A.: From IT leveraging competence to competitive advantage in turbulent environments: the case of new product development. Inf. Syst. Res. **17**, 198–227 (2006)

14. Rai, A., Pavlou, P.A., Im, G., Du, S.: Interfirm IT capability profiles and communications for cocreating relational value: evidence from the logistics industry. MIS Q. **36**, 233–262 (2012)

15. Roberts, N., Galluch, P.S., Dinger, M., Grover, V.: Absorptive capacity and information systems research: review, synthesis, and directions for future research. MIS Q. **36**, 625–648 (2012)

16. Sinkovics, R.R., Kim, D.: The impact of technological, organizational and environmental characteristics on electronic collaboration and relationship performance in international customer-supplier relationships. Inf. Manag. **51**, 854–864 (2014)

17. Smith, A.D.: Successfully managing manufacturing supplier integration and procurement issues: case studies in recessionary environments. Int. J. Procure. Manag. **4**, 121–138 (2011)

18. Srivardhana, T., Pawlowski, S.D.: ERP systems as an enabler of sustained business process innovation: a knowledge-based view. J. Strateg. Inf. Syst. **16**, 51–69 (2007)

19. Stark, J.: Product Lifecycle Management: 21st Century Paradigm for Product Realisation. Springer, London (2011)

20. Tai, Y.M.: Competitive advantage impacts of direct procurement management capabilities and web-based direct procurement system. Int. J. Logist. Res. Appl. **16**, 193–208 (2013)

21. Thomas, E.: Supplier integration in new product development: computer mediated communication, knowledge exchange and buyer performance. Ind. Mark. Manage. **42**, 890–899 (2013)

22. Todorova, G., Durisin, B.: Absorptive capacity: valuing a reconceptualization. Acad. Manag. Rev. **32**, 774–786 (2007)

23. Troy, L.C., Hirunyawipada, T., Paswan, A.K.: Cross-functional integration and new product success: an empirical investigation of the findings. J. Market. **72**, 132–146 (2008)

24. Tsai, K.H.: Collaborative networks and product innovation performance: toward a contingency perspective. Res. Policy **38**, 765–778 (2009)

25. Wiengarten, F., Fynes, B., Humphreys, P., Chavez, R.C., McKittrick, A.: Assessing the value creation process of e-business along the supply chain. Supply Chain Manag. Int. J. **16**, 207–219 (2011)

Design and Implementation of Advanced HCI Education

Yi Yang[✉]

Tsinghua National Laboratory for Information Science and Technology, Department of Electronic Engineering, Tsinghua University, Beijing, China
Yangyy@tsinghua.edu.cn

Abstract. Existing HCI courses are usually designed for advanced undergraduates and graduates. And most of them do not have independent lab course. The practical parts are confined to the form of projects in the curriculum. This paper presents a new lab course called Media and Cognition and its lab platform. The new lab course is more appropriate and more general education for junior students with less professional knowledge. By using a larger, scalable and complete design of experiments, included five project modules and thirty-seven knowledge points, the lab platform integrates many contents of existing HCI courses, and offers more knowledge about media expression and human cognition to meet higher requirements of computer education. The other contributions of this work include: provides Open-Educational-Resources (OERs) for short-term foreign exchange students. Now the lab course has served more than one hundred students every semester. Over thirty pieces of achievements are produced in each year. The Statistics of feedback demonstrates that Media and Cognition and its lab platform can improve the students' ability of developing HCI projects.

Keywords: Media and cognition lab course · Human computer interaction · Media expression · Open educational resources

1   Introduction

Human Computer Interaction (HCI) courses are essential in computer education. There are a lot of existed HCI courses [1–3]. In generally, these courses are introduction to high-grade undergraduates or graduates (even Ph.D. level) to HCI research. The practical experience is given by some small research projects. There is no independent lab course offered. This paper presents a new lab course called Media and Cognition which is more suitable for junior students in the lower professional degree and range. And construct a richer scalable HCI lab platform. The Media and Cognition lab course is a flexible and fully experiments platform with five project modules and thirty-seven knowledge points, and has a OERs approach to ensure the self-study and other departments' students get their educational resources.

The contribution of this paper is that a new lab course called Media and Cognition which is more suitable for junior students to HCI research is provided, and an integrated laboratory platform is developed to offer more models about media expression

C. Stephanidis (Ed.): HCII 2016 Posters, Part I, CCIS 617, pp. 84–90, 2016.
DOI: 10.1007/978-3-319-40548-3_14

and human cognition besides HCI contents. Moreover, a collaborative laboratory will be able to access via the network to solve the sync-work issues of short-term foreign exchange students; Finally, some OERs resource for other students are provided to give them an intuitive understanding of this course and platform.

This rest of paper is organized as follows: Sect. 2 illustrates the system's design of curriculum and experiment module, Sect. 3 details the analysis and assessment given from students. Finally, Sect. 4 presents conclusions and future work.

2   Course Architecture

2.1   A. Overview

The overview of Media and Cognition lab course which include five project modules and thirty-seven knowledge points is shown in Fig. 1. These modules are:

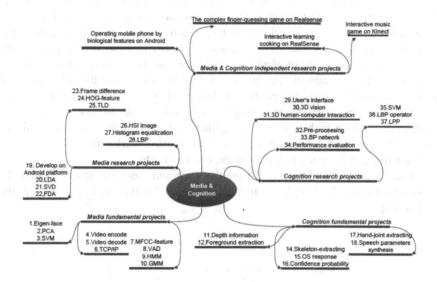

Fig. 1.   Five project modules and thirty-seven knowledge points

- Media fundamental projects.
- Media researching projects.
- Cognition fundamental projects.
- Cognition researching projects.
- Media and Cognition independent researching projects.

After trained and guided by these projects, Students have the ability to propose and complete a series of new projects by themselves. Students are no longer the passive recipients of knowledge. As the subject of the project, they can complete their projects from design to implementation, verification, testing and other related work. These projects include some similar contents to other HCI courses. In contrast, our requirement of professional background knowledge is lower. Because the platform provide a number of ready-made modules which the students only need to combine to achieve the goal. For example, in the project of "Face recognition on Android", the baseline called "X-face" included pre-processing, face detection and face recognition and developed in Eclipse is open to students. They can easily build a basic face recognition program on baseline and further propose their own algorithms to improve the performance of recognition. Undergraduate students can choose to complete some given topics, and complete their final designed HCI topics which can reflect their mastery of the basic HCI knowledge and methods. These contents are suitable for junior students without advanced professional knowledge to generally HCI research.

2.2   B. More Knowledge

In this lab course, there are two types of *Media*: *Media in machine* and *Media in human*. The former means the common digital contents such as text, audio, video and image which can be received and recognized by human. This kind of *Media* is collected by real sensors such as keyboard, microphone, camera or video recorder; the latter means the mental contents such as words, sounds, landscapes and events mapped into the human's brain. This kind of *Media* is collected by human's sensory organs such as eyes, ears, mouth or bodies. But, as before, both of them still have the same and most important function: To carry information. Followed, there are two types of *Cognition*: *Cognition of machine* and *Cognition of human*. The former means the machine's algorithms or methods such as speech recognition, face recognition, video surveillance or any other interaction between machine and the outside world; the latter means the neuronal activity in human's brain about the outside world.

And, as before, both of them still have the same and most important function: To process information. Therefore, the relations between Media and Cognition are displayed in Fig. 2.

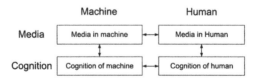

Fig. 2. The relations between media and cognition

–*Media of machine* is the target of *Cognition of machine*, and *Cognition of machine* is to process *Media of machine*; similarly, *Media of human* is the target of *Cognition of human*, and *Cognition of human* is to process *Media of human*.

–*Media in machine* is generated to fit human's organs, which can collect the information and transmit them to *Media in human*; at the same time, *Media in human* is the reflection of *Media in machine* and the outside world. The relation between two *Media* is interdependence and mutually generated each other. For example, film, as a kind of media, utilize the principle of visual staying phenomenon, which belongs to the human's cognitive functions. As an important part of information and entertainment, there is no doubt that film has significant effect on human's life, especially human's cognition and understanding to the outside world.

–*Cognition of machine* is to simulate *Cognition of human*. In fact, almost all the algorithms to process Media are simulating the human's processing mode; at the same time, *Cognition of human* is the maker of *Cognition of machine*. All the algorithms are produced by human until now. Although the machine's ability is stronger than any time, the relation between machine and human is still like children vs. adults. Although children have basic behavior of adults, children's expression ability (*Media*) is limited and the understanding ability (*Cognition*) is smaller than adults. The relation is like mobile-phones vs. smart-phones. Although mobile-phones have basic functions of smart-phones, the media types of mobile-phone is limited and the human-computer interaction module is less than smart-phones.

In fact, the relation between Media and Cognition we presented is: *Media*, as the carrier of external information, preserves and transmits human's cognition to surrounding environment; *Cognition*, as the carrier of internal information, receives and processes the projection from surrounding environment to human's brain. By understanding how they work in this way, students can finally implement their more rich and varied systems than existed.

2.3   C. OERs

OERs has a long history about 14 years. MIT OpenCourseWare [4], one of the most famous and widely used open courseware projects, was started with "the materials used in the teaching of almost all of MIT's subjects available on the Web". Open-CourseWare is "delivering on the promise of open sharing of knowledge". This OpenCourseWare and other well-known open courseware projects such as CMU Open Learning Initiative [5] and MERLOT project [6] are belong to the family of OERs of public fundamental course and professional course which generally included digital high quality academic and educational contents such as courseware, class video or software development platform.

The ordinary remote experiment uses the following forms as: Online Lab Remote Lab and Measurement based Lab [7–9]. Remote Experimental Platform of Media and Cognition is served for overseas exchange students to learn course and obtain credits. The platform help them participate with their local classmates and implement a real-experiment on real devices conducted remotely by Internet. The minimum bandwidth and communication requirements are satisfied by the special network. The students are free to use any developing language(C, C++ or Java) and software that the most suitable for their projects. It is beneficial for students to earlier adapt the remote co-operation mode in their future working environment and cultivate their spirit of cooperation.

3 Analysis and Assessment

We collect both quantitative and qualitative feedback for our courses via unofficial online evaluation system and printed questionnaire. A five point scale survey with 20 online questions collected the local students' evaluation on improving their capacity about this course. The evaluations questions were the following for example:

- How many points you give on promoting your program coding ability?
- How many points you give on improving your system design skills?
- How many points you give on increasing your innovative capacity?
- How many points you give on teacher's responsibility and initiative?

Table 1. Quantitative feedback of local students

Students	Local students		
Year	2013	2014	2015
Number of students	29	56	146
Number of respondents	10	25	92
Percentage of respondents	34.5 %	44.6 %	63.0 %

Table 2. Quantitative feedback of OERs students

Students	OERs students		
Year	2013	2014	2015
Number of students	1	4	4
Number of respondents	1	4	4
Percentage of respondents	100 %	100 %	100 %

Table 3. Quantitative feedback of other departments students

Students	Other departments students		
Year	2013	2014	2015
Number of students	2	5	22
Number of respondents	0	1	16
Percentage of respondents	0.0 %	20.0 %	72.6 %

Table 1 shows the summary of online feedback received from local students for three years. The percentage of respondents grew up from 36.5 % to 63.0 %, which indicates their enthusiasm of participating survey increased year by year. Table 2 shows the summary of online feedback received from overseas exchange students use OERs for three years. The percentage of respondents remained 100 %, which shows overseas exchange students had more and continued enthusiasm of participating survey. Table 3 shows the summary of online feedback received from other disciplines students for three years. The maximum percentage of respondents is 72.6 %, which reflecting in part that other departments students had obviously increasing interest in survey.

The online surveys' results are displayed in Fig. 3. *(Increasing) innovative capacity* item has the most five point which shows that the course has the positive effect on improving students' innovation. On the other hand, *(promoting) program-coding ability* item has the most four and three point, which we assumed the reason is: some projects proposed by students have some ready-made software modules.

As a supplement to the online evaluation, the printed qualitative questions for students were the following for example:

- What is the best point of view you learn from the course?
- Compared with other similar experiments, do you think your development on the virtual platform need more or less time?
- Which item you selected in all the independent optional items?
- What aspects are the main improvement this course needed?

For three years, more than 100 printed feedback were received. These studies indicated that students began to view media and cognition from the perspective of the interactive relationship. The OERs platform is helpful for overseas exchange students to learn and co-work with local students. And the students come from other departments got started to learn HCI with basic principle and feel its charm in this course.

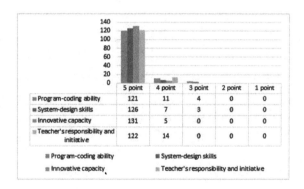

Fig. 3. Analysis of all online survey data in recent three years

4 Conclusion

Media and Cognition lab course, which covers five project modules and thirty-seven knowledge points, hopes to provide the latest and most populous HCI experiments for students. This course provides many different platforms and topics to help students achieve their HCI projects, along with the flexibility for all the students to form teams and create new topics based on their own knowledge structure. The survey for students indicates the students' innovative capacity, improving system-design skills, promoting program coding ability increased year by year.

In the next step, to get more feedback and information, a system-level analysis method will be considered to find the important factors of generating the creativity and imagination in students' mind.

Acknowledgement. Thanks to Intel & Tsinghua teaching projects (202023011) for funding.

References

1. http://hcicourses.stanford.edu/cs376/
2. http://www-inst.eecs.berkeley.edu/cs260/
3. http://www.hcii.cmu.edu/courses/hci-process-and-theory/
4. http://ocw.mit.edu/
5. http://oli.cmu.edu/
6. http://www.merlot.org/
7. Zubla, J.C., Alves, G.: Using Remote Labs in Education-Two little ducks in Remote Experimentation, pp. 102–105. University of Deusto Press, Bilbao, Spain (2012)
8. Kazmierkowski, M.P., Liserre, M.: Advances on remote laboratories and e-learning experiences. IEEE Ind. Electron. Mag. 2(2), 45–46 (2008)
9. Stefanovic, M., Cvijetkovic, V., Matijevic, M., Simic, V.: A lab view based remote laboratory experiments for control engineering education. Comput. Appl. Eng. Educ. **19**(3), 538–549 (2011)

Design and Evaluation Methods, Techniques and Tools

To Err Is Human: Building an Automatic Error Generator System

Luiz Carlos Begosso$^{(\boxtimes)}$ and Marcos Roberto Alves Medeiros

Fundacao Educacional do Municipio de Assis – FEMA Assis, Assis, SP, Brazil
begosso@gmail.com, zxmarcos@gmail.com

Abstract. This paper introduces Human Error Generator (HEG), an erroneous human performance simulator which considers that the errors emerge from human-computer interaction. HEG, in its current version, has two implemented modules: one that designs the interface in which the simulated user performs a task; and an automatic human error generator module. The system is linked to the cognitive architecture ACT-R and is able to simulate the following errors during the user performance: perceptual confusion, omission, inversion, repetition and intentionality reduction. Furthermore, HEG generates a report with the error-affected human performance showing the information related to the cognitive process involved in the simulated task as output. This paper aims to contribute to the field of human-computer interaction regarding the development of systems that anticipate human error.

Keywords: Error generator · Human error · Human-computer interaction

1 Introduction

Human actions are an essential part of any task execution, particularly when dealing with computational systems. In various situations, even when the human operator is focused on adequately performing the designed task, systematic errors can be committed.

Therefore, efforts are being made to develop tools which can tolerate the occurrence of errors that may emerge from human-computer interaction (HCI). Programmers develop mechanisms for error protection and error recovery from human tasks, whether they are motor, perceptual or decision-making. Naturally, these same mechanisms of protection can increase the complexity of human-computer interaction.

Studies on human factors cannot consider human beings alone, as well as human error cannot be solely seen from the performance of humans, [1]. We believe that human factors investigations should take not only the people involved but also their work environment as the resources for task execution.

This work's goal is to present the current stage of development of Human Error Generator (HEG) software, which can contribute to the study of important consequences for operational reliability, helping human-computer interfaces programmers minimize the chances of errors occurring during the interaction.

C. Stephanidis (Ed.): HCII 2016 Posters, Part I, CCIS 617, pp. 93–96, 2016.
DOI: 10.1007/978-3-319-40548-3_15

2 The Human Error Generator System

In order to develop a flexible platform - graphical user interface (GUI) - for the simulation of human performance that takes into consideration the error, HEG looks like an interfaces editor, as shown in Fig. 1.

HEG is divided into two modules: the task design and registration module; and the automatic human error generator module.

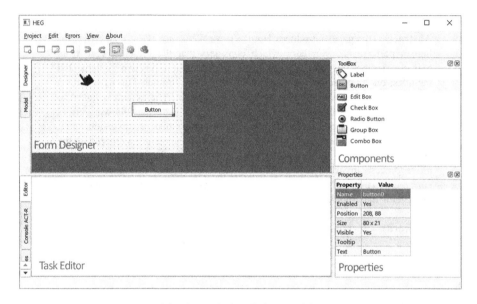

Fig. 1. Task description module

2.1 Task Design Module

In Fig. 1, at Components Box, the items that can be used by the operator to design the GUI are shown. The most common components in computer graphic interfaces were implemented in HEG, enabling the creation of diversified interfaces. Its operation method is based on "drag and drop".

The form is the representation of the GUI where components are arranged and can be subject to the following user operations: change, resize, move and delete. When a component is selected on the form, their properties automatically appear in the Property Editor box. The list of items in a check box can be changed within the form itself by double-clicking the component.

To describe a task it is necessary to use a domain specific language in which the steps to complete the task are informed by elementary actions on the GUI.

A specific language was elaborated for HEG: the Task Description Language (TDL) which to date consists of six reserved words: select, mark, clear, pick, press and fill. In this context, the primary actions planned for HEG are: select radio button, check /uncheck the check box, press button, choose check box and fill the text box.

2.2 Automatic Error Generator Module

The design of HEG is supported by a human information processing model which aims to explain human behavior and is commonly used to study human error activities that were caused during problem-solving processes, [2]. The model is divided into three activity levels performed by a human operator at a certain task: the skill-based level, the rule-based level and the knowledge-based level.

The human error taxonomy adopted by HEG is the theoretical model denominated GEMS (Generic Error Modeling System) which aims to explain human errors, [3]. Such taxonomy is structured according to the performance levels proposed by [2].

HEG is currently prepared to generate skill-based level errors: perceptual confusion, omission, inversion, repetition and intentionality reduction. Also, HEG uses the cognitive architecture ACT-R for the simulation of human performance error. HEG's architecture is shown in Fig. 2.

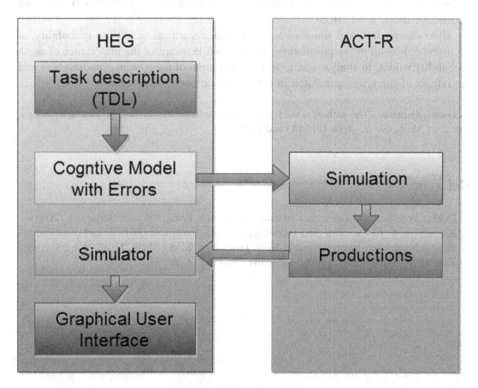

Fig. 2. HEG architecture

The outputs by HEG are models to the aforementioned architecture, i.e., the tasks described in TDL are translated to ACT-R models which can be altered with the errors requested by the operator in one of the steps in the task.

When executing the generated models, a trace is created with the information constituting the entire cognitive process involved in the task, according to ACT-R theory for real-time simulation of these errors.

3 Conclusion

Human errors may be considered contributing factors to a series of accidents and incidents in several areas where people interact with computer systems. Thus, this paper aimed to present HEG, a human performance simulator that takes into account errors that can occur during human-computer interaction.

A point to be made about HEG is its feature of generality, that is, the system can support the design of any user interface, regardless of the domain. On the other hand, the work here presented is prepared only for the automatic generation of skill-based errors. It is known, however, that the complexity of the human cognitive system can trigger user behavior that goes beyond the skill level. Therefore, as future work, we intend to expand the simulation of human errors, implementing rule-based level and knowledge-based level errors.

HEG design is based upon error generation, regardless of its the probability of occurrence. It is up to the programmer of HCI, while aware of the importance of these probability values, to analyze and reflect on the output of the system proposed here and the impact of the errors generated in the human-computer interaction.

Acknowledgments. The authors would like to acknowledge the support of Fundacao Educacional do Municipio de Assis (FEMA) and CNPq.

References

1. Dekker, S.: The Field Guide to Understanding Human Error. Ashgate, Burlington (2006)
2. Rasmussen, J.: Skills, rules, and knowledge; signals, signs, and symbols, and other distinctions in human performance models. IEEE Trans. Syst. Man Cybern. **13**(3), 257–266 (1983)
3. Reason, J.: Human Error. Cambridge University Press, Cambridge (1990)

TAM Reloaded: A Technology Acceptance Model for Human-Robot Cooperation in Production Systems

Christina Bröhl[✉], Jochen Nelles, Christopher Brandl,
Alexander Mertens, and Christopher M. Schlick

Institute of Industrial Engineering and Ergonomics,
RWTH Aachen University, Aachen, Germany
{c.broehl,j.nelles,c.brandl,a.mertens,
c.schlick}@iaw.rwth-aachen.de

Abstract. The cooperation and collaboration between humans and robots is getting ever closer: While the human body was historically protected by a large safety distance, more and more organizations let robots and humans work hand-in-hand. This means that humans and robots are sharing physical space and are engaging in direct contact with each other. One factor that predicts successful human-robot interaction is the acceptance of the robot by the human. In general, only when a product covers human needs and expectations, it is perceived to be useful and hence accepted. This paper aims at presenting an acceptance model with regard to the cooperation between humans and robots that is based on prior acceptance models while also taking ethical, legal and social implications (ELSI) into account.

Keywords: Acceptance model · Human-robot interaction · Human-machine interaction · ELSI · TAM

1 Introduction

Since the middle of the 20th century the field of robotics has kept on growing and has become a vital part of today's production industry [1]. The latest development of robotics leads away from robots as a component of fully automated manufacturing processes towards processes in which human and robots collaborate. This means that while the human body was protected by large safety margins up to now, there are more and more organizations that are designing collaborative workplaces where human and robot can accomplish a task together and at the same time. However, any erroneous behavior of the robot could result in serious injury of the human so the interaction between human and robot has to be designed ergonomically with regard to both hardware components as well as human cognition. One factor which can predict effective and efficient technology usage is the acceptance of the device in question. Technology acceptance in the context of industrial robots has, to our knowledge, not been explored so far. Therefore, this paper aims at building a model to investigate acceptance of human-robot cooperation in an industrial setting.

© Springer International Publishing Switzerland 2016
C. Stephanidis (Ed.): HCII 2016 Posters, Part I, CCIS 617, pp. 97–103, 2016.
DOI: 10.1007/978-3-319-40548-3_16

1.1 History in Technology Acceptance Research

In order to measure acceptance there are a number of different models available. The starting point of this research field is commonly seen in Rogers' theory of diffusions of innovations from 1962. This theory proposes a five-step model from knowledge of a new technology to its validation [2]. The next essential step was the Technology Acceptance Model (TAM) proposed by Davis in 1989 [3] which prognosticates the acceptance and corresponding use of information technologies. Specifically, this model builds on the fundamental assumption that behavioral intention leads to an actual behavior. Behavioral intention in turn is dependent on two variables: perceived usefulness and perceived ease of use. Perceived usefulness is "the degree to which a person believes that using a particular system would enhance his or her job performance" whereas perceived ease of use is defined as "the degree to which a person believes that using a particular system would be free from effort [3].

Several researchers have replicated Davis's original study and added further variables to the model such as social influence (subjective norms, voluntariness, image) and cognitive instrumental processes (job relevance, output quality, result demonstrability, perceived ease of use) (TAM 2 by Venkatesh and Davis [5]) which might be of interest when assessing the acceptance of robots. Another noteworthy approach in this area was the Unified Theory of Acceptance and Use of Technology (Tam 3 by Venkatesh and Bala [4]) that aimed at creating a unified model of user acceptance in information technology. Its successor UTAUT 2 by Venkatesh et al. [6] focused on the consumer's technology acceptance by integrating factors such as hedonic motivation.

1.2 The Present Study

The aim of our research was to build an acceptance model with regard to human-robot interaction that builds on already existing knowledge and takes context-specific factors of the interaction between human and robots in an industrial setting into account. Therefore, we went through four developmental stages. First, a research model based on literature was developed and reviewed in a workshop with associates of robot manufacturing companies, associates of companies which make use of industrial robots, employees working with robots and scientists in the domains of psychology, computer science and engineering. This model took variables of the traditional technology acceptance models, such as TAM [3], TAM 2 [7] and TAM 3 [4] into account and was extended with regard to context specific factors which came up during the workshop. Context specific factors integrated in the model are on the one hand variables for adjustment such as perceived enjoyment, perceived safety, ethical, legal and social implications and on the other hand personal characteristics such as self-efficacy, robot anxiety, affinity towards technology (adapted from Karrer et al. [8]), robot-related experiences (adapted from MacDorman et al. [9]) and perceptions of external control, which are considered as variables with uncertain influence on the predictors. As a second step, a survey based on the emerged variables was developed and iteratively validated with experts. Third, the survey was implemented in an online tool and completed by 322 participants, all of them working in production. Lastly, the model was analyzed statistically by correlation analyses in order to draw conclusions with regard to possible predictors concerning the acceptance of robots for cooperation. As robots can adopt an active role (e.g. handing over heavy components) or a passive role (e.g. hold a component so that the human can work on that component) we built two scenarios for the survey in order to make predictions concerning both ways of interacting. Participants were instructed to base their response behavior on the scenario including the robot as an active partner for interaction or a passive partner for interaction respectively.

2 Method

2.1 Participants

Altogether, 322 subjects participated in the study, recruited via a panel survey. All of them were working in production companies. Thereby, 34.8 % were working in production companies that already deploy robots and 65.2 % were working in companies that do not yet deploy robots. Gender was not well balanced but representative for employees in production: 80 survey participants were female and 242 were male. Age ranged from 21 to 64 years (mean = 46.32, SD = 10.35 yrs).

2.2 Procedure

The survey was structured into explanatory parts, such as the description of the project and questionnaire parts, e.g. for the variables of the model (see Table 1). The mean time to complete the survey was 14.7 min. The software used for the online survey was Unipark, the academic program of Questback. The two scenarios were described as follows:

Table 1. Structure of the online survey

Part	Factors/information
Introduction	Project aim and funding Call for participation
Anchor variables	*Self-efficacy, robot anxiety, robot-related experiences, perceptions of external control*
Scenario 1	Active robot (permuted with scenario 2)
Adjustment variables	*Perceived enjoyment, social implication, legal implications, ethical implications, perceived safety*
Other variables	*Subjective norm, image, job relevance, output quality, result demonstrability, perceived usefulness, perceived ease of use, behavioral intention, use behavior*
Scenario 2	Passive robot (permuted with scenario 1)
Adjustment variables	Same as in scenario 1
Other variables	Same as in scenario 1
Demographical data	Gender, *age*, education
Conclusion	Possibility for final comments on human-robot cooperation and comments on the survey

Active robot: "You are an order picker, working with a robot arm at a shared workstation. Your job is to take a case and the corresponding snap lid and hold these components compatible between you and the robot arm onto the working plate. The robot takes the corresponding screws one after the other and fastens the snap lids to the housing. After mounting the components the robot puts the constructed part in the order picking area next to the workstation and a new process begins."

Passive robot: "You are an order picker, working with a stationary robot arm at a shared workstation. The robot takes an automobile door from the reserve storage and holds it in front of you. You then take individual car components from a shelf and mount these components on the automobile door. After the car components are mounted, the robot puts the door in the order picking area next to the workstation and a new process begins."

2.3   Instruments

The specific items of the survey are presented in Table 2. All items were developed in German to be adequate for the survey participants. The participants rated the degree of consent with the statements on a 7-point likert-scale. In case participants of the survey quoted that they do not deploy robots, items were formulated subjunctively for this group.

Table 2. Items of the survey

Factor	Items
Subjective norm	In general, the organization supports the use of the robot (TAM 2/3)
Image	People in my organization who use the robot have more prestige than those who do not (TAM 2/3)
Job relevance	The use of the robot is pertinent to my various job-related tasks (TAM 2/3)
Output quality	The quality of the output I get from the robot is high (TAM 2/3)
Result demonstrability	I have no difficulty telling others about the results of using the robot (TAM 2/3)
Perceived enjoyment	I find using the robot to be enjoyable (TAM 3/3)
Social implication	I fear that I lose the contact to my colleagues because of the robot
Legal implication (occupational safety)	I do not mind if the robot works with me at a shared workstation
Legal implication (data protection)	I do not mind, if the robot records personal information about me
Ethical implication	I fear that I will lose my job because of the robot
Perceived safety	I feel safe while using the robot
Self-efficacy	I can use the robot, if someone shows me how to do it first (TAM 3/3)

(Continued)

Table 2. (*Continued*)

Factor	Items
Robot anxiety	Robots make me feel uncomfortable (TAM 3/3)
Robot-related Experience	How many times in the past year have you read or watched robot-related news articles, movies or materials on the internet?
	How many times in the past ten years have you had physical contact with a robot? (MacDorman et al. [9])
Perceived usefulness	Using the robot improves my performance in my job (TAM).
Perceived ease of use	My interaction with the robot is easy (TAM).
Behavioral intention	If I could choose, whether the robot supports me at work, I would appreciate working with the robot
Use behavior	I prefer the robot to other machines in the industrial environment
Technology affinity	I like to visit shops for electronic devices. (TA-EG, Karrer et al. [8])
	Electronic devices lead to intellectual impoverishment
	Electronic devices make things cumbersome. (TA-EG)
	I inform myself about electronic devices, even if I do not have the intention to purchase them. (TA-EG)
	Electronic devices make people independent. (TA-EG)
	Trying new electronic devices is fun. (TA-EG)
	I know most of the functions of the devices I own. (TA-EG)
	I am enthusiastic when a new electronic device is launched. (TA-EG)
	Electronic devices cause stress. (TA-EG)
	I know a lot about electronic devices. (TA-EG)
	I find it easy to learn how a new electronic device is working. (TA-EG)

3   Results and Discussion

Correlation coefficients were used to determine the relationships in our model and were calculated by using Spearman's rho. According to Cohen and Cohen (2013), effect sizes can be classified into low ($r = .10$), medium ($r = .30$) and large ($r = 0.50$). The level of significance was set to $\alpha = 0.05$. The complete model is presented in Fig. 1.

Overall, results regarding the robot as an active cooperator compared to the robot in a passive role did not differ significantly, either showing that the area of operation of robots can be ignored when modelling acceptance or that our scenarios did not differ sufficiently. Regarding *perceived usefulness* the most important predictor in our model is *job relevance*, followed by *subjective norm* and *output quality*, which might be caused by the industrial context of the model. Regarding the anchor variables, we found the highest correlation coefficients for the variables of the traditional TAM 3 model *perceptions of external control, self-efficacy* and *robot anxiety*. Against our

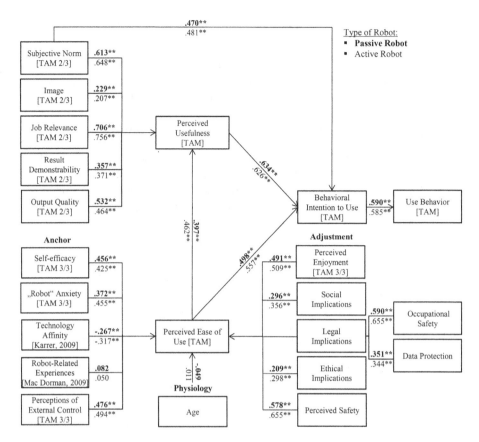

Fig. 1. Robot acceptance model with correlation coefficients as strength of associations between person-specific anchor variables, context-specific adjustment variables, age and the target variable use behavior, *p < .05, **p < .001

expectations, *technological affinity* was negatively correlated with perceived ease of use, maybe because people who have an affinity regarding technology are better informed and may have more prejudices compared to those that shy away from it. Regarding the variables for adjustment we found that *perceived safety* and *occupational safety* are the best predictors for *perceived ease of use* showing high effect-sizes, whereas *social* and *ethical implications* are less important as they show effect sizes which can be classified as medium. With regard to *age*, correlation coefficients showed no significant effect. Therefore, *age* can be ignored in the model. Overall, correlation coefficients between *perceived usefulness*, *perceived ease of use*, *behavioral intention* and *use behavior* reached medium to high levels showing that the original model is transferrable to the domain of human-robot interaction.

The paper presented is a work in progress. As a next step, the model will be analyzed using ordinal regression in order examine the explanatory power of the context-specific variables for the target variable *intention to use* more closely. Furthermore, the model will be evaluated by discriminating between participants who already work with robots on a day to day basis, participants who work with robots sporadically and participants who do not work with robots at all.

Acknowledgements. This publication is part of the research project "MeRoSy", which is funded by the German Federal Ministry of Education and Research (BMBF, Grant No. 16SV7190).

References

1. Ray C, Mondada F, Siegwart R.: What do people expect from robots? IEEE (2008)
2. Rogers, E.M.: Diffusion of Innovations. Free Press of Glencoe, New York (1962)
3. Davis, F.D.: Perceived usefulness, perceived ease of use, and user acceptance of information technology. MIS Q. **13**(3), 319 (1989). doi:10.2307/249008
4. Venkatesh, V., Bala, H.: Technology acceptance model 3 and a research agenda on interventions. Decis. Sci. **39**(2), 273 (2008)
5. Venkatesh, V., Davis, F.D.: A theoretical extension of the technology acceptance model, four longitudinal field studies. Manag. Sci. **46**(2), 186 (2000). doi:10.1287/mnsc.46.2.186.11926
6. Venkatesh, V., Thong, J.Y., Xu, X.: Consumer acceptance and use of information technology: extending the unified theory of acceptance and use of technology. MIS quarterly **36**(1), 157–178 (2012).
7. Venkatesh, V., Davis, F.D.: A theoretical extension of the technology acceptance model, four longitudinal field studies. Manag. Sci. **46**(2), 186 (2000)
8. Karrer, K., Glaser, C., Clemens, C., Bruder, C.: Technikaffinität erfassen–der Fragebogen TA-EG. Der Mensch im Mittelpunkt technischer Systeme **8**, 196–201 (2009)
9. MacDorman, K.F., Vasudevan, S.K., Ho, C.: Does Japan really have robot mania? Comparing attitudes by implicit and explicit measures. AI Soc. **23**(4), 485 (2008)
10. Cohen, J.: Statistical power analysis for the behavioral sciences (2nd ed.). L. Erlbaum Associates. Hillsdale (1988)

On Repairing Generated Behaviors
for Graphical Characters

Andrea Corradini[1](✉) and Manish Mehta[2]

[1] Design School Kolding, 6000 Kolding, Denmark
andrea@dskd.dk
[2] Accenture Technology Labs, San Jose, CA, USA
manish.mehta@accenture.com

Abstract. In this paper, we continue our work on the creation of artificial intelligence (AI) behaviors for graphical interactive characters by novice users. We refer to novice users as any persons who do not have any particular skills, training and experience in both programming and design. The focus of this paper is on the analysis of the needs and requirements that are necessary to identify and repair problems related to the rendering of the behaviors after the authoring stage. We also briefly sketch our strategy for the behavior repair in the behavior authoring system that we are developing.

Keywords: Non-playing characters · AI behavior repair and generation

1 Introduction

In a previous work [1], we addressed the problem of authoring AI behaviors of graphical interactive characters by novice users. This question has been explored also by researchers who have addressed the merit in developing tools for novice users to carry out part of product development and programming activities. We continue on that work by investigating the problem of repairing the behaviors authored by the same kind of users. At this point, it should be noted that we broadly use the term novice users to define users who do not have any skills, training and experience in both programming and design.

The repair of user-authored AI behaviors is an important step in many computing applications populated by graphical agents. Over long game sessions, a character's behavioral repertoire may result in repetitive behaviors that harm the agent's believability. An appropriate repair of the behavior set makes it possible for these characters to autonomously exhibit their author-specified personalities in new and unforeseen circumstances. Proper behaviors also ensure a better player experience. When authored behaviors fail, the player may get annoyed and bored, especially if the problems in the behaviors show up repeatedly. Moreover, each player enjoys different strategies to fight against (in the case of real time strategy games), or varying styles of storytelling (in the case of interactive dramas), different types of story development, different kinds of character behaviors and interactions, etc. Modifying the behaviors according to player's preferences provides a better interactive experience. It is also possible, for authored behaviors not to achieve the games objectives adequately, especially in realistic,

© Springer International Publishing Switzerland 2016
C. Stephanidis (Ed.): HCII 2016 Posters, Part I, CCIS 617, pp. 104–109, 2016.
DOI: 10.1007/978-3-319-40548-3_17

scaled-up domains or applications. These objectives could range from entertainment to education, training, etc. When these objectives are not met on a per-use basis, the AI behaviors should be accordingly modified. Many researchers and game developers hold that game AI is entertaining mainly when it is difficult to defeat [2]. Expert gamers in strategy games can quickly get bored of playing against a built-in AI because they can easily find and exploit flaws in the AI. We contend that modifying the behaviors in response to newer player's tactics would allow for a more challenging AI.

We organize the rest of this paper as follows: Sect. 2 reports on related works and background information. Section 3 briefly sketches the approach we chose to develop a behavior repair layer. Eventually, Sect. 4 summarizes our conclusions.

2 Related Work

The agent's behavior set can be seen as a reactive plan that dictates what the character should do under various conditions. From this perspective, behavior repair becomes a problem of reactive-plan revision. One approach to plan revision is to apply classical planning techniques to re-plan upon encountering failures. Such techniques are still ill suited to the unique requirements of a game domain. They typically assume that the agent is the sole source of change, actions are deterministic and their effects well defined, that actions are sequential and take unit time, and that the world is fully observable. In an interactive, real-time game domain, all these assumptions are violated. Actions are non-deterministic and their effects are often difficult to quantify. Game domains are typically not fully observable either. Some recent work in planning has focused on relaxing these assumptions. Conditional planners such as conditional non-linear planner [3] and sensory graph plan [4] support sensing actions so that during execution, changing environmental influences can be ascertained and the appropriate conditional branch of the plan is chosen based on the sensor values. Unfortunately, as the number of sensing actions and conditional branches increase, the size of the plan will grow exponentially. These techniques are mostly suited to deterministic domains with occasional exogenous or non-deterministic effects, rather than to continuously changing interactive domains. One of the approaches to planning that deals best with exogenous events and non-determinism is based on Markov decision processes (MDP). These approaches, however, require a large number of iterations to converge and only do so when certain conditions are met. In complex game domains, these techniques are intractable for MDP learning algorithms require a prohibitively large amount of time (polynomial to the number of states of the problem [5]). Upon adding game state information, the status level and internal states of various characters, the state space quickly grows untenable. Further, these approaches generalize poorly. An interactive player can significantly change the game world; the learned static policy must be re-trained to accommodate such changes.

In the AI planning community, previous work has investigated techniques for combining deliberative and reactive planning [6, 7]. Unfortunately, to varying degrees, they all make classical planning assumptions and are thus not applicable to real-time interactive games. Furthermore, these approaches treat reactive plans as black boxes;

planning sequences of black-boxed reactive plans, but not modifying the internals of the reactive plans themselves.

In transformational planning, the goal is to re-write the behavior set using a set of plan transformations in order to improve an existing reactive plan [8, 9]. This approach, although promising, is of limited usefulness in game domains because it requires a detailed casual model of the world. In games domains, there is neither the time for extended projective reasoning nor an accurate projection can be performed due to the interactive and stochastic nature of game domains.

Meta-reasoning is the process of monitoring and controlling reasoning. The meta-level control of computational activities deals with the question of when to stop a given computational process. The monitoring part is responsible of figuring out what can fail through the process of introspection also called introspective reasoning. Various approaches to meta-reasoning and more specifically to the task of introspective reasoning have been proposed [10–13, 16, 17].

Another body of related work is in the area of adaptive AI [14]. Dynamic scripting is a technique based on reinforcement learning that is able to generate scripts by drawing subsets of rules from a pre-authored large collection of rules [14]. If the rules are properly authored, different subsets of them provide meaningful and different behaviors. The technique is based on learning which subsets work better under different circumstances. The adaptive AI approach only learns conditions for the applicability of different rules. It assumes that the initial authored rules are perfect and it is unable to identify any problems with the internals of these rules. The Adaptive Behavior Language (ABL) provides an approach towards adaptive AI where the adaptive programming primitives are directly built into the ABL language [15]. The approach supports partial programming, a paradigm in which a programmer needs to specify only the details of behavior known at code-writing time, leaving the run-time system to learn the rest. The approach, though promising, requires novice authors to learn a programming language to allow the characters to be adaptive. Moreover, the adaptation of characters authored in the language to changing circumstances requires many examples.

3   Our Approach

3.1   Identifying and Repairing Failures: General Issues

We assume that a novice author has created an initial set of behaviors. Creating behaviors for graphical characters requires an enormous amount of work to make them properly react to their environment. Despite such efforts, it is however not possible to envision all the possible circumstances that a character would encounter in the game, ultimately leading to authored behaviors that do not reflect an agent's intended personality or do not fit the given interaction context.

There are several dimensions to the task of identifying and repairing failures in user-generated AI behaviors, which make it an especially hard and interesting problem. In general, these are the main questions that arise:

- Which metrics can be used to indicate that the authored AI behaviors need to be improved/modified?

- When does the detection of behavior repair occur?
- How is the feedback on whether the behaviors are performed correctly i.e. on whether they match the specified metrics provided?
- How can feedback be provided?
- When is the actual behavior repair carried out?
- Who has the responsibility for repairing the behaviors?

Performance Metrics. Different game genres present various performance requirements for a repair approach situated within them. For instance, god games usually require the game AI to solve resource allocation problems and long-term strategy problems, while interactive drama require the game AI to adapt the story according to the player interactions in a way that it is more appealing to the player (thus, the latter requires user modeling and story planning). Adventures, interactive dramas and other genres with embodied characters require believable behaviors. These requirements affect the kind of repair approach and results on a set of different metrics. A possible metric is believability when the goal of the repairing task is to have characters behave in accordance with their personality. Another metrics is AI performance when the goal of the repair approach is to provide a more challenging opponent to the player. Other common metrics are defined by player experience and adaptation to different levels of challenge. In both situations, the repair approach has to continuously scale up based on the game difficulty level to the point that a human player is challenged, but not completely overpowered. These metrics are not mutually exclusive. Any AI based repair approach that provides for a stronger AI could possibly provide for a better player experience [2]. Similarly, a believable performance by the characters could result in a more pleasurable experience for the player. In our approach, we use player experience as the performance metric.

Performance Measurement Stage. The performance of the resulting AI behaviors can be measured at different times in the game episode. Roughly speaking, there are two main points when this can occur: either, during the performance of the AI behavior sets in the game episode itself or after the completion of the game episode. In our approach, we detect the need for adaptation after the completion of each interaction episode. Once the player finishes the interaction with the avatar, s/he is asked to provide feedback in order to figure out whether any repair is needed or not.

Feedback Agent. The feedback about whenever the behavior performance does not match one or more of the desired criteria can by provided by the game itself, by the designer of the system, by the player interacting with the system, or a combination thereof. In our approach, we use the player as the feedback agent.

Type of Feedback. The feedback may simply inform the system whether the solution it produced succeeded or failed. In some cases, the feedback consist of a complete trace of the execution of the solution produced by the system, localizing the steps, which need modification. In others, the designer himself provides another preferred solution along with a complete trace of how this solution could be produced. Alternatively, the feedback only specifies the alternative preferred solution. In our current work, the feedback provided by the player is in the form of several numerical ratings about the performance of the avatar.

Behavior Repair. The behavior repair can be carried out during the performance of the AI behaviors or after the completion of problem solving task. We carry out the repair after the completion of the player interaction with the avatar.

Responsibility of Modification. The responsibility of repair can occur either without any designer intervention i.e. lie solely with the underlying AI system (fully autonomous repair) or could be shared between the system and the designers (i.e. novice users) carrying out a mixed initiative repair. In our work, we choose a mixed responsibility shared between the AI system and the designer.

3.2 Overview of Our Repair Approach

The core idea of this work is the addition of a repair layer to the underlying AI system. This layer would allow to identify and to repair the failures in the behavior sets for them to better match the changing context and personality.

One of the key problems in repairing the set of behaviors is to define a metric to measure the success of both the authored behavior sets and the overall interaction. Our strategy is broken down into three main parts. At first, we associated behavioral constraints to authored behaviors in order to provide a metric to measure the success of their rendering. Further, we collected players' feedback about their interaction. Failures are then detected by comparing successful execution traces to unsuccessful ones. Eventually, the repair step involves looking at execution traces (notably, where failures do not occur) to suggest modifications about the failed/wrong behaviors. This is much similar to the work in [10], which focuses on using a library of pre-defined patterns of erroneous interactions among reasoning steps to recognize failures in the story understanding task. Differently from that, we do not require the construction of pre-defined patterns of erroneous interactions and a library of plans to repair the faulty behaviors. This frees the system designer from having to think beforehand of all the possible situations. We were also inspired by the works on model-based diagnosis by [13, 17] where a model of the system is used to localize the errors and to construct alternative traces, which could lead to the desired solution. Our repair approach does however not require a detailed model of the system. Instead, it provides a unique way of detecting the failures through use of knowledge available in successful and unsuccessful traces.

4   Conclusions

We addressed the problem of repairing authored behaviors. After discussing common issues, we introduced several dimensions to take into account when dealing with the task of identifying and repairing failures in user-generated AI behaviors.

The approach consists of three parts (a) constraints that are associated with behaviors that provides a way to measure the success of the behavior sets, (b) player feedback where players provide feedback at the end of their interaction, and (c) failure detection and repair approach through comparison of successful and unsuccessful execution traces [18]. The repair then involves looking at execution traces (where these failures do not exist) to suggest modifications on the failed behaviors to the author.

We evaluated our approach with thirty authors who created a behavior set. To provide the necessary data for the AI repair system, we collected data from sixty-five players who interacted with animated avatars. When asked to compare the original behaviors with the repaired ones, all subjects found these latter smoother and more believable.

References

1. Mehta, M., Corradini, A.: Second mind: a system for authoring behaviors in virtual worlds. In: Proceedings of the Interaction, 16th International Conference on HCI, pp. 345–350 (2015)
2. Buro, M.: RTS games as test-bed for real-time ai research. In: Proceedings of the 7th Joint Conference on Information Science (JCIS 2003), pp. 481–484 (2003)
3. Peot, M., Smith, D.: Conditional nonlinear planning. In: Proceedings of the 1st International Conference on AI Planning Systems (1992)
4. Weld, D.S., Anderson, C.R., Smith, D.: Extending graphplan to handle uncertainty and sensing actions. In: Proceedings of AAAI (1998)
5. Kearns, M., Singh, S.: Near-optimal reinforcement learning in polynomial time. Mach. Learn. **49**(2–3), 209–232 (2002)
6. Gat, E.: Integrating planning and reacting in a heterogeneous asynchronous architecture for controlling real-world mobile robots. In: Proceedings of the AAAI Conference (1992)
7. Bonasso, P., Firby, J., Gat, E., Kortenkamp, D., Miller, D., Slack, M.: Experiences with an architecture for intelligent reactive agents. J. Exp. Theoret. AI **9**, 237–256 (1997)
8. McDermott, D.: Transformational planing of reactive behavior. Technical report, Yale University (1992). Research Report YALEU/DCS/RR-941
9. Beetz, M.: Structured reactive controllers a computational model of everyday activity. In: Proceedings of the 3rd International Conference on Autonomous Agents (2000)
10. Cox, M.T.: Metacognition in computation: a selected research review. Artif. Intell. **169**(2), 104–141 (2005)
11. Cox, M.T., Ram, A.: Introspective multi-strategy learning: on the construction of learning strategies. Technical report, Georgia Institute of Technology (1996)
12. Anderson, M.L., Oates, T.: A review of recent research in metareasoning and metalearning. AI Mag. **28**, 7–16 (2007)
13. Stroulia, E., Goel, A.K.: Functional representation and reasoning in reactive systems. J. Appl. Intell. **9**, 101–124 (1995)
14. Spronck, P., Ponsen, M., Sprinkhuizen-Kuyper, I., Postma, E.: Adaptive game AI with dynamic scripting. Mach. Learn. **63**(3), 217–248 (2006)
15. Simpkins, C., Bhat, S., Isbell Jr, C., Mateas, M.: Towards adaptive programming: integrating reinforcement learning into a programming language. SIGPLAN Not. **43**, 603–614 (2008)
16. Cazenave, T.: Metarules to improve tactical go knowledge. Inf. Comput. Sci. **154**(3–4), 173–188 (2003)
17. Ulam, P., Jones, J., Goel, A.K.: Combining model-based meta-reasoning and reinforcement learning for adapting game-playing agents. In: Proceedings of AIIDE (2008)
18. Mehta, M., Ontanon, S., Ram, A.: Using meta-reasoning to improve the performance of case-based planning. In: Proceedings of the 8th International Conference on Case-Based Reasoning, pp. 210–224 (2009)

Decision Making for Complex Ecosystems: A Technique for Establishing Causality in Dynamic Systems

Ryan A. Kirk[1(✉)], Dave A. Kirk[2], and Peter Pesheck[3]

[1] Kirk Enterprises, LLC, Seattle, USA
info@ryankirk.info
[2] Consul Pack, Inc, Minneapolis, USA
dave.kirkl@comcast.net
[3] Food Biophysics, LLC, Maple Grove, USA
pete.pesheck@gmail.com

Abstract. Understanding naturalistic human use of technology requires accounting for people, processes, and technologies. Modern decision support system strive to facilitate decision making in such ecosystems. However, modeling interaction between people and technology as constrained by explicit or implicit processes quickly becomes a complex spiral of relationships. In order to determine cause and effect in these complex ecosystems we need a form of causal inference that can overcome the limitations of linear cause-effect analysis.

Complex systems are the result of feedback that takes place inside a dynamic systems. In dynamic systems the future values for outcome variables are due to the interactions of causal variables as modified by a shared, often hidden, function. Taken's theorem states that time series variables are causally linked if they are from the same dynamic system. This paper presents the development and application of an approach that examines time-offset relations between variables in order to determine their causal relations. This research examines the effectiveness of this technique through its application to a microwave heating problem.

Keywords: Causality · Decision-making · Decision support systems · DSS · Simulation · Complex systems · Causal inference · Microwave heating

1 Introduction

1.1 Linear Causality

A common form of causal inference examines the effects of changing an independent variable (A) upon the variability in a dependent variable (B). This linear causal inferences requires the change in A to precede the change in B. Statistically significant differences in the distribution of variances signifies to the researcher that the variables are causally related. However, this approach has several drawbacks. First, it is not always practical or ethical to change one variable. Second, this framework only allows the researcher to examine direct, antecedent causal relations. Third, the scientific

C. Stephanidis (Ed.): HCII 2016 Posters, Part I, CCIS 617, pp. 110–115, 2016.
DOI: 10.1007/978-3-319-40548-3_18

community has recently challenged the use of null hypothesis significance testing (NHST) as a tool for determining causal relations [1].

1.2 Complex Systems

Complex systems are the result of feedback that takes place inside dynamic systems. In dynamic systems the future values for outcome variables are due to the interactions of causal variables as modified by a shared, often hidden, function. Granger causality empowers causal inference by examining if historic information in a variable strongly relates to the present information in another. Taken's theorem extends this type of inference to complex systems through examining the time embedded offsets of variables.

Attractors refer to regions within a hyperspace defined by a set of variables from a complex system. The future values of the variables are drawn towards these regions. The force of the attractor depends upon the proximity of the nearby points. Phase shifts are stable states within a complex system where the force of the attractor is similar to the force of the noise within the surrounding system.

1.3 Decision Support Systems

Modern decision-making support systems often makes use of semi or fully automated algorithms [2]. These algorithms outsource some or all of the mental processing required to create an informed decision. As these systems become increasingly advanced and as the underlying systems they strive to model continue to increase in complexity, it will become increasingly difficult to assess causality in coupled systems.

2 Method

2.1 Microwave Heating

Microwave ovens are a popular technology for preparing food. Microwave heating represents an applied environment that includes people, technology, and processes. It is difficult for practitioners to design proper protocols for people to follow when using a microwave to heat a new product that will result in a uniformly heated product. Every product reacts slightly differently to microwave ovens due to factors such as water or fat content, salinity, starting temperature, etc. Microwave ovens add to this complexity by contributing a set of factors such as shape, size, power, turntable rotation rate, etc. For these reasons it is challenging for practitioners to design products or ovens which consistently yield uniform heating results.

Microwave researchers also find it challenging to create a laboratory environment that yields controlled, granular data. For this reason this research makes use of the QWED QuickWave-3D software to simulate electromagnetic wave propagation within the microwave oven and product, the resulting heating of a product, and for data within simulation output files. This study simulated thawing of a $100 \times 75 \times 13.5$ mm block of frozen beef in a microwave oven operating at 2.45 GHz. The output data set contains values of the electromagnetic fields in and near the waveguide that feeds microwave power to the oven cavity, the fields within the cavity, and the product, and the temperature. The sample interval was 0.5 s time steps within a 3D grid of either 15 or 20 cells per wavelength in and around the product. The initial position of the product was either centered on the turntable (X0Y0), moved 5 mm to the right and 5 mm to the rear of the oven (X5Y5), or moved 10 mm (X10Y10). The turntable rotated at 3 rpm.

2.2   Convergent Cross Mapping

Convergent cross-mapping refers to approaches that utilize time embedded relationships between variables to determine their causal influence [3, 4]. CCM tests for causation through examining the extent to which the historic record for one variable can reliably estimate the sates of another. It does this by examining the correlation between predicted and observed variables across time-embedded delayed versions of the original variables. All of these offset dimensions for a variable collectively forms a manifold. CCM uses the points from the manifold for one variable to predict the points on another. It repeats this process several times. Each iteration considers slightly more historic data. The correlation between these predictions and the actual values across sets of various length yields the final CCM result.

This research extends CCM to handle larger data sets. The size of the datasets yielded via QWED were far too large to for direct use within the CCM process due to runtimes exponential to the number of input values. To combat this we modified the approach to use the percentile ranks of individual metrics. Percentile-percentile plots are a common, non-parametric technique for analyzing the similarity in the rate of change between two variables. We used CCM to cross map the independent variables across various percentile cohorts within this 3D space.

2.3   CCM Applied to Microwave Heating Uniformity

A common goal in microwave heating is to improve heating uniformity within the product. Poor heating uniformity can result from a multitude of factors [5–8]. Effects such as multiple field reflections and standing waves within the product and preferential heating at edges and corners often contribute to poor heating uniformity. The temperature-dependent complex permittivity of the food influences reflections at interfaces, microwave wavelength within the food, and the dissipative conversion of electromagnetic energy into heat. When the food undergoes phase change (e.g., thawing of ice), the permittivity can change dramatically over a range of 2–3 °C. When increasing temperature leads to increased absorption of microwave power by any of several mechanisms, runaway heating can result. Runaway heating can lead to rapid, local heating, potentially causing burns, charring, and in extreme cases eruptive boiling or fire. In this work we used thermophysical properties (including permittivity) specified for beef in the food.pmo file distributed with QuickWave-3D. We investigate whether the CCM inference approach can assess the causal effect of initial product position (X0Y0, X5Y5, X10Y10) on heating uniformity.

3   Results

To establish the causality of two variables A and B using CCM, examine their resultant cross mapped (xmap) correlation values (ρ). For A xmap to B, if ρ increases as library length (l) increases then it implies that B drives A and vice versa. This seems counter-intuitive but it takes place because the information from the driving variable is passing through the passive variable. If both lines increase then both variable drive each other. If neither line increase then neither variable drives the other.

3.1   Cross Map Outputs

Load at X0Y0. Because the median of the temperature (T50) xmap with the median of the electromagnetic field (E50) increases as l increases, this implies that the E50 drives T50 (see Fig. 1). This is consistent with expectations. However, because E xmap T also increases with l this is evidence of weak bidirectional causality. E50 xamps T50 with $\rho = 0.96$ and E50 xmaps T50 with $\rho = 0.50$.

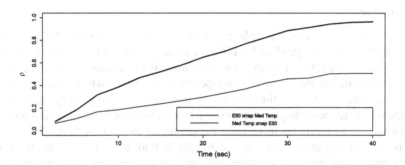

Fig. 1. Load position effects analyzed at X0Y0 using CCM on E50 v. T50

Load at X5Y5. Electromagnetic effect strongly drives temperature. T50 xmaps E50 nearly perfectly with $\rho = 1.0$ (See Fig. 2). Bidirectional causality is more evident at this location. Here E50 xmaps T50 with $\rho = 0.70$. Compare this to 0.50 at X0Y0.

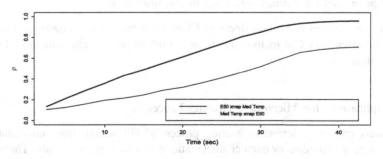

Fig. 2. Load position effects analyzed at X5Y5 using CCM on E50 v. T50

Load at X10Y10. Electromagnetic effect strongly drives temperature. T50 xmaps E50 nearly perfectly with $\rho = 1.0$ (see Fig. 3). Here bidirectional causality is strongly evident; E50 xmaps T50 with $\rho = 0.90$. Compare $\rho = 0.70$ at X5Y5 and to $\rho = 0.50$ at X0Y0.

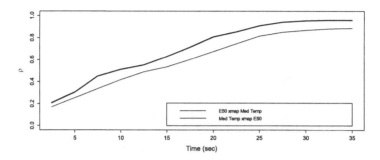

Fig. 3. Load position effects analyzed at X10Y10 using CCM on E50 v. T50

3.2 Analysis

We suspect the bidirectional coupling reflects interactions between the microwave electromagnetic field and product load. Power absorbed from an electromagnetic field is converted to heat (thus, a temperature increase). If the product load is capable of absorbing more power with increasing temperature—as occurs when ice in food thaws —the electromagnetic field in the oven cavity may decrease. Controlling for oven and load type for the range of displacements studied here, moving the product further away from the oven center appears to increase the degree of bidirectional causality.

This method appears to provide a technique to rank the relative strength of two causal relationships within a complex system. Location of a load is a simple but significant variable capable of influencing microwave heating effects and causality relationships across load locations.

4 Discussion

4.1 Implications for Causal Inference in Complex Systems

While [1] has illustrated the usefulness of CCM for establishing causality in complex system, the extended CCM method mentioned in this paper will allow the use of CCM on larger data sets.

4.2 Implications for Microwave Heating Processes

Practitioners creating microwave heating processes will benefit from understanding how differences in product or oven characteristics effect heating uniformity. The results so far suggest that incorporating this technique within microwave simulations would be a step towards transforming such simulations into decision support systems.

4.3 Implications for Decision Support Systems

The need to understand causal relationships between different variables will increase. Decision support systems are increasingly adopting machine-assisted decision-making approaches. These approaches continue to encompass an increasing share of the decision-making responsibilities. Techniques such as those mentioned in this paper will allow researchers to build systems capable of automatically discovering the direction of relationships between variables.

5 Future Work

As mentioned, this is currently a work in progress. We plan to further improve the efficiency of the CCM method. This will allow future work to examine additional design variables such as load geometry, dielectric properties, oven design, rotation or translation rate, packaging design, and packaging materials. Further understanding of the use of these methods to guide system input variables will inform the incorporation of this technique into decision support systems.

Acknowledgements. Our thanks to QWED for use of their QuickWave-3D software.

References

1. Trafimow, D., Marks, M.: Editorial. Basic Appl. Soc. Psychol. **37**, 1–2 (2015)
2. Kirk, R.A.: Evaluating a cognitive tool built to aid decision making using decision making approach as a theoretical framework and using unobtrusive, behavior-based measures for analysis. Doctoral Dissertation, Retrieved from ProQuest (3684297) (2015)
3. Sugihara, G., May, R., Ye, H., Hsieh, C., Deyle, E., Fogarty, M., Munch, S.: Science **338**, 496–500 (2012)
4. Ye, H., et al.: Distinguishing time-delayed causal interactions using convergent cross mapping. Sci. Rep. **5**, 14750 (2015)
5. Risman, P.O.: In: Lorence, M.W., Pesheck, P.S. (eds.) Development of Packaging and Products for Use in Microwave Ovens, pp. 66–105. Woodhead, Cambridge (2009)
6. Wapping-Raaholt, B., Ohlsson, T.: In: Lorence, M.W., Pesheck, P.S. (eds.) Development of Packaging and Products for Use in Microwave Ovens, pp. 38–65. Woodhead, Cambridge (2009)
7. Vadivambal, R., Jayas, D.S.: Non-uniform temperature distribution during microwave heating of food materials—a review. Food Bioprocess Technol. **3**, 161–171 (2010)
8. Murphy, E.K., Yakovlev, V.V.: RBF network optimization of complex microwave systems represented by small FDTD data sets. IEEE Trans. Microw. Theory Tech. **54**(1), 245–256 (2006)

How to Measure Quality of Affordable 3D Printing: Cultivating Quantitative Index in the User Community

Minjae Ko$^{(\boxtimes)}$, Heemoon Kang, Jong ulrim Kim, Yonghyeon Lee, and Jie-Eun Hwang

Department of Architecture, University of Seoul, Seoul, Korea
kmj2653@gmail.com, shhang528@gmail.com,
thoutbox@gmail.com, curiozen@gmail.com,
jongk0795@naver.com

Abstract. Recently, affordable 3d printers have become widely available for personal fabrication. However, the quality of printed outputs often varies aside from printer's machine specifications. It depends on diverse situated factors such as printing materials, slicing algorithm, model layouts, and environment of the printer. In this paper, we examined the related works on popular 3D printing communities in order to find common terminology and to determine the limitations of such experiential evaluation. We suggested a series of the advanced test models and quantitative quality indexes that can be collectively executed and delivered in the community.

Keywords: Affordable 3d printing · Quality index · Quantitative measurement

1 Introduction

Rapid development of 3D printing industry leverages the affordable 3D printer market dramatically. People can easily access 3D printing technology without advanced knowledge. Nevertheless, it is difficult to sustain high quality by using affordable 3d printers, because the quality of printed outputs is not just derived by machine specifications but also various situated factors such as printing mechanism, material properties, slicing algorithm, individual know-how, and so on. Early 3D printer users have conducted the evaluation for the quality of their own 3d printer by printing test models. That has been accumulated useful information about quality factors and models for tests on popular 3D printing communities such as *Thingiverse.com*. Nonetheless, most data of printing quality available is subjective and experiential information [4], because their purpose was to share problems and solutions from the failure, not to achieve objective evaluation. Comparable data of printing quality is essential for end users, HW/SW developers, and engineers in the field of 3d printing. As it enables users to predict the quality of a physical output, users can set an effective design guide or strategies to secure the best quality in advance. Controlling the quality of printed outputs in design process can greatly reduce the cost and time of post-build finishing processes [3]. The quality database would be helpful for a user-to-be or a consumer of the printing service to make

© Springer International Publishing Switzerland 2016
C. Stephanidis (Ed.): HCII 2016 Posters, Part I, CCIS 617, pp. 116–121, 2016.
DOI: 10.1007/978-3-319-40548-3_19

a correct decision as well. In the platform such as 3dhubs.com, a local printing service network, printing quality data could make it more reliable.

In this paper, we examined the related works on popular 3D printing communities in order to categorize common factors more simply and found the limitations and improvements of such experiential evaluation. Then we suggested a series of the advanced test models of the categories and quantitative quality indexes that can be collectively executed and delivered in the community.

2   Case Study

We studied to verify the availability of existing quality evaluation projects of *Thingiverse.com, 3DBechy.com*, and *Make: magazine*. We observed terminologies, shapes, and evaluation methods in used for;

- 378 models categorized "Popular-3d printing-3d printing tests" by *Thingiverse.com*
- a test model of *3dbenchy.com*
- 7 test models of the article "What is Print Quality?" in *Make:* magazine, vol.42 (Table 1).

Table 1. Features and limitations of the cases

Case	Features & Limitations
Thinginverse.com	There is lack of unity among used terminologies on Evaluation methods, quality factors, or test models. However, as the test models have been shared and used for calibration over time, users have started using a common keywords or meanings based on the critical factors or causes of printing quality deviation.
3dbenchy.com	As for shape, *3dbenchy.com* used one model including all elements to be measured, and designed it ship-shaped not typical geometries only for measuring. Although combining test features enables users to save time and materials, failed parts of the model may interfere with the proper compiling of other model features [2].
Make: magazine	Based on the individual knowledge of many open source communities, they tried to reorganize the evaluation items using common terminology. And their 7 different types of test models are more appropriate for objective conditions than that of *3dbenchy.com*. But they couldn't propose the strictly quantitative measurement for each evaluation item except dimensional accuracy. As Its evaluation guidelines include ambiguous words such as "slightly different", "little distinguishable difference" or "any dropped", they are open to arbitrary interpretations. That's because planners did not find any suitable method for measuring or excluded inaccessible measurements in order to enable end-users to evaluate their own print output as a measurers. These limitations may stem from the fact that the printing quality evaluation mainly driven by end-users.

3   The Proposed Category

First, we reorganized quality evaluation items according to the quantitative measurement methods in order to overcome the limitations of existing cases and make new quality evaluation standards. We divided them into 2 groups: Dimensional accuracy and Surface finish. In addition to that, we included build time issues as an important quality factor to be measured, because the time taken for 3d printing indirectly represents various invisible settings of slicers for improving the print quality (Table 2).

Table 2. Grouping evaluation items with quantitative measurement methods

Dimensional Accuracy		Surface Finish	
Accuracy(Backlash)			
LOD (Level of Detail)	Positive fine	Orthogonal surface	**+ Build time**
	Negative space		
	Thickness	Overhang surface	
Bridging			

3.1 Dimensional Accuracy

Dimensional accuracy of the output can be critical for applications where fitting and assemblage are important or when parts have very small feature sizes [5]. Test models belonged to the dimensional accuracy group are measured by using the digital calipers or self-judging. This is a typical way of quantitative measurement used in existing cases, and it measures how accurate the size of the output corresponds to the size of the digital 3d model. Dimensional errors normally occurred because of mechanical issues, extrusion width parameter, material properties and so on.

- Accuracy (Backlash): An accuracy quality factor could be general dimensional errors and the backlash phenomenon of 3d printers. In mechanical engineering, backlash is clearance or lost motion in a mechanism caused by gaps between the parts. It can be seen when the direction of movement is reversed and the slack or lost motion is taken up before the reversal of motion is complete [1].
- LOD (Level of Detail): Capability of the 3d printer to describe more detailed objects accurately is also related to Dimensional Accuracy evaluation. LOD factors could be morphological issues. In this research, each one is focused on: Positive fine, Negative space, and Thickness (Table 3).

Table 3. Shapes of LOD quality factors

Positive fine detail		Negative space detail		Thickness detail	
	Capability to print smaller sections		Capability to print smaller gaps		Capability to print Thinner walls

- Bridging: Bridging is where an otherwise unsupported gap must be crossed by a layer to form the desired structure. Variations in travel speed, extrusion quantity, and cooling will affect the bridging capabilities of the manufacturing processes.

3.2   Surface Finish

Surface finish is an important quality factor that can be recognized intuitively. Low-quality surfaces lead to a direct impact on post-processing costs, aesthetics and functionality of final outputs in production process. Surface roughness is often measured for evaluating surface finish quality. It is quantified by the deviations in the direction of the normal vector of a real surface from its ideal form. The overhang test in existing cases is relevant to the surface finish of 3d printing. The angle between surface to be print and a build plane is a critical factor to determine surface quality. Additionally, we categorized orthogonal surfaces as surface finish group in order to cover surface quality in general forms such as side, top, bottom, and supported surfaces (Table 4).

Table 4. Types of surface

Overhang surface	Orthogonal surface			
Overhang	Side	Top	Bottom on Raft	Bottom on Support

4   Design and Implementation

Based on the proposed category, we designed 7 different test models and collected 17 samples from 8 manufacturers during this research. In this paper, we would verify the possibility to compare quality of 3 samples printed with Ultimaker Original, Ultimaker2, and Flash Forge Creator.

4.1   Test Models with Quantitative Quality Index

According to the evaluation items, we have developed new test model standards as below:

- Challenging features do not interfere with each other. (designing different models for each evaluation item, not an integrated model)
- Test models have unified size and design.
- Test models have appropriate shapes for measuring with a digital calipers and a digital microscope (Tables 5 and 6).

4.2   Comparison of the Printing Quality Index

Conducting the proposed quality evaluation process for 3 outputs from different conditions (printer-materials-slicer-manufacturer), we have verified the possibility of

Table 5. Test models and indexes of dimensional accuracy evaluation

Evaluation item		Design	Dimension	Quantitative index
Accuracy(Backlash)				Main index is average of dimensional errors in the length of outer steps in x, y, z direction. Additionally, depth of holes are used to get the backlash value in x, and y axis.
LOD (Level of Detail)	Positive Fine Detail			Main index is average of dimensional errors in the height of pyramids. Additionally, it can be used for evaluating the retraction performance.
	Negative Fine Space Detail			Main index is the number of pins eliminated from output. Additionally, it can be used for the part fitting tests by using the upper part and remaining pins.
	Thickness Detail			Main index is average of dimensional errors in the thickness of walls.
Bridging				Main index is average of dimensional errors in the thickness of the bridge to evaluate the bridging performance.

Table 6. Test models and indexes of surface finish

Evaluation item	Design	Dimension	Quantitative index
Orthogonal surface			P_a value of roughness and image of the surfaces
Overhang surface			P_a value of roughness and image of the surfaces

getting comparable data. In the evaluation results, outputs from Flash Forge Creator and Ultimaker Original have higher level of accuracy. Flash Forge Creator also produced better surface finishes. However, as we have established the quality indexes of negative value such as dimensional errors or surface roughness, lower index value means higher printing quality. In order for users to figure out the quality index more clearly, it is necessary to collect enough data to get reference value and to redefine the index of positive value in future research.

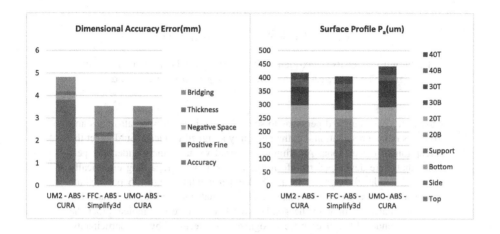

5   Conclusion

We insist the importance of the quantitative data about printing quality and its constructive value within user community. Analyzing related works conducted by *Thingiverse.com*, *3dbenchy.com*, and *Make:*, We found that the user community had autonomously contributed empirical evaluation of the printing quality yet it was insufficient to propose the quantitative index of evaluation for the test models. We reorganized the evaluation items and suggested new test models to measure dimensional accuracy and surface finish. We anticipate these test models evolve as community-cultivated standard. For future study, we are currently planning a printing quality database service that end users and individual manufacturers of affordable 3D printers can feed and refer collectively.

References

1. Backlash (engineering). https://en.wikipedia.org/wiki/Backlash_(engineering)
2. Bastain, A.: What is Print Quality? (2014). http://makezine.com/2014/11/07/what-is-print-quality/
3. Boschetto, A., Giordano, V., Veniali, F.: 3D roughness profile model in fused deposition modelling. Rapid Prototyping J. **19**(4), 240–252 (2013)
4. Brajlih, T., Valentan, B., Balic, J., Drstvensek, I.: Speed and accuracy evaluation of additive manufacturing machines. Rapid Prototyping J. **17**(1), 64–75 (2011)
5. Turner, B.N., Gold, S.A.: A review of melt extrusion additive manufacturing processes: II. Materials, dimensional accuracy, and surface roughness. Rapid Prototyping J. **21**(3), 250–261 (2015)

Evaluation of GenderMag Personas Based on Persona Attributes and Persona Gender

Nicola Marsden[(⊠)] and Maren Haag

Heilbronn University, Max-Planck-Street 39, 74081 Heilbronn, Germany
{nicola.marsden,maren.haag}@hs-heilbronn.de

Abstract. We examined personas to see if (a) gendered persona attributes and (b) the persona presentation, i.e. the randomly assigned gender, would affect the perception of the persona. As stimulus material we used the GenderMag personas that were developed to inform the design process regarding empirically validated gender differences. In a 2×2 experimental design, 36 participants were randomly assigned to evaluate a male or female GenderMag persona either in its original form or with the gender switched. The results indicate that the facets of gender differences were recognized and recalled by the participants. The masculine facets yielded an attribution of higher competence in the personas. The findings can serve as a basis to further discuss what gender-inclusiveness means with regards to personas.

Keywords: Personas · User representation · Social perception · Stereotypes · Usability · GenderMag · Experimental study

1 Introduction

People have the ability to understand others based on a minimum of information about this person. This ability has developed to efficiently process stimuli in the environment. With only a few pieces of information, people can organize and integrate the available material into significant categories. This process is called impression formation [1]: People evaluate social stimuli and then make attributions by inferring traits, intentions, and motivations. To a large extent, these evaluations are automatic processes [2], i.e. they happen without conscious endorsement. Person perception is something that has an imperative flavor; it happens with ease and gives people the feeling of understanding a person.

The persona method makes use of these social intuitions [3]: Personas are fictitious characters created as representatives of users in the design process [4]. They foreground people in the design process and rely on impressions made based on these descriptions. Their appeal lies in the fact that person perception is something familiar to everyone and happening with ease. Yet person perception is prone to numerous biases that can distort social judgment [5]. Since personas are used to inform design, biased social judgments might run the risk of leading to incorrect predictions and implications.

One major source of bias in person perception is gender, leading to numerous effects, e.g. unconsciously devaluing feminine attributes or viewing attributes differently when a male displays them as opposed to a female [6]. Gender is related to the

© Springer International Publishing Switzerland 2016
C. Stephanidis (Ed.): HCII 2016 Posters, Part I, CCIS 617, pp. 122–127, 2016.
DOI: 10.1007/978-3-319-40548-3_20

social attractiveness of an individual and a predisposition to interact with them [7]. Perception of gender is highly linked to role and trait inferences [8]. The two basic dimensions of person perception and social judgment, warmth and competence, are clearly correlated to gender [9]. Development of personas has been shown to rely on gender stereotypes regarding the warmth dimension [10, 11].

2   GenderMag Personas

In an effort to support the development of gender-inclusive software, Margaret Burnett and her colleagues have developed a method for considering existing gender differences [12, 13]. Taking into account actual statistical differences between men and women as they pertain to software tools, they have developed personas representing the different approaches to software that are found more often in males or females. Their method "GenderMag Method – GenderHCI Cognitive Walkthrough with Magnifying Persona" is a kit for software development teams to develop more gender-inclusive software. It consists of a cognitive walkthrough and several personas, including the persona of a female end-user programmer called "Abby", to support analysis especially from a female perspective. The personas can be adapted regarding characteristics of different target user populations, e.g. occupation, age, or geographic location. The authors have carefully designed the personas to not reinforce stereotypes of female versus male users' skills: They are presented as equally good problem-solvers and equally competent with their technical domain. The differences incorporated in the persona descriptions concern five facets: Their motivations to use technology, their information-processing style, computer self-efficacy, risk aversion, and tinkering.

3   Research Questions

With our study we wanted to answer the following research questions:

- Do the gender-specific attributes that the GenderMag Personas are based on make a difference, i.e. is the impression regarding the facets based on the content of the persona description?
- Do gender-specific attributes and/or the presentation as male or female influence the attractiveness of the persona?
- Do gender-specific attributes and/or the presentation as male or female influence the perceived competence or warmth of the persona?

4   Method

Participants. Participants were software engineering students of a large University of Applied Sciences in Germany. They participated in the lab study for course credits. 36 of them completed the questionnaire. The sample consisted of 27 males and 9 females, i.e. the gender ratio in the sample approximates the ratio in the population of IT students and software engineers.

Materials. Independent variables in the experimental design of the study were the persona presentation (male vs. female) and persona attributes (masculine vs. feminine). Stimulus material was the GenderMag Personas "Tim" and "Abby", presented in their original, gender-conforming mode or with the gender switched. These personas are designed to describe the attitudes and behavior found more often in men ("Tim") or women ("Abby"). Thus personas were presented either as male ("Tim") vs. female ("Abby") or with masculine vs. feminine attributes, yielding a 2 × 2 design. The dependent variables were operationalized in a questionnaire comprising the following scales:

- perception of the facets of the GenderMag personas (information processing style, computer self-efficacy, risk aversion, tinkering [12]), operationalized on a scale with two items per facet (e.g. "How confident is this persona in using computers?") and a five-point Likert scale (1 = "not at all", 5 = "extremely")
- ratings of interpersonal attraction (task attraction and personal attraction), using the scale by [7]
- ratings of warmth and competence as basic dimensions of person perception, using the scale by [9].

Procedure. In a between-subjects design, participants were randomly assigned to one of four (persona presented as male vs. female x persona presented with masculine vs. feminine attributes) conditions. They were instructed to peruse the persona description and imagine introducing a new spreadsheet feature to this kind of user. Then they filled out the questionnaire with the scales presented above and basic socio-demographic information.

5   Results

Facets. Regarding the perception of the personas in line with the facets that are used in the GenderMag personas to differentiate male and female approaches, the following results were found:

- Regarding information-processing style no significant effect could be found.
- Regarding computer self-efficacy, the main effect of persona gender was not significant. The main effect of persona attributes was significant, $F(1, 32) = 50.63$, $p < .001$: Computer self-efficacy was significantly higher for personas presented with masculine attributes (M = 8.79) than for personas presented with feminine attributes (M = 4.94). The interaction effect of persona gender and persona attributes was not significant.
- Regarding risk aversion, the main effect of persona gender was not significant. The main effect of persona attributes was significant, $F(1, 32) = 49.38$, $p < .001$: Risk aversion was significantly higher for personas presented with feminine attributes (M = 6.35) than for personas presented with masculine attributes (M = 3.12). The interaction effect of persona gender and persona attributes was not significant.

- Regarding tinkering, the main effect of persona gender was not significant. The main effect of persona attributes was significant, $F(1, 32) = 63.39$, $p < .001$: Tinkering was significantly higher for personas presented with masculine attributes $(M = 9.21)$ than for personas presented with feminine attributes $(M = 4.71)$. The interaction effect of persona gender and persona attributes was not significant.

Interpersonal Attraction. Regarding the interpersonal attraction of the personas evaluated, no significant effect could be found.

Stereotype Content. Regarding warmth no significant effect could be found. There was a significant effect regarding competence, which is visualized in Fig. 1.

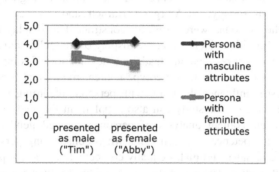

Fig. 1. Competence evaluation – visualization of the main effect of persona attributes on competence. (Color figure online)

Competence was significantly higher for personas presented with masculine attributes $(M = 4.07)$ than for personas presented with feminine attributes $(M = 3.02)$, i.e. the main effect of persona attributes was significant, $F(1, 32) = 14.50$, $p < .01$. The main effect of persona gender and the interaction effect of persona gender and persona attributes were not significant.

6 Discussion

Research into person perception regularly demonstrates gender influences – both in the way that masculine attributes are deemed more important than feminine attributes and that the same attributes are perceived differently when a female versus a male displays them [6]. We replicated some of these effects for personas. A two-by-two analysis of variance yielded a significant main effect for the persona description for most of the facets the gendered descriptions of the GenderMag personas are based on.

The data collected in this study provide evidence that the facets Margaret Burnett and her colleagues [12, 13] based their personas on for a gendered representation of the users were perceived and recalled by the participants. This indicates that they are clearly recognizable in the description. In our study, the descriptions of feminine and masculine attributes were more important than the sole information of a persona being male or female. This can be interpreted as an indicator that the facets actually offer additional information, i.e. although gendered, they cannot be inferred from the information of a personas gender. Rather, they seem to be seen as facets that can actually be displayed by both females and males.

The data yielded regarding the competence dimension of the stereotype content model is disquieting. Presenting the persona as motivated by technology itself, selective in information processing, displaying a high computer self-efficacy, risk-taking, and tinkering made them seem more competent than presenting them as using technology for what it enables one to do, having a comprehensive information processing style, lower computer self-efficacy, be risk averse, and less likely to tinker. The qualities that have been found to be more prevalent in female users thus lead to a depreciation of the persona's competence. The attribution of higher competence to males is prevalent in society, so Margaret Burnett and her colleagues explicitly emphasized that the personas were carefully constructed to display equal technical expertise. Our data provide evidence that the display of masculine attributes overrides the expertise assigned to a persona and leads to a devaluation of competence on other grounds. In line with results on the stereotype content model this further shows how unconscious processes influence the work with personas regarding the dimension of competence. The results of this study can also supplement the study by Marsden and colleagues [10]: Their content analysis of personas showed gender differences in warmth but not in competence – it seems that when constructing personas, designers are careful to create females and males equally competent. The study presented in this paper suggests that even personas carefully constructed to display equal competence may yield a perceived inequality for the people working with the personas.

The participants had evaluated task attraction and personal attraction of the personas, but gendered attributes and persona gender did not yield any differences. This seems to suggest that the two personas that the study was based on are equally attractive.

7   Conclusion

Gender biases in person perception are a comprehensively researched topic in social psychology. So it might come as no surprise that they can also be found in the perception of personas. Nevertheless, the personas used in this study were carefully created to display equal competence and to further an appreciation for the facets that have been shown to be relevant gender differences in the use of technological artifacts. Therefore the results are unsettling: Gender biases might be seen as unavoidable in impression formation of real people one encounters. Yet in the creation of fictitious characters that are developed to base design decisions on they could be seen as a call for action. A solution might be to consider existing gender biases in the development of personas. Designing personas to be impartial and fair might then imply one has to put less emphasis on statistical gender differences in user groups and rather consider statistical differences in the perception of personas. Compensating existing gender biases in person perception would thus be a way to ensure that existing gender biases are not used to inform design of future technological artifacts.

References

1. Asch, S.E.: Forming impressions of personality. J. Abnorm. Soc. Psychol. **41**, 258–290 (1946)
2. Bargh, J.A.: Social Psychology and the Unconscious: The Automaticity of Higher Mental Processes. Psychology Press, London (2013)
3. Marsden, N., Haag, M.: Stereotypes and politics: reflections on personas. In: Proceedings of the SIGCHI Conference on Human Factors in Computing Systems (CHI 2016). ACM, New York, NY, USA (2016)
4. Nielsen, L.: Personas - User Focused Design. Springer, Heidelberg (2013)
5. Fiske, S.T.: Stereotyping, prejudice, and discrimination at the seam between the centuries: Evolution, culture, mind, and brain. Eur. J. Soc. Psychol. **30**, 299–322 (2000)
6. Barreto, M., Ellemers, N.: Detecting and experiencing prejudice: new answers to old questions. In: James, M.O., Mark, P.Z. (eds.) Advances in Experimental Social Psychology, vol. 52, pp. 139–219. Academic Press, New York (2015)
7. McCroskey, L.L., McCroskey, J.C., Richmond, V.P.: Analysis and improvement of the measurement of interpersonal attraction and homophily. Commun. Q. **54**, 1–31 (2006)
8. Kite, M.E., Deaux, K., Haines, E.L.: Gender stereotypes. Psychol. Women Handb. Issues Theor. **2**, 205–236 (2008)
9. Fiske, S., Cuddy, A., Glick, P., Xu, J.: A model of (often mixed) stereotype content: competence and warmth respectively follow from perceived status and competition. J. Pers. Soc. Psychol. **82**, 878–902 (2002)
10. Marsden, N., Link, J., Büllesfeld, E.: Geschlechterstereotype in Persona- Beschreibungen. In: Diefenbach, S., Henze, N., Pielot, M. (eds.) Mensch und Computer 2015 Tagungsband, pp. 113–122. Oldenbourg Wissenschaftsverlag, Stuttgart (2015)
11. Link, J., Büllesfeld, E., Marsden, N.: Genderbewusste Erstellung von Persona-Sets. In: Klemisch, M., Spitzley, A., Wilke, J. (eds.) Gender- und Diversity-Management in der Forschung, pp. 152–165. Fraunhofer-Institut für Arbeitswirtschaft und Organisation IAO, Stuttgart (2015)
12. Burnett, M., Stumpf, S., Macbeth, J., Makri, S., Beckwith, L., Kwan, I., Peters, A., Jernigan, W.: GenderMag: a method for evaluating software's gender inclusiveness. Interact. Comput. **iwv046** (2016)
13. Burnett, M., Peters, A., Hill, C., Elarief, N.: Finding gender-inclusiveness software issues with GenderMag: a field investigation. In: Proceedings of the SIGCHI Conference on Human Factors in Computing Systems (CHI 2016). ACM, New York, NY, USA (2016)

From Acceptability to Acceptance: Does Experience with the Product Influence User Initial Representations?

Nicolas Martin[1,2(✉)], Éric Jamet[2], Séverine Erhel[2],
and Géraldine Rouxel[2]

[1] Uses and Acceptability Lab, b<>com, Cesson-Sévigné, France
`nicolas.martin@b-com.com`
[2] CRPCC, University of Brittany, Rennes, France
`{eric.jamet,severine.erhel,`
`geraldine.rouxel}@univ-rennes2.fr`

Abstract. Adopting a product can be seen as a process that implies some repeated use influencing either positively or negatively judgment over time. Indeed, product judgement is likely to evolve over time and influence the intention to continue using. At yet, little research is available on the evolution of product judgement with use. In this paper, we examined the evolution of User eXperience (UX) and affective-motivational factors between evaluation before and after use. Results showed that interaction with the product significantly influences initial representations with, in our study, more negative judgments after use. Moreover, using Expectation-Disconfirmation Theory, significant influences of initial evaluations (i.e. judgement before use) and disconfirmation (i.e. difference between judgement after and before use) were found on behavioral intention after use.

Keywords: Acceptability · Acceptance · User eXperience (UX) · Comparison before-after use · Expectation-Disconfirmation Theory

1 Introduction

Product adoption is a long term process: it starts from user representations before use and evolves over time with use. Thereby, understanding factors that lead to continued use is a critical point for companies that develop technological products. Consequently, research has been conducted to better understand technology use, with the aim to identify facilitating or inhibitory factors to the adoption of a technological product. Thus, a distinction is made between acceptability (the judgment toward a technology before use [1]) and acceptance (the judgment and the behavioral reactions toward a product after use [1]). Although this distinction exists, majority of research is centered on acceptance. In the following study, we explored the difference between evaluation before and after use in the context of mobile application. Moreover, we tried to understand the factors that explain the pursuit of use of a mobile application through the framework of EDT.

© Springer International Publishing Switzerland 2016
C. Stephanidis (Ed.): HCII 2016 Posters, Part I, CCIS 617, pp. 128–133, 2016.
DOI: 10.1007/978-3-319-40548-3_21

1.1 Acceptance, User eXperience and Affective-Motivational Factors

To understand product adoption, two main models are commonly used: TAM [2] and UTAUT [3]. According to these models, behavioral intention derives from the perception of functional qualities (especially usability and usefulness). Although these models have been tested in numerous studies [4, 5], some limits are now widely recognized. First, inside theoretical field of User eXperience (UX) it was demonstrated that users perceive product beyond their functional qualities [6]. Thereby, UX is defined as "a person's perceptions and responses that result from the use and/or anticipated use of a product, system or service" [7] and incorporates functional and non-functional qualities as predictors of overall judgement [8]. Second, several researchers has highlighted that product's judgement is more complex than a rational evaluation based on quality criteria [9]. Thus, according to previous research, factors as self-image [e.g. 10], intrinsic motivation [e.g. 11] and social influence [e.g. 5] are good predictors of acceptance in addition to usability and usefulness. Nevertheless, aside from a few studies [12, 13], research is only centered on judgement after use. Thereby, we proposed to evaluate the evolution of functional, nonfunctional and affective-motivational variables between evaluation before and after use. Moreover, to understand evolution from acceptability (i.e. judgment before use) to acceptance (i.e. judgement after use), we tried to use the framework of Expectation-Disconfirmation Theory (EDT) [14].

1.2 Expectation-Disconfirmation Theory

To our knowledge, only EDT proposed a framework to explain continued usage [e.g. 12, 13]. Based on Cognitive Dissonance Theory [15], this framework depicts a process model of individual behavior with product over time. According to EDT [14], when consumers purchase a product, they have some prior information on the product (i.e. initial expectations) based on second-hand information, such as vendor claims [12]. Over time and use, users gain more information and experience on the product [13]. Thereby, they compare their prior beliefs to new information gained with experience. If there is some dissonance (difference between one's cognition and reality [12]), they can revise their attitudes and behaviors (e.g. pursuit of use). Lastly, disconfirmations (difference between expectation and reality) and initial expectations determine user satisfaction which explains continued usage [13, 14].

According to previous studies, EDT is a useful framework to understand ongoing use [12, 13]. In the following study, we proposed to rely on EDT framework to study the evolution from acceptability to acceptance. The originality of our work is to include UX and affective-motivational factors in evaluation before and after use.

1.3 Current Study

Today, many people have a smartphone and consequently use mobile applications. Thereby, understanding adoption of applications is a major concern for developers. Nevertheless, in context of mobile application, judgement before use is essential.

Indeed, to choose to install an application, individuals must evaluate it before they can test it. However, to our knowledge, influence of UX and affective-motivational factors on judgement before use has not studied. Thereby, in current study, we evaluated difference between judgement before and after use on usefulness, usability, trust, stimulation, self-image, intrinsic motivation and social influence. Moreover, we used EDT framework to explore adoption of mobile applications. This framework seems to be adapted to mobile application context. Thus, before selecting and downloading an application, individuals have access to little information as the description of the application. From this information, individuals have to form their judgement and attitude toward the application. As soon as the individuals decide to install the application, they will be able to compare their prior judgments with the new representations of the actual application. According to previous studies, individuals should decide to continue their use by taking into account their initial expectations and disconfirmations (difference between expectations and reality).

2 Method

2.1 Material

To test the differences between pre-usage and after-usage on judgement of a mobile application, we have selected a sleeping tracker application "Sleep Better ©" [16]. This application was selected because it is simple, free, designed for repeated use and relatively distributed.

2.2 Measures

To evaluate the influence of UX and affective-motivational factors on acceptability/ acceptance, the following dimensions were measured:

- Assessment of UX factors: Usefulness (4 items), Usability (4 items), Stimulation (4 items) and Trust (3 items)
- Assessment of affective-factors: Motivation (5 items), Self-image (4 items) and Social Influence (3 items)
- Assessment of acceptability/acceptance: Intention to use (4 items)

Some items were constructed specifically for this study and others were based on existing questionnaires as UTAUT [3], Attrackdiff [8] and Engagement Scale [17]. For each item, participants had to answer on an 11 points likert scale (from 0 to 10). Position of each item in the questionnaire was randomly delivered to avoid effects related to order of the items [18]. Lastly, according to EDT, intention to continue using is based on initial expectations (i.e. evaluations before use) and disconfirmations (i.e. differences between expectations and reality). Expectations are measured by evaluating each dimension before use. Disconfirmations are evaluated by calculating the difference between the assessment after and before use for each dimension.

2.3   Procedure

Study involved four main steps: 1/The participants filled out the questionnaire before use after reading a brief presentation of the application. This presentation included text and pictures proposed by Runtastic on market app (Google Play). 2/At the end of the first questionnaire, participants could choose to test the application and participate in the rest of the study. To take part in the following study, participants had to provide their email address. 3/Participants who gave their email address received explanations for installing the application and a link for the post-use questionnaire. 4/After at least one night of use, the participants filled out the after use questionnaire. Only individuals who completed both evaluations were included in our analyses. Data between survey before and after use are linked anonymously with a unique code.

2.4   Participants

318 participants have completed the questionnaire before use. Nevertheless, only 47 participants (39 women), who never used the "sleep better" app, have completed evaluations before and after use. Analyses are realized on these participants. They were recruited on social network: Facebook, Twitter and Linkedin. The average age is 29.19 years (SD = 10.72).

3   Results

To test the effect of use on judgment, we computed comparisons between evaluation before and after user for each dimension. Since evaluation before and after use are completed by the same individuals, we used a statistical method that takes into account non-independence: mixed model [19]. Results (see Table 1) indicated significant decrease between evaluation before and after use on behavioral intention, usefulness, self-image and social influence.

Table 1. Descriptive statistics (mean and standard deviation) and comparison for evaluation before and after use.

Dimension	Before use	After use	Difference
Behavioral intention	6.59 (2.60)	4.89 (2.95)	χ^2 (1) = 17.00, $p < .001$
Usefulness	6.74 (2.19)	5.13 (2.41)	χ^2 (1) = 25.57, $p < .001$
Usability	7.58 (1.61)	7.73 (1.95)	χ^2 (1) = .36, NS
Stimulation	6.80 (2.24)	6.55 (1.74)	χ^2 (1) = .72, NS
Trust	5.56 (1.96)	4.96 (2.40)	χ^2 (1) = 3.42, NS
Self-image	3.77 (2.03)	2.73 (1.96)	χ^2 (1) = 14.58, $p < .001$
Motivation	5.54 (2.19)	5.18 (1.87)	χ^2 (1) = 1.47, NS
Social influence	4.94 (2.32)	2.75 (2.29)	χ^2 (1) = 33.29, $p < .001$

According to EDT, carry on using is based on initial representations (i.e. evaluation before use) and disconfirmation (i.e. difference between initial representations and reality) [12, 13]. To test theses hypotheses, we computed a multiple regression on behavioral intention after use. Results indicated significant influences of initial evaluations of usefulness ($\beta = .85$, $p < .01$), usability ($\beta = .55$, $p < .01$) and stimulation ($\beta = -.49$, $p < .05$). We found also an influence of disconfirmations for usefulness ($\beta = .50$, $p < .05$), usability ($\beta = .36$, $p < .05$), stimulation ($\beta = -.47$, $p < .05$) and trust ($\beta = .35$, $p < .05$). Lastly, among the affective-motivational factors, only intrinsic motivation seem to have an effect ($\beta = .68$, $p < .01$) on behavioral intention after use.

Lastly, we compared two models that explained behavioral intention after use: one model including only variables of TAM and our model introducing UX and affective-motivational factors. Result indicated a significant increasing ($F(7, 47) = 2.69$, $p < .05$) of the explained variance for our model ($R^2 = .67$ vs .74).

4   Discussion and Conclusion

Consistently with previous studies [12, 13], significant influences of use were found on evaluation of several variables: behavioral intention and perceptions of usefulness, trust, self-image and social influence decrease after use. Moreover, we used EDT framework to understand the adoption of this mobile application. To obtain a deeper comprehension than previous studies, we evaluated functional and nonfunctional qualities but also affective-motivational factors. In agreement with EDT, we evaluated the influence of prior judgement and disconfirmation on intention to carry on using. Results showed three main results: firstly, prior perceptions of usefulness, usability and stimulation influence intention to continue using. Secondly, disconfirmation (difference between initial perception and reality) on usefulness, usability, stimulation and trust are significant predictors of intention to continue using. Lastly, the intrinsic motivation is also a significant predictor of intention to continue using. In others words, the initial perceptions of qualities and the difference between these perceptions and reality influenced the intention to continue to use the product. In summary, take an interest to acceptability by evaluating before use functional, nonfunctional qualities and affective-motivational factors seems to be an interesting approach to understand product adoption and continue using.

Nevertheless, several limits can be addressed. Firstly, the sample was relatively small. To confirm our results, it is necessary to carry out new studies on larger samples. Secondly, only one application, which has good functional qualities according to users, was evaluated. For a deeper comprehension of judgement evolution, we should conduct new studies on more applications with several levels of qualities. Lastly, it is necessary to conduct longitudinal study for studying long term use.

Acknowledgements.   This work was carried out within the Institute of Technological Research b<>com and it received support from the French government under the program Future Investments bearing reference ANR-07-A0-AIRT.

References

1. Schuitema, G., Steg, L., Forward, S.: Explaining differences in acceptability before and acceptance after the implementation of a congestion charge in Stockholm. Transp. Res. Part Policy Pract. **44**, 99–109 (2010)
2. Davis, F.D.: Perceived usefulness, perceived ease of use, and user acceptance of information technology. MIS Q. **13**, 319–340 (1989)
3. Venkatesh, V., Morris, M., Davis, G., Davis, F.: User acceptance of information technology: toward a unified view. Manag. Inf. Syst. Q. **27**, 425–478 (2003)
4. King, W.R., He, J.: A meta-analysis of the technology acceptance model. Inf. Manag. **43**, 740–755 (2006)
5. Taiwo, Y.A., Downe, A.G.: The theory of user acceptance and use of technology (UTAUT): a meta-analytic review of empirical findings. J. Theor. Appl. Inf. Technol. **49** (2013)
6. Bargas-Avila, J.A., Hornbaek, K.: Old wine in new bottles or novel challenges? A critical analysis of empirical studies of user experience. In: Proceedings of the SIGCHI Conference on Human Factors in Computing Systems, pp. 2689–2698. ACM, New York (2011)
7. ISO: ISO 9241-210:2010 - Ergonomics of human-system interaction – Part 210: Human-centred design for interactive systems (2010)
8. Hassenzahl, M., Diefenbach, S., Göritz, A.: Needs, affect, and interactive products–facets of user experience. Interact. Comput. **22**, 353–362 (2010)
9. Venkatesh, V., Morris, M.G.: Why don't men ever stop to ask for directions? Gender, social influence, and their role in technology acceptance and usage behavior. MIS Q. **24**, 115–139 (2000)
10. van Schaik, P., Ling, J.: An integrated model of interaction experience for information retrieval in a web-based encyclopaedia. Interact. Comput. **23**, 18–32 (2011)
11. Lee, M.K.O., Cheung, C.M.K., Chen, Z.: Acceptance of Internet-based learning medium: the role of extrinsic and intrinsic motivation. Inf. Manag. **42**, 1095–1104 (2005)
12. Bhattacherjee, A., Premkumar, G.: Understanding changes in belief and attitude toward information technology usage: a theoretical model and longitudinal test. MIS Q. **28**, 229–254 (2004)
13. Venkatesh, V., Thong, J.Y.L., Chan, F.K.Y., Hu, P.J.-H., Brown, S.A.: Extending the two-stage information systems continuance model: incorporating UTAUT predictors and the role of context. Inf. Syst. J. **21**, 527–555 (2011)
14. Oliver, R.L.: A cognitive model of the antecedents and consequences of satisfaction decisions. J. Mark. Res. **17**, 460 (1980)
15. Festinger, L.: A Theory of Cognitive Dissonance. Stanford University Press, Palo Alto (1962)
16. Sleep Better App. https://www.runtastic.com/en/apps/sleepbetter
17. O'Brien, H.L., Toms, E.G.: Examining the generalizability of the user engagement scale (UES) in exploratory search. Inf. Process. Manag. **49**, 1092–1107 (2013)
18. Benton, J.E., Daly, J.L.: A question order effect in a local government survey. Public Opin. Q. **55**, 640–642 (1991)
19. Bates, D., Mächler, M., Bolker, B., Walker, S.: Fitting linear mixed-effects models using lme4. J. Stat. Softw. **67**, 1–48 (2015)

The Use of Emojis as a Tool to Measure Conceptual Design Artefacts

Rosamelia Parizotto-Ribeiro[✉] and Cayley Guimarães

Department of Industrial Design, Federal University of Technology – Parana,
Curitiba, Parana, Brazil
rosamelia@utfpr.edu.br, cayleyg@urfpr.edu.br

Abstract. This paper describes the development of a conceptual product aiming to support social awareness among people from two different generations and a tool to evaluate the potential emotional effect that this artefact could have on its users. The study was carried out during the Conceptual Design course at the Federal University of Technology – Parana. The students taking part of the course were students from the Design course. The results show that the emojis were perceived as a modern and quick way to evaluate conceptual products.

Keywords: Design · Social awareness · Conceptual product · Emojis

1 Introduction

This paper reports an empirical study that was carried out during the Conceptual Design course at the Federal University of Technology – Parana. The students taking part of the course were students from the Design course. They had to develop a conceptual interactive product aiming to support social awareness and a tool to evaluate the emotional effect of it on its users.

For the first part of the study the students had to develop the design of an artefact aiming to connect and create the sense of awareness among people from two different generations – granddaughter or grandson with their grandfather or grandmother – that lived far apart from each other but that were emotionally attached. Therefore, they had to design an artefact that would connect them through a predetermined message delivered by it and understood by the user. This artefact would be an aesthetically beautiful and pleasing product in order to create a more interesting and engaging interaction.

For the second part of the course they had to develop a simple, friendly and modern tool to evaluate the conceptual design artefact that they have developed.

In order to develop the evaluation tool they had to study the effects of positive and negative emotions (Norman 2004) on the user during the interactive experience. They also studied the non-verbal self-report instrument called PrEmo (Desmet and Hekkert 2007). This measurement instrument was developed to measure the mixed emotions that are elicited by an artefact.

C. Stephanidis (Ed.): HCII 2016 Posters, Part I, CCIS 617, pp. 134–137, 2016.
DOI: 10.1007/978-3-319-40548-3_22

2   Literature Review

During the last 15 years there were a lot of interest in the field of emotion and design. That brought a lot of research in the area, such as the research on how the brain works, giving evidence that emotions and cognition are very close related. This motivated several researches from different areas of interest to research about the role that emotion plays on how the user perceives an interactive product.

The students started their work by studying the three levels of emotional design (Norman 2004), the basis of design and emotion (Desmet and Hekkert 2009) and the experience during the product interaction (Desmet and Hekkert 2007).

The emotional design theory (Norman 2004) presents a model of design with three levels. The visceral level is concerned with appearances and it is not culturally dependent. The behavioural level has to do with the product usability. The reflective level considers the status given by the product. These three levels of design motivated him to state that *"aesthetically beautiful objects enable you to work better"*.

Objects are able to influence the occurrence of certain emotions, influencing the process of the design. Desmet (SusaGroup 2015) claims that emotion is part of human nature and everything in the world has a constant influence on the emotions, in this way it is impossible to ignore the emotional side of product experience. It would be like denying that products are designed, bought and used by humans.

Desmet (Blythe et al. 2004) establishes that the major advantage of non-verbal instruments is because they are language independent, so it's possible to use them in different cultures. Besides they are often claimed to be, as Desmet (Blythe et al. 2004) aims, *"less subjective than self-report instruments because they do not rely on the participants' own assessment of the emotional experience"*.

In order to develop the evaluation tool the students had to study the effects that positive and negative emotions (Norman 2004) had on the user during the interactive experience. They also studied the non-verbal self-report instrument called PrEmo (Desmet and Hekkert 2007). This measurement instrument was developed to measure the mixed emotions that are elicited by an artefact. Instead of relying on the use of words, respondents can report their emotions with the use of expressive cartoon animations. In the instrument, each of the 14 measured emotions is portrayed by an animation by means of dynamic facial, bodily, and vocal expressions (Desmet 2004; Blythe et al. 2004).

3   Development of the Work

After completed the literature review the students started with the brainstorming in order to generate the first alternatives for the artefact. Apart from the main criteria – socially connect people from different generations – the students also have to observe that the artefact should not interrupt the persons from their daily tasks and there should be some sort of feedback to reassure the sender that the message was delivered with success.

It was given the same briefing to the entire class but each group was free to develop their own concept of what would be an artefact to create social awareness. The students did not have to worry with the technology used or manufacturing process because the artefact did not have to be feasible at this point. There were some ideas like the message could be sent through a single action or event and it could have two different design so that they would suit their users preferences. One issue that was observed by all groups was that the artefact should be an object of desire, something that the user would feel proud to own and to use.

The next step of the project was to develop a tool to evaluate their artefact. The tool developed by the students to evaluate the conceptual design of the artefact for social awareness was based on emojis and used the same 14 emotions from PrEmo. PrEmo is a non-verbal self-report instrument that measures 14 emotions that are often elicited by product design. Of these 14 emotions, seven are pleasant (i.e. desire, pleasant surprise, inspiration, amusement, admiration, satisfaction and fascination), and seven are unpleasant (i.e. indignation, contempt, disgust, unpleasant surprise, dissatisfaction, disappointment and boredom). Instead of relying on the use of words, respondents would report their emotions with the use of expressive cartoon animations. In the instrument, each of the 14 measured emotions is portrayed by an animation by means of dynamic facial, bodily and vocal expressions (Desmet 2004; Blythe et al. 2004).

Emojis are well known and have a widespread use among users. It would bring a contemporary approach to the evaluation tool as well as a common language for the user providing a familiar interaction. The advantage of using emojis as a tool to evaluate a conceptual design is that they are flexible and easy to adapt.

The students started by looking at the most popular emojis in use today and then narrowing down to three of them for each emotion. They had to combine or adapt those emojis in order to design a single emoticon that would better express the emotion. Those emotions where then developed further to translate into emojis. They had to do it for each one of the 14 emotions. Figure 1 shows the emojis used for eight out of the fourteen emotions.

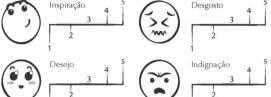

1 - Discordo totalmente; 2 - Discordo; 3 - Neutro; 4 - Concordo; 5 - Concordo totalmente.

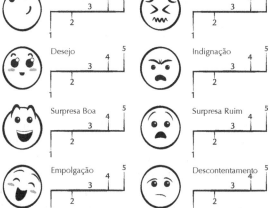

Fig. 1. Thumbnail of the emojis

The evaluation tool was then used to evaluate their conceptual artefact. The pilot evaluation of the tool took place at the university and the participants were students. The emojis were presented to them using two A4 posters, one for the artefact and the other for the emojis. The poster for the artefact was presented as a narrative of the intended usage of the product (Carroll 1999). The narrative was presented in the form of photoplay to help illustrate the interaction of the user with the conceptual product. After that the participants would see a labelled emoticon and rated their emotion towards their artefact in a scale ranging from 1 (does not evoke) to 5 (evoked a lot). The participants had to rate all the emojis in order to complete the task.

4 Considerations

The artefacts developed during the Conceptual Design classes were perceived to be aesthetically pleasing to look at and their interfaces were almost imperceptible to the user. All of them used a single message to create the sense of awareness indicating that someone was not very far away.

The preliminary results of the evaluation tool showed that the use of emojis were well understood and accepted by the public. It was seen as a modern, simple and quick way to evaluate conceptual products. However, as a novel tool to evaluate emotions it must be used in other projects and also with a larger number of participants to verify its suitability for this purpose.

References

Blythe, M.A., Monk, A.F., Overbeeke, K., Wright, P.C.: Funology: From Usability to Enjoyment. Kluwer Academic Publishers, Dordrecht (2004)

Carroll, J.M.: Five reasons for scenarios-based design. In: Proceedings of the 32nd Hawaii International Conference on System Sciences. IEEE (1999)

Desmet, P., Hekkert, P.: Framework of product experience. Int. J. Des. 1(1), 57–66 (2007)

Desmet, P., Hekkert, P.: Special issue editorial: design & emotion. Int. J. Des. 3(2), 1–6 (2009)

Norman, D.: Emotional Design: Why We Love (or Hate) Everyday Things. Basic Books, New York (2004)

SusaGroup: About SusaGroup (2015). http://www.susagroup.com. Accessed 26 October 2015

Distributed Unity Applications

Evaluation of Approaches

Anton Sigitov[1]([⊠]), Oliver Staadt[2], and André Hinkenjann[1]

[1] Institute of Visual Computing, University Bonn-Rhein-Sieg of Applied
Sciences, Sankt Augustin, Germany
{Anton.Sigitov,Andre.Hinkenjann}@h-brs.de
[2] Institute of Computer Science, University of Rostock, Rostock, Germany
Oliver.Staadt@uni-rostock.de

Abstract. There is a need for rapid prototyping tools for large, high-resolution displays (LHRDs) in both scientific and commercial domains. That is, the area of LHRDs is still poorly explored and possesses no established standards, thus developers have to experiment a lot with new interaction and visualization concepts. Therefore, a rapid prototyping tool for LHRDs has to undertake two functions: ease the process of application development, and make an application runnable on a broad range of LHRD setups. The latter comprises a challenge, since most LHRDs are driven by multiple compute nodes and require distributed applications.

Unity engine became a popular tool for rapid prototyping, since it eases the development process by means of a visual scene editor, animation libraries, input device libraries, graphical user interface libraries etc. However, it will charge developers with a high fee in order to make an application LHRD compatible. In our previous work, we developed an extension for Unity engine that allows to run Unity applications on LHRDs.

In this work we consider different static vs. dynamic camera/world conditions of distributed applications; and propose and evaluate different Unity specific approaches within the scope of 2D and 3D applications for these scenarios. The primary focus of the evaluation lays on world state synchronization, which is a common issue in distributed applications.

Keywords: Unity · Distributed rendering · Large, high-resolution displays

1 Introduction

Rapid prototyping tools are of substantial value for researchers since they lower overhead of hypothesis/concept evaluation significantly. Unfortunately, a choice of the rapid prototyping tools for large, high-resolution displays is scarce. To address this issue, we developed a lean, easy to use extension [1] for Unity game engine[1]. It enables developers to create and build Unity applications for different LHRD setups. For the purpose of world state synchronization, we developed a set of routines. These differ mainly in how visibility of virtual objects is determined for a particular application instance.

---

[1] http://unity3d.com, last access on 7.04.2016.

© Springer International Publishing Switzerland 2016
C. Stephanidis (Ed.): HCII 2016 Posters, Part I, CCIS 617, pp. 138–143, 2016.
DOI: 10.1007/978-3-319-40548-3_23

In this work, we evaluated three Unity specific approaches for world state synchronization in distributed applications. We considered different scenarios, e.g. dynamic/static camera, 3D/2D world, different rendering and lightning conditions, in order to achieve more expressive evaluation results.

2 Related Work

Chung et al. [2] classified software frameworks for LHRDs in two categories based on task distribution models: distributed application and distributed renderer. Another way to discriminate these tools is by focusing on the type of information that they distribute across individual application instances. Here we highlight three types: draw-call, pixel data, and change list.

Using a draw call distribution approach, a framework intercepts draw commands executed by a *manager instance*. It processes and subdivides them into sub draw-calls in appliance with the system configuration. Next, it conveys the sub draw-calls to *output instances*. The representative frameworks that implement this approach are: Chromium [3], ClusterGL [4], and CGLX [5].

Within the scope of a pixel data distribution approach, one or more remote nodes generate image data. Based on the LHRD configuration, the *manager instance* splits data and distributes it among *output instances*. The frameworks SAGE [6] and DMX[2], to name but a few, implement this approach.

Following a change list distribution approach, the *manager instance* submits changes made on virtual objects to *output instances*. Using this information individual *output instances* become able to update the state of their virtual world replicas. Implementations of that approach could be found, for instance, in OpenSG [7], Garuda [8], and DRiVE [9].

Our extension [1] combines both task distribution models. The extension requires multiple application instances with each having its own copy of a virtual world. One instance undertakes a manager functionality and becomes responsible for event and world state synchronization. Such configuration reflects the distributed application model. At the same time, the *manager instance* takes on all world simulation routines, thus decoupling rendering from simulation and making other application instances to pure *output instances*. This is characteristic for the distributed renderer model. In addition to its hybrid task distribution model, our extension makes use of the change list approach for world state synchronization. Thanks to Unity's inherent abilities and our extension, we created a promising rapid prototyping tool for LHRDs.

3 Approaches

We developed three Unity specific approaches for world state synchronization in distributed Unity applications: *Naïve*, *Adaptive_F* (Frustum-based), and *Adaptive_C* (Camera-based). The approaches handle virtual objects that own an *MPIView*

---

[2] http://dmx.sourceforge.net/, last access on 7.04.2016.

component. This component tags an object as distributable and encapsulates a unique object ID that ensures a proper object match across individual application instances.

Naïve. The *Naïve* approach broadcasts state information of all distributable objects. It does not matter if a particular application instance requires this information for a current frame. The approach provides the highest integrity level for applications, as all instances have the same world state at any time. This, for instance, allows correct shadow calculation (for objects that lay outside the instance's partial frustum, but their shadows within) on *output instances*. However, *Naïve* causes high network overhead, which depends on both number of virtual objects and number of application instances.

Adaptive_F. The *Adaptive_F* approach tests distributable objects against each virtual camera's frustum. It conveys state information of an object to an application instance only if the object lays within a frustum of the instance's camera. *Adaptive_F* lowers network overhead. Dependences on number of virtual objects and number of application instances remain though, since each object undergoes the frustum check for each virtual camera. This in turn increases computational overhead on the *manager instance*. The approach does not ensure proper shadow calculation, as it cannot detect shadows within a frustum.

Adaptive_C. The *Adaptive_C* approach enforces the manager instance to create and maintain replicas of all virtual cameras. Each camera replica will raise the Unity callback *OnWillRenderObject* for each virtual object it is going to render in a current frame. In this way, *Adaptive_C* determines object visibility for a particular camera. Hence, application instances receive state information of only visible distributable objects. *Adaptive_C* abolishes dependence on number of virtual objects. Dependence on number of application instances remains due to virtual camera replicas. Also, overhead on the *manager instance* rises, since each camera replica renders an image. *Adaptive_C* and *Adaptive_F* have equal network overhead. Similar to *Adaptive_F*, *Adaptive_C* does not safeguard correct shadow generation.

At the heart of our extension lies the centralized control model [10]. The entire world simulation process takes place only on the *manager instance*. The m*anager instance* distributes a new world state across *output instances* at the end of each frame. The *output instance* is responsible for state receiving, state applying, rendering, and output to a connected display unit.

4   Evaluation Setup

The evaluation was performed using a large curved tiled display wall comprising 35 LCD displays (Fig. 1), ordered through a seven (column) by five (row) grid. Each of the columns has a relative angle difference of 10 degrees along the Y-axis to adjacent columns, as such creating a slight curvature. The LCD displays are 46" panels with a 1080 p resolution, resulting in a total of 72 megapixels. The installation is driven by a cluster of three PCs, each equipped with three GeForce GTX 780 Ti, providing a total of twelve outputs per PC.

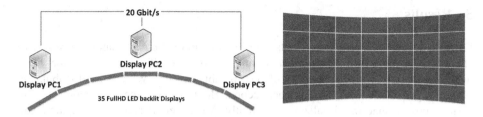

Fig. 1. The Hornet system: (left) view from above; (right) frontal view

We implemented two types of 3D evaluation scenarios (static (s) and dynamic (d)) with three conditions (standard (1), shadow (2), and multiple lights (3)) each. In the standard condition, there was one directional light, which had a random position in a virtual scene and cast no shadows. This was the only difference to the shadow condition, where the directional light cast shadows. In the multiple lights condition, there were one directional light and eight point lights. Neither of them cast shadows.

There were five stages in all type-condition combinations. There were 64 distributable virtual objects at the beginning of the first stage. The number of objects doubled with each subsequent stage. For every stage, we logged lowest frame time, highest frame time, average frame time, and total stage time. We ignored stage preparation frames in order to avoid interference of administrative overhead. Also, we turned the dynamic batching and occlusion culling methods off in order to mitigate impact of Unity's inter routines on the evaluation results.

The static scenarios comprised static, not synchronized virtual cameras. The cameras shared the same origin and orientation. Each camera's frustum made up a part of a large mutual frustum. Distributable virtual objects (cubes of the same size and different colors) appeared at random position and with random orientation within the bounds of the mutual frustum. Each object revolved one degree per frame around its local Y-axis.

The dynamic scenarios had a camera setup comparable to one in the static scenarios. However, the cameras were dynamic and synchronized. The mutual cameras' origin lay at the local center of a ring-shaped volume. Distributable virtual objects emerged within the ring-shaped volume. Each object had a random position and orientation. The objects and the cameras rotated one degree per frame around their local Y-axis. Hence, only a subset of the objects lay within the cameras' mutual frustum at a time.

For a 2D case, we implemented only one type-condition combination, namely static-standard. The 2D scenario incorporated a set of cameras with an orthogonal projection instead of perspective projection, like in the 3D scenarios. It also made use of Unity Sprites instead of 3D cubes.

We determined two baselines for every type-condition variation. The baseline (B1) reflects the application's performance at the standard condition with frame synchronization only. Additionally, *MPIView* components were disabled in order to prevent Unity to make any calls on them. The baseline (B2) shows the performance at a specific condition with frame synchronization and enabled *MPIView* components. Although *MPIView* components were active no world state synchronization took place, as class methods contained no logic.

5   Results

Figure 2 depicts the evaluation results. At every condition the *Naïve* approach was less efficient in comparison to *Adaptive_F* and *Adaptive_C*. The average frame time increased linearly with the number of distributable objects. With 1024 distributable objects it performed with 4 frames per second. However, it is the only approach that ensures proper shadow visualization currently. Moreover, it adds no computational overhead on the *manager instance*.

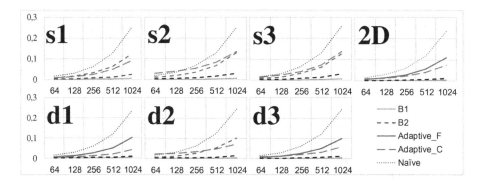

Fig. 2. Evaluation results: (s1) static – standard; (s2) static – shadow; (s3) static – multiple lights; (d1) dynamic – standard; (d2) dynamic – shadow; (d3) dynamic – multiple lights; (2D) static – standard – 2D. The X-Axis shows number of distributable virtual objects. The Y-Axis shows the average frame time in seconds (Color figure online)

Likewise, *Adaptive_F* depends on number of distributable objects strongly. It performed at least twice as fast as the *Naïve* approach though. This ascribes to lower visibility computation overhead in comparison to synchronization overhead. By small numbers of distributable objects, it outperformed the *Adaptive_C* approach too. However, the approach is incongruous if shadow visualization is desirable.

With a low number of distributable objects, *Adaptive_C* performed less efficient than the *Naïve* and the *Adaptive_F* approaches. This is due to rendering overhead caused by virtual camera replicas. The effect is well observable at the shadow conditions (s2) and (d2). It is more resistant to a number of distributable objects in a virtual scene though. As a result, with increased number of objects it performed significantly better in comparison to other two approaches. The transcendence is less apparent in the variations (s2) and (s3). However, inspection of logged data for both variations disclosed that average frame time of the *Adaptive_F* approach had been increasing at a faster pace. Similar to *Adaptive_F*, *Adaptive_C* ensures no proper shadows.

6 Conclusion

In this work, we evaluated three Unity specific approaches for world state synchronization in distributed applications. We applied the approaches to the different scenarios and to the different virtual world conditions to make the evaluation more comprehensive and expressive. The evaluation revealed that the *Naïve* approach performs worst. It is the only alternative to ensure correct shadow generation on *output instances* though. The comparison between *Adaptive_F* and *Adaptive_C* elucidated that *Adaptive_F* is more due for applications with a small number of visible distributable objects, while *Adaptive_C* behaves better with a large number of distributable objects.

References

1. Sigitov, A., Scherfgen, D., Hinkenjann, A., Staadt, O.: Adopting a game engine for large, high-resolution displays. Procedia Comput. Sci. **75**, 257–266 (2015)
2. Chung, H., Andrews, C., North, C.: A survey of software frameworks for cluster-based large high-resolution displays. IEEE Trans. Vis. Comput. Graph. **20**, 1158–1177 (2014)
3. Humphreys, G., Houston, M., Ng, R., Frank, R., Ahern, S., Kirchner, P.D., Klosowski, J.T.: Chromium: a stream-processing framework for interactive rendering on clusters. ACM Trans. Graph. **21**, 693–702 (2002)
4. Neal, B., Hunkin, P., McGregor, A.: Distributed OpenGL rendering in network bandwidth constrained environments. In: Eurographics Symposium on Parallel Graphics and Visualization (2011)
5. Doerr, K., Kuester, F.: CGLX: a scalable, high-performance visualization framework for networked display environments. IEEE Trans. Vis. Comput. Graph. **17**, 320–332 (2011)
6. Jeong, B., Renambot, L., Jagodic, R., Singh, R., Aguilera, J., Johnson, A., Leigh, J.: High-performance dynamic graphics streaming for scalable adaptive graphics environment. In: SC 2006 Conference, Proceedings of the ACM/IEEE, pp. 24–24. IEEE (2006)
7. Roth, M., Voss, G., Reiners, D.: Multi-threading and clustering for scene graph systems. Comput. Graph. **28**, 63–66 (2004)
8. Nirnimesh, H.P., Narayanan, P.J.: Garuda: a scalable tiled display wall using commodity PCs. IEEE Trans. Vis. Comput. Graph. **13**, 864–877 (2007)
9. Sigitov, A., Roth, T., Mannuss, F., Hinkenjann, A.: DRiVE: an example of distributed rendering in virtual environments. In: 6th Workshop on Software Engineering and Architectures for Realtime Interactive Systems (SEARIS), pp. 33–40. IEEE (2013)
10. Chalmers, A., Davis, T., Reinhard, E. (eds.): Practical parallel rendering. AK Peters, Natick (2002)

Formal Specification of Multi-Window User Interface in PVS

Kalyani Singh[1(⊠)] and Brent Auernheimer[2]

[1] Department of Computer Science, California State University, Fresno, CA, USA
kalyanisingh@mail.fresnostate.edu
[2] Department of Computer Science, California State University, Fresno, CA, USA
brent@csufresno.edu

Abstract. Safety critical systems are life protecting systems and specification languages like ASLAN and PVS can be used to better protect and analyze the functioning of these systems. A multi-window user interface already specified in ASLAN is converted to PVS. This paper briefs about the system in hand, newly added input focus functionality and the differences between ASLAN and PVS as inferred from the research.

1 Introduction

Safety Critical Systems are life saving systems consistently used by engineers and commoners. Examples of safety critical systems vary from high budget systems like nuclear power plants and airplanes to low budget yet life critical systems like fire alarms, railway signaling and traffic control. Their failure may lead to death, damage to an equipment or environmental harm [1]. For example, Therac-25 [2,3] was a medical equipment whose malfunctioning gave massive overdoses of radiation to patients. This can be overcome by writing specifications for a system.

Specifications are required to analyze a system and to aid its design by verifying the key properties of interest [4]. Specification languages namely, ASLAN [5] and Prototype Verification System (PVS) [6] can be used to achieve this goal. Although, specifications are not readily used in software development(in spite of the presence of advanced language like PVS), [7] gives an example of a system that is critical to the safety of an animal keeper and proposes specifications for the system.

This research focuses on formally specifying a multi-window user interface in PVS which has already been specified in ASLAN [8]. PVS system is based on the idea of a window manager used for control and monitoring of a critical system such as NASA's space shuttle [9].

The ASLAN specification has a limitation as it does not elaborate on issue of losing input focus [10] but the resulting PVS specification has been modified to include input focus functionality. In addition, this research incorporates the differences between PVS and ASLAN. [11] contains detailed description of PVS and ASLAN codes.

© Springer International Publishing Switzerland 2016
C. Stephanidis (Ed.): HCII 2016 Posters, Part I, CCIS 617, pp. 144–149, 2016.
DOI: 10.1007/978-3-319-40548-3_24

This paper is structured as follows: Sect. 2 describes the system being used for writing specifications, Sect. 3 contains the results and additions made in the previous specification along with the differences in ASLAN and PVS specification [12] languages. Section 4 concludes the paper.

2   PVS System Description

Figure 1 gives a basic flow chart of PVS system displaying blocks of types, variables, constants, definitions, invariants, transitions and initial state of the system with an overview of their contents. The fundamental parts of PVS specification are explained further. There are three main states of windows namely, OPEN, CLOSED and UNUSED. All the windows are accessible to the user except one SPECIAL window. SPECIAL window has imperative critical programs running in it and thus, cannot be closed (iconified), moved or covered by other windows or icons. A structure has been defined with Locations, Sizes and Representations to keep a track of Layout of a window [8]. Constant functions like OVERLAPS deduce if a windows is at the front of another window. BACKGROUND gives information about the layouts of background windows and SPECIAL returns a boolean value if the window is a SPECIAL window. Variable functions like input_focus and output_focus take window as the argument and return the Layout of the open or close window. The specification has a set of functions that update the display when a window is opened, closed, created, destroyed or moved.

Initially, all the processes in the system are set to UNUSED state and input focus of all the states is FALSE. There are a few critical correctness criteria that have to be true at all times in the system e.g. if the window is in OPEN or CLOSED state then it should have open or closed layout. Also, SPECIAL window should not be overlapped at any time in the system.

In the PVS system, each user has a powerful display processor (DP) as their interface to the system. DP is capable of multiple sessions with remote applications and supports a mouse and window (direct manipulation) environment. This system is also required to use commercial off the shelf (COTS) [13] hardware and software wherever feasible.

3   Results

The new system designed in this research, implements the functionality of input focus. Input focus concept is an important part of multi-window user interface because it determines which window is active when the user has not explicitly selected any window. This section also briefs the main differences between ASLAN and PVS as inferred from the translation.

3.1   Input Focus

A process is said to have input focus [10], if it is active and data can be read from and written to it. The formal specification in ASLAN, partially handles the focus by shifting it.

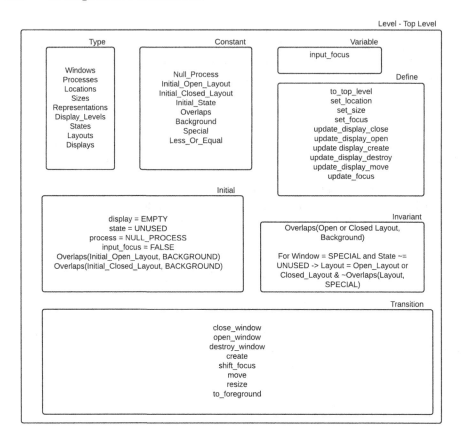

Fig. 1. Block diagram of PVS Specification

```
TRANSITION shift_focus (w: Windows)
EXIT
(state'(w) = OPEN | state'(w) = CLOSED)
& FORALL w1: Windows (input_focus(w1) = (w1 = w))
ALT NoChange
```

This transition states that for a window w1 that has input focus, make the input focus of window w, the same. The previous state of the window to which the focus has been shifted was open or closed. Focus is being handled here by shifting from all the windows to the entry window/input window that is given as argument. This transition does not completely control input focus. For example, assume that the user is working in window w1 and clicks outside of the window boundary. In that case, it is hard to determine the focus of window unless shift_focus is explicitly called to shift the focus to a particular window.

There are two cases to be taken care of:

– When focus is lost e.g. user clicked out of the window
– When a function changes focus from a window to another

The proposed solution to the first problem is that whenever the user clicks out of the window, the focus should be transferred to the most recent open window where the user was working unless he explicitly clicks on another window.

```
set_focus (w1:WINDOWS, s: STATE) :
[( FORALL (w2: WINDOWS ) :
IF (input_focus(w2) ~= TRUE
& open_layout(w1))
THEN input_focus(w1)
ELSE
IF (s = UNUSED) THEN
open_layout(w2) & input_focus(w2) )]
```

It checks if the focus was not true for any of the windows i.e. the user clicked out of the window and a window has previous layout open then the focus is set to that open window. ELSE part of this assertion handles UNUSED and performs the same function of setting the focus to previous open layout. Special windows are usually the UNUSED ones but there could be other windows with UNUSED status in the system.

Below function handles the transitions from one state to another. It sets the input focus to calling window depending on its state. If the state is UNUSED i.e. the window could be a special window, then it's focus is handled by set_focus function.

Here, it has been assumed that closed windows may have input focus. update_focus works on this assumption as it gives input focus to closed window in Case 2.

```
update_focus(w1: Windows, s:State): BOOLEAN ==
/* Case 1 */
((((s = OPEN) & (state(w1) = CLOSED))
input_focus(w1))
/* Case 2 */
| (((s = CLOSED) & (state(w1) = OPEN))
(input_focus(w1))
/* Case 3 */
| (((s = UNUSED))
(set_focus(w1)) )
```

3.2 ASLAN V/s PVS

PVS and ASLAN have a significant difference in their formal foundations [5], structure, backend development, and logic. Figure 2 lists the main differences between ASLAN and PVS.

ASLAN	PVS
Based on the concept of state transitions	Based on higher order logic
Uses SET_DIFF, UNION for addition and subtraction i.e. it follows set theory	Used addition operator(+) and subtraction operator (-) for addition and subtraction i.e. it performs arithmetic operations
Large functions can become complex because of the state transitions	PVS is succinct as subtypes, function types and variable types compress the definitions
ASLAN does not support recursion	PVS supports recursion
Creates different blocks for types, constants, variables, invariants, definitions etc.	Declares a single BEGIN block which contains types, constants, variables, invariants and definitions without division
ASLAN has transitions from previous state to next	PVS only has functions with mappings from domain to range. Domain and range can be seen as analogous to previous and next state in case of transitions
Loosely typed as every constant or variable does not have a type related to it	Strongly typed as every constant, variable, theory and function has a type related to it
Does not support data structures and a structure is expressed as a set	Supports data structures like list, stack, queue and have them pre-defined in prelude.
Does not have a concrete proving system	Specifications can be proved using a combination of PVS and Emacs,
Does not facilitate reusability	Facilitates reusability with theories and partial functions

Fig. 2. Differences between ASLAN and PVS

4   Conclusion

This research specifies the concept of input focus in a multi-window user interface and provides differences between ASLAN and PVS specification languages. It can be concluded that PVS is practically more powerful than ASLAN with robust techniques to verify specification. PVS is easy to understand and can be readily applied for verifying and formulating safety critical system prototypes. PVS is very close to any other programming language like Java or C++. Features like allowance of partial implementation play as an advantage, giving user the power of abstraction. Since PVS has in built functions it reduces the lines of specification unlike ASLAN which operates on the concept of state machines and thus becomes un-manageable for declaring complex functions.

References

1. Knight, J.C.: Safety critical systems: challenges and directions. 2002. In: ICSE 2002 Proceedings of the 24th International Conference on Software Engineering, pp. 547–550 (2002)
2. Leveson, N.G., Turner, C.S.: An investigation of the Therac-25 accidents. Computer **26**, 18–41 (1993)
3. McCormick, J.: We Did Nothing Wrong. http://www.baselinemag.com/c/a/Projects-Processes/We-Did-Nothing-Wrong 27 March 2004
4. Bolton, M.L., Bass, E.J.: Formally verifying human automation interaction as part of a system model: limitations and tradeoffs. Innovations Syst. Softw. Eng. **6**, 219–231 (2010)
5. Auernheimer, B., Kemmerer, R.A.: RT-ASLAN: a specification language for real-time systems. IEEE Trans. Softw. Eng. **SE–12**, 879–889 (1986)
6. Computer Science Laboratory, (2016). http://www.csl.sri.com/
7. Blake, S.A., Auernheimer, B.: Ensuring the safety of animal-keeper protocols, presented at the Zoo Tech Workshop (2016)
8. Auernheimer, B.: Formalisms for user interface specification and design, NASA-NGT-60002 Supplement : 2. NASA Kennedy Space Center, University of Central florida, August 1989
9. Lutz, R.: Software engineering for space exploration. IEEE Comput. **44**, 41–46 (2011)
10. Clow, J.A., Garside, A.J., Winkler, D.V.: Systems and methods for processing input data before, during, and/or after an input focus change event, Washington DC, USA Patent. U.S. Patent 7,461,348, Dec 2008
11. Singh, K., Auernheimer, B.: Comparison of Two Formal Specification Languages to Specify a Simple User-Interface, M.S. thesis, California State University, Fresno (2016)
12. Owre, S., Shankar, N., Rushby, J.M., Stringer-Calvert, D.W.: PVS system guide, Computer Science Laboratory, SRI International, Menlo Park, CA, vol. 1, p. 7 (1999)
13. Basili, V.R.: COTS - based systems top 10 list. Computer **35**, 91–95 (2001)

Optimization for UI Design via Metaheuristics

Ricardo Soto[1(✉)], Broderick Crawford[1], Boris Almonacid[1],
Stefanie Niklander[2,3,4], and Eduardo Olguín[5]

[1] Pontificia Universidad Católica de Valparaíso, Valparaíso, Chile
{ricardo.soto,broderick.crawford}@ucv.cl, boris.almonacid.g@mail.pucv.cl
[2] Universidad Adolfo Ibañez, Viña del Mar, Chile
stefanie.niklander@uai.cl
[3] Universidad Autónoma de Chile, Santiago, Chile
[4] Universidad Científica del Sur, Lima, Peru
[5] Universidad San Sebastián, Santiago, Chile
eduardo.olguin@uss.cl

Abstract. In recent years, different optimization problems have been arose in the context of UI design. Initially those problems were solved by hand with no computational optimization support since the set of potential design combinations was limited. However, when the space of different possible designs increase, the use of optimization algorithms is mandatory. However, several UI design problems are quadratic, for which guaranteeing the global optimum is not possible in polynomial time. Then the use of classic exact methods may not be feasible. In this paper, we briefly present how metaheuristics can straightforwardly be used to model and solve interesting but complex quadratic problems from UI design. In particular, we employ Cuckoo Search, which is a modern optimization technique to solve a well-known problem concerned to keyboard layout optimization.

Keywords: Keyboard optimization · User interface design · Metaheuristics

1 Introduction

In recent years, different optimization problems have been arose in the context of UI design, most of them related to performance, ergonomics, human-error, learnability, accessibility, and aesthetics, among others. Initially those problems were solved by hand with no computational optimization support since the set of potential design combinations was limited. However, when the space of different possible designs increase (e.g. about 30^{30} possible combinations in the problem of arranging 30 menu items), the use of optimization algorithms is mandatory to identify the best design according to all involved factors. To this end, different techniques have been used to solve such problems which are mainly based on mathematical programming such as linear and integer programming.

In the optimization domain, it is well-known that linear objective functions with linear constraints can surely be handled with linear programming methods

© Springer International Publishing Switzerland 2016
C. Stephanidis (Ed.): HCII 2016 Posters, Part I, CCIS 617, pp. 150–154, 2016.
DOI: 10.1007/978-3-319-40548-3_25

such as the simplex one. However, several UI design problems are quadratic, for which guaranteeing the global optimum is not possible in polynomial time. In this paper, we propose the use of metaheuristics, which are optimization techniques specially devoted to find locally optimal solutions when the global optimum is not reachable in a reasonable amount of time. Most metaheuristic are inspired by interesting processes and phenomenon from nature and they have widely been used to solve real-world problems from various application domains (e.g. medicine, biology, mechanics, mining, gaming, and engineering). Our goal is to illustrate that metaheuristics can be used to efficiently solve different kind of UI problems. To this end we model a classic quadratic problem concerned to keyboard layout design optimization and we describe how it can straightforwardly be modeled and solved with a modern and powerful optimization technique called Cuckoo Search. To the best of our knowledge this concern has not enough been explored yet.

This paper is organized as follows: Sect. 2 presents the problem followed by the optimization technique employed to solve it. Finally, conclusions and some directions for future work are given.

2   The Letter Assignment Problem

The letter assignment problem (LAP) is an interesting problem concerned with the optimal design of keyboards [2]. Keyboard layout optimization is known to be important as slight improvements are able to improve productivity, ergonomics as well as learnability [3]. Particularly, the goal of the LAP is to minimize the average cost c_{kl} of selecting letter l after k, considering n letters and n keyslots, and a probability p_{kl} as depicted in Eq. 1.

$$min \sum_{k=1}^{n} \sum_{l=1}^{n} p_{kl} \cdot c_{kl} \tag{1}$$

The p_{kl} probabilities are provided by a bigram distribution of representative corpus of text [1] and the cost is calculated as $c_{kl} = \sum_{i=1}^{n} \sum_{j=1}^{n} t_{ij} x_{ki} x_{lj}$, where t_{ij} is the movement time from key i to key j (normally computed by Fitts' law as detailed in [4]), and $x_{lj} = 1$ if letter l is assigned to keyslot j and $x_{lj} = 0$ otherwise. The problem is subjected to the following constraints.

$$\sum_{l=1}^{n} x_{lj=1} \qquad \forall j \in \{1, \ldots, n\} \tag{2}$$

$$\sum_{j=1}^{n} x_{lj} \qquad \forall l \in \{1, \ldots, n\} \tag{3}$$

$$x_{lj} \in \{0, 1\} \qquad \forall l, j \in \{1, \ldots, n\} \tag{4}$$

Constraint 2 ensures that each slot contains only one letter. Eq. 3 is responsible for assigning each letter to only one slot and finally Eq. 4 guarantees the binary solutions. In the following section, we describe the technique employed to solve this problem.

3   Cuckoo Search

Cuckoo search (CS) is an interesting and efficient metaheuristic inspired by the obligate brood parasitism of some cuckoo species. Brood parasitism involves the manipulation and use of host individuals either of the same or different species for incubation. Details about this metaheuristic can be seen in [6]. CS was developed using three rules, which are detailed in the following.

1. A cuckoo egg represents a solution to the problem and it is left in a randomly selected nest, a cuckoo only can left one egg at a time.
2. Nests holding the higher quality eggs will pass to the next generations.
3. The nest owner can discover a cuckoo egg with a probability $p_a \in [0, 1]$. If this occurs, the nest owner can left his nest and build other nest in other location. The number of total nests is a fixed value.

The generation of a new solution is performed by using Lévy flight as follows.

$$sol_i^{t+1} = sol_i^t + \alpha \oplus \text{Levy}(\beta) \tag{5}$$

where sol_i^{t+1} is the solution in iteration $t + 1$, and $\alpha \geq 0$ is the step size, which is associated to the range of values that the problem needs (scale value), being determined by the U_b and L_b upper and lower bounds as shown below.

$$\alpha = 0.01(U_b - L_b) \tag{6}$$

The Lévy flight distribution provides the step length in the generation of a new solution.

$$\text{Lévy} \sim u = t^{-\beta}, \quad (1 < \beta < 3) \tag{7}$$

To model the LAP, we employ a binary representation as depicted in Fig. 1, where $x_{lj} = 1$ if letter l is assigned to keyslot j and $x_{lj} = 0$ otherwise. We employ the simple CS form where each nest holds only one egg.

$$\boxed{0|1|1|1|1|0}...\boxed{1|1|0|1|0|1}$$

Fig. 1. Binary solution representation

Algorithm 1 depicts the proposed procedure, at the beginning the CS parameters are initialized (α, β, p_a, size for the initial population and maximum number of generation) and an initial population of n nests is generated. Then, a while loop manages the CS actions which are self-explanatory. The objective function of the problem (Eq. 1) is employed to compute the fitness of each solution. Solutions are produced by using the Lévy flight distribution according to Eq. 5. From this process, a real number between 0 and 1 is generated, which needs to be discretized. To this end, we proceed as follows [5]:

Algorithm 1. Cuckoo Search via Lévy Flights

Initialize CS parameters;
Produce the first generation of n nests;
while $t < MaxGeneration$ **do**
    Obtain a random cuckoo/generate a solution by Lévy Flight distribution;
    Quantify its fitness F_j and then compare with old Fitness F_i;
    if $F_j > F_i$ **then**
        Substitute j as the new best solution;
    end if
    A fraction of worse nest $p(a)$ will be abandoned and new nests will be made;
    Maintain the better solutions (or nests with high quality);
    Rank the better solutions and find the best one;
end while
Postprocess results and visualization;

$$x_j = \begin{cases} 1 & \textbf{if } r < x'_j \quad \textbf{or} \quad x'_j > U_b \\ 0 & \textbf{if } r \geq x'_j \quad \textbf{or} \quad x'_j < L_b \end{cases}$$

where x'_j holds the value to be discretized for variable x_j of the SCP solution, and r is a normal distributed random value. Finally, the best solutions are memorized and the generation count is incremented or the process is stopped if the termination criteria has been met.

4   Conclusion

Different UI optimization problems have been appeared during the last years, most of them related to performance, ergonomics, human-error, learnability, accessibility, and aesthetics, among others. In this paper, we have dealt with an interesting problem concerned to keyboard layout optimization called The Letter Assignment Problem. We have illustrated how metaheuristics can straightforwardly be used for solving this problem. Particularly, we have employed Cuckoo Search, which is a modern and powerful technique that can rapidly be mapped to the binary nature of the LAP. As future work we expect to solve more UI problems with different metaheuristics such as for instance artificial bee colony, firefly optimization, and bat algorithms.

References

1. Bi, X., Smith, B.A., Zhai, S.: Multilingual touchscreen keyboard design and optimization. Hum. Comput. Interact. **27**(4), 352–382 (2012)
2. Karrenbauer, A., Oulasvirta, A.: Improvements to keyboard optimization with integer programming. In: The 27th Annual ACM Symposium on User Interface Software and Technology (UIST), pp. 621–626. ACM (2014)
3. Lewis, J., Potosnak, K., Magyar, R.: Handbook of Human-Computer Interaction, chapter Keys and keyboards, pp. 1285–1315 (1997)

4. MacKenzie, I.S., Zhang, S.X.: The design and evaluation of a high-performance soft keyboard. In: Proceedings of the CHI 1999 Conference on Human Factors in Computing Systems: The CHI is the Limit, pp. 25–31. ACM (1999)
5. Soto, R., Crawford, B., Olivares, R., Barraza, J., Johnson, F., Paredes, F.: A binary cuckoo search algorithm for solving the set covering problem. In: Vicente, J.M.F., Álvarez-Sánchez, J.R., López, F.P., Toledo-Moreo, F.J., Adeli, H. (eds.) Bioinspired Computation in Artificial Systems. LNCS, vol. 9108, pp. 88–97. Springer, Heidelberg (2015)
6. Yang, X-S., Deb, S.: Cuckoo search via lévy flights. In: World Congress on Nature & Biologically Inspired Computing (NaBIC), pp. 210–214. IEEE (2009)

A "User-Flow Description" Method
for Usability Investigation

Akira Takahashi[✉]

Faculty of Informatics, Shizuoka University, Hamamatsu, Japan
akirtaka@inf.shizuoka.ac.jp

Abstract. This study proposes user-flow (UF) description, a new method for investigating usability. UF is defined as a series of user operations. A delay in flow in one part of a task procedure can reveal the interface problem in that part of the task. A UF description is a method for investigating usability by measuring and describing a user's operation flow. The method has three parts: (1) a time-series description consisting of a table that lists user's operation along the time series; (2) a personal UF description summarizing the time line for a flow diagram of the operation and describing each individual's UF; and (3) a population UF description integrating the individual UF description for one figure to measure the usability of the all user's operation. This study describes the method's purpose and explains the procedure of the UF description method. Finally, we discuss a problem and its solution using the method.

Keywords: Usability measurement · User-flow · Qualitative and quantitative analysis

1 Introduction

Using a tool or system for achieving a goal requires the user to learn how to operate the tool or system. Typically, the user's purpose is not to learn the system, but to use it to achieve some goal. However, sometimes fatigue or lack of resources (attention, motivation, or time) for using complex and difficult to learn tools, such as computers or smart phones, can prevent the user from achieving the goal. This results in the low usability of complex systems.

Usability is defined in ISO9241-11 as "The extent to which a product can be used by specified users to achieve specified goals with effectiveness, efficiency and satisfaction in a specified context of use." We are able to measure these three elements of usability both quantitatively and qualitatively. Qualitative measurement data might be obtained through a user test, but such data are difficult to summarize. In contrast, a quantitative measurement has the advantage of being able to summarize multi-user data in a single index. However, despite this advantage, quantitative data are difficult to obtain from large subject samples.

Qualitative and quantitative measurement each has its own advantage. We have developed a new measurement method, the user-flow (UF) description, to combine the advantage of each type of measurement. The goal of the UF description method is to measure effectiveness and efficiency of a usability definition both quantitative and qualitative terms.

C. Stephanidis (Ed.): HCII 2016 Posters, Part I, CCIS 617, pp. 155–160, 2016.
DOI: 10.1007/978-3-319-40548-3_26

2 User-Flow (UF)

We consider a series of procedures that a user is follows to achieve a task as a continuous stream, because the series of actions involved in such procedures are not independent from each other. In general, actions taken to achieve a goal are dynamic and continuous. When a succession of acts has stalled for some reason, then we notice a discrepancy in the task performance process. Accordingly, we regard a user's performance as a flow-like structure, UF.

UF is a series of user operations taken towards achieving a purpose, the sequential steps of a procedure that a user actually performs. It has following features:

1. A user aims to achieve the goal through a minimum number of steps, but this might not succeed in some situations. UF follows a straight path from the user's point of view, but the actual path might deviate in practice.
2. UF is restricted by cognitive resources such as attention, motivation, and memory, and by such physical resources as time. Once these resources are exhausted, the UF interrupts the task sequence, preventing the user from achieving the goal.
3. The structure of UF evolve from the skill level toward the rule revel before finally reaching the objective level. For example, in the event that the user is learning to use a computer system to write a report, s/he must first learn how to use the physical devices (e.g., keyboard, mouse, and printer). Once these skills are acquired, the user's attention would shift to how to use the application. When the user has learned the rules of the application (e.g., for a word processing software), then s/he can concentrate on the content of the purpose (e.g., report). The user must perform the task only on this objective level, not in the skill or rule level.
4. UF develops toward maximum efficiency with minimum cost as the user users the system repeatedly. When the learning of the UF is completed, the UF can proceed automatically without consuming further user resources.
5. UF becomes nested. On the way to the goal, sometimes a user must solve another "lower-level" problem of the task. The new lower level's operation is called "sub-flow." The user can not return to the primary UF until the sub-flow is resolved (see Fig. 1). If the nested sub-flows become sufficiently deep, the UF could not return to the primary level because the user's resource become exhausted along the way.
6. UF emerges from the interaction between user interface and the user's previous experience. Hence, UF is created by the user, not by a designer or engineer.

In contrast, work-flow (WF) is defined as the operational steps set up by a system or user interface designer. For example, the procedure represented in user operation manuals comprise WF. WF is the ideal operation procedure that is considered to be the most effective and efficient. WF provides the foundation for analyzing UF.

3   How to Describe UF

The UF description method involves four stages. First, a user's operations are recorded using video or operation capture software (when the target to be measured is a computer system).

The second stage involves observing the user's behaviors and describing them step by step in a table, along with a time series, in accordance with the rules (Table 1). Each column of the table contains nine slots, each of which is filled by analysts (and if possible) with the cooperation of the participant. The detailed information in the table is the basis for the further analysis. The detailed information in the table is the basis for further analysis.

Table 1. Time-series description

Categories	Explanation	Example of description
Time	Elapsed time for user's operation	1"58
Handled object	An object that the user has actually used	Floating menu
Object to operate	An object that the user aims to use	Graph
Real action	An observed action	D (drag)
Purpose	Purpose of an act in the task	To focus on graph
Result (success, S or failure, F)	Whether the act is a success or failure	S
Operation level (1, 2, 3 ...)	Depth of flow: primary flow is 1, sub-flow is 2, and so on.	2
Contribution to the purpose in principal level (Y or N)	Whether the act contributes to achieving the task or not	N
Comment	Noteworthy relevant information (if necessary)	Moving the menu to operate the graph under the menu

1. Time: The start time of the described event relative to the begging of the task.
2. Handled object: An object that the user actually touched. In this example, the user moved the floating menu of the software.
3. Object to operate: The object that the user actually wants to work on. In this example, although the user has moved the floating menu, the real purpose of that behavior was to focus on the graph behind the menu. In this case, the object to work is not the menu but the graph. The contents of this slot is determined by reasoning from the next movement or from an introspective report from the participant.
4. Real action: The observed specific action that a user has performed. Abbreviations are used in this slot, for example, "d" standing for "drag", "dc" standing for "double click."

5. Purpose: The meaning of an act in the task described using a phrase that indicates the purpose of the behavior. This slot is filled based on the contents of slot 3.
6. Result: A record of whether the act ended in success ("S") or in failure ("F"). If the user failed to click the object, the result is "F."
7. Operation level: A number here indicates the depth of the flow level. The primary flow level is "1" and the numbers increase incrementally with sub-flow levels.
8. Contribution to the purpose in main level ("Y" or "N"): In a simple case, the user failed to click the object, and it is recorded as "N" (marked as "F" in slot 6). In a more complex case, when the entire sub-flow was incorrect, all the steps in the sub-flow are judged as "N", even if not every operational procedure failed. This is because the judgement "Y" in this slot would indicate the progress on the UF to the goal, whereas the incorrect sub-flow did not contribute to reaching the goal at all. In the same sense, the steps involved in reading the manual are necessary but are not considered to be contributing to the task and thus are judged as "N."
9. Comment: Describe any notable information meriting further analysis.

The third stage involves drawing the UF diagram for each participant based on the time-series table created at the second stage. Figure 1 is a conceptual drawing that explains the UF description. To draw a diagram, the analyst takes the WF as the foundation. The WF consists of only primary-level flow. The information in the table is further broken down into some units relating to each operation object in the task. In this stage, the order information in the operating was discarded and the all steps are rear-ranged in order of WF for comparison of each UF diagram.

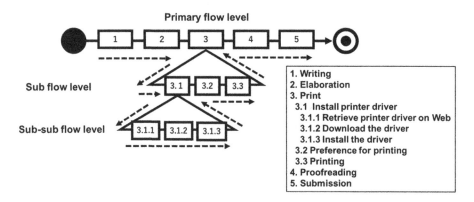

Fig. 1. Conceptual diagram of UF for submitting a report

For the sample in Fig. 1, the user wants to submit a report. Although the first and second steps on the primary level (1 and 2) were proceeding smoothly, a problem with printing the paper has occurred in the third step. To print the paper, the user had to install a printer driver (down to the sub flow level); furthermore, the printer driver is distributed on the Internet, requiring the user to find the driver by searching the network (down to the sub-sub flow level). It is important to note that we designate these sub-flow and sub-sub flow actions as not contributing to achieving the task, as noted previously, since the user's purpose is to submit the report, not to install or search for the printer driver. Certainly, installing the printer driver was a necessary step in the printing procedure, but it is not an essential work directly related to submitting the report. Ideally, these sub-flows and sub-sub flows should be performed automatically by the computer or the printer itself. Users would prefer working towards task goals by proceeding only on the primary level of the UF without needing to dive into sub-flow level. Consequently, the tools must assist the user in achieving the task's true purpose. Procedures not contributing to the purpose itself are essentially useless. This analysis illustrates the qualitative aspects of a user's operations.

We can also use this diagram for measurement of the quantitative side. Figure 2 is an actual analysis example of the UF diagram for a participant. The triangles comprise sub-flow (and sub-sub flow) levels. The numbers separated by slashes in each triangle are the total number of actual steps, the number of the effective or contributed steps, and the number of ideal steps (WF), in order. These values represent the efficiency of the procedure that the particular participant performed.

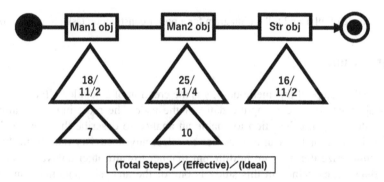

Fig. 2. Example of a participant's UF diagram for a poster construction task on graphic software

In the following procedure, the all users' full diagram is summarized by individual diagrams in Fig. 3. The shape of the full UF diagram is almost consistent with the individual diagrams but differs in two points. First, the meaning of each user operating in sub-flow levels is abstracted, showing only the number of procedures, as we focus only on the number of steps in sub-flows to measure unnecessary steps, regardless of their cause. Second, for each actual step, the minimum and maximum number among all of the user operations are described in parentheses. This indicates the magnitude and the range of the number of actual steps from all users. The description is also adopted for effective steps (but the WF steps are constant). As a result, the full users' combined diagram contains the distribution of the users' operational steps for specific conditions. These values are used, for example, for estimating the quality of a user's manual. When the range is narrow, the procedure may be represented clearly in the manual and much of the users will follow the procedure in the same way. Conversely, in the case where the range is wide, that may suggest that the manual represents ambiguous expressions or multiple procedures, causing different users to follow the procedure in different manners.

If an operation problem is found in total users' diagram, an analyst is able to refer backs to each of the user's diagram for detailed analysis and if necessary return to the time-series table of each participant to dissect the problem.

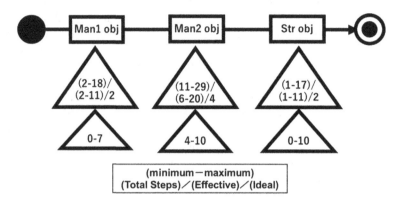

Fig. 3. Example of all users' full UF diagram for a poster construction task on graphic software

4 Conclusion

The principal concept of this methodology is the creation of a detailed UF table from an operational video (or screen capture data) of the user. The most important aim is to infer the intent of a user's action to enable an analyst to describe the user's behavior more exactly. The analyst can also access or select any necessary data from the table and can summarize the diagram in different manner toward other analytical purposes. The UF diagram explained in this study is one of the analysis tools that can derived from the data summarized in the UF table.

Since this methodology is still under development, the details of the technique are likely to change as work progress. In addition, we have found some inherent problems in this method.

This UF description method has three problems. First, it requires substantial effort. For example, transcribing the user's operational video to a time-series table requires more than an hour, even if the video itself is only a few minutes long. Second, the meanings of a user's behaviors are difficult to infer, even if we can obtain information from the participant during the analysis stage. Because many user behaviors are unconscious, users themselves might not able to explain their behavior. Third, the descriptions tend to become ambiguous. Analyses by multiple analysts sometimes do not quite match.

We plan to (semi)automate the description process to solve a portion of these problems, especially in transcription from the recorded data to UF table. Although this tool can only support describing the time-series table from a user's operational log data, we have checked that using it reduced the required effort to some extent. We would like to improve this methodology by introducing more automation and process that require less effort.

COSSplay: Validating a Computerized Operator Support System Using a Microworld Simulator

Thomas Ulrich[1(⊠)], Steffen Werner[1], Roger Lew[1],
and Ronald Boring[2]

[1] University of Idaho, Moscow, ID, USA
{ulrich,swerner}@uidaho.edu,
rogerlew@vandals.uidaho.edu
[2] Idaho National Laboratory, Idaho Falls, ID, USA
ronald.boring@inl.gov

Abstract. Our computerized operator support system microworld simulator with student operators approach is called COSSplay. COSSplay allows testing of specific interface elements such as alarm visualizations without the constraints of the surrounding nuclear control room elements typically associated with full-scope simulation studies. Approaches like COSSplay are ideal for first principles research in human factors and human-computer interaction. This paper highlights the uses of COSSplay as a complimentary approach to full-scope simulation studies for complex interface design.

Keywords: Microworld · Simulation · Process control · Interface design

1 Introduction

Computerized operator support systems (COSS) exist in numerous complex work environments in aviation, maritime navigation, space exploration, medicine, and nuclear process control [1]. Within the context of nuclear process control, a COSS consists of automatic plant control features and a decision support system to aid operators while they monitor and control the plant. A prototype COSS was developed to demonstrate and empirically evaluate added capabilities afforded by automating operator actions for plant transients as described in [2]. The report recognized that managing certain plant upsets is sometimes limited by the operator's ability to quickly diagnose the fault and to take the needed actions in the time available. The COSS provides rapid assessments, computations, and recommendations to reduce workload and augment operator judgment and decision-making during these fast-moving, complex events.

The prototype COSS also provides advanced visualizations to aid the operator in understanding the current state of the plant. Furthermore, the automated prognostic system intelligently detects faults and prescribes procedures, which reduces the cognitive burden placed on the operator. Automating these tasks can lead to an overall improvement in system performance by reducing human error and allowing cognitive

© Springer International Publishing Switzerland 2016
C. Stephanidis (Ed.): HCII 2016 Posters, Part I, CCIS 617, pp. 161–166, 2016.
DOI: 10.1007/978-3-319-40548-3_27

resources to be dedicated to other supervisory tasks. However, adding automation can lead to decreased system performance as evidenced by the operator out-of-the-loop performance problem [3], in which the automation precludes the operator from maintaining situation awareness. Prior to implementation in an actual nuclear power plant control room, the human-computer interactions with the COSS must be carefully evaluated. Any issues associated with the human-computer interactions must be eliminated through an iterative design process in order to create a useful operator support system. Furthermore, a COSS must undergo a verification and validation process as required by NUREG-0711 for any significant control room modification [4].

Two separate simulation approaches will continue to be used to support COSS development. Specifically, a microworld simulation has been used to support COSS development during the iterative design stages to vet and identify usability issues with novel interface display and control schemes. A full-scope simulation has also been extensively used to test and develop the COSS system within the context of a nuclear control room. The full-scope simulation will also be used to perform the verification and validation process required to approve the COSS system prior to its implementation in an actual nuclear control room. Advantages and disadvantages associated with each type of simulation will be discussed in the subsequent sections.

2 Full-Scope Simulations

Simulations serve as a primary method to generate and gather performance data needed for iterative design [5]. Nuclear utilities could potentially use their control room simulators to explore design changes proposed for their control rooms, but plant simulators are ill-suited for these activities. Significant demands for simulator time to conduct operator training and requirements to maintain an exact replica of the actual plant control room preclude plant simulators from much use for design purposes. Dedicated research simulators, such as the Human Systems Simulation Laboratory (HSSL) at Idaho National Laboratory, provide a simulation platform to develop and test complex interface designs for control rooms [6]. The HSSL is a full-scope, fully reconfigurable simulator capable of displaying various virtual nuclear power plant control rooms across its bays of large glasstop touch screen displays. The HSSL has been used extensively to evaluate digital control room upgrades. As control rooms age, obsolete analog components require digital replacements. The digital interface replacements largely embody the original functionality of the analog system being replaced. The resulting "digital islands" replace only a small subset of the original analog indicators and controls found across the control room; therefore, they require the extensive use of neighboring analog indicators and controls for operators to perform their duties. As such, a full-scope simulation is required to test and evaluate the digital replacement within the context of the surrounding control room.

Dedicated research simulators, like the HSSL, circumvent issues associated with the inability to modify plant simulators to test designs. The HSSL is also sufficiently flexible that designs and modifications can be rapidly mocked-up and tested within a virtual representation of a nuclear control room. Dedicated research simulators also alleviate the availability issue with plant simulators due to their extensive use for training; however, there are only a handful of research simulators across the world and their use still poses a significant financial and time investment. There are many instances in which a full-scope research simulator is the most appropriate tool to generate performance data needed for iterative design, but there are also instances in which another simplified approach is more appropriate.

When performing simulations, the amount of the real world elements included in the simulation must be addressed based upon the intended goals of the simulation. For example, simulators used by nuclear utilities are intended for training purposes and therefore require a high level of fidelity to provide learner engagement, suspension of disbelief, and transferable skill acquisition from operator training to the actual real world operation of the plant [7]. In research, the goal of a simulator is fundamentally different because the aim is to acquire human-computer interaction data to better understand how an operator performs the nuclear process control task and translate that understanding into effective interface designs that improve performance. As such, a high level of fidelity is not necessarily required to capture the underlying human-computer interactions needed for the design and testing of new digital interfaces.

3 Microworld Simulations

A microworld is a simplified part-task simulation of a real-world process. The educational value of microworld simulations has been established in a large volume of empirical work [8, 9]. The value of a microworld simulation in the context of complex interface design research is much less established, though a number of studies exist [10–13]. In terms of nuclear process control interface design, microworld simulation offers a complimentary approach to full-scope simulation. Microworld simulation offers a number of advantages particularly during the early design phase. The reduction in scope embodied by the microworld simulation adds experimental control to the evaluations of the interface design [14]. The interface can be evaluated alone without any potential confounds of the control room associated with full-scope research simulations. Specific interface design elements can also be examined in isolation. A detailed evaluation of specific interface elements, such as a new widget, can aid the design process by focusing the human-computer interaction evaluation on that interface element. Each new interface element can undergo this type of testing to determine its effectiveness before undergoing evaluation within the context of the overall new interface. From these detailed control level examinations, first principles for advanced visualization designs can be explored and evaluated under strict experimental control.

The microworld simulation's reduction in scope also expands the applicant pool of participants beyond experienced nuclear operators and condenses the scenario simulation timespans [14]. Individuals without extensive process control training and experience can serve as participants because the reduced scope of the simulation reduces the complexity of the simulated process control task. Inexpensive student participants or plant personnel in training can be quickly trained on the operation of the microworld *and* perform numerous scenario simulations, all within a relatively short timeframe, such as a single experimental session. With a larger participant pool and shorter time required to conduct the simulation scenarios, the central questions surrounding the human computer interaction can receive more focus. During any simulation there are periods of uninformative dead time between events containing useful diagnostic data. Simplified simulations that focus on upset conditions can eliminate some of this dead time, and the scenario simulation can focus on the key human-computer interactions for a particular task. For example, a subset of the system containing the interface element of interest can comprise the entire microworld scenario simulation and focus on that particular interface element to evaluate human-computer interaction dynamics.

Microworld simulations are particularly well suited for addressing research questions for novel designs. Unlike the digital interface replacements comprised of the same or similar functionality found within the original analog system, advanced digital interfaces contain novel design schemes that are outside the current concept of operations found at existing nuclear power plants. Since there is little similarity between the existing analog control room operations and operations proposed in the new advanced digital interface, there is less need to include peripheral components for design and testing. The advanced digital interfaces are also self-contained in the sense that all necessary information from the various sensors throughout the plant and the necessary controls to manipulate all aspects of plant components are present within the interface. There is little need to simulate surrounding analog indicators and controls because they are obsolete and redundant to those found within the advanced digital interface.

The manner in which information is presented in advanced digital interfaces follows a multi-window view scheme in which subsystems of related component information and associated controls are presented at a given time. The operator and the automation within the interface drive which system is presented based on the current plant status and operator task. As a result, the interface can be displayed in a much smaller space on as little as a single visual display unit. For evaluation purposes the relevant windows can be included in the microworld simulation in order to examine how particular visual elements convey information or support operator actions. Including only relevant portions of the system not only isolates the components, but as mentioned previously, it restricts the scope of the simulation to enable novice participants to perform short operator tasks without being overwhelmed by complexity. Since the perceptual capabilities of operators are comparable to that of students, novice participants can provide valid usability data given a sufficiently low-complexity task simulated in the microworld. Additionally, the novice participants are unbiased by prior operating experience and may reveal advantageous novel human-computer interactions that experienced operators may not exhibit. Enhancing aspects of the advanced digital interface to support or strengthen these novel interactions could improve operator performance.

Though microworlds provide a number of advantages, there are some limitations since they are simplified simulations and the novice participants are not nuclear operators. Aspects of the interface that work well in a microworld context may not scale to larger contexts found within a full-scope simulation or actual control room. Some aspects of the interface might prove advantageous with novice users, but those advantages may not translate to advantages for experienced nuclear operators. As a result, it is important to also use a full-scope simulation to ensure that the results and conclusions from the microworld scale to the full-scope simulation context with nuclear operators.

4 Continued COSS Development

In our approach the available pool of student operators for the microworld is extensive, allowing more statistically conclusive design studies to refine COSS. Our COSS microworld simulator with student operators is called *COSSplay*. COSSplay is a word play on cosplay, a term used to describe dressing up like famous characters. COSSplay in this sense is the microworld dressed up to perform key functions of the actual COSS. COSSplay allows testing of specific interface elements such as alarm visualizations without the confounds of the surrounding control room elements [15]. COSSplay therefore is ideal for first principles research in human factors and human-computer interaction. The limitation of this approach is that experimental tasks requiring the skill of professional reactor operators are not possible in COSSplay. Such tasks can, however, be performed by actual operators on the COSS implemented in the full-scope simulator. COSSplay complements COSS and serves as a useful testbed for research.

5 Conclusion

Full-scope and microworld simulations offer complementary approaches to design and evaluate interfaces for nuclear process control. Microworld simulations should be used for novel designs and during early design phases to leverage the expanded participant pool and small cost of operating a microworld simulation. The interface should then undergo testing in the full-scope simulator to ensure any lingering usability issues or context sensitive issues are addressed prior to installation of the new interface in the plant control room.

References

1. Ulrich, T., Lew, R., Medema, H., Boring, R.: A computerized operator support system prototype. INL/EXT-13-29651. Idaho National Laboratory, Idaho Falls (2015)
2. Quinn, T., Bockhorst, R., Peterson, C., Swindlehurst, G.: Design to achieve fault tolerance and resilience. INL/EXT-12-27205. Idaho National Laboratory, Idaho Falls (2012)
3. Endsley, M.R., Kiris, E.O.: The out-of-the-loop performance problem and level of control in automation. Hum. Factors J. Hum. Factors Ergon. Soc. **37**(2), 381–394 (1995)
4. OHara, J., Higgins, J., Stubler, W., Goodman, C., Eckinrode, R., Bongarra, J., Galletti, G.: Human factors engineering review program model (NUREG-0711 rev. 3). US Nuclear Regulatory Commission, Washington. DC (2011)
5. Boring, R.L.: The use of simulators in human factors studies within the nuclear industry. In: Skjerve, A.B., Bye, A. (eds.) Simulator-based Human Factors Studies Across 25 Years, pp. 3–12. Springer, London (2010)
6. Boring, R., et al.: Digital full-scope simulation of a conventional nuclear power plant control room, phase 2: installation of a reconfigurable simulator to support nuclear plant sustainability. Technical report INL/EXT-13-28432, Idaho National Laboratory, Idaho Falls (2013)

7. Hamstra, S.J., Brydges, R., Hatala, R., Zendejas, B., Cook, D.A.: Reconsidering fidelity in simulation-based training. Acad. Med. **89**(3), 387–392 (2014)
8. Rieber, L.P.: Seriously considering play: designing interactive learning environments based on the blending of microworlds, simulations, and games. Educ. Technol. Res. Dev. **44**(2), 43–58 (1996)
9. Romme, A.G.L.: Perceptions of the value of microworld simulation: research note. Simul. Gaming **35**(3), 427–436 (2004)
10. Vicente, K., Pawlak, W.: Cognitive Work Analysis for the DURESS II System. Cognitive Engineering Laboratory, Department of Industrial Engineering, University of Toronto, Toronto, Canada CEL, pp. 94–03 (1994)
11. Boring, R., Kelly, D., Smidts, C., Mosleh, A., Dyre, B.: Microworlds, simulators, and simulation: framework for a benchmark of human reliability data sources. In: Joint Probabilistic Safety Assessment and Management and European Safety and Reliability Conference, 16B-Tu5-5, June 2012
12. Dyre, B.P., Adamic, E.J., Werner, S., Lew, R., Gertman, D.I., Boring, R.L.: A microworld simulator for process control research and training. Proc. Hum. Factors Ergon. Soc. Ann. Meet. **57**(1), 1367–1371 (2013)
13. Lew, R., Boring, R.L., Ulrich, T.A.: A prototyping environment for research on human-machine interfaces in process control use of microsoft WPF for microworld and distributed control system development. In: 2014 7th International Symposium on Resilient Control Systems (ISRCS), pp. 1–6. IEEE August 2014
14. Ulrich, T.A., Werner, S., Boring, R.L.: Studying situation awareness on a shoestring budget an example of an inexpensive simulation environment for theoretical research. Proc. Hum. Factors Ergon. Soc. Ann. Meet. **59**(1), 1520–1524 (2015). SAGE Publications
15. Ulrich, T.A., Werner, S., Boring, R.L.: Change detection for measuring attention allocation: a new approach for capturing situation awareness. In: Proceedings of the Human Factors and Ergonomics Society Annual Meeting 60(1). SAGE Publications (in press)

Low-Fidelity Prototyping for Collaborative User Interface Specifications

Jan Wojdziak[1]([⊠]), Bastian Bansemir[2], Bettina Kirchner[1],
Berit Lochner[2], and Rainer Groh[3]

[1] Gesellschaft für Technische Visualistik mbH, Dresden, Germany
jan.wojdziak@tu-dresden.de
[2] BMW Group, Munich, Germany
[3] Technische Universität, Dresden, Germany

Abstract. The paper describes a procedure for requirements engineering workshops where attendees of different expertise are guided to identify and to describe user interface requirements. Based on a workshop structure with user-centered design constraints, participants are assisted in scoping and ideation processes using low-fidelity techniques and the World Café conversation method to determine user and system requirements.

Keywords: Low-fidelity prototyping · World café · Workshop · Requirements engineering · Interface specification

1 Introduction

The specification of user interfaces (UI) is the fundamental prerequisite for the whole UI development process and highly influences all subsequent steps. To identify user demands and system requirements the perspective of both the customer and the developer is needed. Thus, user representatives as well as application domain experts, designers, and developers have to discuss jointly and reach decisions in consensus.

However, all involved parties typically have their own individual terms, use diverse representations, and pursue different objectives. UI specifications tend to be merely textual and lack a common understanding. Thus, it results often in considerable changes in subsequent development steps.

We present a novel method for UI-related requirements engineering that can be used for a wide range of applications. Therefore, we combine principle ideas of low-fidelity (low-fi) prototyping [1, 2] which is a common technique for requirements engineering [3] with the World Café method [4] that is primary used for dialogues in large groups. Our approach results in a more structured and conversational interaction, enables open discussion, links ideas between heterogeneous participants, and benefits from the collective wisdom. Our practical experiences prove the strengths of the proposed method.

© Springer International Publishing Switzerland 2016
C. Stephanidis (Ed.): HCII 2016 Posters, Part I, CCIS 617, pp. 167–172, 2016.
DOI: 10.1007/978-3-319-40548-3_28

2   Related Work

Low-Fidelity prototypes, on the one hand, are an important tool for designers as well as developers to create and test designs and solutions during early design phases [5]. In doing so, low-fidelity prototypes need to be "quick to build and easy to use" [6]. The concept of low-fi prototyping is applied in software and hardware design. In [7, 8], it is shown that low-fi prototyping can be used to enable end users to design mobile systems, whereas in [9], a low-fi rapid prototyping approach is applied to build a tactile vision sensory substitution system. The World Café, on the other hand, is a creative development technique in which medium size groups generate ideas to solve a problem; usually around social issues within a particular community, such as area development policies [10]. In [11], the World Café approach is applied to the conceptual phase of design processes, during which designers try to integrate concepts based on stakeholder information. The Application of the World Café concept can also be utilized to create interactive learning environments [12]. Studies using the World Café method for requirements engineering (e.g. for game design with children [13] or for geographic visualization with a high fidelity prototype [14]) indicate an efficient and successful approach for user interface specifications.

3   Approach

Based on a series of workshops, we developed a workshop structure that can fit many different objectives, purposes, user groups, and technologies in the context of UI requirements engineering. In our approach, we use an advanced toolset based on elements of a facilitator's toolbox to enhance scoping and ideation processes. These processes are guided by the World Café method. Within four incremental sessions of structured debates, the participants are encouraged to write and draw key ideas on paper and handicraft elements, following the basics of Low-Fi prototyping. Every session provides a different perspective on UI aspects, thus allowing the actors to analyze requirements and identify specifications. Therefore, a smooth progression from an abstract point of view to concrete requirements is realized within the workshop. In the following, we present the resulting structure that describes the creative processes involved and the whole workshop as a user-centered design procedure.

3.1   Preliminary Considerations

In preparation for the workshop, the questions "What should be achieved?" and "Who can help with that?" should be answered. Therefore the overall topic needs to be outlined– i.e., the main purpose of the interface to be built. One or more goals for the workshop have to be determined and their extents clarified. The participants should be chosen according to their fields of expertise, preferably including members from different thematic areas such as designers and developers and end users. Additionally, a workshop leader, who moderates each part of the event, has to be chosen. In a preceding step, the workshop room has to be prepared by arranging the World Café tables and laying out the tools (i.e. pens and paper). The workshop itself is designed for 6 up to 12 participants and takes from 3.5 up to 5 h.

3.2   Kick Off

The workshop leader launches the workshop with a short introduction, giving a summary of the purpose and explaining basic rules for debates. Each participant introduces themselves and their field of work shortly. Afterwards, they will be assigned to one of three groups for the following implementation of the World Café method. In our case, this means that the participants move between three tables. At each table, they continue the debates so far and in response to a set of content issues. These questions are predetermined and focus on three specific aspects of requirements engineering, with each table representing one of the main topics: (1) Data and information, (2) Users and (3) Aims of the interface. For every main topic, the ideation and scoping processes are divided into four phases. In the course of the workshop, one participant of each group acts as a designated expert for one of the topics. This person will stay at the initially assigned table throughout the whole workshop. All other participants are carrying out all phases for each main topic.

3.3   Workshop Phases

The workshop begins with the participants joining their group around one of the three tables. Within the first iteration, they are instructed by the moderator to identify relevant influencing factors for the respective main topic (1), (2) or (3). Each identified factor is written on a Post-it note and collected on the table randomly, before being sorted into groups according to their coherences (Fig. 1).

On reaching the end of the first and every following phase, the workshop leader documents each table in its current state (i.e. with pictures) and explains the next round. Participants of one group, except the designated expert, start to move to the next table. The expert shares ideas and results of the previous round with the new members.

The second iteration comprises a translation of the influencing factors into a visual grammar[1]. The members start by picking one up to three factors (Post-it), sticking it onto an element of the visual grammar and therefore creating entities. As a next crucial step, they determine the User Experience (UX) factor (e.g. simplicity or cognitive load) that plays a role concerning this entity. It is combined with the circle holding the Post-it note. Other Post-it notes are added to this entity if they belong to the same UX factor. In the end, each Post-it should be placed on one entity with a UX factor.

Within the third phase, relations between the entities of one main topic have to be identified and drawn on the table as lines between the circles (Fig. 1).

---

[1] In its simplest form, the visual grammar consists of nothing more than a few circular elements which the Post-it notes are placed on following the grammar rules. These grammar rules are predefined by the workshop leader. Depending on the complexity of the workshop topic, the set of plain circles can be extended by differently colored circles or other geometric items, varying in size and texture.

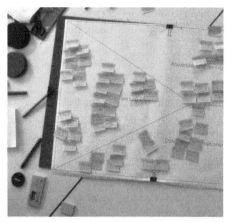

Fig. 1. Cooperative work within different sessions of the requirement engineering process

Once all relevant relations are marked, the groups of all three tables are reunited to start the last phase. There all participants collaborate to define entities across all three main topics and complete the requirements analysis.

3.4   Outcome and Next Steps

Once the main topics are combined in one big picture and connected to each other by the modelled relations, the actual steps of the workshop are finalized. Subsequent to the phases, participants should reflect upon what they have created in the workshop: the completeness of the requirements, the insights they have gained and if this form of collaboration is adequate for their own understanding of the tasks at hand. At the end, the workshop leader gives a summary of the results including a full list of requirements and interface specifications and closes up with a preview of the next necessary steps.

4   Benefits

Three critical factors of UI requirement engineering are addressed by the described approach: (i) Collection of design-critical information, (ii) Kick-start with Ideation and (iii) Participant's buy-in. In the following, the benefits are presented in greater detail.

4.1   Collection of Design-Critical Information

The low-fidelity prototyping methodology puts the objective at the center of all design efforts. Tasks and objectives, the specific users and user groups who have to fulfill them, and the underlying data and necessary information are connected to each other. Establishing these connections is the key to design the aimed UI experience.

With the connections between the three main topics being visible to the participants, it is easy to discover commonalities between them, e.g. all user groups have to fulfill Task A. However, specific requirements of only one user or user group are identified as well. This enables a scrum-based approach in later implementation stages. In addition, user stories can be generated quite effortlessly. The beauty of this method is that the participants gain deep insights about critical design paths to follow-up. By illustrating users in conjunction with objectives as well as information they need, an effective and successful UI design process can be achieved. The described method is distinct in the sense that participants bring-in their knowledge, needs, and experiences and basically do the 'requirements elicitation process' without really knowing it, and all by using their own language.

4.2   Kick-Start with Ideation

Often discussions in the context of requirements engineering emerge around single terms or the meaning of them. Low-fi prototyping substitutes this stage with a motivating, challenging and inspiring ideation stage. At the same time, the utilization of the World Café method creates an open atmosphere where all participants are encouraged to speak up freely and share their thoughts with the group. The massive ideation at the very beginning of the first phase necessitates full concentration and creativity of all participants.

The benefit of this ideation stage on the professional side is that key ideas and requirements are identified quickly and immediately taken further by the next group. Even more importantly, on the motivational side, clear results are produced in the first meeting and lie on the tables in a physically graspable form.

4.3   Participant's Buy-In

Communication during a software development process and interest in its progress can be key factor to failure or success. Developers, designers and end users need to be equally invested in the latter. This can only be the case when everyone has a common interest in reaching this goal, as well as a shared perception of the software's main purpose.

Bringing-in all involved parties in the first stage of the UI design step and letting them work on the requirements jointly puts them on the same page with the project. This creates a closer working atmosphere and enhances the chances of a lively exchange throughout the following processes. This situation is very effective as the personal investment in a successful implementation grows. The participants become promotors, engage in continuously improving the design and will defend the final product.

5   Conclusion

Low-fi prototyping embedded into a workshop structure based on the World Café method improves the requirements engineering process and builds an environment in which users' needs can be identified interdisciplinary. The presented approach was found to be very productive in UI requirements engineering. Especially, guiding non-UI-designers through the process of requirements elicitation in a way that feels natural and motivational to them is a key argument. During the process, an individual common language is formed that is comprehensible to all and encourages collaboration. Using visual abstractions as prototyping elements supports early informal sketching compared to medium or high fidelity prototypes [15]. Furthermore, the World Café method as a guided procedure facilitates the concretion of interface requirements, unleashes broad support for the UI design and an adequate description of UI requirements.

References

1. Coyette, A., Kieffer, S., Vanderdonckt, J.: Multi-fidelity prototyping of user interfaces. In: Baranauskas, C., Abascal, J., Barbosa, S.D.J. (eds.) INTERACT 2007. LNCS, vol. 4662, pp. 150–164. Springer, Heidelberg (2007)
2. Rudd, J., Stern, K., Isensee, S.: Low vs. high-fidelity prototyping debate. Interactions **3**, 76–85 (1996)
3. Nuseibeh, B., Easterbrook, S.: Requirements engineering: a roadmap. In: Proceedings of the Conference on the Future of Software Engineering, pp. 35–46. ACM (2000)
4. Brown, J.: The World Café: Shaping Our Futures Through Conversations That Matter. ReadHowYouWant.com, Sydney (2010)
5. Beyer, H., Holtzblatt, K.: Contextual Design: A Customer-Centered Approach to Systems Designs. Morgan Kaufmann Series in Interactive Technologies. Morgan Kaufmann, Burlington (1997)
6. Virzi, R.A., Sokolov, J.L., Karis, D.: Usability problem identification using both low- and high-fidelity prototypes. In: Proceedings of the SIGCHI Conference on Human Factors in Computing Systems, pp. 236–243. ACM (1996)
7. Svanaes, D., Seland, G.: Putting the users center stage: role playing and low-fi prototyping enable end users to design mobile systems. In: Proceedings of the SIGCHI Conference on Human Factors in Computing Systems, pp. 479–486. ACM (2004)
8. de Sá, M., Carriço, L.: Low-fi prototyping for mobile devices. In: CHI 2006 Extended Abstracts on Human Factors in Computing Systems, pp. 694–699. ACM (2006)
9. Bird, J., Marshall, P., Rogers, Y.: Low-fi skin vision: a case study in rapid prototyping a sensory substitution system. In: Proceedings of the 23rd British HCI Group Annual Conference on People and Computers: Celebrating People and Technology. British Computer Society, pp. 55–64 (2009)
10. Elliott, J.: Participatory methods toolkit: a practitioner's manual. King Baudouin Foundation/Flemish Institute for Science and Technology Assessment (2005)
11. Thompson, W.T.: Designing Together with the World Café: Inviting Community Ideas for an Idea Zone in a Science Center (2015)
12. Anderson, L.: Use the World Café concept to create an interactive learning environment. Educ. Prim. Care **22**, 337–338 (2011)
13. Moser, C.: Child-centered game development (CCGD): developing games with children at school. Pers. Ubiquit. Comput. **17**, 1647–1661 (2013)
14. Opach, T., Rød, J.K.: Cartographic visualization of vulnerability to natural hazards. Cartographica Int. J. Geogr. Inf. Geovisualization **48**, 113–125 (2013)
15. Bansemir, B., Hannß, F., Lochner, B., Wojdziak, J., Groh, R.: Experience report: the effectiveness of paper prototyping for interactive visualizations. In: Marcus, A. (ed.) DUXU 2014, Part I. LNCS, vol. 8517, pp. 3–13. Springer, Heidelberg (2014)

Cognitive Issues in HCI

Evaluation of Colorimetric Characteristics of Head-Mounted Displays

Imad Benkhaled[1]([✉]), Isabelle Marc[1], Dominique Lafon-Pham[2],
and Luc Jeanjean[3]

[1] LGI2P, Ecole des mines d'Alès, Nîmes, France
{imad.benkhaled,isabelle.marc}@mines-ales.fr
[2] C2MA, Ecole des mines d'Alès, Pau, France
dominique.lafon@mines-ales.fr
[3] CHU, Service d'ophtalmologie, Nîmes, France
luc.jeanjean@chu-nimes.fr

Abstract. In order to determine if four HMD offer characteristics that are sufficient for applications that require precise control of colors displayed, we use a method inspired by two tests extensively used for screening of deficiencies in color vision: the Farnsworth Munsell D-15 and the Lanthony test, which are both based on the arrangement of fifteen color caps so as to reduce the color difference between two neighboring caps. After performing colorimetric characterization of the HMD, patches that match for the Farnsworth and Lanthony cap colors are created, and the color differences between two patches are measured in the CIE Lab space. We find out that, for some of the devices, differences in color may become very slight, and reach the perception threshold. It is deduced that these devices would fail to display the color characteristics of an image with a sufficient level of accuracy.

Keywords: HMD · Colorimetric characterization

1 Introduction

Relevant efforts are currently in progress for the development of technologies of virtual reality, with the emergence of new head mounted displays (HMD) that combine wide field of view and high resolution. In order to improve immersive sensation when using these devices, a particular attention must be paid to their colorimetric characteristics: they should give access to images with a large range of lightness, hue and saturation, along with the capability to not distort colors, and give a natural appearance to any object in the scene.

This work is devoted to a comparison of colorimetric properties of four HMD. The comparison of different displays cannot be reduced to the comparison of technical data such as contrast, resolution, brightness; it must include colorimetric data, as well as human perception based evaluation. The choice was made to base our study on psychophysical tests commonly used to detect color blindness. In the so called Farnsworth Munsell D-15 (FM D-15) and Lanthony tests, the task is to arrange 15 colored caps in a

C. Stephanidis (Ed.): HCII 2016 Posters, Part I, CCIS 617, pp. 175–180, 2016.
DOI: 10.1007/978-3-319-40548-3_29

specified order of hues. The question to be answered is then: do these HMD have sufficient resolution in color rendering to allow for discrimination of the cap color?

Precise knowledge of the way they can manage with color is therefore a mandatory milestone. This knowledge is inferred from a thorough colorimetric characterization process, aiming to define the relationship between each point in the device color space, based on its RGB primaries, and the physical properties of the emitted light. Method used for this colorimetric characterization is briefly presented in the first part of this paper. The methods and materials used for colorblindness assessment are explained. Finally, experimental procedure and calculations leading to evaluation of color difference are described.

2 Material

Mainly, two technologies share the market of HMD: the first one, very similar to smartphone displays or computer monitors, is based on liquids crystals (LCD), while the other is based on OLED (Organic Light emitting Diode). The colorimetric parameters of four head mounted devices (Sensics ZSight, Occulus Rift, Vuzix W1200VR and Razer OSVR), whose technical specifications are listed in Table 1 have been evaluated. Technical specifications of these displays are listed in Table 1:

Table 1. Technical specification of HMD

Display	Technology	Resolution	Luminance max cd/m^2
Oculus Rift	LCD	1280 × 800	176
Vuzix WRAP 1200 VR	LCD	852 × 480	4.24
Sensics Zsight	OLED	1280 × 1080	10,41
Razer OSVR	OLED	1920 × 1080	84

3 Colorimetric Characterization

As electronic display characteristics vary considerably in terms of color gamut, white point, and brightness, etc. it is important to be able to control the light emitted in terms of luminance and chrominance. It is then necessary to perform a colorimetric characterization, that is a modeling step aiming to map digital RGB values to device-independent tristimulus CIE XYZ values [1].

Over the years, the characterization of color displays has been widely studied in the literature and several models have been proposed [2]. The first ones have been initially developed for CRT technologies, and rely on two assumptions that are usually verified for this kind of displays: the channel independence (i.e. light emitted by one the three channels is a function of the digital value driving this particular channel, et do not depend on values driving the two others) and chromaticity constancy of primaries (i.e.: for each channel, chromatic coordinates x and y remain constant when driving with various digital counts). Classical linear method which leads to estimate chromatic components as a linear combination of primaries and approximate the tone response curve by a power law has been used for our LCD and OLED displays.

Spectral radiance measurements have been collected using a Konica CS-100 spectrophotometer in a dark room with the apparatus at a fixed distance from the display to be tested, and with a 0° incident angle, in order to ensure evaluation consistency between each display. Any flare resulting from stray residual ambient light or the display itself was corrected for in the calculations.

All colorimetric coordinates are determined using the CIE 1931 Standard Colorimetric Observer (2°).

4 Psychophysical Tests

Numerous methods have been developed for color vision assessment. Arrangement tests, during which people are asked to place small disks or caps according to their hue, have been designed to quantitatively assess the degree of color vision impairment. The Farnsworth-Munsell 100-Hue test appears as a standard, widely used for in the assessment of acquired color deficiencies [3]. It has also been used in studies of color rendering of different light sources, for instance [4]. But it appears to be time-consuming. A shortened version, the Farnsworth-Munsell D-15 test has then been developed for a more rapid assessment: the number of caps is reduced to fifteen plus a reference one, from which the arrangement is started. Subjects with color vision deficiency will arrange the color discs in a different order than a person with normal color vision. Errors in the placement are linked to the type of vision defect, and to its severity. In order to increase the sensitivity for subjects experiencing only slight loss of color discrimination, the Lanthony test, for which the caps exhibit strongly desaturated colors, is often performed along with the FM D-15.

For the both tests, the caps exhibit color of equal saturation, and more or less equal luminance, while the hues are distributed almost uniformly on an oval curve in the CIE xy diagram. These tests are prone to error if lighting conditions are not carefully controlled, and the better accuracy is obtained with standardized C or D65 sources. In this case, the color difference between two adjacent caps is intended to be nearly constant.

5 Experimental Procedure

Our purpose is to investigate if the colorimetric characteristics of our devices make it possible to display the same colors as the Farnsworth and Lanthony test caps. The first step in our experimental procedure is to determine the chromaticity coordinates for each cap. Spectral measurements have been made under daylight conditions, for light reflected by each cap, and for light reflected by a perfect reflecting diffuser: it is then possible to infer the spectral reflectance of each cap, as light is the product of the reflectance spectrum of an object by its illumination spectrum. It is now possible to simulate the light reflected by the caps under any illumination. For each display, a D65 source is simulated by weighting D65 illuminant spectrum by the maximum luminance that can be emitted by the display.

The next step is to evaluate difference between colors of two simulated adjacent caps. This difference has to be calculated in the standardized Lab color space. We use the following equations for CIE Lab color, lightness and chroma difference [5].

$$\Delta E^*_{Lab} = \sqrt{\Delta L^2 + \Delta a^2 + \Delta b^2} \quad \Delta E^*_{ab} = \sqrt{\Delta a^2 + \Delta b^2} \quad \Delta E^*_L = \sqrt{\Delta L^2}$$

6 Results

6.1 Colorimetric Characterization

The difference between the tristimulus values obtained from measured data and those predicted by the model was evaluated using the CIELab color difference. The values of the mean color difference for the three channels are summarized on Table 2.

Table 2. Performance results of characterization model: mean color difference for the three channels.

	Razer	Vuzix	Occulus	Sensics
Average ΔE(Lab)$_{mean}$	5.23	9.23	2.65	9.92

The observed difference can be explained by the fact that for at least two devices, the assumptions of channel independence and chromaticity constancy do not hold. In this case, some more sophisticated methods could be used. For instance, Tamura et al. [6] propose a masking model intended to account for channel interaction.

6.2 Effect of Luminance

All the HMD under test exhibit a low luminance level, that may lead to poor color perception: according to the Hunt effect, it is known that as absolute luminance levels

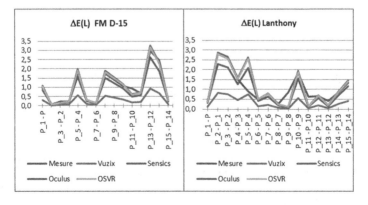

Fig. 1. Lightness difference between two adjacent caps (Color figure online)

decrease, the colorfulness of a stimulus also decreases, with the perceived chromaticity shifting toward white point [7].

Lightness difference between adjacent caps have been calculated for all the HMD, and compared to measured data (Fig. 1). It can be seen that for the Sensics Wrap 1200VR, difference are always behind the detection threshold. For others devices, this happens only between some of the caps, i.e. in some parts of the total gamut, differences are not noticeable.

6.3   Effect of Chroma

Chromaticity coordinates obtained after spectral measurement for each cap and after simulation on a specific display are shown on Fig. 2.

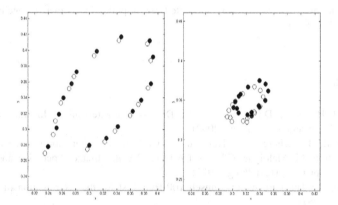

Fig. 2. Cap chromaticity coordinates. Left: FM D-15, right: Lanthony. Black dots: x y obtained from measurements, blank dots: x y obtained by simulation.

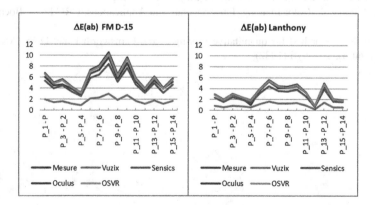

Fig. 3. Chroma difference between two adjacent caps. Left: FM D-15, right: Lanthony

We then evaluate the color difference between two successive caps for a correct arrangement. Results of our calculations are compared to measured values as shown on Fig. 3. Results are coherent with values gained from literature [8]. But once again, the Vuzix HMD exhibits the worst performances for the both tests. All the devices under test do not let the user to discriminate between two colors when they are strongly desaturated.

7   Conclusion

It appears that the HMD under test exhibit somehow different colorimetric behavior: one of them (Vuzix) seems to be definitely inefficient for precise color rendering. The technology (OLED or LCD) is not sufficient for explained such a difference.

Acknowledgements. This work was supported by SopraSteria, Areva, Capgemini, Credit Agricole and SOS Retinite.

References

1. Brainard, D.H., Pelli, D.G., Robson, T.: Display characterization. In: Encyclopedia of Imaging Science and Technology (2002)
2. Thomas, J.-B., Hardeberg, J.Y., Trémeau, A.: Cross-media color reproduction and display characterization. In: Maloigne, C.F. (ed.) Advanced Color Image Processing and Analysis, pp. 81–118. Springer, Heidelberg (2013)
3. Farnsworth, D.: The Farnsworth-Munsell 100-Hue Test for the Examination of Color Discrimination (1957)
4. Rea, M.S., Freyssinier-Nova, J.P.: Color rendering: a tale of two metrics. Color Res. Appl. **33**(3), 192–202 (2008)
5. Tremeau, A., Fernandez-Maloigne, C., Bonton, P.: Image numérique couleur: de l'acquisition au traitement. DUNOD, ISBN **2**(10), 006843 (2004)
6. Tamura, N., Tsumura, N., Miyake, Y.: Masking model for accurate colorimetric characterization of LCD. J. Soc. Inform. Display **11**(2), 333–339 (2003)
7. Reinhard, E., et al.: Color Imaging: Fundamentals and Applications. CRC Press, Boca Raton (2008)
8. Bowman, K.: A method for quantitative scoring of the Farnsworth Panel D-15. Acta Ophthalmol. **60**(6), 907–916 (1982)

An EEG Study of Auditory Working Memory Load and Cognitive Performance

Hsien-Ming Ding[1], Guan-Yi Lu[1], Yuan-Pin Lin[2],
and Yi-Li Tseng[1(✉)]

[1] Department of Electrical Engineering,
Fu Jen Catholic University, New Taipei City, Taiwan
{403216096, 400240577, yltseng}@mail.fju.edu.tw
[2] Institute of Medical Science and Technology,
National Sun Yat-sen University, Kaohsiung, Taiwan
yplin@mail.nsysu.edu.tw

Abstract. Working memory and cognitive performance have received considerable attention in neuroscience research. Most of the studies have demonstrated their interaction over the prefrontal regions while manipulating visual or verbal working memory load. However, less attention has been directed to the impact of musical or auditory input in cognitive performance. In this study, electroencephalography (EEG) of six subjects were measured when they were performing a paradigm of auditory n-back working memory task. EEGLAB and the standardized low-resolution brain electromagnetic tomography (sLORETA) were utilized to parse the scalp EEG signals into source activity. The results revealed that when subjects were engaged in high versus low memory load, there were significantly stronger delta (1–4 Hz) activity in superior frontal gyrus, theta (4–7 Hz) activity in posterior cingulate cortex, alpha 1 (8–10 Hz) and beta 1 (12–16 Hz) activity in insula, but weaker alpha 2 (10–12 Hz) activity in anterior cingulate cortex. These results demonstrated that auditory working memory accompanied distinct brain network modulation to the visual or verbal task.

Keywords: Auditory working memory · EEG · Source reconstruction · sLORETA

1 Introduction

Exploiting the relationship between working memory and cognitive performance has become an important topic in neuroscience research [1, 2]. Most of the studies have demonstrated their interaction over the prefrontal regions while manipulating visual or verbal working memory load. Although these pioneering studies have addressed the pathway of working memory, most of them focused on visual or verbal working memory. Less attention has been directed to the impact of musical or auditory input in cognitive performance.

In the past few years, the anatomical and functional pathway of auditory memory has received growing interests [3–6] using electrophysiological experiment and functional magnetic resonance imaging (fMRI) technique that measure the blood-oxygen-level

© Springer International Publishing Switzerland 2016
C. Stephanidis (Ed.): HCII 2016 Posters, Part I, CCIS 617, pp. 181–185, 2016.
DOI: 10.1007/978-3-319-40548-3_30

dependent (BOLD) activities. For example, Munoz-Lopez *et al.* [4] have shown that the auditory information tends to propagate from rostral superior temporal gyrus to dorsolateral temporal pole and medial temporal cortex, and then to entorhinal cortex and posterior parahippocampal cortex. Musical working memory has been reported to initiate the increased BOLD activities in bilateral superior temporal gyri and inferior frontal and medial superior frontal gyri [9]. The prefrontal region was recently shown to play a critical role in auditory connections for detection, discrimination, and working memory in primate and human [5, 6]. Huang *et al.* [3] further demonstrated that the subregions of anterior dorsal lateral prefrontal cortex were selectively associated with auditory working memory, whereas the areas in more inferior lateral aspects of prefrontal cortex and inferior frontal cortex were selectively related to the auditory attention instead of working memory. Specifically, few studies further accessed the difference in BOLD activities associated with verbal versus tonal (musical) memory. Koelsch *et al.* [7, 8] found the increase in activation in right globus pallidus, right caudate nucleus, and left cerebellum only during tonal working memory task as compared with verbal task.

It is worth noting that although the above fMRI studies can localize the deeper brain structures involved in auditory working memory with high spatial resolution, while the BOLD signals are limited to reflect the rapid changes in temporal characteristics (*i.e.*, poor temporal resolution) with respect to other neuroimaging modalities such as electroencephalogram (EEG) and magnetoencephalography (MEG). This study thus employed the EEG modality to address the temporal dynamics of brain regions in response to a designed auditory n-back working memory task.

2   Materials and Methods

2.1   Auditory n-back Working Memory Task

This study recruited six subjects participating in a paradigm of auditory n-back working memory task that was inspired by [10]. The paradigm was intended to study the emotion regulation during cognitive task by manipulating the memory load and the emotional type of stimuli. This study used an alike protocol to study the auditory working memory processing. Our task has three experimental conditions during music listening: a 1-back (1B) task, a 2-back (2B) task, and a task of passive listening (PL) to the stimuli. Each music stimulation is composed of 12 sound combinations of major, minor, and dissonant chords. The major chords consisted of A, C#, E, A, C#. The minor chords were made of A, C, E, A, C and were considered in music theory as an imperfect consonance. The dissonant chords were made of A, Bb, G, Ab, C, which were thought to be the most dissonant intervals. Following each stimulus, participants were instructed to press the left button in the 1B/2B task when they recognized the chord matching that of the last one/two trials. Otherwise, they needed to press the right button for all other trials or in the PL condition. Each participant underwent a 2-session experiment interleaved with a 2-min rest. Each session consists of 18 blocks with a random combination of task conditions (PL, 1B or 2B) and chord categories (major, minor or dissonant). Each type of block was repeated four times discontinuously during the experiment. Twenty trials were presented in a block with each trial constructed of a sound lasting 1000 ms, followed by a 1500-ms silence before the next trial.

2.2   EEG Recording, Signal Processing, and Source Reconstruction

The EEG signals were recorded using a 32-channel EEG system (Neuroscan, Inc.) and were referenced to the arithmetic average of the left and right mastoids. The electrode impedance was kept below 5 kΩ. The EEG signals were sampled at a frequency of 1 kHz and in a bandwidth of 0.1–100 Hz. For each subject, EEGLAB toolbox (http://sccn.ucsd.edu/eeglab) [11, 12] was adopted to perform independent component analysis (ICA) to remove the artifactual components accounting for eye movement, muscle tension, and electrode artifacts.

This study then employed the time-varying standardized low-resolution brain electromagnetic tomography (sLORETA) [13] to parse the scalp EEG signals into source activity, in which the standardized boundary element head model (BEM) [14] was used for head modeling before source reconstruction. After the source modeling for each individual, group analysis was performed by co-registering the individual source results to a 3D Montreal Neurological Institute (MNI) brain template [15].

3   Results and Discussions

The EEG spatio-spectral dynamics were observed during an auditory working memory task when subjects were engaged in high (2-back) versus low (1-back) memory load. The results of source reconstruction revealed that the high working memory load accompanied stronger delta (1–4 Hz) activity in superior frontal gyrus, theta (4–7 Hz) activity in posterior cingulate cortex, alpha 1 (8–10 Hz) and beta 1 (12–16 Hz) activity in insula, but weaker alpha 2 (10–12 Hz) activity in anterior cingulate cortex as compared to the low counterpart. The locations of cortical regions were adjacent to those recently reported in [3–6].

In addition, this study further explored the temporal profile of the reconstructed source activities in theta frequency band that has been suggested to serve as an indicator of working memory processes [16, 17] and of new information encoding in hippocampo-cortical feedback loops [18]. As compared to the low working memory load task, the high load task exhibited stronger theta activity in temporal region around 335 ms after the stimulation onset (Fig. 1A). The pronounced activations shifted to the frontal (Fig. 1B) and parietal (Fig. 1C) brain regions around 1000 ms. The observed theta modulation in the temporal lobe associated with the auditory working memory indicated the distinction to the pronounced frontal and parietal network involved in visual and verbal task [19, 20]. Future work can be directed to assess the functional coupling (e.g., synchronization) between the temporal and frontal/parietal regions to clarify the auditory working memory network using the EEG neurophysiology.

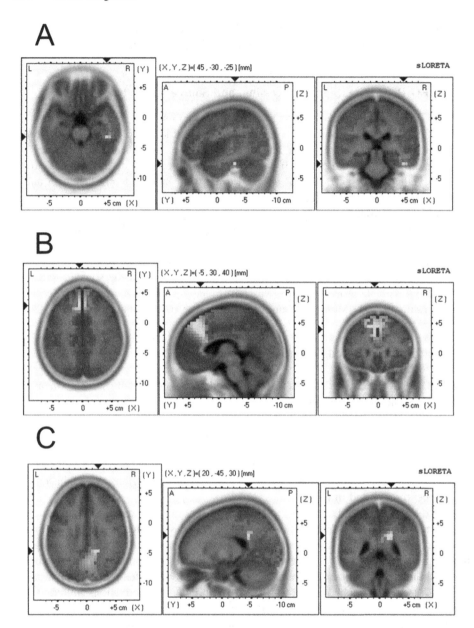

Fig. 1. Averaged source activation when subjects were attending to n-back auditory working memory tasks (2-back versus 1-back). Stronger right temporal activations were observed around 335 ms after the onset of stimuli (A). Activations were more pronounced in frontal (B) and parietal (C) regions around 1000 ms after the music onset.

References

1. Kane, M.J., Engle, R.W.: The role of prefrontal cortex in working-memory capacity, executive attention, and general fluid intelligence: an individual-differences perspective. Psychon. Bull. Rev. **9**(4), 637–671 (2002)
2. Ma, L., et al.: Working memory load modulation of parieto-frontal connections: evidence from dynamic causal modeling. Hum. Brain Mapp. **33**(8), 1850–1867 (2012)
3. Huang, S., et al.: Distinct cortical networks activated by auditory attention and working memory load. Neuroimage **83**, 1098–1108 (2013)
4. Munoz-Lopez, M., et al.: Anatomical pathways for auditory memory II: information from rostral superior temporal gyrus to dorsolateral temporal pole and medial temporal cortex. Front. Neurosci. **9**, 158 (2015)
5. Plakke, B., Ng, C.-W., Poremba, A.: Neural correlates of auditory recognition memory in primate lateral prefrontal cortex. Neuroscience **244**, 62–76 (2013)
6. Plakke, B., Romanski, L.M.: Auditory connections and functions of prefrontal cortex. Front. Neurosci. **8**, 199 (2014)
7. Koelsch, S., et al.: Functional architecture of verbal and tonal working memory: an FMRI study. Hum. Brain Mapp. **30**(3), 859–873 (2009)
8. Schulze, K., et al.: Neuroarchitecture of verbal and tonal working memory in nonmusicians and musicians. Hum. Brain Mapp. **32**(5), 771–783 (2011)
9. Groussard, M., et al.: The neural substrates of musical memory revealed by fMRI and two semantic tasks. Neuroimage **53**(4), 1301–1309 (2010)
10. Pallesen, K.J., et al.: Cognitive control in auditory working memory is enhanced in musicians. PLoS ONE **5**(6), e11120 (2010)
11. Makeig, S.: Auditory event-related dynamics of the EEG spectrum and effects of exposure to tones. Electroencephalogr. Clin. Neurophysiol. **86**(4), 283–293 (1993)
12. Delorme, A., Makeig, S.: EEGLAB: an open source toolbox for analysis of single-trial EEG dynamics including independent component analysis. J. Neurosci. Methods **134**(1), 9–21 (2004)
13. Pascual-Marqui, R.D.: Standardized low-resolution brain electromagnetic tomography (sLORETA): technical details. Methods Find. Exp. Clin. Pharmacol. **24**, 5–12 (2002)
14. Oostenveld, R., Oostendorp, T.F.: Validating the boundary element method for forward and inverse EEG computations in the presence of a hole in the skull. Hum. Brain Mapp. **17**(3), 179–192 (2002)
15. Talairach, J., Tournoux, P.: Co-planar Stereotaxic Atlas of the Human Brain. 3-Dimensional Proportional System: An Approach to Cerebral Imaging (1988)
16. Düzel, E., Penny, W.D., Burgess, N.: Brain oscillations and memory. Curr. Opin. Neurobiol. **20**(2), 143–149 (2010)
17. Knyazev, G.G.: Motivation, emotion, and their inhibitory control mirrored in brain oscillations. Neurosci. Biobehav. Rev. **31**(3), 377–395 (2007)
18. Klimesch, W.: EEG alpha and theta oscillations reflect cognitive and memory performance: a review and analysis. Brain Res. Rev. **29**(2–3), 169–195 (1999)
19. Sauseng, P., et al.: Theta coupling in the human electroencephalogram during a working memory task. Neurosci. Lett. **354**(2), 123–126 (2004)
20. Crespo-Garcia, M., et al.: Functional neural networks underlying semantic encoding of associative memories. NeuroImage **50**(3), 1258–1270 (2010)

Effects on Auditory Attention and Walking While Texting with a Smartphone and Walking on Stairs

Shigeru Haga[✉], Kanae Fukuzawa, Eri Kido, Yoshinori Sudo, and Azuri Yoshida

Rikkyo University, Niiza, Saitama, Japan
haga@rikkyo.ac.jp

Abstract. Effects of texting with a smartphone while walking on stairs in a building were investigated. Twenty-four students performed an auditory detection task for 60 s while using (texting condition) or not using (holding condition) an iPhone 5s. Half of the participants (walking group) performed the signal detection task while walking up the stairs and half of the participants (standing group) performed the task while standing still. Results showed that participants in the texting condition responded significantly more slowly to the targets and missed more targets than in the holding condition. Participants in the walking group missed more auditory targets. We also found a large effect size of smartphone use on a walking performance. Results of our present study can be used as evidence to show the risk of using smartphones, especially on stairs.

Keywords: Cell phone · Texting · Pedestrian · Inattention · Safety

1 Introduction

Our previous studies provided empirical evidence of inattention by pedestrians using cell phones.

Among them, Masuda et al. [1] compared reaction time to visual and auditory stimuli while walking with a cell phone (feature phone or smartphone of their own) in hand under four experimental conditions: texting, conversation, orally repeating words heard, and control (just holding a phone). Results showed that reaction times to either visual or auditory stimuli were significantly longer under the three cell phone-use conditions than under the control condition. Moreover, participants who used smartphones responded more slowly to visual stimuli under the texting condition than those using feature (standard cell) phones.

Haga et al. [2] requested university students with an iPhone 5s to text a message, watch a video, play a game, or just to hold the phone (control condition) in addition to performing visual and auditory detection tasks at the same time. The number of right footsteps that missed the line marking the walking route was greater under cell phone-use conditions than under the control condition. Mean reaction times for both visual and auditory targets were significantly longer under cell phone-use conditions than under the control condition.

© Springer International Publishing Switzerland 2016
C. Stephanidis (Ed.): HCII 2016 Posters, Part I, CCIS 617, pp. 186–191, 2016.
DOI: 10.1007/978-3-319-40548-3_31

Injury reports show the occurrence of a number of accidents involving cell phone users in railway stations. Commuters use smartphones on board and continue to use them after getting off the train. Some people check the train schedule by phone while walking through stations before getting on a train. Others use the phone in a waiting room or on a platform for communication or amusement, and then start walking to get on a train. Many people now use their smartphones to communicate with others by email, LINE, Facebook, Twitter, etc., all of which involve texting.

The purpose of this study was to measure quantitatively the effects of texting with a smartphone on auditory attention and walking. In this study, we asked our experimental participants to walk on stairs. This differs from previous studies that dealt with cell phone use while walking on a flat floor or a treadmill (e.g. [1–4]).

2 Methods

Twenty-four undergraduate students participated in the experiment and were divided into two groups according to whether they walked up stairs or stayed still while they performed an auditory detection task for 60 s while using (texting condition) or not using (holding condition) a smartphone (APPLE iPhone 5s). The detection task was to respond to designated target signals as quickly as possible by clicking the button held in the hand that was not holding the phone. Auditory stimuli were presented through a pair of earphones (Pioneer SE-E11-Z1) once every second for a duration of 500 ms. The target stimulus for reaction was a higher pitch (460 Hz) among the tones (440 Hz). The button for reaction (Kokuyo ELA-FP1) was connected wirelessly to a laptop computer (SONY VAIO Fit 11) that controlled the stimulus presentation. Every reaction time was recorded. After a 60-s trial, the participants rated the subjective workload of the task with the Japanese version of NASA-TLX [5]. As with the original NASA-TLX [6], the rating scale consisted of 6 subscales: mental demand, physical demand, temporal demand, participant's performance, effort, and frustration.

Participants were asked to describe their travel in detail from their house to the university on the Notes of the iPhone under the texting condition. Under the holding condition they just held the phone in hand.

The experiment took place on a staircase in an 8-story building with a landing between floors. Participants in the walking group were instructed to walk up the stairs at a safe speed and to step with the right foot on the white line drawn in the middle of the stairway. We recorded participants' steps as they walked on the stairs with a video camera (SONY HDR-SR8). The participants wore a hard hat such as worn by cyclists and knee and elbow pads to prevent injury. Figure 1 is a photo taken of a walking trial.

3 Results

3.1 Data Analysis

Data obtained from two participants in the walking group were excluded from analysis due to noncompliance to the instructions. In order to match the number of subjects, two participants in the standing group were chosen at random and removed from our data pool. Hence, data from twenty participants were used for analysis. Within each behavior (walking or standing) group, five participants performed the texting condition followed by the holding condition, and the remaining five performed the task in the opposite order.

Two-way analysis of variance (ANOVA) was applied for dependent variables observed in the detection task and workload ratings. The factor of smartphone use was a within-subject independent variable and the factor of behavior was a between-subject independent variable. Student's t-test was used for variables related to walking performance in the walking group. Cohen's d for walking performance and partial eta-squared (ηp^2) for the detection task and the workload ratings were calculated to evaluate the effect size of independent variables.

Fig. 1. Photo of a walking trial

3.2 Results of Detection Task

Mean reaction times to auditory targets are shown in Fig. 2. Interaction between the two factors was not significant. Main effect of behavior was not significant but that of smartphone use was significant ($F(1, 18) = 10.64$, $p < .001$, $\eta p^2 = .37$). The participants responded significantly more slowly to the targets in the texting condition than in the holding condition.

Mean number of missed targets is shown in Fig. 3. Interaction between the two factors was not significant ($F(1, 18) = .16$, $p > .05$, $\eta p^2 = .11$). Main effects were significant both for behavior ($F(1, 18) = 15.84$, $p < .01$, $\eta p^2 = .47$) and smartphone use ($F(1, 18) = 10.68$, $p < .01$, $\eta p^2 = .37$). The participants in the walking group missed more targets than those in the standing group, and they missed more targets under the texting condition than under the holding condition.

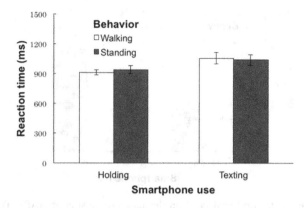

Fig. 2. Mean reaction time to auditory signals. Error bars show standard errors

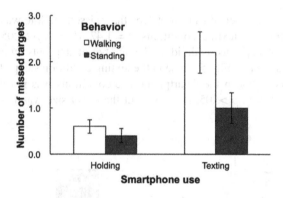

Fig. 3. Mean number of missed auditory signals. Error bars show standard errors

3.3 Results of Workload Ratings

The AWWL score [7] was calculated from ratings on 6 subscales of the Japanese version of NASA-TLX [5] using the weight of 6 for the highest-rated subscale, 5 for the second highest, etc. The result is shown in Fig. 4. Interaction between the two factors was not significant ($F(1, 18) = .01$, $p > .05$, $\eta p^2 = .001$). Main effect of behavior was not significant but that of smartphone use was significant ($F(1, 18) = 58.58$, $p < .001$, $\eta p^2 = .77$). Participants rated the task more demanding after trials with texting than after trials in the holding condition.

3.4 Results of Walking Performance

There were significant differences in the number of floors walked up ($t = 3.34$, $df = 9$, $p < .01$, $d = .80$) and the number of total footsteps taken ($t = 3.13$, $df = 9$, $p < .05$, $d = .51$) between the texting and holding conditions. Participants walked a shorter distance and took fewer steps when they texted with a phone while walking.

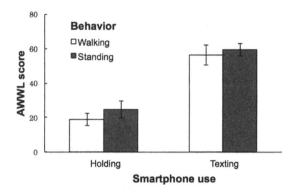

Fig. 4. Subjective mental workload rated on the Japanese version of NASA-TLX. Error bars show standard errors

Difference in the number of right footsteps that missed the line was not significant between the holding and texting conditions ($t = 1.47$, $df = 9$, $p > .05$, $d = .69$). We calculated the rate of step-outs by dividing the number of step-outs by the total number of steps taken. As shown in Fig. 5, those in the texting condition stepped out at a higher rate. The difference between the smartphone use conditions was not statistically significant ($t = 1.83$, $df = 9$, $p > .05$, $d = .89$), but the effect size was large.

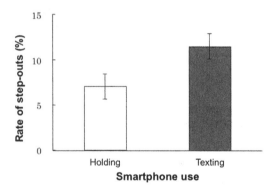

Fig. 5. Rate of steps that missed the line out of total number of steps walked. Error bars show standard errors

4 Discussion

As shown above, participants responded significantly more slowly to auditory targets, missed more stimuli, and felt the task more demanding when they were texting with a phone than when they were just holding a phone. These results demonstrated deterioration of the user's attention when smartphone texting. The facts that participants in the walking group missed more targets and the effect size of smartphone use was large regarding the number of step-outs suggested that walking on stairs makes people less attentive to auditory stimuli and to their own actions. However, the effects were not amplified when walking on stairs since no significant interaction between smartphone use and behavior was found. Smartphone use seemed to equally deteriorate attention no matter whether participants were standing or walking. It might be a consequence of our instruction to walk safely. Participants walked slowly.

Since the risk of injury caused by inattention is much greater for people walking on stairs than people standing still, our present results can be used as evidence to show the risk of using smartphones, especially on stairs.

References

1. Masuda, K., Takahashi, H., Haga, S.: Hokouchuuno keitaidenwa shiyouga chuuito hokouni oyobosu eikyou (Effects of cell phone use while walking on pedestrians attention and walking). In: Proceedings for the 53rd Annual Meeting of the Japanese Ergonomics Society, pp. 206–207 (2012). (Japanese)
2. Haga, S., Sano, A., Sekine, Y., Sato, H., Yamaguchi, S., Masuda, K.: Effects of using a smart phone on pedestrians' attention and walking. Procedia Manuf. **3**, 2574–2580 (2015)
3. Nasar, J., Hecht, P., Wener, R.: Mobile telephones, distracted attention, and pedestrian safety. Accid. Anal. Prev. **40**, 69–75 (2008)
4. Hyman Jr., I.E., Boss, S.M., Wise, B.M., Mckenzie, K.E., Caggiano, J.M.: Did you see the unicycling clown? Inattentional blindness while walking and talking on a cell phone. Appl. Cogn. Psychol. **24**, 597–607 (2010)
5. Haga, S., Mizukami, N.: Japanese version of NASA task load index: sensitivity of its workload score to difficulty of three different laboratory tasks. Japan. J. Ergonomics **32**, 71–80 (1996). (Japanese with English abstract)
6. Hart, S.G., Staveland, L.E.: Development of NASA-TLX (task load index); results of empirical and theoretical research. In: Hancock, P.A., Meshkati, N. (eds.) Human Mental Workload, pp. 139–183. North Holland, Amsterdam (1988)
7. Miyake, S., Kumashiro, M.: Subjective mental workload assessment technique: an introduction to NASA-TLX and SWAT and a proposal of simple scoring methods. Japan. J. Ergonomics **29**, 399–408 (1993). (Japanese with English abstract)

How Coping Strategies Influence Cyber Task Performance in the Hybrid Space

Kirsi Helkala[1(✉)], Benjamin Knox[1], Øyvind Jøsok[1], Ricardo Lugo[2], and Stefan Sütterlin[2]

[1] Norwegian Defence Cyber Academy, Lillehammer, Norway
{khelkala, f-bknox, ojosok}@mil.no
[2] Lillehammer University College, Lillehammer, Norway
{ricardo.lugo, stefan.sutterlin}@hil.no

Abstract. This paper combines two previous studies concerning how the applied use of specified coping strategies can improve performance, and, how knowledge of task importance affect performance in cyber cognitive tasks. The participants self-evaluated their application of coping strategies after a period of time for reflection having completed the cyber cognitive tasks. The results show how applying 'Control' and drawing on 'Self-confidence and belief in oneself' can influence performance in cyber cognitive tasks amongst cyber officer cadets.

Keywords: Coping strategies · Cyber tasks · Performance · Self-efficacy

1 Introduction

Performing Cyber Cognitive Tasks in the Hybrid Space [8] requires high order cognitive capabilities that are aligned with automated technical solutions. As cyberspace and the physical domain merge and command levels converge, managing multiple simultaneous interactions demand humans apply context adaptive coping strategies for improved decision-making and performance to affect cognitive processes and resulting behavior [3].

The actual 'ability to control' had the strongest positive effect on cyber officer cadet's performance in both military and academic contexts [4]. Further, motivation gained by understanding the reason and the importance of the cyber task, had a positive effect on the performance of the cyber tasks [5].

In this study, we combined these two previous studies by Helkala et al. in an attempt to find out which Coping Strategies (see Sect. 2.2) cyber officer cadets of the Norwegian Defence Cyber Academy (NDCA) used when conducting Cyber Cognitive Task Performance tests.

2 Experiment

The experiment took place during Exercise Cyber Endurance 2015: a two-week long military exercise held annually. Total of 35 cyber officer cadets of the NDCA self-evaluated their use of pre-determined coping strategies (see Sect. 2.2) and their

© Springer International Publishing Switzerland 2016
C. Stephanidis (Ed.): HCII 2016 Posters, Part I, CCIS 617, pp. 192–196, 2016.
DOI: 10.1007/978-3-319-40548-3_32

perceived performance (on a scale of 1–6) in the Cyber Cognitive Task tests (see Sect. 2.1). The self-evaluation questionnaire was completed alongside a Reflections Log. Detailed descriptions of the earlier experiments can be found in [4, 5].

2.1 Cyber Cognitive Performance Test

Cyber Cognitive Performance Test contained five tasks.

- *1st task:* The participants were told to monitor continuously moving network traffic and raise an alarm when they observed a traffic peak taller or equal to 3000. This task took 20 min to complete.
- *2nd task:* The participants were told to detect different states of different network devices in a very unstable environment. Basic geometric figures were presented for one second, then a 2 × 2 matrix appeared for 3 s and the cadets had to identify and locate the figure in the matrix. In total, 75 single figure and corresponding matrix pairs were presented.
- *3rd task:* The participants used trial-and-error method to memorize a random 12 digit long encryption key. The same sequence had to be completed 15 times.
- *4th task:* The participants were given one chance to enter the complete encryption key from the 3rd task.
- *5th task:* The participants were instructed to memorize coded messages sent from a terrorist grouping. The messages contained three Norwegian sentences with a total of 13–14 words and a picture of five single-color basic geometric figures. The message was visible for one minute. Subsequently, they had to write down the sentences and draw the figures.

2.2 Coping Strategies

Coping strategies are a series of universal tools to support performance.

- *Situational Understanding:* a person's ability to gain a comprehensive overview of current challenges to support understanding tasks and possible future challenges.
- *Accept the situation:* a person's ability to accept and work purposefully within the operational environment and with the resources available.
- *Use of knowledge and tools:* active cooperation and performance tracking. Application of logic and common sense to support theoretical and practical knowledge.
- *Ability to be proactive:* to be forewarned and prepared for changes. Constantly revise and trust intuition.
- *Finding alternatives and solutions:* a person's ability to be open to others' input and applying creative or logical thought.
- *Ability to prioritize:* set priorities among assignments, personnel, material and intellectual resources to support decision-making.

- **Ability to control:** manage levels of oversight and detail concerning resources, responsibility, risk, capacities and capabilities in any given context. Awareness of the relative power and agency of those around you (internal and external).
- **Ability to influence:** an individual's ability to cut through complexity and tension to find suitable and effective means of affecting positive outcomes.
- **Self-confidence and belief in oneself:** a feeling of trust in one's abilities, skills, knowledge, and judgement.
- **Ability to handle uncertainty:** to focus on one's own reactions and take steps to actively manage behavior.

3 Results

The cyber officer cadets self-evaluated their performance with scale from one to six, where six was the best performance score. The t-test showed that the average rate of self-evaluated performance was significantly higher among students who reported usage of ability to control-strategy than among the students that did not use the strategy, see Table 1. Similar result applied the students that used self-confidence and belief oneself strategy. There were no significant differences with usage of the other strategies.

Table 1. The average rates of self-evaluated performance

Cyber Cognitive Task Test	Ability to control strategy			Self-confidence and belief oneself strategy		
	Using	Not using	p-value	Using	Not using	p-value
Test I	4.8	4.0	0.01	4.8	3.7	0.002
Test II	4.6	3.5	0.008	4.5	3.3	0.006

4 Discussion

In this small study students self-evaluated their own performance in Cyber Cognitive Task Performance tests. Before the students answered the Coping and Performance questionnaire they were able to reflect and discuss with colleagues concerning performance. In addition, submitting the self-evaluation questionnaire with a Reflection Log was a pedagogic method introduced for personal development throughout the entire semester. This made the self-evaluated performance scores more reliable.

The results showed significantly better performance rates among participants who stated using the ability to control and self-confidence and belief in oneself strategies. These results support earlier research findings as both strategies (as defined in Sect. 2.2) contribute to self-efficacy; an individual's belief about his capabilities to complete a task with certain performance levels [1].

Stajkovic and Luthans [9] found that situational self-efficacy is a predictor for performance in different domains. Judge et al. [7] showed that high self-efficacy predicts task-related performance. Hepler and Feltz [6] connected high self-efficacy to better decision-making strategies and therefore better task performance. Choi, Levy and Hovav [2] showed that in cases were cyber task demands and their relevance are defined self-efficacy can enhance cyber oriented performance.

Our findings, together with earlier research, suggests that motivation gained by task-related information, increase one's belief in the ability to control the situation and therefore empowers performance.

5 Conclusion

In this study, the cyber officer cadets from the NDCA were asked to self-evaluate their overall performance when conducting Cyber Cognitive Tasks tests during a military exercise, and, report usage of Coping Strategies and own performance.

Cyber Cognitive Performance tests included password recalling, net traffic and state monitoring, memorizing a message and a key. The coping strategies were; situational understanding, accept the situation, use of knowledge and tools, ability to be proactive, finding alternatives and solutions, ability to prioritize, ability to control, ability to influence, self-confidence and belief in oneself and ability to handle uncertainty.

The results showed the average rate of self-evaluated performance was significantly higher among students who reported usage of ability to control-strategy and/or usage of self-confidence and belief oneself- strategy. This, combined with the earlier finding relating to motivation gained by understanding the reason and the importance of the cyber task having a positive effect on the performance of the cyber tasks [5], supports research showing that; in cases when cyber task demands, and their relevance are defined, then self-efficacy can enhance cyber oriented performance [2].

This suggests that motivation gained by task-related information can increase beliefs in the ability to control the situation and therefore empowers the performance.

References

1. Bandura, A.: Self-efficacy: The Exercise of Control. Freeman and Co, New York (1997)
2. Choi, M., Levy, Y., Hovav, A.: The role of user computer self-efficacy, cybersecurity countermeasures awareness, and cybersecurity skills influence on computer misuse. In: pre-ICIS Workshop on Information Security and Privacy (SIGSEC) (2013)
3. Gutzwiller, S., Fugate, R., Sawyer, B., Hancock, P.: The Human Factors of Cyber Network Defense (2015)
4. Helkala, K., Knox, B., Jøsok, Ø.: How the application of coping strategies can empower learning. In: Frontiers in Education, pp. 1–8 (2015a)
5. Helkala, K., Knox, S., Lund, M.: Effect of motivation and physical fitness on cyber task. In: International Symposium on Human Aspects of Information Security & Assurance, pp. 108–119 (2015b)
6. Hepler, T.J., Feltz, D.L.: Take the first heuristic, self-efficacy, and decision-making in sport. J. Exp. Psychol. Appl. **18**(2), 154 (2012)

7. Judge, T., Jackson, C., Shaw, J., Scott, B., Rich, B.: Self-efficacy and work-related performance: the integral role of individual differences. J. Appl. Psychol. **92**(1), 107–127 (2007)
8. Jøsok, Ø., Knox, B.J., Helkala, K., Lugo, R.G., Sütterlin, S., Ward, P.: Exploring the hybrid space - theoretical framework applying cognitive science in military cyberspace operations. In: International Conference on Human-Computer Interaction (2016, in press)
9. Stajkovic, A.D., Luthans, F.: Self-efficacy and work-related performance: a meta-analysis. Psychol. Bull. **124**(2), 240 (1998)

Predicting Performance in Space Teleoperation Tasks Through Vernier Acuity

Yu Hongqiang, Ting Jiang, and Chunhui Wang[✉]

National Key Laboratory of Human Factors Engineering, China Astronaut
Research and Training Center, Beijing 100094, China
50984684@qq.com, jtingx@aliyun.com, chunhui_89@163.com

Abstract. In order to analyze whether vernier acuity index can predict space teleoperation performance or not, twelve subjects participated in the experiment. A simulated robotic arms teleoperation task was adopted to detect space tele-operation capability and four kinds of vernier acuity were also measured. Pearson correlation test was conducted between teleoperation task performance and four patterns of vernier acuity, results showed two significant positive correlations. One correlation was between position difference and vertical center vernier acuity ($p < 0.01$), and the other one was between angular difference and horizontal center visual acuity ($p < 0.01$). The positive correlations indicating that better vertical center vernier acuity meant smaller position difference in the horizontal direction and better horizontal center visual acuity caused smaller pitch deviation in space teleoperation tasks.

Keywords: Teleoperation · Vernier acuity · Robotic arms · Rendezvous and docking

1 Background

Teleoperation means a manually operation method which control the target with the physical distance between the operators and operands [1]. In this process, operators need to sensor the camera image feedback to get relevant information [2, 3]. Space teleoperation tasks means either or both of operator and operands are in special space environment. Many features of robot machine and spatial environment as well as human capacity may affect performance in space teleoperation tasks [4]. There are two key factors associated with human capacity which named remote sensing and remote operation considering the system in the perspective of ergonomics [5]. For the effective operation of the robot to perform the task, the operator needs to obtain sufficient information from the Human-Computer Interface to percept working conditions and send control commands accurately. Perceptual ability is the cognitive basis of excellent operating performance in a certain extent [6]. Visual stimuli accounted for more than 80 % in the amount of information used by human to percept external environment, so the information provided by image from Human-Computer Interface, which reflects real physical scene and other data of machine, are the most important information to ensure the completion of operation.

© Springer International Publishing Switzerland 2016
C. Stephanidis (Ed.): HCII 2016 Posters, Part I, CCIS 617, pp. 197–202, 2016.
DOI: 10.1007/978-3-319-40548-3_33

There are two important aspects of Human-Computer Interface in space teleoperation tasks. One aspect is input interface from system to human, which contains distal environmental information, machine motion and sensor information transmitted to the operator from a display device. The other aspect is output interface to system from human, such as a mouse, keyboard and handles interface through which control commands are assigned to the computer system by operator [7]. Two aspects constitute the teleoperation interactive display and control interface and details on this interface are very pivotal for mission completing.

Vernier acuity is one of effective test indicators to reflect discrimination ability of spatial detail clues both in central vision field and peripheral vision field and it is a representative index in perceptual learning effect [8]. In a vernier acuity test, observers need to detect an offset between two abutting grating segments. It is thought to be a hyperacuity index mediated by fairly low-level visual mechanisms. Different purposive training methods can improve vernier acuity just like that training can improve performance in space teleoperation tasks [9, 10].

So the purpose of this research is to check the correlation between space teleoperation performance and vernier acuity. We assumed that operators with higher vernier acuity could perform better in space teleoperation tasks.

2   Method

2.1   Subjects

Twelve male participants with an average age of 23.75 years (ranging from 23 to 25) participated in this study. The participants were all right-handed. None of the participants suffer from eye diseases except eight of them are myopic and their visual acuity or corrected visual acuity was 1.0 or more. All subjects were gave informed consent prior to their participant in the study and received reward after participation.

2.2   Measurements

A typical task which named simulated robotic arms teleoperation task was adopted to detect space teleoperation capability. It is a simulated mission that request subjects to control a robotic arm with six joints to complete insert task. All the six joints suffer restricting rotational angle, but their cooperation can make the terminal of arm achieve six motion degree in the workspace. The six motion degree includes three position degree (front - back, left - right, and up – down) and three postural degree (roll, pitch and yaw). The simulation software platform was shown in Fig. 1. In the experiment, subject operator needs to observe image information provided by a liquid crystal display in perspective of a fixed camera, and then control two different handles (one for position degree and one for postural degree) with both hands to complete docking tasks.

Fig. 1. Simulation software platform of robotic arms

Vernier acuity test was generated using Psychtoolbox Packages in Matlab 2012b. In the test, subjects need to detect an offset between two abutting grating segments (Fig. 2). There are two types of stimuli with different arrangements of two gratings (horizontally or vertically aligned), and the contrast of gratings were 45 % in both types. In addition, there are two positions (center and top left of the screen) for stimulus presentation. In order to ensure that subjects gaze at center of the screen, a letter H or N would present at the center of the screen simultaneously with gratings which presented at top left and subjects were asked to response letter name firstly before detect offset of gratings. So we measured four kinds of vernier acuity values from each subject using limit method in psychology.

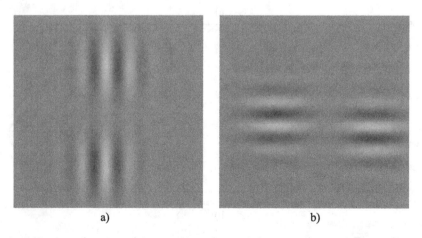

a)   b)

Fig. 2. Different arrangements of two gratings for vernier test. (a) vertically aligned for vertical vernier acuity measurement; (b) horizontally aligned for horizontal visual acuity measurement.

2.3   Procedure

In the experiment, subjects need to complete six teleoperation tasks with same difficulty through simulation software platform and then underwent vernier acuity test. In the test, the subject viewed the stimuli binocularly from a distance of 4 m with darkroom environment. A chinrest was used to ensure that the central visual field was in the center of the display screen. The whole process lasted for about one hour.

3   Results

Cumulative position difference and angular difference of four teleoperation tasks excluding the worst two operations were chosen to represent for teleoperation performance. Four kinds of vernier acuity were represented by minimum viewing angle value. Data of twelve subjects was shown in Fig. 3.

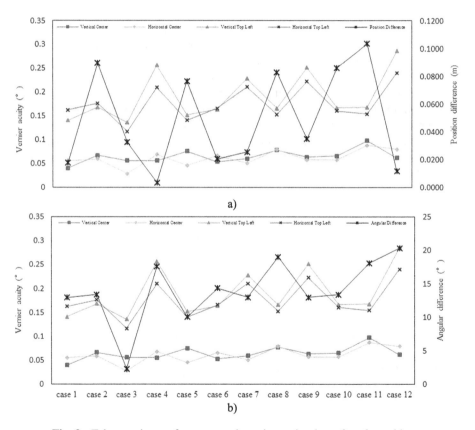

Fig. 3. Teleoperation performance and vernier acuity data of twelve subjects

Average value of subjects' data was calculated. Average position difference was 0.04866 m and average angle difference was 10.34°. Four kinds of vernier acuity average value were shown in Fig. 4.

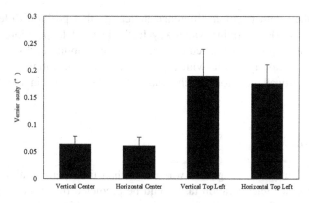

Fig. 4. Average value of subjects' four kinds of vernier acuity

Pearson correlation test was conducted between teleoperation task performance (positional difference and angle difference) and four patterns of vernier acuity, results were shown in Table 1.

Table 1. The correlation coefficient by pearson correlation test

Vernier acuity	Vertical center	Horizontal center	Vertical top left	Horizontal top left
Position difference	0.793[a]	0.196	−0.499	−0.499
Angular difference	0.311	0.947[a]	0.517	0.562

[a]Correlation is significant at the 0.01 level (2-tailed).

4 Discussion

In order to check the correlation between space teleoperation performance and vernier acuity, twelve subjects participated in simulated robotic arms teleoperation tasks and vernier acuity measurement. Subjects' teleoperation performance and four kinds of vernier acuity were generally similar except case 3's angular difference (2.31°) indicating their operating capacity and visual ability was approximately the same to a certain degree. Comparison between four kinds of vernier acuity showed that central vernier acuity (0.0645° and 0.0613°) was better than peripheral vernier acuity (0.1904° and 0.1763°), which was consistent with human visual characteristics.

There are only two significant positive correlations through pearson correlation test conducted between teleoperation task performance and vernier acuity. One correlation was between position difference and vertical center vernier acuity (p < 0.01), and the other one was between angular difference and horizontal center visual acuity (p < 0.01). The interesting result indicated that center vernier acuity did affect teleoperation performance while peripheral vernier acuity did not, and different kinds of center vernier acuity influenced different aspects of teleoperation performance. Vertical center vernier acuity which measured ability to distinguish horizontal differentiation was closely linked with position difference indicating that position difference in the horizontal direction (left – right) was a key factor in the teleoperation performance. Similarly, horizontal center visual acuity which measured ability to distinguish vertical differentiation was closely linked with angular difference indicating that angular difference in the vertical direction (pitch) was also a key factor in the teleoperation performance.

5 Conclusion

Central vernier acuity of young men was better than their peripheral vernier acuity. Performance in space teleoperation task could be predicted by vernier acuity to some extent. Operators with higher center vernier acuity could perform better in space teleoperation tasks. Specifically, better vertical center vernier acuity meant smaller position difference in the horizontal direction and better horizontal center visual acuity caused smaller pitch deviation.

Acknowledgments. This work was supported by the Foundation of National Key Laboratory of Human Factors Engineering (SYFD140051806).

References

1. Sheridan, T.B.: Space teleoperation through time delay: review and prognosis. IEEE Trans. Rob. Autom. **9**(5), 592–606 (1993)
2. Sheridan, T.B.: Telerobotics. Automatica **25**(4), 487–507 (1989)
3. Menchaca Brandan, M.A.: Influence of spatial orientation and spatial visualization abilities on space teleoperation performance. Massachusetts Institute of Technology (2007)
4. Forman, R.E.: Objective performance metrics for improved space telerobotics training. Massachusetts Institute of Technology (2011)
5. Fong, T., Thorpe, C., Baur, C.: Advanced interfaces for vehicle teleoperation: collaborative control, sensor fusion displays, and remote driving tools. Auton. Robots **11**(1), 77–85 (2001)
6. Wang, C., Tian, Y., Chen, S., et al.: Predicting performance in manually controlled rendezvous and docking through spatial abilities. Adv. Space Res. **53**, 362–369 (2014)
7. Jankowski, J., Grabowski, A.: Usability Evaluation of VR Interface for Mobile Robot Teleoperation. Int. J. Hum. Comput. Interact. **31**(12), 882–889 (2015)
8. Sayim, B., Westheimer, G., Herzog, M.H.: Contrast polarity, chromaticity, and stereoscopic depth modulate contextual interactions in vernier acuity. J. Vis. **14**(1), 29 (2014)
9. Owsley, C., Ball, K., Keeton, D.M.: Relationship between visual sensitivity and target localization in older adults. Vis. Res. **35**(4), 579–587 (1995)
10. Saarinen, J., Levi, D.M.: Perceptual learning in vernier acuity: what is learned? Vis. Res. **35**(4), 519–527 (1995)

Outside the Head Thinking: A Novel Approach for Detecting Human Brain Cognition

Insoo Kim[1(✉)], Miyoung Kim[2], Taeho Hwang[2], and Chang W. Lee[1]

[1] Samsung Research America, Richardson, TX, USA
insoo3.kim@samsung.com
[2] Samsung Electronics, Seoul, South Korea

Abstract. Electroencephalography (EEG) is one of the most commonly used measures in neuroscience and psychophysiology research for studying functional information of brain activity such as cognition and emotion. However, because of lack of convenient methods to measure EEG, it is difficult to use in everyday situations. The electrodermal potential (EDP) can be used to monitor brain activities. This study investigated the correlation between scalp acquired EEG and EDP from the body below the head, for two distinctive cognitive statuses of relaxation and attention. The results showed that theta power decreases while beta power increases in the attention state compared to relaxation from EDP. We also obtained 84.2 % of classification accuracy to discriminate attention-relaxation states using EDP signals, while obtaining 83.9 ~ 89.3 % of the classification accuracy using a single channel EEG.

Keywords: Electroencephalography · Electrodermal potential · Brain-machine interfaces · Relaxation · Attention · Cognition

1 Introduction

EEG (Electroencephalogram) often provides interfaces for controlling machines or computers due to recent developments in inexpensive, easy-to-wear, and low power acquisition systems [1, 2]. Thus, EEG-based Brain Computer Interface (BCI) is one of the most promising technologies for device interaction and detection of cognitive and emotional activities. As a result, abundant studies have been performed to investigate the BCI-based interfaces: event-related synchronization/desynchronization (ERS/ERD), steady-state visual evoked potentials (SSVEP), slow cortical potentials (SCP), visually evoked P300 potentials, movement-related potentials (MRPs), and changes in brain rhythms [3, 4].

However, current EEG-based BCI headsets are ill-suited for daily use owing to challenges with hardware positioning/placement, requisite device knowledge, training, and skills. In fact, the current EEG-based BCI technology usually takes anywhere from a few minutes up to 45 min to configure EEG electrodes on a person's scalp depending on the types of electrodes (e.g., dry and wet electrodes) used, which is one of major obstacles for the technology to be widely adapted in daily living. Additionally, consumer based EEG headsets have not been widely accepted by the public due to design and their obtrusive nature.

© Springer International Publishing Switzerland 2016
C. Stephanidis (Ed.): HCII 2016 Posters, Part I, CCIS 617, pp. 203–208, 2016.
DOI: 10.1007/978-3-319-40548-3_34

To overcome these issues, we explored the possibility of estimating the brain's cognitive states using electrodermal potentials (EDP), which characterize the skin's electrical activity by measuring potential differences between two separate electrodes similar to measuring surface electromyogram, from non-scalp areas in the body. In this study, we developed a wrist-worn device (Fig. 1) by collaboration with Freer Logic (Skyland, NC, U.S.A.), and verified the feasibility of classifying an individual's attention and relaxation states by comparison with EEG.

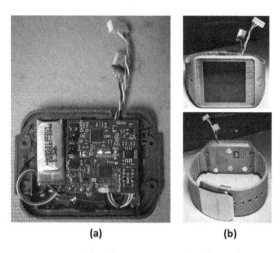

(a)   **(b)**

Fig. 1. The proposed wrist-worn device to measure EDP. The printed circuit board (a) measures 1 × 1 inch in size and the device has four electrodes in the back (b); two electrodes are for signal sensing, one is for ground and the other one is for electrode-off detection.

2 Methods

2.1 Signal Acquisition

Simultaneous EDP and EEG recordings were performed in 5 healthy subjects (4 males, 1 female) using the proposed device and commercially available EEG recording system as shown in Fig. 2. The EDP device incorporating two recording electrodes and one reference electrodes was positioned in the middle of anterior left forearm where bra-chioradialis and flexor carpi radialis muscles reside. For the EEG recording, an Avatar EEG recording amplifier (Electrical Geodesics Inc., OR, U.S.A.) with g. SAHARA dry electrodes (g.tec Medical Engineering, Gmbh, Austria) was used. Six electrodes (Fz, Cz, C5, C6, PO3, and PO4) were positioned based on the international 10–20 system, while the reference and ground were placed at the right and left mas-toids, respectively. The recorded data were transmitted to the same host computer for signal processing via on-board microcontrollers and Bluetooth modules.

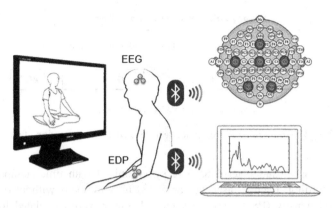

Fig. 2. Two acquisition systems were used: EEG and EDP. An electrode cap was positioned as International 10–20 electrode placement, and the activity was recorded at Fz, Cz, C5, C6, PO3, and PO4. EDP was collected via the wrist-worn device.

2.2 Experimental Protocol

Participants were tested in multiple sessions over 40 min. They were requested to avoid any stimulants such as coffee, tea, and cigarettes in the 2 h preceding the recording period. We educated the participants on the entire experimental procedure and guided them during the recordings. No training and/or calibration were provided to the subjects prior to the recordings. The participants sat down in a comfortable chair wearing both EDP and EEG recording systems described in Sect. 2.1 during the recording. A host computer was connected to both, the EDP and the EEG recording systems for simultaneous data storage.

The participants were asked to be comfortable and to refrain from moving to minimize motion and EMG artifacts during recording. The experiments were conducted with the following protocol: First, a monitoring session was performed for eyes-closed resting EEG with no stimulus. Second, the participants were asked to relax while closing their eyes to obtain the status of relaxation. Third, for the attention state, the Continuous Performance Test (CPT) was used to induce sustained attention level of the participants. The CPT was designed to present the randomized sequence of letters on the computer screen for 0.5 s with 1-s intervals. Participants were instructed to continuously pay attention to the computer screen for about 2 min and mentally count the total number of appearances of a designated target letter (e.g. 'G') (Fig. 3). At the end of the CPT session, the participant was required to input the total number of such appearances. We assessed the attentiveness of each participant by verifying the correctness of the answer.

2.3 Signal Processing

The recorded EEG and EDP data were analyzed using MATLAB (MathWorks Inc., Natick, MA). The EEG signal was low-pass filtered under 45 Hz (with digital Butter-worth filter) and 5th-order band-pass filtered with 0.5 to 50 Hz. Under human

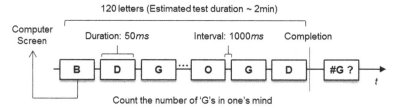

Fig. 3. Continuous Performance test devised for the attention state.

supervision, the EDP and EEG data were synchronized with time stamps generated during the recording. Each dataset was analyzed in 5-s epochs without overlap. The Power spectral density (PSD) and the averaged power were calculated for four frequency bands: theta $(4 \sim 8$ Hz), alpha $(8 \sim 12$ Hz), beta1 $(12 \sim 15$ Hz), and beta2 $(15 \sim 20$ Hz).

For the attention classification analysis, we extracted a more diversified set of features from both the spectral domain and the time domain. A total of 80 features were composed of the statistical variables in time-domain signals (e.g. mean, standard deviation of amplitude), the spectral powers (both absolute and relative) of each frequency bin (e.g. theta, relative theta, theta/alpha, $4 \sim 12$ Hz, $12 \sim 20$ Hz), and signal entropy and complexity (e.g. permutation entropy, Higuchi fractal). The classification between the relaxation and attention states was analyzed with the linear kernel Support Vector Machine (SVM) in a 10-fold cross-validation for each subject. We balanced the number of samples of the relaxation and attention states by resampling for unbiased error estimation.

3 Results

Figure 4 represents the signal trend analysis results from the EDPs. We compared average powers of each frequency band when the subjects were asked to change their cognitive states (e.g., attention to relax, quiet attention to relax, and attention to quiet attention). In the comparison between attention and relax states, we observed theta power decreases in 14 epochs (93.3 %) out of 15 epochs and an increase in beta2 power in 12 out of 15 epochs (80 %). On the other hand, for comparisons between attention and quiet attention states, no significant difference was observed.

We carried out 10-fold cross-validation to estimate classification accuracy in each subject (Fig. 5). As expected, the 8-channel EEG showed the highest accuracy (91.1 %). However, the classification performance varied in single EEG channel analysis, ranging from $83.9 \sim 89.3$ %. EDP achieved 84.2 % of classification accuracy on average, which is comparable to that of any single EEG channel, but with large standard deviation (17.0 %) relative to EEG $(3.3 \sim 7.8$ %). We believe EDP is a valuable signal for studying an individual's attentional state, although it requires improvements in signal reliability for general use.

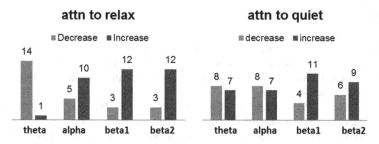

Fig. 4. Comparisons of the average power of each frequency band with different cognitive states. (Color figure online)

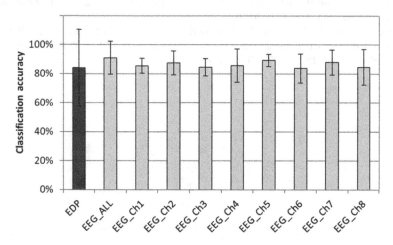

Fig. 5. Comparative analysis of the EDP and EEG in classification accuracy of attention-relaxation state (N = 5). (Color figure online)

4 Conclusion

We have introduced a technique for unobtrusive measurements of cognitive responsiveness in the body. We hypothesized that body locations other than the traditional scalp area can also represent a cognitive activity in bio-potentials such as EDP. To verify this hypothesis, we performed simultaneous EDP and EEG recording at six scalp locations of Fz, Cz, C5, C6, PO3, and PO4 and the body location of the middle of the anterior left forearm. As shown in the results, there are similar trends in EDP and EEG responses to the cognitive status of relaxation and attention. Although many challenges exist in the field, our results illustrate the considerable potential of this technology. Further investigation on EDP and development of the acquisition system will enhance usability of the EEG-based BCI system. In addition, this study initiates further investigation to unveil EDP and EEG correlation for other brain functionalities such as event-related potentials responding to sensory, cognitive, or motor events.

References

1. Carrino, F., Dumoulin, J., Mugellini, E., Khaled, O.A., Ingold, R.: A self-paced BCI system to control an electric wheelchair: evaluation of a commercial, low-cost EEG device. In: 2012 ISSNIP Biosignals and Biorobotics Conference: Biosignals and Robotics for Better and Safer Living (BRC), pp. 1–6 (2012)
2. Lin, C.-T., Ko, L.-W., Chang, C.-J., Wang, Y.-T., Chung, C.-H., Yang, F.-S., Duann, J.-R., Jung, T.-P., Chiou, J.-C.: Wearable and wireless brain-computer interface and its applications. In: Schmorrow, D.D., Estabrooke, I.V., Grootjen, M. (eds.) FAC 2009. LNCS, vol. 5638, pp. 741–748. Springer, Heidelberg (2009)
3. Dehzangi, O., Nathan, V., Zong, C., Lee, C., Kim, I., Jafari, R.: A novel stimulation for multi-class SSVEP-based brain-computer interface using patterns of time-varying frequencies. In: 2014 36th Annual International Conference of the IEEE Engineering in Medicine and Biology Society, pp. 118–121 (2014)
4. Allison, B., Lüth, T., Valbuena, D., Teymourian, A., Volosyak, I., Gräser, A.: BCI demographics: How many (and what kinds of) people can use an SSVEP BCI? IEEE Trans. Neural Syst. Rehabil. Eng. 18(2), 107–116 (2010)

An Eye-Tracking Approach to Evaluating Decision-Makers' Cognitive Load and Need-for-Cognition in Response with Rational and Emotional Advertising Stimuli

Min Hee Hahn[1], Kun Chang Lee[2([⊠])], and Seong Wook Chae[3]

[1] SKK Business School, Creativity Science Research Institute,
Sungkyunkwan University, Seoul 03063, Republic of Korea
[2] SKK Business School, SAIHST (Samsung Advanced Institute of Health
Sciences and Technology), Creativity Science Research Institute,
Sungkyunkwan University, Seoul 03063, Republic of Korea
kunchanglee@gmail.com
[3] Department of Business Administration, Hoseo University,
Cheonan 31066, Republic of Korea

Abstract. This study is concerned with using rational and emotional stimuli and analyzing changes of our visual attention responses with the aid of eye-tracking method. Those rational and emotional stimuli were designed in a form of advertising copies and images. To add rigor to our study, we organized heterogeneous stimuli and homogeneous stimuli to make appropriate stimuli, where heterogeneous stimuli consist of either emotional copies and rational images, or rational copies and emotional images. Homogeneous stimuli are designed to consist of either emotional copies and emotional images, or rational copies and rational images. By using those stimuli, we measured respondent's cognitive load and need-for-cognition by taking advantage of the eye-tracking technique. 80 respondents were invited to our experiments, and their physiological responses were measured in a form of cognitive load and need-for-cognition. We analyzed fixation length data from the participants' eye-movement with the stimuli. Participant's cognitive load increased more when they were exposed to heterogeneous stimuli, while participant's fixation length changed significantly only when there exists interaction effect between cognitive load and need-for-cognition in response to the stimuli.

Keywords: Eye-tracking · Cognitive load · Need-for-cognition · Rational copy · Emotional copy · Fixation length

1 Introduction

It is customary that we are exposed to a lot of advertising copies and images everyday. In our daily lives, we are forced to make some decisions on products and services which are advertised in various types of advertising copies and images. It is true that

© Springer International Publishing Switzerland 2016
C. Stephanidis (Ed.): HCII 2016 Posters, Part I, CCIS 617, pp. 209–215, 2016.
DOI: 10.1007/978-3-319-40548-3_35

advertising copies and images affect our decision-making to some extents. Besides, we know that some of our cognitive efforts are needed to process those advertising copies and images before making decisions.

However, there are no studies investigating how much our cognitive load (CL) and need-for-cognition (NFC) are needed to understand many types of information from a physiological view. Understanding advertising copies and images is working as tasks on our brain. Processing such tasks require our mental resources which are interpreted as CL and NFL. In literature, CL was investigated from the eye-tracking approach [12]. In creativity literature, those people with high NFC are known to exhibit higher performance on recall and recognition tasks [9]. They tend to also actively seek new information to accomplish their goals.

It is well known in neuroscience that working memory is critically required when we work on tasks [2]. The size of individual working memory is closely related with CL (Cognitive Load). In our physiological responses, CL can be measured pupil expansion [3, 10].

Meanwhile, NFC is related to reflecting individual differences in cognitive motivation to enjoy effortful cognitive endeavours [5]. Therefore, it is no surprise that NFC affects cognitive elaboration and recall of various advertising stimuli [16]. Besides, NFC has influence on formation and changes in attitude [7] and problem solving [14].

In this study, we adopt an eye-tracking approach to measuring CL and NFC. Physiological approach like eye-tracking has many advantages compared to perceived approach such as survey method. It can reduce people's psychological, minimizing distortion of discretionary evaluation of participants' results. The physiological data is very hard to modify intentionally [19]. Especially, among the physiological metrics, eye movement data have a long tradition. A human's eye gathers the largest amount of information of all the sensory systems. People obtain more than 70 % of external information through visual processing. Also, in working memory, more than 90 % of information used for cognitive activity is obtained from visual information [19]. Eye movements triggered by visual stimuli indicate that an individual perceives selectively and actively [1]. Therefore, eye movement is considered an important measurement for understanding cognitive activity triggered by visual stimuli [6].

Literature review tells us that there is no study attempting to measure the effects of CL and NFC on decision-maker's visual attention responses when they are exposed to advertising copies and images which are designed as rational stimuli and emotional stimuli. Main objectives of this study are as follows. Firstly, this study aims to introduce the need of understanding CL and NFC in order to improve the quality of decision-making by using rational stimuli and emotional stimuli which are used to trigger CL and NFC. Secondly, this study tackles aims to investigate the effects of CL and NFC on our physiological system. Eye-tracking method is adopted to handle CL and NFC in response to rational and emotional stimuli.

2 Experiments with Eye-Tracking Method

2.1 Eye-Tracking Method

Eye-tracking methods were used for various applications. Noh et al. [14] used eye-tracking method to measure the effects of multimedia elements on learning achievements in digital contents. Buchmann et al. [4] also applied eye-tracking method to analyze semantic processing. Krishnasree et al. [10] developed a driver fatigue monitoring system based on eye-tracking mechanism. Eye-tracking enables automatic chasing and exploration of information without interrupting the automatic process of eye movement. It also provides a measure of fixation duration through which we can achieve a better grasp of cognitive processing [20]. Eye-tracking has proven to be a strong approach to measure performance in the interaction between products, services and customer, and its use is expanding to help better understand the reception of visual stimuli in information handling processes [13].

2.2 Stimuli

We used advertising messages and images as stimuli to check the level of NFC and CL. We set up experimental stimuli that were expected to have different levels of CL and NFC. Experiment participants were exposed to the stimuli. By using an eye-tracker device, we obtained eye movement tracking data and then conducted a survey to assess participants' self-reports about the level of CL and NFC that they perceived through the stimuli. To secure rigorous validity of our experiment results, the experiment stimuli were composed of rational and emotional copies and images. Those stimuli consist of advertising copies and images.

Advertising Copies. We prepared 20 examples of advertising copies (10 "emotional copies", and 10 "rational copies") to carry out the eye-tracking experiment. To secure validity of the stimuli, a professional market research company was recruited to produce those advertising copies. To obtain qualified advertising copies, two filtering sessions were carried out. At first, 474 copies (227 for iPhone and 247 for Galaxy) provided by the company were submitted to 1 professor, 6 doctoral students for the sake of further proof-reading and double-check. They assess the copies to check whether they possess adequate messages from the perspective of being rational and emotional. Here, a rational copy indicates that it appeals to facts and reasoning, and an emotional copy means that it appeals to our feeling.

After the first session, a survey was carried out to divide the qualified copies into rational copy and emotional copy. 50 raters were asked to rate, on a scale from 1 to 9, how appealing a copy was, with 1 being "emotional very much" and 9 being "rational very much". These measures were adapted from Rosselli et al. [17]. The raters received no more than 40 copies, considering their capability to rate without mental fatigue. Finally, 376 advertising copies (179 for iPhone and 197 for Galaxy) were rated as qualified to be either rational or emotional. If copies have a rating score less than median, they were classified as emotional ones. If rating score is greater than median, the copies were categorized as rational ones. As stated previously, we selected 10 rational copies and 10 emotional copies to conduct the eye-tracking experiments.

Advertising Images. 10 advertising images were organized with the professional support of graphic designers. Also, 40 raters were invited- 24 male (60 %) and 16 female (40 %) to determine validity of the images. They were categorized into two groups of 20 each. One group was shown only emotional images, while the other group was exposed to only rational images. We asked them to rate each image on a seven-point Likert scale, with one being "emotional very much" and seven being "rational very much". There exists significant difference ($p < 0.05$) between the two groups. Therefore, we were convinced that those advertising images are qualified to be used as proper stimuli for our experiments.

Stimuli Group. For the sake of rigorous experiment design, we organized stimuli into four groups- "emotional image × emotional copy", "rational image × rational copy", "emotional image × rational copy", "rational image × emotional copy." Then the two groups such as "emotional image × emotional copy" and "rational image × rational copy" are classified as homogeneous stimuli, and the two groups "emotional image × rational copy", "rational image × emotional copy" are termed as heterogeneous stimuli.

2.3 Results

From Fig. 1, we found that the level of CL was lower in the group exposed to homogeneous stimuli compared to the group exposed to heterogeneous stimuli. This means that if two heterogeneous stimuli ("emotional image × rational copy", "rational image × emotional copy") are presented, the participant's CL to process that information increases. Such mental workload may be understood in terms of the relationship between demand for mental resources required for the task and the capability of individuals to supply such resources [13]. This indicates that, because there are limits on cognitive processing, the amount of information that can be activated or processed and the degree of cognitive processing that can be handled is also limited. However, there was no interaction effect with NFC in terms of CL. Regardless of the level of NFC, the heterogeneous stimuli increase CL.

From Fig. 2, when participants have high NFC, the fixation length increases as CL increases. However, neither the main effect of NFC nor that of CL on fixation length was statistically significant. In the end, we could demonstrate that fixation length changes only when interaction effect between NFC and CL exists. Therefore, we reject hypotheses 1 and 2, but accept hypothesis 3. Human gaze is related to obtaining information and cognitive processing [8]. When individuals find it difficult to extract information or are interested in an object, the length of eye fixation increases (Just and Carpenter 1976). People with high NFC have the tendency to accept cognitively effortful situations naturally, and therefore, when they are presented with heterogeneous stimuli, as in this experiment, they will process that information willingly, accepting the CL. As a result, their fixation length increases as they try to deal with the CL derived from NFC. On the other hand, if homogeneous stimuli are presented

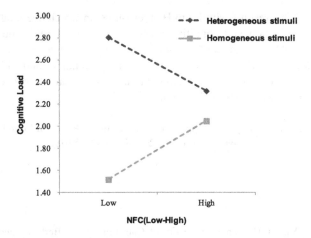

Fig. 1. Cognitive Load in line with NFC (Color figure online)

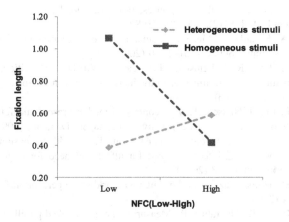

Fig. 2. Fixation length (Color figure online)

(low CL condition), there is no need to handle the problem caused by discord among stimuli. This results in straightforward decrease of fixation length as a result.

3   Concluding Remarks

Decision-makers may show different metrics of CL according to the characteristics of situation. We found that heterogeneous stimuli increase participant's CL. One of interesting results was that there is no significant change in participant's fixation length even when there are changes in either CL or NFC level. However, participant's fixation length changes significantly under 90 % confidence level only when there exists interaction effect between CL and NFC. Another result worthy of being mentioned was that when participants with high NFC were exposed to heterogeneous stimuli, fixation length increased. This result is similar to Henderson [8] in which eye fixation is related to information acquisition and cognitive processing. Future study issues include the following topics. First topic is that EEG and ECG analyses are necessary to investigate more serious research topics by using rational and emotional stimuli. Second topic is that fMRI test results can be used to strengthen our view towards how decision makers will react to rational and emotional stimuli.

Acknowledgments. This study was supported by the National Research Foundation of Korea Grant funded by the Korean Government (NRF-2014S1A3A2038108).

References

1. Arnheim, R.: Visual Thinking. University of California Press, Berkeley and Los Angeles (1969)
2. Baddeley, A.: Working Memory. Clarendon Press, Oxford (1986)
3. Beatty, J.: Task evoked pupillary responses, processing load and structure of processing resources. Psychol. Bull. **91**(2), 276–292 (1982)
4. Buchmann, R.A., Mihaila, A., Meza, R.: Semantic processing based on eye-tracking metrics. WSEAS Trans. Comput. **8**(10), 1701–1710 (2009)
5. Cacioppo, J.T., Petty, R.E., Feinstein, J.A., Jarvis, W.B.G.: Dispositional differences in cognitive motivation: The life times of individuals varying in need for cognition. Psychol. Bull. **119**(2), 197–253 (1996)
6. Glenstrup, A.J., Engell-Nielsen, T.: Eye controlled media: present and future state. Ph.D., DIKU (Institute of Computer Science), Univ. Copenhagen, Denmark (1995)
7. Haddock, G., Maio, G.R., Arnold, K., Huskinson, T.: Should persuasion be affective or cognitive? The moderating effects of need for affect and need for cognition. Pers. Soc. Psychol. Bull. **34**(6), 769–778 (2008)
8. Henderson, J.M.: Human gaze control during real-world scene perception. Trends Cogn. Sci. **7**(11), 498–504 (2003)
9. Klingner, J., Kumar, R., Hanrahan, P.: Measuring the task-evoked pupillary response with a remote eye tracker. In: Proceedings of ETRA 2008, pp. 69–72. ACM, Savannah (2008)
10. Krishnasree, V., Balaji, N., Rao, P.S.: A real time improved driver fatigue monitoring system. WSEAS Trans. Sig. Process. **10**, 146–155 (2014)
11. Kun, A.L., Paek, T., Medenica, Z., Memarovic, N. and Palinko, O. Glancing at personal navigation devices can affect driving: experimental results and design implications. In: Proceedings of Automotive UI 2009, pp. 129–136. ACM (2009)
12. Levin, I.P., Huneke, M.E., Jasper, J.D.: Information processing at successive stages of decision making: Need for cognition and inclusion-exclusion effects. Organ. Behav. Hum. Decis. Process. **82**(2), 171–193 (2000)
13. Moray, N.: Mental Workload: Its Theory and Measurement. Plenum, New York (1979)
14. Noh, K.B., Song, K.S., Nam, S.C., Park, S.Y.: The effects of multimedia elements on learning achievements in digital content. WSEAS Trans. Comput. **13**, 361–367 (2014)
15. Peltier, J.W., Schibrowsky, J.A.: Need for cognition, advertisement viewing time and memory for advertising stimuli. Adv. Consum. Res. **21**(1), 244–250 (1994)
16. Ravaja, N.: Contributions of psychophysiology to media research: Review and recommendations. Med. Psychol. **6**(2), 193–235 (2004)

17. Rosselli, F., Skelly, J., Mackie, D.M.: Processing rational and emotional messages: the cognitive and affective mediation of persuasion. J. Exp. Soc. Psychol. **31**(2), 163–190 (1995)
18. Solso, R.L.: Cognition and the Visual Arts. MIT Press, Cambridge (1997)
19. Verplanken, B., Hazenberg, P.T., Palenéwen, G.R.: Need for cognition and external information search effort. J. Res. Pers. **26**(2), 128–136 (1992)
20. Wickens, C.D.: Multiple resources and performance prediction. Theor. Issues Ergon. Sci. **3**(2), 159–177 (2002)

The Evaluation of Visual Fatigue
in 3D Televisions

Po-Hung Lin[✉]

Department of Industrial Engineering and Management Information,
Huafan University, New Taipei City, Taiwan
phlin@cc.hfu.edu.tw

Abstract. This study explores the effects of 3D film types, watching time and ambient illumination on users' visual fatigue through experimental design. A three way mixed factorial design was used to investigate the effect of ambient illumination, the film type and the watching time on the change of critical fusion frequency (CFF) and simulator sickness questionnaire (SSQ). The ANOVA results indicated that watching time was significant on change of CFF and SSQ, where watching 15 min has more visual fatigue than 5 min and 10 min for subjects. In addition, the interactions between watching time and film type were also found on change of CFF and SSQ.

Keywords: Visual fatigue · 3D television · Film type · Watching time

1 Introduction

With the advancement of technology and maturing of techniques, 3D displays have been the mainstream of the market. The 3D technology is applied in many areas, such as 3D televisions and notebooks. Compared to traditional 2D displays, 3D displays contain better image qualities. Kalich et al. [1] pointed out that three-dimensional displays provide a wider field of vision. Kooi and Toet [2] proposed that binocular viewers may pass uncorrelated noises easily to see relevant signals which represent the objects in the scene. Therefore, the issue of 3D displays is an interesting topic.

Ambient illumination is a critical factor affecting participants' visual fatigue when watching 3D TVs. For smaller size displays, Jeng et al. [3] found that the legibility of electronic paper increased with the illumination level in the range of 200–1500 lx, but decreased at a higher illumination level. In addition, dark room is also an alternative for watching 3D TVs since people currently consider TVs with large screens as home theaters. In addition, Obrist et al. [4] had investigated the four types of movies including skiing, space jumping, breakdance, and body painting on 3D screens. Actually, video types with different visual effects may bring the impacts on partici-pants' visual fatigue and it's also worthy to be investigated. Finally, duration time for participants' watching was also an important consideration. Obrist et al. [4] set about 3 min for people watching the four types of movies. Lambooij et al. [5] conducted the questionnaire survey after participants' watching 3D movies for 15 min. Based on above arguments, ambient illumination, video type and watching time were the three independent factors with corresponding levels considered in this study.

© Springer International Publishing Switzerland 2016
C. Stephanidis (Ed.): HCII 2016 Posters, Part I, CCIS 617, pp. 216–219, 2016.
DOI: 10.1007/978-3-319-40548-3_36

2 Method

Forty college students took part in this experiment. All had corrected visual acuity better than 0.8 and passed the Stereo Fly Test (Stereo Optical Co., Inc., U.S.A). A three way mixed factorial design was used to investigate the effect of video type (sport and travel), watching time (5, 10, and 15 min), and ambient illumination (dark room, 200, 1500 and 3000 lx) on subjective visual fatigue and change of critical fusion frequency (CFF). Analysis of variance (ANOVA) was conducted with repeated measures on subjective visual fatigue and change of CFF. The Least Significant Difference (LSD) test was used to find the significance among the levels of independent variables. All statistical analyses were calculated with the Statistical Products Services Solution (SPSS).

3 Results and Discussion

The ANOVA results for subjective visual fatigue indicated that watching time ($F = 7.737$, $P < 0.05$) and the interaction between watching time and video type ($F = 7.635$, $P < 0.05$) were the significant factors. The significant interaction was needed to test the simple main effect (see Fig. 1). Therefore we focused on each video type, investigating its effect on watching time. The results indicated that sport video was significant in watching time ($F = 7.562$, $P < 0.01$), where significant differences ($P < 0.01$) were found among 5, 10, 15 min through LSD test. The results also indicated that travel video was significant in watching time ($F = 8.915$, $P < 0.01$), where significant differences were found between 5 and 10 min ($P < 0.01$), and between 5 and 15 min ($P < 0.01$). We then studied the effect of each watching time on video type. The results indicated that no matter in which level of watching time, the results were not significant ($P > 0.05$).

The ANOVA results for change of CFF indicated that watching time ($F = 9.384$, $p < 0.01$) and the interaction between video type and watching time ($F = 6.906$, $p < 0.05$) were the significant factors. The significant interaction was needed to test the simple main effect (see Fig. 2). Therefore we focused on each video type, investigating its effect on watching time. The results indicated that sport video was significant ($F = 11.322$, $P < 0.01$), where the significant differences were found between 5 and 15 min ($P < 0.01$) and between 10 and 15 min ($P < 0.01$). The results also indicated that travel video was significant in watching time ($F = 6.5$, $P < 0.05$), where significant differences were found between 5 and 10 min ($P < 0.05$), and between 5 and 15 min ($P < 0.01$). We then studied the effect of each watching time on video type. The results indicated that no matter in which level of watching time, the results were not significant ($P > 0.05$).

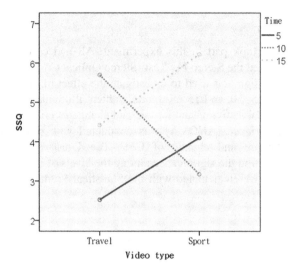

Fig. 1. The interaction between video type and watching time for SSQ (Color figure online)

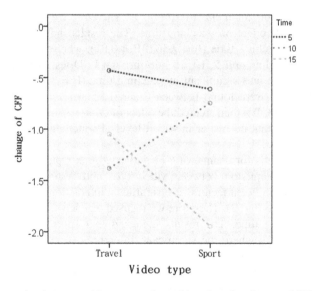

Fig. 2. The interaction between video type and watching time for change of CFF (Color figure online)

4   Conclusion

This study explores the effect of file type, watching time and ambient illumination on subjective visual fatigue and change of CFF. The results for the interactions between watching time and video type on change of CFF and subjective visual fatigue indicated that for travel video, the difference between 10 and 15 min can't be distinguished. The reason may be that travel videos may bring less visual fatigue than sport videos, especially for long time watching.

References

1. Kalich, M.E., Rash, C.E., van de Pol, C., Rowe, T. L., Lont, L.M., Peterson, R.D.: Biocular image misalignment tolerance. In: Rash, C.E., Reese, C.E. pp. 284–295. (2003)
2. Kooi, F., Toet, A.: Visual comfort of binocular and 3D displays. Displays **25**, 99–108 (2004)
3. Jeng, S.-C., Lin, Y.-R., Liao, C.-C., Wen, C.-H., Chao, C.-Y., Lee, D.-S., Shieh, K.-K.: Effect of character size and lighting on legibility of electronic papers. In: SID 06 Digest, pp. 1316–1319 (2006)
4. Obrist, M., Wurhofer, D., Meneweger, T., Grill, T., Tscheligi, M.: Viewing experience of 3DTV: An exploration of the feeling of sickness and presence in a shopping mall. Entertain. Comput. **4**, 71–81 (2013)
5. Lambooij, M., Murdoch, M.J., IJsselsteijn, W.A., Heynderickx, I.: The impact of video characteristics and subtitles on visual comfort of 3D TV. Displays **34**, 8–16 (2013)

The Experiment Research of Pupil Change for the Evaluation of Mental Workload

Zhongqi Liu[1], Bhao Xing[1], Qianxiang Zhou[1], and Xin Zhang[2(✉)]

[1] Key Laboratory for Biomechanics and Mechanobiology of the Ministry of Education, School of Biological Science and Medical Engineering, Beihang University, Beijing 100191, China
[2] China National Institute of Standardization, Beijing 100191, China
zhangx@cnis.gov.cn

Abstract. To investigate whether the motivation or interesting can take effect on the change of pupil size and whether pupil size reflect mental workload differences in a situation with different task difficulties. Twelve subjects participated in the experiment and they were asked to make target search task of three different difficulty level. The task difficulty levels were controlled through searching different number of differences between pictures. The experiment was done in two different conditions: the subject did the searching task only with basic rewards without time limited; the subjects received different additional rewards according their performance. The pupil size was recorded with eye movement tracking system. The results of the pupil size change showed the common characteristic and also difference for all the subjects. The same characteristic of pupil size change for all subjects was that the pupil size was larger in the second experiment condition than of the first corresponding condition. The difference were reflected on that some subjects pupil size first dilated and then constricted, and some first constricted and then dilated, while some others continuously constricted. Conclusions can be made from the results: the increasing of task difficulty will make pupil dilate, the positive motivation or interesting also dilate the pupil size, while the visual fatigue constrict the pupil size.

Keywords: Mental workload · Pupil size · Eye movement · Fatigue · Ergonomics

1 Introduction

The visual system of human obtains external information through the pupil. The role of pupil is to adjust its size to change the amount of entering the eyes. The pupil will dilate when light is strong and it will constrict while the light is weak. Pupil size is determined by a balance between the competing forces of two smooth muscle systems, controlled by the parasympathetic and sympathetic nervous system, respectively [1]. The pupil is constricted by parasympathetic nervous system (PNS) activity which is responsible for the light reflex and near response. Pupil dilation is effected by the sympathetic nervous system (SNS). Certain mental process (such as perception, memory, thinking, language, and processing, motivation, emotion and other senior

© Springer International Publishing Switzerland 2016
C. Stephanidis (Ed.): HCII 2016 Posters, Part I, CCIS 617, pp. 220–225, 2016.
DOI: 10.1007/978-3-319-40548-3_37

psychological activities), will also affect the size of the pupil. Because of pupils' important role to people, it has attracted the interest of many researchers.

One of the earliest researchers to examine pupil size variations was Bumke, who, in 1911 (as cited in the document of Hess), stated that intellectual processes, psychical effort, active mental images, and all affect the pupil size [2]. Today the measurement of pupil size was use to evaluate mental workload (MW), they think that the pupil size was related to task difficulties and it can effetely reflect the fluctuation of the MW which was closely related to the change of task difficulty. The pioneer work measuring pupil size changes relating to mental workload and task difficulty should be Hess and Polt who studied the pupil in a mental arithmetic experiment [3]. They found that the pupil size of the subjects gradually dilated along with the time elapse of presentation of a multiplication problem and reached a peak immediately before the production was orally reported; then constricted rapidly back to the original size. Following their work, extensive studies showed that the changes of pupil size reflect mental workload and the level of difficulty in different tasks and pupils dilate as task difficulty increases [4–7]. The relationship between increments in pupil diameter and mental workload is a very well known and it can be found from the investigations of Ahlstrom and Friedman-Berg [8] or Jainta and Baccino [9].

Numerous studies have shown the high sensitivity and validity of this index in providing an adequate measure of the cognitive demands imposed by a task (e.g. LeDuc et al. [10]). However, some authors casted doubts on the validity of pupil size as an appropriate index of mental workload. Schultheis and Jameson have evaluated the validity of pupil size in adaptive hypertext systems and the results showed no significant differences in pupil diameter in relation to text difficulty [11]. Conati and Merten also found that pupil size was not a reliable predictor of self-evaluation when the user interact with an environment for exploration-based learning [12].

In this study, target search task was made to investigate whether pupil size reflect mental workload differences in a situation with different task search difficulties and whether the motivation or interesting can take effect on the change of pupil size. We expected that the pupil size would be more cognitively demanding, reflecting the task demands.

2 Method

2.1 Participants

The experiment was completed by 12 male undergraduate students who were recruited through the internet from the Beihang University and their ages ranged form 18 to 23 (the average age was 20). Each was tested by a standard near-visual chart to ensure that they had a near fovea acuity that was normal. Participants provided informed consent and received RMB 100 yuan in compensation.

2.2 Apparatus

Pupil size were recorded using a eye tracking system of Eyelink II measuring system manufactured by Canada's SR Research CORP.

2.3 Stimulus Material

Thirty pictures were prepared. They were modified by drawing software with three ways. In the first way, there was one difference to the corresponding raw picture after each picture was modified; in the second condition, there were two differences between the modified picture and the corresponding raw picture; there were three differences to the corresponding picture of the modified picture. So there were four groups of pictures: the raw pictures group(RG), one difference group(OG), two differences group (TG) and three differences group(TDG) (Fig. 1). There were 30 pictures in each group. The subjects' task was to find difference between the modified pictures and raw pictures.

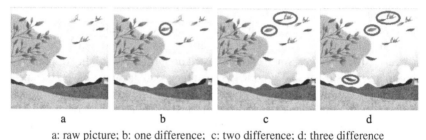

a   b   c   d

a: raw picture; b: one difference; c: two difference; d: three difference

Fig. 1. Experiment pictures

The searching of picture differences was done in two experimental conditions. The first condition(FC) was that the subjects were asked to find these differences as soon as possible without time limited. The second condition(SC) was that the subjects were given additional rewards except the basic remuneration according their searching performance that the more quickly they found the differences, the more rewards they would get and the slowest 3 people would only get the basic payment of RMB 100 yuan. The pupil data of subjects were recorded with the eye movement measuring system in the experiment.

2.4 Procedure

At first, the subjects searched difference according FC and sequence was as follows.

(1) To find the difference between RG and OG and have a rest for 5 min.
(2) To find the difference between RG and TG and have a rest for 5 min.
(3) To find the difference between RG and TDG and have a rest for 5 min.

After finishing the experiment of FC, the subjects made the searching task of SC as the same sequence of above.

3 Result and Discussion

The same characteristic of pupil size change for all subjects was that the pupil size of the OG, TG and TDG was larger in FC than that of the corresponding in SC. There were also different characteristics of pupil change among subjects and. The first difference: the pupil size dilated from one difference to two differences while constricted at three differences (e.g. subject 1, Fig. 2) and two subjects were in this condition. The second difference: the pupil size constricted from one difference to two differences while dilated at three differences (e.g. subject 2, Fig. 3) and four subjects were in this condition. The third difference: the pupil size continuously decreased from one difference to three differences (e.g. subject 5, Fig. 4) and six subjects were in this condition.

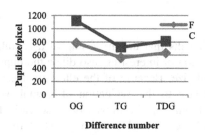

Fig. 2. Changes of pupil size of subject 1 (Color figure online)

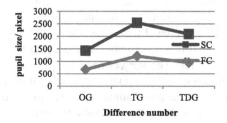

Fig. 3. Changes of pupil size of subject 2 (Color figure online)

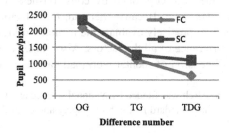

Fig. 4. Changes of pupil size of subject 5 (Color figure online)

With the SC, the additional rewards might be an encouragement to drive subjects try their best to search the differences between the pictures, so all the subjects' pupil size was larger than the corresponding FC and it could be shown that motivation or interesting could take an effect on pupil size. After the experiment, we have asked the feeling of visual fatigue of all subjects, they all reported that they feel tied with their vision in different experiment stage. Some subjects reported their fatigue when they search the TDG (e.g. subject 1) while the most subjects reported their fatigue when they search the TG (e.g. subject 2 and subject 5). So it could been seen that if the subject don't feel tied of their eye, the pupil size will dilate when the task become more difficult (Fig. 2). When the subjects felt tired of their eye, the pupil size will constrict (Fig. 4), but the results didn't always show such trend, some subjects the pupil size will dilate in the final of the experiment session (Fig. 3). It might be an interesting phenomenon and perhaps it could be named as "the terminal effect". When the subject saw the terminal of the task, they be excited and they will spend more effort to perform the task, so the pupil size in Fig. 3 dilated at the final session.

In this experiment, difficulty level was according to the difference number, it was more difficult with the more difference number. It was easier for subject to find the one difference between the pictures. The subject need to spend more time and pay more attention to the more difference to discriminate the detail of the pictures, so it was easier to cause the feeling of visual fatigue. Fatigue will lead to the decrease of pupil size while the increasing of the task difficulty will make the pupil size dilate and they have been proved by researchers. In this study, the results agreed to the present research.

4 Conclusion

It can be seen from the results that the increasing of task difficulty will make pupil dilate, the positive motivation or interesting also dilate the pupil size, while the visual fatigue constrict the pupil size. Because of the effect of these factors, it is hard and complicate to use pupil size to the evaluation of mental workload. Thought it is difficult, controlling or eliminating the impact of these variables, the pupil size is a reliable index of a person's mental workload change. The terminal effect that may have influence on pupil size may be an interesting phenomena and it worth to make a further study.

As a physiological index not controlled by consciousness, pupil size can reflect well the people's mental workload. Because there are more factors affecting the pupil size and mental workload, to precisely evaluate the mental workload with pupil size, it need to eliminate the interference of all the factors. Also the experiment task need to be refined, so only single dimension of mental workload can be evaluated.

Acknowledgement. This research was funded by National science and technology support plan "User evaluation technology and standard research of display and control interface ergonomics" (2014BAK01B04).

References

1. Wilhelm, B., Giedke, H., Luèdtke, H., Bittner, E., Hofmann, A., Wilhelm, H.: Daytime variations in central nervous system activation measured by a pupillographic sleepiness test. J. Sleep Res. **10**, 1–7 (2001)
2. Hess, E.H.: Pupillometrics: Handbook of Psychophysiology, pp. 491–531 (1972)
3. Polt, J.M., Hess, E.H.: Pupil size in relation to mental activity during simple problem solving. Science **132**, 349–350 (1964)
4. Brouwer, A.M., Hogervorst, M.A., Holewijn, M., van Erp, J.B.: Evidence for effects of task difficulty but not learning on neurophysiological variables associated with effort. Int. J. Psychophysiol. **93**(2), 242–252 (2014)
5. Kun, A. L., Palinko, O., Medenica, Z., Heeman, P.A.: On the feasibility of using pupildiameter to estimate cognitive load changes for in-vehicle spoken dialogues. In: INTERSPEECH, pp. 3766–3770 (2013)
6. Niezgoda, M., Tarnowski, A., Kruszewski, M., Kamiński, T.: Towards testing auditory-vocal interfaces and detecting distraction while driving: A comparison of eye-movement measures in the assessment of cognitive workload. Trans. Res. Part F: Traffic Psychol. Behav. **32**, 23–34 (2015)
7. Palinko, O., Kun, A.L., Shyrokov, A., Heeman, P.: Estimating cognitive load using remote eyetracking in a driving simulator. In: Eye Tracking Research and Applications Symposium, pp. 141–144 (2010)
8. Ahlstrom, U., Friedman-Berg, F.J.: Using eye movement activity as a correlate of cognitive workload. Int. J. Ind. Ergon. **36**, 623–636 (2006)
9. Jainta, S., Baccino, T.: Analyzing the pupil response due to increased cognitive demand: an independent component analysis study. Int. J. Psychophysiol. **77**, 1–7 (2006)
10. LeDuc, P.A., Greig, J.L., Dumond, S.L.: Involuntary eye responses as measures of fatigue in U.S. Army Apache aviators. Aviat. Space Environ. Med. **76**, 86–92 (2005)
11. Schultheis, H., Jameson, A.: Assessing cognitive load in adaptive hypermedia systems: physiological and behavioral methods. In: Bra, P.M., Nejdl, W. (eds.) AH 2004. LNCS, vol. 3137, pp. 225–234. Springer, Heidelberg (2004)
12. Conati, C., Merten, C.: Eye-tracking for user modeling in exploratory learning environments: an empirical evaluation. Knowl. Based Syst. **20**, 557–574 (2007)

ATHENA – A Zero-Intrusion No Contact Method for Workload Detection Using Linguistics, Keyboard Dynamics, and Computer Vision

Tammy Ott[⊠], Peggy Wu, Amandalynne Paullada, Derek Mayer, Jeremy Gottlieb, and Peter Wall

Smart Information Flow Technologies, LLC, Minneapolis, USA
{tott, pwu, apaullada, dmayer, jgottlieb, pwall}@SIFT.net

Abstract. We describe preliminary evaluation data for ATHENA (Appraisal of Task Health and Effort through Non-intrusive Assessments), a completely no contact, zero-intrusion workload measurement method which harnesses multi-modal metrics (e.g. linguistic markers, keyboard dynamics and computer vision). Preliminary results reflect the existence of different types of workload, with our zero-intrusion metrics demonstrating respectable classification accuracies when the variable causing workload (e.g. time) is matched with the type of workload assessed (e.g. temporal). By not requiring extra equipment or interrupting workflow, ATHENA represents a valuable step forward in providing automated workload support tools as well as a tool for understanding the workload concept.

Keywords: Human factors · Zero-Intrusion workload measure · Linguistic analysis · Cognitive workload · Machine learning · Keyboard dynamics

1 Introduction

The current work discusses the initial validation and preliminary results for ATHENA (Appraisal of Task Health and Effort through Non-Intrusive Assessments); a workload sensor with the ability to automatically assess and evaluate human workload. Once workload level is known performance can be optimized through adaptable automation [1] and task scheduling. Our machine learning enabled software sensor uses a variety of human behavioral features (such as linguistic analysis, keyboard dynamics and computer vision), all obtained with zero-intrusion and at little cost since the underlying behaviors contributing to the metrics are naturally exhibited during task completion.

ATHENA is ideally suited for NASA's expected long duration space missions as well as other high criticality domains due to its zero-intrusion nature and use of a variety of metrics. By collecting naturally occurring behavioral metrics as well as information obtained through no contact sensors, ATHENA allows workload estimates to be obtained without modification or interruption of workflow, which can affect the crew's workload and confound results (as seen with self-reports or additional equipment attached to the operator [2]). The variety of metrics allow an appropriate subset to

C. Stephanidis (Ed.): HCII 2016 Posters, Part I, CCIS 617, pp. 226–231, 2016.
DOI: 10.1007/978-3-319-40548-3_38

be applied as the current context allows. This is important given the wide variety and multimodal nature of tasks will make some metrics useful during some tasks but not others (e.g. keyboard dynamics are not useful if typing is not occurring). We have shown a subset of our metrics can provide accurate classification, but the best classification rates are obtained when all available metrics are used [3].

2   Materials and Methods

2.1   Surveys

Ground truth workload data was obtained through surveys administered after the completion of each game. We used the Bedford Scale as a uni-dimensional rating scale to measure spare mental capacity [4]. The hierarchical scale guides users through a ten point decision tree, with each point having an accompanying descriptor of the workload level. For classification purposes we divided the Bedford into 4 levels following natural divisions provided by the scale itself: 1–3, 4–6, 7–9, and 10. We also used the NASA-TLX as a multi-dimensional rating scale to provide additional diagnostic information about experienced workload [5]. We divided the TLX into three levels such that 33 % of the data fell into each of a high, medium, and low category. This was done to provide us with the discrete categories needed for classification and maintain the nature of the TLX as a way to determine relative workload levels.

2.2   Procedure

We developed a NASA relevant testbed scenario by reframing the codebreaking game of Mastermind [6] as a task for astronauts performing a wiring reconfiguration to support the docking of future commercial crew and cargo vehicles. Nine professionals in the Minneapolis, MN area played the game. Linguistic data was collected through "mission control" texts using a pre-defined protocol, allowing for the collection of structured text and keyboard dynamic data, as well as unstructured linguistics via "think aloud" [7]. We believe workload is a multi-dimensional concept for which different types of workload can be manipulated independently. Therefore, Workload was manipulated 'cognitively' by using different in-game feedback mechanisms (that either made the task harder or easier) and requiring memory usage for previous guesses; and 'temporally' by adding various time constraints. The effect of a consistent audio background noise recorded from onboard ISS was also explored, see Fig. 1.

We developed proprietary software to collect and analyze keyboard and mouse dynamics, and augmented techniques available in open source software to derive heart rate using the RGB video stream. The collected data was processed to obtain desired metrics such as heart rate [8], typing pauses and errors [9], as well as task performance [10]. Metrics were chosen based on a literature review and internal brainstorming.

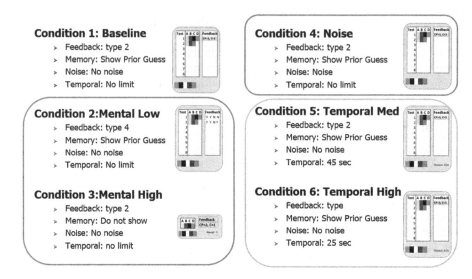

Fig. 1. ATHENA pilot test conditions. Condition 1: Baseline for all comparisons. Additional conditions used: Mental workload 2 & 3, Temporal workload 5 & 6, and noise 4.

3   Results

We used Simple Linear Regression as our supervised machine learning approach, via an interface with the WEKA toolkit [11], to classify each game played. Each participant played six games, each game divided into thirds for analysis. We performed 10-fold cross-validation using the survey scores as classification targets. We expected the total TLX to best classify all games, the Bedford and TLX mental subscale to best classify our Mental Low/Baseline/High conditions, and the TLX temporal subscale to best classify our Baseline/25/45 time limits. Noise was included as an exploratory variable.

Under these assumptions our classification accuracies ranged from 57 %–100 % (lower bound was 48 % accuracy when looking at a full cross between game type and survey result used for classification, but 75 % when removing the all games assumption), see Fig. 2. The TLX mental subscale (78 %), TLX total (100 %), and Bedford (79 %) had the highest classification accuracies for our Mental Low/Baseline/High conditions. The TLX temporal subscale (75 %) had the highest classification accuracy for our Baseline/25/45 time limits.

To determine if the other TLX subscales could be of additional diagnostic value, we completed classifications using each TLX subscale, see Fig. 3. The TLX mental (78 %), frustration (100 %), and performance (88 %) subscales had the highest classification accuracies for our Mental Low/Baseline/High conditions. The TLX temporal subscale had the highest classification accuracies for our Baseline/25/45 time limits. The TLX effort (85 %) and physical (68 %) subscales had the highest classification accuracies for our Baseline/Noise conditions.

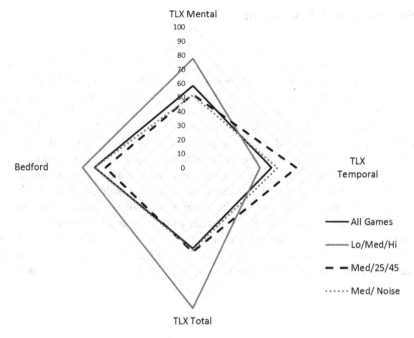

Fig. 2. Classification accuracies, with larger shapes indicating greater overall accuracy

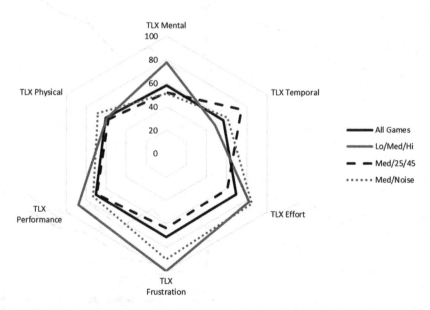

Fig. 3. Classification accuracies of TLX subscales, with larger shapes indicating greater overall accuracy.

4 Summary and Conclusions

Our preliminary results reflect the existence of different types of workload, with our zero-intrusion metrics demonstrating respectable classification accuracies when the variable causing workload (e.g. time) is matched with the type of workload assessed (e.g. temporal). For example, the TLX temporal subscale best classifies manipulations due to temporal demands but performs the worst for mental manipulations, as would be expected. Also, the similar classification accuracies for the Bedford and TLX mental subscale support the Bedford as a cognitive workload scale, while the increased classification accuracy seen with the TLX total supports the idea of workload being more complex than purely cognitive in nature and our 'cognitive' manipulations were not purely cognitive in terms of workload dimensions. Finally, our results indicate noise affected the perceived effort and physical aspects of workload, while our cognitive manipulations affected perceived mental, frustration and performance aspects of workload. Using our zero-intrusion metrics, no survey or subscale produced highest accuracy levels for all our conditions combined (i.e. all games) even though there were marked differences in subjective reporting, see Fig. 4. While our work points to the

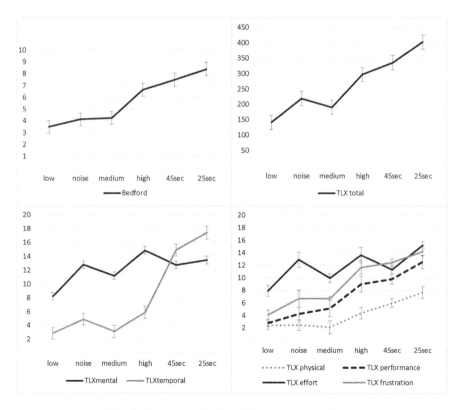

Fig. 4. Survey results for different game conditions

existence of different workload types more work is needed to fully understand them and the multi-dimensional concept that is workload.

Overall, ATHENA has demonstrated that accurate assessments of workload can be achieved by a sensor that solely utilizes zero-intrusion metrics. Thus, ATHENA represents a valuable step forward in providing for automated workload support tools that can be used on long-duration space missions as well as a tool for understanding the workload concept.

Acknowledgments. Concepts described above were developed with support from US AF (Contract # FA8650-06-C-6635), NIST (Contract # 70NANB0H3020), ONR (Contract # N00014-09-C-0265) and NASA (Contract # NNX12AB40G). ATHENA was sponsored by NASA SBIR (Contract # NNX15CJ18P), undertaken by SIFT, LLC. We would like to thank Mai Lee Chang, Kristina Holden, Brian Gore, Gordon Voss, Aniko Sandor, Alexandra Whitmire, and Mihriban Whitmore for oversight, guidance, and support.

References

1. Miller, C.A., Funk, H., Goldman, R., Meisner, J., Wu, P.: Implications of adaptive vs. adaptable UIs on decision making: Why "automated adaptiveness" is not always the right answer. In: Proceedings of the 1st International Conference on Augmented Cognition, Las Vegas (2005)
2. Chen, F., Ruiz, N., Choi, E., Epps, J., Khawaja, M.A., Taib, R., Yin, B., Wang, Y.: Multimodal behavior and interaction as indicators of cognitive load. ACM Trans. Interact. Intell. Syst. (TiiS) **2**(4), 22 (2012)
3. Wu, P., Ott, T., Paullada, A., Mayer, D., Gottlieb, J., Wall, P.: Inclusion of linguistic features to a zero-intrusion workload assessment technique. In: Proceedings of the 7th AHFE Conference, 27–31 July 2016. CRC Press, Inc. (accepted)
4. Roscoe, A.H: Assessing pilot workload in flight. In: AGARD Conference Proceedings Flight Test Techniques, Paris (1984)
5. Hart, S.G., Staveland, L.E.: Development of NASA-TLX (Task Load Index): Results of empirical and theoretical research. In: Hancock, P.A., Meshkati, N. (eds.) Human Mental Workload. North Holland Press, Amsterdam (1988)
6. Meirowitz, M.: Mastermind (1970)
7. van Someren, M.W., Barnard, Y.F., Sandberg, J.A.C.: The Think Aloud Method: A Practical Guide to Modelling Cognitive Processes. Academic Press, London (1994)
8. Miller, S.: Literature review workload measures. Document ID: N01-006. National Advanced Driving Simulator. http://www.nads-sc.uiowa.edu/publicationStorage/200501251347060.N01-006.pdf (2001). Accessed 7 Jan 2014
9. Vizer, L.M., Zhou, L., Sears, A.: Automated stress detection using keystroke and linguistic features: An exploratory study. Int. J. Hum Comput Stud. **67**(10), 870–886 (2009)
10. Tsang, P.S., Vidulich, M. A.: Mental workload and situation awareness. In: Handbook of Human Factors and Ergonomics (2006)
11. Hall, M., Frank, E., Holmes, G., Pfahringer, B., Reutemann, P., Witten, I.H.: The WEKA data mining software: an update. SIGKDD Explor. **11**(1), 37–57 (2009)

Influence of Display Resolution on Brain Activity and Task Workload

Kiyomi Sakamoto[1]([✉]), Yutaka Tanaka[1], Kuniko Yamashita[2], and Akira Okada[2]

[1] Groupwide CTO Office, Panasonic Corporation,
1006 Kadoma, Kadoma City, Osaka 571-8501, Japan
{sakamoto.kiyomi,tanaka.mame}@jp.panasonic.com
[2] Department of Human Life Science, Osaka City University,
3-3-138 Sugimoto, Sumiyoshi-ku, Osaka 558-8585, Japan
{yamasita,okada}@life.osaka-cu.ac.jp

Abstract. We experimentally investigated the influence of the use of a high-resolution 4K tablet on participants' physiological and psychological state while engaged in searching tasks, to evaluate their associated mental and physical workloads. The results showed NIRS, an index of nervous system activity, to be significantly higher during searching tasks with 4K content than with 2K content, whereas LF/HF (level of sympathetic nerve activity) during searching tasks was significantly lower for 4K content than for 2K content, although no significant differences were observed in subjective assessments between 4K and 2K displays.

Keywords: Physiological and psychological measurements · High-resolution 4K tablet · NIRS · LF/HF

1 Introduction

Developments continue in high-definition displays, with 4K products already in production and 8K displays in prospect; and various types of viewing styles, using TVs, PCs and Smartphones, make it increasingly important to consider the effects of these changes on human physical and mental health. Our view that improvements in picture quality and presence should be accompanied by reduced viewer stress and visual fatigue prompted us to investigate the influence of the use of high-resolution 4K display devices on participants' physiological and psychological state while engaged in various types of tasks, to evaluate their associated mental and physical workloads. In a prior study [1], we conducted an investigation into the effects on the physiological and psychological states of eight participants in their 20s of using a high-resolution 4K tablet while viewing various types of video content that included scenic content and video material with movement and action. The results showed the scores along the scales of "precise–coarse," "feeling of invigoration–no feeling of invigoration" and "enjoyable–boring" when viewing 4K scenic content to be significantly higher than those for 2K scenic content. Moreover, their NIRS (near infrared spectroscopic topography) values, an index of nervous system activity, during viewing tests of 4K

© Springer International Publishing Switzerland 2016
C. Stephanidis (Ed.): HCII 2016 Posters, Part I, CCIS 617, pp. 232–237, 2016.
DOI: 10.1007/978-3-319-40548-3_39

scenic content, were significantly higher for 4K content than for 2K content. However, further studies using various types of task will be needed to confirm whether, physiologically and psychologically, 4K viewing is superior to 2K for doing such tasks. We therefore explored and evaluated the influence of a high-resolution 4K tablet on participants' physiological and psychological state while engaged in searching tasks, which are likely to be very typical activities when using a tablet as a PC. As interim results, we reported the NIRS figures from a previous study [2]. The authors report here the results for heart rate variability (LF/HF) in addition to the results for NIRS during searching tasks, and discuss the general pattern of the results.

2   Methods

Participants: Eight adults aged in their 20s participated in this experiment. Visual acuity under 0.8 in any participant was corrected using contact lenses or glasses. Each participant gave his or her written informed consent to take part in this experiment according to the protocol approved by the Osaka City University Research Ethics Committee at the Graduate School of Human Life Sciences.

Measurements: The following items were investigated.

1. Subjective assessment: The participants gave a subjective assessment of their psychological state using a "subjective symptoms report" [3] before and after each task and by filling in questionnaires after each task that included inquiries as to their state on the scales of "stressed–relaxed," "comfortable–uncomfortable," "no visual fatigue–visual fatigue," etc., giving each a score of 3 to –3 (Table 1).
2. Task performance (rate of correct answers) for text-searching tasks was also calculated.
3. NIRS: Brain activity, based on total hemoglobin or oxyhemoglobin, was obtained using NIRS detectors placed on the left and right side of the participant's forehead.
4. Heart rate (HR) and heart rate variability (LF/HF; level of sympathetic nerve activity): LF/HF is defined as the ratio of the low-frequency band (LF: 0.04–0.15 Hz) to the high-frequency band (HF: 0.15– 0.5 Hz) [4, 5], calculated by FFT analysis using the R-R interval based on heart rate variability obtained by electrocardiogram.
5. Blinking rate, obtained using an electrooculogram (EOG).

Apparatus: The display device was an A3-size 4K tablet (Panasonic UT-MB-5015SEZ).

The viewing distance was set at 1.5H (45 cm). Screen-to-eye distance was defined in relation to screen height (H). The recommended viewing distance for a 4K TV, defined as 1.5 times the display's height, was 45 cm for the A3 tablet.

Test room illumination was set at 200 lx to simulate the light level of an average Japanese living room, based on JIS standardization.

Table 1. Subjective assessment items

Subjective assessment items (including 15 items)
The appearance of the characters
"easy to read–difficult to read,"
"precision–lack of precision,"
"precise–coarse,"
"natural–artificial,"
"feeling of congruity–feeling of incongruity,"
"clear–not clear,"
"slight blurring–significant blurring,"
"feeling of worry–no feeling of worry,"
"kind to the eyes–not kind to the eyes, "
"no visual fatigue–visual fatigue"
The impression of the whole display and emotional state
"bright–dark,"
"not dazzling–dazzling,"
"comfortable–uncomfortable,"
"relaxed–stressed,"
"aroused–sleepy"

Procedure: Figure 1 shows the process of the searching task, which was to count the number of target *kanji* characters in a scrolling line of *kanji* or a stationary *kanji* layout image. Each scrolling *kanji* line included 26 Japanese *kanji* characters, taking 35 s for the whole set to scroll continuously from right to left of the screen (Fig. 2 left). Each *kanji* layout image included 25 Japanese *kanji* characters, displayed for 10 s (Fig. 2 right). One task comprised 12 scrolling lines and 12 layout images, displayed alternately. Each task comprised 10 min each of 4K or 2K content. Before and after each searching task, the participants gave a subjective assessment of their psychological state. One minute of rest time was given before each searching task, and two minutes of rest time was given afterwards. A 10-min rest was given between the 4K and 2K tasks. Physiological indices were monitored while the participants underwent the searching tests. To eliminate the order effect, the order of resolutions was made unique to each participant. Moreover, the resolution or current content was not informed to the participant, since it might have influenced their evaluation score.

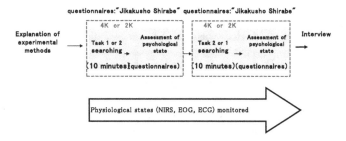

Fig. 1. Content of searching task

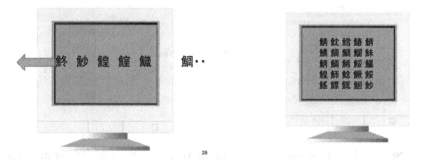

Fig. 2. The task was to count the number of target *kanji* characters in a scrolling line of *kanji* (left-hand figure) and in a *kanji* layout image (right-hand figure).

Statistical analysis: A paired t-test was performed to analyze the influence of the display resolution. The level of significance was set at $p = 0.05$.

3   Results and Discussion

The results showed that during searching tasks, NIRS, an index of nervous system activity, tended to be higher for 4K content than for 2K content [2]. The graphs illustrate the results for NIRS for participant S1 as a typical example (Figs. 3 and 4). However, the LF/HF (level of sympathetic nerve activity, calculated by monitoring an electrocardiogram (ECG)) during the rest time after the task, tended to be lower for 4K content than for 2K content (Fig. 5). There was a significant difference between LF/HF for 2K content during the rest time before the task and that during the searching task, and between LF/HF for 2K content during the rest time before the task and that during the rest time after the task (Fig. 5). However there was no significant difference between LF/HF for 4K content during the rest time before the task and that during the searching task, or between LF/HF for 4K content during the rest time before the task and that during the rest time after the task (Fig. 5).

Moreover, HF/(LF + HF) (level of parasympathetic nerve activity) was significantly higher for 4K content than for 2K content during the rest time after the task (Fig. 6). There was a significant difference between HF/(LF + HF) for 2K content during the rest time before the task and that during the searching task, and between HF/(LF + HF) for 2K content during the rest time before the task and that during the rest time after the task (Fig. 6) However, there was no significant difference between HF/(LF + HF) for 4K content during the rest time before the task and that during the searching task, and between HF/(LF + HF) for 4K content during the rest time before the task and that during the rest time after the task (Fig. 6). On the other hand, no significant differences were observed in subjective assessments between 4K and 2K displays. Furthermore, no significant differences were observed in task performance (rate of correct answers) between 4K and 2K displays.

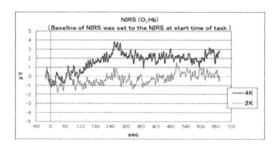

Fig. 3. NIRS (O₂Hb) at 4K and 2K for participant S1. X-axis: resolution (4K or 2K); Y-axis: NIRS (O₂Hb). (Color figure online)

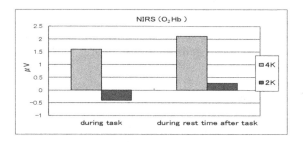

Fig. 4. Time course of NIRS (O₂Hb) during searching tests at 4K and 2K for participant S1. X-axis: Time (sec); Y-axis: NIRS (O₂Hb). (Color figure online)

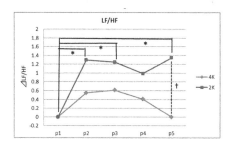

Fig. 5. LF/HF during searching tests at 4K and 2K (Average value of eight participants). +: $p < 0.1$, *: $p < 0.05$; X-axis: Time (period; p1, p2, p3, p4, p5); p1 = rest time before task; p2 = first half of searching task; p3 = second half of searching task; p4 = first half of rest time after task; p5 = second half of rest time after task; Y-axis: LF/HF

In summary, the NIRS and LF/HF data on use of a 4K tablet for searching tasks agreed with our prior study results on viewing content [1]. The current results suggest that searching tasks at 4K can cause a surge in brain activity but a lower task workload, such as physical and mental stress, although subjective assessments might not exactly mirror the scientific data. Further investigations will be needed to gain a more precise picture of the influence on psychological state of high-resolution 4K displays.

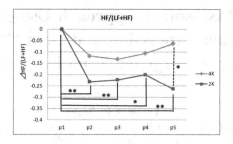

Fig. 6. HF/(LF + HF) during searching tests at 4K and 2K (Average value of eight participants). *: $p < 0.05$, **: $p < 0.01$; X-axis: Time (period; p1, p2, p3, p4, p5); p1 = rest time before task; p2 = first half of searching task; p3 = second half of searching task; p4 = first half of rest time after task; p5 = second half of rest time after task; Y-axis: HF/(LF + HF)

References

1. Sakamoto, K., Sakashita, S., Yamashita, K., Okada, A.: The effect of a high-resolution 4K tablet on physiological and psychological state while viewing various types of content. In: Stephanidis, C., Tino, A. (eds.) HCII 2015 Posters. CCIS, vol. 528, pp. 138–143. Springer, Heidelberg (2015). doi:10.1007/978-3-319-21380-4_25
2. Sakamoto, K., Tanaka, Y., Yamashita, K., Okada, A.: Effect of display resolution on brain activity and task performance rate. In: Proceedings of the 2016 IEICE General Conference, H-2-2, p. 264 (2016)
3. Sakai, K.: Revice 2002 for "Jikakushô Shirabe". In: Digest of Science of Labour, 57th edn. By the Japan Society for Occupational Health, Tokyo, pp. 295–298 (2002). (in Japanese)
4. Ishibashi, K., Kitamura, S., Kozaki, T., Yasukouchi, A.: Inhibition of heart rate variability during sleep in humans by 6700 K pre-sleep light exposure. J. Physiol. Anthropol. **26**(1), 39–43 (2007)
5. Ishibashi, K., Ueda, S., Yasukouchi, A.: Effects of mental task on heart rate variability during graded head-up tilt. J. Physiol. Anthropol. **18**(6), 225–231 (1999)

Objects Assessment Approach Using Natural Language Processing and Data Quality to Support Emergency Situation Assessment

Matheus F. Sanches, Valdir A.P. Junior, Jessica O. Souza,
Caio S. Coneglian, Fábio R. Jorge, Natália P. Oliveira,
and Leonardo C. Botega[✉]

Computing and Information Systems Research Lab (COMPSI),
Marília Eurípides University (UNIVEM), Marília, São Paulo, Brazil
{matheusferraroni,valdir.junior,fabio_jorge,
nataliaoliveira,botega}@univem.edu.br,
osz.jessica@gmail.com, caio.coneglian@gmail.com

Abstract. Situation Awareness (SAW) is a cognitive process that is defined by the perception of relevant elements present in a monitored environment (e.g., people, objects, vehicles, places), the understanding of their meaning (i.e., what they are doing) and the projection of their statuses in the near future. In the domain of emergency management, the data employed to the process of acquisition and maintenance of SAW are provided by several sources, using different formats and different classifications, such as: images from security cameras, reports made to the emergency response center, posts in social networks and several physical sensors, such as: positional, altitude and movement. Data from this sources, if well processed and understood by a specialist, may contribute to the decision-making process, supporting the establishment of emergency response tactics and a better allocation of operational resources. The acquisition of SAW demands the characterization of the ongoing situation. Typically, knowing exactly what is going on demands exhaustive routines of intelligent data assessment. In the emergency management domain, it means to better explore and analyze what the humans say about the events. This paper presents a general architecture that integrates objects and situational assessment for the emergency management domain and a specific process for the objects assessment using natural language processing (NLP) and semantic practices, to better identify relevant elements that may be useful for the situation assessment routines, such as information fusion. Known approaches are limited due to the absence of data quality analysis as part of the process, undesirable when decision makers need to rely on emergency information. Preliminary results of a case study of an intelligent object assessment of a robbery situation reported in Brazilian Portuguese demonstrate the advantages and practical particularities of our solution.

Keywords: Situational awareness · Emergency situational assessment · Natural language processing

© Springer International Publishing Switzerland 2016
C. Stephanidis (Ed.): HCII 2016 Posters, Part I, CCIS 617, pp. 238–244, 2016.
DOI: 10.1007/978-3-319-40548-3_40

1 Introduction

To acquire and to maintain SAW demands the characterization of the current situation, that is, what is going on with the entities of interest in the environment.

The process of situation assessment typically starts with routines of objects assessment (also known as acquisition of data for situation assessment) to perform an initial analysis of input data to find the first entities, their attributes and the relationships among them, which may be of interest to start the SAW process. In the emergency management domain, such analysis may be triggered by a crime report made by the victim or a witness (from Human Intelligence - HUMINT).

To accomplish this, HUMINT data must be retrieved and compared with known information to help systems to identify incoming useful information. However, HUMINT data are typically imperfect, due to the influence of several internal and external factors, since the level of stress until variables of the physical environment where the reporter is. Such imperfections inherent to information may introduce uncertainties into human's mind.

To mitigate the problem of dealing with imperfect reports from humans, data must be qualified and quality meta data be used as criteria for mining and processing.

This paper presents the organization of a objects assessment process that involves techniques of Natural Language Processing (NLP) to better acquire and to process information from humans in benefit of SAW.

The paper is organized as fallow: Introduction, Related Works, The Process of Object Assessment using NLP and Information Quality Awareness, Conclusion and References.

2 Related Work

Identification of entities of interest inhuman reports is a challenging task. The acquisition of terms while performing NLP is not just about retrieving and matching a specific word or sequence of words from a data model, but it is also the assignment of a meaning to sentences in order to obtain gain more useful information that helps to describe objects of interest, their relationships and also their statuses.

Regarding semantic approaches, Reckman et al. [8] show a way to get the natural speech and attributes to the collected words, applying meaning using machine learning. Using a virtual restaurant game, they developed a technique to perform the analysis and the association of meaning to the words that was considered as unknown. Hence, they were able to develop patterns to identify items of the menu. Variations of the AI Technique developed in Recman's works may be used to future works to improve the results of the data acquisition step.

Paralic and Kostial [9] show a different way to use ontology to perform information retrieval. According to this work, it is possible to link the information that is being analyzed with the ontology, using association of words. This work tends to be a very related to our work because to perform a good acquisition and preliminary assessment of information coming from human reports, depends on the vocabulary, that can vary frequently and have lots of different meanings to the same words. Using this technique, it may be possible to perform the identification of relevant elements even when the word was just acquired and presented with a different meaning than it was expected. This works proposes a process that may contribute to the acquisition and preliminary assessment of information provided by natural language, using techniques of natural language processing (NLP) and then identify relevant items and objects to support the other assessment routines of situations in the emergency management domain.

Known solutions proved that is possible to improve the results provided by the acquisition using ontologies that are able to specify the meaning of the words present into textual reports. However, through a quality-aware ontology, it is possible to improve the assessment by quantifying sentences while identify words and meanings and hence acquiring trustfulness to the results provided by NLP.

The preliminary assessment process is the main port to entry data to be analyzed. Incomplete or erroneous information coming from the NLP may cause problems to the situational awareness and jeopardize decision-making, resulting in threat to life and property.

2.1   General Architecture for Objects and Situation Assessment

To accomplish the objective of providing means to assess emergency situations under imperfect and ever-changing data and information, a new situation assessment architecture was proposed. The architecture is an integrated approach of syntactic and semantic objects and situation assessment routines to the emergency management domain. Figure 1 describes the process to perform objects and situation analysis starting from HUMINT data. HUMINT data are prone to failure, once they can be incomplete, incorrect and imprecise. Each failure that persists may propagate through the system and jeopardize decision-making.

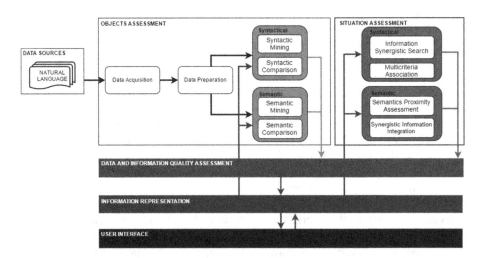

Fig. 1. The general architecture for objects and situation assessment to improve emergency situation awareness.

To solve this problem this architecture is based on a Data And Information Quality Assessment layer, since the firsts steps until the user interface. Performing this, the information that is currently being managed, if uncertain, will be know by all phases of the assessment process, including the human operator at the user interface. The new architecture for objects and situation assessment in the context of situational awareness has the following modules:

- Data Sources (acquisition of data): the module in charge of the acquisition of HUMINT data from the environment to feed the process. The acquisition is performed aiming data information from human reports made to the emergency response center and also from social networks.
- Object Assessment: the main module of this work (red part of Fig. 1), regarding the identification of relevant objects, their attributes and properties which define their actions and activities among them. Such assessment is performed through a syntactical (for further information about the syntactical analysis the reader must refer to Sanches *et al.* [13]) and a semantic perspective to verify similarities by object's grammatical form and also by means of their meaning. This module is better described in the next section.
- Data and Information Quality Assessment: every assessed object pass through this module to acquire indexes that quantify them under data quality dimensions, such as completeness, precision, timeliness, consistency, relevance and uncertainty. Hence, it's possible to verify what information is better than others and choose the best ones to feed the following modules of the process. The results of this parts are also used to improve the next evaluations of the Object Assessment. For further information regarding data quality assessment, the reader should refer to [12].
- Situation Assessment: is the module where the qualified objects (objects with quality indexes) are analyzed to verify the synergy among to compose relations that define situations. Such analysis, as the Objects Assessment, is also performed under syntactical and semantic perspectives.
- Information Representation: In order to improve the results from the object assessment this step give meanings to the words and sentences that are being analyzed. This stage is responsible for the representation of the semantic of all objects, attributes and their relation.

3   The Process for Objects Assessment

In this Section, the internal methods for the objects assessment approach is described, as also shown in Fig. 2.

3.1   Data Acquisition and Preparation

The acquisition of the data coming from the Data Sources, that are text transcripts from natural language speech or posts in social medias, are received for a web server and unpacked from a JSON and transformed into an object. The preparation of the

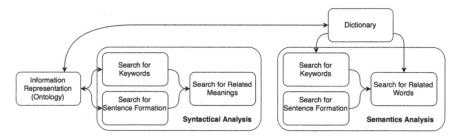

Fig. 2. The process of object assessment using NLP and information quality awareness

information is responsible for clean the data and add specific information that are necessary to search important information into the data. Each step is described below.

As soon as the information is acquired it need to be cleared to remove slangs and words that can harm the final analysis. In order to resolve this, it was developed an application that continues the flow of the acquisition. This application receives the data at the moment that the acquisition finish the process.

Comparing each of the words received with a dictionary predefined when a slang is find it will be replaced with the right word. For instance when the letter "u" is found it is replaced with the word "you".

The second step of preparation of the information is add to the sentence and words important information. To perform this action it was used a software called Cogroo [6], that is a parser. The entire sentence is submitted to Cogroo, after this every word will become a block of information. The result of Cogroo analysis will be similar to this: "{ "tokens":[{ "features":"F=S", "POSTag":"n", "lemmas":["moto"], "lexeme":"moto" }], "TAG":"NP" }".

Every word in the sentence will receive this information, "features" is compost by the genre and number of the word, male or female and singular or plural. "POSTag" is the class of the word, in this example is a "noun". "lemmas" are the variations of the word and "lexeme" is the word that was analyzed.

3.2 Semantic Analysis

Different from the Syntactic Analysis [15] that check each word, grammar class and their combination inside the text, the function of the Semantic Analysis is give meaning to the words and sentences. This step work aside to the Syntactical Analysis, for this reason they are executed at the same time.

Words and words related to a certain keyword are submitted to an ontology created for this propose that will return the in semantic representation. Utilizing this semantic representation, it's possible to better understanding the meaning of the sentences and words. The ontology received a word and return the words that are related to the word received.

Later, the word "guy" is submitted to the ontology, that will return words related to it, and this way causing to be possible to identify what the word "guy" mean. Once its know that this may mean the criminal, words close to this are send to the ontology, the word "stole" is sent to the ontology and then it will say that this word is related to the criminal and the action of stole something. After this analysis its possible to identify the criminal in the sentence and his action in the report.

4   Conclusion

This work proposed a new general architecture and specific objects assessment process for guiding the development of new solutions regarding the identification of objects that may be useful for situation assessment routines. Preliminary and promising results indicate a great applicability of our approach in this context.

After the Objects Assessment, the results are always submitted to the Data and Information Quality Assessment to receive data and information quality scores.

The full path of our approach to asses the information about objects for the emergency management domain can be simplified by: acquisition of the information from reports made to the police emergency response center and social networks. Then, this information is sent to the information preparation. The Information Preparation removes slangs and replace them with the complete words and remove words that can perturb the analysis. With the data prepared, they are sent to the Syntactic and Semantic Analysis.

As the last step of this process, after all the information already acquired, they are transformed into a JSON object and structured in a way that allows the next stage to understand and handle this data. The results are saved on a database and the next stage are informed with the identification of this analysis.

References

1. Endsley, M.R.: Designing for Situation Awareness: An Approach to User-Centered Design. CRC Press, Boca Raton (2011)
2. Kokar, M.M., Endsley, M.R.: Situation awareness and cognitive modeling. IEEE Intell. Syst. **27**(3), 91–96 (2012)
3. Botega, L., Ferreira, L.C.N., Oliveira, P., Oliveira, A., Berti, C.B.: User interface for enhancing situational awareness in emergency management system. In: 17th International Conference on Human-Computer Interaction, Los Angeles. Lecture Notes in Computer Science (2015)
4. Souza, J., Botega, L.C., Santarém Segundo, J.E., Berti, C.B., de Campos, M.R., de Araújo, R.B.: Conceptual framework to enrich situation awareness of emergency dispatchers. In: Yamamoto, S., Oliveira, N.P. (eds.) HIMI 2015. LNCS, vol. 9173, pp. 33–44. Springer, Heidelberg (2015). doi:10.1007/978-3-319-20618-9_4
5. Ciprian, C., Dan, B., Maria, S., Patrick, N., Shankar, K.: Large Scale Language Modeling in Automatic Speech Recognition
6. Kinoshita, J., Salvador, L.N., Menezes, C.E.D: CoGrOO1 – Um Corretor Gramatical para a língua portuguesa, acoplável ao Open Office

7. Rao, K., Peng, F., Beaufays, F.: Automatic pronunciation verification for speech recognition. In: 40th International Conference on Acoustics, Speech and Signal Processing 2015 (2015)
8. Reckman, H., Orkin, J., Roy, D.: Learning meanings of words and constructions, grounded in a virtual game. In: 10th Conference on Natural Language Processing (KOVENS)
9. Paralic, J., Kostial, I.: Ontology-based information retrieval. In: Information and Intelligent Systems, Croatia, pp. 23–28 (2003)
10. Ranwez1, S., Ranwez, V., Sy, M., Mortmain, J., Crampes, M.: User centered and ontology based information retrieval system for life sciences. In: Semantic Web Applications and Tools for Life Sciences
11. Souza, J., Botega, L., Segundo, J.E.S., Berti, C., Araújo, R.B.: A methodology for the assessment and representation of the quality information from robbery events for acquiring situation awareness in decision making system
12. Sanches, M.F., Botega, L.C, Oliveira, A.C.M.: Processamento de Linguagem Natural para a Avaliação de Situações de Emergência com Interface de Realidade Virtual at WRVA 2015 (2015)

Fixation-Related EEG Frequency Band Power Analysis: A Promising Neuro-Cognitive Methodology to Evaluate the Matching-Quality of Web Search Results?

Christian Scharinger[✉], Yvonne Kammerer, and Peter Gerjets

Leibniz-Institut für Wissensmedien, Schleichstr. 6, 72076 Tübingen, Germany
{c.scharinger, y.kammerer, p.gerjets}@iwm-tuebingen.de

Abstract. We used fixation-related EEG frequency band power analyses to study the evaluation of web search results. Participants were presented thirteen search queries, each followed by a Google-like list of six search results. One of the search results was a complete match (i.e., having strong lexical and semantical overlap with the search query), one a complete mismatch (i.e., having neither lexical nor semantical overlap with the search query), and four were partial matches, having either only semantical or only lexical overlap with the search query. We analyzed the EEG alpha frequency band power for individuals' fixations during the initial viewing of each search result. We observed that on average the EEG alpha frequency band power at parietal electrodes was significantly lower for the complete match than for the other search results. Thus, this decreased alpha power might reflect participants' detection of the hit in a list of search results.

Keywords: EEG · Alpha · Eye-tracking · Web search

1 Introduction

Using web search engines like Google has nowadays become the typical starting point for any information gathering process. Despite the importance and prevalence of using web search engines in our daily life, research to date has only rarely addressed the cognitive aspects of conducting web searches by means of the electroencephalogram (EEG). In the current study we were interested in one of these cognitive aspects, namely cognitive load (CL, cf. [1]). We assessed CL during participants' evaluation of web search results by means of EEG alpha frequency band power.

Previous research showed that for increasing CL (i.e., increasing demands on executive functions and working memory), the EEG alpha frequency band power at parietal electrodes decreases [2, 3]. Especially, a decrease of alpha frequency band power in the range between 10 to 13 Hz (i.e., the upper alpha) has been associated with semantic processing demands [4, 5]. Importantly, EEG alpha power might be used as a reliable measure of CL in the context of hypertext reading and link selection [6, 7].

The use of fixation-related EEG frequency band power analysis (see Sect. 2.4) in the current study provided participants a normal reading situation during the web

© Springer International Publishing Switzerland 2016
C. Stephanidis (Ed.): HCII 2016 Posters, Part I, CCIS 617, pp. 245–250, 2016.
DOI: 10.1007/978-3-319-40548-3_41

search evaluation. We manipulated the manner of overlap between different search results and the search queries, thus creating search results of different matching-quality [7]. We used four different matching conditions: A complete match, showing sematic and lexical overlap with the search query (the HIT), partial matches, showing either semantic or lexical overlap (SEM and LEX), and a no-match (MISS), showing neither sematic nor lexical overlap with the search query. We expected that depending on the amount of semantical and lexical overlap between search query and search result the induced CL would vary. The MISS should be easily identified as irrelevant for the current search query, thus resulting in lower CL as compared to the CL during reading of search results that had semantic and/or lexical overlap with the search query (i.e., potential matches that therefore had to be more thoroughly processed).

2   Methods

2.1   Participants

Twenty-two healthy university students (age mean = 22.41, sd = 3.43, 17 f/5 m) participated in the study and received a payment of 8 €/h. They were all native speakers of German, right-handed, and had normal or corrected-to-normal visual acuity. The study was approved by the local ethic committee. Participants gave their written informed consent at the beginning of the study. Due to technical problems, one participant had to be excluded from further data analysis.

2.2   Materials and Procedure

We designed the task material and procedure in analogy to a study described in [8]. We used thirteen different fact-finding search queries addressing a variety of topics. Each query was formulated as a whole-sentence question presented at the center of the screen (see Fig. 1). Each search query was followed by a search engine result page (SERP), i.e., a Google-like list of six search results. One of the search results was a HIT, one a MISS, and four were partial matches (SEM, LEX). While the SEM search results – like the HIT – would provide an answer to the search query, the LEX search results – like the MISS – would not. The order of the different search result categories varied between SERPs to avoid list sequence effects (e.g., [9]). Furthermore, the order of the search queries was varied between participants.

Each search result consisted of one line of a blue-colored heading (Arial, 26 pts) and a content-summary of two to three lines (Arial, 16 pts, black color). The search results consisted of only textual content information, and no source information was provided. This was because we were specifically interested in participants' evaluation of search results based on content information only.

Participants were instructed to read the search results and then to evaluate the matching between the search query and each search result by mouse-clicking first on the best matching search result and then in descending relevance-order on the other search results. The presentation speed of search queries and SERPs was self-paced. A button labeled "To the search results" was positioned below the search query. By

Controlling Airplane Trade? Only a few companies build all of the large airplanes in the world. Other businesses are beginning to face...	LEX
Kids Domain - Holiday Fun - Summer Guide Summer's here and the time is right for kids crafts, BBQ's, outdoor games, camping trips, picnics and much more! Check out Kaboose for more ideas.	MISS
Airplane Aeronautics: Wings Lift and Drag are considered aerodynamic forces because they exist due to the ... The special shape of the airplane wing (airfoil) is designed so that air ...	HIT
Curvature of Oars Plays a Large Role In Propulsion The relative movement between the oar blades and water during the drive phase of the stroke was modeled, and the forces affecting the direction and velocity of movement...	SEM

Fig. 1. Exemplary sequence of a search query ("why do airplanes have differently shaped wings?") followed by a corresponding SERP (showing four out of six search results). The task materials were originally presented in German.

clicking on this button, participants reached the corresponding SERP. Here, after a mouse-click on a search result, the blue-colored heading changed to a dark red to indicate that the mouse-click had been registered. Participants always stayed on the SERP until they clicked on a button labeled "Next search query" at the bottom of the SERP.

The task procedure was identical for all participants. At the beginning of the web search evaluation, after the calibration of the eye-tracker, written task instructions were presented as the first page on the screen, which was then followed by the first search query (see Fig. 1 for exemplary task materials).

2.3 Apparatus

The experiment was run in a quiet, dimly lit room. Participants sat in a comfortable chair in front of a 22-in. Dell monitor (1680 × 1050 pixels screen resolution) while their EEG and eye-tracking data were recorded. We used a light-gray background-color on all displayed web pages to provide a constant and pleasant brightness value to minimize eye-strain.

Eye-tracking data were recorded using a 250 Hz SMI (SensoMotoric Instruments) infrared remote eye-tracking system that was positioned below the monitor. A chin rest was used to avoid head movements during data recording and to guarantee a fixed distance of about 70 cm between the eyes and the eye-tracking device. The eye-tracking data were recorded at a sampling rate of 250 Hz (SMI iView X 2.7.13). The eye-tracker was calibrated using the built-in calibration routines (SMI Experiment Center, 9-point calibration) before the written task instruction appeared on the screen.

EEG data were recorded from 27 electrode sites (Fp1, Fp2, F7, F3, Fz, F4, F8, FC5, FC1, FC2, FC6, T7, C3, Cz, C4, T8, CP5, CP1, CP2, CP6, P7, P3, Pz, P4, P8, O1, O2) positioned according to the international 10/20 system. The right mastoid served as reference during recording. Ground electrode was positioned at AFz. Three additional electrodes were placed around the eyes for recording of the electro-occulogram (EOG). EEG data were recorded (PyCorder 1.0.2) at 500 Hz sampling rate (ActiCHamp, Brainproducts, Inc.) using active electrodes (ActiCap, Brainproducts, Inc.). Impedances were kept below 5 kOhm.

2.4 Analysis Procedure

Eye-tracking and EEG data were preprocessed and synchronized as described in [7]. For each SERP six equal-sized rectangular areas of interest (AOIs) were defined, one for each of the six search results (SMI BeGaze 3.41). The AOIs were used to analyze the EEG data eye-fixation related. We collapsed the data of the two semantic and the two lexical search results, resulting in four AOI categories that reflected the four different categories of search results (i.e., HIT, SEM, LEX, and MISS). Using these four AOI categories, portions of the EEG data were selected for further analyses that were related to fixations of these AOIs. Specifically, we analyzed the EEG data for individuals' fixations during the initial viewing of each search result. The initial viewing was defined as the first sequence of fixations of an AOI that in sum lasted longer than 500 ms. The EEG data was epoched in one-second-long data epochs, time-locked to the onset time of the first viewing of the AOI and labeled with the corresponding AOI category. In total, for each participant and each category thirteen epochs (HIT, MISS) respectively 26 epochs (LEX, SEM) were created.

Mean EEG frequency band power was then calculated for the one-second EEG data epochs using fast-fourier transforms (FFTs) for the upper alpha frequency band spectrum (10 Hz to 13 Hz). The alpha power was then averaged for each participant over all epochs of each of the four AOI categories (i.e., the matching-conditions).

3 Results

Participants' average reading times for the SERPs were 39.15 s ($sd = 11.91$). The average initial viewing durations were: HIT, 2.84 s ($sd = 1.44$), SEM, 2.64 s ($sd = 1.36$), LEX, 1.92 ($sd = 0.97$), and MISS, 1.42 s ($sd = 0.63$). A one-factorial repeated measures ANOVA revealed a main effect of matching-condition, $F(3,60) = 24.43$, $p < .001$, $\eta_p^2 = .55$. Paired-sample t-tests (two-way, Bonferroni-corrected) confirmed a significant decrease in viewing durations from HIT to LEX to MISS as well as from SEM to LEX to MISS (all $p < .001$), whereas there was no significant difference in viewing durations between SEM and HIT ($p > .99$).

Interestingly, the EEG alpha frequency band power data (see Fig. 2) showed a different result pattern. A one-factorial repeated measures ANOVA also revealed a main effect of matching-condition, $F(3,60) = 7.91$, $p < .001$, $\eta_p^2 = .28$. The mean upper alpha power at electrode Pz for the conditions SEM (8.50^1, $sd = 0.50$), LEX (8.43, $sd = 0.62$), and MISS (8.22, $sd = 0.48$) did not differ ($p > .88$). However, the HIT showed significantly lower upper alpha power than the other three conditions (HIT vs. MISS, $p = .036$, HIT vs. SEM, $p = .001$, HIT vs. LEX, $p = .028$). Topoplots (see Fig. 2, right part) showing the upper alpha frequency band power expressed as ERD/ERS%-values [6] at all electrode sites over the scalp underlined the parietal-central localization of the decreased alpha for the HIT. This is in line with literature on CL [3, 6] and justifies our selection of Pz as indicative electrode.

---

[1] EEG alpha power is expressed in $10*\log_{10} \mu V^2/Hz$. For reasons of readability we omitted writing the unit in the text.

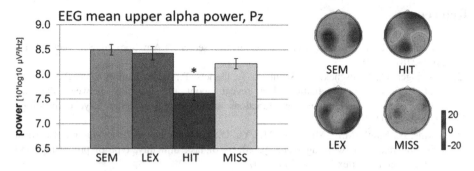

Fig. 2. Left: bar plots showing the mean alpha frequency band power (10–13 Hz) at parietal electrode (Pz) for the partial matches (SEM, LEX), the complete match (HIT), and the mismatch (MISS). Note. * = p < .05. Right: Topoplots showing alpha ERD/ERS% values [6]. As baseline for the ERD/ERS% served the mean alpha frequency band power of all conditions.

4   Discussion

We used a methodology of fixation-related EEG frequency band power analysis to study users' cognitive load (CL) during the evaluation of web search results. With respect to CL, our initial hypothesis was not supported by the EEG data. EEG alpha frequency band power did not differ between the no-match and partial matching search results. Instead, we observed a significantly decreased upper alpha frequency band power – indicating increased CL – for the search result that had semantical and lexical overlap with the search query (i.e., the HIT), as compared to the other search result categories. Importantly, this outcome could not be simply attributed to confounding factors like different viewing times of the four AOIs, as the result pattern of mean AOI fixation durations was different from the EEG outcomes. The observed EEG pattern indicates that when readers encounter a hit for their current search query, they might process this search result more thoroughly. This might lead to increased CL and hence decreased EEG alpha frequency band power. This interpretation is corroborated by studies showing EEG alpha to reflect semantic processing demands [4] and also by studies showing decreased alpha frequency band power as indicative for complex decision making [10]. However, it is an open question why the processing of the search results with only semantic overlap (SEM) did not cause a similar or even higher CL.

Clearly, the current study might only serve as a starting-point for a more thorough examination of cognitive aspects of web search evaluation in future research. Nonetheless, it might indicate that the methodology of fixation-related EEG frequency band power analyses can provide important insights into these cognitive aspects that are not covered by other measures. Especially, alpha frequency band power might be a good measure to cognitively evaluate the matching-quality of search engine results and thus add an important factor to traditional methods of web search evaluations.

Acknowledgements. This research was funded by the Leibniz ScienceCampus Tuebingen Informational Environments (http://www.wissenschaftscampustuebingen.de/www/en/index.html).

References

1. Gwizdka, J.: Distribution of cognitive load in web search. J. Am. Soc. Inf. Sci. Technol. **11**, 2167–2187 (2010)
2. Scharinger, C., Soutschek, A., Schubert, T., Gerjets, P.: When flanker meets the N-back: what EEG and pupil dilation data reveal about the interplay between the two central-executive working memory functions inhibition and updating. Psychophysiology **52**, 1293–1304 (2015)
3. Gevins, A., Smith, M.E., McEvoy, C.L., Yu, D.: High-resolution EEG mapping of cortical activation related to working memory: effects of task difficulty, type of processing, and practice. Cereb. Cortex **7**, 374–385 (1997)
4. Klimesch, W., Doppelmayr, M., Pachinger, T., Russegger, H.: Event-related desynchronization in the alpha band and the processing of semantic information. Brain Res. Cogn. Brain Res. **6**, 83–94 (1997)
5. Klimesch, W.: Alpha-band oscillations, attention, and controlled access to stored information. Trends Cogn. Sci. **16**, 606–617 (2012)
6. Antonenko, P., Paas, F., Grabner, R., van Gog, T.: Using Electroencephalography to measure cognitive load. Educ. Psychol. Rev. **22**, 425–438 (2010)
7. Scharinger, C., Kammerer, Y., Gerjets, P.: Pupil dilation and EEG alpha frequency band power reveal load on executive functions for link-selection processes during text reading. PLoS ONE **10**, e0130608 (2015)
8. Keil, F.C., Kominsky, J.F.: Missing links in middle school: developing use of disciplinary relatedness in evaluating internet search results. PLoS ONE **8**, e67777 (2013)
9. Pan, B., Hembrooke, H., Joachims, T., Lorigo, L., Gay, G., Granka, L.: In Google we trust: users' decisions on rank, position, and relevance. J. Comput. Commun. **12**, 801–823 (2007)
10. Davis, C.E., Hauf, J.D., Wu, D.Q., Everhart, D.E.: Brain function with complex decision making using electroencephalography. Int. J. Psychophysiol. **79**, 175–183 (2011)

Information Presentation
and Visualization

Organization Schemes in Institutional Repositories from Federal Universities

Ronnie Fagundes de Brito$^{(\boxtimes)}$, Milton Shintaku, Diego José Macedo,
Priscila Paiva Castro, Ingrid Schiessl, and Andrea Fleury

Instituto Brasileiro de Informação em Ciência e Tecnologia,
Rio de Janeiro Area, Brazil
{ronniebrito, shintaku, diegomacedo, priscila,
ingridschiessl, andreafleury}@ibict.br

Abstract. In Brazil, institutional repositories have been adopted by universities with the purpose of disseminating their intellectual production. However, very little is discussed about the organization of these repositories, as it directly affects the classification and location of the documents. The objective of the study is to analyze the various forms used in the organization of university repositories maintained by the government. A study to support the discussion on a relatively unexplored subject, but that affects the usability and accessibility of the archives. Results show that most repositories represent the hierarchical structure of the university in the repository, with little use of thematic organizations. This reveals the need for studies to support the organization of academic systems on such systems.

Keywords: Institutional repository · Organization scheme · User navigation

1 Institutional Repositories

Institutional Repositories (IR) are adopted by colleges and universities as a way to provide greater visibility to their academic work. With this, many authors have discussed about these tools, Bjork [1] in his scholarly communication model, places the IRs as access facilitators; Leite and Costa [2] see IRs as knowledge management tools; Harnad et al. [3] consider the IRs as the green way to open access. Usually, content stored in an IR can be indexed and structured recovered from different search engines. However, word searching is one of the different interaction strategies for discovery of documents and materials deposited in these repositories. Among other strategy for the discovery of documents in IRs is browsing by links and categories organized under an organizational scheme, such as task-oriented, audience, topic, alphabetical, chronological, geographical, metaphors or even hybrid schemes [4].

In the case of browsing, the organizational scheme used in IR content structuring influences the document recovery processes, requiring the user knowledge over such structure in order to retrieve the content. The more representative the organization scheme is for the user, the easier are navigation and content retrieval tasks. In this context, the study investigates the organization schemes of information present in

© Springer International Publishing Switzerland 2016
C. Stephanidis (Ed.): HCII 2016 Posters, Part I, CCIS 617, pp. 253–258, 2016.
DOI: 10.1007/978-3-319-40548-3_42

institutional repositories of federal universities and analyzes them on principles of web information architecture.

2 Methods

This is an exploratory study aimed to identify repositories organization schemes. Thirty-five (35) IRs were identified linked to universities geographically distributed across the country, a sample that represents 55 % of Brazilian federal universities.

All repositories analyzed are using DSpace, an open-source software widely used in Brazil [5]. DSpace allows hierarchical organization of content grouping items into Communities, Subcommunities and Collections. This organization guides local navigation, it is complemented by contextual navigation systems such as facets filtering, where metadata fields can be used as filters in the items list, and also search mechanisms.

3 Results

In the analyzed repositories it was identified the prevalence of organization schemes driven by topics, with three main patterns of schemes for organizing information: oriented by institutional structure; guided by the knowledge areas and oriented by document's types, besides the significant presence of hybrid scheme, mixing elements of different schemes of representation on the same hierarchical levels (Fig. 1).

Fig. 1. Navigation oriented by organizational scheme based on administrative structure at http://www.repositorio.ufop.br/.

The frequency of different schemes found in the repositories are shown on Table 1.

Table 1. Document organization schemes found in institutional repositories of Brazilian federal universities.

Community	Subcommunity	Collection	#	Example
Campus	Program/department	Document type	12	http://repositorio.unb.br/
	College/course	Document type	3	http://repositorio.bc.ufg.br/
	Document type	Course	1	http://200.129.241.122/
Center	Program/course	Document type	1	http://guaiaca.ufpel.edu.br/
College	Program/course	Document type	2	http://repositorio.ufjf.br/
Occupation Field	–	Document type	2	www.utfpr.edu.br/riut
Document Type	Campus	Center	1	http://www.repositorio.ufal.br/
	Knowledge area	Course	1	http://www.locus.ufv.br/
	Great knowledge area	Knowledge area	1	http://dspace.unipampa.edu.br: 8080/xmlui
	Document subtype	Knowledge area	1	http://www.lume.ufrgs.br/
	Program	Course	1	http://repositorio.uft.edu.br/
Knowledge area	College/department/Course	Document type	3	http://ri.ufs.br:8080/
Hybrid	Hybrid	Hybrid	6	http://dspaceprod02.grude. ufmg.br/

Another form of organization found was by document type, where the user chooses between the kind of academic work, and then choose the area of knowledge or the associated institutional program. Figure 2 shows an example of this organization scheme.

A third type identified was navigation guided by organization schemes based in knowledge areas, where the user initially selects the area of knowledge wanted to access, then the administrative department, and finally the type of document. As illustrated in Fig. 3.

In some cases, form of hybrid organization was identified, using schemes of different natures in the organization of communities, sub-communities and collections, as presented in Fig. 4.

A summary of the survey is shown in Fig. 5: three different organization schemes of collections in repositories were identified, with prevalence of the schemes representing administrative structures. In universities such organization schemes are almost unanimously, considering that universities have stable administrative structures, known and accepted by academia, with intrinsic thematic representation, having a disciplinary organization based on knowledge classification, as in mathematics, physics or chemistry departments. However, classification of scholar works from interdisciplinary courses can be problematic under this approach.

Fig. 2. Navigation by document type at http://www.locus.ufv.br/

Fig. 3. Navigation area of knowledge at https://ri.ufs.br/

Fig. 4. Navigation oriented by hybrid schemes at https://repositorio.ufma.br/

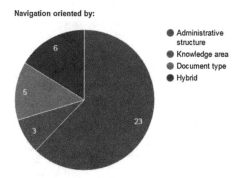

Fig. 5. Distribution of content organization schemes in repositories (Color figure online)

4   Conclusion

Hybrid organizational schemes appear in the survey in the intent to concile categories belonging to different organizations, in order to better classify institutional work. According to [4] "it is often difficult to agree upon any one scheme, so people throw the elements of multiple schemes together in a confusing mix" (p. 68). This reveals the need for studies aimed at organizing collections in such repositories.

Finally, the representation of the institutional structure in the organization of repositories can reveal the urgency in taxonomy studies for classification of items, since many users may not be familiar with institution's structure. Also, in some cases, a course and its intellectual production may be linked to different faculties or departments, complicating documents recovery under this structure, lowering usability.

References

1. Björk, B.C.: Scientific communication life-cycle model (2005). http://oacs.shh.fi/publications/Model35explanation2.pdf
2. Harnad, S., et al.: The access/impact problem and the green and gold roads to open access (2004). http://eprints.soton.ac.uk/265852/2/serev-revised.pdf
3. Leite, F.C.L., Costa, S.M.S.: Repositórios institucionais como ferramentas de gestão do conhecimento científico no ambiente acadêmico. Perspectivas em Ciência da Informação **11** (2), 206–219 (2006)
4. Morville, P., Rosenfeld, L.: Information Architecture for the World Wide Web, p. 504. Sebastopol, O'Reilly Media (2006)
5. Murakami, T.R.M., Fausto, S.: Panorama atual dos Repositórios Institucionais das Instituições de Ensino Superior no Brasil. InCID: Revista de Ciência da Informação e Documentação, Brasil, 4(2), pp. 185–201, dez. 2013. ISSN 2178-2075. http://dx.doi.org/10.11606/issn.2178-2075.v4i2p185-201

A Practical Approach to Icon Taxonomy

Teemu Korpilahti[✉]

Aalto University, Helsinki, Finland
`teemu.korpilahti@aalto.fi`

Abstract. There have been various studies and attempts for classifying icons according to semiotic principles. Comparing these systems with each other, it seems the discussion is verging on semantics as much as it is on semiotics. What is needed is a more concrete and practical system. One that can be adopted by designers, even without a very profound understanding of semiotic theory. This paper proposes a practical approach to icon taxonomy and presents survey data that has been gathered to validate some of the basic assumptions of the system.

Keywords: Interface · Icon · Interface design · Taxonomy · Semiotics

1 Background

According to Charles Sanders Peirce all signs can be classified into **icons, symbols** and **indexes** based on the signs relation to the referent. In this system an icon is limited to a representation that resembles its object. An index carries an actual connection to its object. A symbol in contrast has no visual connection to its object [1].

In the context of interface design the icon has acquired a more general meaning where it stands for any visual representation that denotes an action, a setting or a content type. Compared to semiotics it covers all the three major phenomenological categories.

There have been various studies and attempts for classifying icons. Webb et al [2] wrote an article about potential ways for evaluating icons already in 1989. The authors recognized three main icon categories:

1. **Picture** – Realistic depiction of system object or function. These are most detailed and easiest to interpret and remember.
2. **Symbol** – Emphasize critical feature by analogy or symbolism. These are simplified and most affected by context.
3. **Sign** – No intuitive connection between icon and referent. These are abstract, simple and association must be learned.

Wang et al. [3] compare this system with others such as Rogers [4], who recognized four main types **resemblance, exemplar, symbolic** and **arbitrary**, or Lidwell et al's [5] system of **similar, example, symbolic** and **arbitrary.** All-in-all they compare nine different existing systems and propose one of their own. But categories overlap and different researchers use different terminology sometimes to describe what in essence is the same thing. What is needed is a more concrete and practical system. One that can be

© Springer International Publishing Switzerland 2016
C. Stephanidis (Ed.): HCII 2016 Posters, Part I, CCIS 617, pp. 259–263, 2016.
DOI: 10.1007/978-3-319-40548-3_43

adopted by interface designers and professionals even without a very profound understanding of semiotic theory.

2   A Practical Approach to Icon Taxonomy

Per Mollerup [6] has devised a system for classifying trademarks that is a good benchmark for designing a practical approach to icon taxonomy. To build this system Mollerup has defined the following five rules a functional taxonomy must comply with.

1. It must consist of classes that are distinct. The differences between the classes must be clear so there is no room for misunderstanding to which class an item belongs to.
2. The characteristics the classes are based on should be used consistently and each step in the classification should be based on a single principle of division.
3. There should be no overlapping between classes. Parallel (co-ordinate) classes should be exclusive.
4. Co-ordinate classes should be able to collectively cover all possible entries.
5. The classes should be relevant to the purpose of the taxonomy.

Proposed Basis for a Classification System. Following these rules, two basic classifications for icons can be proposed:

1. Is the icon abstract or concrete?
2. Is the icon logical or arbitrary?

The next step is to figure out how these two classifications could relate to each other, and can they somehow be used to construct a taxonomy tree. To clarify these relations following assumptions need to be considered:

1. An **arbitrary** icon can be either **concrete** or **abstract.**
2. A **logical** icon can only be **concrete.** And therefore an **abstract** icon can not be **logical.**

The second assumption is the weaker one, since the interpretation of whether or not something is concrete can be very subjective. For instance – is a geometric arrow concrete or abstract?

3   Survey Results

The functionality of the proposed main classifications and their relations were tested in an online survey. The purpose of the survey was not to collect extensive data from a variety different user demographics. The majority of the participants were designers, design students and IT professionals, with just a few exceptions. 119 participants took part in the survey, 79 of which were Finnish. In all there were participants with 22 different nationalities ranging from United States and Germany, to Iran and China.

58 % of the participants were male and 42 % Female. The majority of the respondents (49 %) were 30 to 40 years old, with the entire range being between 10 and 57 years.

The participants were asked to describe their skills in using digital devices on a five step range: very good, good, average, poor, or very poor.

66 % of the respondents described their skills as very good, 28 % good, and the rest 6 % average.

They were also asked how often they found it difficult to understand the meaning of interface icons or buttons. This was also measured on a five step range: very rarely, rarely, occasionally, often, or very often.

29 % of the respondents replied very rarely, 40 % rarely, 29 % occasionally, and 2 % often. So it seems, that even skillful users sometimes encounter problems in understanding interface icons.

Importance of Context. The survey asked the participants to classify a set of twenty icons (Fig. 1) through two questions:

1. Is the icon abstract or concrete?
2. Is the icon logical or arbitrary?

In addition to this, they were asked to shortly name what they thought each of the icons stands for, i.e. what is its meaning or function. The purpose of this question was to verify, that the user had correctly recognized the icon. It was clear from the answers, that some of the icons could be understood in a variety of ways, and others were not always recognized at all. The lack of context is one important factor in this. For instance, the magnifying glass was recognized as both a search and magnifying tool. Similarly, the cross icon that stands for closing or deleting, was also recognized as the symbol for irritating substances.

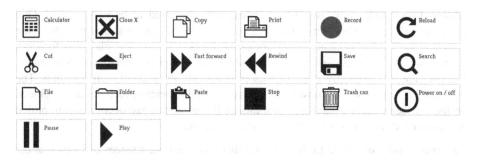

Fig. 1. The icon set that was used in the survey

Accuracy of the Classification. The total number of icon classifications was 2380 (119 participants classified 20 icons). Out of these, there were 242 cases where the icon had not been correctly recognized. Therefore, 89.8 % percent of the data was valid, and this part of it was analyzed further.

One of the main motivations for this study was to find out how strong correlation there is in concrete icons being dominantly logical, and abstract ones being arbitrary.

Table 1 shows the percentage of replies that classified each icon as concrete and logical. So that 0 % concrete equals 100 % abstract and 0 % logical equals 100 % arbitrary.

Table 1. Summary of the survey data

Icon	% Concrete	% Logical	Icon	% Concrete	% Logical
Calculator	99,1	90,6	Play	14,4	58,5
Close X	2,3	36,8	Power	9,1	24,2
Copy	83,1	77,1	Printer	98,1	91,3
Cut	96,6	94,1	Record	9,1	20,2
Eject	10,7	36,9	Reload	13	59,3
Fast forward	14,3	65,5	Rewind	14,3	65,5
File	94	76,1	Save	94	70,9
Folder	98,2	92	Search	87,8	81,6
Paste	81	58,3	Stop	4,8	21,2
Pause	7	23,5	Trash can	99,2	97,5

The differentiation between concrete and abstract icons is very strong. All of the icons were either below 14.4 % or above 81 % concrete. The differentiation in logical versus arbitrary was not as clear. There was a cluster of strong logical icons, among which the strongest icons were trash can (97.5 %), cut (94.1 %), and printer (91.3 %). There was also a very clear correlation with concrete icons being logical.

Abstract and Arbitrary. In abstract icons, there appeared to be two clusters. One comprised of strongly arbitrary icons. The other cluster of icons was above 58 % in the logical scale. This group consisted of the arrow icons of the survey: play, fast forward, rewind, and reload. It is clear, that arrows were considered as abstract representations. Yet they are so commonly used, that users intuitively understand their meaning. The origin of the arrow symbol most likely derives from the concrete archer's arrow object. So the case seems to be, that the appearance of the arrow has just become so simplified and abstracted, that it is no longer considered concrete.

Arbitrary and Concrete. In this icon set there were no occurrences of icons that are clearly arbitrary and concrete at the same time. The paste icon comes closest to this, being 81 % concrete and only 58,3 % logical. It would seem, that icons are most commonly in this group, if the metaphor or descriptive relation of the icon (signifier) and its signified is weak from the beginning, or becomes unclear over time.

4 Summary and Future Work

The preliminary survey confirmed the proposed main classifications effective in the sense that the data showed clear differentiation between the alternatives. In addition, certain correlations were discovered, such as concrete icons being logical and abstract icons being mostly arbitrary.

Starting to build a clean and simple taxonomy tree from these two main classifications is still a challenge since there was some surprising overlapping in the data, such as the existence of a group of icons that were classified as abstract and logical. Dividing the main classes into subclasses should also be examined. The logical icons could for instance be divided to descriptive and metaphorical ones.

Another interesting aspect and challenge for the classification is how icons can loose their logical meaning over time. This phenomenon is apparent in the case of the classic floppy disk save icon that is still commonly used in some software, despite the fact that it no longer bears no logical meaning to younger users.

The project website www.iconresearch.net provides further information about the surveys and the research topic.

References

1. Rayan, A., Hubner, R.: Pictograms Icons and Signs. Thames & Hudson Ltd., London (2006)
2. Webb, J.M., Sorenson, P.F., Lyons, N.P.: An empirical approach to the evaluation of icons. SIGCHI Bull. **21**(1), 87–90 (1989)
3. Wang, H.-F., Hung, S.-H., Liao, C.-C.: A survey of icon taxonomy used in the interface design. In: Proceedings of the ECCE 2007 Conference, London, pp. 28–31 (2007)
4. Rogers, Y.: Icons at interface: their usefulness. Interact. Comput. **1**(1), 105–117 (1989)
5. Lidwell, W., Holden, K., Butler, J.: Universal Principles of Design. Rockport Publishers, Massachusetts (2003)
6. Mollerup, P.: Marks of Excellence. Phaidon Press Limited, London (1997)

User Interface for Customizing Patents Search: An Exploratory Study

Arthi M. Krishna$^{(\boxtimes)}$, Brian Feldman, Joseph Wolf, Greg Gabel, Scott Beliveau, and Thomas Beach

United States Patent and Trademark Office, Alexandria, VA, USA
{arthi.krishna, brian.feldman, joseph.wolf, greg.gabel, scott.beliveau, thomas.beach}@uspto.gov

Abstract. Prior art searching is a critical and knowledge-intensive step in the examination process of a patent application. Historically, the approach to automated prior art searching is to determine a few keywords from the patent application and, based on simple text frequency matching of these keywords, retrieve published applications and patents. Several emerging techniques show promise to increase the accuracy of automated searching, including analysis of: named entity extraction, explanations of how patents are classified, relationships between references cited by the examiner, weighing words found in some sections of the patent application differently than others, and lastly using the examiners' domain knowledge such as synonyms. These techniques are explored in this study. Our approach is firstly, to design a user interface that leverages the above-mentioned processing techniques for the user and secondly, to provide visual cues that can guide examiner to fine tune search algorithms. The user interface displays a number of controls that affect the behavior of the underlying search algorithm—a tag cloud of the top keywords used to retrieve patents, sliders for weights on the different sections of a patent application (e.g., abstract, claims, title or specification), and a list of synonyms and stop-words. Users are provided with visual icons that give quick indication of the quality of the results, such as whether the results share a feature with the patent-at-issue, such as both citing to the same reference or having a common classification. This exploratory study shows results of seven variations of the search algorithm on a test corpus of 100500 patent documents.

Keywords: Patent similarity · Prior art search · User interface design

1 Introduction

Searching for prior art is one of the most critical, time-intensive aspects of patent examination. Searching is like navigating through ocean waters, using beacons to avoid rough shorelines and to reach the correct destinations. There is an ocean of prior art available today in the form of patents, published applications and non-patent literature. Examiners use beacons in the form of search tools and databases to navigate the prior art ocean. And in doing so, they aim to avoid irrelevant references - i.e. rocky shorelines–and apply the relevant ones - i.e. to reach the correct destinations.

© Springer International Publishing Switzerland 2016
C. Stephanidis (Ed.): HCII 2016 Posters, Part I, CCIS 617, pp. 264–269, 2016.
DOI: 10.1007/978-3-319-40548-3_44

Automatic prior art retrieval algorithms, if accurate, can assist expert examiners by identifying literature that would otherwise take substantial research to uncover. Examiners today have access to an automated search tool, PLUS - the Patent Linguistic Utility Services, which is limited in its usability. PLUS uses a typical approach to automating prior art search, namely determining a select few keywords from the input patent application and retrieving published patent documents that exhibit a high level of textual similarity to these keywords. However, simple keyword searches have limited utility in the patent prosecution context because of the high prevalence of uncommon language patterns [8] and intentional creation by patent applications of 'abstract vocabulary' specific to their claimed invention. Thus, there has been extensive research on how keyword matching can be augmented by various techniques such as using classification systems and citations within references [1, 2, 4].

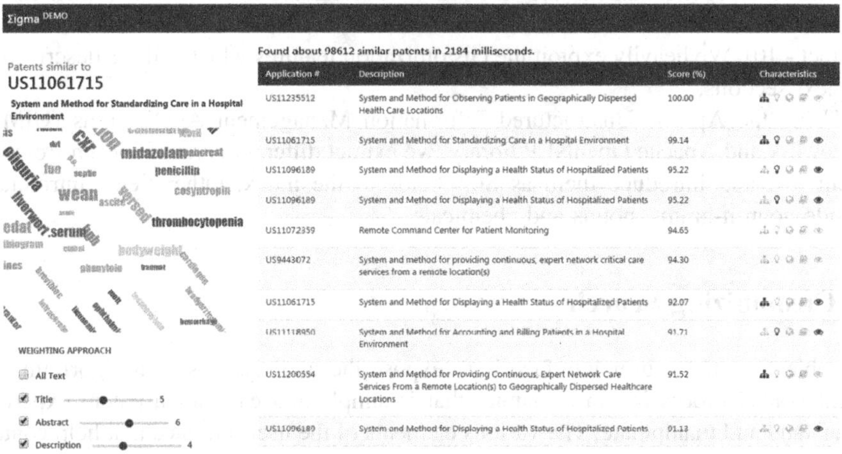

Fig. 1. Interface shows patents results similar to US11061715

Our new approach to building a reliable automated prior art search system is two-fold. Firstly, we build a search system that not only performs the basic keyword searches, but also has several layers of augmented processing techniques that can be controlled and modified as the search progresses. By designing a user interface (Fig. 1) that allows the expert to alter the behavior of search algorithm, for instance defining the relative weights of different sections of the patent (e.g., title, claims, specification and abstract), experts can create strategies of patent retrieval algorithms best suited to examining a particular application. Secondly, the user interface has quick visual cues that provide immediate feedback regarding the quality of the patent search results. For example, visual indicators show whether the input patent belongs to the same "patent family" as the result, thereby helping the user judge the quality of the patents search.

2   Implementation

We use Apache Solr Lucene [6] open source search system with cloud capability (version 5.1) to implement the core of the patent search system tool, which hereafter we refer to as Sigma. The web-based user interface for Sigma is built using AngularJS.

The patent text available in public corpus (http://patents.reedtech.com/) is ingested into Solr indices with the following Solr fields – id, title, abstract, claims, specification and full_text. Lucene uses term frequency – inverse document frequency (tf-idf) [7] calculations for text relevancy and retrieval. Among Solr's various built in query parsers, such as Simple and Field query parsers, the MoreLikeThis query parser, which can take an entire document as the input and retrieve other documents similar to it, is the one we choose for this implementation. The MoreLikeThis parser finds the top unique terms in the input document, and uses these terms to retrieve related documents. A number of customizations are allowed by MoreLikeThis at runtime, such as the number of terms to be searched and the "boost" or importance of Solr fields (e.g. abstract - 10). We heavily exploit the customization features which will be described in the next sections.

Using the Apache Unstructured Information Management Applications (UIMA) framework and Apache OpenNLP library, we extract different parts of speech from the patent text and introduce them as Solr fields to the index. Other fields introduced include noun n-grams, nouns and chemicals.

3   Customizing Search

The objective of the user interface is to expose the underlying search algorithm and patent related processing in a manner that is simple and easy for a patent expert to understand and manipulate. The various elements of the user interface that help control the search algorithm are detailed in this section.

3.1   Weights for Patent Sections

A considerable amount of research has been done on how the words in the different sections of a patent [3] such as claims and abstract, affect the relevancy of the results. By allowing the users to select which sections of the patent they would like to use for matching and how much relative weight to assign to the words in these sections, we are able to allow users to optimize their search.

As shown in Fig. 2, we expose the different sections of the patents—abstract, claims, title and description—as options that can be checked or unchecked, and the sliders next to them control the weights. The option of choosing the patent sections to compare is a powerful tool, as for example the claim-to-claim comparison of patents can provide insights into double patenting, a phenomenon where the same invention is attempted to be patented more than once by the applicant. We can offer this flexibility to the user by indexing the various patent sections as different Solr fields and assigning different boost values to these fields through the payload to the search call.

WEIGHTING APPROACH

☐ All Text

☑ Title ————————●——————————— 4

☑ Abstract ————————————●——— 7

☑ Description —————————●———— 5

☑ Claims ——————————●—————— 5

Fig. 2. Sections of patents are chosen with different weights assigned through sliders

3.2 Natural Language Processing

Gerunds in claims have been studied to be an indicator of the strength of the claims. Other parts of speech, such as noun phrases [10], are shown correlated to the relevancy of patent similarity results. However, the benefits to emphasizing on different parts of speech are not uniform across the different patents subject matters; for example, the business methods patents tend to have a large portion of the invention described in verbs instead of nouns. The user interface exposes the different part of speech and chemical matching as options that the user can control as required by the subject area of interest.

3.3 Input Words

Select words from the patent application are used for matching with the corpus of patents available. As we have seen in the previous sections the weights influence the ranking of these words. The words chosen and their corresponding weights are displayed as a word cloud at the left margin of the interface as shown in Fig. 3. In this initial effort, we are able to let the user choose the number of top words to consider, and we limit it to the 25–500 range in order to avoid overloading the system. Users can explicitly exclude any of the words in the tag cloud in order to restrict the results. Also, a limited list of synonyms can be inputted and WordNet [9] synonym support maybe turned on if desired.

Fig. 3. Tag cloud of interesting terms in the patent US11061715

4 Validation Indicators

To follow up on our approach of letting patent experts to fine tune the patent search algorithm, we expose visual cues that make it easy for the experts to judge the quality of the results. Each result has a number of indicators which show signs of how the result is related to the patent application. If a patent is listed as being in the same family as the patent application, ⚱ indicator is colored in. Patent documents within a family tends to be the most related to each other with a high degree of similarity. The CPC (Cooperative Patent Classification) ♀ and USPC (United States Patent Classification) ⊘ indicators are shown active if the patent application shares at least one CPC or USPC class respectively with the patent application. Any overlap in the patents cited by the result and the patents cited by the patent application results in the reference indicator ⊟ being on. The shared art unit indicator ☙ reflects if the input patent application and the result have been assigned to examiners in the same art unit.

5 Preliminary Results

The United States Patent Office created a test corpus of 100500 patent documents with 60300 granted patents and 40200 pre-grant publications. 8 sample searches across the different technical domains has been conducted by specialists in the fields, and the handpicked best references has been made available for testing.

The Sigma tool has been stood up on one Amazon Web Services (AWS) m3 server with 2 CPU, 3.75 GB RAM and 32 GB attached storage. We used 6 different settings of the search algorithm to do preliminary analysis of the performance. The table shows the PRES [5] results across the different technology areas.

Though on average algorithm 3 seems to do the best, as shown in Fig. 4, no one algorithm has shown to be superior across all the various technology areas (areas C & H do well on algorithm 4). These are preliminary results were obtained on a limited dataset, and a small subset of the algorithms available; future work is needed to verify.

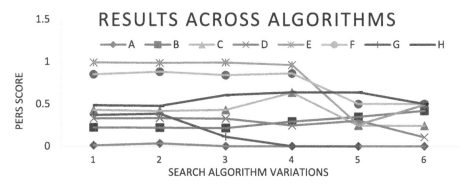

Fig. 4. The chart shows the scores of technology areas A through H on 6 variations of the search algorithms.

6   Conclusions and Future Work

Automated prior art search systems are useful to patent examiners when they are highly accurate. By augmenting simple keyword search algorithms with features that the experts can manipulate, our early results show promise that we can improve one of the most critical, time-intensive aspects of patent examination.

Our preliminary findings are based on a limited corpus of only patent applications. Given the importance of navigating the entire ocean of prior art, we will soon be expanding this corpus to include non-patent literature such as scientific research papers and foreign documents. We will investigate ways to leverage established linkages between prior art references and patent applications to improve the search algorithm results. These results also suggest that the customized algorithms have different optimizations for different settings. Future research will involve exploring how examiners alter the behavior of the search algorithm and ways to validate how examiners use the results. By capturing these settings, we will explore the development of a feedback loop to optimize the behavior of the search algorithm using a "committee of experts" approach and to facilitate knowledge transfer between examiners.

Acknowledgements. We would like to thank David Chiles, Joseph Bailey, Jamie Kucab, Aaron Pepe, Zoin Amir, Arva Adams, Jamie Simpson, Brigit Baron, Terrel Morris and Britt Hanley for their support.

References

1. Bashir, S., Rauber, A.: Improving retrievability of patents in prior art search. In: European Conference on Information Retrieval, pp. 457–470 (2010)
2. Fujii, A.: Enhancing patent retrieval by citation analysis. In: Proceedings of SIGIR 2007 (2007)
3. D'hondt, E., Verberne, S.: Conference and Labs of the Evaluation Forum and Intellectual Property (CLEF-IP) 2010: Prior Art Retrieval using the different sections in patent documents. In: Braschler, M., et al. (2010)
4. Herbert, B., Szarvas, G., Gurevych, I.: Prior art search using international patent classification codes and all-claims-queries. In: Peters, C., Di Nunzio, G.M., Kurimo, M., Mandl, T., Mostefa, D., Peñas, A., Roda, G. (eds.) CLEF 2009. LNCS, vol. 6241, pp. 452–459. Springer, Heidelberg (2010)
5. Magdy, W., Jones, G.J.: PRES: a score metric for evaluating recall-oriented information retrieval applications. In: Proceedings of the 33rd International ACM (2010)
6. Smiley, D., Pugh, E., Parisa, K., Mitchell, M.: Apache Solr 4 Enterprise Search Server, 1st edn. Packt Publishing, Birmingham (2014)
7. Wu, H.C., Luk, R.W.P., Wong, K.F., Kwok, K.L.: Interpreting TF-IDF term weights as making relevance decisions. ACM Trans. Inf. Syst. **26** (2008)
8. Verberne, S., D'hondt, E., Oostdijk, N., Koster, C: Quantifying the challenges in parsing patent claims. In: Proceedings AsPIRe (2010)
9. Fellbaum, C.: WordNet: An Electronic Lexical Database. MIT Press, Cambridge (1998)
10. Andersson, L., Mahdabi, P., Hanbury, A., Rauber, A.: Exploring patent passage retrieval using nouns phrases. In: Serdyukov, P., Braslavski, P., Kuznetsov, S.O., Kamps, J., Rüger, S., Agichtein, E., Segalovich, I., Yilmaz, E. (eds.) ECIR 2013. LNCS, vol. 7814, pp. 676–679. Springer, Heidelberg (2013)

Identification of Food Allergens by Using Relief Pictograms in Food Packaging

João Mesquita[1](✉), António Silva[2], and Bruno Giesteira[3]

[1] University of Porto, Porto, Portugal
joao.m.m.mesquita@gmail.com
[2] University of Porto - Disabled Students Support Services, Porto, Portugal
amcsilva@letras.up.pt
[3] University of Porto - Design Department, Porto, Portugal
bgiesteira@fba.up.pt

Abstract. Many of the 17 million Europeans who suffer from food allergies could benefit from a more direct information system in the identification of the 14 allergens regulated by the Parliament and Council Regulation (EU) n° 1169/2011 in packages of food products. This study aimed at creating pictograms representing these 14 allergens along visual and tactile lines, through relief printing. Based on Inclusive Design approach, the project meant to overcome restrictions such as sight impairment or illiteracy. Making use of User Centered Design (UCD) methodology, and with the support of the SAED (Disabled Students Support Services of the University of Porto) and GAENEE-UP (Support Office for Students with Special Educational Needs of the University of Porto), it employed field observation processes, in which potential users recorded their tactile perception of basic elements of visual communication. The result is the creation of a universal code, which is meant to satisfy the expectations and needs of potential users, namely people with impaired sight.

Keywords: Food · Allergens · Pictograms · Relief · Packaging

1 Introduction

Accessibility is the creation of products or services for people with disabilities and/or for multiple use contexts. The concept of accessible design is both the creation of products or services that can be used by the disabled without the need of external help, but also creating a compatibility with the technology they already use.

This project was developed in this scope, with the purpose of creating a unique and universal code that could help two specific groups of disabled people: The 2–4 % adults and 6 % children under three (Europe)[1] and 2 % adults and about 5 % children (USA)[2] that suffer from food allergies and the visually impaired. The main objective

---

[1] http://ec.europa.eu/research/infocentre/article_en.cfm?id=/research/star/index_en.cfm?p=64&item=All&artid=&caller=SuccessStories, 30/03/2016.

[2] http://www.fda.gov/Food/GuidanceRegulation/GuidanceDocumentsRegulatoryInformation/Allergens/ucm106187.htm, 30/03/2016.

© Springer International Publishing Switzerland 2016
C. Stephanidis (Ed.): HCII 2016 Posters, Part I, CCIS 617, pp. 270–275, 2016.
DOI: 10.1007/978-3-319-40548-3_45

was the creation of signs that represented the 14 allergens regulated by the European Union, under the Parliament and Council (EU) Regulation n° 1169/2011. Moreover, after careful consideration, this project was based on Inclusive Design, since we wanted it to be of use to everyone, thereby overcoming possible consumer restrictions, such as blindness and/or visual acuity deficit, reduced knowledge of more technical vocabulary, or even illiteracy.

According to the World Health Organization, there are 285 million people estimated to be visually impaired worldwide: 39 million are blind and 246 have low vision. Furthermore, 82 % of people living with blindness are aged 50 and above.[3]

In this paper we will explain how the process of creating these signs was conducted, as well as the framework that underlies it.

In Sect. 2 "Problem and Methodology" we have focused on the fact that the visually impaired struggled with the problem of not being able to identify any components in a food package, because they are not inclusive. Moreover, we will explain the methodology used in the creation of the 14 pictograms and the problems that arose from this.

In Sect. 3 "Preliminary Results" we will focus on the results obtained with the tests undertook and explain how we finally decided on a viable model for these pictograms to work for everyone that uses it.

Section 4, the Conclusion, reflects the results we obtained with the tests we undertook and the explanation of how we overcame the issues that arose.

2   Problem and Methodology

Systems are frequently designed without taking into account what is really important – the end-user.

User-Centered Design (UCD) is the process of designing a system or a tool considering the needs and expectations of the end-user, with his intervention along the development process of the end-user. Instead of requiring the user to adapt to the referred tool or system, the system is created in order to correspond to the users' needs or existing behaviors. The result of applying User Centered Design to a system is a product that is user-friendly, potentially more inclusive, supporting the user with a better experience and helps the user in their experience with the product.

In this sense, the main purpose of this study is to aid the user who buys packages of food products identify the allergens in each food product.

Thus, our first approach to this issue implied undertaking tests with blind people in several aspects, through structured and unstructured interviews, focus-groups, and questionnaires.

Initially we set up a survey with the purpose of identifying the kind of blindness the users had, for how long had they been blind, if they had food allergies, and if they experienced difficulties identifying the presence of food allergens in the packages of the products they bought.

---

[3] http://www.who.int/mediacentre/factsheets/fs282/en/, 31/03/2016.

The group that participated in the survey consisted mainly of people with acquired blindness as an adult, caused by different diseases. However, we concluded that the majority of the participants is unable to read braille, making it almost impossible to include the information using that writing system.

In a second phase of the study, the users were presented with the 14 allergens in solid form, in order to register their tactile perception, namely at the level of the basic elements of visual communication (e.g., point; line; texture; scale) relative to each of the substances. The idea is to identify the parts (tactile identification) in order to transpose them to a visual and tactile whole, the pictogram, thus basing this study in the theory of Gestalt that states that "The whole is greater than the sum of the parts".

The results of these tests differ, depending on weather the user was born blind or had acquired blindness.

The purpose of this test was to understand which tactile characteristics of each product were identified by the users, thus starting with a tactile approach.

The main purpose of this test was to gather as many tactile characteristics reported by the users as possible, and understanding which ones are repeated among themselves and which are the most relevant ones. After this, we intend to apply the reported characteristics to the relief pictograms.

In the third phase of the project, we tested 14 pictograms printed in relief, which represent the 14 allergens. These pictograms were built based on simple geometric shapes, using only five elements: the square, the circle, the triangle, lines and dots.

Following this, the 14 allergens were divided into three categories: animal origin, plant origin and chemical origin. Each geometric shape corresponds to one category. The square corresponds to the elements of animal origin, the circle corresponds to the elements of plant origin, and the triangle corresponds to the elements of chemical origin.

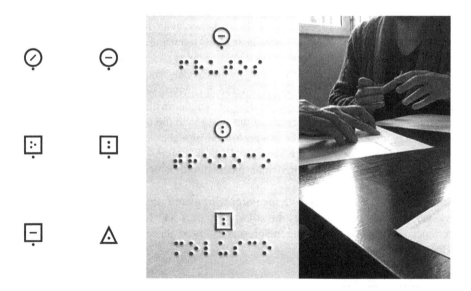

Fig. 1. Project evolution – creation, printing, and tests

The lines and dots compose the inner part of each pictogram, thus identifying the allergen intended.

These pictograms were tested in several sizes: 2 cm, 1 cm and 0.5 cm.

The purpose of testing the size of the test was to understand which minimal size was perceived by the users.

The size that caused the best reaction among the users was 1 cm.

After having categorized the allergens in the three origins, we asked the users to identify which of the identified geometric shapes (circle, square, and triangle) they associated to each origin.

Similarly, we tried to understand which type of printing was most perceivable by the users. We tested two types of printing: one version with dots (very similar to braille) using the Viewplus Spotdot Embosser technology and one version with continuous printing using the Zy-Fuse technology. We had the support of the Office for Inclusion - GPI of University of Minho with the printing with the Zy-Fuse technology (Fig. 1).

3 Preliminary Results

In a first experience we created multiple geometric shapes, such as the circle, the ellipsis, the square, the rectangle, and the hexagon. We also created several organic shapes, such as a tree, a man, an egg, and an apple.

All of these shapes had several sizes between 2 cm and 0,5 cm and with various strokes, between 1 mm and 0,35 mm, all of them fully filled in.

We concluded that the organic shapes are too complex in order to be sensed through the tactile experience and the attempt to read them is very time-consuming.

As for the geometric shapes, the rectangle, the ellipsis and the hexagon did not work for the users. All of the participants said that they thought the ellipsis was a circle and the rectangle was a square. The hexagon did not receive any positive feedback, as none of the users had a mental image of this shape.

This was very conclusive as it made us base this project in the use of geometric shapes the least complex as possible.

The reason why we made a correspondence between the allergens and the geometric shapes was a matter of simplicity. In fact, we associate, maybe in a rather emotional way, the geometric shapes to sensations and signs. In this sense, it was normal to relate these shapes with the three divisions we created. Moreover, we also wanted to make a symbolic link between the elements. In fact, we naturally make an association between the *Forbidden* sign and a triangle. On the other hand, the circle is by definition the representation of Nature, the organic, which makes sense in the categorization. Finally, although the square is more the representation of precision and stability, this is an advantage for this code, because it makes it perceivable.

The tactile test caused some constraints to the participants, since they were asked to identify characteristics in allergens such as crustaceans, fish or molluscs. These allergens often caused some discomfort due to their strong odor and to their consistency.

On the other hand, we had some difficulties in presenting some of the allergens to the group. Allergens such as soy, mustard, milk or sulphite exist in many possible forms, including in a liquid state. For this reason, these four allergens were not used in the following tactile approach.

As for the tests with the relief printing, results have shown that the use of continuous printing has a more positive reaction from the users, as well as simple shapes, such us the above mentioned geometric shapes and the line.

The dots do not seem to be viable, because due to the thickness of the paper, in the final printing, they might turn into lines, thus creating a wrong pictogram or one very similar to an existing one. This situation is liable to mislead the consumer.

4   Conclusion

A pictogram code has an advantage over braille language for three main reasons. On the one hand, braille is a language that requires much space in order to be written. Also, the information in the packages has been growing to a point that there is not so much room left to insert new information. And at last, maybe the most important reason, is that most blind people, especially the ones with acquired blindness in their adulthood, are actually incapable of reading braille.

This project has the capacity of creating new codes as needed. It has a framework under which it is very simple to include any new allergen that is regulated in the future. This happens through an increasingly better system of questions that allows identifying the most important tactile characteristics for the creation of a new pictogram.

By asking the user about the shape, texture, volume and size of the solid product we are making a results-oriented approach that enables us to avoid questions that do not have a direct answer and that might lead the investigators to an error. The parameters being analyzed are rather simple and allow us the fast creation of new pictograms without the hassle of having to create a new code.

The pictograms follow the production of the products with braille. In what refers to the packaging, one of the solutions being analyzed to avoid increasing the price of production is using already existent techniques, in order to avoid to high an investment in production.

Also, this code has the potential to be used in computational contexts, following the new 3D techniques, which makes it very adaptable in the future.

At the moment, this project is focused in the 14 allergens regulated in Europe by the EC. However, the project intends to create pictograms for new allergens that might be regulated in the future, which is the case of natural latex in Brazil, mango in Thailand and royal jelly in Australia and New Zeland.

References

1. The European Parliament and the Council of the European Union. L 304/18. Official Journal of the European Union (1169), 18–63 (2011). http://eur-lex.europa.eu/legal-content/EN/TXT/PDF/?uri=CELEX:32011R1169&from=pt. Accessed

2. Center for Food Safety and Applied Nutrition (n.d.). Allergens - Food Allergen Labeling and Consumer Protection Act of 2004 (Public Law 108-282, Title II). Center for Food Safety and Applied Nutrition. http://www.fda.gov/Food/GuidanceRegulation/GuidanceDocumentsRegu latoryInformation/Allergens/ucm106187.htm. Accessed
3. WHO | Visual impairment and blindness. (n.d.). http://www.who.int/mediacentre/factsheets/ fs282/en/. Accessed
4. Information Centre - Food allergies. (n.d.). http://ec.europa.eu/research/infocentre/article_en. cfm?id=/research/star/index_en.cfm?p=64&item=All&artid=&caller=SuccessStories. Accessed 7 Apr 2016

Enhancing Data Visualization Modes Through a Physical Representation: The "Makerometer" Solution

Antonio Opromolla[1,2], Massimiliano Dibitonto[1(✉)], Stefania Barca[1],
Sergio Frausin[1], Claudia Matera[1], and Carlo Maria Medaglia[1]

[1] Link Campus University, Rome, Italy
{a.opromolla,m.dibitonto,s.barca,s.frausin,
c.matera,c.medaglia}@unilink.it
[2] ISIA Roma Design, Rome, Italy

Abstract. In this work we investigate how a physical representation of a large amount of data could increase not only their value but also their understanding by the final users. Indeed, the use of visual metaphors related to a three-dimensional environment, specific of a physical representation, makes the access to the related information easier and "natural" if compared to those used in an only-digital environment. In this context, digital fabrication tools can be useful for fast prototyping and testing of different tools. In this work, we show one application of these concepts, "Makerometer", a solution installed at Maker Faire Rome 2015, which collects and visualizes the data related to this exhibition.

Keywords: Data visualization · Digital fabrication · Physical representation

1 Introduction

Data are an important patrimony of our contemporary society. Technologies play an important role in producing, managing and analysing them. One of the central challenges is to bring out the information from data, so that people are able to better understand specific events and to make right choices. The academic literature concerning the managing of data focuses on identifying data visualization methodologies and tools that aim to obtain an intelligible and usable information [1]. The main purpose is exploring how it can effectively reach people and meet their (different) needs.

The aim of our work is to explore how a physical representation of data can increase their value and improve their understanding. Such a representation allows to use visual metaphors different from the ones employed in an only digital environment. They use space and movement related elements, resulting more natural and easy to understand [2, 3], unlike the representations based only on digital tools that use more abstract (and so, more difficult to understand) metaphors. In this contest, the digital fabrication, which consists in creating solid and three-dimensional objects through the use of different manufacturing techniques and "open" software and hardware, can be used to make prototypes in a fast way, allowing the test of different tools for the data visualization [4].

© Springer International Publishing Switzerland 2016
C. Stephanidis (Ed.): HCII 2016 Posters, Part I, CCIS 617, pp. 276–281, 2016.
DOI: 10.1007/978-3-319-40548-3_46

2 The "Makerometer" Solution

In this work, we show one application of physical representation of big amount of data: the "Makerometer". It is designed and implemented for the Maker Faire Rome 2015 [5]. Through this solution, the visitors can express their mood related to their exhibition experience and check the moods of all the visitors of the five areas of the event. It allows to know the real time situation (e.g.: which the most crowded area is, which the most frequent mood is, etc.) and to make right choices concerning their movement within the exhibition (e.g.: to avoid the most crowded areas, to move towards the area which recorded the most positive moods, etc.). The visitors can express or consult six moods, split in three couples of opposite adjectives: inspired – bored; satisfied – unsatisfied; serene – stressed. Each of them is identified by an emoticon [6] and a characteristic colour (inspired: yellow; bored: red; satisfied: green; unsatisfied. violet; serene: blue; stressed: orange) basing on the definitions of the von Goethe's theory of colours [7]. The "Makerometer" solution consists in four components: mobile native application, web-based application, physical application and central server. They are available on three kinds of devices: smartphone, totem, and physical installation that allow to access to different visualization of the same data, depending from different needs and contexts of use.

The mobile native application (available for iOS and Android), which is the official application of the Maker Faire Rome 2015, allows the visitors to share their mood in a specific moment (Fig. 1), also sending their GPS position during their visit. The server collects these data, operates some calculations (e.g. geographical segmentation of the data, time series, and percentage calculation), and offers them to the other components through RESTful web services. Once the user accepts to use the app his/her GPS position is constantly sent. The system considers the user "active" if he/she is in the exhibition area. Moreover his/her vote is considered in the "real-time" percentage as long as he/she is in the area where the mood was expressed, while in the time series it is considered according to the sampling rate (5 min).

The web-based application allows to visualize the moodboard of the event visitors, split in the five different exhibition areas ("Next Tech", "Home, Cities and Environment", "Makers for Culture", "People&Life", and "Learning by Doing"). The Fig. 2 shows this representation. In this visualization, the light blue spheres represent the different areas. The percentage related to each area represents the "active" visitors tracked in that specific area in a specific interval of time (sampling rate 5 min). For each light blue sphere, the different moods are represented by six different spheres having the colour of the related mood. The size of the single sphere for each "area sphere" represents the number of visitors that have expressed that single mood and that are still in the area. Another sphere shows the total amount of people in the exhibition in that moment (according to the 5 min sampling interval).

The moodboard data can be also visualized on an interactive totem that allows to access to other statistics and visualizations concerning the same data (Fig. 3), including the heat map showing the concentration of people (Fig. 4), the time lapse (during the 3 days of the event) and the segmentation per area. This is made with a web-app optimized for touch interaction.

Fig. 1. Mobile native application: the choice of the moods

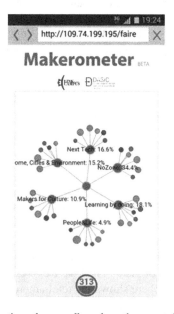

Fig. 2. Web-based application: the moodboard on the smartphone (color figure online)

The core of the "Makerometer" solution is the physical installation (Fig. 5), realized with an Arduino board and servomotors. This device, that we can define a "physical display", is composed by five rows, representing the five areas of the exhibition, and for

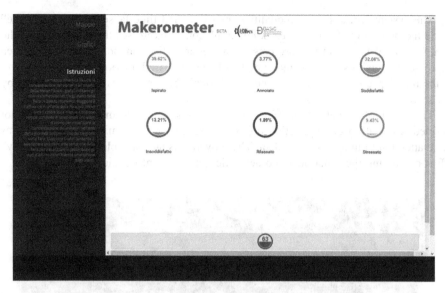

Fig. 3. Web-based application: a different visualization of the data related to the collected moods

Fig. 4. Web-based application: the heat map showing the concentration of people

each row there are seven physical spheres, representing the six moods plus the percentage of people present in that area (the "area population" sphere). These spheres can move up and down, according to the expressed percentage of moods. The higher the percentage, the more the single sphere is at the bottom. So, the user can fast note in real time the most populated area and for each area the prevalent mood.

The system works in two modalities: real-time and time lapse. In the "real-time" mode the percentage for the "area population" sphere expresses the percentage of the total visitors of the event that are present in that area. Each mood sphere of each area expresses the visitors of the single area that have expressed a mood and are still there. In the time lapse mode the devices go fast through the time series of data recorded by the server.

This kind of visualization offers a more immediate information, although not detailed, while the web application offers a more detailed information, but it requires more attention to understand the data. The movements and the colours create a "wow" effect combining the functional and aesthetic quality of information visualization.

Fig. 5. The physical installation of the "Makerometer" solution

3   Conclusions and Future Work

The prototype of the "Makerometer" solution used during the Maker Faire Rome 2015 event has been useful to collect the evaluations and the remarks of the visitors. Going beyond the positive results concerning the ease of use and the usefulness of a "physical" visualization of the data, a particular attention has been given to the identification of the fields of application of this solution. In particular, the visitors would use this solution also in the city environment (e.g.: to send and receive feedback from the different city areas), in the work environment (e.g.: to see the mood of the colleagues), and in the customer satisfaction sector (e.g.: to see the product's customers evaluations). In the future work we will apply this solution in one of these fields.

References

1. Zhao, J., Vande Moere, A.: Embodiment in data sculpture: a model of the physical visualization of information. In: Proceedings of the 3rd International Conference on Digital Interactive Media in Entertainment and Arts, pp. 343–350. ACM, New York (2008)
2. Vande Moere, A.: Beyond the tyranny of the pixel: exploring the physicality of information visualization. In: Proceedings of the 12th International Conference Information Visualisation, pp. 469–474. IEEE Computer Society, Washington (2008)
3. Spindler, M., Tominski, C., Schumann, H., Dachselt, R.: Tangible views for information visualization. In: International Conference on Interactive Tabletops and Surfaces, pp. 157–166. ACM, New York (2010)
4. Alexander, J., Jansen, Y., Hornbæk, K., Kildal, J., Karnik, A.: Exploring the challenges of making data physical. In: Proceedings of the 33rd Annual ACM Conference Extended Abstracts on Human Factors in Computing Systems, pp. 2417–2420. ACM, New York (2015)
5. Maker Faire. http://www.makerfairerome.eu/en/what-is-maker-faire
6. Park, J., Barash, V., Fink, C., Cha, M.: Emoticon style: interpreting differences in emoticons across cultures. In: Proceedings of the 7th International AAAI Conference on Weblogs and Social Media, pp. 466–475. AAAI Press, Palo Alto (2013)
7. von Goethe, J.W.: Zur Farbenlehre, Tubinga (1810)

Grid and Typography Guidelines to Inform Design of Digital Art Magazines

Ana Paula Retore, Cayley Guimarães(✉), and Marta Karina Leite

Federal Technological University, Curitiba, Parana, Brazil
aretore@alunos.utfpr.edu.br,
{cayleyg,martaleite}@utfpr.edu.br

Abstract. There is a lack of graphic design studies for grid and typography for digital objects. This paper presents grid and typography guidelines to inform the design of art magazines considering the usability aspects of the web. The research was comprised of bibliographical review and the analysis of the best and worst practices of how principles of grid and typography are applied on digital medias. The results of these analyses were compiled into the proposed guideline found to be valuable for designers.

Keywords: Grid · Typography · Guidelines · Web design

1 Introduction

Graphic Design has long studied grid and typography, but there are very few studies of such variables on digital artifacts [1]. A Grid organizes the page, giving it structure, hierarchy and consistency [2] in a very different manner on the web than on paper [3]. Typograpy is "[…] the means by which a visual form is given for a written idea […] a visual language that enhances power and clarity" [4]. Both typography and grid are vital to the final usability of a digital site [5]. This research proposes Grid and Typography Guidelines to inform the design of digital art magazines considering the usability aspects of the website media.

2 Methodology

The authors selected three variables: for Grid the variables are: Structure, Hierarchy, and Constancy and Variation; For Typography the variables are: Legibility, Hierarchy, and Identity. The authors analyzed five art magazines for their best and worst practices: three Brazilian magazines (DASartes, Select, and Zupi), one American (Triple Canopy), and one British (Aesthetica Magazine).

Figure 1 shows the methodology used: the authors selected from the theoretical references the Design principles and their variables regarding their application on the Web. Then the authors performed an expert evaluation of the websites of the selected art magazines as per best and worst practices. The overall findings were compiled into a set of Guidelines. The guidelines were user-tested and validated as per the UTAUT methodology, proposed by Venkatesh et al. [6].

© Springer International Publishing Switzerland 2016
C. Stephanidis (Ed.): HCII 2016 Posters, Part I, CCIS 617, pp. 282–286, 2016.
DOI: 10.1007/978-3-319-40548-3_47

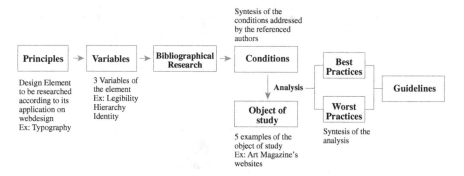

Fig. 1. Methodology

3   Elaboration of the Guidelines

The first step consisted of a thorough bibliographical research to identify design best practices and recommendations. With said recommendations, the authors analyzed the sites of the five Magazines. A total of 30 analyzes was performed, crossing six variables (three for grid plus three for typography) with five art magazines. Worst and best practices were found, as well as their recurrence in the studied websites. Worst practices were thus categorized due to lack of following the indicated conditions. The authors then compiled a series of ideas to help solve the problems. Best practices were considered as such because they met the pre-established requirements or because they have been shown to be functional and well applied in the design of websites.

As an example, Fig. 2 shows Triple Canopy Magazine as a successful illustration of how the guidelines can be implemented. The website has coherent alignments relating the header with the image at the bottom. It has a visible navigation, with the three lines fixed menu at the left top of the page. The images are fully shown on the screen, the grid of the pages vary in order to respect the different contents but also maintains consistency in order to keep the reference of the website. Regarding the typography options we can perceive that the font respects the text's function, calling for attention when necessary and being informative if it needs so. It has an identity coherent with the magazine's style, has a clear hierarchy, legibility and readability. The type size is accordant with the medium (in this case, a desktop screen).

The guidelines were derived by a compilation of the results into a series of best practices to be followed by designers to inform their future design. The guidelines related to grid are the following: (a) Coherent alignments (the grid must be coherent with the content); (b) Visible Navigation (important elements should be "on display"; (c) Visual elements arrangement (random display of content may prevent a good layout); (d) Proportions (make your images responsive); (e) Variation according to each page (grids should follow content and platform specificities); (f) Logical constancy (menu, footnotes and margins may have a fixed location); (g) Responsiveness. Guidelines for Typography: (a) Understand the function of the text (legibility, form etc.); (b) Typography has identity (it communicates subjective impressions);

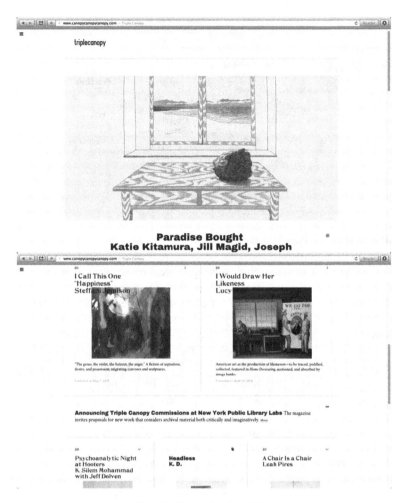

Fig. 2. Example of website

(c) Balance; (d) Hierarchy for organization; (e) Value Legibility and Readability; (f) Consider type size according to the medium; and (g) Adequate spacing.

4   Validation of the Guidelines

Initial validation came from the literature review that provided the theoretical base with which to create the guidelines. Then the authors used those guidelines to perform heuristic evaluation of websites of art magazines; the heuristics are presented elsewhere. Finally, an Intent of Use validation was performed, as per the UTAUT (Unified Theory of Acceptance and Use of Technology) proposed by Venkatesh et al. [6]. For this evaluation, the construct "Social influence" was not considered because the user research was completely voluntary.

The intent of use validation followed an online survey format with the questionaire available for a 10-day period (from July 14th to July 25th, 2015). There were 23 responses from designers. For each construct of the UTAUT model, a hypothesis and its related questions can be found on Fig. 3.

The Student t distribution was used in order to measure the answer's confidence interval and to validate the hypothesis. Figure 3 shows the construct, its related hypothesis and questions, the means the confidence interval. According to the results, all the hypothesis for the proposed guideline have a 99.95 % of confidence interval, thus validating the guidelines.

Construct	Hypothesis	Questions	means t		C.I.
Performance Expectancy	H1: The guidelines offer resources to make user's performance better	Question 1a: This guide is useful for new site's creation	17.77	16.04	99.95 %
		Question 1b: This guide is useful for existing site's evaluation	14.71		
		Question 1c: I would use this guide before creating a website	16.73		
Effort Expectancy	H2: The guidelines offer conditions that make its use easier	Question 2a: This guide is easy to understand	13.23	12.77	99.95 %
		Question 2b: I found new information on this guide	8.07		
		Question 2c: The content is complete	14.20		
		Question 2d: There are repeated information	15.58		
Facilitating conditions	H3: The guidelines offer support for the user	Question 3a: The images were helpful as examples	15.42	15.51	99.95 %
		Question 3b: The guide uses its own directions correctly	17.61		

Fig. 3. Hypothesis confidence interval

The Guidelines were written in an informal language to appeal to young designers. The final guide is freely available online, on the following address: http://annaretore. wix.com/guideline#!home/c1dmp.

5 Conclusion

This research considers the digital media as its own language, respecting it as being separate from the printed media. The guidelines derived after the analysis will help designers in their task of creating digital art magazines that take into consideration design and usability aspects. During the research, a process for analyzing variables was created (see Fig. 1): such process can be used in future studies for other variables. This paper makes the guidelines available to the design community.

There is a natural limitation on these guidelines. They address a very specific field and the results may not be transferred to all web sites and other scenarios. However, they can be the beginning for future studies.

References

1. Lynch, P.J., Horton, S.: Web Style Guide, 2nd edn. Yale University, New Haven (2002)
2. Franz, L.: Typographic Web Design: How to Think Like a Typographer in HTML and CSS. John Wiley & Sons, Chichester (2012)
3. Vinh, K.: Ordering Disorder: Grid Principles for Web Design. New Riders, Berkeley (2011)
4. Ambrose, G., Harris, P.: The fundamentals of Typography. G. Ambrose paperback, 6 (2011)
5. Spiekermann, E.: The Invisible Language of Typography. Blucher, São Paulo (2011)
6. Venkatesh, V., Morris, M.G., Davis, F.D., Davis, G.B.: User acceptance of information technology: toward a unified view. MIS Q. **27**, 425–478 (2003). Lynch, P.J., Horton, S.: Web Style Guide, 2nd edn. Yale University, New Haven (2002)
7. Triple Canopy (2016). https://canopycanopycanopy.com/
8. Retore, A.: Proposal of guidelines elaborated after research on grid and typography applied to art magazines websites' design. Completion of course work – Degree of Technology in Graphic Design, Federal University of Technology – Parana, Curitiba (2015)

Quantitative Evaluation for Edge Bundling by Difference of Edge Lengths and Area Occupation

Ryosuke Saga[✉]

Department of Computer Science and Intelligent Systems, Graduate School
of Engineering, Osaka Prefecture University, Sakai, Japan
saga@cs.osakafu-u.ac.jp

Abstract. There are a lot of information visualization techniques to utilize and analyze big data. Network visualization as node-link diagrams is one of techniques, which can visualize the relationship of multidimensional data, but when the data become very large, the visualization becomes obscure because of visual clutter. In order to solve this problem, a lot of edge bundling techniques have been proposed. However, although graphs may have some attributions, previous techniques don't reflect these attributions. In this paper, we propose a new method of edge bundling for attributed co-occurrence graph. Electrostatic force works between each pair of edges, but if edges are different attribution, repulsion works between the pairs. By bundling edges by same attribution, the graph shows relationships of data more clearly.

Keywords: Edge bundling · Network visualization · Evaluation

1 Introduction

Network visualization is one of the visualization methods that can express the data and the relationships between data. Network visualization is based on graphical representation in mathematics. Hence, a network consists of vertices and edges, which also exhibit attributes. The vertex set is V, the edge set is E, and a network G is presented as $G = G(V, E)$.

Several methods can be used to visualize networks [1]. Recently, edge bundling has drawn attention as a new approach to improve visual clutter. This method enables observers to recognize the main stream of edges through bundle edges in accordance with certain standards. For example, several methods based on the hierarchical structure of nodes [2], parallel coordinates [3], mechanical models [4], spring force-based approach [5] have been proposed. However, visualization results are qualitatively evaluated using questionnaires and other similar materials. Although researchers evaluate the calculation times for visualization, the efficiency or effect of edge bundling is not evaluated quantitatively.

Therefore, this study proposes a new evaluation strategy for edge bundling by using three measurements on the basis of edge lengths before and after edge bundling, area occupation, and edge density. Overall, this research will help develop an evaluation

© Springer International Publishing Switzerland 2016
C. Stephanidis (Ed.): HCII 2016 Posters, Part I, CCIS 617, pp. 287–290, 2016.
DOI: 10.1007/978-3-319-40548-3_48

method to conduct studies on edge bundling without qualitative measurement. Therefore, this study proposes a new evaluation strategy for edge bundling by using two measurements on the basis of edge lengths before and after edge bundling, area occupation. The first measurement, Mean Edge Length Difference (MELD) (Fig. 1), is based on the length in edge bundling, less change in edge lengths is assumed to indicate better edge bundling result. The second measurement, Mean Occupation Area (MOA), is based on occupation area in screen. Generally, the area of edges before edge bundling is larger than that after bundling. Given this phenomenon, a better bundling can compress the area occupied by the edges (Fig. 2).

2 Measurement of Edge Bundling

2.1 Edge Length

The first measurement is based on the length. In edge bundling, less change in edge lengths is assumed to indicate better edge bundling result. In fact, edge bundling changes the lengths of the edges and tries to bundles them. However, over-bundling often loses the meaning of the original network. Therefore, the above assumption can be considered reasonable. From this assumption, an evaluation measure called Mean Edge Length Difference (MELD) is proposed, as shown in Eq. (1) and Fig. 1. Spring force F_s working at p_i is the following:

$$MELD = \frac{1}{n}\sum\nolimits_{e \in E} |L'(e) - L(e)| \tag{1}$$

where n is the number of edges, $L'(e)$ is the length of edge e after edge bundling, and $L(e)$ is the original length of e.

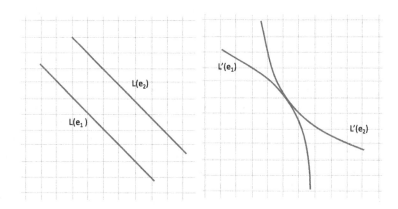

Fig. 1. Concept of Edge Length Difference (MELD) Left: before edge bundling, Right: after edge bundling.

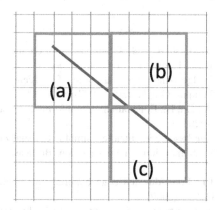

Fig. 2. Occupied area by edge (Unit Size: 4)

2.2 Divided Edge Bundling

Generally, the area of edges before edge bundling is larger than that after bundling. Given this phenomenon, a better bundling can compress the area occupied by the edges.

To calculate the area occupied by the edges, two parameters are used: the size of unit area and the occupation degree. The size of unit area or unit size defines the areas by separating canvas, and the value is given as pixel size. The occupation degree is an integer number used to determine whether an edge occupies the given area.

For example, as shown in Fig. 2, the unit size is 4, and the occupation degree is set to 2. The edges pass through three areas (a), (b), and (c). Areas (a) and (c) are identified as occupied but area (b) is as not occupied because only one pixel is passed by an edge.

By using the above parameters, a measurement called Mean Occupation Area (MOA) is proposed, as shown in Eq. (2).

$$MOA = \frac{1}{N} \left| \bigcup_{e \in E} O(e) \right| \tag{2}$$

where N is the number of total areas, O(e) is the set of occupied areas by edge e, and | | shows the number of elements contained by a set.

3 Conclusion

This research proposes two measurements to quantitatively evaluate edge bundling. The measurements are developed using the features of edge bundling and can use it to optimize the parameters to do edge bundling. For future works, the measurements will be extended for multi-type edge bundling [6].

Acknowledgement. This research was supported by MEXT/JSPS KAKENHI 25420448.

References

1. Herman, I., Melançon, G., Marshall, M.S.: Graph visualization and navigation in information visualization: a survey. IEEE Trans. Vis. Comput. Graph. **6**(1), 24–43 (2000)
2. Holten, D.: Hierarchical edge bundles: visualization of adjacency relations in hierarchical data. IEEE Trans. Vis. Comput. Graph. **12**(5), 1077–2626 (2006)
3. Zhou, H., Xu, P., Yuan, X., Qu, H.: Edge bundling in information visualization. Tsinghua Sci. Technol. **18**(2), 145–156 (2013)
4. Telea, A., Ersoy, O.: Image-based edge bundles: simplified visualization of large graphs. In: Eurographics/IEEE-VGTC Symposium on Visualization, Bordeaux, vol. 29(3), pp. 843–852 (2010)
5. Holten, D., van Wijk, J.J.: Force-directed edge bundling for graph visualization. Comput. Graph. Forum **28**(3), 983–990 (2009)
6. Saga, R., Yamashita, T.: Multi-type edge bundling in force-directed layout and evaluation. Procedia Comput. Sci. **60**, 1763–1771 (2015)

Knowledge Extraction About Brand Image Using Information Retrieval Method

Fumiaki Saitoh[✉], Fumiya Shiozawa, and Syohei Ishizu

Department of Industrial and Systems Engineering,
College of Science and Engineering, Aoyama Gakuin University,
5-10-1 Fuchinobe, Chuo-ku, Sagamihara, Kanagawa, Japan
saitoh@ise.aoyama.ac.jp

Abstract. The purpose of this study is to extract characteristic words as the information of expression pertaining to a brand's image, from the language resources that have accumulated by users on Twitter. In this study, we analyzed Twitter data related to brands extracted the characteristic representations by using Okapi BM25, which is a ranking function that has been recently introduced in information retrieval. To confirm the validity of our approach, we conduct comparative experiments on the Twitter data of several Japanese automobile brands using BM25 and TF-IDF. By using the BM25, the extraction of keywords that are meaningful and buried in high frequency terms can be expected.

Keywords: Twitter · BM25 · Brand image · Text-mining

1 Introduction

Social media, in particular Twitter, has become one of the most important sensors for information about the trends, reputation, and climate for products and events in the real world. Twitter users transmit personal information tweeting about personal events and their interest within the constraints of 140 characters. This results in a large amount of information originating from the real world being stored on Twitter, and it includes a wide variety of topics, such as the trivial daily events, political claims, and reviews of products and services.

Twitter has been widely used in recent years for a variety of subjects such as observing the mood of the consumers and their response to marketing strategies. The analysis of the reviews on e-commerce sites is suitable for the acquisition of a direct evaluation of products and services; however, it is not suited for extracting the impression and evaluation of companies and brands from a consumer point of view. Therefore, we consider that information available on social media is effective for investigating the impression and reputation for companies and brands in the real world.

The purpose of this study is to extract characteristic words as the information of expression related to a brand's image from the language resources accumulated by Twitter users. In this study, we analyze brand related data obtained from users' tweets, and we extract the characteristic representations, by weighting the query terms using

© Springer International Publishing Switzerland 2016
C. Stephanidis (Ed.): HCII 2016 Posters, Part I, CCIS 617, pp. 291–295, 2016.
DOI: 10.1007/978-3-319-40548-3_49

Okapi BM25, which is a ranking function in information retrieval. To confirm the validity of this study, we compare the word extraction using TF-IDF and our approach.

2   Characteristic Keywords Extraction Based on Information Retrieval

2.1   The Conventional Method Using TF-IDF

The extraction target features on the internet from a language resource perspective is regarded as important in various fields. For example, in the feature extraction and analysis from a company Web site, weighting based on the frequency of the query word is widely used; TF-IDF and IDF are widely used in such tasks.

IDF and TF-IDF are determined by the following equations:

$$IDF_i = \log(N/DF_i) \tag{1}$$

$$TFIDF_{ij} = TF_{ij} \times IDF_i \tag{2}$$

Where i and j indicate the indexes of word and document, respectively. TF_{ij} is the term frequency of the j-th word in the i-th document, and DF_i is the number of documents that include the i-th word.

2.2   BM25

BM25 is a relatively new ranking function that has gained traction in recent years. Different to TF-IDF, BM25 takes the document length into consideration. Therefore, negative effects of high-frequency words due to long documents can be avoided and keywords can be extracted that are truly characteristic. The value of BM25 for word Q contained in document D is calculated as

$$BM25(D,Q) = \sum_{i=1}^{n} IDF(q_i) \frac{f(q_i,D)(k_1+1)}{f(q_i,D) + k_1\left(1 - b + b\frac{|D|}{avg\_dl}\right)} \tag{3}$$

where $f(q_i,D)$ is the term frequency for the i-th word q_i in the document D, $|D|$ is the length of the document D (the total number of words), and avg_dl represents the average document length of all documents. k_1 $(1 < k_1 < 2)$ and b $(0 < b < 1)$ are parameters for weighting the effect of term frequency and document length, respectively.

2.3   Processing Procedure in the Analysis Using BM25

In this study, we focus on adjectives as characteristic words. As extraction method, we adopted BM25. TF-IDF is the most popular method for extracting keywords, but it extracts many irrelevant words because it is proportional to the document length.

BM25, on the other hand, takes the document length into consideration and extracts keywords that are more characteristic and that would otherwise get mixed up with high-frequency words when using TF-IDF. Therefore, BM25 is better suited than TF-IDF for extracting knowledge to help corporate management. We believe the pro-posed method helps to understand a brand's strengths and weaknesses and to compare it with its competitors.

The process flow of the proposed method is as follows.

Step. 1:	Construct document matrix for tweet data, including each brand name using the morphological analysis.
Step. 2:	Weight the document matrix that has been acquired in Step.1 by using BM25.
Step. 3:	Extract keywords for each brand from the weighted document matrix from Step.2. The words with highest BM25 value are extracted.

3 Comparative Experiment

3.1 Experimental Settings

We collected the documents that were tweeted in Japanese, including the brand names, as experimental data. We applied morphological analysis to construct a document matrix and then applied BM25 and TF-IDF to calculate a data frequency matrix. For our study, the part of speech that we are interested in are adjectives.

As parameters for BM25 we used $b = 0.75$ and $k_1 = 1.2$, which are the generally recommended values. In this study, we analyzed the tweets and brand names of 14 different Japanese automobile companies. For publication purposes, we anonymized the brand names and represent them as A - N.

3.2 Experimental Results

The top five keywords for brands A, B, and C are shown as an example of the experimental results. Tables 1 and 2 show sample results of BM25 and TF-IDF, respectively. In these tables, words that were extracted for more than one brand are shaded. To evaluate the results quantitatively, we determined the precision and recall for tweets retrieval using the extracted keywords. Precision and recall values were calculated through a retrieval experiment using the keywords extracted for brand A.

Figure 1 compares the retrieval results of BM25 and TF-IDF. The vertical axis in Subfigure (a) shows precision for retrieval of brand keywords, and the vertical axis in Subfigure (b) shows recall for retrieval of brand keywords. The horizontal axes rep-resent the number of words used for the retrieval in descending order. Black dotted lines and gray solid lines correspond to BM25 and TF-IDF, respectively.

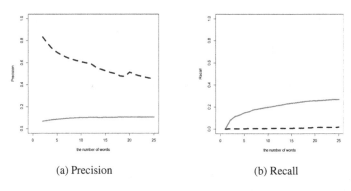

(a) Precision   (b) Recall

Fig. 1. Comparison of retrieval results

Table 1. Brand-related keywords extracted by BM25

Brand A		Brand B		Brand C	
Keyword	BM25	Keyword	BM25	Keyword	BM25
interesting	4.630	dear	4.552	sinful	5.449
frightening	4.078	rugged	4.552	comfortable	5.449
dangerous	4.078	lonely	4.552	red	5.220
cool	4.078	troublesome	4.552	young	5.099
ugly	4.078	brave	4.552	lonely	5.099

Table 2. Brand-related keywords extracted by TF-IDF

Brand A		Brand B		Brand C	
Keyword	TFIDF	Keyword	TFIDF	Keyword	TFIDF
not	125.081	detailed	408.452	nice	90.767
detailed	112.905	great	117.895	detailed	59.773
nice	96.302	deep	97.597	not	58.667
many	59.773	want	43.170	good	56.457
good	58.667	nice	34.314	want	27.673

3.3 Discussion

In our study, we compare BM25 and TF-IDF for extracting brand keywords. Table 1 lists various keywords extracted with BM25. Table 2 lists keywords extracted with TF-IDF. While BM25 extracts keywords of special loans in the target brand, TF-IDF extracts common purpose words relating to the purchase of goods in general and to other brands in particular, such as "want," "detailed," and "good." Because with TF-IDF-based extraction the characteristic words are mixed with high-frequency words, we conclude that our BM25-based approach is better suited for brand keyword extraction.

BM25-based extraction delivers descriptive adjectives for representing each brand image, such as "rugged," "red," and "good-looking." We compared the extracted adjectives with the brands ourselves and argue that they represent the characteristics of each brand very well. To provide an objective evaluation, we plan to conduct a questionnaire-based survey.

Precision of BM25 is significantly higher than the precision of TF-IDF, while recall of TF-IDF is higher than recall of BM25 (see Fig. 1). Because it can be argued that TF-IDF weights against a wider range of keywords than BM25, this supports the results of Tables 1 and 2.

4 Conclusion

This study presented a text analysis for extracting brand keywords using BM25, a relatively new ranking function from information retrieval that has gained traction in recent years. In the experiment, keywords related to a brand's image in Japan were extracted from corresponding Twitter data. The study results confirmed that our BM25-based approach is better in extracting characteristic words than the traditional TF_IDF-based approach, which mixes characteristic words with high-frequency words.

References

1. Sakamoto, M., Ueda, Y., Doizaki, R., Shimizu, Y.: Communication support system between Japanese Patients and Foreign Doctors using onomatopoeia to express pain symptoms. J. Adv. Comput. Intell. Intell. Inform. **18**(6), 1020–1025 (2014)
2. Komatsu, T.: Choreographing robot behaviors by means of Japanese onomatopoeias. In: Proceedings of the Tenth Annual ACM/IEEE International Conference on Human-Robot Interaction, pp. 23–24 (2015)
3. Lertsumruaypun, K., Watanabe, C., Nakamura, S.: Onomatoperori: recipe recommendation system using onomatopeic Words. IPSJ SIG Tech. Rep. **73**(6), 1–7 (2009). (in Japanese)
4. Fukushima, H., Araki, K., Uchida, Y.: Disambiguation of Japanese onomatopoeias using nouns and verbs. In: Sojka, P., Horák, A., Kopeček, I., Pala, K. (eds.) TSD 2014. LNCS, vol. 8655, pp. 141–149. Springer, Heidelberg (2014)
5. Kato, A., Fukazawa, Y., Sanada, H., Mori, T.: Extraction of food-related onomatopoeia from food reviews and its application to restaurant search. J. Adv. Comput. Intell. Intell. Inform. **18**(3), 418–428 (2014)

Analysis on Historical Periods of Architectural Visualization Under the Perspectival Consciousness

ZhenDong Wu[1,2(✉)] and WeiMin Guo[1]

[1] School of Design, Jiangnan University, Wuxi, China
wzd888@gmail.com
[2] College of Mechanical Engineering and Automation, Huaqiao University,
No. 668 Jimei Avenue, Xiamen, Fujian, China

Abstract. Visualized images of buildings have been important means of representing and studying architectural space all the time. Their histories may be traced back to the period from prehistoric civilization to introduction of modern digital image technologies. From the spatial perspective, this paper briefly introduces technologies and logics of evolving visualized images by practical cases according to theories of iconology and visual perception. Summing up the characteristics of the era when such images evolved, it also summarizes three development stages of architectural visualization under the perspectival impacts.

Keywords: Architectural visualization · Perspectival · Space consciousness

1 Contemporary Concept and Significance of Visualization of Architectural Space

Spatial visualization specifically reflects "iconized media" in architectural and spatial representation. The significance of visualization consists in its visual recording, presentation, analysis and communication of artificial space where people live and all activities they conduct in that space. Regardless of recording spatial events on rock paintings or porcelains in the period of prehistoric civilization or today's visual representation of virtual heritages and space, human beings have been closely integrating visualized images with architectural space.

Nevertheless, cognition about visualized images of architectural space is a little vague. In other words, architectural visualization is a visual tool or a visual method of spatial cognition afterall. Has it gone through a relatively clear and identifiable development process in human development history of visual images? Have new pertinent practices and theories emerged with the development of times. In this paper, an attempt is made to conduct the research based on perspectival consciousness.

C. Stephanidis (Ed.): HCII 2016 Posters, Part I, CCIS 617, pp. 296–301, 2016.
DOI: 10.1007/978-3-319-40548-3_50

2 Using Perspective as Image Tool or Spatial Consciousness

2.1 Utilizing Perspective as Spatial Image Tool

Traditionally, perspective is understood as a terminology of image drawing theory for three-dimensional space on two-dimensional space. As a product of the renaissance era, narrow perspective (i.e. linear perspective) means that actual spatial location of objects is represented by basic geometric perspectival drawing. Leone Battista Alberti, an Italian painter of the 15th century, illustrated mathematical foundation of painting and importance of perspective in his work titled On Painting. As a German painter, Albrecht Durer applied geometrics in arts, so that the discipline theoretically developed. Up till now, perspectival painting has become a watershed of architectural images. By now, such linear perspectival painting based on vanishing points is still applicable to expressing most spatial images.

2.2 Considering Perspective as Spatial Consciousness

In the mean time, the German thinker Jean Gerser summed up three stages for the development of human consciousness, including pre-perspectival, perspectival and aperspective. Although these three stages are neither chronological nor have any clear boundaries of time, they have distinct characteristics of times. Jean Gerser didn't reckon perspective as a drawing method, but summarized it as a methodology for reflecting on space. From the perspective of this methodology, it may be found that human beings' abilities to perceive images of architectural space have been always in a stage of compound and progressive growth of being educated and guided by represented media. Some of their abilities like cognition of directions have come into being in the prehistoric times. However, their abilities have been mostly trained throughout the development of image-related means. For instance, three-dimensional space is observed from perspectival images.

3 Analysis on Historical Stages of Visualizing Architectural Space and Pertinent Characteristics

3.1 Pre-perspectival Visualization Stage

After a case analysis of Yunnan Cangyuan rock paintings and paintings of the ancient Egypt, it may be discovered that human beings made original records of space-related information such as architectural construction and residence by visual means in the period of prehistoric civilization. As shown in Fig. 1, prehistoric human beings visualized production, life and living processes of their villages through intuitive perception. There is an oval circle in the center of the picture that represents the aboundary of a village or possibly a wall or moat for defense. All buildings above and beside are depicted by inverted or lateral painting. Size of objects isn't defined by vertical space representation of perspectival painting that objects are small in distant places, but large nearby. In contrast, it is arranged pursuant to importance of people or buildings.

This drawing method is pretty consistent with "law of frontality" (Fig. 2). Non-perspectival features of the planes are evident. In form, location of architectural space could be reflected from representation of image space in the pre-perspectival era to certain extent. Nevertheless, space is rendered by an empirical two-dimensional method with graphic and non-perspectival visual characteristics on the whole.

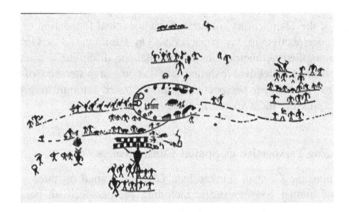

Fig. 1. Zhaofu Chen, Xueming Wu, Cangyuan petroglyphs, 《Complete Works of Chinese Fine Arts Painting series》, People's Fine Arts Publishing House, P11 [1].

Fig. 2. Rudolf Arnheim, Art and visual perception [J]. University of California Press, 2001 [2]

3.2   Perspectival Visualization Stage

The perspectival method developed and systematized by Leone Battista Alberti in the period of Renaissance is used for constructing space of graphic painting. It includes some basic hypotheses, assuming a scene as a window, and hypothesizing that the standpoints are separate and fixed that project a view cone to the world, where the scene deemed as a window is a section that perpendicularly cuts the cone. It has a visual characteristic that corresponding two-dimensional sections of three-dimensional space are geometrically and homogeneously obtained.

In Albrecht Dürer's prints, methods of Rennaisance painters for studying perspectival painting techniques for space were depicted in detail (Fig. 3). The painters determined position of points of three-dimensional space on a two-dimensional glass panel by connecting lines. Ropes connected three-dimensional objects with two-dimensional scenes. Once the ropes are removed, the power of such mapping may be clearly felt through scenes. With the maturity of such spatial visulization technique that "looks" through "windows" via interpretation of geometric paintings, frames have become corresponding two-dimensional sections of three-dimensional space, developed into a new cognitive spatial consciousness and formed a sharp epoch-making contrast with pre-perspectival spatial consciousness.

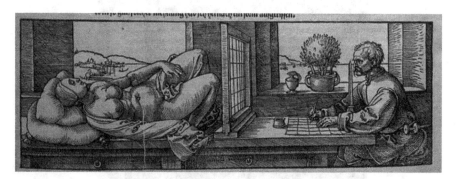

Fig. 3. Filippo Brunelleschi Peephole device authentication perspective relations (Source: https://maitaly.wordpress.com/2011/04/28/brunelleschi-and-the-re-discovery-of-linear-perspective/).

In opinions of Rennaisance painters, space was orderly, homogeneous and fixed. It could be best described by techniques of geometric analysis. They converted perceptual space into geometric space based on visual observations and geometric foundations.

3.3   Aperspective Visualization Stage

If preperspectival visible spatial painting techniques draw space intuitively and perspectival painting techniques mean fragmented representation of two-dimensional to three-dimensional space, scientific progress of the early 20th century has been reviewed and a new advance has been achieved in people's spatial consciousness known as aperspective consciousness. After the launch of Einstein's theory of relativity and quantum mechanics, people have regarded time and space to be static and absolute. The space people face is so-called four-dimensional space composed by three-dimensional space and time. Thus, aperspective consciousness is the consciousness upgraded after people's understanding of four-dimensional time-space where they are.

Gebser considered that time and space were divided by perspective. In their opinion, time dimensions are concealed that purely static sense of space was created, and visual perception thus became a dominant way of spatial experience. The newly emerged aperspective wasn't an opposite of perspective, but revealed a new attitude. Time became the fourth dimension to supplement original dominating spatial conciousness. The time and space consciousness thereby combined over again updated previous spatial consciousness.

Zaha Hadid attempted to reflect multi-dimension and superposition of time-space in her architectural images. Such image visualization technique presenting numerous languages of lens such as wide angles, slow motions, closeups and quick connection fully reflected her spatial design ideas of ignoring morphology, order and gravity (Fig. 4).

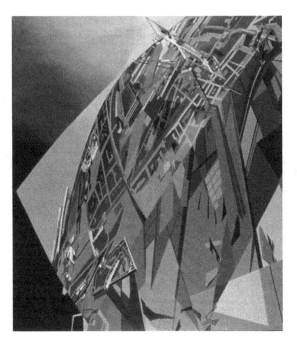

Fig. 4. Zaha Hadid, the world (89 degrees) (Source: http://www.zaha-hadid.com/design/the-world-89-degrees/).

Without attaching importance to center of gravity and stability like traditional architecture, Greg Lynn created buildings by simultaneously considering time, motion and combined multi-directional forces. He designed buildings according to detailed topographical and environmental materials by procedures of automotive design and animated movies. It seemed as if motions of fields could be felt in these buildings. Having become a type of flowing digital media, buildings are filled with rhythms. The new visual techniques explored by him have played critical roles in architecture and modern urban communications (Fig. 5).

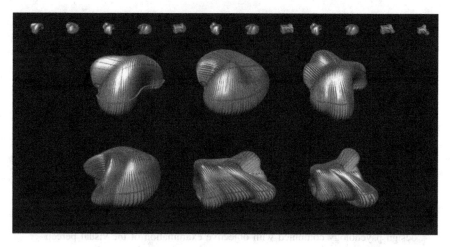

Fig. 5. Greg lynn embriological housing (Source: http://static.digischool.nl/ckv2/ckv3/kunstentechniek/lynn/greglynn.htm).

4   Conclusion

Above all, changes to human beings' space representation are attributed to the evolution of their spatial consciousness and improved abilities to understand space. The appearance of perspective tools is a critically important technical variable that has led to their changes. It is worthy of efforts to constantly explore how paradigms of image generation, representation and analysis for architectural space have evolved and developed with the rapid advancement of informatization and digital technologies in the post-industrial times.

References

1. Chen, Z., Wu, X.: Cangyuan petroglyphs, Complete Works of Chinese Fine Arts Painting series. People's Fine Arts Publishing House.
2. Arnheim, R.: Art and visual perception: A psychology of the creative eye. University of California Press (1954)

Comparative Study on Visual Differences of Poster Designs Based on Design Psychology

Tian-yu Wu[✉] and Yan Liu

School of Design Art and Media, Nanjing University of Science and Technology,
Nanjing, Jiangsu, People's Republic of China
1031063471@qq.com

Abstract. Objective. This paper is to offer relevant theoretical basis and experimental method for future Chinese ink poster designs through the information on differentiation obtained from an in-depth analysis of the concept of design psychology combined with objective examination of the visual perception of Chinese ink poster designs of both professionals and nonprofessionals by means of eye movement experiments. **Method.** Methods of questionnaire and eye movement experiments were adopted to extract the differentiated information on the visual perceptions of Chinese ink posters of both design professionals and nonprofessionals with the aim of studying and understanding their visual focus and visual perception of poster designs and realizing the "customer-oriented" concept of Chinese ink poster designs. **Conclusion.** Through data gathering, assessment and analysis, conclusion has been reached that professionals are more concerned about the cultural connotation and aesthetic imagery while nonprofessionals focus more on the information transmission through the hieroglyphs in the posters. The paper argues that Chinese ink poster designs are based on certain psychological theories and tested and evaluated via scientific experiment.

Keywords: Eye tracker · Poster · Design · Visual · Psychology

1 Overview of Design Psychology

Design psychology is a science which studies the law of occurrence and development of psychological activities of designers in modern design acts based on general psychology with an aim to meet the basic requirements and application psychology of users [1]. As a borderline science at the crossroad of artistic design and psychology, design psychology is both a sub-branch of applied psychology and a major component of artistic design. As modern technologies are experiencing continuous development, the values of "people-oriented" and "design for the real world" are now the theme of modern social activities, which require that designers take the physical and psychological demands into full consideration in the creative process and incorporate them into the whole design practice.

It is undeniable that human visual activity is a complicated social activity, and a part of human psychological activity. As for the designers, the methodologies required to study the patterns of the psychological activities of user communities are no different

C. Stephanidis (Ed.): HCII 2016 Posters, Part I, CCIS 617, pp. 302–307, 2016.
DOI: 10.1007/978-3-319-40548-3_51

from the general psychology research methodologies. The reform and development of human psychology itself has provided a scientific theoretical foundation for the development of design psychology practices and applications [2]. However, human behavior and mindset belong to a distinct field. Therefore, a series of new questions and challenges will be raised when certain approaches of psychology study are applied to investigate the visual behavioral patterns of the audience. As a result, an in-depth analysis of design psychology research methods will not only contribute to the integrity of the specific design project operation but also enrich the experience of major psychology research methods. Conventional approaches adopted in design psychology research include observation, interviews, questionnaires, projection, experiments, the summative rating scale, the semantic differential scale, case study, etc. Among them questionnaires and experiments are generally combined with e-questionnaires and eye movement experiments to repeatedly test and evaluate the stage achievements of artistic design practices so as to achieve the exact purpose of "people-oriented" design.

2 Design Psychology and Poster Design

From the perspective of design psychology, human reception and recognition of information have two important stages: perception and consciousness. Perception is the most basic and simplest psychological phenomenon, since there is no consciousness or other psychological activities without perception. Visual sense accounts for 87 % of the all five senses, leaving 13 % to the rest four sense organs [3]. Undoubtedly, poster design is one of the most representative forms in graphic designs. Freehand poster design crosses various disciplines and even till now, Chinese traditional freehand posters still possess the distinctive feature of oriental charm and symbolization, which are not only the inheriting of traditional culture but also pay respect to the expression techniques of traditional art [4]. Unfortunately, at the time of economic globalization, large amounts of Chinese-style poster designs have overlooked the manipulation of design psychology concept, resulting in some specious and superficial works. For this reason, certain scientific theoretical principles should be followed and the core connotations of the poster art should be conveyed from the perspective of design psychology, customer consciousness and the aesthetic form of design, so that poster designs may bring their intended functions into play in public activities and art appreciation.

Among all the fine poster design works, those of Kan Tai-Keung's are exemplary in graphic art. The success of his design lies more in the assimilation of traditional cultural elements and a profound understanding of the audiences' visual perception with the assistance of psychological theoretical framework than in his personal artistic style of the "fusion of China and the west". Hence this paper tries to offer the objective evaluation and repetitive tests of audiences' visual differences toward the "Feelings of the Brush" poster series (Fig. 1) by conducting eye movement experiments with the aim of extracting some concise and proper points of design.

Fig. 1. Poster design series "Feelings of the Brush" by Kan Tai-Keung

3 Design Psychology Tests in Posters

This experiment adopted psychological research methods to test and evaluate the feasibility of designs. The object was poster design series "Feelings of the Brush" by Kan Tai-Keung. Eye trackers were used to analyze behavior reactions of the audience from different professional backgrounds after their visual cognitions of posters. Reliable information on users' visual variation was obtained at a relatively low cost. This experiment involved college students with bachelor or above degrees in design majors and in non-design majors. 28 subjects were divided into two groups, each with 14. In addition, the experiment was conducted in a behavior analysis lab with noise-resistant and lucifugal conditions. Each subject entered the lab alone to avoid any distraction during the experiment [5]. The evaluation process had two stages: In the first stage, visual heat maps were generated according to the operational process of eye movement tests on selected subjects. In the second stage, subjects who went through the eye movement test should complete a questionnaire. Therefore, subjective information was collected to complement objective information from the eye movement test, and to enable data analysis and summary. The two research modules will be elaborated in the following text. Please refer to the overall flow chart, the flow chart for experimental evaluation (drawn by the author) (Fig. 2).

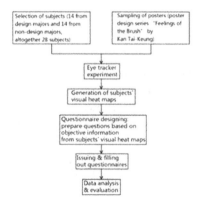

Fig. 2. The flow chart for experimental evaluation (drawn by the author)

3.1 Eye Movement Experiments

TobiiStudio eye tracker and its eye-tracking technique were applied in the eye movement experiment to record the movements of users' visual tracks when browsing the source materials (poster design series "Feelings of the Brush" by Kan Tai-Keung). Eye movements during the process were recorded to track their patterns and spatial positions that users took interest in, and their attention shifting process was also acquired in order to identify the visual focus of different groups [6]. Fixation duration, tracks, sequence, regression times as well as other eye movement data were used in the eye movement experiment analysis. The experimental results can even be demonstrated via intuitive graphs and videos, so human psychology and behavior were evaluated to achieve objective results of users' subconscious. The experiment therefore is an applicable evaluation approach to assess the final product of design practices (Fig. 3).

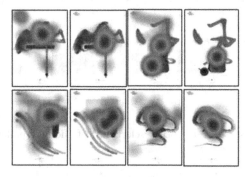

Fig. 3. Heat map of poster design eye movement experiment (left: design professionals; right: nonprofessionals).

From the heat map, we can see the fixation duration and concentration of the subjects on certain areas. Red indicates fixation and green means a shorter duration. In the poster design series "Feelings of the Brush" by Kan Tai-Keung, Chinese elements are properly applied. Combined with a modern touch, a design concept of cultural continuity with innovation as well as application of both the ancient and modern have been realized. The poster designs are pervaded with aesthetic features of the unity of fiction and reality, along with form and spirit, fully displaying the oriental design style and artistic creation. By observing the eye movement experiment results of 27 subjects, a conclusion has been reached that differences exist between design professionals and nonprofessionals: the visual focuses of professionals are mainly centered on the visual focus of the posters while the nonprofessionals focus more on a certain area of the poster, especially the real item pictures on the poster.

3.2 Questionnaire Survey

After the data gathering of eye movement experiments, subjects were asked to fill in the questionnaires to identify the sources of test data. Possible reactions to the various design elements in the above-mentioned posters were looked into and collected, and 9 representative questions were devised with one linking another in a progressive manner. Questions were edited and questionnaires were typeset, with multiple choice questions with one or more answers, along with subjective questions. After the eye movement test, subjects were asked to write down their subjective feelings about the posters. Data have shown that 56 % of subjects from design majors would pay attention to the ink font, and 30 % of them would focus on the overall layout. It suggests that subjects with a design background often have visual aesthetic demands in terms of the overall layout and special techniques of expression, and obviously they prefer posters of this category (Tables 1 and 2).

Table 1. Bar chart of "poster focus selection" of design professionals & design nonprofessionals

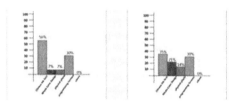

Table 2. Bar chart of "reason focus selection" of design professionals & design nonprofessionals

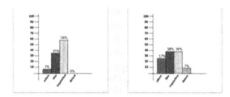

3.3 Data Analysis and Result Discussion

In this experiment, posters with distinct features were selected. The spiritual connotation of their imagery and traditional aesthetic charm served as the inspiration for designers. Therefore the final manifestation of the posters is more abstract compared to the usual realistic ones. So experimentation and questionnaire methods of design psychology were adopted to provide the scientific assessment and evaluation of the poster series "Feelings of the Brush". The experimental data indicate that the visual focuses on different subjects clearly differed from each other and so did the objective information reflected. Design professionals among the subjects instantly noticed the words in Chinese ink on the posters and then their focuses fluctuated between the words and the overall color, and then wandered in the center of the poster for some time before they took notice of the picture of real items. On the contrary, nonprofessionals immediately cast their sight to the most realistic pictures on the posters and finally paid attention to the ink brushwork by the end of their observation. It is therefore clear that the series of visual elements in the posters have effects on audiences' visual perception to different degrees, including images and symbols, decorative color, font and size, typeset and layout, as well as techniques of expression. In addition, target users from a variety of educational and professional backgrounds also have different judgments and aesthetic preferences toward poster designs of typical styles.

4 Conclusion

As the most expressive creative form of graphic design, poster design has been exerting constant effects on modern designers for them to make continuous innovations and elevations. Its cultural charm and aesthetic consciousness have also inspired love for graphic art in modern people. Through the analysis and study of the posters "Feelings of the Brush" by Kan Tai-Keung, it is evident that designers should base their works on certain theoretical foundation of design psychology, grasp the aesthetic preferences of the audience with the assistance of psychology, avoid the self-centered design habit and convey the unique cultural connotations and imagery charm of the artistic posters. On top of that, to be closer to the visual perception experience of target customers, after completing stage design practices, test approaches to design psychology should be actively adopted to offer viable tests and objective evaluations on current designs. There is no doubt that eye movement studies are the most effective evaluating method of graphic art and provide more proofs to explain how different tasks affect cognitive processing in real time [7]. User groups of various backgrounds display obvious value discrepancy concerning the visual perception of posters, which indicates that designers should adhere to the "people-oriented" principle and create poster designs in line with users' aesthetic preferences, spiritual needs and visual perceptions in a scientific manner.

References

1. Pieters, R., Wedel, M.: Attention capture and transfer in advertising: brand, pictorial, and text-size effects. J. Mark. **68**(2), 36–50 (2004)
2. Zhang, Z.-S., Shen, D.-L.: General psychology. Educational Science Publishing House, Bei Jing (2001)
3. Dai, R.-X.: Design psychology study method and application. Art Des. (11), 13 (2007)
4. He, P.-J., Chen, P.: Comparison and analysis of poster design between Kan Tai-Keung and Tanaka. Packag. Eng. **31**(10), 62 (2010)
5. Shi, B.-Y.: On Usability Design Evaluation of Product Packaging Based on Eye Movement Research. Human University of Technology, Human (2012)
6. Chang, F.-Y.: Usability evaluation of smart phone application graphic user interface based on eye-tracker. Packag. Eng. **36**(8), 55 (2015)
7. Pieters, R., Wedel, M.: Goal control of attention to advertising: the yabus implication. J. Consum. Res. **2**, 224–233 (2007)

Visual Analysis of Soccer Match Using Player Motion Data

Miohk Yoo and Kyoungju Park[✉]

GSAIM, Chung-Ang University, Seoul, South Korea
vogue90l@naver.com, kjpark@cau.ac.kr

Abstract. Sports data analysis has come to play a significant role in improving player performances as these analytics proved to aid in reversing the fortunes of ailing sports teams. With tremendous advancement of digital devices such as cameras, sensors, and wearables, analytic providers are now able to record many aspects of player performance. However, soccer data obtained through these devices are of a complex structure and not provided in a standardized format. Thus finding effective ways to manage and comprehend massive player feature data has become an inevitable problem to solve. Therefore, we suggest a method of analysis system to allow the users to easily analyze and comprehend the context of soccer game by visually portrayed player aspect data based specifically on player movements throughout the game.

Keywords: Soccer match data · Visualization · Visual analytics system

1 Introduction

Since soccer data is based on the movement of twenty two players, soccer match data contains massive movement information of players and consists of complex properties and structures. Especially, regarding the fact that players move in the field constantly during the game, both spatial complexity and time complexity are high. Meaningful analysis of such complex data is able to help in figuring out characteristics of the team and establishing appropriate strategies for the team [1]. Also, patterns of attacks and defenses can be seen through players' movement data as well, which serve as the key in understanding semantics of the game. Therefore, it is important to understand intuitively these data and analyze them contextually [2].

Hence, we propose a system that visually represent the movements of players during a match, by comparatively visualizing the different movements of players during attacks and defenses and the differences according to the formation or positions of the player such as 1 vs1 marks. Our system is as follows. First, we structuralize the player movement data and create metadata per position. Next, we visualize 2D movements, divide them into offensive and defensive patterns, and provide a user interface so that the user is able to select which information to visualize. Lastly, we determine the most frequently occurred information area by dispersion pattern of players based on the metadata, draw the determined area for each player, and assign distinct colors to these areas depending on the team of players. This enables comparative visualization.

© Springer International Publishing Switzerland 2016
C. Stephanidis (Ed.): HCII 2016 Posters, Part I, CCIS 617, pp. 308–312, 2016.
DOI: 10.1007/978-3-319-40548-3_52

2   Motion Data of Player During Soccer Match

Sample data are extracted from whoscored.com [3] which are recorded by very famous English professional soccer analyzers to design and develop a soccer game data visual analysis system. First, data scraping method and direct record methods are used to classify data as characteristics for design and removal of unnecessary data during data extraction process. Collected data are structured through data management system construction; then, the data are saved. By considering formation which consists team and position of players, player movement position in space of stadium is categorized and set as metadata. Then, data are selected for visualization and re-arranged due to that. Finally, it will be saved into a file as CVS format to read arranged data for development of visualization. These segmentation methods make users to recognized information from visualization more intuitive [4].

3   Match Content Visualization Analysis

We suggest a visualization analysis system that analyzes game content based on movement data of players. Motion data will be the core of figuring out game content since it shows patterns of offense and defense. Each meta data is created by each position of players from structured data. Each data is expressed as distribution graph by categorizing the data based on the formation of a team. Offense direction of the team is set to increase understanding of game content analysis. Movement and location information functions from each position area are developed for comparable other players' movement data. These can make to figure out player movement data easily

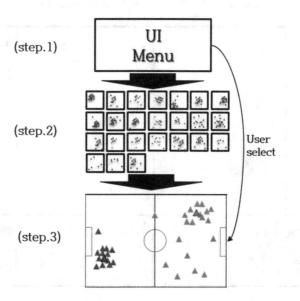

Fig. 1. Match content visualization analysis system procedures

even the formation is not matched and convenient to compare players' movement when the strategy of each team is different. From Fig. 1, visualization due to team, player and positions are created by configuring control panel (step. 1). Visualization image data (step. 2) which corresponds to relative factors are constructed. Finally, required game content data are visualized from the request of users to be analyzed (step. 3).

4   Comparison by Positions of Players

It is necessary to figure out the formation of players for each team to express the movement of players. 2D movement location data are figured out and saved into patterns of offense and defence by categorizing them. Users select optional data to visualize the movement of a player due to offense and defence of the player. Data forms are decided by player movement frequency location and location which are gathered as coordination of x, y in the 2D soccer field. By categorizing these forms of data, players and positions are constructed and confirm offense and defence patterns by each team. Offense and defence pattern are expressed by visualizing location value and movement for each position in each team's base. The color of the team is expressed as #ffcc66 for A team and #ff9933 for B team. High-frequency location of players is colored into more primary color. If it is not, it has the color of 10 % saturation. As a result, the density of data, in other words, when the location of players' movements is more duplicated into a certain location, the location will be closed to 100 % saturation of color. If not, it is expressed as minimum 10 % saturation. Visualization expressed into the corresponding color of team based on the most occurred information field by

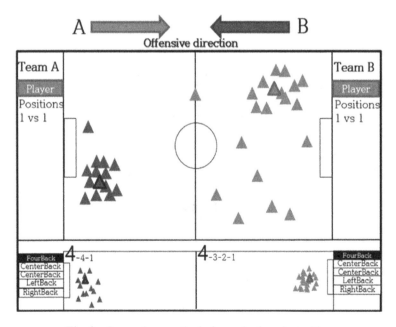

Fig. 2. Comparison methods for each player's position

changing the movement of players into distribution form. We changed saturation value based on one color to compare more than two data property patterns of teams so that it is possible to compare with two patterns (Fig. 2).

5   Experiment and Discussion

Actual game data are used to deduce result from visualization analysis system and compare the movement of players and movement of defence due to the formation of A team and B team were compared. A team had 4-4-2 formation, and B team had 2-3-1 formation. The most important role of defence from soccer game is lowering instability to defence core regions [5]. The result of the defense line visualization is shown in Fig. 1(b). At the moment when the user selects a player or position, movement data is formed with use of the meta-data as shown in the Fig. 1(a) and the result is visualized Fig. 1(b). In our result the both teams use different formations, A teams plays in a 4-4-1 formation and B team plays 4-3-2-1 formation. Although both teams use different formations the use a back-four based defense line and that is why it is easy to compare and analyze our visualization result. In the enlarged image (b) different states of player distribution for both teams. Players in team A are more widely distributed and team B players are concentrated in the center. By analyzing player movement we can say that team A uses a more man-to-man defense tactic since the movement is widely distributed, while team B uses a defense tactic for a particular player. Our system can analyze offense as well. From the result of analyzing FIFA world cup in 2010, successful teams often conducted more side attack rather than center attack [2]. Our visualization analysis system can be used as a tool to confirm the correlation between a team winning and offense from a certain location. Of course, it can't decide winning team from these analysis result. However, it is possible to figure out characteristics such as offense tendency and defense tendency of the team through this data analysis.

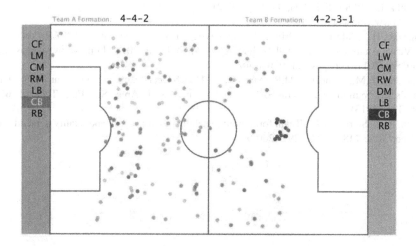

Fig. 3. Comparative visualization analysis by formation of A and B team

Therefore, it is possible to bring good result by increasing the efficiency of a team from training players based on setting strategy which can increase the efficiency of team formation and encourages the potential of players into maximum [6] (Fig. 3).

6 Conclusion

By visualizing variety and complex soccer match data, it is easy to access information. So we designed and built a system which is convenient to a user by providing visual analysis. Only necessary data are primarily extracted from a large amount of game data to structure and arrange data to be accessed easily through the interface. Based on converted data, movements of players during a game are compared through visual analysis interface to conduct an experiment. The suggested visualization analysis system is not enough to implement in real. So, it needs a supplementary process by applying various visualization methods and analysis methods, as well as evaluation by experts. If the system is continuously developed through visualization methods of other information which is related with winning of soccer including data about player movements through modification and supplement process, the system can be applied to other team sports including soccer. Furthermore, it is possible to expect that this visualization analysis system can be provided as content to figure out the flow of games for public, as well as professional game analyzers.

References

1. Bernard, M.: How big data and analytics are changing soccer. LinkedIn, 25 March 2015. Web. Anderson, R.E.: Social impacts of computing: codes of professional ethics. Soc. Sci. Comput. Rev. **10**(2), 453–469 (1992)
2. Clemente, F.M.: Study of successful soccer teams on FIFA world cup 2010. Pamukkale J. Sport Sci. **3**(3), 90–103 (2012)
3. http://www.whoscored.com/
4. Janetzko, H., et al.: Feature-driven visual analytics of soccer data. In: 2014 IEEE Conference on Visual Analytics Science and Technology (VAST). IEEE (2014). http://www.variousways.com/blog/2011/03/happyrain-twitter-art/
5. Clemente, F.M., Couceiro, M.S., Martins, F.M.L.: Soccer teams behaviors: analysis of the team's distribution in function to ball possession. Res. J. Appl. Sci. Eng. Technol. **6**(1), 130–136 (2013)
6. Boon, B.H., Sierksma, G.: Team formation: matching quality supply and quality demand. Eur. J. Oper. Res. **148**(2), 277–292 (2003)

TimeTree: A Novel Way to Visualize and Manage Exploratory Search Process

Yin Zhang, Kening Gao, Bin Zhang[✉], and Pengfei Li

School of Computer Science and Engineering,
Northeastern University, Shenyang, China
{zhangyin,gaokening,zhangbin}@cse.neu.edu.cn

Abstract. Methods have been proposed to assist activities in exploratory search processes, but few allow the users to appropriately manage their own search processes. In this paper, we present the *TimeTree* workspace provided in our process-oriented search system *CiteXplore* that supports visualized management of search processes and enables reviewing and retrospecting of information during long-term exploratory search. Formal user experiments with 16 participants have been proposed to evaluate the proposed methods. We also discuss possible research directions to use *TimeTree* to reuse search experiences by enabling collaborative search and providing visualized recommendations.

Keywords: Exploratory search · Search process visualization · Search process management · *TimeTree*

1 Introduction

Exploratory search refers to a specific type of information seeking in which uses with unclear information needs search in probable unfamiliar domains. This leads to a series of queries and clicked documents, establishing long search processes with perhaps branching and retrospecting. New methods have been proposed to assist search actions in exploratory search processes [1–5]. However, to the best of our knowledge, few attentions have been paid to helping users manage the search processes themselves.

Search processes of exploratory search tasks may require hours, days or even weeks to finish. Under these circumstances, users will need to suspend and resume their undergoing search tasks multiple times. Meanwhile, to reduce complexity, a user usually gradually divides an exploratory search task into several subtasks, and may need to review previous queries and clicks frequently to plan new subtasks. These managing works for search processes cost users extra cognitive load, which should be reduced by taking new designs.

Graph is an intuitive way to organize search processes and to present the relations between queries and clicks [3, 5, 6]. With a search process graph, a user could easily remember the origin of a query, and what he or she did after the query. However, the key disadvantage of organizing search processes as graphs is that the chronological information which can be used to inference the chronological order of past search actions is only available for adjacent queries and clicks. This might not be a problem for a simple search task, but for a long-term exploratory search task, the search process

© Springer International Publishing Switzerland 2016
C. Stephanidis (Ed.): HCII 2016 Posters, Part I, CCIS 617, pp. 313–319, 2016.
DOI: 10.1007/978-3-319-40548-3_53

graph could quickly become too complex for the use to tell the sequence of queries and clicks, making it hard to remember and organize subtasks.

List is a more traditional way to store search histories [2, 4]. A chronological list of search actions could help a user quickly go over the past search efforts. However, a main shortcoming of search history lists is that they are unable to show the relations between queries and clicks, which is important to supporting sense making in exploratory search.

The purpose of this work is to create and evaluate a new process-oriented exploratory search system. Our system supports task-level search process management, facilitating users to save and reopen search processes. Especially, our system provides a tree-based workspace named *TimeTree* for logging and managing queries and clicks. In *TimeTree*, queries and clicks are visually organized for users to review the clicks and the origin of a query. The relative order of all the queries and clicks are also preserved, helping users quickly remember the sequence of queries and clicks in subtasks. Users could also rate and comment on tree nodes to highlight important queries and clicks or to take notes. By these means, we seek ways to help users organize and manage long-term exploration search processes.

2 Methods

In this section, we present our process-oriented open-source exploratory search system *CiteXplore* and its tree-based workspace *TimeTree*. Currently, based on third-party search APIs, *CiteXplore* has been tuned to work as a scholar search engine, but a general purpose version is also under active development.

2.1 The *CiteXplore* User Interface

As shown in Fig. 1, the user interface of *CiteXplore* could be divided into three areas: the search area at the left, the *TimeTree* workspace at the right, and the task management area at the bottom right corner. The search area provides a traditional search engine interface: a text box is available for users to enter query keywords, and the search results are shown below. The difference is that, the queries and clicks performed in the search area are automatically synchronized into the *TimeTree* workspace, which will be introduced in detail in Sect. 2.2.

The task management area allows users to save search tasks, create new tasks, and load or delete previous tasks. Tasks are sorted according to their last modification time so that users could easily access their recent tasks. A user could only work on one task at a time, but parallel search could be achieved by opening multiple tabs, windows, browsers or even computers. In this case, actions performed in the *TimeTree* workspace and the task area are synchronized across all the open views.

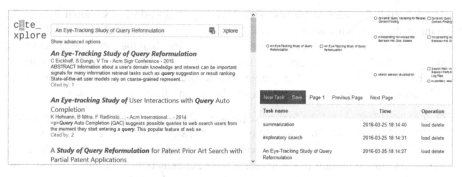

Fig. 1. The user interface of *CiteXplore*

2.2   The *TimeTree* Workspace

Figure 2 provides a detailed view of the *TimeTree* workspace of *CiteXplore*. In *TimeTree*, two kinds of nodes are shown: circles for queries, and squares for clicks. A clamped label, which is limited to no more than 3 lines, of the query text or the title of the search result is located on the right side of a node to help a user quickly remember what a node stands for. Nodes are created when a user submits a new query or makes a click. When a new node (excepted for the root node) is created, a corresponding arc will also be created according to the following rules:

1. An arc from a query node to a click node is created if the click is made in the search result pages of the query.
2. An arc from a click node to a query node is created if the content of the click contains the query text.
3. An arc from a query node to a query node is created if the latter query is a post-query of the former query when Rule 2 fails.

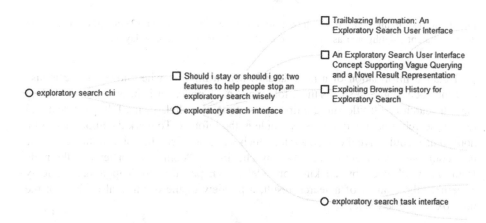

Fig. 2. The *TimeTree* workspace of *CiteXplore*.

Users could also reorganize nodes and arcs by drag-n-drop, as shown in Fig. 3. With these arcs, nodes are arranged in relative chronological order (as shown in Fig. 2): The source node of an arc will have an earlier timestamp than the target node, and will be located to the left of the target node; sibling nodes with later timestamps are always located below the others, with their parent node located at the center; nodes at the same level lie along a straight line. Such a layout brings the following advantages:

- Quick identifications of the logical sequences of search actions: Since all the nodes are located in relative chronological order, it is always easy to determine the logical sequence of two search actions. If one node is an ancestor of the other node, then the action corresponding to the ancestor node happens before the other action. If it is not the case, then the action of the node located above the other node logically happens before the other action. The latter case does not follow strict chronological order, but it does reflect the logical sequence of a user performing exploratory search: try different search directions on-by-one, and may need to go back to continue a previous search direction.

- Quick reviews of search sub-tasks: With *TimeTree*, a user could quickly go over a sub-task. Starting from a specific query node, all the subsequent search actions are located on the right side of the node, and will not be interrelated with nodes from the other sub-tasks. The logical sequences of performing the sub-tasks could also be determined easily, as mentioned above.

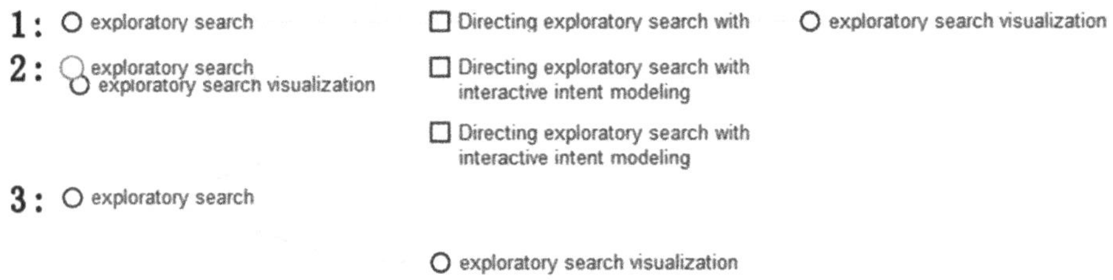

Fig. 3. Reorganizing nodes using drag-n-drop: (1) the original layout, (2) dragging the child to the new parent (highlighted as the orange circle), (3) forming the new layout.

Detailed information of a node is shown in a infobox when hovering the mouse over the node. Figure 4 shows the infobox of a click node. Basic information, including the full search result title and the first access time of a click, or the full query text and the first search time of a query, is available in the infobox. To mark the importance of a node, a user could give the node a rate, which will also affect the color of the node. The user could also comment on the node by clicking on "comment" or remove the node from the workspace by clicking on "delete". Especially, to help a user quickly remember the content of a search result, a preview of the result is also given in the infobox on the left side.

Fig. 4. The *TimeTree* infobox for clicks

3 Experimental Design

Experiments are designed to answer the question: If and how could the search process management mechanisms provided by *CiteXplore*, especially the *TimeTree* workspace, help users conduct long-term exploratory search. For the experiments, 16 participants affiliated with the Northeastern University campus will be recruited.

The participants will be asked to work on a long-term exploratory search task in a controlled environment with all the interactive actions logged. 8 members will be working with a fully functional version of *CiteXplore* and the others with a version that has the *TimeTree* workspace disabled. To simulate the situation of conducting real-life long-term search tasks, the participants will be limited to search for related topics only at specific time periods which will across several days. Subjective metrics such as opinions from the participants, objective metrics such as patterns and statistics of the interactive actions, and expert evaluated metrics such as the relevance of the clicked documents as well as the quality of the final reports written by the participants will be collected to show if and how could *CiteXplore* help users perform long-term exploratory search.

4 Future Works

Our top priority is to finish the user experiment to examine the potential positive and negative influences of the proposed methods on exploratory search. We also argue that the *TimeTree* workspace provides a novel way to record and reuse search experiences. We discuss two possible directions to use *TimeTree* to reuse search experiences.

Collaborative search is a direct and real-time way to reuse search experiences. By working on a same task collaboratively, users could see what the other co-searchers are doing, so as to share search progresses, to avoid duplication of work and to learn new searching skills from their teammates [7, 8]. To enable collaborative search in *CiteXplore*, users could join groups to work as group users. Users in a group share a same workspace, and by leveraging the same mechanism used in the synchronization of actions across views of a same user, operations in the *TimeTree* workspace and the task area are also synchronized to all the users in the group. This feature brings users real time collaborative search experiences.

Beyond exploratory search, given the tree representations of search processes saved by the users, we could seek to provide visualized recommendations to reuse search experiences in a more generous way by suggesting users what to do and the possible gains from the next step. It has been proved that representations built by the other searchers could be used by users to handle the undergoing tasks [9]. To achieve this, two kinds of visualized recommendations extracted from previous search experiences could be provided directly in the *TimeTree* workspace: Query recommendations with their top-clicked search results, and click recommendations along with possible post-click queries. Similar to the Intent Radar [1], query recommendations provided in *CiteXplore* could be diversified to show possible search directions to users. But moreover, the top-clicked search results of each recommended query could also be attached to give users a quick preview of what they can get by following a search direction. The same idea could be also applied to click recommendations by providing post-click queries so that users could know what they could possibly do after reading a document.

Acknowledgements. This work is supported by the National Natural Science Foundation Program of China (61572116, 61572117, 61502089) and the Special Fund for Fundamental Research of Central Universities of Northeastern University (N140404016).

References

1. Ruotsalo, T., Jacucci, G., Myllymäki, P., Kaski, S.: Interactive intent modeling: information discovery beyond search. Commun. ACM **58**(1), 86–92 (2014)
2. Andolina, S., Klouche, K., Peltonen, J., Hoque, M., Ruotsalo, T., Cabral, D., Klami, A., Głowacka, D., Floréen, P., Jacucci, G.: IntentStreams: smart parallel search streams for branching exploratory search. In: Proceedings of the 20th International Conference on Intelligent User Interfaces, pp. 300–305. ACM, New York (2015)
3. Park, H., Myaeng, S.H., Jang, G., Choi, J., Jo, S., Roh, H.: An interactive information seeking interface for exploratory search. In: Proceedings of the Tenth International Conference on Enterprise Information Systems, HCI, pp. 276–285 (2008)
4. Chen, W.-L., Teng, W.-G.: Exploiting browsing history for exploratory search. In: Smith, M. J., Salvendy, G. (eds.) Human Interface, HCII 2009, Part I. LNCS, vol. 5617, pp. 355–364. Springer, Heidelberg (2009)
5. Sarrafzadeh, B., Vechtomova, O., Jokic, V.: Exploring knowledge graphs for exploratory search. In: Proceedings of the 5th Information Interaction in Context Symposium, pp. 135–144. ACM, New York (2014)
6. Lamm, K., Mandl, T., Koelle, R.: Search path visualization and session performance evaluation with log files. In: Peters, C., Di Nunzio, G.M., Kurimo, M., Mandl, T., Mostefa, D., Peñas, A., Roda, G. (eds.) CLEF 2009. LNCS, vol. 6241, pp. 538–543. Springer, Heidelberg (2010)
7. Jiang, T.: Exploratory search: a critical analysis of the theoretical foundations, system features, and research trends. In: Chen, C., Larsen, R. (eds.) Library and Information Sciences, pp. 79–103. Springer, Heidelberg (2014)

8. Morris, M.R.: Interfaces for collaborative exploratory web search: motivations and directions for multi-user designs. In: Proceedings of the CHI 2007 Workshop on Exploratory Search and HCI, pp. 9–12 (2007)
9. Fisher, K., Counts, S., Kittur, A.: Distributed sensemaking: improving sensemaking by leveraging the efforts of previous users. In: Proceedings of the SIGCHI Conference on Human Factors in Computing Systems, pp. 247–256. ACM, New York (2012)

Interaction Design

Unframes: Extendible Interface and Investigations of Its Usages

Taichi Hisatsune$^{(\boxtimes)}$ and Kiyoshi Tomimatsu

Graduate School of Design, Kyushu University, Fukuoka, Japan
taichi.hisatsune@gmail.com,
tomimatu@kyushu-u.design.ac.jp

Abstract. In this paper, we propose the extendible Tangible User Interface and investigate usages and the possibilities of extendible user interface. Recently the shape changing user interface is focused on the field of Tangible User Interface. It can be changed its shape to express the digital data and physical interactions. Based on this idea, we are making Unframes: the extendible module-based user interface that can be assembled. Unframes consists of 4 cm cubic modules that can extend 4 cm in one direction. Users can make their own user interface like a visualizer, a data manager and a controller by assembling these modules. Each module have a date and synchronize each other, so it's possible to recognize the existence of data physically.

This research is a work in progress. Now on, we investigated the interfaces with only 4 units and we suppose there are still design spaces to expand and study. In the poster sessions, we will present the Unframes and investigations of its usages.

Keywords: Tangible User Interface · Interaction design · Extendible system · Shape changing user interface · Organic user interface

1 Introduction

Recently, the shape changing user interface is focused on the field of Tangible User Interface. It is not to project a GUI to objects and a table but to change the shape of the objects in order to express the digital data in an actual world. There are three differences between it and other TUI. One is that it can be a more expressive by using not only sounds and colors but also a changing of shapes. Second, from a point of an input device, an interaction of the shape changing user interface is so primitive and there is not any rules such as a pointing device. If user wants to interact with it, the only thing he should do is that he applies a force as he wants. The last is that even if a computer is turned off, it keeps its shape and the shape is based on the digital data, so the data is maintained. To connect the shape changing and digital data is able to make a new expression in a field of user interface (Fig. 1).

Before implementing our devices, first we explored what the shape changing is. The above picture shows some kinds of the shape changing. The thing like water and clay can change its shape freely without changing its volume. Rubber can expand it by applying a force or a pressure of an air. A movement of rotation like a robotic arm is

C. Stephanidis (Ed.): HCII 2016 Posters, Part I, CCIS 617, pp. 323–328, 2016.
DOI: 10.1007/978-3-319-40548-3_54

Types of shape chanings

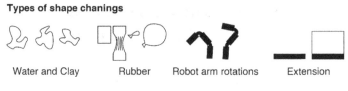

| Water and Clay | Rubber | Robot arm rotations | Extension |

Fig. 1. Types of shape changings

also a kind of the shape changing. In this paper, we focused on an extendible shape changing and developed a device that consisted of extendible cubes. Each cube can be connected each other and we can make one user interface as we want. The reason why we made is that the past shape changing user interfaces are mostly a table-top user interface and there are not enough considerations for a module-based user interface. Also, in the case of the table-top interface, an interface can only extend in upward. On the other hand, our module-based user interface can extend in not only upward but also other directions and it enables to make new expressions. Still this paper is work-in-progress, but we are exploring the usages and the design spaces of our interfaces and what we can express with it.

2   Unframes

2.1   First Prototype

First, we proposed module-based cubes that can extend in three directions. The name is Unframes. Each cube can be expanded to X, Y and Z directions to double. By assembling these cubes, it enables to express the digital data. As a first prototype, we made four cubes. The cube has three cylinders inside and the air pressures in these cylinders control its shape. All cylinders have an own valve that can be connected with a computer controlled air pump. Users can connect each cube with its magnetic joints. The picture below is our device (Fig. 2).

Fig. 2. First Prototypes

Through developing this prototype, we found that horses are obstacles to use the devices as the user interface. Because of the horses, at least one side of the cube cannot be used as the joint and if all cubes have three horses, it's too hard to recognize the totally shape. As a solution of this problem, we changed the futures of Unframes, for example, it extends in only one direction and we changed the cylinder to a servomotor.

2.2 Second Prototype

For second prototype, we developed module-based cubes that can only extend in one direction with servomotor. The size of the cube is 4 cm and it can extend 4 cm. Each cube can be connected with pins and pins also can be as the connector to a computer. To watch how the cubes are connected and control the extensions of all modules in the software, all cubes have a circuit inside and each circuit always communicate each other (Fig. 3).

Fig. 3. Second prototype

2.3 Implementations

Unframes consisted of three components: a connector, the cubes and the software.

Connector. Due to connect the cubes and the computer, the connector has a USB connector, an FTDI driver and an Attiny44 to control the serial data. It can also supply the electric power and convert the signal from the cubes to the serial data. Its size is same as the cube (Fig. 4).

Fig. 4. Connector of unframes

The Cubes. Each cube module has an LED, a servomotor and an ATtiny44 to communicate each other and control the servomotor and the LED. Its lid goes up and down when the servo rotates and an attached gears work. All surfaces have a pin to connect other cube modules. A resolution of the servo rotation is 180 /1024 degrees, so considering of its size, it can control its lid up to 0.04 mm (Fig. 5).

Fig. 5. The cubes

Software. The software is developed by C ++ and we use OpenFrameworks as a library. In the software, it watches the connections of all cubes and how the lid of all cubes up. Also, it detects directions of cubes. Users can set usages of Unframes and attach data to the cubes. Currently we didn't develop any input systems so users need not only to connect the cubes, but also to set how they use in the software. However, our goal is that to use Unframes only by interacting with the cube modules (Fig. 6).

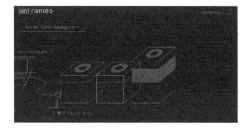

Fig. 6. Software of unframes

2.4   Usages

We explored the design spaces of Unframes. Mainly usages can be divided into three: data management, visualizer and robotics.

Usages for 1 Cube. By connecting one cube to the connector, it enables to see a digital value physically as a height of the cube. The cube can keep the data and when it has the data, its lid goes up. Furthermore, we proposed that it can be as a storage of the data like a USB flash drive. Even if it's removed from connections, it maintains the data and when it's connected to Unframes again, it shows the data inside of it. Also, everyone seeing Unframes can recognize the cube has a date because of the height of the lid.

Additionally, we proposed a specific usage: a notification. For example, by connecting the height of the module and a reception status of new mail, not only a person, but also other nearly people can recognize the shape changing as an amount of new emails (Fig. 7).

Fig. 7. A notification system

Usages for 2 Cubes. By assembling two cubes, it enables to express the differences between the two data. About the relations of two data, we developed a gravity-based system to move data in one cube to the other one. The system is that when a cube is on the other cube, the upper data drops down to the lower cube. This expression gives users an existence of digital data (Fig. 8).

Fig. 8. The gravity-based system to transport data

Usages for 3 Cubes. Assembling three cubes enable visualization. Physical visualization enables users not only to see, but also to touch. Because of a lack of the input part, we haven't developed yet, but consider about a usage of modeling.

Usages for 4 and More Cubes. When it's assembled 4 and more cubes into squares, it can express a physical screen as the digital data. Also, we proposed a robotic usage, but still we haven't developed yet.

3 Future Works

We already described above, but it still doesn't have the input part so we cannot use it as TUI. About the input part, we consider two ways to express, one is to push and withdraw lids of modules, and the other one is to touch in right rotation to down the lid and in left rotation to up the lid. We also considered deeply about the advantages of module-based user interface. If Unframes is supported Bluetooth communication and connects to mobile, it could be more useful and interact smoothly.

Additionally, we need to do a user test to find problems in the second prototype. From now on, we first will do the user test and evaluate and reveal what kinds of usages are useful for Unframes.

References

1. Niiyama, R., et al.: Sticky actuator: free-formplanar actuators for animated objects. In: Proceedings of the Ninth International Conference on Tangible, Embedded, and Embodied Interaction. ACM (2015)
2. Ishii, H., et al.: Radical atoms: beyond tangible bits, toward transformable materials. Interactions **19**(1), 38–51 (2012)
3. Yao, L., Niiyama, R., Ou, J., Follmer, S., Della Silva, C., Ishii, H.: PneUI: pneumatically actuated soft composite materials for shape changing interfaces. In: Proceedings of the 26th annual ACM symposium on User interface software and technology - UIST 2013, pp. 13–22. ACM Press (2013)
4. Harrison, C., Hudson, S.E.: Providing dynamically changeable physical buttons on a visual display. In: Proceedings of the SIGCHI Conference on Human Factors in Computing Systems. ACM (2009)
5. Bdeir, A.: Electonics as material: littleBits. In: Proceedings of the 3rd International Conference on Tangible and Embedded Interaction – TEI 2009, pp. 397–400. ACM Press (2009)

Collaboration Strategies for Drag-and-Drop Interaction with Multiple Devices

Stephen Hughes[(⊠)], Marc Davenport, and Dalton Ott

Coe College, Cedar Rapids, USA
{shughes,mdavenport,ddott}@coe.edu

Abstract. ManyMouse is a software tool that revisits the ability of multiple users to collaborate by connecting their personal independent mouse hardware to a shared computer. This tool, implemented at the system level, assigns each input device to its own simulated mouse cursor, extending the potential for collaboration to any application. ManyMouse is currently being used as a platform to explore various coordination strategies and assess their impact on learning potential. Previous work on this topic has largely focused on inferring a group's intention from the relative positioning of the mouse pointers. This work attempts to extend those ideas to include coordination of direct actions such as drag-and-drop.

Keywords: Single display groupware · Collaborative input · Collective interaction · Mice · Drag-and-drop

1 Introduction

Single Display Groupware systems have demonstrated benefits in educational settings by enriching collaboration opportunities, opening communication channels among participants, and encouraging peer-teaching [1]. Numerous studies have explored a range of different approaches for managing collaborative input – from enforced turn taking while sharing a single mouse [2] to simultaneous control of a single mouse pointer [3]. The vision for single display groupware calls for each user to have their own private, independent input channel, but this is at odds with the way that operating systems behave when multiple devices are attached. Typically, inputs generated by movements from multiple mice are aggregated to adjust the position of a single on-screen mouse pointer. Therefore, when users wish to operate their own physical hardware in a collaborative setting, specialized software, such as described in [4, 5], is needed to create and manage multiple on-screen pointers. With this software in place, it is relatively easy to recognize and respond to basic group behaviors such as "swarming" or "convergence" which are based strictly on the position of multiple mouse pointers. However, more complex behaviors, such as synchronizing clicks and drag-and-drop operations have proven more difficult [5]. In order to capitalize on the benefits of multi-device collaboration with popular drag-and-drop programming environments such as Scratch, MIT AppInventor and other Blockly-based languages, it is important to develop strategies and recognize behaviors that can support this level of interaction.

© Springer International Publishing Switzerland 2016
C. Stephanidis (Ed.): HCII 2016 Posters, Part I, CCIS 617, pp. 329–333, 2016.
DOI: 10.1007/978-3-319-40548-3_55

2 ManyMouse

2.1 Design

Like other software solutions, ManyMouse is a tool that enables multiple users to have control of their own independent mouse cursor in a shared environment. However, this tool was explicitly designed to serve as a test bed for various interaction strategies to support drag and drop operations. As shown in Fig. 1, ManyMouse intercepts raw input coming from any number of connected mice and filters the input according to the state of the mouse. This allows the program to not only determine how to display and position a customized mouse icon, but also affect the behavior of the device by deciding which system messages to pass through to the operating system.

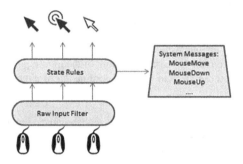

Fig. 1. ManyMouse schematic

Problems arise from the fact that "dragging" is not an explicit action in most systems; rather it is a derived from a temporal series of system messages. The system understands that it is dragging if it detects a MouseDown message followed by a sequence of MouseMove events; it exits the dragging state when it receives a MouseUp message. Without the intervention of a tool like ManyMouse, most systems will not discriminate the origin of system messages. Therefore one user's attempt to drag an icon can be routinely interrupted by another user clicking; the second user's MouseUp message forces the first user to drop their icon. However, solving this problem is not as simple as associating system messages with a specific input device; drag-and-drop problems arise from both the system level and the user interaction level.

2.2 Strategies

The ManyMouse system provides the flexibility to implement a variety of interaction strategies by simply altering the state rules. At the most basic level, users might be allowed to designate a "primary" device which is capable of performing unrestricted actions, while other devices are allowed to perform only actions that don't interfere with the primary device's actions. This delegates authority to the user of a particular device to act on behalf of the group. This technically works as a system-level solution, however, it can be problematic if authority is given to a domineering personality who doesn't ever want to relinquish control. Participants with limited capabilities are likely to feel alienated and disengaged and will not find value in this kind of system. Another strategy might attempt to democratize the role of the primary device by allowing access to sensitive actions to be granted on a First-Come, First-Serve basis. With respect to drag-and drop operations, this strategy can be implemented by simply ignoring all MouseDown and MouseUp events from other devices until an initial MouseDown event is completed with a corresponding MouseUp event from the same device. Numerous other strategies (such as turn-taking or timeouts) for ManyMouse can be imagined and implemented as a set of state transitions. From a user experience perspective, strategies that are both transparent and equitable are likely to be more successful.

3 Collective Interaction

One intriguing variation for managing collaborative drag-and-drop activities is known as Collective Interaction – a term coined by [6] to describe the natural phenomenon of individuals deliberately coordinating their input to achieve more complicated tasks. For example, when moving a heavy piece of furniture; there is an active dialogue about where to lift, how quickly to move or if a break is needed. In this paradigm, the operators must focus their attention on the input that is needed to produce a result and its rationale rather than strictly on the end result. In the context of drag-and-drop interfaces, elements may be perceived as 'too heavy' for one user to manipulate by themselves; they would need to coordinate with a peer to collectively manipulate the object. This constant negotiation of user input may prove quite valuable in a collaborative setting. As the collaborators attempt to collectively come to agreement on a course of action, individuals would need to justify their strategies in attempts to persuade others to participate in the collective behavior.

To implement collective drag-and-drop in ManyMouse requires the implementation of six states, as outlined in Fig. 2, with transitions outlined in Table 1.

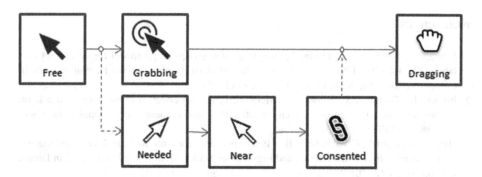

Fig. 2. Collective drag-and-drop states

Table 1. State transitions

State	MouseDown	MouseUp	MouseMove
Free	Grabbing; others to needed	Ignored	Passed through
Grabbing	N/A	Free (all)	Ignored
Needed	Ignored	Ignored	Passed through
Near	Consented	Ignored	Passed through
Consented	N/A	Near	Ignored
Dragging	N/A	Free (Drop)	Passed through

The intuition for this strategy is as follows. All pointers are considered "Free" until the first mouse button is pressed. If the button is immediately released, the act is counted as a "click" and all pointers are Free again. However, if the user holds the button down, it indicates that they have grabbed an icon, and need to wait in that location until some collaborators come to help to drag it elsewhere. Whenever another user comes to help they can agree to the actions of the "dragger" by holding down their mouse button. However they can withdraw their consent at any time by simply releasing the mouse button. The position of the consenter's mouse pointer moves relative to the dragging pointer; this eliminates the need to synchronize movements. The implication is that the dragger ultimately decides where to drop, but they must have the consent of their collaborators to perform any repositioning.

4   Evaluation

A functional prototype of ManyMouse has been developed and tested with the first-come, first-served and collective interaction strategies. Initial and informal evaluations of the system continue to suggest refinements before a formal evaluation can be performed. However, the design for that evaluation is currently being explored and expected to be conducted in the near future.

References

1. Stewart, J., Bederson, B., Druin, A.: Single display groupware: a model for co-present collaboration. In: CHI 1999 Proceedings of the SIGCHI Conference on Human Factors in Computing Systems, New York, pp. 286–293 (1999)
2. Inkpen, K., Booth, K.S., Klawe, M., McGrenere, J.: The effect of turn-taking protocols on children's learning in mouse-driven collaborative environments. In: Graphics Interface, pp. 138–145 (1997)
3. Hughes, S., Bardell, C., Schafer, J.B.: Human performance with multiple devices influencing a single cursor. In: Human Factors and Ergonomics Society 57th Annual Meeting, San Diego, CA, pp. 808–812 (2013)

4. Moraveji, N., Inkpen, K., Curtrell, E., Balakrishnan, R.: A mischief of mice: examining children's performance in single display groupware systems with 1 to 32 mice. In: CHI 2009 Proceedings of the SIGCHI Conference on Human Factors in Computing Systems, New York, pp. 2157–2166 (2009)
5. Heimerl, K., Vasudev, J., Buchanan, K., Parikh, T., Brewer, E.: MetaMouse: improving multi-user sharing of existing educational applications. In: ICTD 2010 Proceedings of the 4th ACM/IEEE International Conference on Information and Communication Technologies and Development, New York (2010)
6. Krogh, P., Petersen, M.: Collective interaction: let's join forces. In: COOP 2008 (2008)

Timbre Image Scale for Designing Feedback Sound on Button Operation

Shota Imai[1](✉), Sanae H. Wake[2], Megumi Mitsumoto[1],
Mitsuyasu Noguchi[3], Yoshitaka Uchida[3], and Noriko Nagata[1]

[1] Graduate School of Science and Technology,
Kwansei Gakuin University, Hyogo, Japan
imachu-shota@kwansei.ac.jp
[2] Information Media, Doshisha Women's College, Kyoto, Japan
[3] Kojima Industries Corporation, Aichi, Japan

Abstract. The purpose of this study is to build an image scale for operation feedback sound. When a sound designer designs the operation feedback sound, the scale could be used as a tool to share the sound image with the product developers. We evaluated the impression of the sound using the semantic differential method. Then, we carried out factor analysis, and obtained four factors: (1) artificiality, (2) liveliness, (3) gorgeousness, and (4) gentleness. From this result, we built two image scales, an artificiality-liveliness scale and a gorgeousness-gentleness scale, and put the 72 feedback sounds on these scales. These could be used to design or choose feed-back sounds that could be adapted to the product design image.

Keywords: Sound · Feedback sound · Touchscreen · User interface · Sound design · Factor analysis

1 Introduction

Operation feedback sounds are used on a lot of electric devices. When you operate a button on a touchscreen, these sounds are heard. Several studies reported these operation feedback sounds can improve the operational feeling and reduce a number of operating errors [1]. We carried out experiment to develop the sound design guideline for improving the feeling of button press [2].

Almost all feedback sounds used on contemporary electronic devices are "beeps." Regarding these sounds, we propose the use of various timbres on feedback sounds. We think they can express product's own unique images and make it easier for users to distinguish between products, allowing users to feel that certain products are better to operate than others.

The purpose of this study is to build a timbre image scale for designing feedback sounds for operation. It can be useful for adapting sound image to product design, which means it can be a tool to share the timbre image between a product designer and a sound designer. We build the image scale based on an impression evaluation experiment.

© Springer International Publishing Switzerland 2016
C. Stephanidis (Ed.): HCII 2016 Posters, Part I, CCIS 617, pp. 334–339, 2016.
DOI: 10.1007/978-3-319-40548-3_56

2 Impression Evaluation Experiment for Building Image Scale

2.1 What Is an Image Scale?

An image scale [3, 4] is a visual representation of the relationship between stimulus and its impression. The procedure of building an image scale begins with the participants evaluating each of stimulus (e.g., color, sound) image using the semantic differential method. Then, a factor analysis is conducted on the obtained data to extract some factors of the underlying image. And then, rectangular coordinate system could be made using these factors, and the stimulus are plotted on the system.

As an example, Kobayashi et al. built the color image scale [3]. They made connections between colors and adjectives and mapped them on a rectangular coordinate system. The vertical axis of the color image scale is "SOFT-HARD" and the horizontal axis is "WARM-COOL". The scale was built using 180 pairs of adjectives for color. The scale works as a color design support tool for designers who deals with color design.

We think that operation feedback sounds are part of product design, and the timbre image scale could work for the product designers.

2.2 Stimuli

In general, sounds consist of loudness, pitch, and timbre. In this research, we focused on timbre and prepared 72 feedback sounds that were different in timbre.

Sounds Designed by Sound Designers. We asked three sound designers to design operation feedback sounds using various timbres.

We showed the designers the acoustic guideline [2] (see Fig. 1). The guideline indicates the conditions of amplitude envelope: attack time is between 0 ms and 20 ms, decay time is between 50 ms and 100 ms, and total time is between 60 ms and 110 ms. When you hear the operation feedback sound which meets the conditions, you can get the good operation feeling.

Each of the designers had his own plan for designing sounds. One designer designed simple and plain sounds, another designer designed the sounds like sound-effects used in video games, and the third designer designed sounds using recorded material, such as beating or knocking on something. They designed 45 feedback sounds in total.

Sounds Designed by Authors. We designed feedback sounds based on sin wave given the following our rules.

1. Fundamental Frequency: 500 Hz, 1000 Hz, 1500 Hz
2. Harmonics:
   (a) Adding 2nd harmonic tone with 1/2 amplitude to the fundamental frequency
   (b) Adding 3rd harmonic tone with 1/3 amplitude to the fundamental frequency
   (c) Adding 4th harmonic tone with 1/4 amplitude to the fundamental frequency

3. Attack time and decay time of the amplitude envelope:
   (a) Attack time: 20 ms, Decay time: 50 ms
   (b) Attack time: 5 ms, Decay time: 70 ms
   (c) Attack time: 0 ms, Decay time: 90 ms

We designed 27 feedback sounds in total by combining these parameters.

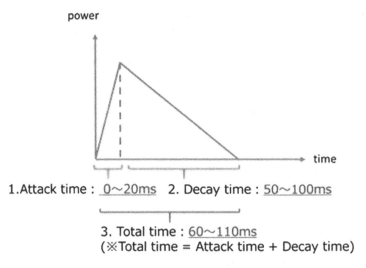

Fig. 1. Guideline for designing feedback sounds

2.3 Bipolar Adjective Pairs for Evaluation

As already mentioned, we think that operation feedback sounds are part of product design. Therefore, we decided to use the adjectives, which are used in design process, for semantic differential method. Saito et al. told that there were 12 clusters of adjectives related to design: "functional beauty," "sense of accuracy," "kindness, cuteness," "sense of quality, soft feeling," "sense of color," "elegance," "strength, familiarity," "traditional beauty," "creation and satisfaction," "modernity, fresh beauty," "luxury," and "noticeability" [5]. We selected 15 adjectives from these 12 clusters, at least one adjective from one cluster, and added another 5 adjectives. Then, we established pairs of adjectives by adding an antonym adjective to each. Table 1 shows the bipolar adjective pairs for evaluation.

2.4 Participants and Procedure

We used semantic differential method for the evaluation. 26 participants (17 men and 9 women) took part in the experiment. Participants evaluated the sound stimuli by just listening to them (they did not operate the button.) 72 stimuli were presented randomly, and the time for evaluation was one minute per stimulus. While a stimulus sound was

Table 1. Selected bipolar adjective pairs

Decorative	Functional	Plain	Gorgeous
Rough	Accurate	Modest	Noticeable
Cold	Mild	Disagreeable	Likable
Bold	Delicate	Not tire of	Tire of
Matte	Glossy	Mature	Childish
Wild	Refined	Calm	Lively
Serious	Airy	Formal	Casual
Classical	Futuristic	Masculine	Feminine
Natural	Artificial	Cheap	Expensive
Complex	Simple	Inappropriate	Appropriate

being replayed 20 times, the participants evaluated it with 20 bipolar adjectives on a 7-point scale using a semantic differential method.

3   Result and Discussion

We conducted a factor analysis to confirm the impression structure. When we conducted the last factor analysis, the items "appropriate-inappropriate," "not tire of-tire of," and "likable-disagreeable," were excluded. Principal factor analysis and varimax rotation were carried out as the method of factor analysis.

Table 2 shows the calculated factor loadings. Specifically, adjectives that had high loadings for factor 1 were "wild-refined," "rough-accurate," "matte-glossy," "masculine-feminine," "classical-futuristic," "modest-noticeable," "cheap-expensive," "natural-artificial," and "decorative-functional." Those with a high loading for factor 2 were "mature-childish," "calm-lively," and "formal-casual." Those with a high loading for factor 3 were "plain-gorgeous," "complex-simple," and "serious-airy," and those for factor 4 were "cold-mild" and "bold-delicate." We named these four factors; artificiality, liveliness, gorgeousness, and gentleness.

4   Building Timbre Image Scales

We built two timbre image scales using the four factors we had gotten from the analysis. The first (and the main) scale is shown in Fig. 2. We used the artificiality factor as a horizontal "NATURL - ARTIFICIAL" axis, and the liveliness factor as a vertical "LIVELY - CALM" axis. We call this scale the "artificiality-liveliness scale" (see Fig. 2). We also made the second scale which is "gorgeousness-gentleness scale" by using the third and fourth factors as the "SIMPLICITY - GORGEOUSNESS" axis and the "MILDNESS - COLDNESS" axis.

We mapped the sounds on the scales using the factor scores as the coordinate values, and also mapped the adjectives using the factor loadings.

Table 2. Factor loadings of each of 17 bipolar adjective pairs in the semantic differential

Bipolar adjective pairs	Factor 1	Factor 2	Factor 3	Factor 4	Communality
Artificiality					
Wild - refined	**0.765**	−0.165	−0.086	0.223	0.333
Rough - accurate	**0.723**	−0.137	−0.004	−0.096	0.551
Matte - glossy	**0.703**	0.044	0.127	-0.01	0.575
Masculine - feminine	**−0.668**	−0.029	0.128	−0.155	0.575
Classical - futuristic	**0.657**	0.155	0.415	−0.096	0.512
Modest - noticeable	**0.609**	0.263	0.181	−0.077	0.669
Cheap - expensive	**0.605**	−0.328	0.2	0.123	0.384
Natural - artificial	**0.552**	0.161	0.459	−0.127	0.637
Decorative - functional	**0.528**	−0.172	−0.09	−0.131	0.558
Liveliness					
Mature - childish	−0.061	**0.732**	−0.095	0.057	0.339
Calm - lively	0.089	**0.686**	0.159	−0.116	0.557
Formal - casual	−0.417	**0.544**	−0.032	-0.021	0.479
Gorgeousness					
Plain - gorgeous	0.397	0.042	**0.621**	0.114	0.551
Complex - simple	0.068	0.005	**−0.573**	−0.077	0.517
Serious - airy	−0.282	−0.307	**0.405**	−0.215	0.472
Gentleness					
Cold - mild	-0.1	−0.046	−0.017	**0.75**	0.487
Bold - delicate	0.084	−0.006	0.091	**0.748**	0.529
Factor contribution ratio	4.244	1.705	1.426	1.352	8.727
Cumulative contribution ratio	24.967	34.997	43.388	51.342	

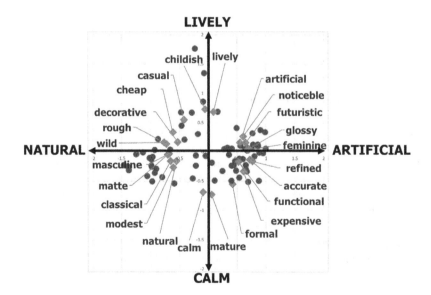

Fig. 2. Artificiality-liveliness scale

5 Conclusion and Future

In conclusion, we built two timbre image scales. These could be useful for selecting or designing operation feedback sounds, the sound images of which are adapted to the product design.

In the future, we will integrate these image scales in the iPad application "Sign Sound Selector (SSS)" [6]. SSS is a tool to share the timbre image between a client (ex. a product developer) and a sound designer. It could be used for designing sound sign and UI sounds.

References

1. Seebode, J., Schleicher, R., Moller, S.: Investigation multimodal feedback in a mobile interaction paradigm. In: Proceeding CD of Forum Acusticum 2014, Krakow, CD: ISSN 2221-3767, pdf No. SS26_3 (2014)
2. Imai, S., Wake, H.S., Mitsumoto, M., Noguchi, M., Uchida, Y., Nagata, N.: Conditions of operation feedback sound that imparts pressing feeling in touch screen. In: Proceeding of Autumn Meeting of Acoustical Society of Japan, 1-5-5 (2015)
3. Kobayashi, S.: The aim and method of the color image scale. Color Res. Appl. 6(2), 93–107 (1981)
4. Sangenya, T., Fujisawa, T.X., Nagata, N.: Creation of a sound-image scale - quantification of the images of chord progressions with impression evaluation used. In: 2008 IEEE International Conference on Systems, Man and Cybernetics (SMC 2008), pp. 1905–1909 (2008)
5. Saito, E., Tagawa, K.: Selection of sensory evaluation terms on design, and effectiveness of those terms by sensory evaluation on design of article. Japan. J. Sens. Eval. 3(2), 105–114 (1999)
6. Wake, S.: "SIGN SOUND SELECTOR" in the AppStore. https://geo.itunes.apple.com/us/app/sign-sound-selector/id1087232439?mt=8

Effect of Navigation Methods on Spatial Awareness in Virtual Worlds

Makio Ishihara[1]([✉]), Saki Higuchi[1], and Yukio Ishihara[2]

[1] Fukuoka Institute of Technology, 3-30-1 Wajiro-higashi,
Higashi-ku, Fukuoka 811-0295, Japan
`m-ishihara@fit.ac.jp`
[2] Kyushu University, 3-1-1, Maidashi, Higashi-ku, Fukuoka 812-8582, Japan
`iyukio@redoxnavi.med.kyushu-u.ac.jp`,
`http://www.fit.ac.jp/~m-ishihara/Lab/`,
`http://hyoka.ofc.kyushu-u.ac.jp/search/details/K004222/english.html`

Abstract. This manuscript discusses navigation methods which would help users to build and maintain their own mind map so that they do not lose their awareness in a virtual world. An experiment in an impact of three navigation methods of **Key**, **Click** and **Auto** on spatial awareness is conducted. **Key** is a method that enables the user to hit keys and/or manipulate the mouse to control the player freely. **Click** is a method that enables the user to click on each of pre-defined viewpoints in order to let the player jump onto it. **Auto** is a method that the player walks automatically at a constant speed along a pre-defined path. The result shows that **Key** or **Auto** methods have a better performance for spatial awareness.

Keywords: Navigation methods · Spatial awareness · Virtual worlds · Interface design

1 Introduction

A virtual world is now commonplace in games. It is a three dimensional computer-generated space and players can move around freely in it. A consumer game of Grand Theft Auto is a good example. In the game, there is a tremendously big virtual city where a lot of buildings, roads, bridges, restaurants, shops, bars, gas stations, factories, harbors, theme parks and other things exist. The sun rises in the morning and sets in the evening. Rivers flow into the sea and smoke rises from chimneys, and transportation like cabs, buses, trains and ships runs across the city. Players can walk along the sidewalk, ride a bicycle in the park, and drive a car on the highway. Other applications of virtual worlds include distance learning, open house, rehabilitation of claustrophobia, and therapy of communication disorders. Thus there are a wide range of applications.

A common device to display a virtual world to users is a high-definition wide screen. A sequence of images (screen images) to be displayed on the screen is

© Springer International Publishing Switzerland 2016
C. Stephanidis (Ed.): HCII 2016 Posters, Part I, CCIS 617, pp. 340–344, 2016.
DOI: 10.1007/978-3-319-40548-3_57

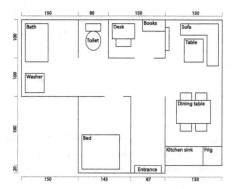

Fig. 1. A virtual house used in our experiment. A floor layout of the house (left) and a screen shot that is taken from the kitchen (right).

taken by a virtual camera in the virtual world. The virtual camera functions as a user's viewpoint. In other words, the user sees what the virtual camera sees. Another device is a head-mounted display. A head-mounted display is a goggle-type display and it gives users a highly immersive environment. Users perceive as if there was an ultra-wide screen before their eyes. In addition, a built-in head-tracking sensor is usually attached to the head-mounted display and it enables users freely turn their heads in order to look at something they want to see in the virtual world. These two devices are now mainstream.

As regards navigation techniques in a virtual world, computer mice and keyboards are often used. To control players, there are several options of mouse-key combination. One example is that the player turns when the user moves the mouse horizontally. The player also moves forward/backward when the user hits W/S keys. Another is that the player turns left/right and moves forward/backward when the user hits A/D/W/S keys. These navigation techniques and the display devices mentioned above are generally accepted by a wide range of applications that utilize virtual worlds.

One concern is a lack of spatial awareness that stems from discrepancy between the user's physical movement and the player's virtual movement. For example, the player moves around in the virtual world while actually the user is in a real chair and looking at his/her computer screen, resulting in unaware of the player's current position in the virtual world. This is called the getting-lost problem. Paraskeva et al. [1] discussed properties of spatial awareness and showed that there is a significant impact of gender on it. This poster discusses three navigation methods which would help users to build and maintain their own mind map so that they will not lose awareness of the player's current position.

2   A Virtual House and Navigation Methods

Figure 1(left) is a floor layout of a virtual house used in our experiment. The floor is 530 cm by 400 cm, and there are everyday things such as a dining room,

Fig. 2. Design of navigation methods. The pre-defined viewpoints for **Click** method are shown to the left and they are rendered as green cubes as shown in the screenshot in the center. The pre-defined path for **Auto** is shown to the right. (Color figure online)

Table 1. Elapsed time to complete sketches.

Navigation methods	Elapsed time
Key	08 min 30 s
Click	11 min 09 s
Auto	07 min 29 s

a study, a bedroom, home furniture and home appliances. Figure 1(right) shows a perspective view from the kitchen. Using this virtual house, three navigation methods are evaluated.

Three navigation methods are **Key**, **Click** and **Auto**. **Key** is a method that enables the user to hit W/A/S/D keys to let the player move forward/step left/move backward/step right, respectively and manipulate the mouse to let him/her look around. **Click** is a method that enables the user to click on each of pre-defined viewpoints in order to let the player jump onto it. **Auto** is a method that the player walks automatically at a constant speed along a pre-defined path.

Figure 2(left) shows the pre-defined viewpoints used in **Click** method. Each viewpoint is represented by an arrow in the figure, which is rendered as a green cube in the virtual house shown in Fig. 2(center). The user can click on the cube to jump onto it. Figure 2(right) shows the pre-defined path used in **Auto** method. The path starts at the entrance and goes through rooms, and comes back to the entrance.

3 Experiment and Results

Twelve subjects between the ages of 22 and 24 were asked to move around freely in the virtual house with the given navigation method. At the same time, they were asked to figure out and sketch the floor layout as precisely and fast as possible. After that they were asked to complete a questionnaire with a five-level scale (strongly yes 5 to strongly no 1):

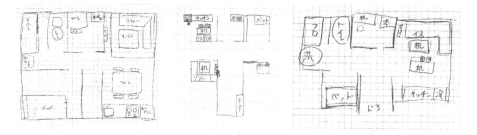

Fig. 3. Three representative sketches of the floor layout drawn by subjects given **Key** method, **Click** method and **Auto** method in order.

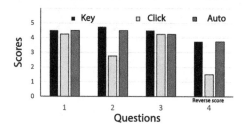

Fig. 4. Questionnaire result. (Color figure online)

Q1 Did you feel as if you were moving in the virtual house?
Q2 Was it easy to locate yourself in the virtual house?
Q3 Was it easy to remember spatial relations between home furniture?
Q4 Did you feel you were lost?

Table 1 shows the average of the elapsed time for subjects to finish their sketches. From the table, subjects given **Auto** method draw sketches more quickly than the others. Figure 3 shows three pieces of representative sketches drawn by subjects. The left one was drawn by a subject given **Key** method. The center and the right ones were done by ones given **Click** and **Auto** methods, respectively. From the sketches, subjects given **Key** method draw a more precise floor layout than the others. Figure 4 shows scores obtained from the questionnaire and it shows **Key** method has greater scores on average than the others.

Above all the results, **Key** or **Auto** methods have the potential for helping users to build and maintain their own mind map.

4   Conclusions

This manuscript discussed navigation methods which would help users to build and maintain their own mind map so that they do not lose their awareness in a virtual world. An experiment in an impact of three navigation methods of **Key**, **Click** and **Auto** methods on spatial awareness was conducted. The result showed that **Key** or **Auto** methods have a better performance for spatial awareness.

In the future work, we are going to conduct further experiments using various virtual houses and floor layouts.

Reference

1. Paraskeva, C., Koulieris, G.A., Coxon, M., Mania, K.: Gender differences in spatial awareness in immersive virtual environments: a preliminary investigation. In: Proceedings of the 11th ACM SIGGRAPH International Conference on Virtual-Reality Continuum and its Applications in Industry (VRCAI 2012), New York, USA, pp. 95–98 (2012)

Beyond Human Factors: The Role of Human Centered Design in Developing a Safety-Critical System

Nicholas Kasdaglis[1](✉) and Kimberly Stowers[2]

[1] Florida Institute of Technology, Melbourne, FL, USA
nkasdaglis@my.fit.edu
[2] University of Central Florida, Orlando, FL, USA
kstowers@ist.ucf.edu

Abstract. This paper describes the utility of Human Centered Design research as an extension of the human factors approach to developing safety-critical technology for human use. A case study is provided that illustrates how this paradigm can be employed during innovation efforts of the Trajectory Recovery System (TRS). The research paradigm in this project is organized around four nodes: understanding; conceptual development; prototyping; evaluation and analysis. Founded in creative exploration of a user-centered solution to In-Flight Loss of Control (ILOC), a multi-disciplinary effort was organized around a mixed methods research design. Human Centered Design, with its emphasis on examination of activity in larger contexts, is the organizing principle which serves to balance the technical engineering of systems with the complex needs of humans.

Keywords: Human centered design · Human factors · Tangibility · Contextual design · Aviation · Aerospace · Display

1 Introduction

Human Centered Design (HCD) may be envisioned as a simple process to aid in design [1]. The literature is replete with characterizations of HCD as a synonym for User-Centered Design (UCD), making it difficult to determine whether these areas of focus are the same or simply overlapping. ISO 9241-210:2010 generally defines HCD as: "an approach to systems design and development that aims to make interactive systems more usable by focusing on the use of the system and applying human factors/ergonomics and usability knowledge and techniques." While this definition highlights the utility of HCD as an extension of Human Factors, it also limits HCD to a focus on the user.

Even where some have implicitly acknowledged HCD as a discipline, explicit claims of it being simply a focus on the user remain [2]. Norman has suggested that HCD may actually be harmful due to what he believes is a focus upon user needs in a task to the exclusion of the larger activity [2]. He envisions that HCD is simply the process that includes a creation of personas, scenarios, and designs to make the

© Springer International Publishing Switzerland 2016
C. Stephanidis (Ed.): HCII 2016 Posters, Part I, CCIS 617, pp. 345–351, 2016.
DOI: 10.1007/978-3-319-40548-3_58

intended system adapt to the human. Instead, he favors Activity Centered Design (ACT). In a clarification to his provocative statements, Norman went so far as to say that HCD requires a revision: to include an activity-centered approach. This is unfortunate, as Boy has long argued for a systemic view that transcends a focus on the user; he has articulated an activity centered view of task in context, being influenced by organizational, technological, and situational constraints [3]. The Cognitive Functional Analysis Method (CFA) stands as a foundational construct of what Boy envisions as good HCD [4, 5]. Aside from simply a focus on the activity to be done, CFA argues that the designer must understand the underlying mechanism present, which Boy calls cognitive functions (see Fig. 1).

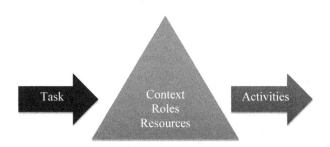

Fig. 1. Cognitive function transforms a task into an activity [3]

This paper asserts that HCD is very much concerned with "activity." In fact, safety-critical tools that are developed—in this case the Trajectory Recovery System (TRS)—are concerned more with the "activity" than with isolated discreet tasks. Furthermore, focus transcends the user and activities to include a broader context. Knowledge that is elicited from an examination of the activity, user input, human factors, and domain expertise will inform conceptual design, prototyping and evaluation.

The functional approach is especially useful in the engineering of complex systems. Early HCD discerned that a more holistic understanding of work was required in order to produce reliable work systems [3]. Characteristically complex systems are organized around multiple agents in dynamic contexts, utilizing various resources to produce reliable work. Engineers and traditional human factors practitioners have been slow to realize this. Those who conduct design are more often than not absolved from responsibility when a system fails. Instead, when a complex system fails, they might blame "human error" or – in the case of systemic issues – "automation surprises" [6]. While many solutions have been suggested to address these issues, none have considered the emergent properties of systems in the design process. Engineers, be it human or technological, had failed to understand what they had created was part of an emergent phenomenon. Designers, operators, and organizations utilized systems that they failed to fully understand the underlying principles and practice of its operation [7]. Thus Leveson could rightly state: *"The problem is that we are attempting to build systems that are beyond our ability to intellectually manage...* [8].

The result of this ignorance was building systems we could not control [7, 9]. The consequence was wide spread—accidents or failures of life critical systems could be described as "normal" [10]. This is the gap that HCD offered when it insisted on elicitation of system functions. For with this focus upon functions, task, tools, and agents could be understood in the context of operation.

2 Summary of the Trajectory Recovery System Design

The TRS is a safety-critical system that seeks to address the problem of in-flight loss of control (ILOC) due to a stall in commercial or general aviation aircraft. To find a solution to the problem of ILOC, which is the number one cause of fatalities in commercial aviation, we conducted an examination of how the ILOC recovery task is performed in varying contexts, human/machine roles, and resources [11]. HCD was utilized to understand the context of use, elicit user requirements, innovate, prototype, test empirically, and iterate for improvement [12].

The TRS research project proposed an innovative display that guides a pilot to avoid terrain. HCD methods were critical to its development, as TRS built upon interaction design research. Prior work suggests that environmental cues can be leveraged to offer affordances for action [13–15]. The TRS concept advanced prior investigation of eco-logical displays in aviation by reducing the distance between interpretation of aircraft angle of attack and the required angle of attack for recovery [16]. Additionally TRS addressed the danger of cognitive tunnelling through application of advanced interaction media principles, namely cognitive countermeasures [17, 18].

3 Application of a Human Centered Design Method

The TRS HCD research paradigm is composed of four nodes organized around "activity": *understanding; conceptual development; prototyping; evaluation and analysis*. This organization bridges the gap between abstract and tangible concepts. Furthermore, the TRS project leveraged these four HCD-based nodes to make possible the synthesis of tangibility, creativity and context in order to produce a feasible, viable, and usable solution to the problem of ILOC.

3.1 Understanding

Understanding of principles that are gathered during literature review, user surveys of Human Factors or Cognitive Engineering principles, and ethnographic observations were synthesized and made tangible a priori. This progression of tangibility continued into the TRS conceptual design and prototyping. At the focal point of these design milestones was the activity of the user. For example, the understanding phase was made tangible through the semantic structures. Such structures required anchoring to the real world. Thus, the design process was an effort to anchor semantic structures to the tangible world for the purpose of pragmatic operations.

3.2 Conceptual Development

In the conceptual development phase, understanding continued to an "imagined" world of what is possible and nominal. This is the place that creativity was set free to explore within the real world for which the system must be constrained. The way that the TRS project envisioned this being accomplished was through the development of scenarios and storyboards. Scenarios provide a contextual environment for requisite imagination and creativity in the design process. Likewise, storyboards provide an anchor for planning how scenarios occur in the "real world."

3.3 Prototyping

The junction between creativity, contextual design, and tangibility is prototyping. This is where the TRS project has continually validated what has been understood and conceptually developed with the real world. Yet the real world or the world of activity is a complex one with interactions between technology, organizations and people [3] (see Fig. 2). The goal of prototyping is to validate the design realized in conceptual development, and thus create a tangible, testable system.

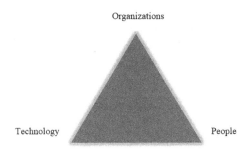

Fig. 2. Systems comprise interactions between technology, organizations, and people [3]

3.4 Evaluation and Analysis

The evaluation and analysis phase is not a discreet event within the research paradigm but an ongoing activity that occurs in each of the prior milestones. In the development of the TRS, understanding was continually evaluated against new data acquired, the conceptual model was validated against learning that occurred in the understanding phase; and prototyping naturally led to validation studies with users in context. Thus the process of validation was updated until a desired outcome was reached.

The final question of course is: "when do we know we have arrived"? In the case of the TRS project, the goal was to demonstrate that the system proposed actually worked. Therefore, it is acknowledged that maturity in context is still an ongoing activity, which will continue beyond the boundaries of the TRS project.

4 Application of Human Factors Methods

To supplement and assist in the application of a synthesized HCD research paradigm, multiple human factors methods were applied to maximize the development and successful implementation of the TRS. After all, HCD has blossomed to address paradigms not found in the field of Human Factors itself. Likewise, Human Factors approaches involve paradigms not typically used in HCD. Throughout the stages of developing and testing the TRS, more traditional human factors methods were employed, such as performing interviews with expert pilots, and implementing a research study in a high fidelity flight simulator.

4.1 Interviews with Experts

Interviews with experts are important to the field of Human Factors in that they provide researchers with a complete picture of the end user population. Where HCD provides the backbone of the system being developed in a context, completing interviews based in traditional human factors methods allows researchers to delve deeper into specific paradigms relevant to humans involved. Interviews with pilots played an integral role in the development of the TRS.

4.2 Research Study

As the final stage of design and development, a human factors research study with pilots was implemented to examine more deeply the human reaction to the TRS system. Measures tracking human performance, including eye data, workload data [19], situation awareness [20], and successful scenario completions were collected to gain a complete picture of the human condition while using the TRS. This information not only validated the use of the TRS, but provided additional details to understand the utility of the TRS for pilots. Final results are currently being generated [21].

5 Beyond Human Factors

The development of the TRS was an effort to propose, design, create and test an innovative solution to ILOC. The chosen research method, while including many human factors methods, was ultimately a product of HCD. Several concepts were joined in a complete research paradigm that led to the successful HCD development and Human Factors testing of the TRS. In this way, it can be said that HCD and Human Factors were joined in a symbiotic relationship in accomplishing the joint goal of developing a truly usable and desirable system. Indeed, we argue that these two foci complement each other and should be used in tandem to create the most effective systems for human use in complex environments.

The use of TRS can be applied to many contexts, including operational recovery guidance and/or training prompts for use during simulated upset recovery events by providing scaffolded learning. Furthermore, because the development of the TRS took into account the end user, the technology itself, and the context in which it can be used, it may carry a degree of external validity that many systems don't have. This can, once again, be attributed to the combined approach of HCD (for considering the larger realistic context that the system exists in) and Human Factors (for iterative assessment). In future work, we encourage others to take a similar approach to designing and testing systems that will ultimately be used in real-world, safety-critical systems.

References

1. HPOD.: Air Force Human Systems Integration Handbook: Planning and Execution of Human Systems Intergration. AFD-090121-054 (2009)
2. Norman, D.A.: Human-centered design considered harmful. Interactions **12**, 14–19 (2005). CACM
3. Boy, G.A.: Cognitive Function Analysis. Ablex Publishing Corporation, Norwood (1998)
4. Boy, G.A.: The Handbook of Human-Machine Interaction: A Human-Centered Design Approach. Ashgate, Burlington (2011)
5. Boy, G.A.: Orchestrating Human-Centered Design. Springer, New York (2013)
6. Sarter, N.B., Woods, D.D., Billings, C.E.: Automation Surprises. Handb. Hum. Factors Ergon. **2**, 1926–1943 (1997)
7. Hollnagel, E.: Coping with complexity: past, present and future. Cogn. Technol. Work **14**, 199–205 (2012)
8. Leveson, N.: Engineering a Safer World: Systems Thinking Applied to Safety. The MIT Press, Cambridge (2011)
9. Woods, D., Branlat, M.: Hollnagel's test: Being 'in control' of highly interdependent multi-layered networked systems. Cogn. Technol. Work **12**, 95–101 (2010)
10. Perrow, C.: Normal Accidents: Living with High-Risk Technologies. Basic Books, New York (1984)
11. Boeing Commercial Airplanes. Statistical Summary of Commercial Jet Airplane Accidents, Worldwide Operations. Worldwide Operations (2011). http://www.boeing.com/news/techissues/pdf/statsum.pdf
12. Boy, G.A.: What do we mean by human-centered design of life-critical systems? Work J. Prev. Assess. Rehabil. **41**, 4503–4513 (2012)
13. Gibson, J.J.: The Theory of Affordances. Hilldale, USA (1977)
14. Hutchins, E.L., Hollan, J.D., Norman, D.A.: Direct manipulation interfaces. Hum. Comput. Interact. **1**, 311–338 (1985)
15. Norman, D.A.: The Design of Everyday Things. Basic Books, New York (2002)
16. Temme, L.A., Still, D. and Acromite, M.: OZ: a human-centered computing cockpit display. In: 45th Annual Conference of the International Military Testing Association, pp. 70–90 (2003)
17. Dehais, F., Tessier, C. and Chaudron, L.: Ghost: experimenting countermeasures for conflicts in the pilot's activity, pp. 163–168 (2003)
18. Dehais, F., Tessier, C., Christophe, L., Reuzeau, F.: The perseveration syndrome in the pilot's activity: guidelines and cognitive countermeasures. In: Palanque, P., Vanderdonckt, J., Winckler, M. (eds.) HESSD 2009. LNCS, vol. 5962, pp. 68–80. Springer, Heidelberg (2010)

19. Hart, S.G., Staveland, L.E.: Development of NASA-TLX (task load index): results of empirical and theoretical research. Adv. Psychol. **52**, 139–183 (1988)
20. Selcon, S., Taylor, R.: Evaluation of the situational awareness rating technique (SART) as a tool for aircrew systems design. In: Situational Awareness in Aerospace Operations (AGARD-CP-478, pp. 5/1–5/8). Neuilly-Sur-Seine, France (1990)
21. Kasdaglis, N.: Angle of attack visualization: a proposal for a tangible interactive in-flight loss of control recovery system. Dissertation, Florida Institute of Technology, Melbourne, Florida (in progress)

Tele-Immersion: Virtual Reality Based Collaboration

Muhammad Sikandar Lal Khan[1]($\boxtimes$), Haibo Li[2], and Shafiq Ur Réhman[1]

[1] Department of Applied Physics and Electronics, Umeå University,
901 87 Umeå, Sweden
muhammad.sikandar.lal.khan@umu.se
[2] KTH Royal Institute of Technology, 100 44 Stockholm, Sweden

Abstract. The 'perception of being present in another space' during video teleconferencing is a challenging task. This work makes an effort to improve upon a user perception of being 'present' in another space by employing a virtual reality (VR) headset and an embodied telepresence system (ETS). In our application scenario, a remote participant uses a VR headset to collaborate with local collaborators. At a local site, an ETS is used as a physical representation of the remote participant among his/her local collaborators. The head movements of the remote person is mapped and presented by the ETS along with audio-video communication. Key considerations of complete design are discussed, where solutions to challenges related to head tracking, audio-video communication and data communication are presented. The proposed approach is validated by the user study where quantitative analysis is done on *immersion* and *presence* parameters.

Keywords: Tele-immersion · Virtual reality · Embodied telepresence system · Presence · Distal attribution · Spatial cognition

1 Introduction and Background

Virtual Reality (VR) headsets are becoming more popular due to cheaper prices, more immersive experience, high quality, better screen resolution, low latency and better control. According to statistics, around 6.7 million people have used VR headsets in year 2015 and it is expected to grow to 43 million in year 2016 and 171 million in year 2018 [1]. The most valuable application for these headsets could be video teleconferencing to enhance a personal and social experience by more 'immersive' and 'presence' feelings [3]. Among other problems, for example, gaze perception and nonverbal communication; 'different-environmental-spaces' poses a big problem in standard video teleconferencing [4]. This problem leads to a lack of immersiveness and presence experience in standard conferencing setup. Immersion is a key feature of virtual reality headsets. Immersion is a phenomenon of *getting lost, involved or drawn into something*. Teleimmersion is when *geographically distant located participant immerse himself to be located in a new environment, where he shares a same space with his collaborators* [3].

© Springer International Publishing Switzerland 2016
C. Stephanidis (Ed.): HCII 2016 Posters, Part I, CCIS 617, pp. 352–357, 2016.
DOI: 10.1007/978-3-319-40548-3_59

One-to-many video teleconferencing setups are quite common in many applications, where *one* person (called a 'remote user') collaborates with his/her *many* collaborators (called a 'local collaborators') using audio-video modalities. The standard video teleconferencing setups pose certain problems at remote user end. The remote user cannot (i) take turns, (ii) do side-conversation, (iii) make an eye-contact, (iv) explore the distant environment, etc. [4,5]. This affects a conferencing experience of the remote person which results in lack of participation, immersion, engagement and involvement in in-meeting discussions [7].

Over the years, number of solutions have been proposed which varies from software algorithms to hardware platforms. The software solutions apply computer graphics, image processing, computer vision and augmented reality techniques to solve the above mentioned problems in standard video teleconferencing [8]. The most common example of hardware based solution is mobile robotics telepresence (MRP) systems. The basic construction of almost all MRPs consist of a mobile robotic base, an LCD screen, a camera, a microphone and some non-verbal gestures, like hand gestures, etc. The review on MRPs can be found in [7]. The other types of hardware solutions can be broadly categorized into (i) an anthropomorphic design and (ii) a non-anthropomorphic design. The characteristics and appearance of anthropomorphic video teleconferencing systems (AVTS) are similar to real-human characteristics and appearance. On the other hand, the appearance of non-anthropomorphic video teleconferencing systems (NAVTS) are not like human but they still possess some human skills. The review on AVTS and NAVTS can be found in [4].

Despite all these solutions, a remote person still feels *disconnected* with his local collaborators. The major reason is that the above mentioned solutions did not address an important issue of '*different environmental spaces*' between the remote and local participants. This work aims to provide a solution to minimize the distance between the remote person and the local collaborators.

2   System Overview

The system diagram of our virtual reality (VR) based video teleconferencing setup is shown in Fig. 1. As compared to a traditional conferencing setup, our setup employs a virtual reality headset at a remote-user end. This work uses a google-cardboard [2] in combination with smartphone, but it can be extended to other VR devices. The VR headset displays local environment/participants to the remote user.

The right side of Fig. 1 shows our embodied telepresence system (ETS), which is placed among the local collaborators. The ETS is 3-DOF neck robot which actuates an attached tablet-PC. The tablet-PC is used for audio-video communication and a neck robot is used for presenting head gestures. The ETS embodies the remote user's head movements at the local site. The details of ETS can be found in [6].

We have proposed two head tracking algorithms to map the remote person's head movements to ETS mechatronic platform. Our first solution uses external

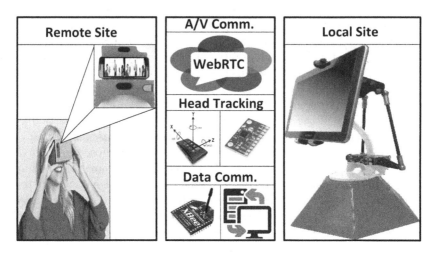

Fig. 1. Virtual Reality based video teleconferencing setup: On the left, we have a remote site and on the right we have a local site. The remote person uses VR headset (in our case google cardboard with mobile phone). Remote person is represented by our Embodied Telepresence System (ETS) at the local site. The ETS embodies the remote person head with a mechatronic robot where tablet-PC is used for audio-video communication. The audio-video communication is implemented through WebRTC. The head tracking of remote person is done by (i) orientation sensor of mobile phone and/or (ii) external IMU sensor. The data communication is done through (i) Xbee for short range and/or (ii) client-server application for long range.

IMU sensor to record 3 orientation angles, i.e., yaw, pitch and roll angles [9]. Our second solution uses an orientation sensor of a smartphone to capture these head rotations. The data communication between the remote site and local site is done by using (i) a XBEE for short range communication and (ii) a client-server application for long range communication.

The final step in our design is an audio-video communication. The traditional conferencing software (e.g. skype) cannot be used here as these software does not allow a stereo view for VR headsets. Therefore, we have proposed our own audio-video communication technique, which is based on webrtc [13]. Our webrtc based solution is a peer-to-peer connection between the remote and local sites, and the local video can be edited to make it a suitable input for a VR headset.

3   User Study: Remote User Perspective

A user study is conducted to compare our proposed virtual reality (VR) based video teleconferencing setup with the setup given in [9]. The setup in [9] uses embodied telepresence system (ETS) and the study with this setup shows promising results as compared to standard video teleconferencing softwares (e.g. skype).

3.1   Participant and Procedure

Seven participants, aging from 18–40 were recruited from the campus of Umeå University-Sweden, including both the students and staff members. For each round of an experiment we have one remote person and six local participants (one-to-many video teleconferencing scenario). The remote participant is asked to collaborate with local participants/environment based on a flexible-script provided by us. There are two conferencing scenarios for each remote person; collaboration performed with (i) the ETS-only setup (ETS) [9] and (ii) our proposed VR in-combination with ETS setup (VR-ETS). At the end of the experiment, the participants are asked questions related to an immersion and presence parameters, attention, mental construction, emotional state, engagement, ease-of-interaction and being-there [10,11].

- **Attention:** Which system increases the attention level during collaboration?
- **Mental Construction:** Which system helps you in creating a mental representation of a local environment?
- **Emotional State:** Which system has more affect on an emotional state of a person?
- **Engagement:** Which system makes you believe that your actions are interdependent, connected to and responsive to the others?

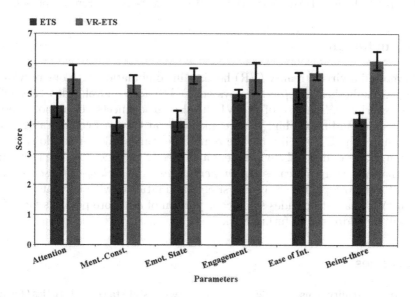

Fig. 2. Comparative results of the ETS vs the VR-ETS on immersion and presence parameters. The participants' response are presented in the form of mean and stad. dev. on a 7-point likert scale. The blue bars show responses for the ETS and the red bars show responses for the VR-ETS. (Color figure online)

- **Ease of Interaction:** Which system provides a better quality of experience (QoE)?
- **Being-there:** Which system creates a sense of spatial presence in a local environment?

We have used a likert style 7-point rating system (1 to 7) [12] to compared ETS with VR-ETS, where 1 represents strong disagreement (negative) and 7 represents strong agreement (positive).

3.2   Results and Discussion

The comparative results (ETS vs VR-ETS) of above mentioned questions are shown in Fig. 2. These results are presented in the form of means and standard-deviations of participant responses. The blue bars show the responses for the ETS and the red bars show the responses for the VR-ETS. The results clearly show that VR-ETS outperforms ETS on all immersion and presence parameters. Among all parameters, *being-there* got the highest score for the VR-ETS. This is because of immersion capability of a VR headset. Furthermore, the quality of interaction and level of engagement is also improved with an introduction of the VR headset. The movement capability of ETS in combination with a VR headset helps a remote user to get aware of the local environment and increases his level of attention which in-turn affects the emotional state of the remote person.

4   Conclusion

We have used a virtual reality (VR) headset in combination with our previously developed Embodied Telepresence system (ETS) for a novel video teleconferencing experience. The use of the VR headset disconnects the remote person from his space and makes him/her feel-like to be at the local collaborator space. Furthermore, the ETS facilitates the remote person to take turns, do side conversation, explore the local environment and specify his gaze, etc. The user study shows that our setup increases the *immersiveness* and *feeling-of-presence* experience of a remote person at a local site. The limitation with current system is that the VR headset occludes significant portion of a remote person's face. This issue will be addressed in future work.

References

1. Virtual reality users (2016). http://www.statista.com/statistics/426469/active-virtual-reality-users-worldwide/
2. Google Cardboard (2016). https://www.google.com/get/cardboard/
3. Perry, T.S.: Virtual reality goes social. IEEE Spectrum **53**(1), 56–57 (2016)
4. Khan, M.S.L., Rehman, S.: Distance communication: trends and challenges and how to resolve them. In: Handbook: Strategies for a Creative Future with Computer Science, Quality Design and Communicability. Blue Herons (EDs) (2014)

5. Fischer, K., Tenbrink, T.: Video conferencing in a transregional research cooperation: Turn-taking in a new medium. Technical report. http://nats-www.informatik.
   unihamburg.de/fischer/VKfischertenbrink.pdf
6. Khan, M.S.L., Li, H., ur Réhman, S.: Embodied Tele-presence System (ETS):
   designing tele-presence for video teleconferencing. In: Marcus, A. (ed.) DUXU 2014,
   Part II. LNCS, vol. 8518, pp. 574–585. Springer, Heidelberg (2014)
7. Kristoffersson, A., Coradeschi, S., Loutfi, A.: A review of mobile robotic telepresence. Adv. Hum. Comput. Interact. **2013**, 17 pages (2013)
8. Eisert, P.: Immersive 3D Video conferencing: challenges, concepts, and implementations. In: Proceedings of VCIP 2003, pp. 69–79 (2003)
9. Khan, M.S.L., et al.: A pilot user's prospective in mobile robotic telepresence
   system. In: 2014 Annual Summit and Conference on Asia-Pacific Signal and Information Processing Association (APSIPA). IEEE (2014)
10. Heeter, C.: Being there: the subjective experience of presence. Presence: Teleoper.
    Virtual Env. **1**(2), 262–271 (1992)
11. Diemer, J., et al.: The impact of perception and presence on emotional reactions:
    a review of research in virtual reality. Front. Psychol. **6** (2015)
12. Likert, R.: A technique for the measurement of attitudes. Arch. Psychol. **22**, 55
    (1932)
13. Johnston, A.B., Burnett, D.C.: WebRTC: APIs and RTCWEB Protocols of the
    HTML5 Real-Time Web. Digital Codex LLC, St. Louis (2012)

A Suitable Design for Natural Menu Opening Manipulations When Note-Taking on Tablet Devices

Atsushi Kitani[1] and Takako Nakatani[2](✉)

[1] University of Tsukuba, 3-29-1 Otsuka, Bunkyo-ku, Tokyo 112-0012, Japan
atsushi.kitani@gmail.com
[2] The Open University of Japan, 2-11 Wakaba, Mihama-ku, Chiba 261-8586, Japan
tinakatani@ouj.ac.jp

Abstract. There are various handwriting applications available for tablet devices. The chances of using those applications for the purpose of note-taking is increasing. When we use handwriting applications, we want to take notes naturally as if we are using a real pen and paper notebook. Therefore, handwriting application menus will also be required to accommodate natural manipulations.

With regard to natural menu manipulations, menus on existing handwriting applications and past researches have signaled some drawbacks. We propose a better menu manipulation named "Palm lift manipulation (PLM)". PLM opens context menus naturally by means of unintended touches while notes are being taken. This menu manipulation will contribute to the diversity of multi-touch interactions with regard to handwriting applications. In this research, we evaluate past research on menus, as well as our menu from the view point of natural manipulations.

1 Introduction

As tablet devices become more and more popular, various handwriting applications are developed and evaluated. When those handwriting applications are used in class or in meetings for note-taking, users iteratively change colors, stroke weights and other functions by means of menus. It is certain that the users want to take notes as if they are using real paper notebooks. Thus, they do not want to change their writing hand posture in order to open menus, and do not want to select items through several steps of touches or gestures. Such unnatural manipulations to open menus and select items are not adequate for note-taking applications.

To the extent at which users can select menus in a more natural way while taking notes is rather important for note-taking applications and their menu manipulations. Thus, we list natural note-taking criteria below.

1. The writing space should be as large as possible
2. Users can put their writing hand on a touch display when taking notes

© Springer International Publishing Switzerland 2016
C. Stephanidis (Ed.): HCII 2016 Posters, Part I, CCIS 617, pp. 358–363, 2016.
DOI: 10.1007/978-3-319-40548-3_60

3. Users do not have to change their writing hand posture to open menus
4. No stumbles while taking notes

Various research has been done with regard to menu design and menu manipulations. Most of the research focuses on rapidity and accuracy. Both rapidity and accuracy are important for menu manipulations, though they are not the only criteria of good note-taking applications.

From the view point of our criteria, we review menus with regard to general handwriting applications and menus of past researches. Then, we evaluate their adequacy in relation to natural note-taking. In terms of usability for note-taking, there are several drawbacks which we list below.

1. Occupying writing space
2. Opening menu manipulations
3. Hindering contents underneath menus
4. Being covered by manipulating hand

Most handwriting applications [2,4,9] routinely place their menus on either side of or at the top or bottom end of a display. Although those menus can be selected easily, they occupy writing space. This is drawback 1, and will be in conflict with our criteria 1. In addition, when there is a menu on a display at all times, users will be forced to keep their hand above the display, because, if they put their hand on the display, the hand accidentally touches the menu and selects items. This will be in conflict with our criteria 2.

In order to keep the writing space large, context menus (also called pop-up menus) [7,8] will be a reasonable option for handwriting applications. Context menus appear near the manipulation point of a stylus pen through specific manipulations such as a long tap or double taps. Because they only appear while selecting items and will disappear after the selection, they do not occupy the writing space at all times.

Context menus also contain the drawback 2. Some handwriting applications already have embed context menus and those menus are mostly opened by the long tap manipulation; however, the activity of taking notes will stumble due to the long tap manipulation. Thus, it is inconsistent with our criteria 4. Other operations initiated through single touch interactions to open menus conflict with drawing manipulations.

Multi-touch interactions require complicated touch manipulations and thus, will disturb the posture of holding a stylus pen. This goes against our criteria 3.

When context menus appear close to the manipulating stylus pen, the menus tend to hinder contents underneath themselves. If something similar were to occur while taking notes in a real paper notebook, it would be like a small piece of memo paper suddenly appearing on the notes, and thus disturbing our recognition of the written contents. This is drawback 3.

There are several shapes of context menus. The general shape of menus are square and rectangular. Also, there are round shaped context menus such as Pie menu and Tracking menu [3,5]. When selecting items, the manipulating stylus

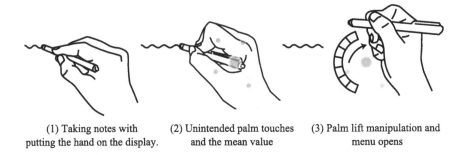

(1) Taking notes with   (2) Unintended palm touches   (3) Palm lift manipulation and
putting the hand on the display.   and the mean value   menu opens

Fig. 1. The flow of palm lift manipulation

pen and hand tend to cover parts of those menus. This is drawback 4, and is inconsistent with our criteria 4.

Context menus solve the drawback of occupying writing space. We consider that context menus for note-taking applications still have drawbacks with regard to the positions in which they appear, and further, with regard to opening manipulations.

2 Approach

We adopt context menus as our menus of note-taking applications, and attempt to meet our criteria and overcome their drawbacks. To achieve our criteria 2, a function called "Palm rejection" [10] is needed. Palm rejection enables non-purposed palm touches to avoid accidental inking, which is mostly produced by unintended touches [1].

Furthermore, in order to meet our criteria 3 and 4, we make use of the unintended touches to open our menu.

2.1 The Way of Opening Menus Naturally

In general, unintended touches are considered as unnecessary. Though we recognize all touches as variable. Most unintended touches are generated by a writing hand and those touches indicate where the writing hand is. We consider making use of this indication when opening menu manipulation.

In order to design our menu manipulation, we developed a simple handwriting application. The application is a web application and is developed by Javascript and HTML Canvas. When we use the web application on general multi-touch tablet devices such as iPad, the application detects multiple touch information.

For the purpose of distinction of intended touches and unintended touches, we embed a simple palm rejection function within our application. When there are multiple unintended touches, the mean value of the unintended touch-coordinates will be regarded as the center. Because unintended touches move rapidly with very short touch periods and are unstable, we include 20 bits of historical data in order to set a stable mean value.

Once the position of the manipulating hand becomes certain, there are no specific manipulations to open our menu, except lifting up the dominant hand from the touch display. Then, our context menu will pop-up at the recorded point. We named it "Palm lift manipulation (PLM)" and Fig. 1 shows the flow of the manipulation.

Most of other applications and researches embed long tap or multi-touch interaction to open their context menus. Whereas, long tap manipulation will be inconsistent with our criteria 4, and multi-touch interaction will be also inconsistent with our criteria 3: PLM on the other hand, does not have to do any specific manipulation to open the menu and, will be able to allow natural note-taking.

2.2   Representation of Our Menu

In this research, we adopt a characteristic arc shaped menu design [6] and call it "Arc menu". When the menu is opened by PLM, the arc shaped design will contribute to the following points:

Because of the arc shaped design, when selecting items from the menu, users can recognize all items. This will help to overcome the drawback 4. If the menu was a different design such as Pie menu, users would need to move their hand more extensively than with the Arc menu to select items. The extra movement is inconsistent with our criteria 4. Figure 2 shows the comparison of the distance of the movement.

In addition, other context menus completely cover the underneath space and users cannot see the next writing place at all. Whereas, the middle of the Arc menu is empty, and thus, helps to recognize the place that will most probably

Arc Menu   Pie Menu

Fig. 2. The comparison of the distance of the movement

Arc Menu   Pie Menu

Fig. 3. The comparison of the recognition of the writing place

receive writing. The slight difference may have a positive influence in achieving our criteria 4. Figure 3 shows the comparison of the recognition of the writing place.

3   Discussion

In this section we discuss our menu according to the following view points: adequacy of PLM and variability of the menu design.

3.1   Adequacy of Palm Lift Manipulation

We have adopted PLM in order to open menus naturally while taking notes. PLM overcomes drawbacks 1 and 2. With regard to general applications, users open menus through specific manipulations such as a long tap, double taps, or, multi-touch interactions. Such manipulations will add extra operations for users.

PLM has no specific operations to open the menu except lifting up a note-taking hand. When we are using a real pen and paper notebook, we often lift up our hand and choose other stationery from our pen case. Also while taking notes, we often lift up our hand to move to the next blank space. Therefore, we do not regard PLM as a specific manipulation.

PLM meets all our criteria 1, 2, 3 and 4. On the other hand, the disadvantage of PLM is that the menu does not appear when users do not put their hand on the display. This will happen when users take notes near the edge of the display. Under such circumstances, they are not able to put their hand on the device. To avert this disadvantage, we need to consider other supplemental options when users take notes near the edges.

We have arranged several positions with regard to opening the menu. The menu position around the writing stylus pen seams to be the fastest position for item selection. However, sometimes the writing contents will be hindered by the menu. In addition, the incompatibility between the position of the lifting palm and the position in which the menu may appear will cause confusion.

Although we have tried the opening position below the palm as well, a basic note-taking flow moves horizontally from left to right. Thus, the opening position below the palm will compel the user to move in zigzags which would conflict with our criteria 4. Under the palm on the other hand, does not lead to incompatibility, and further, does not disturb the note-taking flow. Thus, opening menus under the palm is a reasonable and adequate position.

3.2   Variability of the Menu Design

We have adopted the Arc menu, which is an arc shaped context menu. The Arc menu overcomes drawbacks 3 and 4.

The angle, size and number of items are heuristically decided. Thus, we should analyze each of them and bring out the best combination of them. We do not take into our account the difference of hand size. Children have smaller hands than adults, and those differences should be considered.

4   Conclusion

In this research we propose the novel manipulation technique named "Palm lift manipulation (PLM)" and applied the Arc menu. PLM makes use of unintended touch coordinates to set the opening position of the menu. PLM enables users to concentrate on what they are writing and lets users naturally open the menu. The Arc menu overcomes drawback 3 and 4, and thus it enables users to select items naturally. The combination of PLM and the Arc menu meet all our criteria and overcome all drawbacks.

However, there is an additional drawback, in which, the menu only appears when users are putting their manipulating hand on a display.

Since we have not had experiments, comparisons between PLM and other manipulation techniques will be needed. That will be the future topic of discussion.

References

1. Annett, M., Gupta, A., Bischof, W.F.: Exploring and understanding unintended touch during direct pen interaction. ACM Trans. Comput. Hum. Interact. **21**(5), 28:1–28:39 (2014)
2. BambooPaper. Wacom. http://www.wacom.com/ja-jp/jp/everyday/bamboo-paper
3. Callahan, J., Hopkins, D., Weiser, M., Shneiderman, B.: An empirical comparison of pie vs. linear menus. In: Proceedings of the SIGCHI Conference on Human Factors in Computing Systems, CHI 1988, pp. 95–100. ACM, New York (1988)
4. Evernote. Penultimate. https://evernote.com/intl/jp/penultimate/
5. Fitzmaurice, G., Khan, A., Pieké, R., Buxton, B., Kurtenbach, G.: Tracking menus. In: Proceedings of the 16th Annual ACM Symposium on User Interface Software and Technology, UIST 2003, pp. 71–79. ACM, New York (2003)
6. Kitani, A., Shiraishi, M., Nakatani, T.: A proposal of arc palette for a hand writing application used on a tablet device. In: Proceedings of the 5th International Congress of International Association of Societies of Design Research, pp. 2389–3498 (2013)
7. Kurtenbach, G.P., Sellen, A.J., William, A.S.: Buxton: an empirical evaluation of some articulatory and cognitive aspects of marking menus. Hum. Comput. Interact. **8**(1), 1–23 (1993)
8. Lepinski, G.J., Grossman, T., Fitzmaurice, G.: The design and evaluation of multitouch marking menus. In: Proceedings of the SIGCHI Conference on Human Factors in Computing Systems, CHI 2010, pp. 2233–2242. ACM, New York (2010)
9. Paper. Fiftythree. https://www.fiftythree.com/paper
10. Schwarz, J., Xiao, R., Mankoff, J., Hudson, S.E., Harrison, C.: Probabilistic palm rejection using spatiotemporal touch features and iterative classification. In: Proceedings of the 32Nd Annual ACM Conference on Human Factors in Computing Systems, CHI 2014, pp. 2009–2012. ACM, New York (2014)

The Interaction in an Interactive Exhibition as a Design-Aesthetics-Experience Relationship

Humberto Muñoz[✉]

Universidad Nacional de Colombia, Bogotá, Colombia
Humberto.munoztenjo@gmail.com

Abstract. This paper is the result of a ethnographic based research process, with the objective of identifying the design issues that intervenes and defines the interaction in an exhibition. The research takes as theoretical reference, phenomenology, embodied cognition and pragmatist aesthetics, based on them, a fieldwork was done, documenting through a semester several users from school level. As a result of the analysis of the obtained records at fieldwork, there were identified the main factors to take into account in the design process of a new exhibition. Understanding that interaction, and its possibilities, is a key resource that allows that design, as a disciplinary activity, make a contribution for social appropriation of science. Clarifying the role of design in the knowledge management in the creation of interactive exhibitions.

Keywords: Interactive exhibitions design · Interaction · Aesthetics experience · Embodied cognition · Phenomenology · Affordances · Science appropriation

1 Introduction

Some strategies for social appropriation of science, are related to museums and interactive centers which are scenarios where design is able to manage a quantity of implicit thinking; strategies that design supports through the different representation and materialization ways that constitute the designed exhibition.

Several disciplinary fields have had an approach to the interaction concept, having a special evolution when talking in education and communication, motivated by the changes that technology advance impulse, making new environments available, media and channels to make it possible, register and save informational contents[1]; new technologies, which characteristics are interactivity and diversity, as a result, people are not passive receptors anymore, they are active actors that manipulate and decide the order, complexity and quantity of information they want to receive, taking into account that information is received by different senses, and its is not just about the written information, as it is now presented as a spectacle issue.

An interactive exhibition is the one that reacts to the visitors acts, and at the time, motivates an answer from them, establishing a dependence between the visitors and the exhibition itself. That is why it has to be designed, understanding that the visitors'

---

[1] Ministerio de Cultura de España, 1986, pág. 12.

© Springer International Publishing Switzerland 2016
C. Stephanidis (Ed.): HCII 2016 Posters, Part I, CCIS 617, pp. 364–370, 2016.
DOI: 10.1007/978-3-319-40548-3_61

learning process is not unidirectional and can include affective and social way, or even psychomotor skills. The success of an interactive exhibition is related to the fact that when a person is motivated for learning, emotions and feelings are involved in a significant way, also the thoughts. (Léonie 1996).

In that way, and relating it to the design of interactive exhibitions, it appears the question how interactivity is understood and how it has to be defined in the design process, because that would allow a greater success and harmony in the communicational goals that is looking for, as it is to approach people to knowledge.

In the field of design there are several interpretations or definitions to the interaction concept. In the case of interaction design (IxD), is an interdisciplinary field that has the purpose of defining the behave of products and systems that interact with people. The interaction design products are normally developed with interaction analysis and users tests. Interaction designers prioritize users' goals and experiences, and evaluate the design in terms of "usability" and affective influence.

In the case of interactive centers, the concept is used to motivate visitors to use and manipulate objects, as a way to propitiate experiences about science, where they are disposed as a particle, that when used by a visitor, this one at the time becomes one, activating the phenomenon and propitiating the interactivity. Traditional museography has taken the concept in recent decades, in a centered communicational process way, where, according to Alejandro G. Bedoya, interactivity is the capacity of the receptor to control a non-lineal message to the grade establish by the emisor, within the limits of asynchronous communication via (Mestre and Piñol 2008). This definition refers to the idea of hypertext, convergence or randomness in communication processes.

In a full-scale way and having said, interaction, then, refers to the intervention of senses, because through them the communicational fact takes place, where cognitive activity is involved.

2 Main Hypothesis

The interaction in an exhibition is established by the relation between the design, as a material result of a thinking and planning process, the aesthetics, as the expressive external qualities of the exhibition, and the knowledge that can be potentiated in the visitors through the exhibition.

The exhibition is characterized as changing a group reality/space/time, where a link is established, that in one hand, achieves the goal of making a contribution to the learning process and the knowledge appropriation, on the other hand, the exhibition's visitor, who, thought the interaction and the aesthetics embodied experience, creates a cognitive relation to the knowledge, making their learning process possible. The design as a process that originates the exhibition, creates the physical world for the visitors to interact. A hybrid physical media created, where the control in the design process is possible in order to stimulate the interaction.

Interaction appears when visitors react with emotional basic acts to that physical environment that the exhibition is, the aesthetics interaction is a result of the visceral emotional reaction that the visitor has, face to the phenomenon or reality that catches his/her attention. Taking into account that the aesthetics interaction is only possible related to external conditions or events that, as the exhibition, can characterize the relation that people has with the world. Design has to take it as a reference to understand and propose interaction and materialize that physical external and artificial environment to be created.

3 Development

To create a new interactive exhibition, from design, to propose an experience in the visitors that has to have place thanks to the physical and representation environment, those materialize the exhibition, however the exhibition itself is not just they; without ignoring the attractiveness and pleasure that has to characterize it as a gateway to the cognitive process that is established in the pleasure and fun that visitors find in the physical phenomenon that they experience.

The research is systematic, its main purpose was to inquire how the interaction takes place in an interactive exhibition, and how the objects and all the physical environment act and are assumed by the visitors. Thus, the research is based, among others, in the Maurice Merleau-Ponty approaches, and phenomenological philosophy, who proposed that it is not possible to understand and assume the world but for its "faculty", and the "sensitivity" can only take place linked to a physical specific context (Merleau-Ponty 1994; Calvo Garzón 2007; Sacrini and Ferraz). In the same way, the approaches in the pragmatic aesthetics of Richard Shusterman, who ensures that the world can only be justified as a "aesthetic phenomenon" ((Shusterman, Aesthetic experience) (Kul-Want, 2007), and that body, mind and instrumentation are the core of the experience, being this an approach different from the analytic aesthetics which understands the aesthetics denying the aesthetic qualities as natural (Shusterman, 2002).

Such a theoretical frame allowed to understand the interaction in an exhibition as an aesthetic experience, product of perception and temporary hookup of visitors; an experience that gives a place to a continuous interaction-cognition of body/mind/media. Considering that aesthetics acts not as a contemplation issue, but as a result of interaction, that is to say that thinking is dynamic and implies a continuous link between sensation and action, between the internal and external world, between subject and exhibition.

The systematic approach realized in this research from the design perspective, was methodologically based in the recourses and tools of the ethnographic work, such as conversation analysis, immersion in context, coexistence and observation, for giving place to explanation and interpretation, as they show the questions that took place while analyzing the interaction in an interactive exhibition.

After the field work and relating it to the theoretical frame it was possible to conclude that the interactive exhibition can be understood as a "dynamic form", its expressive qualities are tridimensional material objects, bidimensional and digital tools that may vary in dimension and technological complexity that enable interaction and aesthetic experience in people. A designed dynamic form that establishes a complex and hybrid atmosphere, were people have a link or a ludic approach to the phenomenons and science knowledge that compose the exhibition, and propitiating their learning. People that through the continuous interaction body/mind/brain build their own perception about the exhibition. Where socio-cultural approach, values and behaviors happen, thus, the aesthetic experience is favorable from the atmosphere of the interactive exhibition, that implies that people are known from cognitive dimension, embodied, perceptual-motor, emotional and socio-cultural.

With the methodology and after a six month fieldwork in two different scenarios, during a semester, using technological tools as eye tracking, and filming of the visitors' experience, it was possible to analyze how the aesthetic experience in the interactive exhibition is built in different levels.

Those levels happen from the espatial-architectual dimension of the space where the exhibition is, followed of access to knowledge areas and the general scenography, and direct interaction with activation areas or interaction interfaces. Those levels act simultaneously and responding to the users diversity that are in the exhibition at the same time, they constitute a whole dynamic form, that sensitize and prepare visitors for free and open interaction with the phenomenon and information that they can find in the exhibition.

School visitors arrive to the exhibition formally and disciplined by the school rules and the influence of teachers, but when students get into the exhibition atmosphere they leave that formalism and act as themselves, they create groups by affinity and fellowship, creating spontaneous groups that plan their route through the exhibition. This sets the mood and the emotional attitude for visiting the exhibition.

The areas or interfaces that use high tech, weird objects or in movement equipment attract visitors' attention. They move thought the exhibition in disorder, a non established route, in a funny way. When visitors face interaction areas they do not read instructions, they do not try to understand the order or logic or the way to use the equipment, they just push buttons, pull handles or go directly to interfaces. They are especially attracted to activities, phenomenon and equipment where their own body is used as part of the explanation, because the challenge and the opportunity to make a comparison with their mates is funny for them.

They try to make everything work at the same time if they do not receive any feedback they immediately abandon it or try interaction in other part, they just wait for a few seconds. The elements information, and the aids that exhibition offers for communication they just ignore them. When a specific area or phenomenon catches their attention, curiosity and anxiety for discovering, identifying and understanding what happens, is what keeps their attention and interest and gives a place for them to build or create theories and interpretations.

When a phenomenon or action area that they use is nice they try to make it last longer, it is about the aesthetic experience as a result of the interaction with the exhibition and the reaction is to try to make it last for "pleasure", this kind of situation enables the appropriation of the information and potentialities some learning. Interaction and aesthetic experience are evident in conversations, attitudes, expressions and visitors' behavior.

After visiting the exhibition, visitors recreate it from the experience, they do not relate specific aspects or aesthetic qualities, they describe the visit relating it to their daily life. In some cases they relate some learning or reference information in the exhibition, they keep in mind that exhibition was about science and they do not forget the funny moments at the exhibition.

In a rigorous and focused on design way, five factors were identified, for taking into account in the creative process, this factors act simultaneously and mold the aesthetic experience and the interaction in the exhibition, they are:

1. Social an physical **context**, they create the atmosphere. All the situations and aspects that are "sensitization ways" or the environment that pushes people to interact. This is about social and the collectiveness that people visit the exhibition with, and the physical environment that works as a scenography, an external world that can be done, modified and proposed from design.
2. The **movement**, as an extension of events in time. Is the main factor that determinate interaction and builds the experience in the exhibition, visitors make their tour through the space related to external references as they are the activities and the physical characteristics of the space. The different experiences of the exhibition are related to the displacement that visitors make in the space and the events that happen while touring, and also some aspects of the interaction itself.
3. The **attractiveness**, which is related to all the things that motivate or attract visitors to interact in certain activities or spaces, most of attractiveness is about the aesthetic appearance or the expressive qualities of the form of the exhibition module, as also the motivations that appear from the relations and social situations at the moment of interaction.
4. The **activity**, referred to all those individual and collective situations that happen while people are interacting with the exhibition and the physical environment. They are: behaviors, habits, displacements, search, they constitute the dynamic relation between people-people and people-objects. The exhibition as a chain of "events" that integrate visitors, some of them structured and planned, others spontaneous and unpredictable, they all constitute the interactivity.
5. The **demonstration** is the factor that creates the expectation in people, they expect a result after the activation of a phenomenon, or the interaction with the exhibition model. The experience that is produced by the interaction is centered in the verification of something (a principle, concept, data, etc.) from the own experience of visitors (Fig. 1).

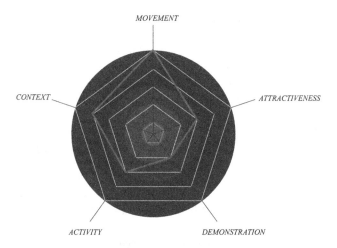

Fig. 1. Design factors that determine the interaction

4 Conclusion

An interactive exhibition acts as a learning environment. It has the physical conditions that make possible all sensitize to the aesthetic experience. It is a dynamic form that enables interaction, from expressive qualities, which gives place to the aesthetic experience understood as the emotional state of the subjects. They, the visitors of the exhibition, through the embodiment of sensations that the form inspire, and attracted by the expressive qualities give a sense to their emotions, interact and access to knowledge. That interaction is the result of the link of design, as the creator of the exhibition, the aesthetics, as expressive qualities of this, and knowledge as a result of the interaction of people there. The exhibition is an external world where visitors are conscious of this world, so they can understand and judge it. Those levels of the interactive exhibition, and due to the design process are the resource that can control the design in the creation of the interactive exhibition. The five identified factors understood in a conscious and systematic way can contribute to a higher efficiency an impact of the exhibition.

References

Calvo Garzón, F.J.: Arquitectura de la Cognición, pp. 1–64. Fundación Séneca, Murcia-España (2007)

Danilov, V.J.: Science and Technology Centres. MIT Press, Cambridge (1982)

Boer, T.: Global User research methods. In: Handbook of Global Research, pp. 145–201 (2010)

Dewey, J.: El Arte Como Experiencia. Paidós, Barcelona (2008)

Dorfles, G.: El diseño Industrial y su estética. Labor, S.A., Barcelona-España (1968)

Falk, J.: Learning from Museums, Visitor Experiences and Making of Meaning. Altamira Press, USA (2000)

Flórez Ochoa, R.: Hacia una pedagogía del Conocimiento. Mc Graw-Hill, Bogotá-Colombia (2000)

Gomila, C.: Handbook of Cognitive Science, 1ª edición. Peter Slezak, USA (2008)

Hartson, R., Pardha, S.P.: The UXBook. Elsevier Morgan Kaufman, USA (2012)

Hummels, C.: Special issue editorial: aesthetics of interaction. Int. J. Des. 4(2), 1–2 (2010)

Kul-Want, C.: Introducing Aesthetics. Icon Books U.K., Cambridge (2007)

Léonie, J.R.: Science centres and science learning. Stud. Sci. Educ., 387–423 (1996)

Mc Lean, K.: Planning for People in Museum Exhibitions. Association of Science-Technology Centers, Washington (1993)

Mc Manus, P.: Topics in museums and science education. Stud. Sci. Educ. 20, 157–182 (1992)

Merleau-Ponty, M.: Fenomelogía de la Percepción. Ediciones Península, Barcelona-España (1994)

Michel, R.E.: Design Research Now. Birkhäuser Verlag AG, Berlin (2007)

Muñoz Tenjo, H.: Algunas consideraciones de diseño en los Centros Interactivos. Universidad Nacional de Colombia, Bogotá-Colombia (2004)

Norman, D.: El diseño Emocional. Paídos, Barcelona-España (2007)

Not, L.: Las pedagogías del conocimiento, 1ª reimpresión. Fondo de Cultura Económica, Bogotá-colombia (1994)

Perry, D.L.: What Makes Learning Fun? Altamira Press, Plymouth (2012)

Press, M.: El diseño como experiencia. Gustavo Gilli, SL, Barcelona-España (2009)

Rambla Zaragozá, W.: Estética y Diseño. Universidad de Salamanca, Salamanca- España (2007)

Rickenmann del Castillo, R., Angulo Delgado, F., Soto Lombana, C.: El Museo como medio didático. Editorial Universidad de Antioquia, Medellín-Colombia (2012)

Ross, P.R.: Designing behavior in interaction: using aesthetic experience as a mechanism for design. Issue Des. **4**, 3–13 (2010)

Sacrini, M., Ferraz, A.: (s.f.) La fenomenología practicada por Merleau-Ponty, pp. 143–166. Universidad de Sao Paulo, São Paulo

Saffer, D.: Designing for Interaction: Creating Innovative Applications and Devices. New Riders Publishing, New York (2009)

Santacana i Mestre, J.: Manual de Museografía interactiva. EdicionesTrea, S.L., Oviedo- España (2010)

Sawyer R.K.: The Cambridge Handbook of Learning Sciences. Cambridge University Press, Washington (2006)

Screven, C.G.: The Measurement and Facilitation of Learnign the Museum Environment: An Experimental Analysis. Smithsonian Institution Press, Washington (1974)

Semper, R.J.: Science museums as environments for learning. Phys. Today **43**, 2–8 (1990)

Shapiro, L.: Enbodied Cognition. Routledge, New York (2011)

Shusterman, R.: Estética Pragmatista. Idea books, S.A., Barcelona-españa (2002)

Shusterman, R.: (s.f.) Aesthetic experience

Sommerer, C.: The Art and Science of Interface and Interaction Design. Springer, Vienna (2009)

Van Dijk, J.: Cognition is not what it used to be: Reconsidering usability from an embodied. Hum. Technol. Interdisc. J. Hum. ICT Environ. **10**, 29–46 (2009)

Van Dijk, J.: Creating traces, sharing insight, explorations in embodied cognition design (tesis Doctoral). Technische Univesiteit Eindhoven, Eindhoven (2013)

Visser, W.: The Cognitive Artifacts of Design. Lawrence Eribaum Associates, Publishers, London (2006)

User-Centered Tile Menu Selection Technique in Large Scale Display

Katsuhiko Onishi[(⊠)] and Yamato Gomi

Osaka Electro-Communication University, 1130-70 Kiyotaki,
Shijonawate, Osaka 575-0063, Japan
{onishi,mt14a004}@oecu.jp

Abstract. In this study, we describe about our approach for the selection technique by using user-centered region to define selection state. It is a mainly subject to realize the efficient selection gesture by user's arm for any position on the screen. we designed selection region and pointer fixed region by using relative position of the user's arm joints. Our method uses user's hands, elbows and shoulder position at each arm. And it recognized user's selected points by the relative position of these joints. We make the prototype system which has been implemented our method. And we confirm behavior of our technique from the prototype system. Through the experiment of our selection method, it is confirmed that our method allows users to perform smooth selecting operation regardless of objects position.

Keywords: 3D pointing · Selection technique · Gesture · User-centered region

1 Introduction

Large display systems have become popular recently. It has been also used in many public space as the signage system or the information system and so on. These systems also have some interaction system which allows users to select object by using direct/indirect manipulation like hand/finger gesture. These gesture manipulation techniques are very common in human computer interaction [1–3]. The system which is implemented this technique has been measured user's hand/finger position and execute selection tasks. It is not generally need an assistance such kind of manuals and so on. Therefore, it is used many kinds of systems which are able to use in public places. But in some case, especially indirect manipulation, it is difficult to select objects depending on the object position. Many systems define the selection state by finger position from the display or the measure device. Therefore, it is sometimes difficult to select objects which is closed to the corner of display. Because, it keeps a distance from user's position in comparison with the other position of objects.

In this study, we describe about our approach for the selection technique by using user-centered region to define selection state. It is a mainly subject to realize the efficient selection gesture by user's arm for any position on the screen. We designed a selection method which uses selection region and pointer fixed region by using relative position of the user's arm joints. Our method uses user's hands, elbows and shoulder position at each arm. And it recognized user's selected points by the relative position of

© Springer International Publishing Switzerland 2016
C. Stephanidis (Ed.): HCII 2016 Posters, Part I, CCIS 617, pp. 371–375, 2016.
DOI: 10.1007/978-3-319-40548-3_62

these joints. We make the prototype system which has been implemented our method. And we confirm behavior of our technique from the prototype system. Through some experience of our selection method, it is confirmed that our method allows users to perform smooth selecting operation regardless of objects position.

2   User-Centered Tile Menu Selection Technique

The selection technique by using 3D gesture motion is generally used raycasting method. It is selected objects by expanding the user's arm to the object. However, in the large display environment, it is sometimes difficult to select the object according to the position on the screen. Because it becomes out of movable range of the arm. Therefore, our method is focused a user-centered region for selection task. The region is a circle area and the center of it is defined user's shoulder. Figure 1 shows our method summary. As our former study discussion [4], Our method uses two kind of operation status. One is selection and another is pointer fixed status. These statuses are defined by user's hand position. If the user's hand is interfered in the selection region, it is defined as selective operation. And if the user's hand is interfered in the pointer fixed region, it is defined as fixing the pointer in a screen.

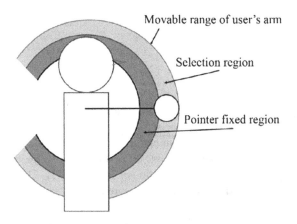

Fig. 1. User-centered region for selection task

To measure the interference between user's hand and these regions, our method measures the hand, elbow and shoulder positions. Figure 2 shows a summary of our method. It calculated two vectors, shoulder-elbow and shoulder-hand. And it uses the angle by the two vectors to determine these statuses. Since the orientation of the two vectors in our extended arms becomes almost same, the angle is close to $0°$. The results were verified by preliminary experiments, the θ when fully extended arms had a value of less than $15°$. Therefore, our method uses $15°$ as the threshold of selection region.

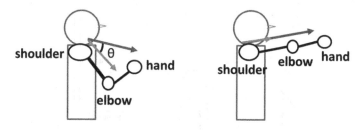

Fig. 2. A method of interference decision by using user's arm joints position

3 Implementation

We developed the prototype system which is implemented our method. Our system is developed at Windows PC and measure the user's each joint position by using Microsoft Kinect. Figure 3 shows an image of our system.

Fig. 3. An image of our prototype system

To confirm the usability of our method, we make experiments with a conventional selection method which uses just user's hand position from a screen. Figure 4 shows our experimental environment. We prepared four kinds of a parameter β which defines a threshold between selection region and pointer fixed region. As an experimental task, it is prepared that participant selects all objects randomly which are set 3 × 3 on the screen. And the task completion time is measured at each method. At first, the participants are introduced each method by performing the operation. And they practice each method in 2 times. Then, they execute each task 2 times by using all methods and the completion time is measured. The participants were intended for 4 students.

Figure 5 shows an average of task completion time. It is confirmed that the time of our proposed method is less than that of the conventional method which does not have parameter β. And it is confirmed that the participant can select all objects easily.

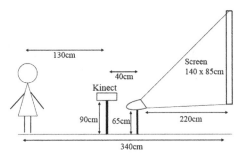

Fig. 4. An experimental environment

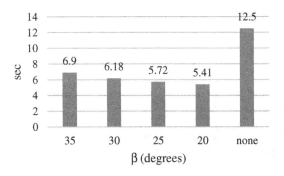

Fig. 5. Average of task completion time

4 Conclusion

In this study, we designed the selection technique by using user-centered region to define selection state. Our technique uses a region which is around the user's shoulder. And two statuses are defined, selection region and pointer fixed region. Our method uses the user's three arm joint position to manipulate the pointer. We developed the prototype system which is included our proposed technique. As a result of the experiment, we confirmed the efficiency of our method. In the future work, it is needed to study of the gestures pattern which is adequate to our method.

References

1. Vogel, D., Balakrishnan, R.: Distant freehand pointing and clicking on very large, high resolution displays. In: Proceedings of the 18th Annual ACM Symposium on User Interface Software and Technology, pp. 33–42 (2005)
2. Cheng, K., Pulo, K.: Direct interaction with large-scale display systems using infrared laser tracking devices. In: Proceedings of the Asia-Pacific Symposium on Information Visualisation, vol. 24, pp. 67–74 (2003)

3. Pfeiffer, M., Stuerzlinger, W.: 3D virtual hand pointing with EMS and vibration feedback. In: Proceedings of IEEE Symposium on 3D Use Interfaces 2015, pp. 117–120 (2015)
4. Gomi, Y., Onishi, K.: Study of tile menu selection technique using the relative position of joints for gesture operation. In: Stephanidis, C., Tino, A. (eds.) HCII 2015 Posters. CCIS, vol. 528, pp. 481–484. Springer, Heidelberg (2015). doi:10.1007/978-3-319-21380-4_81

Common-Awareness Artifacts
Conceptual Elements to Designing and Evaluating Collaboration in CVE

Wilson J. Sarmiento[1,2(✉)] and César A. Collazos[2]

[1] Multimedia Research Group, Military Nueva Granada University,
Bogotá, Colombia
wilson.sarmiento@unimilitar.edu.co
[2] IDIS Research Group, University of Cauca, Popayán, Colombia

Abstract. This paper present the common-awareness artifacts, interaction elements that support the activities of workspace awareness. These artifacts are tools to design and evaluation of interaction and immersion components of a CVE, through a set of ten guideline/indicators. A case study shows how to design and evaluate a common-awareness artifact using the guidelines and indicators. The guidelines allowed building a suitable component to support a collaborative navigation activity in a CVE. A test with user provided that quantitative metrics of indicators may found the difference between two collaborative conditions.

1 Introduction

Collaborative Virtual Environments (CVE) are systems that allow a team work in a common task inside a virtual world. The main goal of these systems is to provide an optimal integration of two kind of systems, collaborative software (groupware) and multi-user virtual reality (VR) environments [1]. This implies challenges in how to design, build and evaluate a CVE, where the collaboration must be the center of attention; and the immersion and interaction elements are the way to generate a suitable team cohesion [1]. Collaboration is a complex activity that involves many key processes such as communication, information sharing, coordination, negotiation, and awareness i.e. a high-level process related to the ability to recognize a surrounding reality, e.g. objects, events, task or another person.

When a user interacts in a virtual environment (VE), several awareness levels can be observed. So, He/She must be able of to recognize technological elements that mediate all interaction, must feel that is in a VE and forget the real world (presence), must perceive his/her partners, must be part of a team (co-presence), must have aware that he/she is executing a task, and it is part of collaborative

C.A. Collazos—Thanks are due VRI and IPET of Cauca University of University, Colombia. Wilson J. Sarmiento is supported by the Military Nueva Granada University, Colombia. We finally thank to test team formed by students of University of Cauca.

© Springer International Publishing Switzerland 2016
C. Stephanidis (Ed.): HCII 2016 Posters, Part I, CCIS 617, pp. 376–381, 2016.
DOI: 10.1007/978-3-319-40548-3_63

work [5]. However, most of the awareness models in CVEs are only oriented to physical interaction between a user and other elements in the VE, included other users [5]. Therefore, they leave outside the other aspects of awareness.

Awareness has been highlighted as necessary to reach a desirable collaboration, however *"there are few developers of CVEs who have given many thoughts to awareness aspect while designing collaborative virtual worlds"* [5]. This work introduces the concept of the common-awareness artifacts (CAA), which are mechanisms that integrate elements of interaction and immersion in a unique design component in order to facilitate users to reach the most high awareness levels.

2   Background and Related Works

The concept of common-awareness artifacts proposed in this work is based on two concepts defined in computer supported cooperative work (CSCW): the common artifacts [6] and the workspace awareness framework [2].

Common or shared artifacts, are interactive elements designed to facilitate a group activity [7]. The correct design of a common artifact is a complex task due that this must involve all processes that affect the collaboration. Robinson defines five desirable characteristics that could to allows to determine the correctness of a common artifact (1) predictability; (2) peripheral awareness; (3) implicit communication; (4) double level language; and (5) overview [6]. By definition, these characteristics only involve interaction aspect, leaving out the immersion component, which is fundamental in a CVE. A related term, proposed by Tee et al. [8], is the artifact awareness, defined as *"one persons up-to-the-moment knowledge of the artifacts and tools that other distributed people are using as they perform their individual, ongoing work"* [8]. The main difference between a common artifact and an artifact awareness is that the first act when the team interaction starts, and the second may act before the interaction, because promotes it [8]. But, they neither include immersion aspects.

On the other hand, the workspace awareness is a framework that defines how the awareness supports the collaboration through processes and activities developed following the perception-action cycle of Neisser [2], which is composed of three stages. The first one, is the information that makes up awareness, which answers questions *"who, what, where, when, and how"* [2]. The second one, involves the mechanisms that allow gathering awareness information [2]. And the last one, correspond to the awareness activities that support collaboration i.e., (1) management of coupling, (2) simplification of communication, (3) coordination of actions, (4) anticipation and (5) assistance, which must arise naturally in a collaborative work [2]. Although, these concepts were not proposed specifically for CVEs, It will allows to explain the relationship between awareness and immersion and how they affect the collaboration in a CVE.

The design of artifacts to support interaction or immersion tasks in a CVE is a recurrent topic [3,4], but only few authors include the concept of common artifacts, shared artifacts or artifacts awareness. Besides, as Nguyen and Duval assert, there are a lack of moment to include awareness aspect in the design of CVE [5]. This scarcity in design affect also the evaluation of a CVE, because if there are not guideline to build an CVE considering awareness aspects, is very difficulty verify these aspects.

3   Common-Awareness Artifacts

As was explained above, common artifact concept disregards the immersion aspects of the interaction elements, which are fundamental in a CVE. So, we introduce the concept of common-awareness artifacts as interaction elements that support the activities of workspace awareness, allowing keep proper immersion senses.

In a CVE, at the first stage of the workspace awareness cycle, information relates to the state of surrounding reality perceived by the user. Information quality, given through CAA, affects awareness level reached by the user, and consequently immersion senses. At the second stage, the way as the user interact in 3D must be designed to permit see, listen, speak, and others kinds of communicating and perceiving. So, CAA have the responsibility of providing the channels for sending and receiving awareness information. To close the cycle, at the last stage, CAA allow the user carry out tasks in a CVE. If the interaction is correct, the individual work evolves in workgroup, and the awareness activities arise. These activities fortify the senses of presence, co-presence and all immersion senses.

The design and the evaluation of common-awareness artifacts must be included factors of interaction and immersion. In the design moment, the guidelines are composed of five desirable characteristics of collaborative interaction and five behaviors expected to facilitate that generation of awareness activities. In this way, the artifacts will be developed considering aspects of interaction and immersion. In the evaluation moment, is possible define ten indicators, five of interaction and five of immersion, which allows a diagnosis of how this artifact affects the collaborative work. Table 1 shows the set of ten design guidelines and evaluation indicators of a common-awareness artifact.

4   Case Study

In order to exemplify how common-awareness artifacts could be designed and evaluated, a case study is herein described. In a CVE an interaction artifact must be oriented to one of four basic 3D interaction tasks: selection, manipulation, navigation or system control. The navigation task is maybe the more cognitively rich; two subtasks compose it, the physics locomotion and the cognitive wayfinding. So, the focus of the case study was an artifact to support a traditional collaborative wayfinding activity, capture the flag. The activity was defined as follows: *"The team (two users) must capture eight flags at a maze in time limited. Only one flag is available at the same time, when the team wins*

Table 1. Design guidelines and evaluation indicators of a common-awareness artifact

Interaction	Immersion
IT^1 Predictability	IM^1 Management of coupling
Users predict how to use it	Users may couple with partners
IT^2 Peripheral awareness	IM^2 Simplification of communication
Users interact using peripheral attention	Users may send messages more simples
IT^3 Implicit communication	IT^3 Coordination of action
Users communicate on alternative channels	Users may suggest how improve the work
IT^4 Double level language	IM^4 Anticipation
Users have information to negotiate	Users may predict partners intentions
IT^5 Overview	IM^5 Assistance
Users have an overview of the work	Users may help their partners

the current flag, the next is available. All team members must walk over flag's neighborhood for catch it."

In brainstorming sessions, the design team discussed each guideline and how to implement it. The design looks for to accomplish the Robinson's characteristics and to facilitate waking up of awareness activities. The intermediate stages of the design included drawing, sketches and paper prototypes. Figure 1 shows the final artifact. It is a head-up display placed in the right bottom corner screen. Two minimaps, one side other. The left minimap shows the relative current flag position, which is a known radar view where the interest object is around of relative user position (radar center). The right minimap is a global view of the maze in which the user can to see himself (green point) and his partner (white point). Another important cue is the user orientation (green arcs), which allows to user identify his partner relative position. This artifact has predictable and easy use, it allows user is focused on the main task, it also provides alternative communication channel (users movements), it gives the required information to negotiation and provide an overview of the collaborative activity. Additionally, the artifact provides necessary elements to generate and maintain team cohesion; it simplifies the communication between users; allows coordination actions and allows that a user anticipates and assists a partner.

The evaluation team designed an experiment for measuring how a team develops the collaborative task in two different collaboration conditions, normal and constrained. At the constrained condition, some elements of CAA were removed to generate restrictions in the collaboration i.e. each user see only a partial view of artifact, one user sees the radar view and the other the global map. This view is swapped when a team captured a flag. The experiment also included a locomotion constraint that avoided users move away than a limited distance.

Within-subject design was followed, swapping the test (normal, constraint) between two consecutive teams. Two different scenes (mazes), one for each test, allowed eliminating memory bias. The experiment included 32 subjects, assorted

Fig. 1. Design of common-awareness artifacts in the case study. (Color figure online)

Table 2. Results of statistical analysis of calculation to metric set.

Interaction				Immersion			
	Normal		Constrained		Normal		Constrained
IT^i	$\mu \pm \sigma$	p	$\mu \pm \sigma$	IM^i	$\mu \pm \sigma$	p	$\mu \pm \sigma$
IT^1	1−(Relative velocity between users / Maximum velocity)			IM^1	Team velocity / Maximum velocity		
	0.395 ± 0.083	**<0.000**	0.6345 ± 0.082		0.540 ± 0.136	**<0.000**	0.381 ± 0.150
IT^2	1−(Activity time / Maximum possible time)			IM^2	Sum of (Current capture communication time / Previous capture communication time)		
	0.258 ± 0.023	**<0.000**	0.131 ± 0.113				
IT^3	Users distance / Maximum users distance.				0.123 ± 0.167	**0.041**	0.275 ± 0.092
	0.793 ± 0.143	0.795	0.731 ± 0.235	IM^3	1- Mean for users of User rotation differences		
IT^4	1−(Users distance to ideal path/ Length of ideal path)				0.881 ± 0.934	**0.003**	0.895 ± 0.028
	0.928 ± 0.071	0.437	0.909 ± 0.059	IM^4	Mean for users of User flag distance.		
IT^5	1−(| Length of ideal path - Length of team path|/ Length of ideal path)				0.154 ± 0.783	**<0.000**	0.084 ± 0.063
				IM^5	Communication time / Activity time		
	0.878 ± 0.113	0.234	0.802 ± 0.197		0.223 ± 0.101	**<0.000**	0.328 ± 0.105

in 16 teams. The CVE ran on two machines, with the same technical specifications, over a private LAN network. Each machine had a passive stereoscopic TV of 42 in., for immersive visualization; a MS Kinect sensor, for tracking user limbs movements that were mapped in the avatar for generating proprioceptive sense; a traditional gamepad for allowing locomotion; and a headset to spoken communication.

A set of quantitative metrics was defined, one metric for each indicator. Metrics were calculated for the two collaborative conditions (normal and constraint) and a statistical analysis was processed looking for significant differences between the activity performed by a team over two conditions. Statistical data analysis included a test of t-student paired or a Wilcoxon signed-rank, according to result of a normality test (Shapiro-Wilk). The Table 2 shows data results. Columns include the metric set to interaction and immersion. Rows show a metric description and data, i.e., mean (μ), standard deviation (σ) and *p-value* (p) of statistic test. Values with significant difference ($p < 0.05$) are highlighted.

5   Conclusions

This paper presented the concept of common-awareness artifacts, which are interaction elements that support the activities of workspace awareness. The proposal defines how these artifacts allow the design and evaluation new components of a CVE that include interaction and immersion components from a perspective of collaboration theory. The proposal includes 10 aspects, guidelines/indicators, 5 relates to interaction and 5 to immersion. A study case showed a concrete example of how to design and to evaluate a common-awareness artifact, which supports a way-finding collaborative activity in a CVE. The evaluation with users included a comparison of two collaboration conditions. The analysis of results showed that set of metric are suitable to identify differences between the two conditions. As a future work, we intend to conduct new studies case which involves a strong relation between interaction, immersion and awareness.

References

1. Churchill, E.F., Snowdon, D.: Collaborative virtual environments: An introductory review of issues and systems. Virtual Real. **3**(1), 3–15 (1998)
2. Gutwin, C., Greenberg, S.: A descriptive framework of workspace awareness for real-time groupware. Comput. Support. Coop. Work (CSCW) **11**(3), 411–446 (2002)
3. Hrimech, H., Alem, L., Merienne, F.: How 3D interaction metaphors affect user experience in collaborative virtual environment. Adv. Hum. Comput. Interact. **2011**, 11 (2011). (Article ID 172318)
4. Landauer, C., Polichar, V.E.: More than shared artifacts: collaboration viashared presence in MUDs. In: Seventh IEEEInternational Workshops on Enabling Technologies: Infrastructure forCollaborative Enterprises, 1998, (WET ICE 1998) Proceedings, vol. 1, pp. 182–189. IEEE (1998)
5. Nguyen, T.T.H., Duval, T.: A survey of communication and awareness in collaborative virtual environments. In: IEEE VR 2014 Workshop on 3D Collaborative Virtual Environments (3DCVE), pp. 1–8. IEEE Computer Society Press, Minneapolis (2014)
6. Robinson, M.: Design for unanticipated use... In: ECSCW 1993 Proceedings of the Third Conference on European Conference on Computer-Supported Cooperative Work, pp. 187–202. Kluwer Academic Publishers (1993)
7. Spillers, F., Loewus-deitch, D.: Temporal attributes of shared artifacts in collaborative task environments. In: Workshop on the Temporal Aspects of Tasks (HCI 2003), pp. 1–11 (2003)
8. Tee, K., Greenberg, S., Gutwin, C.: Artifact awareness through screen sharing for distributed groups. Int. J. Hum. Comput. Stud. **67**(9), 677–702 (2009)

Sensing Grasp Force Using Active Acoustic Sensing

Buntarou Shizuki[✉]

Department of Computer Science, University of Tsukuba,
1-1-1 Tennodai, Tsukuba, Ibaraki 305-8577, Japan
shizuki@cs.tsukuba.ac.jp

Abstract. We present an active acoustic sensing technique for sensing grasp force. With this technique, using machine learning, an existing solid object can be made grasp-sensitive by attaching a vibration speaker and a contact microphone to the object. After learning, the technique estimates how the object is grasped, along with the grasp force. Our technique estimates the grasp force based on the change in the resonant frequency response of an object with the strength of the grasp: the steepness and power of the response generally decrease when thejapa grasp force increases.

Keywords: Touch sensing · Pressure · Prototyping · Acoustic classification · Piezo-electric sensor

1 Introduction

Many techniques (e.g., [4,7,8,11,12,17]) give designers the chance to prototype touch-sensitive objects: objects with touch interaction including grasp; the capability of sensing touch force, including grasp force, will further enrich the vocabulary of touch interaction. Such capability would allow designers to prototype objects with a rich set of touch interactions. For example, designers can prototype a grasp-sensitive controller and test its usability, where the user must grasp it strongly in an appropriate position to use it.

Previously, we reported a technique to estimate touch force based on active acoustic sensing [13]. The technique applied our active acoustic sensing [12] and support vector regression (SVR) to estimate how an existing solid object is touched, along with the touch force, by simply attaching a vibration speaker and contact microphone to the object.

In this paper, we applied our active acoustic sensing to sense grasp force. This technique estimates the force *without machine learning*, and thus is simpler and more lightweight than our previous technique [13]. We also implemented a prototyping tool based on the technique (Fig. 1). With this tool, a designer can make an existing solid object grasp-sensitive by attaching a vibration speaker and contact microphone to the object by using machine learning, as we did in [12]. After learning, the tool shows how the object is grasped, along with the grasp force.

© Springer International Publishing Switzerland 2016
C. Stephanidis (Ed.): HCII 2016 Posters, Part I, CCIS 617, pp. 382–387, 2016.
DOI: 10.1007/978-3-319-40548-3_64

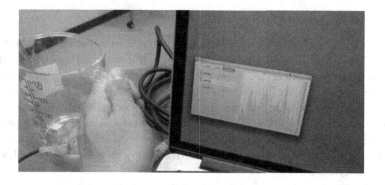

Fig. 1. Tool for sensing the grasp force.

2   Related Work

Various techniques for building force-sensitive surfaces have been researched, especially for prototyping.

2.1   Circuit-Based Approaches

PrintSense developed by Gong et al. [4] is a sensing technique for planar, curved, and flexible surfaces; it allows for single-layer printing of sensors that can sense multi-touch input, hover, several levels of touch pressure, and deformation. Rosenberg and Perlin used a matrix of force-variable resistors to build UnMousePad [15], which is a pressure-sensitive flexible multi-touch touchpad; such a matrix had been used previously to build a thin flexible pressure sensor [10]. PyzoFlex by Rendel et al. [14] used a ferroelectric material to form a pressure-sensitive bendable surface, which can even sense hover. While these devices can perform a wide range of stable pressure-sensing on surfaces, the sensitive area is located on the devices themselves. By contrast, our technique makes the surface of an existing object grasp- and force-sensitive.

2.2   Vision-Based Approaches

A touch sensing technology [5] based on frustrated total internal reflection (FTIR), which is widely used for prototyping multi-touch surfaces, can be used to estimate the touch force (e.g., [1,3,6,16]). RetroDepth by Kim et al. [9] used a stereo camera and retro-reflective surfaces to estimate the three-dimensional (3D) contours of interacting objects on and above the surfaces precisely; the precision is so high that subtle changes in the 3D locations of the fingertips can be identified when the user presses the surface of a malleable object; the locations can be used to estimate the touch pressure. In contrast to the above techniques, our acoustic-based technique can sense grasp force on existing solid objects.

2.3   Acoustic Approaches

A resonant pressure sensor [2] is a fluid pressure sensor consisting of the following three elements: a diaphragm with a variable self-resonant frequency characteristic, a drive transducer to vibrate the diaphragm, and a pickup transducer to capture the vibration. The sensor estimates pressure by exploiting the fact that the vibration frequency of the diaphragm depends directly on the pressure applied to the diaphragm. While our technique uses a similar sensing principle to make the surface of an object grasp- and force-sensitive, the technique also observes the steepness and power of the frequency response of the object to estimate the grasp force.

Our previous technique [13] estimates how an existing solid object is touched using support vector classification (SVC), as well as the touch force using SVR, through attachment of a vibration speaker and contact microphone to the object. While the technique we present in this paper uses the same hardware, it estimates the grasp force without machine learning, and thus is simpler and more lightweight than our previous technique.

3   Sensing Grasp Force Using Active Acoustic Sensing

Our technique estimates the grasp force based on the principle that the resonant frequency response of an object, which can be observed by vibrating the object and performing spectrum analysis of the signal captured from the attached microphone using fast Fourier transform (FFT), changes with the strength of the grasp.

Fig. 2. Test object: a ceramic bowl.

To test this, we observed the changes in the resonant frequency response of a ceramic bowl, observing the responses when we did not grasp it, grasped it weakly, or grasped it strongly, as shown in Fig. 2.

In these observations, we used the same hardware as in [13]. As the two piezoelectric elements, we used a bimorph piezo-electric element (THRIVE K2512BP1, 25 mm × 12 mm × 0.23 mm) after cutting it into halves to reduce the footprint. Both elements were attached to the bowl by using double-sided adhesive bonding tape (3M SPG-12). The signal currents to and from the elements were amplified and sent to a computer (Apple MacBook Air, CPU: Intel Core i7 1.7 GHz, RAM: 8 GB) via a USB audio interface (Native Instruments Audio Kontrol 1). The computer plays sinusoid sweep signals repeatedly from 20 kHz to 40 kHz, whose frequency increases linearly in 20 ms, at a 96 kHz sampling rate through the speaker. In parallel, the computer also converts the signal captured by the microphone into the resonant frequency response using FFT.

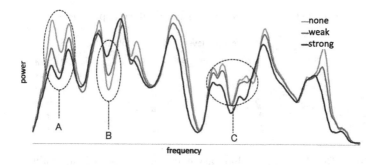

Fig. 3. Changes in the resonant frequency response with grasp. (Color figure online)

We found the following in the resonant frequency response (Fig. 3) when the grasp force increased:

- The power of the response generally decreases.
- The steepness of the response generally decreases.
- The power decreases at some frequencies (e.g., Fig. 3A), while it increases at other frequencies (e.g., Fig. 3B).
- The number of peaks decreases at some frequencies (e.g., Fig. 3C).

Therefore, we tested the following four metrics to estimate the grasp force:

- The sum of the resonant frequency response (sum_af),
- The variance of the resonant frequency response (var_af),
- The sum of the spectrum of the resonant frequency response (sum_sp), and
- The centroid of the spectrum of the resonant frequency response (g_sp).

Estimating the grasp force using one of the above metrics is simple; if the metrics decreases, we can conclude that the force should be strong.

4   Preliminary Experiment

We tested the four metrics on three objects: a knob, control lever, and plastic toy, as shown in Fig. 4. We used the same hardware as in the previous section. In this experiment, we grasped each object 20 times. For each grasp, we changed the grasp force according to the animated guide [13], which we used as the ground truth of the grasp force.

The results are illustrated in Fig. 5. In this figure, "guide" means the ground truth. We found that all of them performed well, since these metrics increase monotonically in accordance with the ground truth. Therefore, we used sum_af, which has the lowest calculation cost, to implement the tool shown in Fig. 1.

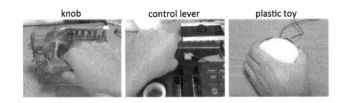

Fig. 4. Objects tested in our preliminary experiment.

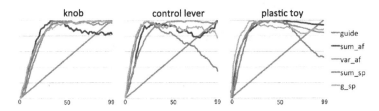

Fig. 5. Results of the preliminary experiment. (Color figure online)

5   Conclusions and Future Work

We presented an active acoustic sensing technique for sensing grasp force. With this technique, using machine learning, an existing solid object can be made grasp-sensitive by attaching a vibration speaker and a contact microphone to the object. After learning, the technique estimates how the object is grasped, along with the grasp force. Our technique estimates the grasp force based on the change in the resonant frequency response of an object with the strength of the grasp: the steepness and power of the response generally decrease when the grasp force increases.

In future work, we plan to conduct a user study to examine how our technique will perform with multiple users. We also plan to increase the number of piezo-electric elements to examine how the performance of our technique increases.

References

1. Augsten, T., Kaefer, K., Meusel, R., Fetzer, C., Kanitz, D., Stoff, T., Becker, T., Holz, C., Baudisch, P.: Multitoe: High-precision interaction with back-projected floors based on high-resolution multi-touch input. In: Proceedings of the 23nd Annual ACM Symposium on User Interface Software and Technology, pp. 209–218. ACM (2010)
2. Blanchard, W.C.: Resonant pressure sensor, uS Patent 3,745,384 (1973)
3. Desai, S.S., Eckert-Erdheim, A.M., Hoover, A.M.: A large-area tactile force sensor for measuring ground reaction forces from small legged robots. In: Proceedings of the 2013 IEEE/RSJ International Conference on Intelligent Robots and Systems, pp. 4753–4758. IEEE (2013)

4. Gong, N.W., Steimle, J., Olberding, S., Hodges, S., Gillian, N.E., Kawahara, Y., Paradiso, J.A.: PrintSense: A versatile sensing technique to support multimodal flexible surface interaction. In: Proceedings of the 32nd Annual ACM Conference on Human Factors in Computing Systems, pp. 1407–1410. ACM (2014)

5. Han, J.Y.: Low-cost multi-touch sensing through frustrated total internal reflection. In: Proceedings of the 18th Annual ACM Symposium on User Interface Software and Technology, pp. 115–118. ACM (2005)

6. Hennecke, F., Berwein, F., Butz, A.: Optical pressure sensing for tangible user interfaces. In: Proceedings of the ACM International Conference on Interactive Tabletops and Surfaces, pp. 45–48. ACM (2011)

7. Hudson, S.E., Mankoff, J.: Rapid construction of functioning physical interfaces from cardboard, thumbtacks, tin foil and masking tape. In: Proceedings of the 19th Annual ACM Symposium on User Interface Software and Technology, pp. 289–298. ACM (2006)

8. Kawahara, Y., Hodges, S., Cook, B.S., Zhang, C., Abowd, G.D.: Instant inkjet circuits: Lab-based inkjet printing to support rapid prototyping of UbiComp devices. In: Proceedings of the 2013 ACM International Joint Conference on Pervasive and Ubiquitous Computing, pp. 363–372. ACM (2013)

9. Kim, D., Izadi, S., Dostal, J., Rhemann, C., Keskin, C., Zach, C., Shotton, J., Large, T., Bathiche, S., Nießner, M., et al.: RetroDepth: 3D silhouette sensing for high-precision input on and above physical surfaces. In: Proceedings of the 32nd Annual ACM Conference on Human Factors in Computing Systems, pp. 1377–1386. ACM (2014)

10. Malacaria, C.F.: A thin, flexible, matrix-based pressure sensor. Sensors Mag. **15**, 102–104 (1998)

11. Olberding, S., Gong, N.W., Tiab, J., Paradiso, J.A., Steimle, J.: A cuttable multi-touch sensor. In: Proceedings of the 26th Annual ACM Symposium on User Interface Software and Technology, pp. 245–254. ACM (2013)

12. Ono, M., Shizuki, B., Tanaka, J.: Touch & Activate: Adding interactivity to existing objects using active acoustic sensing. In: Proceedings of the 26th Annual ACM Symposium on User Interface Software and Technology, pp. 31–40. ACM (2013)

13. Ono, M., Shizuki, B., Tanaka, J.: Sensing touch force using active acoustic sensing. In: Proceedings of the Ninth International Conference on Tangible, Embedded, and Embodied Interaction, pp. 355–358. ACM (2015)

14. Rendl, C., Greindl, P., Haller, M., Zirkl, M., Stadlober, B., Hartmann, P.: PyzoFlex: Printed piezoelectric pressure sensing foil. In: Proceedings of the 25th Annual ACM Symposium on User Interface Software and Technology, pp. 509–518. ACM (2012)

15. Rosenberg, I., Perlin, K.: The UnMousePad: An interpolating multi-touch force-sensing input pad. ACM Trans. Graphics **28**, 65:1–65:9 (2009)

16. Sakamoto, Y., Yoshikawa, T., Oe, T., Shizuki, B., Tanaka, J.: Constructing an elastic touch panel with embedded IR-LEDs using silicone rubber. In: Proceedings of IADIS International Conference Interfaces and Human Computer Interaction, pp. 263–268 (2012)

17. Savage, V., Zhang, X., Hartmann, B.: Midas: Fabricating custom capacitive touch sensors to prototype interactive objects. In: Proceedings of the 25th Annual ACM Symposium on User Interface Software and Technology, pp. 579–588. ACM (2012)

The Use of Wearable Technologies and Body Awareness: A Body–Tool Relationship Perspective

Ayoung Suh, Ruohan Li[(✉)], and Lili Liu

School of Creative Media and Department of Information System,
City University of Hong Kong, Hong Kong, China
{ayoung.suh, ruohanli2, llili2}@cityu.edu.hk

Abstract. Wearable technologies—innovative and multi-functional media technologies that can be attached to our body—have received a great deal of attention by the digital media industry. The wearability of technology brings new affordances that may significantly change the way humans interact with technological objects. However, little is known about how such emerging technologies can shape our perceptions of the body and the interactions associated with technology use. Focusing on users' experience of wearable technologies, this study explores the influence of wearable technologies on individuals' perceptions of their body–tool relationship and body awareness. A series of in-depth interviews was conducted to investigate how users' interactions with wearable technologies affect their perceptions. Our findings indicate that perceptual properties (materials, weight, battery life, and vibration) influence users' body-tool relationship, whereas motor activity properties (monitoring, tracking, and real-time feedback) influence users' body awareness.

Keywords: Wearable technologies · Body–tool relationship · Body awareness

1 Introduction

Recently, a new trend in digital media technologies typified as wearable technologies (hereafter: wearables), including iWatch, Fitbit, and Pebble, has received a great deal of attention in the digital media industry. Prior research has found that the proliferation of diverse wearables affects the ways in which people communicate with others and view the world [2, 4]. Some scholars argue that these wearables will significantly change our perception of body awareness by providing hands-free features, ubiquitous computing, and real-time biofeedback [2]. Despite the increasing scholarly and industrial focus on novel user experiences enabled by wearables, few empirical studies have been conducted to investigate the interactions between the human body and the technologies attached to it. Our knowledge about how the specific technological functions of wearables influence our body concept remains limited. This research thus seeks to shed light on emerging issues regarding the influences of wearables on body awareness from a body-tool relationship perspective.

© Springer International Publishing Switzerland 2016
C. Stephanidis (Ed.): HCII 2016 Posters, Part I, CCIS 617, pp. 388–392, 2016.
DOI: 10.1007/978-3-319-40548-3_65

2 Literature Review

2.1 The Body–Tool Relationship

In the present study, the body–tool relationship is framed using Heidegger's philosophical illumination of the "disappearance of a tool": when people skillfully manipulate a tool, that tool disappears from their perception during use, which makes them more focused on the task rather than the tool [5, 8]. In this study, "disappearance of a tool" refers to the extent to which a tool becomes an extension of the human body, disappearing from them in their perception [1]. Unlike unwearable technologies, such as computers and hand-held devices, the most distinctive characteristic of wearables is their close proximity to the body, which can make users unconsciously forget their existence. Even though users perceive wearables as having disappeared, they still receive informational feedback that introduces real-time computation to the body. However, when the tool fails to function as expected, it re-appears as an object in people's perception. Hence, it is important to understand how people perceive breakdown when using wearables.

> *RQ1: How does the use of wearable technologies influence the body-tool relationship?*

2.2 Body Awareness and Wearable Technologies

Leder argues that our bodies experience a "disappearance" from our perception [6]. For example, we gaze at the world, but we rarely notice the existence of our own eyes until we experience pain in them [6]. In light of Leder's notion, body awareness can be defined as the reflection of the body's condition, here used to explore how the use of wearables influences this "awareness." Scholars assert that wearables will significantly change our perceptions of our bodies because we are reminded of our bodily state through reviewing the information the wearables record [2]. In this research, body awareness refers to humans' perception of bodily states, processes, and actions [7]. Given that users' body awareness could be influenced by interacting with wearables [8], it is important to understand the specific functions of wearables and their roles in shaping users' body awareness.

> *RQ2: How do specific technological functions of wearable technologies influence body awareness?*

3 Methods

This study employs a qualitative approach to answer the questions. In-depth interviews were used to ascertain participants' experience of using wearables. At the preliminary stage, 10 users of wearable technologies who were using different kinds of wearable devices for fitness (e.g., iWatch, Fitbit, Pebble, Misfit Shine, and Mi Band) were recruited as interviewees. The rationale for the inclusion of diverse wearables was to generate a comprehensive understanding of user experience. All of the interviewees were members of an online wearable technologies forum (age range: 20–30 years old). Interviews with participants were conducted individually using online chat software with audio chat function, Tencent QQ, which is similar to Skype. Each interview lasted for approximately 30 min. All of the interviewees were active users who used wearables daily and for almost 24 h per day. They had an average of more than six months of user experience.

4 Findings

4.1 Perceptual Properties and Body–Tool Relationship

A perceptual property refers to how humans sense artifacts using bodily sensory systems [3]. Based on the interviews, we extracted four perceptual properties of wearables that influenced users' perception of the body–tool relationship.

Materials. Participants indicated that the materials used to make wearables, such as mental, silicon rubber, and fluoroelastomer, influenced their perception of the body–tool relationship. For example, participant A stated the following: "Sometimes I forget that I am wearing the device. However, I develop skin allergies after wearing the device for a long time because of the materials used to make it. Then my attention will be drawn by the wearable device." Participant G added, "You won't intentionally notice the existence of the device when you are using it. It is part of the body, and it is very comfortable to wear. But I still remember that one time it caused an allergy on my left wrist, so I had to move it to my right wrist."

Weight. Participants emphasized that the weight of the wearable was important in eliciting the disappearance experience. Participant E stated the following: "I treat [my] wearable device as my extended body, especially when I use Fitbit Flex. As it is very light, most of the time I don't realize I am wearing it. However, it is very powerful in providing body information." On the contrary, participant H reported the following: "Fitbit Surge is too heavy and too big to be forgotten, especially when I am wearing clothes that have tight sleeves. I feel uncomfortable during the night and sometimes it disturbs my sleep. Thus, I don't think it is a part of my body."

Battery life. The interview results implied that battery life affected whether the users perceived wearables as disappearing. Participant D explained this: "When I need to recharge my wearable, I treat it as an object rather than a part of my body." Participant J added, "The battery of Jawbone Up is short and the charging method is stupid: I have to use an audio cable. It is so inconvenient that I never consider it as disappearing. However, I do not need to charge Misfit Shine for several months because the battery life is very long. It is also waterproof. I wear it every day for 24 h and I don't feel it. It disappears. I feel that it is like a part of my own body."

Vibration. Vibration also influenced users' perception of the body–tool relationship. Participant I explained this: "Well, our own organs will not vibrate, so when the device starts to vibrate, it attracts my attention and I do not consider it as my body." Participant J added, "Vibration of wearables seems like a reminder that enables your communication with your body and forms an information loop. Although it makes you realize the existence of the tool, you still feel it is powerful, like a cyborg plug-in that extends your abilities."

4.2 Motor-Activity Properties and Body Awareness

A motor activity property is defined as what humans do with their bodies in order to interact with an artifact [3]. Based on the interview results, we identified three motor activity properties that affected users' body awareness.

Monitoring. Monitoring functions of wearables enhanced the users' body awareness. Participant G stated the following: "The heart rate monitoring function is quite useful. I was sick one time; however, I didn't realize that I was running a low-grade fever until I found that my heart rate was abnormal, which was 180 times/min from the data on the wearable device." Participant B added, "Wearables can record my sleep quality in detail. For instance, it provides information about how many times I have woken up or turned over as well as the length of deep sleep time. I have never learned about these data before. Being aware of the above-mentioned data totally changes my understanding and my behavior about my own body." Participant C remarked, "I think the most useful function is heart rate monitoring, which helps me to learn about the physical changes of my body. Previously, when I was running, sometimes I felt that my heart was uncomfortable. Since I started using the wearable device, I was able to better control my exercise intensity based on my heart rate."

Tracking. Activity-tracking functions also enhanced their body awareness. Participant E said, "Previously, it took five minutes for me to run one kilometer. I felt extremely uncomfortable during running. After using the wearable device, I set up a lot of plans for exercise. I have improved my vital capacity, physical stamina and running speed (as shown by the wearable device data). Wearable devices are able to record my activities during a long period and display the data with a tendency chart. Given the improvement of my body condition, which is implied by the data, I am motivated to continue exercising in order to sustain the condition." Participant I added, "The activity-tracking function of wearable devices is very useful because it helps to record users' activities over a long period of time. It is difficult for us to memorize our activities one month ago, or even one week ago. Wearable devices store all of our data, which is accessible whenever and wherever we like. It makes us learn more about our bodies in the long term."

Real-time feedback. Our findings implied that real-time feedback enhanced users' body awareness. Participant A said, "I can receive real-time feedback from my body, informing me of how many miles I have walked or run and how many calories I have burned. The more I know about my own body, the more I want to set up a goal to maintain a healthy lifestyle." Participant D added, "It is very helpful when my iWatch recommends some activity to me, which reminds me of my body condition. Normally, I would follow the recommendation and do some exercise, such as standing for a while." Participant B remarked, "I feel very happy when I receive real-time feedback about achieving a specific goal (e.g., competing 10,000 steps per day). It seems like I am healthier than before."

To sum up, our findings indicate that perceptual and motor activity properties need to be considered when designing a wearable in order to provide an enhanced user experience.

Acknowledgement. This paper was supported by the National Research Foundation of Korea Grant funded by the Korean Government (NRF-2013S1A3A2054667).

References

1. Hansen, T., Dirckinck-Holmfeld, L., Lewis, R., Rugelj, J.: Using telematics to support collaborative knowledge construction. In: Collaborative Learning, Cognitive and Computational Approaches (1999)
2. Ferraro, V., Ugur, S.: Designing wearable technologies through a user centered approach. In: Proceedings of the 2011 Conference on Designing Pleasurable Products and Interfaces, p. 5. ACM (2011)
3. Lakoff, G., Johnson, M.: Metaphors We Live By. University of Chicago Press, Chicago (2008)
4. Park, S., Jayaraman, S.: Enhancing the quality of life through wearable technology. IEEE Eng. Med. Biol. Mag. **22**(3), 41–48 (2003)
5. Heidegger, M.: Being and time (trans.). In: Macquarrie, J., Robinson, E. (eds.) Harper, New York (1962)
6. Leder, D.: The Absent Body. University of Chicago Press, Chicago (1990)
7. Mehling, W.E., Gopisetty, V., Daubenmier, J., Price, C.J., Hecht, F.M., Stewart, A.: Body awareness: construct and self-report measures. PLoS One **4**(5), e5614 (2009)
8. Nunez-Pacheco, C., Loke, L.: Crafting the body-tool: a body-centred perspective on wearable technology. In: Proceedings of the 2014 Conference on Designing Interactive Systems, pp. 553–566. ACM (2014)

Design for Older Users

An Information-Centric Framework
for Mobile Collaboration Between Seniors
and Caregivers that Balances Independence,
Privacy, and Social Connectedness

Yomna Aly[1(✉)] and Cosmin Munteanu[1,2]

[1] Technologies for Aging Gracefully Lab, Department of Computer Science,
University of Toronto, Toronto, Canada
yomna.aly@mail.utoronto.ca, cosmin@taglab.ca
[2] Institute of Communication, Culture, Information and Technology,
University of Toronto Mississauga, Mississauga, Canada

Abstract. Participating in intellectually and socially complex activities provides cognitive benefits to older adults [9]. Socially engaged seniors tend to live longer [8], experience fewer depressive symptoms, self-report lower disability levels, and demonstrate higher levels of cognitive function [1] and lower incidence rates of dementia [3]. However, as complexity of knowledge, size of caregiver circle, and reliance on computers are all increasing, seniors need to maintain their sense of control and independence in their information-centered activities, as well as be able to access reliable trusted information sources. Therefore, our research goal is to develop a theoretical framework for intelligent assistive technologies that provide information-managing support and autonomy to older adults while alleviating the burden on caregivers. This framework will be tested and deployed as a collaborative mobile tool that facilitates information seeking and sharing, increases seniors' confidence in the information presented, and satisfies their need of privacy and independence.

Keywords: Collaborative · Independence · Assistive technology · Socio-technical environments · Social connectedness · Aging · Caregiving

1 Introduction

Home care and support technologies are receiving increasing attention commercially [7]. Transition of care for seniors from well-structured facilities and centers to the unpredictable environment at home can be challenging for both seniors and their caregivers whether family or professionals. The main research approach in the last two decades is to focus on technologies that support seniors to be self-dependent enough to independently live comfortably and safely in their preferred environment. This can improve the quality of life while delaying the onset of institutionalization. At the same time, it may reduce the burden family caregivers often experience. For this, technologies have been developed to monitor seniors' activities and interactions around their house to help maintain awareness and allow for intervention at times of crisis.

© Springer International Publishing Switzerland 2016
C. Stephanidis (Ed.): HCII 2016 Posters, Part I, CCIS 617, pp. 395–400, 2016.
DOI: 10.1007/978-3-319-40548-3_66

Technology is integrated into most aspects of life and is increasing the scope of communication and care delivery across conditions such as declining cognitive and motor abilities We review here the state of the art in research on technologies for helping older adults remain independent, productive, and socially engaged and connected to family and friends. We discuss some of the factors increasing the adoption of these technologies such as perceived usefulness to both seniors and caregivers. We also discuss how privacy and increased stress on caregivers may hinder the technology adoption.

1.1   Background

Health care and health management are increasingly being carried out in the home with the assistance of caregivers who could be professionals or family members or by the seniors themselves [7]. Often this is complicated by conditions that affect daily living, such as physical frailty or cognitive decline. Mobile health technologies such as smartphone applications and home support systems have been growing rapidly and these can improve collaboration with caregivers and increased independence for seniors. However, Prasad et al. [7] studied aspects related to seniors' willingness to share private health information and what type of information is being captured and shared from such technologies to caregivers. The study revealed that the sharing behavior is dependent on the type of information shared and with whom it will be shared with. This brings forth the need to balance seniors' desire for independence and control over the normal running of their lives with keeping what is private or confidential away from those they do not feel comfortable sharing with. The post study interviews carried out in [7] revealed interesting findings regarding the factors that influence the sharing of health information: seniors are less willing to share location information than sensed information, they are more concerned with disclosure of diet and exercise information than medication tracking, they are more comfortable sharing information about health and weight with healthcare professionals rather than their family caregivers, and they are worried that sharing illness details with family or caregivers will burden them and worry them. This illustrated how the relationship with the sharing recipient and the perceived benefit from sharing with others influences how and with whom sharing happens.

Carmien and Fischer [2] have studied the challenges in supporting the healthy, independent lifestyle of seniors. The study reveals that the home environment, unlike a retirement or senior care facility, includes coordination between multiple groups of people with shared (sensitive) knowledge about the senior's life. However, seniors reported decline in levels of control over their lives due to a wide variety of people acquiring information about their daily running without their permission. Seniors desire to live independently without the help of caregivers. Research efforts have thus focused on developing and adopting new technologies that would meet the seniors' needs for control over their private information. Tixier et al. [10] have proposed a framework to allow for successful adoption of such technologies for seniors. The proposed framework emphasizes that a successful assessment of the senior's life using ADL (Assessment of Daily living) is required when developing technologies for seniors.

By this, technologies developed are set to be tailored to the individual senior based on the level of independence they acquire [10]. Therefore, the likelihood for adoption of a technology and what needs it targets is proportional to the ability of a senior to perform the basic daily tasks independently [10].

Seniors vary in their health conditions, wellbeing, motor capabilities and healthcare needs. On the other end of the spectrum, caregivers are greatly impacted by their care giving roles in maintaining supervision over seniors. Hence, Consolvo et al. [4] proposed the notion of Computer Supported Coordinated Care (CSCC), which shifts the focus of technologies on keeping the healthy life style of both seniors and caregivers. In addition to continuous updating and monitoring of seniors' activities, CSCC systems also consider the caregiver and senior's mental, emotional and overall wellbeing. Among these, two systems introduced four years apart are representative of the potential to address those challenges. Care Net [4] and MAPS [2] are systems that attempt to create a socio-technical environment supporting customization, personalization and effective collaboration between both seniors and caregivers through the use of Meta Design and Distributed Intelligence approaches.

The Care Net Display [4] consists of an interactive picture frame that surrounds the digital photograph of the senior with relevant information about their daily lives. This digital frame provides caregivers updates throughout the day about the senior's activities, calendar, mood and medication tracking. This technology is still widely used and accepted due to its unique characteristics being the focus on seniors, not only from a health perspective but an emotional perspective as well. It ensures that the whole caregiver network is updated instantaneously, which improves on having a single designated member to share all relevant information and news – hence everyone has equal access to crucial information. Caregivers are updated instantaneously which helps satisfy their roles of monitoring the day to day lives of their beloved elder but at the same time seniors have no knowledge on the type of information caregivers receive. User studies in [4] present increased acceptance by seniors of this technology due to the increased level of independence and autonomy afforded to the functioning of their lives. However, they reported loss of privacy and control over the information shared about them. Care Net system provides automatic updating from monitoring seniors without the need of caregivers initiating any actions or tasks nor seniors providing information about themselves [4].

The second proposed system known as the Memory Aiding Prompting System (MAPS) [2] creates an environment that allows caregivers to create scripts for seniors that enables them to carry out task independently. This would satisfy the independence requirements of seniors and give caregiver full control and awareness of the normal functioning of the elderly life [2, 10]. MAPS was designed to help seniors achieve more independence through a distributed intelligence approach. This allows the limited internal scripts created by caregivers to be complemented by more powerful external scripts from professional caregivers [2]. Hence, MAPS is integrated with the capability for personalization and customization to tailor the settings in regards to the specificities and particular capabilities of the senior. In addition, MAPS is contextually aware of the current situation through the use of a panic button, which can help when immediate help is needed and help recover from any errors introduced by the system. A participatory design study during the development of MAPS revealed that such a feature is essential for caregivers who are anxious about not being able to intervene in situations where seniors need immediate help and support [2, 10].

The systems and research approaches presented here illustrate that technology interventions can improve the management of information that is essential to both older adults and caregivers. However, as we have highlighted in our analysis, this is not without disadvantage, mainly in the form of seniors' potential loss of control and privacy. The following section discusses a proposed approach to address these shortcomings.

2 Proposed Solution

Although there has been much research and commercial activity in the last two decades on technology for knowledge acquisition and sharing, little of this has considered seniors and their sense of independence and control as the primary target. In addition, few have considered how design must take into consideration deteriorating cognitive abilities and alleviating care giving burden. Moreover, where research has targeted older adults, it has predominately studied them as consumers of content, knowledge and care, rarely focusing on their capacity to manage and even contribute to knowledge creation (e.g. such as in the case of an older adults caring for a spouse and customizing health information for his/her). As such, what is needed is a more integrated approach to acquiring, managing, and sharing increasingly-complex information.

Our research project aims to focus on the digital independence afforded by collaborative platforms to help support better quality of life for both seniors and caregivers. Seniors struggle in finding accurate sources of information and with understanding the medical terminology discussed in medical articles. We hypothesize that a digital platform that allows collaboration while maintaining seniors' control over the flow of information may address such challenges. We envision that this can be achieved through the use of semi-automated information and collaboration tools such as summarizing, annotating, and the placement of virtual sticky notes. The use of the natural language component together with the visual representation of sticky notes will help assist the knowledge acquisition task. This framework will be assessed and validated through the creation of a mobile based multi-modal interface that helps older adults increase their digital independence with respect to information-centric tasks.

We are currently witnessing an increase research focus in developing formal requirements that will inform the development of assistive technologies for seniors [6]. Methods such as automatic speech processing and gesture processing are expected to enhance the intelligence of mobile assistive interfaces by increasing the ability to support older adults' information acquisition tasks. Furthermore, collaborative digital artifact creation has been employed in many design projects such as the Post Card Memories application proposed in [5]. Based on the promising results of such prior work, we aim to contribute a unique research direction to this space, which relies on combining speech and natural language technology and integrating them into assistive interfaces that make use of annotation techniques and sticky notes to better meet seniors' information and knowledge needs.

3 Proposed Methodology and Evaluation

We plan to evaluate the proposed framework in four phases. The first phase (pre-deployment stage) consists of one-on-one sessions with older adults and caregivers using contextual inquiry to gain further understanding of how older adults seek new information relevant to their health. The second phase (pre-development) is conducted as a participatory design workshop that will bring in the seniors in the early prototyping and development stage. The third stage (development stage) consists of the development of the tool that will integrate natural language processing techniques such as summarization and annotations together in an elder-centric collaborative mobile tool. This tool will be designed to enable seniors to easily seek and research health-related information online. Furthermore, through crowdsourcing and collaborations among the caregiver circle, the collaborative platform will provide discussions and annotations that will allow older adults to better assess the reliability and trustworthiness of each information source they find. The final stage is carried out as a usability evaluation of the tool together with an extensive qualitative interview to gain further insight into future developments.

4 Conclusion

Accessing new information, continuing to learn and be engaged in the society is always a priority for seniors, but with limited eyesight and dexterity, simple tasks such comprehending health information could be a great struggle. This leads to the need of caregivers to assist them. However, with family members often serving as caregivers (and often from a distance), the potential for immediate assistance can be a struggle, leaving socially- and physically-isolated older adults without much needed support. At the same time, seniors need to maintain their privacy and independence with respect to managing their health. Intelligent assistive technologies based on mobile, collaborative and multimodal interfaces (speech, natural language and gestures) offer the potential to fill this gap and provide seniors support for accessing and comprehending critical information while staying connected to their family and beloved ones. The goal of our project is to facilitate older adults' digital independence by addressing the challenges faced by them when seeking health information while maintaining an optimal balance between privacy and support. For this, we will propose a theoretical framework for better collaboration between seniors and caregivers. We hypothesize that such a framework will enhance older adults' independent living, encourage social participation with their care network, and reduce the burden and stress caregivers face. The framework will be practically implemented as a collaborative, natural and interactive annotation tool. This will support and connect seniors and family caregivers during the management of health-related information.

References

1. Bassuk, S.S., Glass, T.A., Berkman, L.F.: Social disengagement and incident cognitive decline in community-dwelling elderly persons. Ann. Intern. Med. **131**(3), 165–173 (1999)
2. Carmien, S.P., Fischer, G.: Design, adoption, and assessment of a socio-technical environment supporting independence for persons with cognitive disabilities. In: Proceedings of the SIGCHI Conference on Human Factors in Computing Systems, pp. 597–606. ACM, April 2008
3. Crooks, V.C., Lubben, J., Petitti, D.B., Little, D., Chiu, V.: Social network, cognitive function, and dementia incidence among elderly women. Am. J. Public Health **98**(7), 1221–1227 (2008)
4. Consolvo, S., Roessler, P., Shelton, B.E., LaMarca, A., Schilit, B., Bly, S.: Technology for care networks of elders. IEEE Pervasive Comput. **3**(2), 22–29 (2004)
5. Ludlow, B.A., Ladly, M.J.: Postcard memories: developing a mobile postcard application using a novel approach to multi-level system design (2014)
6. Neves, B.B., Franz, R.L., Munteanu, C., Baecker, R., Ngo, M.: My hand doesn't listen to me!: adoption and evaluation of a communication technology for the 'oldest old'. In: Proceedings of the 33rd Annual ACM Conference on Human Factors in Computing Systems, pp. 1593–1602. ACM, April 2015
7. Prasad, A., Sorber, J., Stablein, T., Anthony, D., Kotz, D.: Understanding sharing preferences and behavior for mHealth devices. In: Proceedings of the 2012 ACM Workshop on Privacy in the Electronic Society, pp. 117–128. ACM, October 2012
8. Reblin, M., Uchino, B.N.: Social and emotional support and its implication for health. Curr. Opin. Psychiatry **21**(2), 201 (2008)
9. Stine-Morrow, E.A., Payne, B.R., Roberts, B.W., Kramer, A.F., Morrow, D.G., Payne, L., Janke, M.C.: Training versus engagement as paths to cognitive enrichment with aging. Psychol. Aging **29**(4), 891 (2014)
10. Tixier, M., Gaglio, G., Lewkowicz, M.: Translating social support practices into online services for family caregivers. In: Proceedings of the ACM 2009 International Conference on Supporting Group Work, pp. 71–80. ACM, May 2009

Speech-Enabled Intelligent Mobile Interfaces to Support Older Adults' Storytelling Around Digital Family Pictures

Benett Axtell[1(✉)] and Cosmin Munteanu[1,2]

[1] TAGlab, University of Toronto, Toronto, Canada
{benett, cosmin}@taglab.ca
[2] Institute of Communication, Culture, Information and Technology,
University of Toronto Mississauga, Mississauga, Canada

Abstract. Seniors' needs or interests are often ignored in the design and development of new technologies, causing many new applications that may benefit them to be overlooked. Digital storytelling is one such emerging application that is based on oral, written, or artefact-based storytelling, which in its traditional format has been shown to increase socialization in older adults. In our work we propose a new multimodal interface that incentivizes seniors to tell stories from family photos. The proposed authoring tool is based on speech interaction, and allows for the creation of unstructured, free-flowing stories by older adult users as guided by the app. This tool is intended to act as a trigger for storytelling by being enjoyable to use and by having shareable outputs (i.e. multimedia stories and robust photo tags) that preserve family memories. This solution is expected to increase socialization among seniors and preserve family knowledge without undue effort.

Keywords: Digital storytelling · Multimodal interaction · Speech and audio interfaces · Technologies for ageing · Social connectivity

1 Introduction

Oral storytelling is the oldest form of sharing stories. It continues to be an excellent way to encourage socialization and communication for seniors and people with dementia, and has been found to increase life satisfaction and self-esteem [3]. A common form of modern oral storytelling is family narratives around family photographs. In recent years, digital storytelling has been growing as a field and using photos to frame that storytelling has been a common thread. Many different modes for digital storytelling have been explored; tablets, projected tabletop displays, cell phones, and digital paper and pen, to name a few, but many structure or limit the story. We hypothesise that placing a focus on free-flowing, independent oral digital storytelling will increase older adults' motivation to tell and document their stories and will add a new range of possibilities to the existing digital storytelling work.

© Springer International Publishing Switzerland 2016
C. Stephanidis (Ed.): HCII 2016 Posters, Part I, CCIS 617, pp. 401–406, 2016.
DOI: 10.1007/978-3-319-40548-3_67

1.1   Background Information

Photo Storytelling for Seniors. Several projects have already explored the area of storytelling with family photographs specifically for seniors. These solutions aim to increase socialization or memory in their older adult users. Recent research shows that a mobile application is useful in encouraging seniors with early-stage dementia and their families to engage in storytelling from photographs in the form of digital or physical postcards [7]. These postcards use photos annotated with a written, typed, or spoken message which the recipient can respond to in kind. Video-enhanced speech recognition is used to support speaking messages to be written onto the postcard, and speech or video media can be added to the digital postcards, a feature reported by users to be the most meaningful. This suggests that seniors may benefit from multimodal interfaces for storytelling.

Other research has explored how tools designed for family and caregivers can improve a senior's socialization. One such intuitive approach researched a digital annotation system using paper photos and a digital pen that allows family and caregivers to collaboratively create an interactive photo album comprised of audio-enhanced photos to be viewed by seniors [9]. Family members can annotate family photos for the senior, through both written text and recorded audio, with memories of the photo or other details. Seniors are encouraged to share their memories by going through the album and playing the recordings. This use of pen and paper is familiar to seniors, but limits how far the system can go compared to using a tablet.

Picgo [5] is another system that is designed for caregivers that simplifies the work of annotating family photos by prompting for answers to five general questions (who, what, where, when, and why) about each photo and adding tags that correspond to the given answers. These annotated and tagged photos are meant to be used by the caregiver to design and implement reminiscence activities with the senior, so it is not meant to be a tool for creating and telling stories.

These examples all focus on brief messages or memories around a single photo. They enhance communication and socialization in a back-and-forth conversation, but do not encourage a user to spend a longer time to tell a complete story.

Audio-Enabled Digital Storytelling. Other work has been done more generally into the field of digital storytelling around photos without a focus on older adults as users or recipients. These works provide more examples of how speech can be used to enhance digital storytelling, but much of the research is older and recent technological changes leave much room for improvement. Moreover, increased recent awareness of issues related to social isolation for older adults [8] and storytelling's potential to reduce social isolation [3], demand that efforts be focused on the usability aspects of authoring tools that support older adults' creation of complete oral stories augmented with photos.

Among projects that exploit the audio track of stories is an eavesdropping system that uses audio recording to derive information from storytelling [2]. As a story is being told, audio capture derives keywords, themes, and other metadata for the displayed photo. The main purpose of this is to index the photos for future text searches, and stories are saved so they can be shared through email. This research was solely into the speech-processing system that leverages storytelling for the user's gain. This tool runs as a part of a thumbnail gallery and photo viewer that is built into the computer, so a user must choose to view their photos through that system in order for the audio capture to occur. Unfortunately, the system is not designed to support complete authoring.

Other work includes a custom-built tablet-like device [1] to build and view stories with the option of recording audio, a table-top projected interface [11] that supports telling a collective past with a focus on natural conversation and flexible storytelling, and the Cherish system [4] that uses digital photo frames to prompt storytelling based on visiting guests or special events. These systems all create a larger story across multiple photographs, and allow more freedom as to the story's structure. Our research plans to bring a similar flexibility to digital storytelling for seniors and leverage such previous advances to improve the authoring process for complete multimedia stories.

Storytelling Design for Seniors. This research is motivated by previous studies into how seniors want to document their stories and that propose guidelines for designing solutions for seniors' reminiscence. One study found that seniors do enjoy reminiscing in the form of storytelling and that, though they often do not feel like they have knowledge worth sharing, a trigger (such as a photo or verbal prompt) would help to remind them and to make them feel comfortable in telling [12]. Similarly, another field study into the different ways that older adults are recording memories found a need for a malleable way to create stories that allows users to have control over their own content [6]. Both studies found that seniors want to construct narratives around their stories, and call for simple, intergenerational solutions that create story artefacts.

Opportunities to Focus on the Authoring Process. Despite the research that shows a desire for ownership and flexibility in storytelling, most existing storytelling tools use a very structured approach in which a user is prompted to build a set of photos or answer a set of questions for a story, and often the user is a caregiver, not the senior. Based on the previous work surveyed here, we can hypothesize that a flexible, free-flowing, and independent approach will match older adults preferred storytelling methods by giving them more control over their stories and artefacts. Motivating an older adult to tell a story is a common problem as well. Therefore, our aim for this project is to research whether suggesting clusters of family photos, built from the user's own stories, as triggers can encourage self-directed, free-flowing oral storytelling. Once a story has started, that speech can be leveraged to guide the user through a longer, unstructured story.

2 Proposed Solution

This research will investigate the needs of older adults with respect to supporting the capture of storytelling from photographs and how best to support these with advanced multimodal and automatic speech recognition interfaces. It is hypothesised that such storytelling will require a tool that is free-flowing, without enforcing any strict story structure. As well, such a tool should be designed for user independence so the senior can own the process and use it on their own, and should be speech-enabled so the themes of a story will motivate further stories suggestions. The large goal is that these features will create a tool to motivate seniors not only to tell and share their stories, but to encourage them to continue to tell that story and to create a larger narrative arc.

Design Motivation. As surveyed earlier in this paper, research shows that seniors desire full control and independence over their own histories [6], but much previous work researches tools that family members or caregivers can use along with or to guide seniors. A storytelling tool that is designed with the older adult as the sole user and content producer/curator is an area that is still largely unexplored. Although storytelling is a collaborative process, the fact that the senior owns their stories and curates their own artefacts provides a stronger motivation. Ownership will also likely lessen the chore or obligation around documenting family history as they will choose when and how to use the tool.

Another common trend in existing applications of digital storytelling is to provide a forced structure for the story [1, 4, 5]. This can take the form of a set of basic questions to be answered or by requiring the user to manually build an ordered set of photos from which a story will be told. These structures limit how a story can be made. Telling stories as personal narrative is a culturally ingrained act, with a standard outline that is generally followed [10]. Therefore, it is not necessary to provide, for example, generic questions that would be answered organically if a complete story were encouraged. Instead, a more free-flowing approach can provide an initial trigger, built from information gained from previous stories told, and guide the user with suggestions of how to continue the story. This will allow for an open-ended story with no fixed beginning or ending beyond the user's shared memories and will work well with natural human interactions such as speech.

Remembrance almost always involves speech. Stories are shared orally, and through oral storytelling, family histories are preserved and moral values passed on. This makes speech interaction a logical mode for digital storytelling, but also suggests that it must be a natural interaction that is inspired by how stories are shared between people. These oral stories can create rich multimedia artefacts through explicit recording and post-processing to determine story themes, for example. These themes become apparent as speech about a photograph can reveal much about the content of that photo.

Storytelling Artefacts. The multimedia artefacts resulting from these stories create sharable outputs in the form of individual stories or a larger multimedia biography. The senior, as independent curator of their stories, is responsible for the management and sharing of these artefacts. Individual stories can be modified or rearranged in the larger story. One or multiple stories can be shared with others to encourage communication between distant family members. Together, digital stories create a living artefact that encompasses one overarching story holding the complex framework of a family's history.

Motivation in Storytelling. This research will bring together the concepts of free-flowing storytelling, senior user independence, and speech-enabled interfaces to investigate a tool that promotes storytelling in older adults. As the owner and curator of their storytelling process, they will be motivated to share their stories. This may leverage a sense of responsibility to document family history while lessening the work usually required to do so.

Another impediment to older adults sharing stories is a sense that others are not interested in their memories and so those memories are not valuable [12]. Providing a memory trigger, based on recently told stories, is a reminder of their stories' value and will strengthen the original motivation.

That initial trigger will aid a senior to start a story. Continuing this story across a complete narrative arc will be done through the suggestion of new triggers based on the current story. This continues the motivation of the story on a longer, open-ended path, and it is believed that a free-flowing, independent, speech-enabled solution will achieve this goal of motivation across the entirety of a story.

3 Proposed Methodology

Older adults' current methods of storytelling, family history documentation, and photograph organization will be investigated in one-on-one sessions using Contextual Inquiry to gain further understanding of common practices, desired outcomes, and physical interactions with these items. This will support previous research done in similar areas [6, 12] and will give insight into both how photographs are organized physically (e.g. in photo albums, boxes, digitally) and how the content is organized (e.g. by time, event, people). Also of interest is how people naturally cluster photos when telling a story and what gestures are used to interact with the physical photographs.

The information gathered in these sessions will be used to define the design for a tool using natural touch and speech interactions, based on what was observed from and reported by the participants, and leveraging the observed ways that the participants store, organize, and cluster their photos. The acceptance of the tool's design will be measured in user studies conducted with each user's own photographs and stories.

4 Conclusion

This research investigates how a speech-based tool can assist seniors with the production and editing of rich multimedia stories that can be shared with family members. A main focus of our fieldwork is discovering what will best motivate a senior to choose to tell a story, start telling that story, and continue it across a full narrative arc. There is an emphasis on independent and free-flowing storytelling, in agreement with the findings of previous research tools for seniors' remembrance, and supporting speech interaction for oral storytelling is the preferred modality for sharing memories. These underexplored research areas show much promise for future work and contributions to reducing older adults' social isolation through digital storytelling.

References

1. Balabanović, M., Chu, L.L., Wolff, G.J.: Storytelling with digital photographs. In: Proceedings of the SIGCHI Conference on Human Factors in Computing Systems, pp. 564–571. ACM, April 2000
2. Fleck, M.: Eavesdropping on storytelling. Technical report HPL-2004-44, HP Laboratories Palo Alto (2004)
3. Harrand, A.G., Bollstetter, J.J.: Developing a community-based reminiscence group for the elderly. Clin. Nurse Spec. **14**(1), 17–22 (2000)
4. Kim, J., Zimmerman, J.: Cherish: smart digital photo frames for sharing social narratives at home. In: CHI 2006 Extended Abstracts on Human Factors in Computing Systems, pp. 953–958. ACM, April 2006
5. Lee, H.C., Cho, S.Y., Cheng, Y.F., Tang, H.H., Hsu, Y.J., Chen, C.H.: Picgo: a reminiscence physical-digital photo annotation service for the elderly. Gerontechnology **13** (2), 236 (2014)
6. Lindley, S.E.: Before i forget: from personal memory to family history. Hum. Comput. Interact. **27**(1–2), 13–36 (2012)
7. Ludlow, B.A., Ladly, M.J.: Postcard memories: developing a mobile postcard application using a novel approach to multi-level system design (2014)
8. Nicholson, N.R.: A review of social isolation: an important but underassessed condition in older adults. J. Prim. Prevent. **33**(2–3), 137–152 (2012)
9. Piper, A.M., Weibel, N., Hollan, J.D.: Designing audio-enhanced paper photos for older adult emotional wellbeing in communication therapy. Int. J. Hum. Comput. Stud. **72**(8), 629–639 (2014)
10. Robinson, J.A.: Personal narratives reconsidered. J. Am. Folklore **94**(371), 58–85 (1981)
11. Shen, C., Lesh, N., Vernier, F., Forlines, C., Frost, J.: Building and sharing digital group histories. In: CSCW Videos, p. 3, November 2002
12. Thiry, E., Rosson, M.B.: Unearthing the family gems: design requirements for a digital reminiscing system for older adults. In: CHI 2012 Extended Abstracts on Human Factors in Computing Systems, pp. 1715–1720. ACM, May 2012

Designing ICTs for Elders: Considering a Taxonomy of Dignity

Julie Buelow[1]([⊠]), Ben Migotto[2], and Lia Tsotsos[2]

[1] Faculty of Arts and Design, Sheridan College, Oakville, Canada
julie.buelow1@sheridancollege.ca
[2] Centre for Elder Research, Sheridan College, Oakville, Canada
{migottob, lia.tsotsos}@sheridancollege.ca

Abstract. The consideration of dignity in computer design for elders seems almost non-existent; however, in the medical field, a patient's dignity is a key consideration. As the world's population ages and the trend is toward more computerized care, a taxonomy for dignity for healthcare (such as proposed by Jacobson [3]) could be extended and applied to the design of computer and mobile health care systems for older adults. Including dignity into human computer interaction and design could strengthen current design approaches and improve adoption of ICT technologies by older adults. This paper provides a case study where Jacobson's taxonomy is used to guide an evaluation of a computerized health system.

Keywords: Aging · Dignity · ICTs

1 Introduction

The phenomenon of the world's aging population is "unprecedented, pervasive, and enduring with profound implications" [1]. As the World Health Organization reports that the number of people over age 60 will double by 2050, it also calls for a fundamental shift in the way governments deal with acute and long term health care in order that older people can "live their last years with dignity" [2].

Jacobson [3] conducted a study that produced a theory explaining a form of "social dignity" that is based on interactions and interpretations. The study also produced a set of vocabulary for describing dignity promotion and violation that allows dignity to be addressed empirically in a healthcare setting. This paper explores whether Jacobson's theory and taxonomy can be utilized for designing healthcare technologies and to what extent. Successful employment of the theory could enhance current approaches to dignity for health technologies, and potentially improve adoption of technologies by older adults.

1.1 ICTs and Aging

Research with older adults and Information and Communication Technologies (ICTs), such as email and the Internet, explores the technology experiences and needs of older adults [4]. Previous research has shown that ICTs may positively impact the quality of

© Springer International Publishing Switzerland 2016
C. Stephanidis (Ed.): HCII 2016 Posters, Part I, CCIS 617, pp. 407–412, 2016.
DOI: 10.1007/978-3-319-40548-3_68

life of older adults ([5] as cited in [4]) by improving social support and psycho-social well-being ([6–8] as cited in [4]). Despite the potential benefits of ICTs, many older adults remain reluctant to adopt technologies, especially when compared with younger cohorts [9]. One way to interpret these trends is that older adults are willing to use ICTs but may experience various barriers to learning and using them. In a review by [4], the most commonly cited barriers included: age-related issues (e.g. health, mobility, cognitive changes), characteristics of existing technologies, attitudinal and financial issues, and training and support issues (as cited in [4]). Furthermore, researchers such as Baecker et al. [10] have identified the need for "identity, self-reliance, and self-worth" to be addressed when designing technologies for older adults and use Maslow's hierarchy of needs [11] as a framework. The framework suggests that physiological needs (ex. health) must be addressed first, with safety and social inclusion to follow, thus enabling the pursuit of self-actualization.

1.2 Dignity and ICTs

When one considers the important role technology plays (and will continue to play) in the health care field, it raises the question of how a patient's dignity can be preserved in the face of the impersonal nature of interactions with, or mediated by, technology. The discussion of dignity, especially in an ICT context, is very often avoided due to a myriad of definitions and interpretations in addition to Jacobson's. For instance, Sharkey [12] chooses the capabilities approach [13] to evaluate how the dignity of older people is affected by robot care. In a study of technology-based support groups for people with advanced stage cancer, Street et al. [14] use dignity and deferral narratives. Hosking et al. [15] propose a conceptual framework for designers that links 'empathy tools' with increased patient dignity in the development of medical devices. And while they do not refer specifically to dignity, Schulz et al. [16] propose a classification for 'Quality of Life Technologies' with a life-span approach to facilitate communication between various stakeholders. These differing methodologies result in a less cohesive approach to ensuring dignified design of technologies.

Jacobson's taxonomy [3] helps explain links between health care and human rights. The finding that "every human interaction holds the potential to be a dignity encounter" could be used to augment an inclusive design process [17, 18] for ICTs for older adults. Jacobson describes dignity violation interactions in terms of social processes such as rudeness, indifference and condescension. Dignity promotion interactions are described as contribution, empowerment, independence, and advocacy. Examining whether an ICT encounter promotes dignity and/or could predict potential adoption.

For the current study, mixed methods were used to investigate a taxonomy of dignity and ICT use, in conjunction with an inclusive design process to enable older adults to provide insights on a health computer system. Findings from this case study begin an exploration around how to implement a discussion of dignity in the ICT design process, specifically with a goal of designing a taxonomy of dignity for this space.

2 Methods

The Centre for Elder Research at Sheridan College recruited two focus groups composed of four older adult participants each (3 men total; avg. age = 74.75). Participants were recruited through the Centre's research database, and individuals were considered for inclusion if they were (as self-described) cognitively well and are currently, or have had experience, dealing with a medical condition. All participants provided informed consent to take part in the study, and the study was approved by Sheridan's Research Ethics Board. The sessions each lasted approximately an hour and data collection was done via note-taking and audio recording. The focused conversation method [19], in which questions progress from objective to increasingly reflective, interpretive and decisional, was used to begin the sessions with questions about technology use, experienced barriers, and the impact of technology on daily life.

Since there is evidence of positive results for pre-screening of cancer symptoms via computer technology [20], participants were then introduced to a computerized tool that allows cancer patients to assess their symptoms prior to seeing their clinical care team. As part of the cognitive walk-through of the system that followed, participants were introduced to a persona [21] and asked to assist the persona to use the symptom-reporting portion of the software prior to receiving chemotherapy. The persona in this case was a fictional gentleman named Bob Proctor; the participants 'helped' Bob use the system (by signing in, reporting on the severity of his symptoms, etc.), and then provided feedback on the software interface, specifically as it related to dignity.

Following this guided discussion, additional interpretive and decisional questions were posed to the participants. These included asking them to define dignity, describe how the computer system impacted their dignity (positively or negatively), and their general thoughts on the interface of design and dignity for health care technologies.

3 Results

The older adults we spoke to were relatively tech-savvy; all have regular access to cell phones and computers, and some mentioned using tablets, fitbits, and advanced technologies in their cars. Online activities with respect to health and well-being were: searching for general health/medication information, monitoring exercise and activity levels, and communicating with others. Barriers to using technology were: privacy, security, obsessive use of technology, frustration with difficult-to-use applications, platform changes/updates, increasing complexity, cost, lack of help/support, and more fast-paced living with the feeling one must respond immediately to a text. Benefits of technology, particularly mobile, were stated as useful and comforting for emergencies, reducing loneliness, increasing communication with younger family members, allowing information at their fingertips and downloading books without carrying them. Everyone agreed that their daily lives had been affected by technology.

During the cognitive walk-through of the software, the participants noted many similar issues that had been observed during a previous round of usability testing conducted on the system [22] such as the instruction screen needed to be further simplified, the symptom scale from 1 to 10 was difficult to quantify as to what constituted different levels, the definitions of each symptom needed to be more clear and visible, and there was concern for people whose first language was not English. In addition, other suggestions made were: enable patients to sign in with their name instead of a number, provide smiley happy or sad face emoticons for symptom reporting instead of a 1 to 10 scale, and ask if extra time is needed to complete the questionnaire instead of announcing that the system would time out within seconds. It was felt that completing the questionnaire at home could enhance security and privacy; however, the "human touch" would need to be built-in to the process by the clinic/hospital showing the patient how to download and use the home app, provide a time frame for symptom reporting, pre-program the location of the appointment for the patient, and provide a friendly "how-to" video explaining the app's use and purpose. Participants stated dignity could be enhanced by acknowledging that this is a stressful time, making it clear that "all is not lost" if an answer is completed incorrectly, and using the patient's name to provide messages of encouragement (ex. "only four more questions, 'Bob'").

The participants viewed the technology as making more efficient use of the clinician's time. They also noted a downside of this being that "Doctors don't look at you if they are looking at their laptops. The technology removes human contact". When asked about their feelings of evaluating the system, one participant said, "Glad to have the opportunity. Often nobody asks". Another participant said, "It's empowering", and another provided the caveat, "as long as they consider our answers and use them".

Participants defined dignity as "respect that is not demeaning or patronizing", "respect for privacy", "respect of the individual" and "you are not a number; you are a person". When describing dignity loss when technology doesn't work as expected, the words/feelings were: frustrated, angry, "feel like an idiot", annoyed, threatened (if privacy is breached), lack of control, time-consuming, and "want to cry".

4 Discussion

How was exploring a taxonomy for dignity based on Jacobson's work useful? Although we were not able to create a taxonomy specific to ICTs and older adults in this study, we discovered that opening up the conversation about dignity enabled deeper discovery and new insights. Perhaps the greatest value of this study was the realization that starting a discussion of dignity alongside technology could be a method to improve healthcare (not unlike that proposed by [15]). It seemed awkward at first to explore both dignity and an application in the same session but the focused conversation method provided a bridge to gradually deepen questions from objective to interpreting concepts of dignity in relation to a computer system. This also led the participants to reconsider the self-evident; something so basic to dignity, a patient's name to sign in, had never come up, even with prior usability studies. Thus, this approach can reveal insights that may not always be uncovered using more traditional techniques.

In this study, the taxonomy that Jacobson uses for dignity violation did not seem to apply. Participants spoke of dignity violation and technology more in terms of frustration, wasted time through loss of data or system failure, feeling like a disaster had occurred via harsh error messages, issues of loss of privacy or loss of security. These strong feelings coincided more with Jacobson's description of the *consequences* of dignity violation where there are "strong language and vivid examples" where "the individual may experience many emotions, including shock, fear, disbelief, hurt, mortification or embarrassment, discomfort or pain, indignation, frustration, or anger".

Participants spoke freely using concepts of dignity promotion, in contrast with Jacobson's findings, where the participants had to be prompted. Our participants felt they were making a "contribution" and "empowered" through their participation in the study. They made suggestions toward "independence" of use, and places where human "presence" could be enhanced. They were "advocates" for better patient outcomes and more efficient use of a clinician's time. They talked about giving "control" to the patient and discussed privacy and security issues as a baseline necessity for system use. This is very much in line with Maslow's hierarchy of needs [11]; technology adoption could be strengthened by ensuring that safety is inherent in the system.

5   Conclusion

While Jacobson's taxonomy for dignity violation seemed too strong to describe computer interaction, the complimentary taxonomy for dignity promotion was applicable to the positive suggestions that participants provided for system improvement. The potential for increased dignity promotion for patient care through consideration of small changes to an application's interface seems promising. The limitation of this particular study was that it only involved a small group of older adults. Involving older adults in future studies may yield further useful insights that contribute towards the development of a possible taxonomy of dignity for health-care applications.

Acknowledgements.   Thanks to Cancer Care Ontario and the Centre for Elder Research for their participation. We are extremely grateful to the older adults who participated in this study.

References

1. United Nations Department of Economic and Social Affairs Population Division. World Population Ageing: 1950–2050 (2002). http://www.un.org/esa/population/publications/worldageing19502050/
2. World Health Organization. WHO | World report on ageing and health, September 2015. http://www.who.int/ageing/publications/world-report-2015/en/
3. Jacobson, N.: A taxonomy of dignity: a grounded theory study. BMC Int. Health Hum. Rights 9, 3 (2009). doi:10.1186/1472-698X-9-3
4. Blaschke, C.M., Freddolino, P.P., Mullen, E.E.: Ageing and technology: a review of the research literature. Brit. J. Soc. Work 39, 641–656 (2009)
5. Eastman, J.K., Iyer, R.: The elderly's uses and attitudes towards the internet. J. Consum. Mark. 21(3), 208–220 (2004)
6. Adler, R.: Older Americans, broadband and the future of the net. SeniorNet (2006). www.seniornet.org/research/SeniorNetNNPaper060606.pdf

7. Czaja, S.J., Lee, C.C.: The impact of the internet on older adults. In: Charness, N., Schaie, K. W. (eds.) The Impact of Technology on Successful Aging. Springer Publishing, New York (2003)

8. White, H., McConnell, E., Clipp, E., Branch, L.G., Sloane, R., Pieper, C., Box, T.L.: A randomized controlled trial of the psychosocial impact of providing internet training and access to older adults. Aging Mental Health **6**(3), 213–221 (2002)

9. Charness, N., Boot, W.R.: Aging and information technology use: potential and barriers. Curr. Dir. Psychol. Sci. **18**(5), 253–258 (2009)

10. Baecker, R.M., Moffatt, K., Massimi, M.: Technologies for aging gracefully. Interactions **19** (3), 32–36 (2012)

11. Maslow, A.H.: Motivation and Personality. Harper & Row, New York (1954)

12. Sharkey, A.: Robots and human dignity : a consideration of the effects of robot care on the dignity of older people. Ethics Inf. Technol. **16**(1), 63–75 (2014)

13. Nussbaum, M.C.: Creating Capabilities: The Human Development Approach. Belknap, Cambridge (2011)

14. Street, A.F., Wakelin, K., Hordern, A., Bruce, N., Horey, D.: Dignity and deferral narratives as strategies in facilitated technology-based support groups for people with advanced cancer. Nurs. Res. Pract. **2012**, 1–7 (2012)

15. Hosking, I., Cornish, K., Bradley, M., Clarkson, P.: Empathic engineering: helping deliver dignity through design. J. Med. Eng. Technol. **39**(7), 388–394 (2015)

16. Schulz, R., Wahl, H., Matthews, J.T., De Vito Dabbs, A., Beach, S.R., Czaja, S.J.: Advancing the aging and technology agenda in gerontology. Gerontologist **55**(5), 724–734 (2015)

17. Bontoff, M., Pullin, G.: What is an inclusive design process? In: Clarkson, P.J., Colemean, R., Keates, S., Lebbon, C. (eds.) Inclusive Design: Design for the Whole Population, pp. 520–531. Springer, London (2013)

18. Treviranus, J.: Leveraging the web as a platform for economic inclusion. Behav. Sci. Law **32**, 94–103 (2014)

19. Stanfield, R.B.: The Art of Focused Conversation: 100 Ways to Access Group Wisdom in the Workplace, p. 30. New Society Publishers, Vancouver (2000)

20. Barbera, L., Sutradhar, R., Howell, D., Sussman, J., Seow, H., Dudgeon, D., Krzyzanowska, M.K.: Does routine symptom screening with ESAS decrease ED visits in breast cancer patients undergoing adjuvant chemotherapy? Support. Care Cancer **23**(10), 3025–3032 (2015)

21. Hanington, B., Martin, B.: Universal Methods of Design: 100 Ways to Research Complex Problems, Develop Innovative Ideas, and Design Effective Solutions. Rockport Publishers, Beverly (2012)

22. Healthcare Human Factors University Health Network. Insights on ISAAC Usability & Service Design (2014)

Distributed User Interfaces for Luria's Tests for Older Adults

Pedro Cruz Caballero[1]([⊠]), Amilcar Meneses Viveros[1],
and Erika Hernández Rubio[2]

[1] Departamento de Computación, CINVESTAV-IPN, México, D.F., Mexico
pcruz@computacion.cs.cinvestav.mx, ameneses@cs.cinvestav.mx
[2] Instituto Politécnico Nacional, SEPI-ESCOM, México, D.F., Mexico
ehernandezru@ipn.mx

Abstract. Luria's tests can be used, mainly by psychologists, neuropsychologists or any other mental specialist, to analyze mental decline in older adults. The application of Luria's tests in older adults using mobile devices may encounter different obstacles, not only because of visual, cognitive, and physical limitations but also when using devices with limited screen attributes or touch space. One of the most typical solution includes the implementation of contextual plasticity, which provide the applications with the possibility of use the best interface modality based on the user's capabilities or to take advantage of closer devices like secondary screens. In this work we present a distributed graphic user interface for three Luria's visual perceptual tests for older adults. This distributed graphic user interface is implemented in a prototype for iOS, using iPad and appleTV.

1 Introduction

The study of memory as part of the analysis of pathological changes, is one of the areas most researched by mental health specialists. In these studies, tests are applied to evaluate the level of cortical functions of patients such as, attention, language, movement and action, perception, memory, and learning

Beta II-R and Wais tests [1,2] are based on research made by the neuropsychologist Alexander R. Luria [3] and are some of the most used in older adults. These tests are applied using pencil, paper, graphic resources such as images, recordings and in some cases by analyzing body movements. Currently, there have been researches and implementations on mobile devices aimed at older adults [4,5] with the intention to help those who can not travel to a clinic [6,7]. These developments must consider user's physical and mental impairments as well as the limitations of hardware.

Existing solutions use responsive design, contextual plasticity and multimodal interaction, all this to provide a better user interface [8]. Our solution includes the development of a distributed graphic user interface for three Luria's visual perception tests using a tablet and SmartTV [9,10]. The purpose of joining these devices is to have a larger viewing area (appleTV) and use the different

© Springer International Publishing Switzerland 2016
C. Stephanidis (Ed.): HCII 2016 Posters, Part I, CCIS 617, pp. 413–419, 2016.
DOI: 10.1007/978-3-319-40548-3_69

modes of interaction that provides the tablet (iPad), this could facilitate the usage to older adults.

2   Related Work

This work is based on previous work related to design of interfaces for older adults, Luria's tests and distributed user interfaces (DUIS). Design of user interfaces is an essential part of software development, which involves concepts such as usability, modalities of interaction and context of use. Design process should usually take three following steps. (1) Know what the user will do and what kind of tasks are executed on the device. (2) Recognize the characteristics of the user and which of these can affect user performance when using the system. For example, age or physical disabilities such as blindness. (3) It should recognize the environment in which the user will make use of technology (use of context) in order to identify advantages or disadvantages that might affect user performance when using a mobile device or any application. Publications related to the design of displays for older adults suggest changes in applications to support visual and auditory weaknesses [11–13]. For example, screens are recommended to have between 5 and 9 in.. The text should be displayed in capital letters, with a size of at least 12 points and a Sans Serif font type (for example Arial or Times New Roman). Use a contrasting font-color to the background, such as white letters on a black background. When audio is used, it should not exceed 4000 Hz and male voice is recommended to give instructions.

Luria's Tests, corresponding to the ability of learning and memory, have been developed and analyzed using mobile devices, multimodal interaction, and contextual plasticity [4,5,14,15]. In our case, we use tests associated with visual capabilities using a distributed user interface, which is a resource that provides alternatives to expand the capabilities of an application, one of them, sharing the display area with a bigger-screen device or adding new functions from external devices. Whenever using a DUI, is important to understand the principles of distribution [9] and distinguish what would be the possible improvements we could get when using it in our application [10,16]. It is also important to determine the level of acceptance by older adults [17,18].

3   Design

In order to assess our proposed solution, we developed an application using a DUI, on a device with iOS, referred to Luria's visual tests (Poppelreuter and Raven tests)

3.1   Luria's Vision Test

These tests are applied when visual perceptual research is performed. First phase consists on showing a set of clear images to the patient and request to watch them and remember. In the second phase, the patient watch more complex or blurry images, these images begin to display visual noise that can be obtained by combining original images with random stripes. In the last phase, noise in the images increases (Poppelreuter test) and new complex images are shown to patient to identify particular characteristics, such as size, color, and geometric patterns (Raven test).

The Poppelreuter test starts showing drawings of objects from everyday life (e.g. bottle, spoon, an apple) to the patient. Then, series of images are displayed with the same object but overlapped with more strokes, or lines (Fig. 1a). The patient must distinguish the object from the rest of the strokes by pointing its silhouette. The test becomes more difficult when more silhouettes are in the same drawing. (Fig. 1b)

The Raven test begins presenting an image with a certain visual vacuum to the patient, the gap must be completed by choosing between six options. The test belongs to the space series test in which the patient must observe a certain visual structure and differentiate from others and, in special cases, grasp the complex principle in which its structure was built. (Fig. 1c)

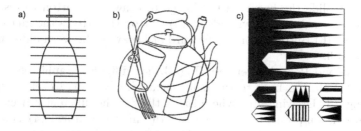

Fig. 1. (a) Poppelreuter test 1 (b) Poppelreuter Test 2 (c) Raven Test

3.2   Architecture

The application has two options for testing, one uses iPad and the other uses the union with the iPad and AppleTV. We used an iPad Mini 2 (Retina Display 2048 × 1536, 16 GB, A7 Chip, Wi-Fi, 1.3 GHz, 1 GB RAM, iOS 9.1) and appleTV 4th generation (H.264 video up to 1080 p, 32 GB, A8 Chip, Wi-Fi, Ethernet, 2 GB RAM, tvOS 1.2, Siri Remote[1]).

The communication between devices uses Airplay, which is a wireless streaming service from Apple designed to allow users to stream content from Macs and iDevices (Fig. 2). This service provides all the necessary mechanisms for communication and iOS offers classes and functions to work with a second display device. Therefore, one must code functions (using Swift 2.1) that modify the user interface and update the graphic elements of the second screen.

---

[1] Currently, Siri is only available in US, Canada, Australia, France, Germany, and U.K.

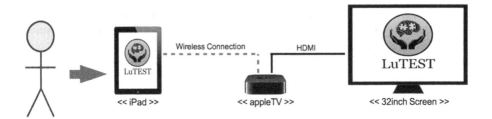

Fig. 2. Distributed User Interface

3.3   Test Design

The following images show the design of the application, which consists of an initial menu with three possible options to perform tests (Poppelreuter 1, Poppelreuter 2, and Raven Test). When starting any of the tests, instructions on how to do it will be heard and at the same time a message is displayed with instructions. In the first Poppelreuter test (Fig. 3a) six different graphic elements are identified. (1) Button back to the main menu. (2) Image with the original object. (3) Drawing area where the outline of the original object should be recognized, simply slide the finger on the image to draw. (4) Button to restart the drawing area, deletes all drawing done. (5) Button that stores the image on the drawing area. (6) Buttons to move forward or backward between different tests. This updates 3.

In the second Poppelreuter test (Fig. 3b) six different graphic elements are identified. (1) Button back to the main menu. (2) Buttons to select the color for drawing. (3) Drawing area where the outline of the different objects should be recognized, simply slide the finger on the image to draw. (4) Buttons to move forward or backward between different tests. This updates 3. (5) Button to restart the drawing area, delete all drawing done. (6) Button that stores the image on the drawing area.

In Raven test (Fig. 3c) four different graphic elements are identified. (1) Button back to main Menu. (2) Main picture, which is shown incomplete. (3) Buttons to move forward or backward between different Raven tests. (4) Solution Options.

When distributing the application to a larger display device (appleTV connected to a 32-in. screen), display of the tests will be as follows (Fig. 4). For Poppelreuter tests, the drawing area is moved to AppleTV and iPad will remain the same elements. When drawing on the iPad, it will be seen immediately on the screen. For Raven test, appleTV shows the image with the gap and the iPad shows solution options and navigation buttons. Solution options are displayed at a larger size as the image on the AppleTV is also shown on a larger scale.

The application also modifies the text and audio depending on the language in which you set the iPad (for the moment only the Spanish language and English is contemplated).

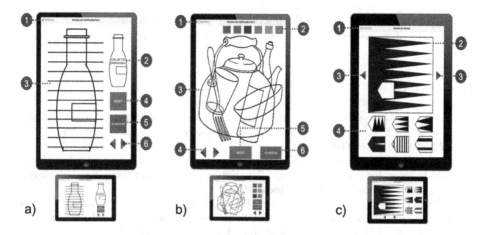

Fig. 3. Tests in Portrait and Landscape orientation

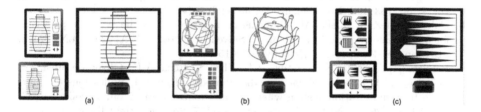

Fig. 4. Tests using DUIs (Portrait and Landscape orientation)

4 Results

The prototype allows to perform the three tests previously described. Each screen
has an adaptive design related to device's orientation (Portrait and Landscape)
to take advantage of the screen dimensions and give the user the option of testing
as deemed best. Even when distributing the interface, all the tasks are executed
on the iPad because it allows user to save locally images from his tests and the
use of a touch screen helps him to draw just using his finger. These are not
possible using AppleTV where storage is restricted to be online (iCloud) and
touch is not necessarily related with the screen and its coordinates X Y.

5 Conclusion

Implementation of Luria visual tests using a mobile DUI is feasible and provides
various modalities of interaction. An appleTV application was contemplated to
be developed, but finally we used iPad as the main device and appleTV as
secondary screen because of the interaction modalities that tests required, they
suit best with iPad functions. Application only has to be installed on iPad. The
prototype must be validated with the help of a specialist (neuropsychologist)

and then testing usability and effectiveness with older adults. In the future, recognition of voice instructions will be added to run navigation, restart, and save actions.

References

1. Neiva, K.: Manual de pruebas de inteligencia y aptitudes. Plaza y Valdés (1996)
2. Kaufman, A.S., Lichtenberger, E.O.: Essentials of WAIS-III Assessment. John Wiley, New Jersey (1999)
3. Luria, A.: Las funciones corticales superiores del hombre: (y sus alteraciones por lesiones locales del cerebro). (Breviarios de conducta humana. Psicología, Psiquiatría y salud). Martínez Roca (1983)
4. Miranda, J.A.H., Hernàndez Rubio, E., Meneses Viveros, A.: Analysis of luria memory tests for development on mobile devices. In: Duffy, V.G. (ed.) DHM 2014. LNCS, vol. 8529, pp. 546–557. Springer, Heidelberg (2014)
5. Viveros, A.M., Rubio, E.H., Hijar Miranda, J.A.: 8. In: Design of Luria Memory Test for Older Adults on Mobile Device. Horizons in Computer Science Research, vol. 9, pp. 183–198. Nova Science Publisher Inc. (2014)
6. Calero Valdez, A., Ziefle, M.: Older users' rejection of mobile health apps a case for a stand-alone device? In: Zhou, J., Salvendy, G. (eds.) ITAP 2015. LNCS, vol. 9194, pp. 38–49. Springer, Heidelberg (2015)
7. Pereira, C., Almeida, N., Martins, A.I., Silva, S., Rosa, A.F., Oliveira e Silva, M., Teixeira, A.: Evaluation of complex distributed multimodal applications: evaluating a telerehabilitation system when it really matters. In: Zhou, J., Salvendy, G. (eds.) ITAP 2015. LNCS, vol. 9194, pp. 146–157. Springer, Heidelberg (2015)
8. Sears, A., Jacko, J.A.: Human-Computer Interaction: Development Process. CRC Press, Boca Raton (2009)
9. Vanderdonckt, J.: Distributed user interfaces: How to distribute user interface elements across users, platforms, and enviroments. In: Proceedings of XIth Congreso Internacional de Interacción Persona-Ordenador Interacción'2010, pp. 3–14 (2010)
10. Brown, A., Evans, M., Jay, C., Glancy, M., Jones, R., Harper, S.: Hci over multiple screens. In: CHI 2014 Extended Abstracts on Human Factors in Computing Systems, CHI EA 2014, pp. 665–674. ACM, New York (2014)
11. Pak, R., McLaughlin, A.: Designing Displays for Older Adults. CRC Press, Boca Raton (2010)
12. Fisk, A.D., Rogers, W.A., Charness, N., Czaja, S.J., Sharit, J.: Designing for Older Adults: Principles and Creative Human Factors Approaches, 2nd edn. CRC Press, Boca Raton (2009)
13. Jang, W.: An ipad application prototype to enhance memory of older adults. In: Stephanidis, C., Tino, A. (eds.) HCII 2015 Posters. CCIS, vol. 528, pp. 299–304. Springer, Heidelberg (2015). doi:10.1007/978-3-319-21380-4_51
14. Fernando, L.M.R., Vazquez, R.I.: Sistema interactivo de ejercitación de memoria para personas mayores. Bachelor's thesis, Escuela Superior de Cómputo ESCOM-IPN, May 2010
15. Mancera Serralde, E.I., J.O.F.: Estudio comparativo de interfaces plásticas para pruebas del test luria. Master's thesis, Escuela Superior de Cómputo (ESCOM-IPN), February 2015
16. Luyten, K., Coninx, K.: Distributed user interface elements to support smart interaction spaces. In: Seventh IEEE International Symposium on Multimedia, p. 8, December 2005

17. Bobeth, J., Schmehl, S., Kruijff, E., Deutsch, S., Tscheligi, M.: Evaluating performance and acceptance of older adults using freehand gestures for tv menu control. In: Proceedings of the 10th European Conference on Interactive Tv and Video, EuroiTV 2012, pp. 35–44. ACM, New York (2012)
18. Best, R., Souders, D.J., Charness, N., Mitzner, T.L., Rogers, W.A.: The role of health status in older adults' perceptions of the usefulness of ehealth technology. In: Zhou, J., Salvendy, G. (eds.) ITAP 2015. LNCS, vol. 9194, pp. 3–14. Springer, Heidelberg (2015)

Are Google Office Applications Easy for Seniors?: Usability Studies with 120 Elderly Users

Javier Diaz and Ivana Harari[✉]

Computer Science School, National University of La Plata UNLP,
La Plata, Argentina
{jdiaz, iharari}@info.unlp.edu.ar

Abstract. The Computer Science School of the UNLP, constantly works with the area of education, bringing ICTs to sectors that are excluded from the information society. Since 2010, it began working with the senior citizen sector. In 2015 they took the GDocs and GDrive course with the possibility to participate in a usability research. The students, about 120 seniors between 68 and 90 years of age, belonged to PAMI, the National Institute for Retirees and Pensioners of Argentina. The main objective of this poster is to share this experience for which usability studies were developed in order to find out if Google collaborative office apps are easy to learn and use by seniors. These form a broader research work, of great value to the discipline of HCI, where the focus of study is a community of people that are not usually considered as potential users of the products that are being developed today.

Keywords: Seniors · Usability · Web · CSCW · Applications · GDrive · GDocs · ICT training

1 The Initiative

During the academic year 2015, we imparted training on GDocs and GDrive applications to about 120 elderly between 68 and 90 years old.

This learning process was conducted with two objectives– to enable seniors in the use of widely used applications, and to use the same resources to study the user interaction between these people and Google Apps in an appropriate framework of usability evaluation [1]. Google products are of massive use; the subjects had certainly heard of them but were still strangers to these technologies, with no real knowledge of what they mean and what they were for.

The courses consisted of a weekly three hour encounter for a period of 8 weeks, totaling 24 learning hours plus six extra hours for the usability evaluation. 5 courses were offered, each to groups of 20 to 25 people with a PC for every student. The courses were offered at the Computer Science School [2].

The evaluation methodology used basically consisted of the following stages:

© Springer International Publishing Switzerland 2016
C. Stephanidis (Ed.): HCII 2016 Posters, Part I, CCIS 617, pp. 420–425, 2016.
DOI: 10.1007/978-3-319-40548-3_70

- Initial Stage: presentation of the group of students and teachers. At this stage, personal interviews were conducted to learn about students' prior knowledge, expectations, and motivations, among others.
- Training Stage: presentation of the product to study, investigation of the product, theoretical and practical teaching on the product. This stage was conducted in two parts. In the first part, prior to the winter break, the basic concepts and uses of GDocs and GDrive were covered. A second part was conducted after usability testing; which covered more advanced features.
- Assessment Stage: This process consisted of a usability test and took place after the winter break, when students had already become acquainted with basic applications. In the test, students were designated a series of activities to develop. These practical activities of increasing complexity were monitored by the method of direct observation and registered in spreadsheets [3].

After practical experience, interviews were held in order to find out the degree of satisfaction of the students after the activities. Then, small focus groups were implemented for students to better express themselves, reflecting on what they learned and experienced.

This paper addresses only the usability testing process developed at the assessment stage.

2 The Usability Testing

The usability testing conducted with senior citizens took place during the assessment stage of the training process. Students were informed that this evaluation would have a different objective: it was going to evaluate the software, not the students' knowledge.

They reported feeling at ease understanding that difficulties and mistakes taking place during interaction with the products could originate not in age-related limitations as they tended to think, but in usability-related design flaws in the products, and that this would be the object of the assessment.

The term usability refers to the degree of effectiveness, efficiency and satisfaction with which specific users can achieve specific goals in specific contexts of use [4]. The best way to determine if a system is usable is to monitor users attempting to perform real tasks using the product. Usability tests are essential for this purpose [5].

In our case, the observed performance of senior citizens interacting with GDocs and GDrive applications is valuable information to determine how easy it is for them to learn and use these programs with remote and collaborative features.

The sections that follow will deal with the sample of participants, the development of the assessment and its results.

2.1 Sample of Participants

The sample of participants that participated in the Google applications usability testing consisted of 120 people between 68 and 90 years of age affiliated with the PAMI national entity [6].

An initial survey was carried out during the course registration, aiming at the level of education of the students, their current activity and the previous experience in Google applications. This survey yielded the following results:

- 73.33 % were women.
- Only 6.66 % had university level studies; 26.66 % were working.
- 40 % had no basic skills in computer use. The rest had used a PC because they had attended one of the previous offered courses such as an introductory course on Computer Literacy, Facebook, Internet and Word Processors. Only 15 % used the PC frequently after this training.
- Although most had heard of Google, only 1.66 % knew about GDocs and GDrive apps before the announcement of the course. The majority did not know what they were and did not understand that Google brings a collaborative office application.

They were reportedly motivated by a desire to learn and to thrive. Yet another interesting motivation that drove them was the desire for a closer relationship with young people, in the sense of improving dialogue, as well as understanding the technical slang used by them and their new habits.

2.2 Developing the Test

The usability testing consisted of 10 development activities on GDocs and GDrive applications. These were carried out in two encounters so students would have time to spare. The activities, with different degree of difficulty, were the following:

1. Login to GDrive, create a document.
2. Write an invitation to an event in GDocs and name it "InvitacionDeJuanPerez". Replace Juan Perez with your full name.
3. Insert an image related to the subject.
4. Share the note with two people– one with editing permissions and another with commenting permissions.
5. Create a folder named "Notas" in GDrive.
6. Move the note you made to this folder.
7. Download the note you made to the hard drive.
8. Find notes a particular student made and find out who else the works were shared with.
9. Leave a comment in a shared work where you have permissions to do so.
10. Exit the application.

The spreadsheet recording the results of the interaction between the seniors and the software observed in these activities consisted of two parts. The first stating whether the activity was completed easily, with difficulty or not at all. The average completion time was also included. A second section stated the difficulties encountered, either because the activity was carried out in an overly complicated manner or could not be completed. Reasons cited were that the user was disoriented, the object was not found or the activity was not understood.

2.3 Results of the Usability Test

The results of the usability evaluation are shown in Table 1. These findings come from analyses of the data recorded in Part 1 and 2 of the spreadsheets.

Table 1. Results of activities in GDocs and Gdrive. Values are expressed in %

#Task	Performance				Difficulties encountered			
	Easily	With some difficulty	Not completed	Average completion time	Number of users with difficulties	Was disoriented	Did not find it	Did not understand
1	31.66	46.66	17.5	16' 54"	66	39.39	42.42	18.18
2	30	19.16	59.16	14' 33"	94	22.34	67.02	10.63
3	27.50	35.83	45	7' 16"	87	62.06	13.79	24.13
4	15	25.8	64.16	23' 49"	108	44.44	23.14	32.40
5	10	32.5	55.83	21' 21"	106	42.45	19.81	37.73
6	15.83	23.33	60.83	18' 56"	101	42.57	38.61	18.81
7	25.83	22.5	51.66	9' 16"	89	44.94	20.22	34.83
8	12.5	30	57.5	20' 25"	105	37.14	29.52	33.33
9	15	29.16	55.83	19' 11"	102	47.05	17.64	35.29
10	10.83	20	69.16	21' 56"	107	51.40	10.28	38.31

Analyzing these results we can conclude that:

- In the first activity, the students were disoriented in trying to login to GDrive. Several tried using the Start button of Windows. Although they were in the Google page they did not associate the ⦂⦂⦂ Google applications icon with the task at hand. Few people who knew Android applications icons could recognize it.
- Editing a document and changing the file name was not associated with clicking on Untitled. It took them some time and they were confused as regards the file name.
- Activity 3 featuring image insertion was quick but students were confused when prompted with an incompatible format error after searching and selecting it, as it appeared to be accepted, checked in green.
- Activity 4 caused them to confuse file and link sharing. It took students a while to add users with different permissions (Fig. 1).

Fig. 1. Delays in sharing a file with multiple users with different permissions (SCR: GDocs)

- Creating a folder took them a while because the option is in the New menu but in the GDrive tab. They have difficulties working with tabs and finding certain features when alternating between the GDrive and GDocs contexts. In GDocs they did not associate the Organize option of the File menu with that task.
- Moving the document to a new folder gave them great difficulties in GDocs because they found it with the Organize term. They generated too many tabs, as the ☑ opening GDrive in a new tab icon can be found in the same location as the ▸ displaying My Unit folders icon (Fig. 2).

Fig. 2. Confusion with the icons on the right of My Unit (SCR: GDocs)

In GDrive, moving is in an ⋮ icon which they did not recognize easily.

- Activity 7 featuring document download differs greatly between the GDocs and the GDrive environment. One has it in the File menu, with a choice of format, and the other with the ⋮ icon, automatically downloaded as .DOCx.
- Finding out the author and who a file had been shared with was complicated in GDrive since there is no author search and the information is in the ⓘ icon, associated more with application information than with file details. GDocs has file and author permissions in sharing. The students were disoriented because they did not intend to share the file but to analyze how it had been previously shared.
- Leaving a comment in a shared file implicates a process they could not understand. They had to go to GDrive, Shared with me, click the file name twice, then click open when they already could see it open (Fig. 3), then click comment. Some of them thought that open meant opening another file, as in File-Open.

Fig. 3. Disorientation in trying to open a file that is already open (SCR: GDrive)

- In activity 10, most students did not exit the application correctly. They did not understand that they had opened multiple tabs. They close their document but not their GDrive session. Other used the x to close the browser entirely. None of them saw that they had been prompted with a warning.

3 Conclusions

This paper explains details of a usability test of popular applications such as GDocs and GDrive with senior citizens in a context where the testing was integrated into a training process. The same people who participated in the course, participated in the test once they had the basic knowledge required. This had a positive impact in the interaction between the students and the HCI evaluators, the testing time and the confidence of the participants. When working with older adults, feelings and emotions play important roles in the interaction and hence the development of the test.

> *"We cannot believe we have learned and even worked in the process of testing!"*, said Gladys, 78 years old. *"We learned that we are not responsible for all the mistakes we make with the software, product developers are also to blame!"*, as mentioned by Jorge, 71 years old.

The usability evaluation process with senior citizens was an enriching experience. There was great interest among the students to explain how they felt, where they made mistakes, where they got to, and what interface elements confused them.

We also aim at going deeper in an almost unexplored disciplinary field, where there is a great lack in studies and background research. We also try to immerse ourselves in a community that is not usually the target that a Web developer has in mind: senior citizens.

References

1. Nielsen, J., Mack, R.: Usability Inspection Methods. Wiley, New York (2004)
2. Diaz, F.J., Banchoff, C., Harari, V., Harari, I., y Ambrosi, V.: Accesibilidad, Brecha Digital y Medio Ambiente: Líneas estratégicas en la Facultad de Informática de la UNLP. XI Taller de Extensión Universitaria, Cuba (2012)
3. Gremillion, B., Chapman, C., y Munroe, L.: A Field Guide to Usability Testing. Samshing Magazine, New York (2012)
4. ISO:9241-11:1998. Ergonomic requirements for office work with visual display terminal. Part 11: Guidance on usability. https://www.iso.org/obp/ui/#iso:std:iso:9241:-11:ed-1:v1:en
5. Rubin, J., Chisnell, D.: How to Plan, Design, and Conduct Effective Tests. Handbook of Usability Testing, 2nd edn. Wiley Publishing Inc, New York (2008)

Design Research of Geriatric Rehabilitation Products Based on Natural Interaction

Qijun Duan[1(✉)], Kai Fang[1], Min Liu[1], and Yilin Pan[2]

[1] School of Design Art and Media, Nanjing University of Science
and Technology, 200, Xiaolingwei Street, Nanjing 210094, Jiangsu, China
pylduan@aliyun.com
[2] Shanghai University of Finance and Economics, 777 Guoding Road,
Shanghai 200433, China

Abstract. Acceleration of the aging process of population urges the research and innovative design of geriatric rehabilitation products. This paper introduces natural interaction technology to geriatric rehabilitation products through analysis of the elderly's physiological and psychological characteristics. This paper aims at exploring new approaches to geriatric rehabilitation products design, approaches that are innovative in both of the two aspects: product function and interactive experiences of using the product.

This paper has established some basic strategies to geriatric rehabilitation product design: (1) Design product functions according to the elderly's demand for body exercise and rehabilitation; (2) Design products' operation and control mode according to the elderly's inherent cognitive habits and living and behavioral ways, simplify operational process, and increase operational efficiency; (3) Emphasize users' experience in product using, design products' interaction process according to the elderly's psychological characteristics and demand, and improve patients' medical rehabilitation experience.

Geriatric rehabilitation products based on natural interaction technology not only could overcome the operational inconvenience caused by pathological factors that the elderly may suffer from, but also could discover potential physiological diseases of the elderly users. Moreover, they can provide the elderly users with better interactive experience through the usage of different channels.

Keywords: Natural interaction · Elderly · Rehabilitation products · Psychology · Behavior · Function · Experience

1 Introduction

At the start of the 21st century, China stepped into an aging society. It is expected that from 2001 to 2020, the elderly population will soar by an average amount of 5.96 million each year, and the average annual growth rate will be 3.28 %; By 2020, the elderly population will reach 248 million, accounting for 17.17 % of the whole population; By 2050, the numbers will be 483 million and 34.1 % respectively [1]. With acceleration of the aging process, the difficulty and high cost of getting medical treatment caused by insufficiency of medical resources and defection of medical care

© Springer International Publishing Switzerland 2016
C. Stephanidis (Ed.): HCII 2016 Posters, Part I, CCIS 617, pp. 426–431, 2016.
DOI: 10.1007/978-3-319-40548-3_71

system are becoming increasingly prominent. However, the promotion of living standard and the changes in people's self-care awareness and ideas about health lead people to attach importance to disease prevention and health care. Therefore, it is inevitable that traditional medical model consisting mainly of clinical therapy progresses towards diversified comprehensive medical system centering on prevention and combining home nursing and rehabilitation. In this social context, an increasing number of medical rehabilitation products (RP) are ranking among household essentials.

Nevertheless, since the household medical product industry in developing countries is far from mature, barely any design optimization aimed at the elderly's psychological and physiological traits and behavioral characteristics has been conducted on medical products there. Currently, there is great demand for design research on the interaction and usability of products targeted at the elderly and development of related products.

2   Elderly Users' Characteristics and Demands for RP Design

- **Physiological Characteristics.** Along with increase in human's age are gradual atrophy of muscles, weakened muscular strength and flexibility of joints, decay in cardiopulmonary function and reduction in exercise endurance, decrease in elasticity and tenacity of bones, and eventually, increase in risk of doing physical exercise. Hence the main purpose of exercises for the elderly should be maintaining endurance and improving stability [2]. Regular limb exercise can postpone the aging process of muscles for the elderly, maintain the flexibility of bones and joints, strengthen blood circulation and improve heart-lung function.
- **Cognitive Function.** In the aging brain, reduced cell activity and decelerated central nervous information transmission can take a toll on memory and ability of thinking, and thus ability of comprehension and expression. Compared with the young, it takes more time for the elderly to evaluate the environment, make decisions and adjust their actions accordingly [3]. Interactive products intended for the elderly should adopt simplification in information presentation, i.e. removal of redundant information and functions, to reduce learning cost. Key words and graphics may help the elderly to understand. Repeated demonstration can certainly deepen the elderly's memory about the interactive process.
- **Psychological Characteristics.** We have conducted interviews to gather the elderly's personal information and information about their family ties, social relationships, rehabilitation training needs and behavioral characteristics. Through analysis of interview results, we have drawn the conclusions that the elderly are generally concerned with their own physical and psychological health, they are inclined to participate in social groups consisting mainly of their peers, they are mentally and physically independent, they are afraid of wide spread of emerging new things, and they sympathize with each other.

Langer from Harvard holds the view that aging is no more than a concept instilled in the minds of the elderly [4]. Her experiments show that one's rate of aging is closely related to environmental implications. If we can give the elderly appropriate mental hints through products' function and/or feedback information, it is not beyond the scope of possibility that declinations in their functions be delayed. This is precisely an indispensable property that rehabilitation products should have.

3 Design Principles for Geriatric RP Based on Natural Interaction

In natural interaction, NATURAL refers to users' feelings when using the products; Natural interaction means operating devices with movements, gestures and language, to ease users of learning and cognition burden and to raise the efficiency of the whole interactive process by appealing to the users' behavioral habits. Applying natural interaction to geriatric RP design is a fundamental approach to meet the elderly's demands.

We have formed four design principles of applying natural interaction to geriatric RP design:

- **Accessibility and Safety.** Target products should be designed according to the elderly's physiological and psychological characteristics in order to prevent the elderly from security incidents or potential risk and make the whole process more flexible, more convenient, more comfortable and safer.
- **Suitability.** Three aspects of suitability should be considered: suitability of rehabilitative exercise mode, suitability of amount of exercise, and suitability of interactive mode.
- **Experience Consistency and Integrity.** Target products should be able to provide users with a complete range of medical diagnostic tests, rehabilitative exercise, healthcare and treatment services through establishment of household medical rehabilitation product system. On the strength of data sharing processes and interlinkages between products, this system should guarantee the users the effective implementation of rehabilitative treatments and offer users with complete and systematic rehabilitative treatment experience.
- **Entertainment and Participation.** Natural interaction between users and target products should help the elderly users ease the boredom, physiological fatigue and pressure of exercise, promote communication with other elderly rehabilitative exercise participants, and develop interest in interactive process and exercise result sharing.

4 Design Practice of Geriatric RP Based on Natural Interaction

According to design principles listed above, we have completed the research and design of a rehabilitation product system.

4.1   Choice of Rehabilitative Exercise

There are 6 forms of body movements: flexion, extension, abduction, adduction, rotation, and circumduction [5]. We choose appropriate exercise mode for our product and control the range and frequency of movement to help the users rehabilitating.

Strolling is a common type of exercise and a kind of rehabilitative exercise that is easy to be accepted by the elderly because the body movements involved in strolling are natural and comfortable. We consider the design of rehabilitative exercise from two expects:

- Convert the joint movements of strolling into rehabilitative exercise based on our product, including the movements of (A) shoulder joint, (B) elbow joint, (C) wrist joint, (D) hip joint, (E) knee joint, and (F) ankle joint as is shown in Fig. 1.
- Adjust, guarantee and control range and frequency of movements and amount of exercise. Since compared with the youth, the elderly probably have weaker sensation of balance and respond more slowly, we adopt this kind of exercise mode that is indoor, fully-monitored and comparatively less likely to bring accidental injury.

Fig. 1. Design of exercise mode for geriatric rehabilitation products

4.2   Function Framework of Rehabilitation Product System

The elderly in rehabilitation have various demands, including rehabilitative exercise, management of health information, participation of social activities and entertainment. Therefore, we propose a product function framework as is shown in Fig. 2.

4.3   Construction of Natural Interaction in Rehabilitation Product System

- **Improve users' perception of elements of human-computer interface.** To attain this goal, we amplify sensory stimuli of elements of human-computer interface by changing the environment, time length, intensity and frequency of information feedback [6]. In the aspect of visual feedback, we enlarge the area of information presentation and enhance the contract of characters and graph [7]. In the aspect of auditory feedback, we increase sound volume. In the aspect of tactile feedback, we

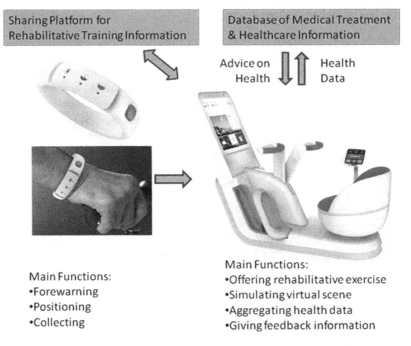

Main Functions:
•Forewarning
•Positioning
•Collecting

Main Functions:
•Offering rehabilitative exercise
•Simulating virtual scene
•Aggregating health data
•Giving feedback information

Fig. 2. Function framework and design proposal of rehabilitation product system

boost the intensity of vibration. Take operation interface of rehabilitation product system, we choose color black and high contrast to make the controls more recognizable, large buttons to allow easier interaction, and voice broadcast when users switch interfaces to offer information via multiple channels.

- **Add cultural and entertaining elements.** By mimicking the color, shape and function design of classic products, our products may give some impact on the nostalgic elderly. Entertaining elements of the product can help the elderly develop interest in rehabilitative process and ease training pressure [8]. Since the main exercise mode offered by target product is based on strolling, we integrate virtual panoramic landscape of multiple scenic spots into the interface to provide the users with different *scene* at every *step* and to realize the interaction between users and virtual scene [9].

- **Interlink products and artificial intelligence.** Sensor technology allows real-time monitoring of physiological conditions of users while Internet of Things and mobile internet enable the sharing of data. Adaptive capacity and self-learning ability make it possible for the product to react timely to the elderly's physiological conditions and operant behaviors, offset, to some extent, the elderly's disadvantage in memorization and reaction [10, 11].

5 Conclusion

Four perspectives should be taken into consideration when designing geriatric rehabilitation products: affordance (relation between an object or an environment and an organism that, through a collection of stimuli, affords the opportunity for that), suitability (form and amount of rehabilitative exercise suit individual users), timeliness of feedback (health data are sent timely to and rehabilitation management system), and entertainment of interactive process (combination of virtual reality and social platform makes rehabilitation interesting). The development and application of natural interaction and digital technology will urge great products that meet fundamental physiological and psychological instead superficial demands to break out.

References

1. Sun, W.: Research on City Community Service for the Old Based on the Home Care Mode. Jilin Agricultural University, Changchun (2008)
2. Fan, S.: Design for Behavior and Cognition. China Electric Power Press, Beijing (2009)
3. Zastrow, C., Kirst-Ashman, K.: Understanding Human Behavior and the Social Environment, 6th edn. Cengage Learning, Boston (2003)
4. Langer, E.J.: Counterclockwise: Mindful Health and the Power of Possibility. Ballantine Books, New York (2009)
5. McCormick, E.J., Sanders, M.S.: Human Factors in Engineering and Design, 7th Revised edn. McGraw Hill Higher Education, New York (1992)
6. Saffer, D.: Microinteractions, 1st edn. O'Reilly Media, California (2013)
7. Spence, R.: Information Visualization: Design for Interaction, 2nd edn. Pearson, New York (2007)
8. Valli, A.: The design of natural interaction. Multimedia Tools Appl. 38(3), 295–305 (2008)
9. Slater, M., Steed, A., Chrysanthou, Y.: Computer Graphics and Virtual Environments, 1st edn. Addison-Wesley, Boston (2001)
10. Johnson, N., Galata, A., Hogg, D.: The acquisition and use of interaction behaviour models. IEEE 38(8), 866–871 (1998)
11. Scarantino, A.: Affordances explained. Philos. Sci. 70(5), 949–961 (2003)

The Persuasive Design for Aged People's Health Behavior Change in the Domiciliary Health-Care Background

Yongyan Guo[(⊠)], Minggang Yang[(⊠)], and Zhang Zhang[(⊠)]

East China University of Science and Technology,
Shanghai, People's Republic of China
{gyymemory, yangminggang}@163.com,
ziziedelweiss@gmail.com

Abstract. Ageing population in China is increasing, which is to be a sorely test to China's pension services industry. Preventive treatment is an important concept of traditional Chinese medicine and keeping a healthy lifestyle is a good way to improve the health of senior citizen. Many elderly people become to pay more attention to improve their health self-management now, but many people don't know how to trigger themselves in keeping daily health. These are the research background of this article. As to improving elders' health behaviors, persuasive technology is applied. Persuasive Tech is broadly defined as the technology that is designed to change attitudes or behaviors of the users through persuasion and social influence, but not through coercion. DWI model is a tool to inspire the user's behavior change. According to this model, we research on the method of persuasion in health-keeping. Then we design different prototypes based on this method about how to persuade elders change their health behaviors in daily routines.

Keywords: Persuasive technology · Aged people · Health behavior

1   Persuasive Design and Persuasive Model

Persuasive Design (PD) is the extension of human centered design [1]. It supports the change of human behavior and attitude in the way of design [2]. Fogg developed a behavioral change model. According to this model three factors of behavior change were brought up, motivation, ability, and trigger [3, 4]. Design intended to influence or improve certain user behaviors [5]. In the field of product design, the subject of health is in particular attractive [6]. Many researchers do research in this area. Four persuasive design models are evaluated, persuasion advices and design guidelines of research are offered [7]. There are two modes in the latest model: "inspiration" and "prescription" [8]. The two modes are divided into six different lens, on behalf of the design to influence the behavior of specific perspectives. It serves to explore the various design patterns [5]. The Design with Intent (DWI) Method helps designers and other stakeholders generate Persuasive Design concepts to investigate further, by putting forward examples and insights from different disciplines [8]. The patterns are grouped into six 'lenses' (Fig. 1).

© Springer International Publishing Switzerland 2016
C. Stephanidis (Ed.): HCII 2016 Posters, Part I, CCIS 617, pp. 432–438, 2016.
DOI: 10.1007/978-3-319-40548-3_72

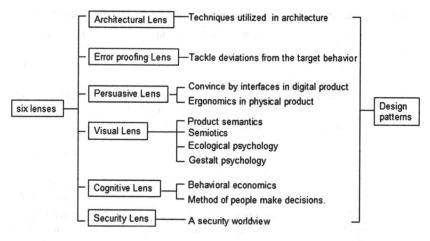

Fig. 1. The six lenses of DWI model [8]

The persuasive design method in this research is as follows (Fig. 2):

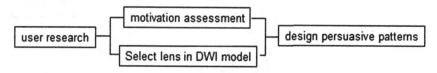

Fig. 2. The persuasive design method

Persuasive Patterns are triggers to promote changes of user behaviors in using products, such as ease of use design, error-proofing design, emotional design, visual semantic design, cognitive decisions design, security design. The PD principle is to encourage users to use the product on the basis of the non mandatory measures, and gradually improve their healthy behavior.

2 Pattern Analysis of Persuasive Design for Health

According to the Maslow's hierarchy of needs, the health needs of elders are analyzed (Table 1). Based on the DWI model, persuasive patterns are designed by the brain-storming. The first design is about the Error Proofing Lens, such as loud whistle, flash of light, limited structures of products. The second design refers to emotional reminders with Visual Lens, such as remainder by human voice or expression symbols, etc. The third design is about Cognitive Lens. It can be identified through the subconscious, and will not bring the offensive force to users.

Table 1. Health behavior classification and health needs analysis of the elderly

User research	Motivation assessment by the Maslow's hierarchy	Health needs in daily life	Select lens and design persuasive patterns (DWI)
Physical health	1. Physiological need 2. Safety need	Healthy diets, drinking water, take medicine, exercise, physical testing, emergency help......	- Time remind - Physical restriction reminder - Easy to use - Physical condition visualization
Mental health	3. Belongingness and love need 4. Esteem need 5. Need for self-actualization	No mood, weakness, no social behavior, loneliness......	- Keep in touch with the outside environment, - To maintain the integrity of personality, - Social relationships - Metaphor design

Fig. 3. Designed by Xiangrong Ye

Fig. 4. Designed by Chenlong Wen

Fig. 5. Designed by Jiayao Chen

2.1 Persuasive Design Based on Error Proofing Lens

The medicine kit (Fig. 3) is designed with structure limits, and elderly people can set the alarm to remind them take daily medication on time. The medicine kit structure constraints the number of drugs by pressing the button, one pill a time, because of taking into account the old man's inflexible fingers. This structure is easy to use and will avoid the pills rolling out, which can reduce the chances of elderly people forgetting to take medicine.

2.2 Persuasive Design Based on Visual Lens

The elderly needs to drink water every day to maintain a healthy body, but because of the memory loss of them, they often can't remember the time and quantity of drinking. Expression cup (Fig. 4) is a design to remind the elderly pay attention to the regular life of healthy drinking. After setting the daily amount and frequency of drinking, the cup will remind the elderly by lights flashing on in time, and show different expressions to let users pay attention to their drinking status. For example, if the user forgot the time, the cup will show the sad face. While users drink water on time, it will show the smiling face. It is found that the elderly are generally like this alert mode according to user tests.

2.3 Persuasive Design Based on Persuasive Lens

Due to their decrease physical function, elderly gradually reduce their social activities. They contact with outside less and less because of the lacking of goals and motivations. Some people are too stubborn to go out, so that psychological symptoms of depression are increased. Because of lack of guidance and trigger, they often hesitate to participate in the activities in the neighborhood. The walking stick (Fig. 5) is designed with a social remind function. When the elderly of neighborhood participate in collective activities outdoors, the crutches will send a flashing signal to remind the elderly to go out together. With the driving force of social relationships, the chance of outdoor activities of elderly is increased. At the same time the social motivation is also enhanced, and the psychological health is improved.

3 Case Study of the Persuasive Design Method

3.1 Background of Health Behavior of the Elderly

After 60 years old, a series of physiological and psychological factors will be changed to elderly. Physical ability and memory will gradually decline. If coupled with the disease, some elderly people will feel sorrow, worry, and fear all the time. In order to maintain a healthy state, they need to improve their physiological and psychological factors. On the one hand, the elderly need to build more social relationships to relieve the psychological depression and do more exercise; on the other hand, because of lack of fitness environment and outdoor weather restrictions, they need do more exercise alone at home. Indoor fitness bicycle is designed to improve elderly health. There are many effects for elderly riding fitness bicycle, such as expand the heart function, reduce the risk of hypertension, make bones strong, lose weight, etc. Although with so many good effects, the exercise alone is very boring and many people can not adhere to exercise at home. That's why Pervasive design is introduced here.

3.2   User Research About the Persuasive Factors

We Released research questionnaire to find whether the elderly loneliness is one of the main factors affecting health. In this study, 22 elderly people were investigated, including 2 people over 75 years old, 11 people over 65 years old, 9 people over 55 years old. The residential areas are 40.91 % in the city center, 22.73 % in the urban and rural area, and 36.36 % in areas far away from the rural area. The elderly live with their spouses accounted for 63.64 %, live alone accounted for 22.73 %. 90. 91 % elderly need more communication with their children about spiritual life. 31.82 % of the old man felt lonely when no one accompanied with them, 54.55 % of the elderly think the lack of spiritual sustenance to make them feel lonely. 63.64 % of the old people hope that they need someone to accompany with them in exercise.

For multiple choice question about what kind of company makes old people feel better, 36.36 % choose the demand of accompanied chat, 27.27 % choose the accompany entertainment, 45.45 % choose the silently accompany, and 77.27 % choose to contact with their children and family, 18.18 % choose to get health counseling knowledge. So our hypothesis is that social factor and physical data visualization will be a positive effect on the elderly health behavior to use the elderly fitness bicycle.

3.3   Persuasive Design for Improving Elders' Health Behavior

After doing the user research, elderly needs are combined in the prototype. According to DWI model, we hold a workshop and discuss the design patterns under different lenses by brainstorming. Then persuasive Lens and Visual Lens are selected to create the persuasive design.

Visual lens: product visual design plays a semantic guiding role, so that the elderly can be easy to identify interface, feel safe and easy to learn how to use it.

Persuasive Lens: in the part of intelligent software product, dashboard data is feedback timely and related social relationships are combined into persuasion mode, encouraging the elderly to do exercise together and feel more enjoyable. The PD model will help to improve the health behavior and experience of elderly.

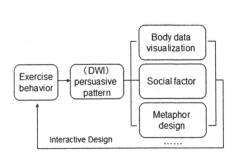

Fig. 6. Persuasive Pattern

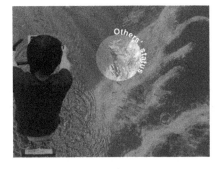

Fig. 7. Prototype, designed by B. Yu, K. Lin, X. Lin, Y. Guo

Based on the preliminary study, the advantages of various persuasive patterns (Figs. 6 and 7) are created, and the persuasive design of the intelligent fitness bicycle is as follows:

(1) Body data visualization. It is the body data visualization that makes the health of the feedback timelier and more vivid to the elderly. The information is projected onto the ground. The size of the ripple in the interface reflects the exercise time and calorie consumption, with the number of ripples reflecting the heart pulse index. The more obvious of the ripples on the interface, the better effect of exercise.

(2) Social factor. To ease the loneliness when the elderly exercise with fitness bicycle, social mode is a trigger to improve the enthusiasm of exercise behavior, such as user collaboration in the health games or chatting with friends or relatives when users riding the bicycle, etc. Social communication between friends or relatives is a mode to encourage the elderly does exercise regularly.

(3) Metaphor design. In the interactive interface of the fitness bicycle, a group of fish is swimming around a user which is the metaphor of the social relationship of their exercise friends. The more friends join the movement, and the more the number and species of fish. He needn't to keep on talking in the movement only feels someone is company with him. User's need of the quiet and entertainment company is met by the metaphor social interactive information. It will be funny to users' health behaviors.

The prototype has been tested by 31 elder people including 14 males and 17 females, and 87 % of them show they like this product and want to do more exercise with social company mode.

4 Discussion

According to the above case study, we sum up the persuasion design methods for the elderly health behaviors change in home care scenario: (1) Analysis of the needs of users health according to the Maslow's hierarchy of needs (2) Based on the DWI model to collect the design samples and technical information, then evaluate the effectiveness of the design patterns. (3) Select proper lens and list out the corresponding interactive methods according to the effectiveness by the brainstorming. (4) In the step of design, user needs and the persuasive model are combined together, which will help to create many ideas. After selecting the proper persuasive design ideas, the prototype will be created to meet the users' needs.

In conclusion, this article studied how to use the persuasive model in design process so that to improve the health motivation and health behaviors of the elderly. The decline of the physiological ability of the elderly and the sense of loneliness will greatly affect their physical and mental health. Moreover, old people are difficult to accept the new technology. The persuasion design in the product and human-computer interaction will be more humanized and interesting to users, which will be easy to accept for elderly.

Acknowledgements. Grateful acknowledgement is made to my supervisor M. Yang. I also owe my sincere gratitude to my friends in TU/e who gave me their help and time in listening to me and helping me work out the prototype. I also want to thank my students in ECUST who help to organize the workshop and do some designs in this topic.

References

1. Redström, J.: Persuasive design: fringes and foundations. In: IJsselsteijn, W.A., de Kort, Y.A. W., Midden, C., Eggen, B., van den Hoven, E. (eds.) PERSUASIVE 2006. LNCS, vol. 3962, pp. 112–122. Springer, Heidelberg (2006)
2. Torning, K., Oinas-Kukkonen, H.: Persuasive system design: state of the art and future directions. In: Proceedings of PERSUASIVE, p. 30 (2009)
3. Fogg, B.J.: Creating persuasive technologies: an eight-step design process. In: Proceedings of the 4th International Conference on Persuasive Technology (Persuasive 2009), pp. 1–6, Claremont, CA (2009)
4. Fogg, B.J.: A Behavior Model for Persuasive Design. Persuasive Technology Lab, Stanford University. www.bjfogg.com
5. Lockton, D.: Design with intent toolkit Wiki. http://www.danlockton.com/dwi/Main_Page. Accessed 14 May 2013
6. Chatterjee, S., Price, A.: Healthy living with persuasive technologies: framework, issues, and challenges. J. Am. Med. Inform. Assoc. **16**(2), 171–178 (2009)
7. Tørning, K.: A review of four persuasive design models. Int. J. Conceptual Struct. Smart Appl. **1**(2), 17–27 (2013)
8. Lockton, D., Harrison, D., Stanton, N.A.: The design with intent method: a design tool for influencing user behaviour. Appl. Ergon. **41**(3), 382–392 (2010)

Designing Smartphone Keyboard
for Elderly Users

Eun Jeong Ryu[✉], Minhyeok Kim, Joowoo Lee, Soomin Kim,
Jiyoung Hong, Jieun Lee, Minhaeng Cho, and Jinhae Choi

UX Lab, Mobile Communication R&D Center, Mobile Communication
Company, LG Electronics, Seoul, South Korea
{ej.ryu,minhyeok0804.kim,joowoo.lee,soomin.kim,
jiyoung.hong,jeun.lee,minhaeng.cho,jin.choi}@lge.com

Abstract. This study aims to explore the cognitive perception by elderly users
when using smartphone keyboard, and to discover the suitable design that
achieves higher satisfaction and perceived usability performance.

A usability test is performed on 30 Korean participants aged between 55 and
70 who use smartphone keyboard frequently for communication. A prototype of
a Smart Keyboard, which user can manually adjust the key's overall height, each
key's width, and font size and bold styling of characters in each key, is installed
in 5.5-inch touch screen smartphone. Participants tested a default smart keyboard and customized the keyboard as they liked, then they tested again with the
newly adjusted keyboard.

The result showed when given the chance of adjustment, all participants
attempted changing the key size and font's readability. This increased satisfaction level and the typing performance within the participant significantly.

Keywords: Smartphone · Keyboard · Elderly users · Age · Usability

1 Introduction

Smartphone started as a new gadget for younger trendy generation, and now it is
distributed across all generations in South Korea. In this growth of consumer pool, it is
especially notable that the population of elderly smartphone users drastically increased
since the beginning. From Gallup Report [1], a population survey by Korean marketing
research agency, it was shown in 2012, only 13 % of seniors (aged 60 or more) were
using smartphones, but in 2015, 49 % of seniors were using smartphones.

Elderly users' usual activities with smartphones includes communicating with
friends and family with instant messenger or SMS. However, due to ageing, elderly
users' typing skill decreases (Salthouse [3]) due to their hand-eye coordination skill
decreases [2, 3]. Their accuracy and speed when tapping a target also decreases that
elderly users should be provided with bigger size targets [4–7]. However, current
smartphone keyboard's keys are in smaller size due to the screen size limitation and
also to make interacting with the screen above easier when the keyboard is on. This
may be a good trade-off for younger users who are good at multitasking and has a good
accuracy in tapping. However for elderly users who are not great in multitasking [8],

© Springer International Publishing Switzerland 2016
C. Stephanidis (Ed.): HCII 2016 Posters, Part I, CCIS 617, pp. 439–444, 2016.
DOI: 10.1007/978-3-319-40548-3_73

and also has lower accuracy, this may not be a good design to serve. Interesting result from Salthouse [3]' research was that elderly users seem to take strategy of focusing on accuracy rather than speed of typing [3], which means such design will cause more discomfort and perhaps frustrations from the elderly users.

Along with the decline of motor skills many elderly users suffer presbyopia, therefore smaller font size on these small keys in smartphone keyboard may as well cause discomfort on elderly users [9].

This study analyzes current smartphone touch keyboard's usability for elderly users in aspects mentioned above, and aims to discover the suitable design that achieves higher satisfaction and usability performance.

2   Experiment

2.1   Participants

30 participants aged between $55 \sim 69$, with touch phone experience with frequent smartphone touch keyboard usage (15 4 × 3 Naratgul users, 15 Qwerty users), were recruited in Seoul, South Korea.

2.2   Method

This experiment was performed in three steps. First, participants tested the default design of a currently selling touch keyboard prototype in Android smartphone. Participants were given writing samples to type in 4 × 3 keyboard and Qwerty. To provide natural typing experience and not to stress participants in experiment environment, participants were allowed to fix errors made while typing. The typing speed and final error rate for each keyboard layout are recorded. For the analysis, typing speed including error fixing time is considered as the main UI performance. Participants then self-rated the satisfaction level in readability of characters on the keys and overall in seven points Likert scale.

After pre-test, participants were given chance to adjust the design of the keyboard: Keyboard's overall height, which changes the key height, key width, font size, and font style (Bold). Participants were allowed to stay with the default settings if they find it comfortable. Adjustment made by participants were recorded and measured.

After adjustment, participants again tested their adjusted keyboard with a new writing samples. New typing speed and error rates were recorded and compared against their previous records. Participants rated on their satisfaction in readability and overall again. This is also compared against ratings they made on the default keyboard.

Writing samples provided to users were counterbalanced for pre-test and post-test, and order or Qwerty and 4 × 3 layout were also counterbalanced.

Assuming participants adjust the key size and font size, the hypothesis of this experiment state as below:

H1: There will be a significant difference of typing speeds between original keyboard and adjusted keyboard.

H2: There will be a significant difference of satisfaction ratings between original keyboard and adjusted keyboard.

2.3   Prototype

A 5.5 inch, 1440 × 2560 QHD android smartphone (LG G3) was used for this study. The keyboard prototype is designed to portray the newest version of LG Smart Keyboard for Android OS. It has two different types of layout: 4 × 3 Naratgul and Korean Qwerty. The key width, height, and font size are set as default size that LG provided for 5.5 inch display size. These are measured on screen in metric system.

The prototype contains a setting that allows participants to adjust key width, overall keyboard height, and key font size (Figs. 1 and 2). It also allowed to apply bold to the key font. The overall keyboard height ranged between 38 mm to 63 mm and default was at 45.2 mm, and the control was in continuous increment. Key width and font size were controllable in 11 levels, and default was set in level 5. As participants adjust the size, the change was applied in real time so the adjustments can be checked right away.

Fig. 1. Adjusting overall keyboard height

3   Result

3.1   4 × 3 Keyboard (Naratgul)

While participants did not have much discomfort with the current 4 × 3 keyboard design, when given the change, they tried to increase the key size and apply bold (Fig. 3). Participants increased overall keyboard height from original 45.2 mm to average of 55.2 mm (20 % increase). This increased each key's height from 8 mm to 9 mm (12.5 % increase).

Participants also increased the key width from 13.5 mm to average of 14 mm (3.7 % increase).

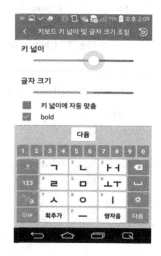

Fig. 2. Adjusting key size, font size and bold style

80 % of participants applied bold style, however, only 40 % of participants changed the font size. Many participants reported that current keys and font size were also big enough to see comfortably. However, there was a significant difference of readability between default keyboard (M = 5.20, SD = 1.49)

and adjusted keyboard (M = 6.10, SD = 1.06); t(29) = −4.161, p < 0.0005, and the overall satisfaction between the default keyboard (M = 4.03, SD = 2.17) and the adjusted keyboard (M = 5.77, SD = 1.22); t(29) = −5.017, p < 0.0005. Participants also showed a significant improvement of typing speed when using the adjusted keyboard (Table 1).

From the survey after session 56.7 % of participant chose to have their 4 × 3 keyboard in bigger size than to see more information above the keyboard.

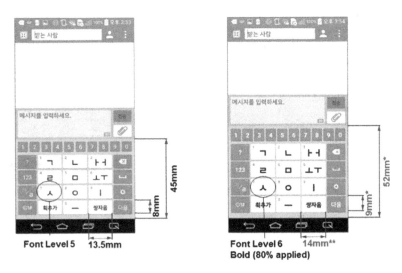

Fig. 3. Change of layout on 4 × 4 keyboard after adjustment

Table 1. Change of satisfaction and performance in 4 × 3 keyboard

Measurement		Default	Adjusted	t	df	Sig (two-tailed)
Satisfaction	Overall (/7)	4.03 (2.17)	5.76 (1.22)	−5.02	29	<0.0005
	Readability (/7)	5.20 (1.49)	6.10 (1.06)	−4.16	29	<0.0005
Performance	Speed (chars/min)	45.18 (29.81)	55.21 (29.82)	−6.09	29	<0.0005
	Error rate (%)	2.50 (4.3)	1.48 (2.24)	1.44	29	0.160

3.2 Korean Qwerty

As more keys take space in one line, the keys were smaller therefore, more attempts to make the keys and font size bigger are made (Fig. 4). Participants tried to increase the overall keyboard height from 45 mm to 54 mm (20 % increase) on average and key width from 5 mm to 6 mm (20 % increase) on average. 93.3 % of participants increased the font size and 90 % applied bold style. There was a significant difference of readability between default keyboard (M = 4.43, SD = 1.81) and adjusted keyboard (M = 6.06, SD = 1.14); t(29) = −5.887, p < 0.0005, and there was a significant difference of overall satisfaction between the default keyboard (M = 4.86, SD = 1.72) and the adjusted keyboard (M = 5.90, SD = 1.21); t(29) = −4.545, p < 0.0005. Again, participants' typing speed improved significantly when using the adjusted keyboard (Table 2).

From the survey followed after session, 63.3 % of participants chose to have their qwerty keyboard in bigger size than to see more information above the keyboard.

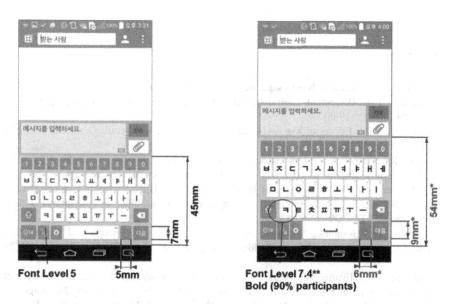

Fig. 4. Change of layout on qwerty keyboard after adjustment

Table 2. Change of satisfaction and performance in qwerty keyboard

Measurement		Default	Adjusted	T	df	Sig (two-tailed)
Satisfaction	Overall (/7)	4.86 (1.72)	5.96 (1.21)	−4.55	29	<0.0005
	Readability (/7)	4.43 (1.81)	6.06 (1.14)	−5.89	29	<0.0005
Performance	Speed(chars/min)	50.97 (17.30)	55.94 (18.89)	−5.42	29	<0.0005
	Error rate (%)	2.92 (7.74)	1.62 (0.34)	0.89	29	0.383

4 Discussion

The result of this study showed that elderly users prefer greater key size and clearer labels on keys. Such change will improve both the UI performance and satisfaction within the user. While this new design does not meet the suggested

Table 3. Suggested button size vs. prototype

Measurement (mm)		Height	Width
Suggested		14	14
Original	4 × 3	8	13.5
	Qwerty	7	5
Adjusted	4 × 3	9	14
(mean)	Qwerty	9	6

size by Leitao and Silva [4, 10] (Table 3), it still appears as a good direction to improve the UI for elderly users in the future smartphones. Also we have to consider how typing requires users to type several keys in sequences, increasing size of keys too much will cause another usability problem. One participants in this study decreased the size of keyboard smaller so he would reach the top keys easier. Further studies should be performed to discover the size that balances the reachability and UI performance in elderly users.

References

1. Gallup Report on Smartphone usage. http://www.gallup.co.kr
2. Salthouse, T.A.: Perceptual, cognitive, and motoric aspects of transcription typing. Psychol. Bull. 99(3), 303 (1986)
3. Salthouse, T.A.: Effects of age and skill in lyping. J. Exp. Psychol. Gen. 113, 345–371 (1984)
4. Leitao, R., Silva, P.A.: Target and spacing sizes for smartphone user interfaces for older adults: design patterns based on an evaluation with users. In: Proceedings of the 19th Conference on Pattern Languages of Programs, p. 5. The Hillside Group, October 2012
5. Han, Y.S., et al.: A Study on elderly for improvement of usability on smartphone. J. Soc. e-Bus. Stud. 17(1), 39–52 (2012)
6. Hertzum, M., Hornbæk, K.: How age affects pointing with mouse and touchpad: a comparison of young, adult, and elderly users. Int. J. Hum.-Comput. Interact. 26(7), 703–734 (2010)
7. Kobayashi, M., Hiyama, A., Miura, T., Asakawa, C., Hirose, M., Ifukube, T.: Elderly user evaluation of mobile touchscreen interactions. In: Campos, P., Graham, N., Jorge, J., Nunes, N., Palanque, P., Winckler, M. (eds.) INTERACT 2011, Part I. LNCS, vol. 6946, pp. 83–99. Springer, Heidelberg (2011)
8. Heo, W.H., Kim, J.Y.: A study of smartphone UI design guideline for the elderly. Des. Convergence Res. 29, 3–14 (2011)
9. Sugimoto, K.Y., Saku, T.: The user interface design for smartphone for elderly users. INTEC Tech. J. 12, 36–43 (2012)
10. Jin, Z.X., Plocher, T., Kiff, L.: Touch screen user interfaces for older adults: button size and spacing. In: Stephanidis, C. (ed.) HCI 2007. LNCS, vol. 4554, pp. 933–941. Springer, Heidelberg (2007)

Breaking Digital Barriers: A Social-Cognitive Approach to Improving Digital Literacy in Older Adults

Kelly S. Steelman$^{(\boxtimes)}$, Kay L. Tislar, Leo C. Ureel II, and Charles Wallace

Michigan Technological University, Houghton, MI 49931, USA
{steelman,cltislar,ureel,wallace}@mtu.edu

Abstract. The ability to navigate the ever-changing world of digital technology is a new form of literacy, one that presents a considerable challenge to older adults. Digital literacy has quickly evolved from an option to a necessity, and the rapid pace of technological change makes it insufficient to simply teach older adults to use a single technology. Rather, they must develop flexible skills and technological self-efficacy in order to maintain their hard-earned digital literacy. For four years, our research group has led a digital literacy program to address older adults' questions about digital tools and applications. Through our work, we have identified numerous socio-technical barriers that older adults encounter as they adopt new technology and explore the digital world. Here, we review these barriers, discuss the Social Cognitive Theory that informs our tutoring approach, and describe our ongoing work to formalize the training program and develop technology to support older adults online.

Keywords: Older adults · Senior citizens · Aging · Digital literacy · Computer training · Cyberlearning · Social cognitive theory · Critical decision making

1 Introduction

From the confluence of two social phenomena—an aging population and an increased dependence on digital technology— a critical need has emerged for older citizens to develop digital literacy. Over the next 35 years, the United States is projected to experience rapid growth in its older population, with nearly 20 percent of the population being 65 or older by 2030 [1]. Although older adults are also the fastest-growing group of Internet users in the United States [2], 41 percent of older adults still do not use the Internet at all [3].

In a review of the literature on computer use and older adults, Wagner, Hassanein, and Head [4] discovered a variety of reasons for the low level of digital adoption. Some have to do with a lack of access to computer hardware or the Internet, and others are related to physical and cognitive changes that people experience as they age. Melenhorst, Rogers, and Bouwhuis [5] argue that while it is widely believed that cost is one of the main factors that deter older adults

© Springer International Publishing Switzerland 2016
C. Stephanidis (Ed.): HCII 2016 Posters, Part I, CCIS 617, pp. 445–450, 2016.
DOI: 10.1007/978-3-319-40548-3_74

from using technology, a larger reason is the lack of perceived benefit: older adults either do not find that the technology meets their needs or do not understand the technology well enough to appreciate what it can do for them. Mackie and Wylie [6] agree that technology acceptance depends on several factors, including the degree to which the technology meets the user's needs and the user's awareness of the technology and its purpose. A study by Czaja, Guerrier, Nair, and Landauer [7] confirms that older adults are more likely to use computers if they perceive the technologies and the tasks for which they can use the technologies to be useful.

2   Barriers to Digital Literacy

Listening to older adults and addressing their learning needs as we develop the technologies of tomorrow is a moral imperative. Since 2011, the Breaking Digital Barriers group at Michigan Tech has run a program called BASIC (Building Adult Skills in Computing) that pairs our students with community members, most of them 60 years of age or older, who are seeking help with computing technology. We have reported on some of the recurring themes in our interactions [8]:

- *Anxiety stifles exploration.* The experience of using a computing device is known to cause anxiety in older people, and our experiences bear this out. A common concern for participants in our group is that something they do will "break" their investment. Even routine activities cause anxiety as users fear accidentally going "off script".
- *Danger online.* Many learners are fearful of going online because of stories of fraud and identity theft they have heard in the media. Without a basis of understanding for how malware and other threats work, they have no model for how to minimize their threat level.
- *Context sensitivity and non-obvious affordances.* A shift toward mobile devices with small displays and a shift toward "clean" design have led to a decrease in affordances and other cues in user interfaces. To use these interfaces effectively, the user must be willing to explore the space and uncover the functionality. A change triggered by an inadvertent action makes older users feel anxious and out of control.
- *Details obscure abstraction.* Not so long ago, users typically accomplished activities like email and word processing through dedicated applications specific to a particular personal computer. The movement toward mobile computing devices and cloud-based storage and applications has abstracted those activities into general "services". For many of our learners, conceiving of computing in this abstract way runs contrary to their script-based style of learning about computers.
- *Functionality across devices.* Most older adults do not use the same services across different devices; rather, they use different devices for different tasks. For example, seniors might not use a tablet to check the weather if they associate that ability with a PC. Also, many older users do not realize that

content on the Internet, especially "cloud" services, is accessible and consistent across devices.

Issues like these cannot be explained satisfactorily through traditional factors like age-related cognitive, perceptual, or motor changes. Usability tests focused purely on external behavior, like eye tracking or measuring response time, are insufficient. In general, a focus purely on end goals ("completing the task") without taking the method of learning into account will hide important cognitive and social barriers to digital adoption.

3 Our Social-Cognitive Approach

Bandura's Social Cognitive Theory (SCT) informs our approach to digital literacy [9,10]. According to this theory, an individual's functioning is the product of an interaction between cognitive, behavioral, and contextual factors. It emphasizes the social context of learning and the importance of observation. In opposition to a behaviorist approach, learning and the demonstration of what has been learned are separate, so learning involves not just the acquisition of new behaviors, but also acquisition of knowledge, cognitive skills, concepts, rules, values, and other cognitive constructs.

SCT provides a foundation for interventions designed to improve people's learning. Below we review several key SCT principles [9,10] and describe how our instructional practices are connected to each.

– *Observational Learning/Modeling.* SCT's most basic instructional implication is that learners require access to models of the knowledge, skills, and behaviors they are expected to learn. Multiple types of models (e.g., instructors, peers) and various forms of modeling (e.g., cognitive, verbal, mastery, coping) should be used. Instruction must support learners' engagement in observational learning.

  Our BASIC program pairs each learner with a tutor who models behaviors and strategies that we hope to reinforce in the learner. The simplest form of modeling is when our tutors demonstrate how to conduct an action. To make their actions and intentions more obvious, they typically vocalize what they are doing while they are doing it.

  Tutors model not only behavior but also problem solving and exploration. We believe it is important for our learners to see that learning the skills to find the answer is often more important than knowing the answer. Tutors also model their emotional reactions to not knowing the solution. It is critical for tutors to demonstrate to learners that, while it is reasonable to feel annoyed when something is not easy to figure out, there is no need to feel anxious; there are ways to find a solution and recover from mistakes.

– *Outcome Expectations.* Instruction should help people see that situated learning and the demonstration of that learning lead to personally valued or important outcomes. Lessons should emphasize real-world applications and the relevance of material to the learners' lives.

Rather than delivering predefined training sessions, we invite learners to come to us with their specific needs. We then tailor our one-on-one tutoring sessions accordingly. Addressing the learner's specific problem often affords opportunities to address specific digital literacy competencies along the way. In this way, the skills we teach are tied to problems of personal value to our learners. We also invite our learners to bring their own devices to our tutoring sessions. This ensures that learners are developing skills on the devices they will be using in their day-to-day lives. To support an understanding of functionality across devices, we often encourage learners to use multiple devices in the same session. For example, when a learner is interested in learning about the cloud, we may work with him or her to synchronize files across devices and access information from the cloud from a variety of platforms and devices.

- *Goal Setting.* Instruction needs to help students set effective goals—goals that are attainable, clear, specific, and moderately challenging. To facilitate progress and self-efficacy, learning goals should be attainable with moderate levels of effort. Goals that learners set or endorse themselves have a bigger effect on their behaviors than do goals that are assigned.

As mentioned above, our tutoring sessions are driven by the requests and goals of our learners. Even in the cases in which learners specify a general goal of "learning about computers", our tutors spend time talking to them about their lives to identify potential computing needs and to choose learning goals that may be most relevant to each learner's life.

- *Perceived Self-Efficacy.* People will be more active, effortful, and effective learners when they are confident in their ability to complete tasks successfully. Instruction should be designed to help learners develop and sustain self-efficacy: the belief in one's capabilities to organize and execute the courses of action required to manage prospective situations.

Our learning sessions are hands on, and whenever possible, we ask the learner to "drive". Although we may model behavior by demonstrating a sequence of steps, our tutors ask the learners to repeat the steps themselves to help ensure they will be able to address the problem on their own at home. As noted above, our tutors do not always know the answers to a learner's problems and may need to seek assistance online or from another tutor. In doing this, we hope to reinforce that even "experts" need help finding the answer and that having questions about how to do things on a computer or handheld device is normal and not something to feel ashamed about.

- *Self-Regulation.* All students should be supported in their efforts to be self-regulated learners. Three processes involved here are self-observation (monitoring one's own behaviors and outcomes), self-judgment (evaluating whether one's actions are effective), and self-reaction (responding to the self-evaluations by changing, rewarding, or discontinuing the behavior). Instructors can promote self-observation by helping people learn how to monitor different aspects of their learning behavior through aids such as checklists.

Our program currently offers only limited support for self-regulation. Tutors provide models of self-observation, self-judgment, and self-reaction, and they can encourage similar behavior in learners, but the limited contact time makes it difficult to practice these behaviors. Future work may include self-guided learning tasks done outside of the group sessions. Also our planned tool support for wayfinding (discussed in the next section) offers an opportunity to record learning progress and present it to the learner.

4 Future Directions

Talking to seniors is important, but so is talking to the tutors with whom they work. Community educators around the world are using novel approaches to address the numerous socio-technical barriers facing older adults, and they have a wealth of knowledge that can be used to improve educational programs. In many cases, however, their knowledge is tacit and must be elicited. We have adapted an incident-based cognitive task analysis technique, the Critical Decision Method (CDM) [11,12], to elicit this tacit knowledge from our own tutors. The CDM uses a three-sweep, semi-structured interview to help experts tell stories from their field. We plan to expand this interview project to tutors from other programs in North America. We will use the experiences of these community educators to formalize our training program, identify opportunities to improve our current program, and motivate the design of technology to support the acquisition and maintenance of digital literacy.

One direction we are pursuing is the development of digital tools to support online *wayfinding* behavior. Wayfinding is the process of "organizing and finding a way through dynamic explorations and analyses [13]". Our observations suggest several barriers that older adults, in particular, may face when wayfinding online. These include the high level of visual complexity in online interfaces, obscure or hidden affordances, and the difficulty of remembering past wayfinding successes.

We propose a socio-technical approach to developing wayfinding skills among older computer users, through a scaffolded adaptive web navigation tool used in conjunction with small-group, active-learning sessions. The technical tool at the heart of this learning activity is a browser plugin that will provide just-in-time guidance, highlighting wayfinding options with a high likelihood of success based on analysis of web page structure and previous navigation activity. The tool will also allow users to annotate their wayfinding actions and share them with other learners.

References

1. Vincent, G.K., Velkoff, V.A.: The Next Four Decades – The Older Population in the United States: 2010 to 2050. U.S. Census Bureau Report #P25-1138 (2010)
2. Hart, T.A., Chaparro, B.S., Halcomb, C.G.: Evaluating websites for older adults: Adherence to 'Senior-Friendly' guidelines and end-user performance. Behav. Inf. Technol. **27**(3), 191–199 (2008)
3. Smith, A.: Older Adults and Technology Use. Pew Research Center, New York (2014)
4. Wagner, N., Hassanein, K., Head, M.: Computer use by older adults: A multi-disciplinary review. comput. hum. behav. **26**(5), 870–882 (2010)

5. Melenhorst, A.S., Rogers, W.A., Bouwhuis, D.G.: Older adults' motivated choice for technological innovation: Evidence for benefit-driven selectivity. Psychol. Aging **21**(1), 190 (2006)
6. Mackie, R.R., Wylie, C.D.: Factors influencing acceptance of computer-based innovations. In: Helander, M. (ed.) Handbook of Human-Computer Interaction, pp. 1081–1106. Elsevier, New York (1988)
7. Czaja, S.J., Guerrier, J.H., Nair, S.N., Landauer, T.: Computer communication as an aid to independence for older adults. Behav. Inf. Technol. **12**, 197–207 (1993)
8. Kumar, S., Ureel, L.C., King, H., Wallace, C.: Lessons from our elders: Identifying obstacles to digital literacy through direct engagement. In: Proceedings of Pervasive Technologies Related to Assistive Environments (PETRAE) (2013)
9. Bandura, A.: Social Learning Theory. Prentice-Hall, Englewood Cliffs NJ (1977)
10. Bandura, A.: Organisational applications of social cognitive theory. Aust. J. Manage. **13**(2), 275–302 (1988)
11. Klein, G.A., Calderwood, R., Macgregor, D.: Critical decision method for eliciting knowledge. IEEE Trans. Syst. Man Cybern. **19**(3), 462–472 (1989)
12. Crandall, B., Klein, G., Hoffman, R.: Incident-based CTA: Helping practitioners "Tell Stories" Working Minds: a Practitioner's Guide to Cognitive Task Analysis, pp. 69–90. MIT Press, Cambridge (2006)
13. Mirel, B.: Interaction Design for Complex Problem Solving: Developing Useful and Usable Software. Morgan Kauffman, San Francisco (2004)

Relation Between Mental Workload and Useful Field of View in Elderly

Kimihiro Yamanaka[1]([✉]), Kohei Shioda[2], and Mitsuyuki Kawakami[2]

[1] Konan University, Kobe, Japan
kiyamana@konan-u.ac.jp
[2] Kanagawa University, Yokohama, Japan
kohe0715@gmail.com,
kawakamim@kanagawa-u.ac.jp

Abstract. The aim of this study is to clarify the relation between mental workload and the useful field of view in elderly. To examine the mental workload relative to the size of the useful field of view, an experiment was conducted with 24 participants (group 1: ages 22–24, group 2: ages 60–75). In the primary task, participants responded to visual markers appearing in a computer display. The useful field of view and the results of the secondary task for mental workload were measured. In the mental workload task, participants solved numerical operations designed to increase the mental workload. The experimental conditions in this task were divided into three categories (Repeat Aloud, Addition, and No Task), where No Task meant no mental task was given. The mental workload was changed in a stepwise manner. The quantitative assessment confirmed that the useful field of view narrows with the increase in the mental workload.

Keywords: Mental workload · Useful field of view · Visual information processing · Comparison of younger and elderly

1 Introduction

In 2015, Japan's aged population (ages 65 and above) reached a historic high of 33,840,000, or 26.7 % of the total population. Therefore, the problem of an aging workforce and the influence on society in general cannot be ignored. We are addressing these issues by comparing visual information processing in the young and the aged, with the aim of examining which processing steps are most affected by aging and clarifying the causes of reduced visual perception in the aged.

Visual information processing is performed on information obtained from not only the center of one's field of view, but also along its periphery. The range of visual information collection that can be effectively used during visual cognitive tasks is called the useful field of view (UFOV), which is an important visual characteristic for recognizing, for example, obstacles and markers [1, 2]. Numerous studies have investigated UFOV with regard to ensuring safety and preventing recognition failures. As a result, the form of UFOV has been determined and methods for its measurement have been proposed. We assume a causal relationship between the increase in mental

© Springer International Publishing Switzerland 2016
C. Stephanidis (Ed.): HCII 2016 Posters, Part I, CCIS 617, pp. 451–456, 2016.
DOI: 10.1007/978-3-319-40548-3_75

workload (MWL) and the increase in cognition of visual information. However, few quantitative studies have dealt with both MWL and UFOV, and previous research focused on only MWL [3, 4].

In this study, we investigated the relationship between mental workload and effective visual field in younger and elderly people.

2   Experimental Methods

Figure 1 shows a diagram of the experiment and visual stimulus. A participant was seated with his or her head secured on a chin rest (HE285, Handaya Co., Ltd.), and visual stimuli were presented on a computer display (LC-60Z9, Sharp) at a point located 225 cm in front of the eyes. The authors developed a program in Microsoft Visual Basic 2008 that generated the visual stimuli. In the presentation, a white, circular marker with 1.0° diameter is shown in the center of the display. In addition, a Snellen chart index is randomly shown at the screen edge in one of three directions (horizontal, diagonal, vertical) at one of several possible distances (between 1.25° and 3.25°) from the center. The participant then presses button to indicate the direction of the edge of the Snellen chart index.

As a secondary task (MWL task), the participant s were required to solve numerical tasks (e.g., repeating aloud a list of numbers or performing simple addition). Thus, three conditions were created as follows:

- Repeat Aloud: A list of numbers was relayed to the subject by voice at 3-second intervals, and the participant repeated the numbers.
- Addition: The participant added two consecutive numbers and answered only the first digit in reply.
- No task: The participants were not given a secondary task.

MWL quantification of the two numerical tasks was already performed in previous research [5] through simultaneous measurement with the event-related potential. Addition had the highest burden followed by Repeat Aloud, then No Task. The numerical tasks were presented through a speaker placed on the top of the display with the volume set at 70 dB.

The experimental schedule is shown in Fig. 2. The participants perform the experiment under one set of MWL conditions per day, and they fill out an NASA-TLX [6] evaluation sheet for a subjective evaluation index at the end of each day.

Twelve university students aged 23.7 ± 1.1 and twelve elderly peoples aged 70.5 ± 3.6 with corrected or uncorrected vision of 0.8 or better participated in the experiment. An eye tracker (EYELINK-II, SR-Research) monitored whether participants continued visual fixation during the experiment, and those who did not were excluded from analysis. We also simultaneously performed experiments with an unmoving focus point as a measure of the UFOV with a fixed gaze.

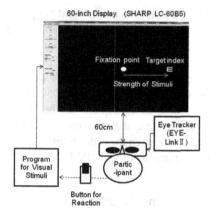

Fig. 1. Experimental setup

First Day (MWL①)			Second Day (MWL②)		Third Day (MWL③)	
Description Practice	Main Task MWL Task	Subjective Evaluation	Main Task MWL Task	Subjective Evaluation	Main Task MWL Task	Subjective Evaluation
10min	18min	NASA-TLX	18min	NASA-TLX	18min	NASA-TLX

Fig. 2. Experimental schedule

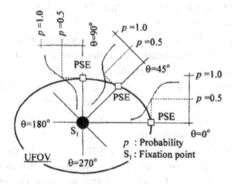

Fig. 3. Definition of useful field of view (UFOV)

3 Measurement of Useful Field of View

The purpose of this experiment is to measure the threshold of recognition when the response category changes from "possible to detect" to "impossible to detect", or vice versa. It is well known that the function linking the possibility of detection and the strength of the stimulus can be obtained as a psychometric curve [7]. Since the distance of the boundary between the "possible to detect" and "impossible to detect" categories indicates the threshold of recognition, the "impossible to detect" category can be estimated by the psychometric curve. Therefore, it may be possible to obtain psychometric curves in any direction from the fixation point. It is also known that the stimulus threshold can be obtained as a probabilistic percentile of the psychometric curve. One of the examples of this threshold with a 50 % probability is the point of subjective equality (PSE), which is equivalent to the threshold of recognition. As shown in Fig. 3, if we can assume that the region plotted within these stimulus thresholds is defined as the UFOV, then the outer limit of the region connected with the PSE for each angle is also defined as the UFOV [8].

4   Experimental Results and Discussion

Figures 4 and 5 show the correct answer rates for the MWL task and the adaptive weighted workload (AWWL) scores [6] calculated by using the responses to the subjective evaluation index, NASA-TLX. Both graphs show the averages for all participant s under all conditions, and the error bars in the graphs indicate the standard deviation. In Fig. 4(a), the correct answer rate in the MWL task is almost 100 % for the Repeat Aloud task, whereas it significantly drops to approximately 70 % for the Addition task ($p < 0.05$, t-test). Moreover, in Fig. 5(a) the AWWL scores were approximately 80 points for Addition, 50 points for Repeat Aloud, and 30 points for No Task. Significant differences were found between No Task and Addition ($p < 0.05$), and between Repeat Aloud and Addition ($p < 0.05$) in an analysis of variance and a multiple comparison test. On the other hand, In Fig. 4(b), the correct answer rate in the MWL task is almost 100 % for the Repeat Aloud task, whereas it significantly drops to approximately 40 % for the Addition task ($p < 0.05$, t-test). Moreover, in Fig. 5(a) the AWWL scores were approximately 70 points for Addition, 50 points for Repeat Aloud, and 70 points for No Task. Significant differences were found between No Task and Addition ($p < 0.05$), and between Repeat Aloud and Addition ($p < 0.05$) in an analysis of variance and a multiple comparison test. The AWWL scores did not differ significantly between the two groups. However, in the correct answer rates, the ability to perform addition, which imposed the highest mental workload among the tasks in this study, was significantly lower in elderly compared with younger people.

Figure 6 shows the measurement results for the UFOV. In the MWL task as shown in Fig. 6(a), the UFOV is the narrowest for the Addition condition, and the widest for the No Task condition. It was found from the analysis of variance and multiple comparison test using the graph values as attributes that the MWL task factor ($p < 0.01$) is the affector. Significant differences were found between No Task and Addition ($p < 0.05$), and between Repeat Aloud and Addition ($p < 0.05$) in the multiple comparison test. On the other hand, In the MWL task as shown in Fig. 6(b), the UFOV is the narrowest for the Addition condition, and the widest for the No Task condition. It was found from the analysis of variance and multiple comparison test using the graph values as attributes that the MWL task factor ($p < 0.01$) is the affector. Significant differences were found between No Task and Repeat Aloud ($p < 0.05$), and between No Task and Addition ($p < 0.05$) in the multiple comparison test.

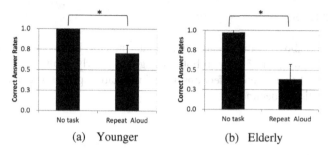

Fig. 4. MWL task and correct answer rate (*: p < 0.05)

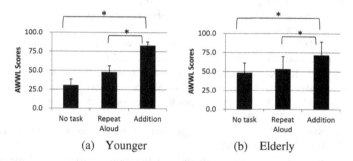

Fig. 5. MWL task and NASA-TLX AWWL scores (*: p < 0.05)

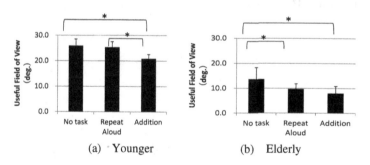

Fig. 6. MWL task and UFOV (*: p < 0.05)

The AWWL score representing subjective workload levels in this study was higher for Addition compared to No Task, and the correct answer rates were also low. Based on these results, we can assume that these tasks formed a high MWL for the participants and so these individuals markedly narrowed their UFOV. However, useful field of view differed significantly between the Repeat Aloud task and the Addition task in young adults but not in elderly adults. These findings suggest that because of a decline in visual function, a small load like the read-aloud task causes narrowing of useful field of view in elderly.

5 Conclusions

In summary, the above findings show that (1) an increase in mental workload causes narrowing of useful field of view in both young and elderly adults and (2) equivalent mental workload has a greater effect on visual information processing in elderly adults because of functional decline.

References

1. Hill, F.S., Walker, S., Gao, F.: Interactive image query system using progressive trans-mission. Comput. Graph. **17**(3), 323–330 (1983)
2. Vivek, D.B.: Ergonomics in the Automotive Design Process, pp. 105–126. Taylor & Francis Group LLC, Boca Raton (2012)
3. Ball, K., Owsley, C.: The useful field of view test: a new technique for evaluating age-related declines in visual function. J. Am. Optom. Assoc. **64**(1), 71–79 (1993)
4. Owsley, C., Ball, K., Keeton, D.M.: Relationship between visual sensitivity and target localization in older adults. Vision. Res. **35**(4), 579–587 (1995)
5. Zuber, B.L., Stark, L., Lorber, M.: Saccadic suppression of the papillary light reflex. Exp. Neurol. **14**, 351–370 (1966)
6. Sharpe, J.A., Sylvester, T.O.: Effect of aging on horizontal smooth pursuit. Invest. Ophthalmol. Vis. Sci. **17**, 465–468 (1978)
7. Alan, H.S., Chan, D.K.T.: Measurement and quantification of visual lobe shape characteristics. Int. J. Ind. Ergon. **36**, 541–552 (2006)
8. Dixon, W.J., Mood, A.M., Ameri, J.: A method for obtaining and analyzing sensitivity data. J. Am. Stat. Assoc. **43**, 109–126 (1948)

Usable Security and Privacy

Privacy Awareness and Design for Live Video Broadcasting Apps

Dhuha Alamiri[1](✉) and James Blustein[1,2]

[1] Faculty of Computer Science, Dalhousie University, Halifax, Canada
dh481896@dal.ca, jamie@cs.dal.ca
[2] School of Information Management, Dalhousie University, Halifax, Canada

Abstract. We investigate the use and privacy perception of applications that allow broadcast of live video to the WWW; and some that allow the video to remain accessible for up to 24 h. We conducted an online survey based on theories of social capital, motivation, network externalities, and uses and gratification, and a model of online self-disclosure. Based on our survey results, we are designing prototypes to increase users' awareness of privacy and to protect the broadcaster's privacy.

Keywords: Live video broadcasting apps · Live streaming video · Broadcaster · Periscope · Meerkat · Temporal social media · Self-destructing · Privacy awareness · Privacy perception · Self-disclosure · Visual privacy · Location privacy

1 Introduction

Transmitted video is a medium of social interaction. Currently, most consumer video (herein, video content generated by individuals) is either VoIP (video over internet protocol) for point-to-point communication (e.g., Skype, Facetime), or pre-recorded user content permanently posted to Internet sites (e.g., YouTube, Instagram). A newer standard consists of live video that can be broadcast, or "streamed", (e.g., Livestream). At a consumer level, a number of products are now available that provide similar functionality (e.g., Periscope, YouNow, Meerkat), for individuals.

Live video broadcasting applications (LVBAs) that do not create (store) permanent materials on the Internet are called temporal-content social media. That term is used because the video is never been accessible on the Internet or that the video is automatically deleted after (up to 24 h [1]). Typically, when using such apps, an event is encoded as it happens and is then broadcast directly to the Internet without editing or review. Research on the usage of such apps is lacking. In particular there are concerns about privacy and security aspects that have not been issues previously.

Studies investigating the use of video chat (e.g., Skype, Facetime) found that people use it to communicate with others who they have close relationship with [2–4]. In workplace, people use it for meetings [2]. Because video chat is mainly used for communication with selected individuals, when used properly there are few or no privacy concerns [2, 3]. On the other hand, people share material on YouTube permanently to a wide international audience, so to demonstrate skills and seeking

© Springer International Publishing Switzerland 2016
C. Stephanidis (Ed.): HCII 2016 Posters, Part I, CCIS 617, pp. 459–464, 2016.
DOI: 10.1007/978-3-319-40548-3_76

popularity [5]. However, such videos are "prepared" (can be edited), and therefore, when used properly those who upload videos do not have privacy concerns [6].

Streaming webcams are another form of streaming video, typically focused on a technology demonstrations, tours, presentations, TV, and social events [7]. It is also used for monitoring, and emergency situations to allow authorities to see events as they occur [8]. No privacy concerns are reported about this type of broadcast.

Temporal content social media (e.g., Periscope, Meerkat) have unique issues. In live video, events occur spontaneously, and actions that are not meant to be shared might be shared. Because the videos are not saved, broadcasters may be operating with an illusion of security and privacy. However, live video increases the likelihood of violating the privacy of others who happen to be caught in the video. A broadcaster could intentionally capture copyrighted material [9]. A broadcaster could be a target for malicious people. Employers might also view such broadcasts, which could create issues for employer-employee relations. Finally, because of the licensing agreement, the companies that supply these apps may capture and use the broadcast for their own marketing purposes without the broadcaster's explicit permission [10]. In addition, privacy-by-design is not considered by many live video broadcasting applications. Periscope, for example, shows the broadcaster's precise location to the public as a default.

As a first phase of this research, we conducted an online survey of live video broadcasters. The survey addressed the patterns of, and reasons for, use, and their perceptions of the privacy and security issues associated with that use.

2 Methodology

Procedure: We used an online, anonymous, international, English language, 33-item survey (which is ongoing) to assess the propensities and activities of users of temporal social media (YouNow, Meerkat, Periscope or other similar apps). The survey design was based on theories of social capital [11], motivation and network externalities [12], uses and gratification [13], as well as models of online self-disclosure. Some questions of the survey were adopted and/or modified from other surveys. We specifically asked participants about their patterns of use, type of content, the time of, and the mood while broadcasting because these may have implications for privacy and self-disclosure. Some questions focus on privacy, but the survey does ask about breaches of privacy/legality that broadcasters may not have considered (e.g., the broadcasting of images of other non-involved persons, re-transmission of copyrighted material).

Participants were recruited by notices on Twitter, Facebook, Google+ and Instagram using #hashtag for YouNow, Meerkat and Periscope. The study was restricted to those who used these apps only for creating broadcasts.

Participants: Age in years was captured in 4 ranges as 18 to 27 ($N = 17$), 28 to 37 ($N = 8$), 38 to 47 (N = 2) and 48 to 57 (N = 2). Education was captured in five ordinal categories as less than high school ($N = 4$), high school ($N = 8$), college ($N = 5$), undergraduate ($N = 10$), and graduate or professional ($N = 6$). Self-reported *comfort with technology* was collected using a five-point scale from 1 ("very comfortable") to 5 ("very uncomfortable"). The mean was 1.65 (SD: 0.95), but the full range was used. Self-reported *knowledge of security* was collected using a three-point scale (0 = "I have no knowledge at all", 1 = "I have minimal knowledge", 2 = "Good: I feel secure". The mean was 1.06 (SD: 0.97; there were two missing values). Participants were generally comfortable with technology and had some knowledge of security.

3 Results and Discussion

The use of YouNow, Meerkat and Periscope or "other apps" was coded on a seven-point scale (0 to 6) from "Never", through "Less than once a month", "Once a month", "Once a week", "Several times a week", "Once a day", to "Several times a day". The number of participants who used Periscope (17), YouNow (8), Meerkat (9), and other apps (6). The mean rating of frequency for Periscope was 3.09 (SD: 2.27, N = 17), YouNow was 1.05 (SD: 1.62, N = 8), Meerkat was 1.50 (SD: 2.28, N = 9), and for other apps was 4.00 (SD: 2.16, N = 6). Six users cited the use of an alternative app but only three identified those as "Blab" or "Snapchat". Only 7 of the 33 participants used more than one app: 12 used Periscope exlcusively, 6 usedYouNow exclusively, 6 used Meerkat exclusively, 2 used some other app exclusively. The use of Periscope was significantly higher than those of YouNow, Meerkat and Other ($\chi^2(3) = 8.8$, p < .049).

Most of the use was to maintain contact with "online friends" (39.4%), "offline friends" (18.2%), or "online strangers" (12.1%). However some use was directed to find "new friends online" (30.2%), or "new followers online" (15.2%). Altruistic endeavors were noted under "advocating for change" (6.1%), "helping people in need" (18.2%), and "advising young people" (12.1%). Finally, business endeavors were noted under promoting "my professional profile" (15.2%), "my business or activities" (12.1%), or "my events" (6.1%). About half the users (45.5%) cited more than one reason. Three participants simply stated "none", "to waste my free time" and "entertainment".

Table 1. Types of broadcasts created by users

Type of BCs	Any of (33)		Private		Public	Planned	
	N	%	Single	Multiple		Yes	No
Formal of self	22	66.7	9.1	22.7	40.9	50.0	40.9
Informal of self	25	75.8	16.0	40.0	32.0	20.0	72.0
Formal of others	20	60.6	20.0	15.0	5.0	50.0	40.0
Informal of others	21	63.6	14.3	33.3	9.5	33.3	52.4
Non-human	19	57.6	5.3	15.8	57.9	15.8	68.4

Participants were asked about the nature of their broadcasts (BC) within five categories (see Table 1), and within three levels of audience type (private single, private multiple and public). The *nonhuman* category explicitly referred to videos that did not contain humans. Values for private, public and planned are expressed as the proportion of individuals within each BC type (i.e., 50.0% of the 22 users who created Formal BCs of Self did so as planned BCs). Table 1 also includes the information about whether the BC was planned or spontaneous (unplanned).

Most participants (69.7%) engaged in a mix of BC types: In fact, 45.5% engaged in all five types (2 participants did not supply a breakdown). Of that, 9.1% engaged in formal BC exclusively, 15.2% engaged in informal BCs exclusively, 21.2% engaged in BCs of self exclusively 6.1% engaged in BCs of others exclusively, and 3.0% engaged in BC of non-human topics exclusively.

Table 2 provides the location of the broadcast. All values are expressed as the proportion of individuals within each BC type. Only five participants created BCs from only one location.

Table 2. Place of broadcast by type of BC

Type of BCs	Work	Home	Public	Parties	Driving
Formal of self	45.5	63.6	40.9	22.7	18.2
Informal of self	24.0	72.0	40.0	28.0	16.0
Formal of others	30.0	35.0	60.0	15.0	15.0
Informal of others	28.6	38.1	42.9	33.3	14.3
Non-human	26.3	47.4	42.1	21.1	21.1

Table 3 provides the mood while broadcasting, again as proportions. The category stims refers to broadcasting while under the influence of stimulants (e.g., alcohol).

Table 3. Mood of broadcasts by type of BC

Type of BCs	Happy	Sad	Angry	Worried	Compelled	Stims
Formal BCs of self	59.1	4.5	4.5	36.4	13.6	4.5
Informal BCs of self	88.0	16.0	20.0	16.0	20.0	0.0
Formal BCs of others	60.0	0.0	5.0	20.0	10.0	10.0
Informal BCs of others	76.2	0.0	14.3	9.5	19.0	4.8
Other BCs	57.9	15.8	15.8	31.6	36.8	10.5

Most BCs are created while happy, but a substantial percent are created when worried, angry or sad, particularly of self, which is a concern. At such times, the broadcaster might not be as careful about privacy or security.

Participants did express concerns in several areas using a four-point scale (1 = "Very Concerned", 2 = "Concerned", 3 = "Not at all Concerned" and 4 = "Never thought about it"). The mean rating of concern for social reputation was 2.07 (SD: 0.94), physical harm was 1.85 (SD: 0.79), economic harm (e.g., ID theft) was 1.81 (SD: 0.80), intellectual property theft was 2.19 (SD: 0.85), unauthorized use of screen shots was 2.07 (SD: 1.01), for the lack of control over who views the material was 2.13 (SD: 0.78), for the lack of control over who views the users location was 1.83 (SD: 0.83), for lawsuits was 2.19 (SD: 0.75), and for potential monitoring by employer was 2.40 (SD: 0.76). Generally, participants were more concerned about legal issues (intellectual property, lawsuits) than about personal harm. "Never thought about it" reaches 37.3%, which implies that many are not thinking about security or privacy.

Using a checklist, participants endorsed several advantages to the ephemeral nature of the videos. It maintains the secrecy of the broadcast (36.4%), and reduces the potential for profiling (41.5%). It also protects the privacy (50.65%), anonymity (24.2%), intellectual property of the broadcaster (24.2%) and others (39.2%), limits unwanted viewers (46.6%), and the ability of companies to learn about the broadcaster (29.1%). Users consider the temporary nature of the video as a protection. It was also considered a drawback because the content could be valuable (50.2%) and would require time to recreate (41.5%). It also limited the ability to identify viewers (47.9%), the chances to view videos (45.2%), the potential for popularity (41.5%), and potential exposure of the broadcaster (33.1%). Note that the endorsement of negatives was higher than that of positives ($p < .001$). The ephemeral nature of the temporal content social media may not last long. In that regard, 72.7% of participants wanted additional feedback about who viewed their locations. Participants indicated their desire to be able to hide face (18.2%), voice (6.1%), exact (54.5%) and approximate location (21.2%), surroundings (9.1%), other people (12.1%), their inappropriate behavior (45.5%) and of others (15.2%). Thus, there is a desire for more control.

4   Conclusion and Future Work

Users of existing video-based social media (e.g., video chat applications, webcam broadcasts, YouTube) have not reported high levels of privacy or security concerns. However, the emerging standard of temporal content video streaming creates additional concerns that broadcasters may not be aware of. Most broadcasters cited numerous concerns for privacy and security, and some wanted specific features to be incorporated into these apps. It would seem that the app developers will need to take responsibility for the inclusion of privacy features.

All significant data that gathered from the online survey will be used to propose context sensitive features to increase privacy awareness and control when deemed necessary. The final goal is to protect the privacy of live video broadcasters. We will apply our proposal designs on Periscope due to showing the broadcasters' location, which makes Periscope more critical. We will provide real-time feedback about the viewers who check the location. In addition, we will provide designs for default visual privacy techniques to protect the privacy of broadcasters who are in atypical mood.

References

1. O'Reilly, T.: What is web 2.0: design patterns and business models for the next generation of software. Commun. Strat. **1**, 17 (2007)
2. Massimi, M., Neustaedter, C.: Moving from talking heads to newlyweds: exploring video chat use during major life events. In: Proceedings of the 2014 Conference on Designing Interactive Systems, pp. 43–52. ACM, June 2014

3. Judge, T.K., Neustaedter, C.: Sharing conversation and sharing life: video conferencing in the home. In: Proceedings of the SIGCHI Conference on Human Factors in Computing Systems, pp. 655–658. ACM, April 2010

4. Wang, J., Mughal, M. A., Juhlin, O.: Experiencing liveness of a cherished place in the home. In: Proceedings of the ACM International Conference on Interactive Experiences for TV and Online Video, pp. 3–12. ACM (2015)

5. Courtois, C., Mechant, P., Ostyn, V., De Marez, L.: Uploaders' definition of the networked public on YouTube and their feedback preferences: a multi-method approach. Behav. Inf. Technol. **32**(6), 612–624 (2013)

6. Misoch, S.: Stranger on the internet: online self-disclosure and the role of visual anonymity. Comput. Hum. Behav. **48**, 535–541 (2015)

7. Juhlin, O., Engström, A., Reponen, E.: Mobile broadcasting: the whats and hows of live video as a social medium. In: Proceedings of the 12th International Conference on Human Computer Interaction with Mobile Devices and Services, pp. 35–44. ACM, September 2010

8. Landgren, J., Bergstrand, F.: Mobile live video in emergency response: its use and consequences. Bull. Am. Soc. Inf. Sci. Technol **36**(5), 27–29 (2010)

9. Vaidya, J.: Sports Broadcast Rights Holders Slowly Adapting to Live-Streaming Apps Such as Periscope [Web log post], 27 July 2015. https://sportsjournalismuk.wordpress.com/2015/07/27/sports-broadcast-rights-holders-slowly-adapting-to-live-streaming-apps-such-as-periscope/

10. Pearson, J.: Periscope Could Have a Privacy Problem, 26 March 2015. http://motherboard.vice.com/read/periscope-could-have-a-privacy-problem

11. Pfeil, U., Arjan, R., Zaphiris, P.: Age differences in online social networking–a study of user profiles and the social capital divide among teenagers and older users in MySpace. Comput. Hum. Behav. **25**(3), 643–654 (2009)

12. Lin, K.Y., Lu, H.P.: Why people use social networking sites: an empirical study integrating network externalities and motivation theory. Comput. Hum. Behav. **27**(3), 1152–1161 (2011)

13. Stanley, B.: Uses and gratifications of temporary social media: a comparison of Snapchat and Facebook. Doctoral dissertation, Cal State University, Fullerton (2015)

Organizational Vulnerability
to Insider Threat

What Do Australian Experts Say?

Justine Bedford$^{(\boxtimes)}$ and Luke Van Der Laan

The University of Southern Queensland,
Toowoomba, Australia
justine@jconsulting.net.au,
luke.vanderlaan@usq.ed.au

Abstract. Approaches to the study of organizational vulnerabilities to intentional insider threat has been narrow in focus. Cyber security research has dominated other forms of insider threat research [1]. However, within the scope of cyber security, the effort is predominantly focused on external threats or technological mitigation strategies. Deeper understanding of organizational vulnerabilities influencing insider threat and responses to insider threats beyond technological security remains limited in Australia. Despite the increasing potential threat and impact of such risk to organizations, empirical studies remain rare. This paper presents an initial study related to identifying organizational vulnerabilities associated with intentional insider threat. A Delphi Method was employed as part of a broader mixed methods study. There was a strong consensus amongst Australian experts as to the primary organizational vulnerabilities to insider threat. These main risks extend across personnel, process, technological and strategic (resource allocation) domains. The organizational vulnerabilities identified by Australian experts is consistent with research, literature, and guidelines, available from other countries. The results confirm the need to look beyond the narrow focus on individuals and technology in order to fully address the insider threat problem. Whilst only preliminary results are presented here, future analysis of data will focus on identifying best practice solutions for the Australian market.

Keywords: Insider threat · Organizational vulnerability · Cyber threat · Risk management · Technological security

1 Introduction

Insider threat has been defined as "…any activity by military, government, or industry employees whose actions or inactions, by intent or negligence, result (or could result) in the loss of critical information or valued assets" [2]. The behaviours associated with insider threat include espionage, sabotage, theft and terrorism [2, 3].

Studies of organizationally enabled insider threats are rare. Historically, research on insider threat has predominantly focused on individually motivated behaviour, psychological predispositions and technological weaknesses. This predominant research

© Springer International Publishing Switzerland 2016
C. Stephanidis (Ed.): HCII 2016 Posters, Part I, CCIS 617, pp. 465–470, 2016.
DOI: 10.1007/978-3-319-40548-3_77

provides a narrow perspective of examining insider threat within the context of organizational vulnerability due to architecture, structure, and processes. The reason for this is most probably a result of underreporting by organizations due to a fear of loss of reputation [4]. It may also be a way to place blame on an individual or technological failure, rather than focus on organizational control and responsibilities.

In the cyber security space, research has concentrated on computer hackers, disgruntled employees, ex-employees and consultants [5]. The research has rarely provided any organization-wide recommendations or managerial decision-making tools as a means for developing countermeasures [1] due to organizational vulnerability as the source of cyber threat. However, researchers are increasingly calling for further studies related to security efforts that account for individual, social, and organizational influences, and that risk management must extend beyond the almost entirely technological detection solutions currently in place [4]. Whilst research to date has been useful it has ignored or undervalued broader organizational dimensions that increase and decrease insider threat.

Colwill [6] confirms that a focus on cyber security and information technology alone does not provide a balanced solution. Certainly this is true when taking into account that insider threats are viewed as more damaging than external threats. Insiders can circumnavigate technical detection and technical detection mechanisms are limited to post-hoc identification of actual insider threat activity [7].

Whilst security is improved by technological assistance and advancement it is not enough [8]. Employers become comfortable and perhaps over reliant on technology. The result is usually missing opportunities to embrace other proactive forms of addressing the insider threat phenomena, including human factors, education and awareness, and crisis response [6].

Given the current status of research on insider threat there is potential to expand understanding of the phenomenon including organizational predispositions and vulnerabilities [9]. This is important as Festa [10] noted that the overall body of research on insider threat is biased, insufficient, and lacking. In summary, the spectrum of insider threat research should embrace a holistic approach that reflects the complexity and convergence of variables that result in damage.

Further attention to broader government, private sector and not-for-profit organizations is warranted especially given that global relevance of research and collaboration has been limited [10]. This is especially clear in Australia where there is a lack of published work and research available in the public and practice domain.

This preliminary study aims to begin addressing some of these limitations in research in the Australian context. It looks to broaden the scope of available research by (a) considering Australian expert opinion, (b) gathering information across private and public sector organizations, (c) providing a diverse focus across individual, organizational, and technological vulnerabilities and (d) identifying first and second-tier mitigation techniques that extend beyond information systems and contribute to warning indicators (although this last point is not addressed in the current poster presentation).

2 Methodology

If insider threat risks are statistically rare [3] or more likely, seldomly reported, then quantitative methods alone cannot provide a full picture of such behaviour. As such the inclusion of qualitative methods, through information provided by subject matter experts is one way to gather relevant and purposeful information on insider threat [1].

The Delphi Method was chosen as an appropriate means of gathering expert opinion through a multi-stage email questionnaire. The Delphi method is an attractive method for researchers as it is a flexible research technique that is suited to addressing problems or phenomenon where limited information exist [11]. It also allows for equality of response thus avoiding dominant (usually prevailing) opinion and allows experts to change their responses. It is a versatile method for exploratory study [12], as is the case with insider threat, where the topic is delicate, sensitive or undocumented [13].

Use of expert opinion in studying insider threat is well established [1, 14]. Consistent with the themes addressed by Okoli and Pawlowski [12] a Delphi Method is considered the most practical and applicable research method as it can investigate a complex issue, provide a group method where experts do not need to meet, is a flexible design that allows for follow up (leading to richer data/deeper understanding), can allow for solicitation of information and, as in this study, ranking importance of organizational vulnerabilities. It also provides a group opinion which may be more valid than an individual opinion [15].

2.1 Choosing Delphi Participants/Experts

For the purpose of the current study, experts were selected based on demonstrated expertise in the field of insider threat and specifically targeted to ensure coverage of the private and public sectors. In addition to at least 10 years of involvement in Justice, National Security, Crisis Management, Counter Intelligence, Cyber Security, Risk Management, and Fraud Investigation, experts also had to meet one of the following recruitment criteria: (1) postgraduate qualifications in insider threat related research, (2) published articles on insider threat or related phenomena, (3) involvement in investigating insider threat cases, or (4) involved in the assessment and mitigation of insider threat within organizations. As such, the experts may be employees or employers or subject matter experts with relevant commentary on insider threat. Given the narrow field of expertise the group was an homogenous sample.

2.2 Participants

The use of convenience sampling and snowball techniques are commonplace in research employing the Delphi method [15]. Using these methods, email requests were sent out to 28 experts inviting participation. Of the 28 experts who were contacted to participate in the study, two declined participation, nine did not respond to the email, and 17 consented to participate in the research. To attempt to enhance participation, follow-up emails were sent to those who had not responded to the initial request for participation. After emailing the first round of the Delphi, two experts withdrew from the process. This left a total of 15 experts participating in round 1 of the Delphi study. Attrition did occur, but was minimal (13 %).

2.3   Delphi Items and Process

The items of the initial Delphi questionnaire were guided by literature review findings. These items were considered to be of high pertinence [15] and the expert panel were required to give feedback and make judgements on these pre-selected issues (on a five-point Likert scale and through free text responses). Experts were also offered the opportunity to raise issues and ideas not already identified in the questionnaire. The questions of the Delphi rounds aimed to gain insight into (1) the experts understanding and definition of insider threat, (2) what organizational vulnerabilities they believe contribute to insider threat behaviour, and (3) how organizations can better protect themselves from insider threat. This paper focuses on point 2 - the organizational vulnerabilities that Australian experts believe contribute to an increased risk of insider threat.

3   Results

Descriptive statistics and P-P Plots were used to assess the responses from the Australian panel experts and determine the level of consensus reached and the identification of any emerging issues or major discrepancies. Consensus on a question was deemed to be achieved if a) at least 70 percent (typically acceptable in Delphi research - see Brewer [16]) of panel members agreed on the direction of the response and b) there was no abnormal distribution of responses i.e. normal distribution, with a low variability and minimal outliers. Where any item achieved at least 70 % agreement and there were no 'polar-opposite' responses of concern it was considered to have reached consensus and eliminated from the next round. This helped reduce the length of subsequent rounds which is also considered a method of reducing attrition in expert participation [15].

Classical content analysis of qualitative data was used to determine emerging themes from responses to open ended questions in rounds one and two of the Delphi. Based on these analytical techniques the panel demonstrated a high level of consensus across the questions during the three rounds of the Delphi Method.

The themes of vulnerabilities were then reviewed to determine those that were of primary importance - where more than 90 % of panel experts agreed or raised an issue/idea and at least one third strongly agreed with that vulnerability. Based on the analyses completed the following were considered primary weaknesses and vulnerabilities that, according to Australian experts, increase the likelihood of insider threat (Table 1).

Table 1. Primary vulnerabilities that increase the likelihood of insider threat

People	1. Ego/sense of entitlement 2. Disgruntlement 3. Ethical flexibility 4. Increase in staff counterproductive workplace behaviour/workplace deviance
Process	5. Poor security practices of leadership 6. Poor application of security 7. No consequences for poor security behaviour
Technological	8. Limited/no auditing and monitoring capabilities 9. Lack of electronic access controls
Strategic	10. Lack of strong and well-defined organizational culture

4   Conclusion

Based on Australian expert opinion, ten primary organizational vulnerabilities that increase the likelihood of insider threat have been identified. These vulnerabilities extend across organizational domains, consistent with research suggesting that addressing insider threat requires more than a narrow focus on technology and/or individual solutions (e.g. [6]). The findings are consistent with previous published works noting that insider threat is a multi-disciplinary concern [8, 17] and demonstrate that organizations need to consider people, process, technology, and organizational strategy in order to adequately address and reduce their risk of insider threat. The latter is closely associated with a leadership predisposition to allocate resources to counter insider threat as a key strategic priority.

It is confirmed that focusing on cyber security and information technology alone does not provide a balanced solution [6] and that broader focus to include weaknesses in the organizational context must be further studied. As Colwill [6] suggested embracing other proactive forms of addressing the insider threat phenomena is necessary. The outcomes of this study suggest that at a minimum a focus on organizational culture and security application and practices must also be part of an overall insider threat solution.

In order to develop a greater understanding of insider threat in Australia, further analysis of the Delphi Method data will be undertaken. Such analysis will provide Australian expert opinion on the top organizational methods and strategies to help decrease the likelihood of insider threat. In the future it is hoped that the Delphi Method information will be distilled into strategies for organizational best practice for the prevention and mitigation of insider threat based on Australian expert opinion.

References

1. Catrantzos, N.: Managing the Insider Threat: No Dark Corners. CRC Press, Boca Raton (2012)
2. Shaw, E.D., Fischer, L.F., Rose, A.E.: Insider risk evaluation and audit (2009). http://www.dhra.mil/perserec/reports/tr09-02.pdf. Accessed 21 June 2014

3. Shaw, E., Fischer, L.: Ten tales of betrayal: the threat to corporate infrastructures by information technology insiders: analysis and observations (2005). http://www.dhra.mil/perserec/reports/tr05-13.pdf. Accessed 21 June 2014

4. Willison, R., Warkentin, M.: Beyond deterrence: an expanded view of employee computer abuse. MIS Q. **37**(1), 1–20 (2013)

5. Brackney, R., Anderson, R.: Understanding the insider threat (2004). http://www.rand.org/pubs/conf_proceedings/CF196/index.html. (cited 22 June 2014)

6. Colwill, C.: Human factors in information security: the insider threat - who can you trust these days? Inf. Sec. Tech. Rep. **14**, 186–196 (2010)

7. Maasberg, M., Warren, J., Beebe, N.: The dark side of the insider: detecting the insider threat through examination of dark triad personality traits. In: 48th Hawaii International Conference on System Sciences, Hawaii, USA (2015)

8. Cappelli, D.M., Moore, A.P., Trzeciak, R.F.: The CERT Guide to Insider Threats: How to Prevent, Detect, and Respond to Information Technology Crimes (Theft, Sabotage, Fraud). Pearson Education, Upper Saddle River (2012)

9. Band, S.R., et al.: Comparing insider IT sabotage and espionage: a model-based analysis. DTIC Document (2006)

10. Festa, J.P.: New technologies and emerging threats: personnel security adjudicative guidelines in the age of social networking. DTIC Document (2012)

11. Skulmoski, G., Hartman, F., Krahn, J.: The Delphi method for graduate research. J. Inf. Technol. Educ. **6**, 1–21 (2007)

12. Okoli, C., Pawlowski, S.: The Delphi method as a research tool: an example, design considerations and applications. Inf. Manag. **42**, 15–29 (2004)

13. Lilja, K.K., Laakso, K., Palomaki, J.: Using the Delphi method. In: 2011 Proceedings of PICMET 2011 Technology Management in the Energy Smart World (PICMET) (2011)

14. Greitzer, F.L., et al.: Psychosocial modeling of insider threat risk based on behavioral and word use analysis. e-Service J. **9**(1), 106–138 (2013)

15. Keeney, S., McKenna, H., Hasson, F.: The Delphi Technique in Nursing and Health Research. Wiley, Hoboken (2010)

16. Brewer, E.: Delphi technique. In: Encyclopedia of Measurement and Statistics. Sage Publications Inc, Thousand Oaks (2007)

17. Nurse, J.R.C., Legg, P.A., Buckley, O., Agrafiotis, I., Wright, G., Whitty, M., Upton, D., Goldsmith, M., Creese, S.: A critical reflection on the threat from human insiders – its nature, industry perceptions, and detection approaches. In: Tryfonas, T., Askoxylakis, I. (eds.) HAS 2014. LNCS, vol. 8533, pp. 270–281. Springer, Heidelberg (2014)

SecureUse: Balancing Security and Usability Within System Design

Saurabh Dutta[1](✉), Stuart Madnick[2], and Ger Joyce[3]

[1] MIT System Design Management, Massachusetts Institute of Technology,
Cambridge, MA 02139, USA
saurabhd@mit.edu
[2] MIT Sloan School of Management and School of Engineering, Massachusetts
Institute of Technology, Cambridge, MA 02139, USA
smadnick@mit.edu
[3] School of Computer Science, University of Hertfordshire,
College Lane, Hatfield, Hertfordshire AL10 9AB, UK
gerjoyce@outlook.com

Abstract. The interdependency of information security and usability has been evident for several years, yet this area is largely under-represented within the Literature. Consequently, no standards yet exist that address the balance between security and usability within system design. To address this gap in knowledge, the authors propose a method that can be used by experts in information security, experts in usability, and by representative users to quickly assess the security and usability of a system. From this assessment, a single metric, known as a SecureUse score, would be derived, which will help to ensure that future systems are both secure and usable.

Keywords: Information security · Cybersecurity · Usability · User experience

1 Introduction

Information security and usability are essential components of most system designs. This will be even more prevalent with the advent of the Internet of Things (IoT), where almost all devices will be connected. Yet, creating a secure, usable system has proven to be a challenge for system designers [1]. There are numerous examples of this in many of the systems that people use. Let's consider just two examples, which are used by millions of people every day:

- **CAPTCHA:** This approach is secure and is widely used on login forms across many websites. Unfortunately, whenever CAPTCHA is utilized web traffic decreases due to the obstructive nature of the method. Consequently, adding an extra layer of security has been shown to degrade usability [2].
- **INSULIN PUMP:** With certain types of insulin pumps, a physician has all the vital information, including the patient's blood glucose level, the moment a patient steps into the clinic. To enable this, the insulin pump has an always-on bluetooth sensor. This convenience comes at the cost of vulnerability to exploitation [3], where it is

C. Stephanidis (Ed.): HCII 2016 Posters, Part I, CCIS 617, pp. 471–475, 2016.
DOI: 10.1007/978-3-319-40548-3_78

possible to tamper with the device remotely with the potential for serious consequences. Subsequently, usability has been shown to degrade security.

2   Related Work

While the importance of both information security and usability have been apparent for some time, no standards yet exist that address the balance between the two within system design. Sets of usability design principles either do not consider security [4, 5], focus on information security management tools [6], or are too specific [7], the latter which focuses only on CAPTCHA's within a mobile context.

Where system design does not consider both information security and usability equally, or offers users a choice, research has shown that users favor usability over security [8–10]. Consequently, people are the weakest link when it comes to information security [11]. This can lead to identity theft, intellectual property theft, loss of consumer confidence, and financial loss [12].

Braz et al. [13] attempted to address this gap with the Security Usability Symmetry, as did Garfinkel [14] with Secure and Usable Design Principles. However, both methods are based on the Heuristic Evaluation model, thus an expert considers both information security and usability. There are two problems with this approach. First of all, it is rare to find people that are simultaneously expert in both security and usability. Secondly, the proposed solutions do not take into account the fact that the perceived usability of a system could differ between experts and users. This is supported by Bevan and Macleod [15], who argue that "reliable measures of overall usability can only be obtained by assessing the effectiveness, efficiency and satisfaction with which representative users carry out representative tasks in representative environments" (p. 132).

3   Approach

To address these issues, the authors propose a method that can be used by experts in information security, experts in usability, and by representative users of a system. A notable aspect of the proposed method is that it can be completed multiple times as needed throughout the software design and development life cycle, from early sketches to interactive prototypes to fully operational software. From an assessment, a single metric, known as a SecureUse score would be derived. The SecureUse score would consider the following elements:

- **Security:** A score from 0 to 15 would be awarded by an Information Security Analyst based on the level of security that the system offers.
- **Usability (all three scores below would be added together):**
  - **Effectiveness:** A score of 0 to 5 would be awarded by a User Experience Designer by observing representative users attempt a task, with 0 for fail, 1 to 4 based on a partially completed task, and 5 for full completion of the task.

- **Efficiency:** A score from 0 to 5 would be awarded by a User Experience Designer by observing how quickly representative users attempted a task, with 0 for failed at a task, and from 1 for slow, up to 5 for quickly completing a task.
- **Satisfaction:** A score from 0 to 5 would be awarded each from one or more representative users within representative environments during a Usability Test, based on their perceived level of satisfaction with the system, from which the sample mean would be calculated.

The resulting quantitative metric is verbally stated in the form of the ubiquitous blood pressure rate. For instance, 30/45 or thirty forty-five would signify that both security and usability levels are high. For ease of comparison with other options, the results would be visualized within a Tornado Chart [16]. The ideal solution being a design that scored highly on both sides of the chart. For instance, within Fig. 1, Option 7 clearly satisfied each evaluator, including representative users, more so than other options.

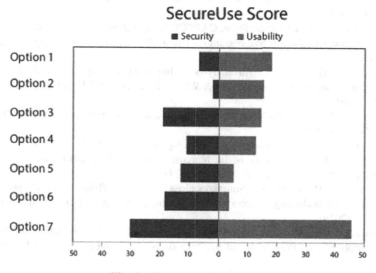

Fig. 1. SecureUse visualization

4 Conclusion

Defeating Cybercrime by creating secure, usable systems has proven to be a challenge in recent years. One of the main deficiencies that has led to this globally-recognized issue is the lack of a standard scoring system that considers both security and usability within system design. The concept proposed within this work is based on research that has shown how a single quantitative metric in the context of usability can quickly inform design decisions [17, 18]. This speed of decision making is vital, especially within fast-paced agile software development environments, where design and development teams may need to react quickly to new insights [19–21].

The contribution of this work is to consider how this single metric, defined by information security experts, usability experts, and representative users, can be used to assess the security and usability of a system or system element. Those responsible for designing secure, usable systems across desktop, mobile, and the Internet of Things will benefit most from this research. As part of the empirical research around the proposed method, semi-structured interviews with potential users of the method are ongoing. These include Information Security practitioners, User Experience practitioners, and diabetes patients that use insulin pumps. Following the information gathering phase, the proposed method will be observed in the field using several case studies.

References

1. Kainda, R., Flechais, I., Roscoe, A.W.: Security and usability: analysis and evaluation. In: ARES 2010 International Conference on Availability, Reliability, and Security, pp. 275–282. IEEE (2010)
2. Yan, J., El Ahmad, A.S.: Usability of CAPTCHAs or usability issues in CAPTCHA design. In: Proceedings of the 4th Symposium on Usable Privacy and Security, pp. 44–52. ACM (2008)
3. Hager, C.T., MidKiff, S.F.: An analysis of bluetooth security vulnerabilities. Wireless Communications and Networking, 2003. WCNC 2003. 2003 IEEE, vol. 3, pp. 1825–1831. IEEE (2003)
4. Nielsen, J., Molich, R., Ballerup, D.: Heuristic evaluation of user interfaces. In: CHI 1990, pp. 249–256 (1990)
5. Joyce, G., Lilley, M.: Towards the Development of Usability Heuristics for Native Smartphone Mobile Applications. In: Marcus, A. (ed.) DUXU 2014, Part I. LNCS, vol. 8517, pp. 465–474. Springer, Heidelberg (2014)
6. Jaferiana, P., Hawkeyb, K., Sotirakopoulosa, A., Velez-Rojasc, M., Beznosova, K.: Heuristics for evaluating it security management tools. Hum. Comput. Interact. **29**(4), 311–350 (2014)
7. Reynaga, G., Chiasson, S., van Oorschot, P.C.: Heuristics for the evaluation of CAPTCHA on smartphones. In: Proceedings of the 2015 British HCI Conference, pp. 126–135. ACM (2015)
8. Herley, C.: So long, and no thanks for the externalities: the rational rejection of security advice by users. In: New Security Paradigms Workshop 2009, pp. 133–144. ACM (2009)
9. Weir, C.S., Douglas, G., Carruthers, M., Jack, M.: User perceptions of security, convenience and usability for e-banking authentication tokens. Comput. Secur. **28**(1), 47–62 (2009)
10. Gunson, N., Marshall, D., Morton, H., Jack, M.: User perceptions of security and usability of single-factor and two-factor authentication in automated telephone banking. Comput. Secur. **30**(4), 208–220 (2011)
11. Sasse, M.A., Flechais, I.: Usable security-why do we need it? how do we get it? In: Cranor, L.F., Garfinkel, S. (eds.) Security and Usability: Designing Secure Systems that People Can Use. O'Reilly Media, Newton (2005)
12. Herr, T., Romanosky, S.: Cyber crime: security under scarce resources. American Foreign Policy Council Defense Technology Program Brief, June 2015

13. Braz, C., Seffah, A., M'Raihi, D.: Designing a trade-off between usability and security: a metrics based-model. In: Baranauskas, C., Abascal, J., Barbosa, S.D.J. (eds.) INTERACT 2007. LNCS, vol. 4663, pp. 114–126. Springer, Heidelberg (2007)

14. Garfinkel, S.: Ph.D thesis, Massachusetts Institute of Technology (2005)

15. Bevan, N., Macleod, M.: Usability measurement in context. Behav. Inf. Technol. **13**(1–2), 132–145 (1994)

16. Abrams, J.B.: Quantitative Business Valuation: A Mathematical Approach for Today's Professionals. Wiley, Hoboken (2010)

17. Sauro, J., Kindlund, E.: A method to standardize usability metrics into a single score. In: CHI 2005 Proceedings of the SIGCHI Conference on Human Factors in Computing Systems, pp. 401–409 (2005)

18. Josang, A., AlFayyadh, B., Grandison, T., AlZomai, M., McNamara, J.: Security usability principles for vulnerability analysis and risk assessment. In: Twenty-Third Annual Computer Security Applications Conference. ACSAC 2007, pp. 269–278. IEEE (2007)

19. Cottingham, H., Snyder, M.: Get your mobile app out the door. In: Stephanidis, C. (ed.) Posters, Part I, HCII 2011. CCIS, vol. 173, pp. 13–17. Springer, Heidelberg (2011)

20. Micallef, A.: UX Matters: Agile Manifesto for Product Management (2015). (Part 1). http://www.uxmatters.com/mt/archives/2015/06/agile-manifesto-for-product-management-part-1.php

21. Maguire, M.: Using human factors standards to support user experience and Agile design. In: Antona, M., Stephanidis, C. (eds.) UAHCI 2013, Part I. LNCS, vol. 8009, pp. 185–194. Springer, Heidelberg (2013)

Implementation and Initial Evaluation of Game in Which Password Enhancement Factor is Embedded

Masahiro Fujita, Mako Yamada, and Masakatsu Nishigaki[✉]

Shizuoka University, Hamamatsu, Japan
nisigaki@inf.shizuoka.ac.jp

Abstract. Embedding a security factor into entertainment instance is an effective approach to improving users' security awareness and/or skills. As an attempt of this approach, we have proposed a password enhancement scheme which enables users to memorize stronger passwords while playing games [5]. In this succeeding paper, we implemented a game instance and evaluated the practical effectiveness of our scheme. We asked five subjects to play our game in their free time for three days. All subjects memorized at least thirteen random characters in this game. After the experiment, we asked subjects to answer a questionnaire. The users' answers suggested that they had positive impression of our game. These results showed the effectiveness of our scheme, i.e. users are able to memorize stronger passwords naturally while playing our game.

Keywords: Entertainment · User authentication · Games · Password

1 Introduction

Consideration of human factors such as cognitive characteristic is indispensable in designing information systems. In this line, researchers have tried to improve security of information systems by combining security with entertainment (e.g. [1–4]). Enjoying entertainment is one of human factors.

There could be two approaches for combining security with entertainment; (i) an entertainment factor is embedded in security technology and (ii) a security factor is embedded in entertainment instances. The aim with approach (i) is to improve security and/or usability of information systems when users use these systems. On the other hand, that of approach (ii) is to improve security skills and/or awareness of users in their daily life. These approaches have different advantages; thus, it is important to investigate both. However, to the best of our knowledge, most previous studies were focused on approach (i). This motivated us to examine approach (ii). In our previous study, as an attempt, we focused on to embed a password enhancement factor (a security factor) into games (entertainment instance) [5]. We designed a password enhancement scheme that enables users to naturally memorize strong passwords while playing games. In this succeeding paper, we implemented a game instance and evaluated the practical effectiveness of our scheme through an experiment.

© Springer International Publishing Switzerland 2016
C. Stephanidis (Ed.): HCII 2016 Posters, Part I, CCIS 617, pp. 476–481, 2016.
DOI: 10.1007/978-3-319-40548-3_79

2 Password Enhancement Through Games

As an attempt of approach (ii), we have proposed a password enhancement scheme that enables users to memorize stronger passwords while playing games [5].

Game players often memorize commands naturally while repeatedly inputting them into games. So, let us consider commands as passwords. This deduces that users can naturally memorize complex commands (passwords) while playing a game if a game system prepares complex commands and requires users to input them at the appropriate time. For example, a roll-playing game prepares a command for using a special attack. While playing the game, users repeatedly input the command for using the special attack. Users will naturally memorize the command in the end, and the command can be later on used as a login password on a Web site or a master password for a password manager.

The idea of "reward" also can encourage users to memorize much stronger passwords. Reward is a factor that helps users play a game or give incentive to users. So, let us consider that the more complex the users' input commands are, the more they can receive a reward. In the example we described above, we can apply the idea of reward to decision regarding the power of a special attack. This works as follows. A user (game player) registers a command (password) on the game system and can use a special attack by inputting it. The user can re-register the command at any time. If he/she registers a short and easy command, the power of his/her special attack is twice the strength of that of an ordinary attack. If he/she registers a long and complex command, the power of his/her special attack is ten times stronger than that of an ordinary attack. Since users want to use a strong attack as possible, they will try to memorize much stronger commands (passwords).

3 Implementation of Game Instance

We implemented a game instance. The game is a simple dungeon exploration game. The dungeon has some floors (1F, 2F, ...) and has a maze in each floor. Users need to explore the dungeon as deeply as possible. This game has three views: Dungeon view (Fig. 1), Battle view (Fig. 2) and Command check view. A Player have status: Current floor, Current level, Needed experience (experience points needed to reach the next level), Accumulated experience points, and The number of gained items. An attack command whose length is N characters is registered on the system.

In Dungeon view, the player moves by pressing up, down, right and left key. Each floor has three items. If the player collects them and moves to stairs, he/she is able to move to next floor. While exploring the dungeon, the player encounters an enemy with a constant possibility (=1.0 %). Whenever encountering an enemy, players automatically move to Battle view.

In Battle view, the player and the enemy have battle status: Hit point, Attack point, and Defense point. The status of the player is set based on the value of the player's

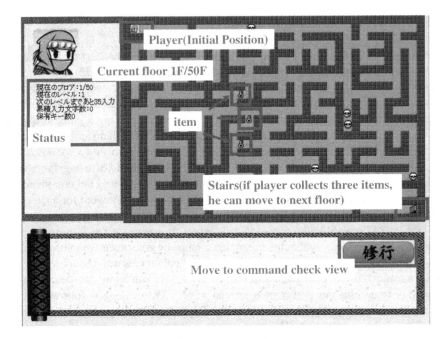

Fig. 1. Dungeon view

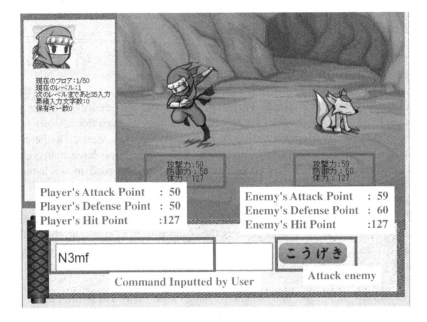

Fig. 2. Battle view

current level. That of the enemy is set based on the value of the current floor. The flow of the battle is as follows:

1. The player attacks the enemy by inputting the k characters from the beginning of the attack command.
2. The attack point of the user will increase depending on the value of k. In this game, we use the following setting: if k is less than four, the point increases by 1.01 times; if k is between five and seven, the point increases by 1.10 times; if k is between eight and ten, the point increases by 1.15 times, and so on. It should be noted that, if the player mistypes the command, the attack point will not increase.
3. The hit point of the enemy will decrease by the player's attack. The damage for the enemy depends on the attack point of the player and the defense point of the enemy.
4. If the hit point of the enemy becomes less than zero, the battle result is win. The game system goes back to Dungeon view.
5. The player is attacked by the enemy.
6. The hit point of the player will decrease. The damage for the player depends on the defense point of the player and the attack point of the enemy.
7. If the hit point of the player becomes less than zero, the battle result is lose. When going back to Dungeon view, the game system sets the number of gained items to zero and moves the player to the initial position.
8. Return to 1.

Players gain experience points when attacking enemies. Specifically, if a user is succeed to input the k characters from the beginning of the attack command, the game system adds k to the user's accumulated experience points. The system, while at the same time, subtracts k from the needed experience (experience points needed to reach the next level). If the needed experience becomes less than zero, the system adds one to the current level of the player and reset the value of the needed experience (the higher the current level of the player is, the bigger value the system sets).

In Command Check view, the player can check the attack command registered on the system. If players click the button at the lower right of Dungeon view, they are able to move to Command Check view (They are unable to move from Battle view to this view).

We have conducted a preliminary experiment beforehand. The parameters and default values used in the game, such as the parameter for damage calculation and the value for the needed experience to reach the next level, are decided empirically by the experiment. The details of them is omitted due to the limitation of space.

4   Experiment

4.1   Method

We asked five university students to play our game in their free time for three days. In this experiment, the command registered on the system was set by the experimenter (i.e., authors) as a random string with thirty characters. The command was "N3mf8-%x

RQkQeV)NMbnn*[sT(WW/". After the experiment, we asked the subjects to answer a questionnaire. The questionnaire includes the following two questions[1].

1. Did you memorize the command positively in our game? (yes/no) And also, please write why you think so.
2. Did you memorize the command naturally in our game? (yes/no) And also, please write why you think so.

4.2 Results

Table 1 shows the result of game play. All subjects were successful in inputting at least thirteen random characters. Surprisingly, four out of five subjects was successful in inputting all thirty random characters. The result of the questionnaire suggested that the subjects had positive impression of our game. In question 1, all subjects answered "yes". They stated the reasons: it gives an advantage in the game; I wanted to increase the current level as soon as possible. In question 2, four subjects answered "yes". They stated the reasons: I was able to memorize the command gradually and naturally; when I encountered an enemy which I didn't beat, I tried to memorize longer command.

Table 1. Results of game play

User A

	Play time [h:m:s]	Number of characters that subject memorized	Number of command inputs
Day 1	0:06:20	11	6
Day 2	0:05:12	23	4
Day 3	0:10:16	30	6
Total	0:21:48		16

User B

	Play time [h:m:s]	Number of characters that subject memorized	Number of command inputs
Day 1	0:53:31	11	58
Day 2	0:29:43	23	26
Day 3	0:14:58	30	14
Total	1:38:12		98

User C

	Play time [h:m:s]	Number of characters that subject memorized	Number of command inputs
Day 1	0:07:06	9	9
Day 2	0:18:19	30	19
Day 3	0:17:44	30	19
	0:43:09		47

User D

	Play time [h:m:s]	Number of characters that subject memorized	Number of command inputs
Day 1	0:14:18	17	13
Day 2	0:21:11	26	19
Day 3	0:14:45	30	46
	0:50:14		78

User E

	Play time [h:m:s]	Number of characters that subject memorized	Number of command inputs
Day 1	0:05:00	8	4
Day 2	0:06:00	12	6
Day 3	0:05:00	13	5
	0:16:00		15

[1] We prepared five questions. But, due to the limitation of space, we in this paper report two questions and their results.

4.3   Discussions

Did subjects memorize stronger password through our game? Bonneau et al. reported that a 56-bit random password is a reasonable strength for most practical scenarios [6]. All subjects memorized at least thirteen random characters, which has an entropy of about 80-bit. In particular, four subjects memorized thirty random characters, which has much bigger entropy than the entropy of 56-bit. These result suggests that our game enables users to memorize an enough strong password.

Did subjects memorize password naturally through our game? All subjects answered "yes" in question 1. According to the reason why the subjects think so, subjects inputted the command (password) for playing the game smoothly or getting an advantage. The results suggest that the subjects recognized the command input not as "memorizing a password" but as "enjoying the game". Once a user can memorize a command while playing a game, later on they will be able to use it as a password. As a conclusion, our game enables users to memorize a stronger password *naturally*. In fact, in question 2, most subjects answered "yes".

5   Conclusion

In this paper, we developed a game instance for the password enhancing game proposed in literature [5] and conducted a user experiment. Its results showed the effectiveness of our scheme, i.e. users are able to memorize stronger passwords naturally while playing our game. This experiment is still initial phase, so we are going to conduct a more comprehensive experiment.

References

1. Yamamoto, T., Suzuki, T., Nishigaki, M.: A proposal of four-panel cartoon CAPTCHA. In: 25th International Conference on Advanced Information Networking and Applications, pp. 159–166. Biopolis (2011)
2. Mohamed, M., Gao, S., Saxena, N., Zhang, C.: Dynamic cognitive game CAPTCHA usability and detection of streaming-based farming. In: Workshop on Usable Security, San Diego (2014)
3. Kojima, Y., Yamamoto, T., Nishigaki, M.: Proposal of an image-based one-time authentication scheme using "Spot the deference". In: IPSJ SIG Technical report, 2007-CSEC-36, pp. 375–380 (2007). (in Japanese)
4. Ur, B., Kalley, P.G., Komanduri, S., Lee, J., et al.: How does your password measure up? The effect of strength meters on password creation. In: 21st USENIX Conference on Security Symposium, Bellevue (2012)
5. Fujita, M., Yamada, M., Arimura, S., Ikeya, Y., Nishigaki, M.: An attempt to memorize strong passwords while playing games. In: The 18th International Conference on Network-Based Information Systems, pp. 264–268 (2015)
6. Bonneau, J., Schecheter, S.: Towards reliable storage of 56-bit secrets in human memory. In: USENIX Security 2014, pp. 607–623 (2014)

Primary Factors of Malicious Insider in E-learning Model

Koichi Niihara[✉] and Hiroaki Kikuchi

Graduate School, Meiji University, Tokyo 164-8525, Japan
{niihara,kikn}@meiji.ac.jp

Abstract. There have been recent incidents in which large amounts of personal information have been leaked by malicious insiders. Organizations are now required to prepare countermeasures to deal with insider threats. To identify the primary causes of malicious insider behavior, an experiment was conducted using a pseudo e-learning website. A total of 100 subjects were recruited by crowd-sourcing and divided into four groups with different hypothesized causes of insider threat. The number of malicious activities in each group was observed. The results show a correlation between the hypothesized causes of insider threat and malicious activities.

Keywords: E-learning · Insider threat · Crowd-sourcing · Information leakage

1 Introduction

In July 2014, an incident occurred [1] in which large amounts of personal information of about 29 million users were leaked by a malicious insider. Subsequently, organizations were required to prepare countermeasures to deal with insider threats. However, the primary causes of insider threats remain unclear because there are so many factors in malicious activities to be considered.

The objective of this research was to identify the primary causes of malicious activities. By identifying the underlying factors involved in malicious activities by insiders, organizations can more effectively tailor their efforts to reduce the risk of malicious insider threats.

However, it is not easy to observe malicious activities because they occur infrequently. Moreover, strict security policies prevent researchers from observing employees performing suspicious behaviors in real organizations.

To address the difficulties in observing malicious activities, we conducted an experiment using a pseudo e-learning website that provided an environment for setting various traps, which corresponded to specific causes of insider threats. Using the crowd-sourcing service, Lancers, Inc., we recruited 100 subjects for our experiment. The results show the correlation between the hypothesized causes of insider threat and malicious activities. The main finding of our study is that a low level of monitoring is the most significant cause of insider threat. An employee

© Springer International Publishing Switzerland 2016
C. Stephanidis (Ed.): HCII 2016 Posters, Part I, CCIS 617, pp. 482–487, 2016.
DOI: 10.1007/978-3-319-40548-3_80

who knows that he or she is not under surveillance is 17.9 times more likely to perform malicious activities than an employee kept under sufficient surveillance by the organization.

The paper is organized as follows: We describe the objectives of the paper and details of our experiments in Sect. 3. We summarize our results and give a discussion in Sect. 4. We provide conclusions and future works in Sect. 5.

2   Related Works

Cohen *et al.* [2] presented the 'routine activity theory', which argues that most crimes have three necessary conditions: a likely offender, a suitable target, and the absence of a capable guardian. Cressey *et al.* [3] proposed the Fraud Triangle model to explain the factors that are present in every situation of fraud: perceived pressure, perceived opportunity, and rationalization. Greitzer *et al.* [4,5] provided some indicators of insider threat based on published case studies and discussions with experienced human resources professionals. The Nikkoso Research Foundation for Safe Society [6] proposed some factors related to insider threat based on investigations of criminal records.

According to these studies, various hypothesized causes of insider threat exist. However, because there are so many potential causes of malicious insider threat, it is unclear which ones have the greatest effect on insider behavior.

3   Primary Factors of Malicious Insider in E-learning Model

3.1   Objective

Our research objective was to identify the primary causes of malicious insider behavior. By identifying these, organizations can focus their efforts on controlling them, minimizing both the cost of compliance and the risk of insider threat.

Based on a recent study [6] we proposed the following three hypotheses related to malicious activities: Let H_1, H_2, and H_3 be the hypothesized causes of insider threats of stress, violence, and low monitoring, defined as follows:

H_1 (stress) states that if an employee is feeling stressed then he/she will be a malicious insider.

H_2 (violence) states that if an employee is treated in a violent manner, he/she will be a malicious insider.

H_3 (low monitoring) states that if an employee finds that no one is keeping him/her under surveillance, he/she will be a malicious insider. An example is a workplace that neglects to monitor its employees.

3.2 Method

To explore the connection between the causes of malicious insider behavior and the malicious activities, we conducted an experiment using a pseudo e-learning website as the environment for observing potential insiders. Using the crowd-sourcing service, Lancers, Inc., we recruited 100 subjects for our experiment. To ensure the quality of workers, we chose Lancers-certified workers with a history of at least 95 % approval rates.

We divided the sample of 100 into four groups, A, B, C, and D, and assigned each group a different malicious insider condition, as follows:

Group A To evaluate H_1, subjects in this group had only 20 min to complete the e-learning task, while subjects in the other groups had more time (average time of 25–45 min).

Group B To evaluate H_2, we gave subjects in this group a threatening warning message with a frightening picture.

Group C To evaluate H_3, we informed all groups except group C that all access and behaviors are logged on the site, and if illegal access was detected they would face a fine.

Group D To evaluate the effects of the insider threat factors in the first three groups, group D was used as a control.

3.3 Definition of Malicious Activities

We defined the following malicious activities as prohibited performances:

(1) Violating a rule of prescribed screen transition, e.g., pressing the back button.
(2) Answering without reading the material and progressing to the next page too quickly to have read the material, e.g., reading speed of 1000 words per 3 or 4 s.
(3) No answer as answering a test with no check.
(4) Reading HTML sources from the browser. This can be detected by fake answers written in source code.

3.4 Result

Table 1 shows the number of malicious activities for each group, where N is the number of users for each group.

Figure 1 shows reading speeds, S_i, with respect to the number of characters of i-th material, where the dashed line indicates the 95 % prediction interval of the regression equation of reading speed. Where reading speed S_i exceeded the dashed line, we determined that the subject performed the malicious activity of (2) (answering without reading).

Table 1. Number of users that caused malicious activities for each group

Malicious activities	group A	group B	group C	group D	Total
1 Breach of screen transition	6	4	9	9	28
2 Answer without reading	5	6	11	1	22
3 No answer	0	0	3	1	4
4 Reading HTML sources	0	0	1	0	1
N	24	22	27	27	100

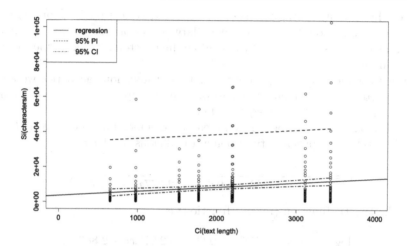

Fig. 1. Scatter plot between reading speed S_i and number of characters C_i

4   Evaluation

4.1   Chi-Square Tests

To measure the significance of our experimental results, we performed chi-square tests on the number of malicious activities of (1) and (2) for some hypothesized causes. We did not investigate malicious activities (3) or (4) further because there were only a few of these (4 cases and 1 case, respectively). In our test, we had:

The null hypothesis (H_0): there is no correlation between malicious activity and the hypothesized causes.
The alternative hypothesis (H_1): there is a correlation between malicious activity and the hypothesized causes.

Table 2 shows the chi-square test results. A statistically significant level of malicious activity (2) occurred when subjects were not monitored in their environment. However, activity (1) did not reach significance, and we were unable to reject the null hypothesis.

Table 2. Results of chi-square tests

Malicious activities	χ^2	df	P value
1 Breach of screen transition	1.921	3	0.589
2 Answering without reading	10.76	3	0.0131**

** significant at P < 0.05

4.2 Logistic Regression Analyses

Subjects have many attributes, such as age, sex, educational history, employment status and so on, that could have a large effect on our results. To identify the primary factors and discard the confounding factors, we performed logistic regression analyses.

In our logistic model, dependent variables of malicious activities were estimated based on independent variables of membership to groups (hypothesized causes of insider threat), defined as follows:

Let x_a, x_b, and x_c be coefficients, meaning membership to Group A, B, and C, respectively. The probability of being a malicious insider p is

$$p = \frac{1}{1 + \exp(3.258 - 1.923x_a - 2.277x_b - 2.883x_c)}, \tag{1}$$

where the logistic function (inverse function) is

$$\log \frac{p}{1 - p} = -3.258 + 1.923x_a + 2.277x_b + 2.883x_c. \tag{2}$$

The odds ratios of groups A, B, and C are 6.84, 9.75, and 17.9, respectively.
Table 3 shows the results of the logistic regression analyses.

Table 3. Results of the logistic regression analyses

Variable	Estimate	Std. Error	Z value	P value
Intercept (D(No cause))	−3.258	1.019	−3.199	0.00138***
A (Stress)	1.923	1.136	1.693	0.09044*
B (Violence)	2.277	1.125	2.023	0.04304**
C (Low monitoring)	2.883	1.091	2.642	0.00824***

* significant at P < 0.1
** significant at P < 0.05
*** significant at P < 0.01

4.3 Discussion

Type (2) malicious activities for each group were significant. Malicious activity types (1), (3), and (4) were observed but the numbers for each group were not statistically significant. Hypothesis H_3 was supported in our experiment: the risk of an insider threat for an employee who knows that he/she is not under surveillance is 17.9 times greater than that for employees who are under surveillance. Based on these results, we suggest that organizations should give more attention to further monitoring to reduce the risk of insider threats. Table 3 shows a statistically significant effect of employee performing malicious activities when a threatening alert was given (group B). H_2 is significant correlation in Table 3.

5   Conclusions

We studied the primary factors of malicious insider behavior by conducting an experiment using a pseudo e-learning website. Our statistical analysis shows a correlation between the lack of monitoring employee and malicious activities. Our future works will focus on methods of surveillance, with real-life testing, to determine why insiders sell personal information.

References

1. Benesse Holdings Inc: Report and response regarding leakage of customers' personal information (2014). http://blog.benesse.ne.jp/bh/en/ir_news/m/2014/09/10/uploads/news_20140910_en.pdf
2. Cohen, L.E., Felson, M.: Social change and crime rate trends: A routine activity approach. Am. Sociol. Rev. **44**(4), 588–608 (1979)
3. Cressey, D.R.: Other People's Money; A Study in the Social Psychology of Embezzlement. Free Press, Glencoe (1953)
4. Greitzer, F.L., Kangas, L.J., Noonan, C.F., Dalton, A.C., Hohimer, R.E.: Identifying at-risk employees: Modeling psychosocial precursors of potential insider threats. In: 2012 45th Hawaii International Conference on System Science (HICSS), pp. 2392–2401 (2012)
5. Greitzer, F., Frincke, D.: Combining traditional cyber security audit data with psychosocial data: Towards predictive modeling for insider threat mitigation. In: Insider Threats in Cyber Security, vol. 49, pp. 85–113 (2010)
6. The Nikkoso Research Foundation for Safe Society: Research report for a measure of human factors threat to information security. The Nikkoso Research Foundation for Safe Society, Technical report (2010) (in Japanese)

Identity Confirmation to Issue Tickets Using Face Recognition

Akitoshi Okumura[✉], Susumu Handa, Takamichi Hoshino,
and Yugo Nishiyama

NEC Informatec Systems Ltd., Nakahara-ku, Japan
a-okumura@bx.jp.nec.com

Abstract. This paper proposes a system of identity confirmation to issue tickets using face recognition software. This has been socially required to prevent illegal resale, such as ticket scalping. Because illegal resale is a critical problem for popular events in Japan, strict steps are followed for identifying people holding tickets at event venues by visual inspection with ID cards. The task is time-consuming for venue attendants. It is also stressful because ticket holders feel uncomfortable when they are kept waiting. The key points in identification are to verify identities efficiently and to prevent people from impersonating others. The system enables securing the identity of the purchaser and holder of a ticket by using face recognition software. It was proven effective for preventing illegal resale by confirming 50,324 attendees at a large concert of a popular music group. The average accuracy of face recognition was 90 %. The average time for identity confirmation was 7 s per person, including guidance to ticket holders, which succeeded in decreasing identity confirmation time by 30 % using visual inspection as well as in reducing the psychological workload of venue attendants.

Keywords: Face recognition · Biometrics · Identity confirmation · Illegal ticket resale prevention

1 Introduction

Preventing illegal resale, such as ticket scalping [1–3], is socially required. Because illegal resale is a critical problem for both ticket users and event companies, strict steps are followed at popular events in Japan from ticket application up to entry admission, as shown in Fig. 1. In advance of an event, ticket users take the following steps: ticket application through fan club membership (step 1) and ticket purchase according to notification of winning (step 2). Tickets are not sent to users to restrain resale. On the event day, attendants take the following steps at the event venue: ticket winning identification by fan club membership cards (step 3), identity confirmation by visual inspection with ID cards or documents (step 4), and admission procedure including ticket issuing (step 5). Step 4 is a time-consuming task for venue attendants because fake IDs are available together with tickets through online auction websites. It is also stressful because ticket users feel uncomfortable when kept waiting.

© Springer International Publishing Switzerland 2016
C. Stephanidis (Ed.): HCII 2016 Posters, Part I, CCIS 617, pp. 488–493, 2016.
DOI: 10.1007/978-3-319-40548-3_81

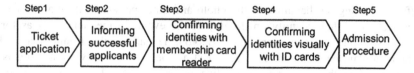

Fig. 1. Example of current ticketholder identification procedure

The key points in identification are to verify identities efficiently and to prevent people from impersonating others.

2 Methods

2.1 Identification System Using Face Recognition Software

We have developed an identification system using face recognition software as a way to improve confirmation efficiency and to prevent people from impersonating others. As shown in Fig. 2, the system registers facial photos when tickets are applied for in Step 1, and it verifies identities by using face recognition software rather than confirming with ID cards in Step 4.

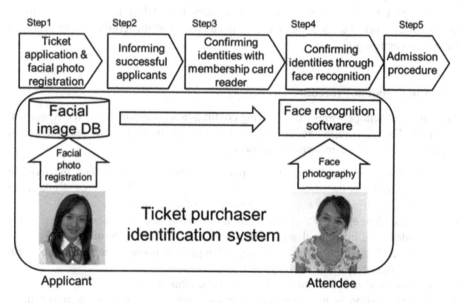

Fig. 2. System's ticket purchaser identification procedure

Our system performs the following steps to identify ticket applicants and ticket holders:

Step 1: People applying for tickets register their membership information as well as their facial photo. At that time, they will read and agree to the privacy policy in effect regarding the handling of the photo and other personal information and the verification of their identity on the day of the event. In the same way as for an ordinary ID photo, the registered facial photo is a clearly visible frontal image taken against a plain background. The face must not be obstructed by a hat, sunglasses, mask, scarf, or the like, or by things like excessively long hair or a flashed peace sign.

Step 2: Successful applicants are notified in the usual manner.

Step 3: Successful applicant identities are confirmed by using a membership card reader in the usual manner.

Step 4: At the event, the attendant uses face recognition software to confirm that the photo taken at the time of application and the registered photo show the same person.

Step 5: The admission procedure is carried out in accordance with the face authentication results.

2.2   Face Recognition Software

The face recognition software the system uses is the internationally reputable commercial product NeoFace [4, 5]. It was implemented in a commercially available AGT10 tablet terminal with a rear view camera [6]. All applicants' facial image information is copied to the tablet terminal in advance, and the terminal alone performs the face recognition process.

2.3   Confirmation Procedure

An event attendant performs the following confirmation procedure using the equipment shown in Fig. 3, comprising a card reader, display monitor, and tablet terminal implemented with face recognition software:

(1) Attendees' membership cards are placed on the card reader, and the monitor screen confirms the attendees are successful applicants. The screen displays the face images that were registered at the time of application.

(2) The attendant explains the identification through a face recognition process to the attendees and instructs them where to stand in front of the terminal.

(3) The attendant executes the face recognition process using the terminal to confirm the attendees are those who applied for the tickets.

(4) If identification is confirmed, the attendee is admitted entry.

(5) If identification is not confirmed, the face recognition process is repeated, or identity is confirmed by direct visual inspection.

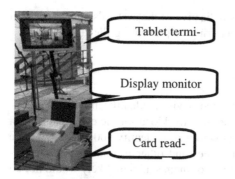

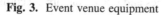

Fig. 3. Event venue equipment

Fig. 4. Attendees being identified

3 Results and Discussion

3.1 Identification at a Concert Venue

The system was utilized for a July 26, 2014 pop music concert at Nissan Stadium in Yokohama. The equipment was installed in 120 locations just behind the baggage inspection site to perform face recognition for 50,324 attendees over two days, as show in Fig. 4. The weather was mostly sunny, but the area became dark temporarily due to a thunderstorm. Face recognition was performed only for ticket applicants and not for people attending with them. The average accuracy of face recognition was 90 %. The recognition failed when the people had their eyes closed, were not looking directly forward, or had hair covering their face. There were also cases where darkness due to the thunderstorm was a factor. The confirming step took 6 s on average or 7 s if we included cases where recognition was not achieved. This was 30 % more efficient than visually confirming identification through comparison with conventional ID cards, the time for which rose to 10 s. No cases of people impersonating others were reported for this event.

3.2 Preventing People from Impersonating Others

People purchasing tickets at websites were well aware that the registered face images of ticket applicants would be matched with the facial images of people attending the event when they entered the venue. Under these conditions, there were no reports about people attempting to impersonate others at the event. The system's performance has been widely reported in the mass media [7, 8]. In addition to the aforementioned pop music concert, it has been used for 26,859 people at the Saitama Super Arena on December 24–25, 2014, for 33,434 people at Fukuoka YAFUOKU! Dome on April 4–5, 2015, and for 38,563 people at Shizuoka Stadium ECOPA on July 31–August 1, 2015. In fact, since the aforementioned pop music concert, it has been used more than 20 times for large scale events [9]. No cases of people attempting to impersonate others were reported for any of these events. This is indicative of the system's effectiveness in improving equity in ticket purchasing and deterring or preventing illegal resale.

3.3   Making Verification More Efficient

The system achieved 30 % more efficiency than a visual identification with a conventional ID card. It also reduced the psychological workload for the event attendants. Most of the attendants were part-time workers who had to identify 500 to 1,000 people per day visually. Verbal exchanges with attendees and other factors put a high psychological workload on the attendants, and many of them said they likely would not do such work at future events because of these exchanges and related factors. According to the event organizers, the identification by a face recognition system makes it easier for them to find part-time attendants who will continue to do such work at future events.

3.4   Future Issues

To make the system's identity confirmation process more efficient, we should consider ways to improve its operating environment and face recognition method. Its operating environment can be improved by installing lighting to compensate for insufficient lighting at the site. We could also make the system more efficient by finding ways that would improve the understanding and cooperation of users. There have been cases at event sites where attendees' photos were taken, but their identity could not be confirmed because they had their eyes closed, because they were not directly facing the camera, or because their hair was obstructing their face. The problem was often compounded because the attendant was unable to give the attendees a good explanation as to why their identity could not be confirmed. Providing prior information relevant to face recognition, at the ticket application time or other times, would enable facial photos to be taken appropriately. In the future, attendee understanding can be expected to increase as the face recognition process and systems such as ours become more widespread. However, event attendants will need to explain to attendees more effectively how their photos taken on the day of the event will be handled to alleviate their concerns.

We plan to study the possibilities of introducing a "walk-through" system as a way to improve face recognition [10]. This would be a system where people are photographed as they approach the system equipment head on and be admitted entry if facial recognition succeeds. Having people photographed as they approach would save them from having to stop to have their photos taken and thus reduce waiting time. We will attempt to develop a practical way in which this can be done.

4   Conclusion

We have developed an identity confirmation system using face recognition software.

The system was proven effective for preventing illegal resale by confirming 50,324 attendees at a large concert of a popular music group. The average accuracy of face recognition was 90 %. The average time for identity confirmation was 7 s per person including guidance to ticket holders, which succeeded in decreasing identity confirmation time by 30 % using visual inspection as well as in reducing the psychological workload of venue attendants. To further streamline the identification procedure, in the future, we plan to improve the performance by introducing ways to explain the procedure to users more clearly and also by introducing a "walk-through" system.

Acknowledgements. The identity confirmation system has been utilized in concerts organized by TAIPIRS Inc. We thank the personnel in the 2nd Government and Public Solutions Division and the Information and Media Processing Laboratories in NEC Corporation for using their face recognition software. We also thank Mr. Jun Tsukumo for his valuable suggestions and comments on this paper.

References

1. Internet auction. The National Consumer Affairs Center of Japan (in Japanese). http://www.kokusen.go.jp/soudan_topics/data/internet3.html
2. Universal studios Japan cracking down on ticket scalping. The Japan Times. http://www.japantimes.co.jp/news/2015/10/19/national/crime-legal/universal-studios-japan-cracking-down-on-ticket-scalping/#.VtgxsZ5f3Sd
3. Johnny's Tracks Illegally Sold Tickets for Arashi's Japonism Tour. http://jnewseng.com/2015/10/25/johnnys-tracks-illegally-sold-tickets-for-arashis-japonism-tour/1
4. NEC face recognition. http://www.nec.com/en/global/solutions/biometrics/technologies/face_recognition.html
5. Sato, A., Imaoka, H., Suzuki, T., Hosoi, T.: Advances in face detection and recognition technologies. NEC J. Technol. 2(1), pp. 28–34 (2005).http://www.nec.com/en/global/techrep/journal/g05/n01/pdf/a028.pdf
6. AGT10 tablet terminal (in Japanese). http://jpn.nec.com/info-square/solution-report/ws/04.html
7. NEC's face recognition prevents illegal reselling of Momoiro Clover-Z tickets. Nihon Keizai Shimbun Electronic Version (in Japanese). http://www.nikkei.com/article/DGXMZO8066-4930Y4A201C1H56A00/
8. PollstarPro: More Face Recognition, 10 December 2014. http://www.pollstarpro.com/NewsContent.aspx?cat=0&com=1&ArticleID=815399
9. Tapirs Inc., Evolution of ticketing systems (in Japanese). https://www.tapirs.co.jp/live-event2015.html
10. NEC article: NEC to strengthen data center operations that serve as a foundation for its "Solutions for Society", 17 February 2015. http://www.nec.com/en/press/201502/global_20150217_01.html

Access Control Is Not Enough: How Owner and Guest Set Limits to Protect Privacy When Sharing Smartphone

Yun Zhou[1]([⊠]), Tao Xu[2], Alexander Raake[3], and Yanping Cai[4]

[1] School of Education, Shaanxi Normal University, 199, South Chang'an Road,
Xi'an 710062, Shaanxi, China
zhouyun@snnu.edu.cn
[2] School of Software and Microelectronics, Northwestern Polytechnical
University, 127, West Youyi Road, Xi'an 710072, Shaanxi, China
xutao@nwpu.edu.cn
[3] Assessment of IP-Based Applications, Technische Universitat Berlin
and Telekom Innovation Labs, Ernst-Reuter-Platz 7, 10587 Berlin, Germany
alexander.raake@tu-ilmenau.de
[4] Xi'an Institute of High Technology, Xi'an 710025, China
Caiyanping502@163.com

Abstract. Even though smartphones are personal devices, phone sharing has proven to be popular at different levels among users. Access control for data is an alternative solution that could let users decide to which degree specific information on the phone should be exposed to a specific person. Although there are a handful of studies that investigate users' behaviors when sharing their phones, how users react to such access control in the app ecosystem has not been figured out. In this paper, we conducted a fine-grained survey with 165 participants, including German and Chinese to investigate users' attitudes towards smartphone sharing as owner and as guest, as well as how they work with such access control mechanism. We also propose four persona guests for the user study, including stranger, acquaintance, close people and kids, which underlie this research, to understand to what extent users expose apps, sensors, and resources for diverse guests.

Keywords: Privacy · Mobile · Access control · Survey

1 Introduction

Even though smartphones are personal devices, phone sharing has proven to be popular at different levels among users [1, 2]. Previous user studies on phone sharing [1–4] were mainly conducted in the form of interviews, semi-interviews, focus groups, etc., covering understanding users' concerns, attitudes and practices when sharing smartphone. These studies have investigated sharing behavior aspects such as the frequency of sharing, location, reasons, and permissiveness by application or data type or the relationships involved. However, mobile phones carry data such as private photos, contacts, and messages, information such as browsing history, and they are equipped

© Springer International Publishing Switzerland 2016
C. Stephanidis (Ed.): HCII 2016 Posters, Part I, CCIS 617, pp. 494–499, 2016.
DOI: 10.1007/978-3-319-40548-3_82

with apps. The way in which these may be configured with personal setting choices, so as to respond to privacy and sharing preferences, is addressed in this paper.

Access control for data is an alternative solution that could let users decide to which degree specific information on the phone should be exposed to a specific person. To address such issues, manufacturers and third-party app providers have incorporated access control into smartphone settings. They provide mechanisms and modes of operations to support access control at different levels, so that people could set limits on who could see or use data, sensors and apps. With iPhone, user could define and block several interactive areas in the settings under the category of accessibility, individually for different apps. The iOS also has a "Restriction" feature that limits specific functions and apps. Although there are a handful of studies that investigate users' behaviors when sharing their phone, how users react to such access control in the app ecosystem has not been figured out. To investigate the user behavior, we divide user into owner and guest, and classify their activities of sharing. Four scenarios indicate sharing behaviors, (1) the owner lends the phone to a borrower; (2) the owner does not give the phone to the borrower, instead, he keeps the phone and navigates it following the borrower's requests; (3) the owner shares the screen with the borrower, and they use the phone together; (4) there is no owner and borrower, that is, a group of people (for example family members) share the (hence "public") phone.

In this paper, we mainly discuss sharing issues of the first and second scenarios. We conducted a fine-grained survey with 165 participants, including German and Chinese to investigate users' attitudes towards smartphone sharing as owner and as guest, as well as how they work with such access control mechanism. We also propose four persona guests for the user study, including stranger, acquaintance, close people and kids, which underlie this research, to understand to what extent users expose apps, sensors, and resources for diverse guests. Based on control mechanisms and the diversity of guests, we explore how phone owners set limits for guests and what phone borrowers expect in terms of privacy protection from the access control provided by the system. In the past, in particular the parental control as one of the sub topics of phone sharing has gained researchers' attentions. Increasingly, children are playing with the smartphone, but parents may be unaware of the dangers faced by children. Therefore, we also explore how adults restrict apps, sensors and resources for the use of a phone by kids. The paper presents a preliminary analysis of the data and discusses the results and implications for usable privacy and interface design.

2 Survey Design and Demography

We recruited 165 participants from Wenjuan website and Prometei, which are influential online crowdsourcing platforms. Participants are required to be the smartphone owner. The questionnaire includes but not limited to four parts: (1) basic demographics; (2) users' attitudes towards phone sharing as owner; (3) users' attitudes towards multiple user account as owner; and (4) users' attitudes towards phone sharing as guest.

In total, we had 69.1 % males and 30.9 % females. Their ages were distributed and covered all age groups but 66.7 % were in the range of 18 to 24. There was a bias towards higher education levels and 94.0 % were under a higher education.

3   Results and Discussion

3.1   Attitudes Towards Phone Sharing as Owner

In this part, we discuss frequency of sharing behaviors, phone owner's concern about the data on phone, lend time, and the data, sensors and resources that the owner would like to block to borrower.

We used the semantic differential technique with paring of Never (score 1)/Always (score 7) to form the answer of sharing behavior frequency in 7-scale with 4 as neutral score. We listed four sharing behaviors, including "lending my smartphone", "borrowing other's smartphone", "sharing screen of my smartphone", "sharing screen of other's smartphone" and "using a public smartphone at home". The median of "using a public smartphone at home" case is 1. Except for this case, the median of other four cases are all 2. Results showed that phone sharing is not that frequent, partly due to participants' no need of sharing (almost everyone owns a smartphone), and partly due to fear of privacy leakage.

To go one step further, we asked participants to describe how much they were concerned about their data on smartphone. The answers were formed using Weak (score 1)/Strong (score 7) pair. From the responses of phone owner's concern about the data on smartphone, we found that they were concerned about the data when lending phone to stranger (median = 7), felt neutral when lending phone to acquaintance and kids (median = 4), but felt weak concern about close people (median = 2).

Besides, the participants were asked to indicate how long they would like to let people use their phone. Most of them (57.6 %) chose to lend phone to stranger for less than 10 min. 25.8 % and 18.5 % of participants chose to lend to acquaintance for less than 10 min and 10 to 30 min respectively, which is similar to lending phone to kids (20 %: 10 min, 13.8 %: 10 to 30 min). With regard to close people like friends or parents, rare of them (1.2 %) did not want to lend the device. 12.7 % and 10.0 % of participants would like to lend the phone to close people for one day and one week respectively.

Finally, we also explored how people restricted resources/sensors and apps for each guest. As shown in Fig. 1, we found that most of participants blocked resources/sensors more strict to stranger, acquaintance, and kids than close people overall, which is similar to the cases of exposing apps (as shown in Fig. 2). Among these resources, people protected call history more than other resources. Among all apps listed, participants gave more protection for four types of apps, including social networking apps (like Facebook, Instagram, and WhatsApp), calendar (also email, notebook, etc.), Settings, as well as photo and video apps.

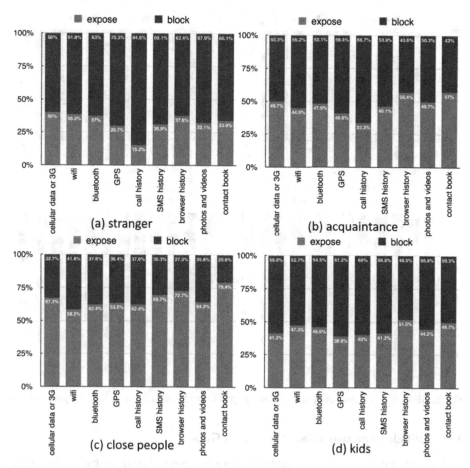

Fig. 1. Responses on restricting and exposing resources/sensors for each guest persona (Color figure online)

3.2 Attitudes Towards Multiple User Account as Owner

We explored users' attitudes as owner towards the necessity of using Multiple User Account (MUA), and their intention to clean guests' trace. In this part, all the answers were formed using Weak (score 1)/Strong (score 7) pair. The median of using MUA for stranger is 7, for acquaintance and kids respectively 5, for close people 2. We found that MUA is necessary for users when lending phone to distant relationships or kids.

When asked how much they would like to use one-button function to clear guests' trace instead of guest clearing trace by themselves manually, more than 67.8 % participants gave scores higher than 4 (The median is 6).

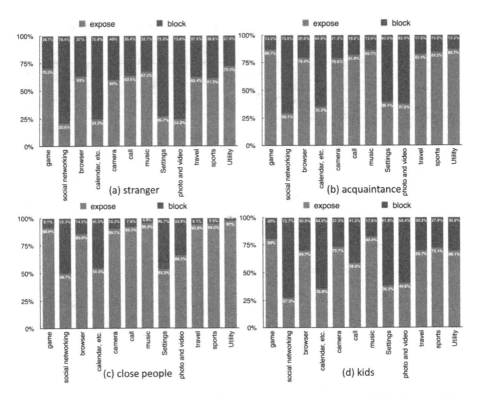

Fig. 2. Responses on restricting and exposing apps for each guest persona (Color figure online)

3.3   Attitudes Towards Phone Sharing as Guest

In this part, we explored users' attitudes towards phone sharing as guest. We asked participants to recall their experience of borrowing a smartphone, and image that they were the guest. We explored their protection actions, concerns about the usage history/log, intention of clearing trace as guest, feelings on the way of other's using multiple user account.

With regard to taking actions to erase their usage trace before they return smartphone, 64.4 % of participants said that they tried to do something, like logging out and deleting the number they dialed. The rest of them expressed that they did not take any actions, partly they thought they did not need to (21.2 %), partly they thought they needed to (6.1 %), and partly they did not become aware of privacy issues (7.9 %).

When asked how much they were concerned about their trace that would be seen by device owner, 37.6 % felt strong concern. The answers were formed using Weak (score 1)/Strong (score 7) pair. The median is 6.

We also asked people to indicate how much they would like to use a one-button function to clear their trace. The answers were formed using Weak (score 1)/Strong (score 7) pair. The median is 6 and most of them (68.4 %) gave scores more than 4. Results showed that people had strong desire to have one click interface to easily protect their privacy as guest.

Finally, we asked how much people felt that they were untrusted by owner (stranger, acquaintance and close people) if the owner used multiple user account in front of them. We did not consider kids since it is not applicable in this case. We used to the semantic differential technique with paring of Weak (score 1)/Strong (score 7) to form answers. The results showed that most of participants (73.4 %) gave scores less than or equal to 4 to stranger owner, and 74.6 % to acquaintance owner. However, 48.5 % participants had negative feelings and gave scores more than 4 to close people owner.

4   Conclusion and Future Work

To investigate users' attitudes towards access control of smartphone, we organize and conduct a survey to understand users' attitudes towards phone sharing as owner, attitudes towards multiple user account as owner, and attitudes towards phone sharing as guest. Results showed that both owner and guest intent to protect their personal data. People gave different protection to resources/sensors and apps. The resources/sensors and apps that contain more personal data have obtained more protection. Multiple user account is necessary for users when lending phone to distant relationships or kids. In the near future, we will compare and analyze people's attitudes towards access control of smartphone and tablet.

References

1. Karlson, A.K., Brush, A.J., Schechter, S.: Can I borrow your phone? Understanding concerns when sharing mobile phones. In: Proceedings of the SIGCHI Conference on Human Factors in Computing Systems, pp. 1647–1650. ACM (2009)
2. Liu, Y., Rahmati, A., Jang, H., Huang, Y., Zhong, L., Zhang, Y., Zhang, S.: Design, realization, and evaluation of xshare for impromptu sharing of mobile phones. IEEE Trans. Mobile Comput. **9**, 1682–1696 (2010)
3. Hang, A., von Zezschwitz, E., De Luca, A., Hussmann, H.: Too much information!: user attitudes towards smartphone sharing. In: Proceedings of the 7th Nordic Conference on Human-Computer Interaction: Making Sense Through Design, pp. 284–287. ACM (2012)
4. King, J.: "How come I'm allowing strangers to go through my phone?" Smartphones and privacy expectations. In: Symposium on Usable Privacy and Security (SOUPS) (2013)

Human Modelling and Ergonomics

Instruction of Digital Human Models Through Interaction in Immersive Virtual Environments

Andreas Geiger[(✉)], Elisabeth Brandenburg, and Rainer Stark

Virtual Product Creation, Fraunhofer IPK,
Pascalstraße 8-9, 10587 Berlin, Germany
andreas.geiger@ipk.fraunhofer.de

Abstract. The use of digital human models is nowadays complex and needs specific knowledge due to its complex user interface. This paper presents a possible approach to instruct digital human models in virtual reality environments. In order to instruct a digital human model we use hand and finger tracking technology to detect virtual grasps. These virtual grasps are used to instruct the digital human model. Furthermore this paper suggests and presents an architecture with a data exchange file format for the communication between digital human models, virtual reality and hand tracking.

Keywords: Virtual reality · Intuitive interaction · Virtual grasping · Digital human models · Usability · Architecture

1 Digital Human Models for Ergonomic Assessment

The use of Digital Human Models (DHM) in major manufacturing companies like the automotive industry is nowadays considered to be state of the art. The type of DHMs depends on the use cases, e.g. ergonomic assessment of assembly stations or new cockpit designs. The primary goal of DHMs is a 3D representation of the human body [1]. Implementations of body parts, muscles and degrees of freedom differ in their level of detail between the DHMs. All DHMs share one advantage they can be used to analyze both, human postures and motions. The DHM IMMA, which we have focused on in this paper, provides a technological approach, which allows "automatic path planning, to find collision free motions of moving objects" [2]. This function increases the usability of the DHM-software regarding instruction expense.

Nonetheless, assessments with DHMs need to include the digital product, its environment and the human model. Typically the user has to use a mouse and keyboard to instruct the DHMs in order to be able to assess the relevant task sequence. Especially the configuration of different grip types is complex and not straightforward. The user has to make various decisions such as whether to use one or two hands and where the grip points on the object are. Furthermore the user has to determine the grip type and the hand aperture. Illustrating one example, the IMMA manikin provides eleven grip types. In fact, basic research has even identified 16 different grip types [3]. A task analysis with IMMA has revealed that it requires at least nine interaction steps

© Springer International Publishing Switzerland 2016
C. Stephanidis (Ed.): HCII 2016 Posters, Part I, CCIS 617, pp. 503–507, 2016.
DOI: 10.1007/978-3-319-40548-3_83

considering a best case scenario, 18 steps in a worst case scenario and furthermore eight decisions are necessary, to define how to grasp the object.

1.1 Objectives

Until now IMMA is instructed via mouse and keyboard. Using these traditional input devices is very ineffective and requires well-trained users that are experienced in working with the software. Especially the instruction of grasping requires experience over time because we need to know how human grasping works [4]. This way the so-called "right" grasp can only be determined through trial-and-error method. Therefore, we need to develop an easier instruction concept for the grasp configuration to instruct DHMs.

This paper introduces a new concept, which enables users to intuitively instruct the digital human model through interacting in a Virtual Reality (VR) environment. The Virtual Reality (VR) environment displays the objects on which the ergonomic assessment is performed. In order to interact with the virtual environment, the software user can either work with a head mounted display (HMD) or a professional multi-sided CAVE (Cave Automatic Virtual Environment [5]). Within these environments a tracking device traces the users' fingers and hands. The user performs the different grip types in relation to the necessary objects.

Subsequently the different performed tasks are exported to an exchange file, which the DHM can read. As a result the manikin simulates the according movements and furthermore analyses them based on standardized ergonomic criteria.

In the following sections of the paper we introduce the statement of problem in more detail. After that we propose a solution, which includes Virtual Reality and the finger tracking device. Furthermore we discuss the recognition of virtual grasps, our suggested architecture and finally we will provide a short outlook, which includes possible steps for the future integration of this technology into working environments.

2   Interactions in Virtual Environments to Instruct the DHM

2.1   Virtual Reality Environments

Head Mounted Displays as well as a professional CAVE provide a VR-environment. There are differences from a technological perspective. While users wear HMDs on their heads like glasses with the display right in front of the eyes, a CAVE can be characterized as a room, which people can enter. In here projectors screen the virtual scene on the five calibrated walls and users can move within the room while wearing active shutter glasses and thus ensuring a stereoscopic view. Additionally an optical tracking system tracks the marker on the glasses for calculating the position and direction of the users' view. This enables the system to render each frame for the individual perspective of the user. For our research we have access to HMDs as well as a five-sided CAVE.

2.2 Hand and Finger Tracking Device

In order to be able to detect different grip types it is necessary to gain information about the hand and finger positions as well as rotational joint information in the VR environment. Our solution uses a Leap Motion with the Orion Beta 3.1.1 software to track the hand and finger position. It is a low-cost optical tracking system, which provides rotational information about the joints as well as translational information about the position of the real hand and fingers. It is also able to map this information in the virtual reality environment (Fig. 1 left side). Furthermore Leap Motion offers an asset for Unity3D, a game development engine, to easily access the hand and finger information in the virtual environment directly.

2.3 Virtual Grasping

There are several works, which describe approaches for virtual grasping [6–8]. Whereas their main objective was to optimize virtual grasping, we want to shift towards an approach, which describes how we can implement virtual grasping as a method to instruct a DHM. To detect the different grip types, we use a pattern-matching algorithm. Currently three different grip types are integrated into the application. It is able to detect a power grip, a finger pinch as well as a lateral finger pinch (Fig. 1 top, right). In order to detect the different grip types we use the following data sets: (1) The distance between the surface of the hands as well as fingers and the objects surface to detect a contact. (2) The orientation of each finger joint.

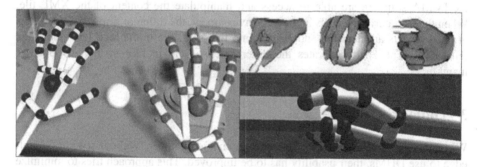

Fig. 1. Left: Leap Motion virtual hands in Unity3D. Top, right: The different grip-types, which are implemented from left to right: Finger Pinch; Powergrap, Lateral Finger Pinch. Bottom, right: Lateral finger pinch grabbing cylinder in VR.

For example, the algorithm to detect the lateral finger pinch (Fig. 1 bottom, right) uses both sets of data. If the distance between the surface of the fingers and surface of the object is smaller than a certain, definable length and if the angle between the tip of the thumb and the tip index finger is bigger than 80°, the algorithm recognizes the lateral finger pinch.

2.4   Software Architecture

We use Unity3D V5.3 as an authoring tool, which the Leap Motion is connected with. Unity3D also has a native HMD (Oculus Rift CV) integration and thus it is possible to display it in the CAVE (Fig. 2).

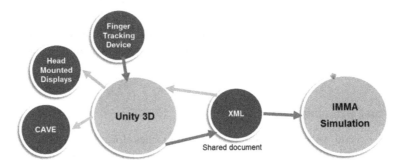

Fig. 2. Architecture with a shared document, which is accessible for both Unity3D as well as the IMMA software. The recognized grip types and the relevant object are written into the xml file.

An HMD as well as a CAVE can visualize the virtual scene. Furthermore, the finger tracking device Leap Motion is connected to Unity3D. Our grip type detection algorithms are implemented in Unity3D. In order to be able to use the developed software with different DHMs we chose an XML file as a shared document. Unity3D as well as the IMMA software are able to access and manipulate the content of the XML file. When the user performs tasks in the VR-environment, the different grip types as well as gripped objects are detected and written into the XML file in the high level language (HLL) [9]. The HLL generates the different tasks and in turn instruct the IMMA manikin.

3   Outlook

Wischniewski [10] suggests that in order to enable engineers without specific knowledge to use DHMs, their usability has to be improved. This approach tries to minimize the complexity to define the different grip types and its configurations for assembly instructions of manikins. Yet, gaps remain in several areas of research.

The software works well for the integrated grip types. Nevertheless the finger tracking device is not accurate and stable enough due to the fact that it is an optical tracking system. This means occlusions occur when all fingers are in the same plane from the tracking device. This leads to partially incorrect finger positions, joint rotations and a twitching of fingers. In addition we have noticed problems with the correct thumb recognition. Thus, the software cannot fully satisfy our demands.

In order to be able to completely use the VR environment to instruct the IMMA manikin, we need to integrate the algorithms for the seven remaining grip types into

Unity3D. Furthermore it is necessary to develop a user interface, which avoids forcing the user to switch between the VR environment and the traditional 2D display.

Additionally we will integrate a feedback system for the user when the software detects a virtual grip. Therefore we plan future research on different feedback systems such as haptic or visual feedback [11]. As already explained the Leap Motion does not provide enough accuracy regarding finger and hand position data. Thus, we will integrate other tracking devices such as data gloves, which should provide more accurate and stable data.

References

1. Duffy, V.G. (ed.): ICDHM 2011. LNCS, vol. 6777. Springer, Heidelberg (2011)
2. Hanson, L., Delfs, N., Gustafsson, S., et al.: IMMA – intelligently moving manikins in automotive applications. In: Proceeding of Third International Summit on Human Simulation (2014)
3. Cutkosky, M.R.: On grasp choice, grasp models, and the design of hands for manufacturing tasks. IEEE Trans. Robot. Automat. **5**(3), 269–279 (1989). doi:10.1109/70.34763
4. Geiger, A., Brandenburg, E., Rothenburg, U.: Ergonomische Montageabsicherung durch digitale Men-schmodelle mit kognitiver Handlungsplanung. In: Wienrich, C., Zander, T., Gramann, K. (eds.) Trends in Neuroergonomics. 11. Berliner Werkstatt Mensch-Maschine-Systeme, Berlin, 7.–9. Oktober 2015, Tagungsband, Universitätsverlag der TU Berlin, Berlin, pp. 289–292 (2015)
5. Cruz-Neira, C., Sandin, D.J., DeFanti, T.A.: Surround-screen projection-based virtual reality. In: Whitton, M.C. (ed.) The 20th Annual Conference, pp. 135–142
6. Wan, H., Luo, Y., Gao, S., et al.: Realistic virtual hand modeling with applications for virtual grasping. In: Brown, J. (ed.) Proceedings of the 2004 ACM SIGGRAPH International Conference on Virtual Reality Continuum and Its Applications in Industry, pp. 81–87. ACM, New York, NY (2004)
7. Ullmann, T., Sauer, J.: Intuitive virtual grasping for non haptic environments. In: Barsky, B. A., Shinagawa, Y., Wang, W. (eds.) The Eighth Pacific Conference on Computer Graphics and Applications, Hong Kong, China, 3–5 October 2000: Proceedings, pp. 373–357. IEEE Computer Society, Los Alamitos, Calif. (2000)
8. Jacobs, J., Froehlich, B.: A soft hand model for physically-based manipulation of virtual objects. In: Hirose, M. (ed.) IEEE Virtual Reality Conference (VR), 2011, Singapore, 19–23 March 2011: Proceedings, pp. 11–18. IEEE, Piscataway, NJ (2011)
9. Mårdberg, P., Carlson, J.S., Bohlin, R., et al.: Using a formal high-level language and an automated manikin to automatically generate assembly instructions. IJHFMS **4**(3/4), 233 (2014). doi:10.1504/IJHFMS.2014.067180
10. Wischniewski, S.: Digitale Ergonomie 2025: Trends und Strategien zur Gestaltung gebrauchstauglicher Produkte und sicherer, gesunder und wettbewerbsfähiger sozio-technischer Arbeitssysteme; Forschung Projekt F 2313; [Abschlussbericht]. Bundesanstalt für Arbeitsschutz und Arbeitsmedizin, Dortmund, Berlin, Dresden (2013)
11. Prachyabrued, M., Borst, C.W.: Visual feedback for virtual grasping. In: Lécuyer, A., Lindeman, R., Steinicke, F. (eds.) IEEE Symposium on 3D User Interface 2014, Minneapolis, Minnesota, USA, 29–30 March, 2014: Proceedings, pp. 19–26. IEEE, Piscataway, NJ (2014)

Image Overlay Support with 3DCG Organ Model for Robot-Assisted Laparoscopic Partial Nephrectomy

Masanao Koeda[1(✉)], Kiminori Mizushino[2], Katsuhiko Onishi[1],
Hiroshi Noborio[1], Takahiro Kunii[3], Masatoshi Kayaki[1],
Atsushi Sengiku[4], Atsuro Sawada[4], Takeshi Yoshikawa[4],
Yoshiyuki Matsui[4], and Osamu Ogawa[4]

[1] Osaka Electro-Communication University, Osaka, Japan
koeda@isc.osakac.ac.jp
[2] Embedded Wings Co. Ltd., Osaka, Japan
[3] Kashina System Co. Ltd., Shiga, Japan
[4] Kyoto University, Kyoto, Japan

Abstract. We have developed a surgery support system for robot-assisted laparoscopic partial nephrectomy. In our system, a 3D computer graphics (3DCG) model, which includes a kidney, arteries, veins, and tumors, is saved separately and overlaid on the surgeon's viewing endoscopic camera image through the operator's console monitor in real time. The position and orientation of the 3DCG model is calculated from the optical flow of the endoscopic camera images, and the model is moved semi-automatically. The display condition of each part of the 3DCG model is independently controlled anytime by using a mouse, rotary controllers, or key board.

Keywords: Surgery · RALPN · 3DCG · Overlay · Transparent

1 Introduction

In recent years, robot-assisted laparoscopic partial nephrectomy (RALPN) has been conducted in several hospitals. From April 2016, RALPN will be covered by the health insurance sector in Japan, and RALPN surgeries are expected to increase sharply. However, the positions of blood vessels, the size of tumors, the amount of visceral fat, etc. differs with each patient, and a proper guide is needed depending on each patient for safe and rapid surgical operation.

Isotani developed a simulator for performing partial nephrectomy by using a 3D computer graphics (3DCG) model of organs. In addition, he developed the RALPN support system by using the 3DCG [1, 2].

We have developed a surgery support system for RALPN. In our system, a 3DCG model, which includes a kidney, arteries, veins, and tumors, is overlaid on the operator's console monitor in real time. The overview of our system is illustrated in Fig. 1. The position and orientation of the 3DCG model is calculated through the optical flow of the endoscopic camera images, and the model is moved semi-automatically.

© Springer International Publishing Switzerland 2016
C. Stephanidis (Ed.): HCII 2016 Posters, Part I, CCIS 617, pp. 508–513, 2016.
DOI: 10.1007/978-3-319-40548-3_84

2 Method

The three phases of the surgical procedure of RALPN are briefly described as follows.

1. Expose important arteries and veins connected to the target kidney, and mark them by using a colored tape (P-1)
2. Remove perinephric fat, and search and identify the tumor (P-2)
3. Pinch the arteries for warm ischemic kidney and remove tumor (P-3)

In each phase, the surgeons focus on particular parts. That is, in P-1, the blood vessels are focused on; in P-2, the arteries are addressed; in P-3, arteries, ureter and renal pelvis are given importance. The renal parenchyma and tumor are considered at all times (Table 1).

However, the parts are buried in a lot of fat tissue. The operators must remove the fat tissue and dig the target areas carefully. For smooth operation, it is important to know the direction for digging, and thus reduce the time for searching each part in each phase. Our system supports the overlaying of the 3DCG model on the surgeon's viewing endoscopic camera image. Figure 1 shows an example of a 3DCG model, which is used in certain cases. The 3DCG model is generated from DICOM images of CT scans, and each generated parts is saved separately. The display condition of each part of the model is independently controlled anytime (Fig. 2). By using a mouse, rotary controllers, or key board, the operator of our system can easily and intuitively change the state of display of each 3DCG model, whether it is displaying, hiding, or making one or all parts transparent.

Table 1. Focused parts in each RALPN phase

	Artery	Vein	Ureter	Organ	Tumor
P-1	✓	✓		✓	✓
P-2	✓			✓	✓
P-3	✓		✓	✓	✓

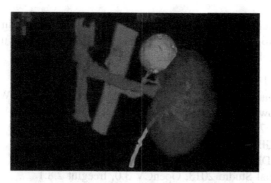

Fig. 1. Example of 3DCG model of a patient's kidney with cancer (Brown: Organ, Orange: Tumor, Red: Artery, Blue: Vein, Yellow: Ureter) (Color figure online)

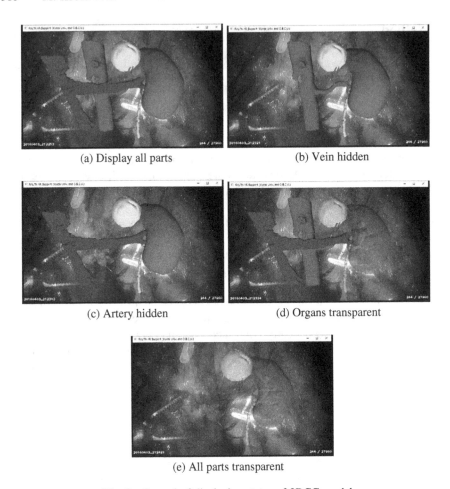

(a) Display all parts   (b) Vein hidden

(c) Artery hidden   (d) Organs transparent

(e) All parts transparent

Fig. 2. Control of displaying status of 3DCG model

3 System Overview

Our support system was practically demonstrated four times in RALPN, from November 2014 to August 2015. Our system was improved and upgraded in each experiment. The following configuration is the latest version of our system (Fig. 3).

Computer and Developing Environment
   Model: MouseComputer, NEXTGEAR-NOTE i420BA3-SP-W7
   OS: Windows8.1 Professional 64 [bit]
   CPU: Corei7-4710MQ
   RAM: 8 [GB]
   GPU: NVIDIA GeForce GTX 860M
   Tools: Visual Studio 2013, OpenCV 3.0, freeglut 2.8.1

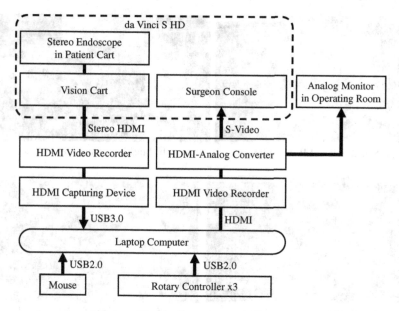

Fig. 3. System overview

HDMI Video Recorder
  Model: Century Corporation, KANROKU-HD
  Resolution and Frame Rate: 1980 × 1080 [px], 30 [fps]
Video Capturing Device
  Model: FEBON, FEBON198
  I/O: HDMI to USB3.0
  Resolution and Frame Rate: 1980 × 1080 [px], 30 [fps]
Rotary Controller
  Model: Griffin Technology, PowerMate
  Interface: USB 2.0

4 Image Processing

In our system, the image is generated as follows.

1. Capture the stereo endoscope video image to the laptop computer and separate the left and right video images (Fig. 4-(a))
2. Convert to hue, saturation, and value (HSV) images, and create a mask for surgical tools based on the saturation value
3. Mask the video image to reduce the noisy flows (Fig. 4-(b))
4. Calculate optical flows (Fig. 4-(c))
5. Overlay the 3DCG model on the video image and move it with the optical flow to x, y, and z translation and vertical axis rotation (Fig. 4-(d))

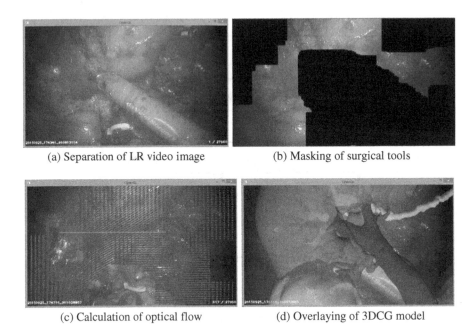

(a) Separation of LR video image   (b) Masking of surgical tools

(c) Calculation of optical flow   (d) Overlaying of 3DCG model

Fig. 4. Image processing

6. Move the 3DCG manually by using a mouse and control the transparency of each part of the 3DCG by using rotary controllers
7. Output the overlaid image to the surgical operator's monitor and operating room's monitor (Fig. 5)

A 3DCG model is created through DICOM by using 3D Slicer [3] under a medical doctor's direction.

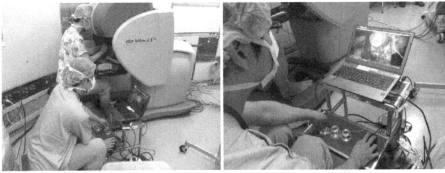

(a) Surgeon using a da Vinci (behind)   (b) Controlling the appearance of 3DCG in
and operator of our system (front)   consultation with the surgeon using rotary
                                             controllers and mouse

Fig. 5. Operation of our system

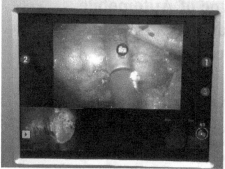
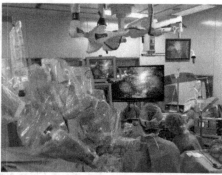

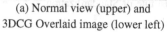

(a) Normal view (upper) and   (b) Analog monitor in operating room
3DCG Overlaid image (lower left)   (rightmost small one)

Fig. 6. Display of our support system

5 Experiment and Conclusion

We conducted four experiments from November 2014 to August 2015. Figures 5, and 6 show the photographs of the experiment. Our support system worked appropriately. According to the surgeon, the system was especially helpful when a tumor is located in a difficult position or when a patient has excess visceral fat. In future, we will aim for robustness and correct tracking of a 3DCG model.

References

1. Isotani, S., et al.: Feasibility and accuracy of computational robot-assisted partial nephrectomy planning by virtual partial nephrectomy analysis. Int. J. Urol. **22**, 439–446 (2015)
2. https://www.youtube.com/watch?v=ZFBKKxZLEeA
3. 3D Slicer. http://www.slicer.org/

Research on the Type of Automobile Controlling Device and Its Ergonomic Design Parameters

Siyuan Liu[1(✉)], Yinxia Li[1], Hui-min Hu[2], and Chaoyi Zhao[2]

[1] School of Mechanical Engineering, Zhengzhou University,
Zhengzhou 450001, China
1216620166@qq.com
[2] Ergonomics Laboratory China National Institute of Standardization,
Beijing 100000, China

Abstract. Automobile controlling device is an important part of the driver - vehicle system. A good ergonomic design of the device can not only provide a convenient and comfortable operation environment, but also greatly reduce any faulty operation and working pressure on the driver. The mainly works on the type of automobile controlling device and its ergonomic design parameters. Firstly, given the extensive domestic and foreign relevant information, we preliminarily categorized the auto control device into manual control, foot control, voice control and eye control in line with the taxonomy of human manipulation. All kinds of specific control device are listed afterwards. We also designed the questionnaire on the classification method, the usage and the influence of corresponding design parameters on drivers' comfort degree. Secondly, by introducing the expert consultation method, we employed fourteen experienced designers in Zhejiang Geely Automobile Research Institute as consulting experts to investigate the preliminary controlling device type and its ergonomic design parameters. According to the investigation result, the type of automobile controlling device and its ergonomic design parameters were determined finally. The research results can provide reference for the design and evaluation of the automobile controlling device. Moreover, it can be model for related ergonomic research in other fields.

Keywords: Ergonomics · Automobile · Controlling device · Expert consultation method

1 Introduction

The ergonomic design problem of vehicle manipulation device can easily cause fatigue driving, which reflects the driving efficiency and even leads to poor health. There are no materials about the classification of vehicle control device and the parameters of its ergonomic design [1–6].

© Springer International Publishing Switzerland 2016
C. Stephanidis (Ed.): HCII 2016 Posters, Part I, CCIS 617, pp. 514–519, 2016.
DOI: 10.1007/978-3-319-40548-3_85

This article mainly investigates the classification of vehicle control device and the parameters of its ergonomic design. The results can provide basic information for vehicle control device types, standards and regulations on parameters of ergonomic design, and reference for the ergonomic design and evaluation of control device.

2   The Determination of Vehicle Control Device Types

Through collecting and organizing the material about the standard and specification of relevant control devices as well as the new control technology [7–10], vehicle control system is initially divide into: manual control device, foot motion control device, voice control device and eye control device according to the human operating part and various types of specific control device are preliminarily listed. The following is an investigation about classification method of the vehicle control devices and the using frequency of each type.

2.1   The Implementation Process of the Expert Consultation Method

Aiming at the classification method of the vehicle control device and the use frequency of each type, an expert consultation method is applied to research. The basic principle of this method is to design a questionnaire according to the initial classification of the vehicle control device and the user frequency of the specific control device in each category; to select senior experts in the relevant fields for anonymous advice; and to determine whether the preliminary scheme is appropriate or not according to the consultation results.

2.2   Results and Analysis

Through analyzing the results of the expert consultation, we can get the results about the use frequency of the vehicle control device. Refer to Table 1.

$\bar{E}$ represents the degree of concentration. σ represents the discrete degree.

Mode on behalf of all the number, said the expert consultation group of data more percentage of the rank.

3   Determination of Ergonomic Design Parameters of Vehicle Control Device

The same as 2 sections.

Table 1. Auto control device using frequency parameters of the statistical tables

Name		$\overline{E}$	σ	Mode
Manual	knob	4.07	0.92	4
control device	button	3.79	0.97	3
	key	3.79	0.97	4
	hand wheel	4.93	0.27	5
	runner	1.50	1.22	1
	toggle switch	1.71	0.83	1
	rocker switch	2.64	1.34	2
	crank	1.36	0.93	1
	key switch	3.64	1.39	4
	handle	3.21	1.48	4
	slide switch	4.93	0.27	5
	thumb wheel	1.93	1.00	1
	label switch	3.07	0.83	3
	Push - pull switch	3.57	1.28	5
	lever switch	2.14	1.10	1
	Touchscreen control	2.21	1.37	1
	gesture control	2.93	1.14	3
	slide switch	1.36	0.84	1
Foot control	Pedal button	1.57	1.34	1
device	pedal plate	4.93	0.27	5
Voice control device		2.14	1.29	1
Eye control device		1.14	0.95	1

3.1   Results and Analysis

Statistical parameters of consulting results refer to Table 2.

Table 2. Auto control device ergonomic design parameters results statistical tables

Name of index		$\overline{E}$	σ	Mode
knob	Diameter D	4.07	0.83	5
	Height H	3.93	0.83	3
	Manipulate force F	3.79	0.97	3
button	Diameter D	3.64	0.74	3
	Displacement S	3.86	0.77	4
	Manipulate force F	3.79	0.97	3
	Nowel N	3.71	0.91	3
key	Length L	3.71	0.73	4
	Width W	3.71	0.73	4
	Displacement S	3.79	0.80	3
	Manipulate force F	3.79	0.97	3
	Nowel N	3.71	0.91	3
hand wheel	The hand wheel diameter D	4.27	0.61	4
	tip diameter d	4.07	0.83	4
	Nowel N	4.21	0.97	5
key	Key height H	3.57	0.65	3
	angular displacement A	3.71	0.73	4
	Nowel N	3.79	0.89	4
hand shank	Diameter D	3.50	1.29	3
	Minimum diameter d1	3.36	1.22	3

Table 2. *(Continued)*

	Maximum diameter d2	3.36	1.22	3
	Length H	3.50	1.22	4
	Manipulation force F	3.79	1.42	5
joystick	Ball diameter D	4.00	0.68	4
	Longitudinal travel A（d-1）	4.07	0.62	4
	cross travel A（d-2）	4.00	0.68	4
	Manipulation force F	4.14	0.95	5
thumb wheel	diameter D	3.64	1.01	3
	High tooth H	3.57	0.85	3
	Tooth spacing L	3.50	0.65	3
	Tooth width W	3.71	0.73	4
	Rim exposed E	3.93	0.92	4
	Nowel N	3.93	1.00	5
label switch	Length L	3.71	0.83	3
	Width W	3.79	0.80	3
	Displacement S	3.71	0.83	3
	Manipulation force F	3.86	1.03	5
The size of the hand	The size of the hand	3.36	1.34	3
Touch screen size	Touch screen size	3.57	1.22	4
touch area	touch area	3.57	1.34	4
Touch time	Touch time	3.71	1.38	4
Pedal plate	Step length L	3.93	1.27	4
	Tread Width W	3.86	1.29	4
	displacement S	4.00	1.30	4
	Manipulation force F	4.14	1.35	5
	Nowel N	4.00	1.36	5

4 Conclusion

In this study, the expert consultation method is used to vehicle ry out consultation on 14 experienced designers and ergonomics, we aimed at the classification method of vehicle steering device and the design problem of ergonomics. The research result showed that, as long as the design of the Advisory table is appropriate, the choice of expert consultants is appropriate. The results can be obtained by the expert consultation approach.

Acknowledgements. Fund program: the 12th five year plan "national science and technology support project" (2014BAK01B02).

References

1. GJB 2873-1997, Human engineering design manual for military equipment and facilities
2. GB/T 14775—93 Ergonomics Requirements for Manipulator
3. ISO 9355-3:2006, Ergonomic requirements for the design of displays and control actuators-Part 3: Control actuators
4. GB_T 15705-1995 Trucks-Operating position dementions of driver
5. Li S.: Fatigue driving characteristics and parameters extraction of. Shandong University (2013)
6. Hu J.: Comfort of manipulate comfort index based automobile clutch. Hefei University of Technology (2014)
7. Sun X.: Tracking and identification technology research video-based gestures. Donghua University (2014)
8. Bin, Y., Zuo, Y., Tan Z., Xie B.: A non-contact gesture control car music player. UXPA Chinese. In: User Friendly 2014 Eleventh China-cum UXPA User Experience Industry Annual Conference Proceedings, vol. 4. UXPA China (2014)
9. Yan, Y.: Design and implementation of audio and video bimodal vehicle voice control system. South China University of Technology (201)
10. Yang C.: Based on near-infrared light non-contact vision technology research tracking. Shandong University (2012)
11. Xiao, J., Douglas, D., Lee, A.H., et al.: A del-phi evaluation of the factors influencing length of stay in Australian hospitals. Int. J. Health Plann. Manag. **12**, 207–218 (1997)
12. Craig, I.R., Burrett, G.L.: The design of a human factors questionnaire for cockpit assessment, pp. 16–20. IEE (1999)
13. Osborne, J., Collins, S., Ratcliffe, M., et al.: What "ideas-about-science" school be taught in school science? A delphi study of the expert community. J. Res. Sci. Teach. **40**, 692–720 (2003)

Comparison of Head and Face Anthropometric Characteristics Between Six Countries

Linghua Ran[⊠], Xin Zhang, Hui-min Hu, Hong Luo, and Taijie Liu

Ergonomics Laboratory,
China National Institute of Standardization,
Beijing 100191, China
ranlh@cnis.gov.cn

Abstract. The head and face dimensions for Japanese, Kenyans, South Koreans, The Netherlands, Americans and Chinese were compared. The Newman-Keuls (N-K) [3] test method was used to compare the difference of the average data between the six countries. The results showed that most of the head and face data between the six countries have significant difference ($p < 0.05$). The comparison shows that Asians' heads can be generally characterized as rounder than Africans', Americans' and European people's heads, and with a flatter back and forehead.

Keywords: Head · Face · Significant difference

1 Introduction

Head and face measurement data are important for technological design. The differences in head and face dimensions among various populations should be studied. The primary purpose of this research is to compare and discuss the presently available data for head and face dimensions among six countries, which covering Asia, South America, Africa and European.

2 Data Resources

The ISO/TR 7250-2:2010 "Basic human body measurements for technological design Part 2: Statistical summaries of body measurements from national populations" [1] provides statistical data for the head and face of the Adults, together with database background information. We select data from six countries to conduct the comparison (Table 1).

Measuring conditions and definitions of measurements in this Technical Report are the same as those described in ISO 7250-1 [2]. All the data were measured by manual. In this Technical Report, the following statistics are described for each measurement: sample size, mean, standard deviation (SD), and 1st, 5th, 50th, 95th and 99th percentile values. Population can be stratified by gender, age, location, occupation or education.

© Springer International Publishing Switzerland 2016
C. Stephanidis (Ed.): HCII 2016 Posters, Part I, CCIS 617, pp. 520–524, 2016.
DOI: 10.1007/978-3-319-40548-3_86

Table 1. Data resources

Countries	Data resource	Sample size	Age	Time period of examination
Japan	Japanese Industrial Standards Committee (JISC)	2880 males 2450 females	20–65	2004 to 2006
Kenya	Kenya Bureau of Standards (KEBS)	133 males 74 females	18–60	2006 to 2007
Korean	Korean Agency for Technology and Standards (KATS)	2613 males 2614 females	18–60	
The Netherlands	Nederlands Normalisatie-instituut (NEN)	560 males 680 females	18–65	1999 to 2000
United States	American National Standards Institute (ANSI)	1120 males 1260 females	18–65	1998 to 2000
China	China National Institute of Standardization (CNIS)	11164 males 11150 females	18–60	1986 to 1987

3 Data Analysis

3.1 Basic Data Statistical Analysis

Three important items including head length, head breadth and face length were selected as data to be compared. The average and standard deviation (SD), see Table 2.

Table 2. Basic data statistical analysis

	Items (mm)		China	Japan	Korea	Netherlands	USA	Kenya
Male	Head length	Average	184	191.4	184.5	197.7	199.9	200.2
		SD	7	6.7	6.9	8	10.4	8.4
	Head breadth	Average	154	163	159.8	153.2	154.5	152.3
		SD	6	6.1	6.1	5.9	6.7	6.4
	Face length	Average	119	122.9	120.3	122.9	121.3	115.7
		SD	7	6.3	7.7	7.4	8	7.7
female	Head length	Average	176	180.5	175.7	187.7	188.5	196.4
		SD	7	6.3	6.5	6.8	7.1	8.6
	Head breadth	Average	149	154.4	151.9	146	146.2	148.2
		SD	5	5.4	6.1	5.5	5.3	7.7
	Face length	Average	109	115.2	114.4	112.8	111.7	109.8
		SD	6	6	6.9	6.5	7.1	7.9

The Newman-Keuls (N-K) [3] test method was used to compare the difference of the average data between the six countries. The results showed that most of the head and face size data between the six countries have significant difference ($p < 0.05$) between different countries. For the head length, there is much larger difference between Chinese and Kenyans, Chinese and Americans than the different between Chinese and Japanese, Chinese and South Koreans (Figs. 1 and 2).

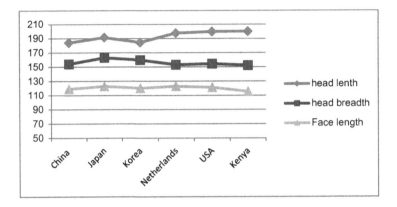

Fig. 1. Head and face data for males in six countries (Color figure online)

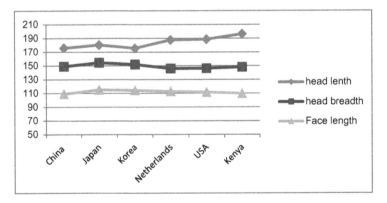

Fig. 2. Basic head and face data for females in six countries (Color figure online)

The two figures show that the head length of male in China, Japan and South Korea are smaller than the head length in Netherland, America and Kenya, but the head breadth in the three Asia Countries are larger than the men in Netherland, America and Kenya. For the female, the data also have the same characteristic with the male data.

3.2   Proportion for Head Data

The proportion of the head length and head breadth could roughly describe the shape of the head. The proportion values see Table 3 and Fig. 3.

Table 3. Proportion for head data

Head length/head breadth	China	Japan	Korea	Netherlands	USA	Kenya
Male	1.19	1.17	1.15	1.29	1.29	1.31
Female	1.18	1.17	1.16	1.29	1.29	1.33

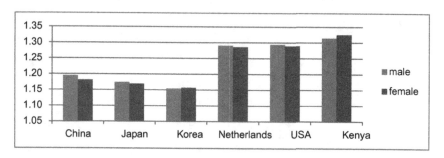

Fig. 3. Proportion for head data in six countries (Color figure online)

The two table and figure above show that the proportion of head length and head breadth in China, Japan and South Korea are between 1.15–1.19 and 1.16–1.18 for male and female respectively, but the the proportion for head data in Netherland, America and Kenya are between 1.29–1.31 and 1.29–1.32 for male and female, which is much larger than the three Asian countries. The comparison shows that Asians heads can be generally characterized as rounder than the people's head in Africa, America and European countries, and with a flatter back and forehead.

4   Results

The quantitative analyses of these head and face shape differences may be applied in many fields, including anthropometrics, product design and so on. When designing the products for the heads and face, such as headgears and headsets, the different anthropological head shape should be taken into consideration.

Acknowledgment. This work is supported by Quality Inspection Industry Research Special Funds for Public Welfare (201510042) and National Science and Technology Basic Research (2013FY110200).

References

1. ISO/TR 7250-2:2010 Basic human body measurements for technological design Part 2: Statistical summaries of body measurements from national populations (2010)
2. ISO 7250-1:2010 Basic human body measurements for technological design. Part 1: cBody measurement definitions and landmarks (2010)
3. Zhang, H., Xu, J.: Modern psychology and educational statistics. Beijing Normal University Press

Some Considerations of Age Estimation Method for "Augmented TV" Based on Posture of Gripping Tablet PC

Yuria Suzuki[1(✉)], Hiroyuki Kawakita[2], Michihiro Uehara[2],
Toshio Nakagawa[2], Hiromitsu Nishimura[1], and Akihiko Shirai[1]

[1] Kanagawa Institute of Technology, Atsugi, Japan
yurry89@gmail.com
[2] NHK Science and Technology Research Laboratories, Tokyo, Japan

Abstract. Augmented TV is an augmented reality system for making TV video to appear to come out of the screen. With Augmented TV, a television program is viewed through the camera of a tablet PC, and related content such as three-dimensional computer graphics (3DCG) is overlaid and displayed on the tablet PC. To provide users with age-targeted content, we have developed a height-estimation method based on the posture estimation method of Augmented TV, in which the height of the user is estimated from the elevation of the tablet PC off the ground. The estimated user height is then used to estimate his/her age. A public testing was carried out with around 90 elementary school students, and the data acquired was used to formulate a relationship between the elevation of the tablet PC and the height of the user. In the age estimation method proposed, the most statistically likely age for a given height was used. Therefore, we created a table containing the most statistically likely age for a given height, and the age of the user was estimated using the table. We evaluated the accuracy of both the height and age-estimations based the results of the public testing. The error in the age estimation based on the height-estimation was about 2 years of age. A rate of the age estimation in the case of using the age estimation method was about 60 %. In addition, developing a prototype application, we confirmed the effectiveness of both methods.

Keywords: Augmented TV · Context aware computing · Augmented reality · Age estimation

1 Introduction

Recent years have witnessed the appearance of services – such as that described in Ref. [1] – that use tablet personal PCs or smartphones (hereafter simply "tablets") as second screens to accompany TV screens. The field of "Augmented TV" [2] is among the areas of research that study this type of audiovisual experience. In Augmented TV, a television is watched through a tablet's built-in camera, thereby allowing the use of AR techniques to display data synchronized to television programs, such as 3DCG, in a way that accounts for position data.

© Springer International Publishing Switzerland 2016
C. Stephanidis (Ed.): HCII 2016 Posters, Part I, CCIS 617, pp. 525–530, 2016.
DOI: 10.1007/978-3-319-40548-3_87

Meanwhile, context-aware computing systems such as that described in Ref. [3] – which automatically deliver content appropriate for a user's current situation – have been a focus of recent attention. This suggests the attractive possibility that Augmented TV methods might be used to automatically estimate a user's age, and then provide age-appropriate content. To this end, we apply an Augmented TV method for posture estimation in order to develop a technique for estimating the height of a user in a standing position, as well as a method for estimating the user's age based on height.

2   Development of Height Estimation Method

In this paper, we report on the development of a height-estimation method that utilizes the elevation of a tablet and is based on the posture-estimation technique described in Ref. [2]. We assume that the elevation of the center of a television screen is known in advance. The elevation of the tablet is defined as the distance from the floor to the tablet's built-in camera. Based on the posture-estimation technique described in Ref. [2], we determine the coordinate of the vertical component of the tablet's built-in camera in a coordinate system whose origin is the center of the television screen, then add the elevation of the television-screen center from the floor in order to compute an estimate of the tablet's elevation.

Using pre-measured values of the tablet elevation in standing positions, together with subject height information, we perform a regression analysis to obtain a formula describing the relationship between the measured values of tablet elevation and subject height, then insert our estimate of the tablet elevation into this formula in order to estimate the user's height. Section 2.1 describes the public test we performed to obtain formulas expressing the relationship between the subject height and tablet elevation. Our results, and the observations drawn from them, are discussed in Sects. 2.2 and 2.3.

2.1   Public Testing

Public test was conducted to obtain formulas expressing the relationship between subject height and tablet elevation. Figure 1 shows a side view of the environment in which our public test was conducted, while Table 1 lists the experimental conditions.

To test our method for estimating height, we require measured values of tablet elevation and webcam images used to compute heights. To generate webcam images, we used two webcams to capture images of the tablet held by the test subject and top of the test subject's head.

When conducting our public tests, we ensured that the posture of test subjects was identical to the posture exhibited while experiencing Augmented TV, and prepared experimental content consisting of a sequence of rapidly switched static images on the television screen.

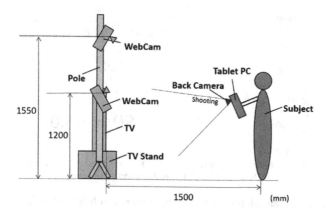

Fig. 1. Side view of public testing environment

Table 1. Experimental conditions

Number of test subjects	90
Age of test subjects	3–21 (70 % between 6 and 12)
Webcam model	Microsoft LifeCam Studio Q2F-00020
Webcam resolution	1280 × 720 (px)
Webcam image angular coverage	60.5 degrees
Distance between TV and test subject	1500 (mm)
Tablet PC model	Acer Iconia W700
Tablet PC dimensions	295 × 191 × 11 (mm)
Tablet PC weight	0.955 (kg)
Resolution of tablet PC built-in camera	2592 × 1944 (px)
Size of television	40 (in.)
Elevation of television screen center	778 (mm)

2.2 Result of Public Testing

Although we conducted public test on a total of 90 test subjects, we could only successfully obtain measurements of both tablet elevation and subject height for 71 of them. This reflects the impact of false identifications in our image processing procedures, which were designed to protect the privacy of test subjects. The results of the public tests described in Sect. 2.1 yielded graphs like that shown in Fig. 2 which characterize the relationship between tablet elevation and measured values of subject height. The regression formula obtained via the least-squares method is given by Eq. (1) below. In this equation, x is the measured value of the tablet elevation and y is the subject height. The contribution ratio was 0.84.

$$y = 1.30x - 84.6 \tag{1}$$

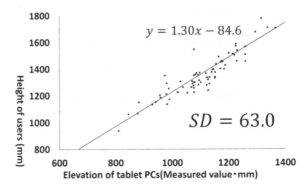

Fig. 2. Relationship between height of users and height of tablet PCs

2.3 Evaluation of Height Estimation Accuracy Supposing the Age Estimation

In this section we discuss the accuracy of our height-estimation procedure method based on the errors in our height estimates. From Fig. 2, the standard deviation of the estimated height values from the predictions of the regression formula using the tablet elevations was 63.0 mm. On the other hand, in the height data tabulated in Ref. [4] for children of ages between 6 and 12, the average height differential between children separated by one year of age is 59.9 mm. Thus, the standard deviation of our formula for the relationship between tablet elevation and subject height corresponds to an age uncertainty of approximately 1.1 years.

Based on this, we conclude that accuracy achieved by our method is sufficient for cases in which estimates are to be attributed certain widths – as is true for estimations of grade levels, which correspond to age ranges segmented by academic mastery based on achievement degree of learning.

3 Development of Age Estimation Method Based on the Height

Next, we will report on the development of an age-estimation method based on height estimates obtained using the procedure of Sect. 2. Our proposed age-estimation method begins by creating a table describing correspondences between heights and estimated ages, then estimates the age of a subject based on an input value of the subject's height. In what follows, highest estimation tables A, B, and C refer to data for male, female, and a mixed-gender population, respectively.

Tables A-C contain age estimates for each of various height values, together with values quantifying the accuracy of the estimates. Our process for constructing these tables is discussed in Sect. 3.1. In Sect. 3.2 we discuss experiments conducted to determine whether or not ages are estimated within a ±1-year accuracy range. Our results are discussed in Sect. 3.3.

3.1   Table that Shows Correspondence Between Height and Estimated Age

We constructed Tables A-C to serve as benchmark values for estimating age from height. First, following Ref. [4], for each of various height values separated by 1-cm intervals, we make test subject age-estimations based on the most common age for particular heights, and then take the ratio of estimated ages for each height value to determine the accuracy of the estimation.

Our procedure for producing age estimates and their accuracy levels are shown in Fig. 3. We augmented the data for the one to four-year age range with numerical values and probability density functions from Ref. [5]. In order to create the mixed-gender data in Table C, we used the average of the values for male and female subjects in the data of Ref. [4].

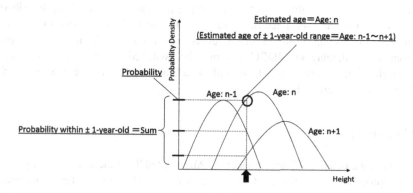

Fig. 3. Definition of estimated age and accuracy

3.2   Experiment of Age Estimation

To test the accuracy of the age-estimation method described in the previous section, we conducted experiments aimed at estimating ages based on heights using tables A-C constructed as described above. For height values, we used the estimated heights of test subjects computed via Eq. (1), as discussed in Sect. 2.2. We then applied these values to Tables A-C and estimated the age of each test subject. For the purposes of these experiments we consider an age estimate to be correct if it lies within ±1 year of the actual age of the test subject. To determine the accuracy needed to estimate ages within ±1 year, we considered the number of subjects of each age who exhibited a given height value in the data of Ref. [4]. Then, for each height value, we totaled the values of the three ages for which that height value appears most frequently.

3.3   Results and Discussion of Age Estimation

The results of the experiments described in the previous section revealed that the fraction of all test subjects for which our age estimates were correct was 60.0 % for cases in which we used the highest estimation tables (A and B), and 61.2 % for cases in which we used the gender-mixed table (C). This level of accuracy cannot be considered adequate for purposes in which accurate ages must be estimated, but we consider it sufficient for the purpose of switching content appropriate for one of three academic grade levels, as discussed in the previous section.

4   Age Estimation Function to Embed in Augmented TV

Next, we developed age-estimation functionality for Augmented TV in which the age-estimation method of Sect. 3 is used to estimate a user's age via a tablet in an Augmented TV system. This age estimate is then used to determine an appropriate academic grade level. We first estimate the elevation of a tablet held by the user, then use this value to estimate the user's height via the height-estimation method described in Sect. 2. From this height estimate, we use the age-estimation method described in Sect. 3 to estimate the user's age in the range from one to 17 years. Finally, we select one of three predefined academic grade levels appropriate for the user. We prepared trial content for display via 3DCG that may be switched in real time based on the results of this determination, and then confirmed that the 3DCG were can be switched based on academic grade level.

5   Conclusion

In this study, we considered an extension of Augmented TV functionality that provides content appropriate to a user's academic grade level. We developed a height-estimation method utilizing an Augmented TV posture-estimation technique and an age-estimation method in which the age of a user is inferred from his or her height. Tests of our two estimation methods demonstrated that they achieve accuracy sufficient to ensure no difficulties for applications requiring estimates of academic grade level. Finally, we demonstrated the effectiveness of our method in an actual implementation of our system by successfully switching trial content through conditional branching based on academic grade levels.

References

1. Disney Second Screen. http://disneysecondscreen.go.com/. Accessed 10 Sep 2015
2. Kawakita, H., Nakagawa, T.: Augmented TV: an augmented reality system for TV programs beyond the TV screen. In: 2014 International Conference on Multimedia Computing and Systems (ICMCS), pp. 955–960. IEEE (2014)
3. Musical Heart. http://wirelesshealth.virginia.edu/content/musical-heart. Accessed 10 Sep 2015
4. MEXT-Japan: School Health Statistic Surveys of 2013 (Japanese). http://www.e-stat.go.jp/SG1/estat/List.do. Accessed 15 Jan 2016
5. The Japanese Society for Pediatric Endocrinology (Japanese). http://jspe.umin.jp/medical/taikaku.html. Accessed 15 Jan 2016

A Computerized Measurement of CROM (Cervical Range of Motion) by Using Smartphone Based HMD (Head Mounted Display)

Changgon Woo and Changhoon Park[✉]

Department of Game Engineering, Hoseo University, 165 Sechul-ri,
Baebang-myun, Asan, Chungnam 336-795, Korea
wcg0916@imrlab.hoseo.edu, chpark@hoseo.edu

Abstract. This paper proposes a computerized measurement of cervical range of motion (CROM) without the help of experts. We aim to develop a reliable and easy-to-use application for CROM by using smartphone based head mounted display (HMD). This healthcare application provides a measuring instrument for 6 cervical motion and tangible visualization for the active cervical ROM data. This computerized approach will increase the accuracy of measurement of CROM by providing real-time feedback for the correct posture during examination.

Keywords: Cervical range of motion · Head mounted display · Computerized measurement · Healthcare application

1 Introduction

According to the Korean National Health Insurance Corporation, the number of patients with cervical disc herniation has increased from 573,912 in 2007 to 784,121 in 2011. The growth rate of patients with the neck disease was 29.7 % compared with 2009, much higher than 18.4 % of increase in spinal herniated disc patients during the same period. In terms of age, patients in their 20 s have seen the largest increase, with those in their teens and 30 s following. Cervical herniated discs, which used to be known as a degenerative disease that occurs in people in their 40 s to 60 s, has become more common in younger generations. In particular, high usage of smartphones and tablets causes a surge of cervical herniated disc patients. When using smartphones, people have their head bowed, which strains the neck and causes herniated discs. Whilst a human head weighs approximately 10 lb, staring at a phone with your head tilted forward will feel more akin to a 20 to 30-pound load.

2 Computerized Measurement of Cervical Spin Motion

2.1 Function

Measuring the active CROM is essential in objective assessment of neck symptomology and the effects of any intervention [1, 2]. The limitations of CROM may

© Springer International Publishing Switzerland 2016
C. Stephanidis (Ed.): HCII 2016 Posters, Part I, CCIS 617, pp. 531–535, 2016.
DOI: 10.1007/978-3-319-40548-3_88

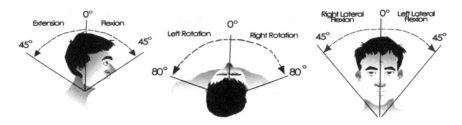

Fig. 1. General cervical range of motion

indicate musculoskeletal disorders, neck pain resulting from trauma or idiopathic [3, 4], headaches [3, 5–7] or some dysfunctions in the temporo-mandibular joints and masticatory muscles [7–9].

In spite of cervical ROM being such a frequently studied impairment, the accuracy of this measure as a diagnostic tool has been controversial due to conflicting evidence concerning its specificity and sensitivity [10, 11]. This paper aims to propose a computerized measurement of cervical range of motion (CROM) by using smartphone based head mounted display (HMD) (Fig. 1).

2.2 System Overview

To develop a reliable and easy-to-use method, we introduce Gear VR, smartphone based HMD. HMD is a display device, worn on the head, that has a small display optic in front of each eye. In order to provide a realistic 360° immersive experience, the HMD must be tracked with fast update rates, low latency with no jitter. Head tracking is used to generate the appropriate computer-generated imagery (CGI) for the angle-of-look at the particular time (Fig. 2).

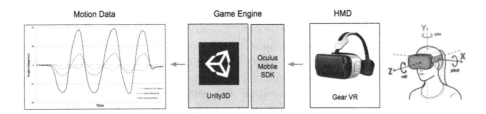

Fig. 2. HMD to data stream

This allows the user to "look around" a virtual reality environment simply by moving the head without the need for a separate controller to change the angle of the imagery. In this paper, we use Gear VR to track the 3-axis orientation of head for the measurement of CROM. Gear VR includes a special IMU for head tracking which updates at a 1000 Hz, where most phone sensors only do 100 Hz or 200 Hz. This IMU is more accurate and well calibrated with lower latency than internal smartphone IMUs.

3 Implementation

We developed a mobile healthcare application by using Unity3D, a commercial game engine. By using head tracking technology of HMD, this application provides measuring instruments for 6 cervical motion the flexion, extension, right lateral inclination, left lateral inclination, right rotation and left rotation. In the application, user interaction is designed for participants to spin his or her head for the measurement of CROM without the help of experts. For the accuracy of measurement, real-time feedback will be presented to maintain the correct posture during examination (Fig. 3).

Fig. 3. Diagnosis flow

The mobile healthcare application aims to provide the active cervical ROM data of the six motion of the cervical spine in a more clear and effective way. To archive this, we design and implement tangible visualization like the figure considering immersive display of HMD. This approach will help the user understand the measurement results of CROM easily comparing with reference values for normal CROM (Fig. 4).

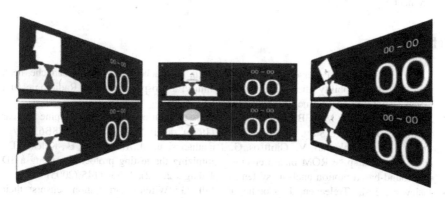

Fig. 4. Representation of diagnosis results using HMD

4 Conclusion and Future Work

In this paper, we proposed a reliable and easy-to-use healthcare application for accessing CROM using smartphone based head mounted display (HMD). This application provides a measuring instrument for 6 cervical motion and tangible visualization for the active cervical ROM data. This computerized approach will increase the accuracy of measurement of CROM without the help of experts. In addition to measuring the limitation in cervical ROM, velocity and smoothness of motion will be also examined. And, we will develop a game like application for exercise as well as measurement of CROM (Fig. 5).

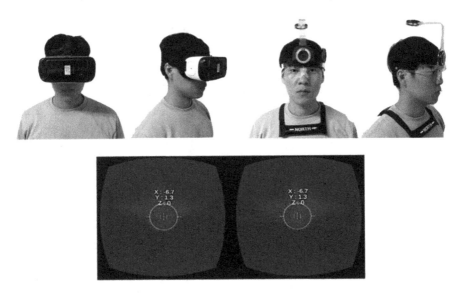

Fig. 5. Computerized measurement using gear VR and CROM3. Screenshots of computerized measurement

References

1. Kasch, H., Stengaard-Pedersen, K., Arendt-Nielsen, L., Staehelin Jensen, t: Headache, neck pain, and neck mobility after acute whiplash injury: a prospective study. Radiologic, and psychosocial findings. Spine **26**(11), 1246–1251 (2001)
2. Squires, B., Gargan, M.F., Bannister, G.C.: Soft tissue injuries of the cervical spine 15 year follow up. J. Bone Jt. Surg. Br. **78**, 955–957 (1996). doi:10.1302/0301-620X78B6.1267
3. Strimpakos, N., Sakellari, V., Gioftsos, G., Papathanasiou, M., Brountzos, E., Kelekis, D., et al.: Cervical spine ROM measurements: optimizing the testing protocol by using a 3D ultrasound-based motion analysis system. Cephalalgia **25**(12), 1133–1145 (2005)
4. Jasiewicz, J.M., Treleaven, J., Condie, P., Jull, G.: Wireless orientation sensors: their suitability to measure head movement for neck pain assessment. Man. Ther. **12**(4), 380–385 (2007)
5. Bevilaqua-Grossi, D., Pegoretti, K.S., Gonçalves, M.C., Speciali, J.G., Bordini, C.A., Bigal, M.E.: Cervical mobility in women with migraine. Headache **49**(5), 726–731 (2009)
6. Solinger, A.B., Chen, J., Lantz, C.A.: Standardized initial head position in cervical range-of-motion assessment: reliability and error analysis. J. Manip. Physiol. Ther. **23**(1), 20–26 (2000)

7. Ferrario, V.F., Sforza, C., Serrao, G., Grassi, G.P., Mossi, E.: Active range of motion of the head and cervical spine: a three-dimensional investigation in healthy young adults. J. Orthop. Res. **20**(1), 122–129 (2002)
8. Sforza, C., Grassi, G.P., Fragnito, N., Turci, M., Ferrario, V.F.: Three-dimensional analysis of active head and cervical spine range of motion: effect of age in healthy male subjects. Clin. Biomech. (Bristol, Avon) **17**(8), 611–614 (2002)
9. Olivo, S.A., Magee, D.J., Parfitt, M., Major, P., Tie, N.M.: The association between the cervical spine, the stomatognathic system, and craniofacial pain: a critical review. J. Orofac. Pain. **20**(4), 271–287 (2006)
10. Dall'Alba, P.T., et al.: Cervical range of motion discriminates between asymptomatic persons and those with whiplash. Spine **26**(19), 2090–2094 (2001)
11. De Hertogh, W.J., et al.: The clinical examination of neck pain patients: the validity of a group of tests. Manual Ther. **12**(1), 50–55 (2007)

Evaluation of Four Eyestrain Recovery Methods for Visual Display Terminal Workers

Hsin-Chieh Wu[1(✉)], Min-Chi Chiu[2], and Jyun-Hao Jian[1]

[1] Department of Industrial Engineering and Management,
Chaoyang University of Technology,
No. 168, Jifong E. Road, Wufong District,
Taichung City 41349, Taiwan
hcwul@cyut.edu.tw
[2] Department of Industrial Engineering and Management,
National Chin-Yi University of Technology,
Taichung City, Taiwan

Abstract. The purpose of this research was to compare four eyestrain recovery methods, and then to find out the best way to eliminate eye fatigue from watching the electronic text. Four visual fatigue recovery methods included a short rest, eye drops, eye massager A (Vibratory), and eye massager B (Pneumatic). We recruited 20 young adults for the experiment. Their ages are between 19 to 25 years. Each participant performed four different experimental trials in four different days. Two visual fatigue indicators were collected before the experiment, i.e., high frequency component (HFC) of accommodative micro-fluctuation waveform and subjective rating (SR) of visual fatigue. The participants performed searching operation firstly, and then, one of the four recovery methods was tested. Experimental results show that the visual fatigue recovery method had a significantly effect on the HFC. The eye massager A had a significantly better effect than the eye drops and a short rest.

Keywords: Fatigue recovery strategy · Eye drops · Eye massager · Short rest

1 Introduction

Proper work and rest time can enhance productivity and prevents fatigue. Previous study [1] tested the combinations of 60 min, 50 min, and 40 min of VDT work and 10 min and 20 min resting time, and found that the optimum combination is 50 min working time and 20 min resting time. Among the combinations of 50 min work and 5, 10, 15, 20, and 25 min resting time, the combination of 50 min work and 15 min rest could reduce fatigue. Boucsein and Thum indicated that a short rest could relieve mental stress and emotion, but a long rest could reduce fatigue and mental strain more effectively [2]. Hayashi proposed that a nap during the day has a positive influence on work [3]. After using the computer for 2 h, a 20 min nap contributes to recovering eye fatigue. Therefore, apps for hand-held intelligent devices can provide work and rest time reminder functions to remind the users to have timely rests during different usage scenarios.

© Springer International Publishing Switzerland 2016
C. Stephanidis (Ed.): HCII 2016 Posters, Part I, CCIS 617, pp. 536–541, 2016.
DOI: 10.1007/978-3-319-40548-3_89

In addition to rest, eye drops and an eye massager can eliminate or relieve eyestrain. Eye drops are a type of lubricant for relieving eye irritation and eye fatigue. In 2002, about 35 % of American families bought eye drops or eye washing prescriptions from pharmacies [4]. Dinslage et al. studied tear substitutes and indicated that eye dryness and grittiness could be significantly improved in subjective sensation by using preservative-free tear substitutes to treat eyes [5]. In addition, using an eye massager to massage around the eyes may relieve eyestrain. However, the effects of some eye massagers require experimental verification. Although there are studies on visual fatigue during computer use, evaluations of eyestrain recovery methods are seldom discussed. Therefore, this study aims to evaluate the extensively accepted eyestrain recovery methods, namely having a nap, using eye drops, and two eye massagers (pneumatic and vibratory), in order to determine the best way to eliminate eyestrain.

2 Methods

2.1 Subjects

This study recruited 20 young volunteers for the experiment, half male and half female. All subjects have naked vision or corrected vision above 0.8, do not have color blindness or other eye diseases, and have English reading ability. They were asked to have adequate sleep the day before the experiment, and avoid reading or performing visual operations 1 h before the experiment. The subjects were informed of the experimental process and purposes before the experiment began. Informed consents were signed.

2.2 Equipments

The iPad, as produced by the Apple Company, was used as the tool for alphabet searching operation. The subjects were asked to use it for 40 min in order to feel visual fatigue. Its screen is 9.7", it adopts LED back light technology, with the LCD wide viewing angle technology of IPS (in-plane switching), and the viewing angle is 178°.

A vibratory eye massager (named massager A) and a pneumatic eye massager (named massager B) were used to massage the eyes for recovery from visual fatigue. The other two recovery methods were eye drops and resting for 20 min. The four methods were compared to determine the most effective method.

The ciliary body accommodative micro-fluctuations analyzer (Righton Speedy-K MF-1, Japan) was used to collect high frequency component (HFC) of accommodative micro-fluctuation waveform. If visual fatigue occurs when the target object is at a long distance, the activity level of the ciliary body is obviously higher than normal vision [6]. Therefore, higher HFC value (above 60) means visual fatigue.

The subjective rating (SR) of visual fatigue was used the scale developed by Heuer et al. [7]. The higher score of SR means higher level of visual fatigue.

2.3 Visual Operation and Control Factors

In order to evaluate the visual fatigue recovery methods, the subjects were asked to perform an alphabet searching operation to reach the fatigue state. The text they viewed was randomly compiled capital English letters, spaces, and punctuations. The font was Times New Roman, the font size was 16pt, the row height was 1.2 times, and each row had 30 ± 5 characters. The font color was yellow, and the target word was "T". The target word randomly occurred in the file, each file contained 1700 ± 10 target words, and there were 4 sets of files.

The file was viewed on the iPad. The iPad was placed on a desk with the dimension of 70 cm high, 70 cm wide and 70 cm long. The chair was 40 cm high, and the seat pad was 40 cm wide and 44 cm long. The illumination around the experimental site was controlled at 500 lx, and there was no other light source. In order to allow the subject to conveniently look at the tablet PC, the tablet elevation was fixed by a bearer at 130°. The screen brightness was 400 cd/m^2, and the resolution was 1024 × 768 (132 ppi). The sight distance measured in this experiment was that the subjects accommodate themselves for viewing the text displayed on the tablet PC. The sight distance was fixed when the experiment begins. The subject could adjust the chair height till feeling comfortable, as shown in Fig. 1.

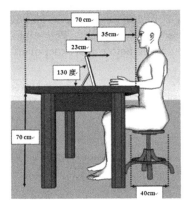

Fig. 1. Experimental arrangement

2.4 Experimental Procedure

In this experiment, the subject used the iPad for 40 min, and then the effects of four fatigue recovery methods were compared. Each participant performed four different experimental trials in four different days. The sequence of the experiment was in random way and it took about 60 min to carry on each experimental trials. The procedure of each trial is described as follows:

1. Environmental arrangement: the experimental display equipment, desk, and chair heights and distances were fixed, and the experimental control factors of the display equipment settings were set.

2. The subjects were informed of the experimental process, adjusted their position to a comfortable state, and rested for 10 min before the experiment.
3. Be acquainted with instrumental operation and how to deal with extreme discomfort during the experiment.
4. The high frequency component (HFC) of accommodative micro-fluctuation waveform and subjective rating (SR) of visual fatigue were collected.
5. The iPad was used for 40-min searching operation. After searching operation, the HFC and SR of visual fatigue were collected again.
6. The subjects used one of the four recovery methods to recover from visual fatigue.
7. Finally, the HFC and SR of visual fatigue were collected again.

3 Results

3.1 Subjects

Originally, 20 subjects participated in this experiment; however, as 5 failed to complete the entire experiment, the final experimental results are the data of 15 subjects. These 15 subjects have an average age of 22.47 ± 2.41 years old, and their naked eye vision or corrected visual acuity is above 0.8; of these 15 subjects, 13 are used to using their right eye, while 2 are used to using their left eye.

3.2 Confirmation of Visual Fatigue

Prior to a comparison of four visual fatigue recovery methods, the subjects first underwent an "alphabet searching operation" for 40 min. All of the collected two visual fatigue indicators (HFC and SR) showed that the subjects after the alphabet searching operation have significant visual fatigue (by the paired t-test, $p < 0.05$).

3.3 Effects of the Visual Fatigue Recovery Methods

The paired t-test was also adopted for comparison of the visual fatigue indicators (HFC and SR) between after the alphabet searching operation and after applying a recovery method. According to paired t-test results, all collected data showed that there was significant difference between after the alphabet searching operation and after applying a recovery method ($p < 0.05$). Therefore, it may be discriminated that these four recovery methods all are able to alleviate the visual fatigue.

One-way ANOVA was used to test whether the effect of recovery method was significant on the changes of subjects' HFC and SR during the recovery period. Recovery method only had a significant effect on the subjects' HFC value changes during the recovery period ($F = 5.761$, $p < 0.05$). Figure 2 shows the HFC means for the four recovery methods in the experiment. Afterwards, the Least Significant Difference (LSD) was further adopted for comparing pairs of treatment means of the subjects' HFC value changes. Table 1 shows that, there was a significant difference between massager A and eye drops (p = 0.000), between massager B and rest (p = 0.018), and between massager B and eye drops (p = 0.029), while there was no significant difference between massager A and massager B (p = 0.065), or between rest and eye drops (p = 0.100). According to the statistical results of the above data, the use of massager A is better than the other recovery methods for recovering from visual fatigue.

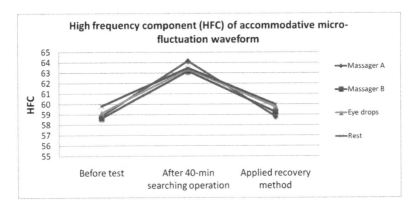

Fig. 2. The HFC means for the four recovery methods in the experiment

Table 1. Comparing pairs of treatment means of the subjects' HFC value changes

Recovery method (I)	Recovery method (J)	Difference between each pair of means (I-J)	p-value
Massager A	Massager B	−1.4000	0.065
	Eye drops	−3.0667	0.000*
	Rest	−1.8222	0.018*
Massager B	Massager A	1.4000	0.065
	Eye drops	−1.6667	0.029*
	Rest	−0.4222	0.537
Eye drops	Massager A	3.0667	0.000*
	Massager B	1.6667	0.029*
	Rest	1.2444	0.100
Rest	Massager A	1.8222	0.018*
	Massager B	0.4222	0.573
	Eye drops	−1.2444	0.100

4   Discussion

In this study, four visual fatigue recovery methods are adopted, namely, eye massagers A and B, eye drops, and rest. The research findings show that the use of an eye massager has better effect than the use of eye drops or rest. After the experiment, through discussions with the subjects, it is known that massager A massages around the eye, but will not directly put pressure on the eye ball, while massager B massages the entire eye, meaning the eye ball may receive pressure under the use of massager B, thus, causing a short phenomenon of blurred vision. In terms of eye drops, the possible side effects caused by the use of eye drops are not considered in this study. Generally, it is not recommended to use healthcare eye drops frequently, as some compositions in eye drops can cause possible adverse reactions after long-term use, or the eyes may become dependent on them. In terms of rest, according to Yoshimura and Tomoda's study [1], through the combination of 50-min of work and 15-min of rest, eye fatigue can be alleviated. This result is similar to the result of this study, and it can be confirmed that visual fatigue will be alleviated after 15-min of rest.

5 Conclusion

This study compared four visual fatigue recovery methods. The experimental results show that massager A (vibration) has better recovery effect than the other methods, followed by massager B (pneumatic), eye drops, and rest, respectively. It is recommended that people with excessive eye use may use a vibration massage for about 15 min, in order to achieve better visual recovery effect. The use of eye drops takes the least time; however, while eye fatigue can be alleviated, eye drops are drugs, and should be used with caution. In this study, the 15-min rest is a no cost method, and has visual recovery effect; however, its effect is not as good as the use of a vibration eye massager. As the subjects in this study were all young people, the results were unable to determine whether these visual fatigue recovery methods apply to the elderly, thus, further experimentation is required for the elderly.

Acknowledgements. The authors thank the Ministry of Science and Technology of Republic of China (Taiwan), for financially supporting this research.

References

1. Yoshimura, I., Tomoda, Y.: A study on fatigue estimation by integrated analysis of psychophysiological function – relating to continuous working time and rest pause for VDT work. Japan. J. Ergon. **30**, 85–97 (1994)
2. Boucsein, W., Thum, M.: Design of work/rest schedules for computer work based on psychophysiological recovery measures. Int. J. Ind. Ergon. **20**, 51–57 (1997)
3. Hayashi, M., Fukushima, H., Hori, T.: The effects of short daytime naps for five consecutive days. Sleep Res. Online **5**, 13–17 (2003)
4. Simmons Market Research Bureau: Brand Tract Report: Eye Drops and Eye Wash (Non-prescription) Spring 2002-full year, Deerfield Beach, Florida, Report BP000799 (2003)
5. Dinslage, S., Stoffel, W., Diestelhorst, M.: Tolerability and safety of two new preservative-free tear film substitutes. Cornea **21**, 352–355 (2002)
6. Collins, G.: The electronic refractometer. British J. Physiol. Opt. **1**, 30–40 (1937)
7. Heuer, H., Hollendiek, G., Kröger, H., Römer, T.: Die Ruhelage der Augen und ihr Einfluss auf Beobachtungsabstand und visuelle Ermüdung bei Bildschirmarbeit. Zeitschrift für experimentelle und angewandte psychologie **36**, 538–566 (1989)

Estimating Carrier's Height by Accelerometer Signals of a Smartphone

Hiro-Fumi Yanai[1]($\boxtimes$) and Atsushi Enjyoji[1,2,P]

[1] Department Media and Telecommunications, Ibaraki University,
Hitachi, Ibaraki, Japan
hfy@ieee.org
[2] Hitachi, Ltd., Ibaraki, Japan

Abstract. The aim of this study is to estimate height of a carrier (owner) of a smartphone by using single three-axis accelerometer signals. We found that the accelerometer signals collected while a carrier goes up the stairs contain features that are correlated with height of the carrier as high as $r = 0.801$. Apart from potentially useful applications of the result, there might arise a privacy issue in using smartphone since approximate height could be acquired in this way. Although, in general, height is not regarded as private information to be worried about, if someone thinks his/her height belongs to privacy, it should be protected against leakage.

Keywords: Stature · Estimation · Smartphone · Accelerometer · Time series · Security

1 Introduction

The scope of our investigation includes two aspects of smartphones (mobile devices). First one is to search for possibilities of accelerometer signal analysis with a view to identification of biological or behavioral information (static or dynamic) of humans. For an example of this direction of studies where accelerometer signal is used among others (including positioning information) to recognize human behavior, refer to Pei et al. [1]. And there are quickly expanding number of medical and health care applications that utilize internal sensors of Apple iOS devices. Second one is related to the security issues of smartphones, that is, if a user takes his/her height or other information for private, and that information could be detectable by smartphone, it should be that the user is able to decide to or not to activate that functionality. Examples of unexpected or unattended privacy issues include extraction of speech from outside of soundproof glass by the use of video camera [2], or recovering text entered on keyboard by monitoring vibration via accelerometer of a smartphone placed on the desk [3].

In our experiment, accelerometer signals were stored while the participants went up the stairs carrying a smartphone with them. We defined features based on the time course of the acceleration. As a result, we found out features that are highly correlated with height of participants.

© Springer International Publishing Switzerland 2016
C. Stephanidis (Ed.): HCII 2016 Posters, Part I, CCIS 617, pp. 542–546, 2016.
DOI: 10.1007/978-3-319-40548-3_90

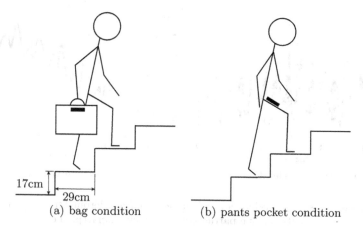

(a) bag condition   (b) pants pocket condition

Fig. 1. Experimental setup. Participants went up the stairs in two conditions, (a) with a smartphone in the bag, or (b) in pants pocket. The small black bar is a smartphone.

2   Experiment and Results

In this section, we describe experimental procedures, specification of the smartphone and the accelerometer, definitions of the features, then we summarize the results.

Procedures. Thirteen participants were instructed to go up the stairs (twelve-step stairs) in their natural ways. They were also instructed to make the first step with their right foot. They did so four times, two times with carrying a bag (2 kg in weight) in their right hand (a smartphone was placed firmly in the bag), the rest two times with a smartphone in their right frontal pants pocket. Figure 1 illustrates the experimental situation.

Smartphone. The smartphone was HTC Desire SoftBank X06HT (60 mm × 119 mm × 12 mm, 135 g, OS: Android 2.2); sampling interval of acceleration was about 20 ms and the range was ±2 g, where g is the earth's gravity, 9.8 m/s^2.

Data selection. In analyzing data, we have omitted the first step and the last two steps (12th and 13th step; note we need thirteen steps to go up twelve-step stairs). The reason why we omitted the first and the last step is that, in those steps, ascending motion is made only halfway. The reason of omission of the second last step was that we wanted to equalize the number of samples from the right and the left steps.

Definition of the Features. The features we adopted are categorized into two groups, group I and group II, with respect to in what way accelerometer signals are used. Group I features are defined directly by the profile of the vertical component of the signal. We thought the vertical component was effective in

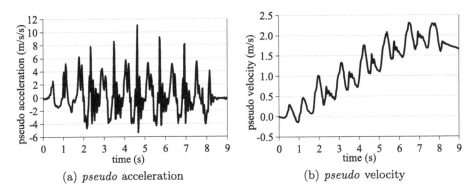

(a) *pseudo* acceleration   (b) *pseudo* velocity

Fig. 2. Example *pseudo* acceleration calculated from accelerometer signal and corresponding *pseudo* velocity for one participant's in-pocket smartphone.

the bag condition since the bag's—hence the smartphone's—direction is approximately fixed and might well represent the participant's vertical motion, which is expected to be more related to the participant's bodily dimension than horizontal motion. Group II features are defined in such a way that they are usable in the situation where smartphone's direction keeps changing in time (this applies to the pants pocket condition). Therefore the features are defined not by specific vector component of accelerometer signal but by the magnitude $a(t)$ of accelerometer signal vector. Yet there remains a serious problem in using the magnitude of accelerometer signal. That is, there is always a bias due to the earth's gravity. To do a workaround on this problem, we defined *pseudo* acceleration at time t, $\tilde{a}(t)$, as $\tilde{a}(t) = a(t) - g$ (see Fig. 2(a)). Then *pseudo* velocity is determined as

$$\tilde{v}(t) = v(t_0) + \int_{t_0}^{t} \tilde{a}(t)dt.$$

This $\tilde{v}(t)$ determined from Fig. 2(a) is shown in (b). Again, there remains a problem in using *pseudo* velocity, that is, there is a drift attributable to the acceleration bias. To overcome this problem, again, we made another workaround. That is, for every single step of participant, right or left, we reset *pseudo* velocity to zero. We denote this new *pseudo* velocity as $\tilde{v}_0(t)$. We defined the beginning of each step as the time at which *pseudo* velocity curve is minimized. Then we defined *pseudo* path length for ith step as

$$L_i = \int_{t_i}^{t_{i+1}} \tilde{v}_0(t)dt.$$

Note that, among thirteen steps in all, as mentioned above, we chose ten steps ($i = 2, 3, \ldots, 11$), where odd number belongs to the right steps and even number the left steps.

Results. We have examined several possible features with respect to their correlation with height. As a result, for vertical acceleration profile in the bag

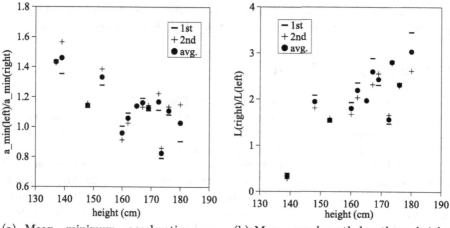

(a) Mean minimum acceleration vs. height in bag condition ($r = -0.745$).

(b) Mean *pseudo* path length vs. height in pocket condition ($r = 0.801$)

Fig. 3. Feature values vs. height for the features highly correlated with carrier's height. Correlation coefficients are calculated using average feature values of the first and the second trials.

Table 1. Correlation coefficients of two features (a_{min} and L) with height or the length of leg for two carrying conditions (bag and pocket). The highest correlations within each condition are printed in bold.

Condition	Feature	Height	The length of leg
Bag	a_{min} : right/left	0.672	0.503
	a_{min} : left/right	**−0.745**	−0.583
	L : right/left	−0.415	−0.207
	L : left/right	0.418	0.213
Pocket	L : right/left	**0.801**	0.728
	L : left/right	−0.695	−0.562

condition, we found that mean minimum vertical acceleration is well related to height. To be specific, the ratio $a_{min}(\text{left})/a_{min}(\text{right})$ is highly correlated with height ($r = -0.745$; see Fig. 3(a)), where a_{min} is mean minimum vertical accelerations, and "right" ("left") stands for the steps with the right (left) foot.

Relationship between *pseudo* path length and height was examined for the bag and the pocket conditions. We found *pseudo* path length is highly correlated, in the pocket condition, with height. In the bag condition, however, correlation is not so high. To be specific, the right-step to left-step ratio of *pseudo* path length $L(\text{right})/L(\text{left})$ is highly correlated with height ($r = 0.801$; see Fig. 3(b)).

Correlations of the features with height are summarized in Table 1. For comparison's sake, features' correlations with *the length of leg* are given in the table.

We defined the length of leg by the difference between height and sitting height, by assuming it approximates the sum of thigh length and lower leg length.

3 Summary and Discussion

We have just made trial and error searching for features that might be correlated with height. We found that the ratio of left to right for mean minimum vertical acceleration is effective for the bag condition, and, for the pocket condition, the ratio of right to left for mean *pseudo* path length is effective.

Although we have found features that have fairly large correlation with height, certainly, estimation error by regression is rather large. One possible approach of reducing the error of estimation would be to use multiple features instead of single features. Also we need deeper understanding of why the particular features have higher correlations with height, preferably by analyzing bio-mechanical model of human walking.

It is interesting to note that the correlation of height with a particular feature derived from accelerometer signals is comparable to, or even larger than, the correlation obtained from anthropometric study, e.g. correlation of height with lower leg length is $r = 0.776$ [4].

Finally we would like to comment on the features' correlation with the length of leg. As can be seen from Table 1, correlations of the features are lower for the length of leg than height. This is a bit strange since the motion of going up the stairs may be thought to be determined mainly by the length of leg. By taking this result for sure, chances are that acceleration is influenced by whole-body motion, so that the length of leg is not the only determinant of acceleration profiles.

References

1. Pei, L., Guinness, R., Chen, R., Liu, J., Kuusniemi, H., Chen, Y., Chen, L., Kaistinen, J.: Human behavior cognition using smartphone sensors. Sensors **13**, 1402–1424 (2013)
2. Davis, A., Rubinstein, M., Wadhwa, N., Mysore, G., Durand, F., Freeman, W.T.: The Visual Microphone: Passive recovery of sound from video. ACM Trans. Graphics (Proc. SIGGRAPH) **33**(4), 79:1–79:10 (2014)
3. Marquardt, P., Verma, A., Carter, H., Traynor, P.: (sp)iPhone: Decoding vibrations from nearby keyboards using mobile phone accelerometers. In: Proceedings 18th ACM Conference on Computer and Communications Security, pp. 551–562 (2011)
4. Nor, F.M., Abdullah, N., Mustapa, A.-M., Wen, L.Q., Faisal, N.A., Nazari, D.A.A.A.: Estimation of stature by using lower limb dimensions in the Malaysian population. J. Forensic Leg. Med. **20**(8), 947–952 (2013)

Experimental Study on Comfort Ranges of Manual Operation in Standing Position

Ai-Ping Yang[1], Wen-Yu Fu[1], Guang Cheng[1], Xin Zhang[2(✉)],
Hui-min Hu[2], and Chau-Kuang Chen[3]

[1] Department of Industrial Engineering,
Beijing Union University, Beijing, China
[2] Ergonomics Laboratory,
China National Institute of Standardization, Beijing, China
zhangx@cnis.gov.cn
[3] School of Graduate Studies and Research,
Meharry Medical College, Nashville, TN, USA

Abstract. The experimental study was conducted to assess the comfort ranges for manual operation in standing position. Twenty healthy young people (10 males and 10 females) were recruited as study subjects. With the example of an index finger push-button operation, the acceptable height ranges (approximately 800–1200 mm) of manual operation in standing position were determined by the experiment. Specifically, the five experimental heights from 800 mm to 1200 mm were set up with the step interval being 100 mm. In the operating plane (workstation), the 50 mm vertical and horizontal spacing buttons were arranged, respectively. The acceptable operating regions of the test height table can be obtained through statistical analysis of the forefinger push-button operations of all study subjects. Thus, the corresponding comfort ranges of manual operation on other experimental height planes can be replicated. The study results yielded certain practical values of mounting position for manual devices in the ergonomic design and assessment.

Keywords: Manual operation · Comfortable range · Ergonomic design and assessment

1 Introduction

Volumes of research results regarding manual operation ergonomics can be found, most of which focuses on the operation of manual push-pull tasks such as the study of the human body strength, analysis of factors affecting the pull-push action forces, and the occupational injury caused by the pushing and pulling force [1–4]. Also, there were some studies concentrating on comprehensive influence analysis on multiple factors which include operation posture, gripping position and load size [5–10]. From a different perspective, this paper emphasized on the study of the comfort ranges of manual operation in standing position.

The role and significance of this study are embodied in the two aspects as follows: (1) evaluating and improving the ergonomics of the manual operating device in the

© Springer International Publishing Switzerland 2016
C. Stephanidis (Ed.): HCII 2016 Posters, Part I, CCIS 617, pp. 547–552, 2016.
DOI: 10.1007/978-3-319-40548-3_91

industrial equipment and infrastructures (i.e., the installation location and operation area being convenient for users to operate correctly for the commonly used key button, knob, handle, control rod, etc.). (2) evaluating and improving the layout of the complex control table (i.e., For the power console, traffic scheduling table, cockpit display control panel used by aircraft, train and car, etc., it is necessary that the most important manual control device is installed in the optimal operation area).

Twenty people (ten males and ten females) from ages 18 to 25 years old with good physical health and no movement impairments were recruited as study subjects. The six main processes were as follows: (1) The adjustable height of the operating platform and button mechanism assemblies were designed and developed; (2) The acceptable operating heights of the operator were preliminarily determined by the experiment (approximately 800–1200 mm); (3) With the 100 mm step size as the interval, five test heights and related press operation regions were set, and the natural standing positions of the trial operation were determined; (4) The subjects were asked to complete the operation of the right index finger button press when test personnel recorded the subject's subjective comprehensive acceptable operating area; (5) Statistical analyses of the test results were performed in order to obtain the acceptable index finger pressing operation regions; and (6) The comfort field chart (table) of standing manual operation was obtained. This research has offered certain practical application values of manual manipulator's positions in the ergonomics design and evaluation.

2   Experiment on Comfort Ranges of Manual Operation in Standing Position

The comfort ranges of manual operation for a single and light load were studied in this paper. A preliminary investigation during the pre-experiment phase led to a discovery of the manual operation being influenced by gender, age, position and operation of the study subjects. This research mainly concentrated on the test methods and technical routes in which twenty healthy young people were recruited as study subjects. The test data were statistically analyzed, and ultimately, the corresponding comfort chart of manual operation in standing position was obtained.

2.1   Determine Height Ranges of Test Table

A test bench device with adjustable height was designed as shown in Fig. 1. The approximate height range of the operating table was roughly set based on the shoulder height and middle finger to ground distance of the vertical arm of the human body measurement dimension in a standing posture. Then the acceptable height ranges of the test surface were determined from 800 mm to 1200 mm by the increment of 100 mm as the step size according to the lowest and highest height of the press operation.

Fig. 1. Adjustable height operation platform

2.2   Experiment Process

1. The two row button mechanism was assembled which consisted of ten sets of buttons on each row in the 800 mm height of the platform. These buttons to the same operating force and operation displacement were adjusted, and the same sizes of the button head were chosen.
2. The ranges of the operating region were roughly determined by the arm length of the people in the 95th percentile, which was divided into the horizontal and vertical regions. As shown in Fig. 2, the left graph indicated a horizontal test table, and the right was a longitudinal test Table
3. The horizontal test was listed as follows: On the horizontal test table shown on the left side of Fig. 2, the subjects completed the pressing operation task on green measurement points in sequence from left to right. The range of the measuring points for the complete task can be achieved, and the press operation comfort zone test in other rows was performed with the same method.

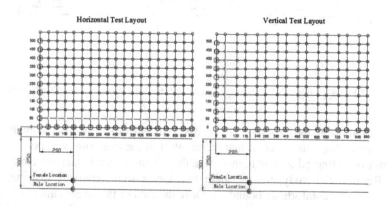

Fig. 2. Test points layouts

4. The specific·process of the longitudinal test was listed as follows: On the vertical test table shown on the right side of Fig. 2, test personnel guided the participants to perceive the comfort of the red point button operation. The comfort ranges of the pressing operation were presented, and the test of other vertical testing points in sequence was completed. The overlap areas of lateral and longitudinal comfort regions mentioned above in steps 3 and 4 were the comfort ranges of manual operation of the study subjects.
5. The comfortable ranges on the other heights were conducted according to the aforementioned steps.

3 Experimental Results

Twenty young people, ten men and women, with good physical health and no movement disorder were tested, respectively. Test scenarios are shown in Fig. 3.

Fig. 3. The index finger pressing operation comfort zone test scenarios (left chart shows the longitudinal test, the right is lateral test)

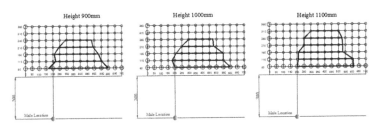

Fig. 4. Ten young male standing manual operation comfortable zone distribution

The results of all the tests showed that 800 mm and 1200 mm were more dispersed. The 800 mm table was lower so that the comfort of the operation was poor while the 1200 mm operating table was higher than that of the general standing elbow height value. Because the study data of these two tables were relatively discrete, it was difficult to find a comfortable boundary. Only the data of the large number of subjects can be clearly defined in the scope of the comfortable boundary, which was only given

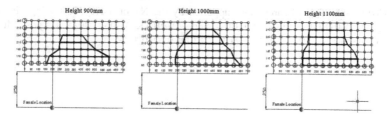

Fig. 5. Ten young female standing manual operation comfortable zone distribution

in the test results of the 900 mm, 1000 mm, and 1100 mm operating height of the male and female on the right hand index finger pressing operation comfort regions. As shown in Figs. 4 and 5, the shape and trend of the male and female graphics were consistent via the trapezoid. The comfort region was located on the front right side of the operator, and the longer operating range was close to the operator. The operating range was shorter when further from the operator. At the left edge of the operating region, the trend was gradually increasing while a gradual decrease was present at the right side of the operating region. The performance of the left and right sides of the boundary line were not smooth due to the small sample size.

4 Conclusions

1. In this paper, the experimental study was undertaken to assess the comfortable location in standing position and light load manual operation. A manual operation test bench with adjustable height was designed and developed. Twenty young men and women were in the operating positions of the right index finger button pressing, testing the operation comfort in standing state under different bench heights. A comfortable region distribution map of three operation positions was obtained. This research demonstrated that certain practical application values of the manual manipulator's position contributed to ergonomics design and assessment.
2. The small sample size of twenty tests might directly affect the accuracy of the test results. As a result, the operation region of the left and right boundary was not smooth. A larger sample would lead to a solid scientific method to obtain a comfortable location region distribution of manual operation in the standing state.
3. Various factors affect the comfort of manual operation, which were only limited to the influence of the test manual operation position on the comfort of operation. Furthermore, the operating force and the operating frequency of the manual operating comfort could have a greater impact via weight analysis of the impact of the main factors on the follow-up plan. Establishing a location comfort assessment model for manual operation would contribute to critical practical values of manual operation in ergonomics design and assessment.

Acknowledgment. This research was supported by the National Key Technology R&D Program (2014BAK01B04, 2014BAK01B02, and 2014BAK01B05), 2015 Beijing Municipal Education Commission Research Project (12213991508101/008).

References

1. Dickerson, C.R., Martin, B.J., Chaffin, D.B.: The relationship between shoulder torques and the perception of muscular effort in loaded reaches. Ergonomics **49**(11), 1036–1051 (2006)
2. Snook, S.H., Ciriello, V.M.: The design of manual handling tasks: revised tables of maximum acceptable weights and forces. Ergonomics **34**, 1197–1213 (1991)
3. Chow, A.Y., Dickerson, C.R.: Determinants and magnitudes of manual force strengths and joint moments during two-handed standing maximal horizontal pushing and pulling. Ergonomics **16**, 1–11 (2015). http://www.tandfonline.com/loi/terg20
4. Hoozemans, M.J.M., van der Beek, A.J., Frings-Dresen, M.H.W., van der Woude, L.H.V., van Dijk, F.J.H.: Pushing and pulling in association with low back and shoulder complaints. Occup. Environ. Med. **59**(10), 696–702 (2002)
5. Al-Eisawi, K.W., Kerk, C.J., Congleton, J.J., Amendola, A.A., Jenkins, O.C., Gaines, W.G.: The effect of handle height and cart load on the initial hand forces in cart pushing and pulling. Ergonomics **42**(8), 1099–1113 (1999)
6. Ayoub, M.M., McDaniel, J.W.: Effect of operator stance and pushing and pulling tasks. Trans. Inst. Ind. Eng. **6**(3), 185–195 (1974)
7. Chaffin, D.B., Andres, R.O.: Volitional postures during maximal push/pull exertions in the sagittal plane. Hum. Factors **25**(5), 541–550 (1983)
8. Olanrewaju, O.O., Haslegrave, C.M.: Ready steady push – a study of the role of arm posture in manual exertions. Ergonomics **51**(2), 192–216 (2008)
9. Waters, T.R., Anderson, V.P., Garg, A., et al.: Revised NIOSH equation for the design and evaluation of manual lifting tasks. Ergonomics **36**, 749–776 (1993)
10. Marras, W.S., Knapik, G.G., Ferguson, S.: Loading along the lumbar spine as influence by speed, control, load magnitude, and handle height during pushing. Clin. Biomech. **24**(2), 155–163 (2009)

Study of Posture Estimation System Using Infrared Camera

Airi Yoshino[⊠] and Hiromitsu Nishimura

Kanagawa Institute of Technology, Atsugi, Kanagawa, Japan
amberofelf@gmail.com

Abstract. In Japan, the number of patients suffering from bedsores has been increasing with the progression of population aging. In this study, we investigated techniques for analyzing posture or motion for the prevention of bedsores. In particular, we propose a method for analyzing the posture of a person lying in bed using depth maps and color images obtained from a Kinect sensor. First, the color images are used to perform color identification of the hair, from which the position of the head is estimated. Hair color by acquiring the color information from each pixel found a part that many belongs. Based on these analyses, it was possible to determine to be the position of the head. Second, the depth maps are divided into four regions: the head region, chest region, abdominal region, and foot region. Based on these analyses, it was possible to determine which of three positions, prone, supine, or sideways, the person was lying down in.

Keywords: Posture estimation · Near-infrared camera · Depth image analysis

1 Introduction

Japan is facing a declining number of registered nurses even as the aging of the Japanese population has led to an increasing number of patients suffering from bedsores [1]. The prevention of bedsores requires the monitoring of changes in the body positions of patients and the detection of cases in which such motion is less or often.

However, some existing monitoring systems require that bodily-detection markers be affixed directly to the bodies of patients, thereby creating (among other difficulties) a burdensome situation for the patients [2]. In this study, as a detection method allowing a reduced burden on patients, we make use of cameras capable of measuring distances via near-infrared radiation. To enable posture estimation for bedridden patients based on near-infrared images, we investigate a technique in which we obtain and make use of a depth map derived from the three most common body positions that we envision for sleeping test subjects.

2 Detection Accuracy Experiment of Kinect Device

To test the suitability of the near-infrared camera used in this study, we first conducted experiments to assess the accuracy of measurements made by a Kinect device. Figure 1 is a schematic depiction of our experimental environment. We then conducted four experimental tests to establish the suitability of Kinect for posture detection.

© Springer International Publishing Switzerland 2016
C. Stephanidis (Ed.): HCII 2016 Posters, Part I, CCIS 617, pp. 553–558, 2016.
DOI: 10.1007/978-3-319-40548-3_92

The first test was conducted to determine if an area of dimensions 2300 × 1500 mm, which are the dimensions of a typical single hospital bed, could be fully captured at the maximum device resolution of 640 × 480. The results confirmed that adequate view angles are available from a distance of 2150 mm, whereupon we assumed that the Kinect device would be installed at a distance of 2150 mm or greater from the measurement subject.

The second test was conducted to determine if the distance values could be obtained at resolutions of 10 mm or less. The results of this test confirmed that such values could indeed be obtained at resolutions below 10 mm, whereupon we concluded that would be possible to detect changes in the positions of body parts.

The third test was conducted to determine if the shape of objects of dimensions less than 10 × 10 mm could be obtained via our depth map. The results demonstrated that the shapes of 10 × 10 mm objects (as determined by the depth map) agree with the actual object shapes, thereby confirming the possibility of identifying the shapes of body parts with fine-grained detail.

Our final test was conducted to determine if the depth map could properly identify objects separated by distances of 10 mm or less as separate objects. The results of this test showed that, at separation distances of 20 mm, the system was capable of identifying the individual objects. Therefore, we could conclude that closely neighboring body parts could be properly distinguished from each other to the necessary extent. In view of these findings, we conclude that the Kinect device allows measurements to be made with an acceptable degree of accuracy.

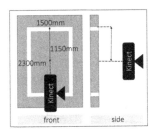

Fig. 1. Relative position of Kinect device and walls

3   Experiments for Posture Estimation

We obtained depth maps for each of the three common body postures we envisioned for the sleeping state – facing upward on one's back (prone), facing sideways, or facing downward (supine) – and scrutinized their features in an effort to identify ideas for use in posture-estimation methods. Assuming a distance between ceiling and bed of approximately 2000 mm, we positioned our equipment at a point 2150 mm off the floor, thereby ensuring that the entirety of the bed would within the area of a single screen image. Figure 2 shows an overview of our experimental environment.

In order to account for differences in male and female bodies, our test subjects initially consisted of one male and one female subject. We confirmed that the entire

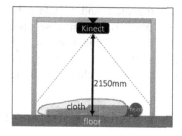

Fig. 2. The experimental situation as seen from the side

bodies of the test subjects fit within the screen area. Next, we analyzed each body posture in order to look for body regions exhibiting prominent variations in distance data values (henceforth termed "characteristic regions").

Figure 3 shows depth maps for a sleeping female test subject in each of the three body postures. Depth data was obtained by scanning in the direction parallel to the short edge of the bed, and then seeking maximal values. This data was plotted with the long edge of the bed taken as the horizontal axis. Here, we focus on the regions of the body surface that exhibit the greatest activity.

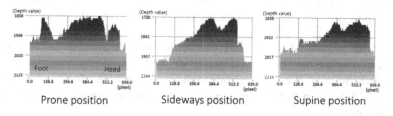

Fig. 3. Depth map for a sleeping female test subject

Comparing the graphs of Fig. 3 for the various body postures reveals high values near the legs, chest, and head of the patient for the prone position. For the side-facing position, values are large near the chest and stomach, while for the supine position values grow progressively larger from the head to the chest. Figure 4 compares graphs for the male and female test subjects in the prone position.

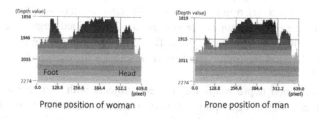

Fig. 4. Comparison of prone position for female and male test subject

Comparing the graphs for the male and female subjects reveals essentially no differences in the shapes of the plots. Based on these findings, we concluded that we had successfully identified the value of characteristic regions for each of the three common body postures. These results were used in our estimation procedure, described below, by focusing on body parts lying in characteristic regions.

4 Body-Part Estimations System of Sleeping Positions

We conducted body-part estimations under a set of conditions chosen based on the characteristic regions identified for sleeping positions. In addition, by identifying the position of the test subject's head, we determined the orientation in which the subject was sleeping, thereby allowing us to make more detailed estimates. In this process, to achieve a more detailed reconstruction of sleeping positions, we augmented the environment of Fig. 2 by having our test subjects sleep on air mattresses.

In identifying the position of the test subject's head, we made use of one piece of data that is characteristic of Japanese individuals: they have black hair. This allowed us to obtain color information from each pixel in a color image and look for regions in which the color of Japanese hair appears frequently, thereby allowing us to determine the position of the test subject's head. For test subjects with long hair, the regions judged to be black in color may extend all the way to the lower portion of the screen, but we expect the majority of regions deemed black in color to appear in the upper portion of the screen.

The depth maps used in our body part estimations are divided into four regions: head, chest, stomach, and legs. In our study, we used a simple equipartition of regions to estimate body parts. We then determined the minimum of the distance values within each subdivided region and used this to establish conditions for estimating the various body positions.

Note that when the patient is in the prone position, values for the legs are small compared to other values, which makes this marker useful for determining if the patient is in that position. More specifically, if values for the screen subdivision associated with the test subject's legs are smaller than other values, we can conclude that the subject is in the prone position. Our criteria for identifying the various body positions are shown in Fig. 5.

Because of our equipartition of regions, disagreements between characteristic regions were found in some portions of the images due to differences in the height, body structure, or sleeping position of the test subjects. For persons in the prone position, the subdivided leg region agreed with the characteristic region, but for persons in the sideways-facing and supine positions, the subdivided regions exhibited disagreements with the characteristic regions. Based on this finding, we concluded that an appropriate subdivision technique used must be chosen for each individual characteristic region.

Next, we obtained depth maps for the test subjects with their bodies in sleeping positions and conducted body-part estimation experiments. Here our test subjects consisted of three male subjects. Figure 6 compares depth maps for a male subject and the female subject of Fig. 3 sleeping in the prone position.

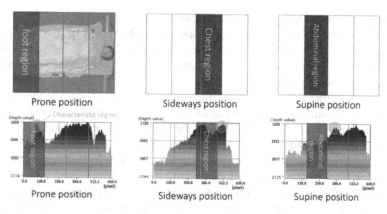

Fig. 5. Judgment condition

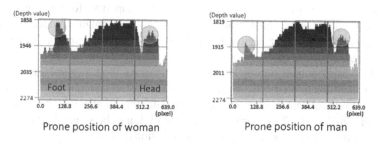

Fig. 6. Comparison of prone positions for female and male test subject

From a comparison with Fig. 3 we see that the highest of the values for the head and leg regions differ, despite the fact that the body postures are the same in the two cases. Similar differences among characteristic regions were found for the side-facing and supine positions. One possible reason for this is that our use of air mattresses ensured that the surface in contact with the bodies of the test subjects was soft and deformable, thereby permitting variations in body postures.

The fact that discrepancies in body contact surfaces can modify observed data – even for otherwise identical body postures – has a significant impact on the accuracy of our method. In our future work, we plan to conduct analyses involving patients and beds in actual hospital environments.

5   Conclusion

The objective of this study was to develop a system to allow efficient modifications of body posture as a means of preventing bedsores. In order to ensure that our method minimizes stress on the test subject, we use a Kinect device to perform non-contact determination of body posture, and used the information obtained to investigate an estimation technique that uses depth maps representing information on the body postures of patients confined to beds.

We began by conducting basic experiments using the Kinect to assess the accuracy with which we were able to measure body postures. The results of these experiments indicated that our measurement setup offered an adequate field of vision and met the conditions we deemed essential for posture estimation, whereupon we deemed it appropriate for use in this research.

Next, we identified characteristic features in depth maps – capturing the three most common body positions we assume test subjects will adopt while sleeping – and then conducted experiments in which we used the depth maps to perform body posture estimation. The results of these tests identified certain characteristic regions associated with each body position, thereby suggesting places in which to look for characteristics associated with particular regions of the body.

We then performed body-part estimation under conditions determined based on the characteristics of each bodily posture. To identify the positions of the heads of test subjects, we used the color information associated to each pixel. Regions containing large numbers of black pixels were deemed to correspond to the subject's head. For body-part estimation we equipartitioned our depth map into four regions – which corresponded to the head, chest, stomach, and legs – and obtained values expressing distance information for each region. From these, we established criteria for identifying body postures.

The four-part equipartitioning of the depth map resulted in some inconsistencies among our identification criteria. Moreover, because we obtained depth maps with test subjects sleeping on air mattresses, different data for identical body postures was obtained in some cases. Thus, our method for subdividing the screen into characteristic regions, and our criteria for identifying body positions, must be improved.

In our future work, we plan to pursue analyses of patients and beds in actual hospital settings. An additional challenge will be to develop a method for identifying the position of the test subject's head without reliance on the assumption that the subject has black hair.

References

1. Japanese Nursing Association (Japanese). http://www.nurse.or.jp/up_pdf/20150331145508_f.pdf. Accessed 21 Jan 2016
2. Toshihiko, T. (Faculty of Engineering, University of Gifu), Member, Osamu, F. (Faculty of Engineering, Nagoya Institute of Technology), Member: A Method for Monitoring the Body Motion in Bed by Using an Infrared Light Emitting Marker System (2005)

Evaluation of Pedal Button Diameter
and Travel Length

Pei Zhou[1(✉)], Yifen Qiu[1], Songtao Zhu[1], Hui-min Hu[2],
and Chaoyi Zhao[2]

[1] Beihang University, Beijing, China
{zhoupei723,18810652420}@163.com,
qiuyifen@buaa.edu.cn
[2] China National Institute of Standardization, Beijing, China
{huhm,zhaochy}@cnis.gov.cn

Abstract. The study was aimed to find the optimal diameter and travel length
of pedal button. People need to feel comfortable and convenient when controlling machine with pedal button. Ergonomic experiments had been done on
81 subjects. Each subjects stepped the pedal button and made assessment on
diameter or travel length. Diameter and travel length were assessed separately.
The results showed that diameter of 55 mm to 70 mm and travel length of
16 mm to 24 mm got the scores closest to "0" which means "suitable". It was
also observed that diameter and travel length are independent variables.

Keywords: Pedal button · Diameter · Travel length · Ergonomic

1 Introduction

Pedal button is a kind of device that moves up and down to finish mechanical transmission. It is widely used in mechanical and medical equipment when it is more
convenient for foot operation or the machines do not need to be controlled accurately.
Travel length refers to the maximal move distance of pedal button during the
up-and-down motion. Diameter is the size of button which contacts with the sole of
foot. Diameter and travel length are the most important factors [2] which affect
operation comfort. Few research has been done on pedal button. Some text books gave
suggest value on diameter and travel length without original data.

2 Methods

Diameter and travel length were the two variables which affected people's feeling
simultaneously, so the experiments adopted control variate method. The two factors
were respectively studied in two parts of experiments research their influences on
subjective assessment. The assessment method adopted subjective method–rating on a
scale [1]. Numerical scales with end points defined by word descriptors. The nine
points from −4 to 4 were symmetric distributed by the midpoint "0" which represented
"suitable", the negative and the positive represented respectively different level of small
and big. Absent descriptors were the median level (Table 1).

© Springer International Publishing Switzerland 2016
C. Stephanidis (Ed.): HCII 2016 Posters, Part I, CCIS 617, pp. 559–563, 2016.
DOI: 10.1007/978-3-319-40548-3_93

Table 1. Assessment on dimension and travel length

−4	−3	−2	−1	0	1	2	3	4
Very small		Small		Suitable		Big		Very big

3 Experiments

Experiments were conducted with 81 subjects (52 males and 29 females). These subjects aged from 18 to 62 and were healthy. Measurements of height, weight, foot length and breadth (right foot) of the subjects had been done before the experiment, stature and dimensions of subjects are shown in Table 2. The subjects included the old and the young, male and female, the 5th percentile female and the 90th percentile male. All the subjects were asked to wear the same kind of shoes which were moderate in hardness to eliminate shoes' effects on subjects' feel of the pedal button.

Table 2. Stature and dimensions of subjects

Stature and dimensions	Minimum	Maximum	Mean ± SD
Height, cm	131.2	194.7	164.1 ± 11.1
Weight, Kg	41.2	112	70.8 ± 13.3
Foot length, mm	195	310	247.5 ± 20.4
Foot breadth, mm	79	119	96.1 ± 8.4
Age	18	62	37.1 ± 11.6

An equipment (shown in Fig. 1) was specially designed for the experiments. There is a platform on the top of this equipment, pedal buttons with different diameter could be installed on the platform. Seventeen pedal buttons were designed, diameter ranged from 10 to 90 mm and the interval was 5 mm, as shown in Fig. 1. Pedal button travel length could be adjusted in this equipment, it ranged from 0 to 40 mm.

Fig. 1. Pedal buttons and equipment for the experiments

Part 1 of the experiments was about diameter evaluation of pedal button. At first, travel length was set to 10 mm. Subject stood on the platform of the equipment and was asked to depress the pedal button down with the right foot and heel kept on the platform, gave the score of pedal button diameter. Seventeen pedal buttons were assessed in random order. Then travel length was changed to 20 mm, 30 mm and 40 mm respectively to evaluate diameters of the 17 pedal buttons. The subjects could depress each pedal for several times if they want to. They were not allowed to see the pedal button during the experiments. Experiment states of this part were shown as the left part of Table 3. AS- assessment. Units of travel length and diameter are millimeter.

Table 3. Experiment states of two parts

Part 1. Assessment on diameter					Part 2. Assessment on travel length					
D	L	L	L	L	D	L	D	L	D	L
10	10	20	30	40	30	8	50	8	80	8
15						16		16		16
...						24		24		24
85						32		32		32
90						40		40		40

D-diameter. L-travel length.

Part 2 of the experiments is about travel length evaluation of pedal button. Experiment states of this part were shown as the right part of Table 3. At first, pedal button of 30 mm diameter was installed to the top platform of the equipment. Subject stood on the platform of the equipment, and was asked to depress the pedal button down with the right foot and heel kept on the platform, gave the score of pedal button travel length, travel length of 8 mm, 16 mm, 24 mm, 32 mm, 40 mm were evaluated randomly during this experiment. Then pedal button of 50 mm, 80 mm diameter were installed to the platform respectively, five travel lengths tested above were evaluated as the same way of 30 mm diameter pedal button.

4   Results and Discussion

Data were analyzed in SPSS (Statistical Product and Service Solutions) and Excel. The scores on each diameter or travel length were averaged as shown in Figs. 2 and 3 Standard deviation was shown on each bar chart.

Data in Fig. 2 shows that evaluation on diameter in four travel lengths of 10 mm, 20 mm, 30 mm, and 40 mm have the similar distribution. Scores changes from negative through '0' to positive when the pedal button diameter changes from 10 mm to 90 mm. When the travel length is 10 mm, absolute value of scores on diameters of 55 mm to 75 mm are less than '1' and close to '0' which means 'suitable'. Similarly, suitable diameters are 55 mm to 80 mm on travel length of 20 mm, 50 mm to 85 mm on travel length of 30 m. 50 mm to 70 mm on travel length of 40 mm. Based on the results, we suggest suitable pedal button diameter of 55 mm to 70 mm.

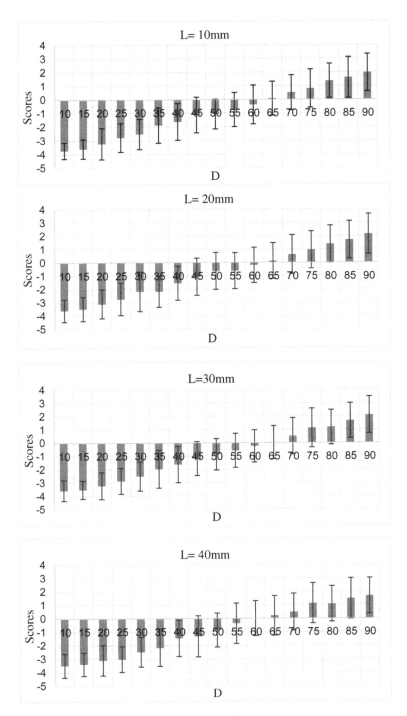

Fig. 2. Results of diameter evaluation in different travel lengths

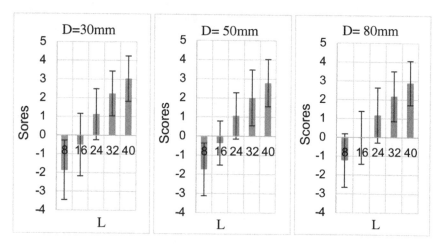

Fig. 3. Results of travel length evaluation in different diameters

Data in Fig. 3 shows that the evaluation on travel length in diameters of 30 mm, 50 mm, and 80 mm have the similar distribution. The scores are close to '−2' which means 'small' when the travel length is 8 mm. Scores get close to '0' which means 'suitable' when the travel length is between 16 mm and 24 mm. Scores are bigger than '2' which means 'big'. So we suggest pedal button travel length of 16 mm to 24 mm.

The averages scores on diameter or travel length are well in distribution. The standard deviations of each average are less than 1.6, the maximum is 1.5026 and the minimum is 0.5919 which are small relatively compared to the bound of assessment. The SD means that the scores fluctuates in a range that we can accept.

The two factors-diameter and travel length ANOVA using SPSS indicates there is no significant difference ($p < 0.05$). As we can see scores of diameter in different travel length has the similar distribution, and vice versa. Thus we can infer that diameter and travel length are independent within limits.

Diameter of 55 mm to 70 mm and travel length of 16 mm to 24 mm are suggested as the most comfort extent. This results are more accurate than the recommend value of Lai [1] and are suitable for Asian. He recommend diameter of 50 mm to 80 mm and travel length of 12 mm to 60 mm. The results can be used to design pedal button to improve operating comfort.

Acknowledgements. Supported by National Key Technology R&D Program (2014BAK01B02) and Quality inspection of public welfare industry research projects (2015QK237).

References

1. Vivek, D.B.: Ergonomics in the Automotive Design Process, pp. 258–260. CRC Press, Boca Raton (2012)
2. Lai, W.: The ergonomics, pp. 205–206. HuaZhong University of Science and Technology Press (1997)

Author Index

Printed in the United States
by Bookmasters

Printed in the United States
By Bookmasters